# Quality of Life Indicators in U.S. Metropolitan Areas

# Ben-Chieh Liu

The Praeger Special Studies program—utilizing the most modern and efficient book production techniques and a selective worldwide distribution network—makes available to the academic, government, and business communities significant, timely research in U.S. and international economic, social, and political development.

# Quality of Life Indicators in U.S. Metropolitan Areas

## A Statistical Analysis

PRAEGER SPECIAL STUDIES IN U.S. ECONOMIC, SOCIAL, AND POLITICAL ISSUES

**Praeger Publishers**   New York   Washington   London

Library of Congress Cataloging in Publication Data

Liu, Ben-Chieh.
    Qualtiy of life indicators in U.S. metropolitan areas.

    (Praeger special studies in U.S. economic, social,
and political issues)
    Includes bibliographical references and indexes.
    1.  Social indicators—United States.  I.  Title.
HN60. L58           309. 1'73        75-42482
ISBN 0-275-56360-X

TO MY BLIND MOTHER IN CHINA

PRAEGER PUBLISHERS
111 Fourth Avenue, New York, N.Y. 10003, U.S.A.

Published in the United States of America in 1976
by Praeger Publishers, Inc.

Recently, more and more people have been commenting on the paradox of affluence. Concern over the quality of life has seemed to increase proportionately with technological progress and increases in income. People have come to realize that "Quality of Life" is not necessarily a simple function of material wealth. The generally accepted national economic health indicator, Gross National Product, often has served as a basis for establishing goals and measuring achievement of the goals at the policy-making level. But growing attention to the social, economic, political, and environmental health of the nation has led to the quest for other indicators which will more adequately reflect the overall "health" of the nation and its citizens' well-being.

In May 1973, Midwest Research Institute published The Quality of Life in the U.S., 1970: Index, Rating and Statistics, an effort to measure and compare the quality of life in the 50 states. Following publication of the state study, numerous people suggested that comparisons of quality of life would be more meaningful if the data were available for geographical areas smaller than a state. Almost three-fourths of the U.S. population live in metropolitan areas. Thus, a metropolitan quality of life assessment seems appropriate. Through a grant awarded to Dr. Ben-chieh Liu, Principal Economist, Midwest Research Institute, by the Washington Research Center, U.S. Environmental Protection Agency, this study of metropolitan quality of life was launched in April 1974. The primary objective of this study is to quantitatively assess the urban quality of life (QOL) variations and to provide statistical information for analyzing the relationships between economic and other QOL components in the 243 SMSA's in the U.S.

This book summarizes the empirical results of the study which covers only one point in time--1970. It is our intent to continue to refine and periodically update the indicators as new data become available. The conceptual model development, the methodology, descriptive analysis, statistical inferences and policy implications, plus the primary statistics collected for all metropolitan areas contained in the book are the opinions of the author, and they do not necessarily reflect those held by the Environmental Protection Agency (EPA) or other public and private agencies associated with Midwest Research Institute.

A summary of this book was published by Midwest Research Institute through a grant from the Kimball Fund, Midwest Research Institute.

John McKelvey
President
Midwest Research Institute

Kansas City, Missouri
May 1975

# ACKNOWLEDGMENTS

The author wishes to express his appreciation to the U.S. Environmental Protection Agency which provided the grant making it possible to undertake this study. The project monitors, Mr. Robert Livingston and Dr. Peter House of Washington Environmental Research Center, EPA, have been extremely cooperative during the entire course of the work. In addition, many suggestions from Mr. Livingston also have resulted in significant improvement in the study.

Messrs. Bruce Macy and Robert Gustafson assisted in theoretical development and made important contributions to the project. Miss Mary Kies capably and efficiently conducted the most painstaking work of data collection, organization, and presentation, and Mr. Raymond Posch developed all computer programs for index construction.

In addition to those of my colleagues at Midwest Research Institute who worked with me, I am deeply indebted to Dr. Charles Kimball, Messrs. John McKelvey, Gary Nuss, Robert Roberts, and Tom Ventresca and Mrs. Mary Lillis for their encouragement during this research effort as well as during the previous state quality of life study. Valuable comments on technical matters from Dr. Murray Aborn of National Science Foundation, Dr. Teh-wei Hu of Pennsylvania State University, Drs. Maw-lin Lee and Ross Shepherd of the University of Missouri, and Drs. Angus Campbell, Wilbur Cohen, and Daniel Tunstall of the University of Michigan are gratefully acknowledged. I have also benefited greatly from frequent discussions and information exchanges with Dr. Clark Abt of Abt Associates, Dr. Michael Flax of Urban Institute, Dr. Robert Foster of the Governmental Studies Programme, Dalhousie University, Dr. O. W. Markley of Stanford Research Institute, Dr. Alex Micheles of the University of Guelph, Dr. Friedhelm Gehrmann of the University of Augsburg, Dr. Robert Parke of the Center for Coordination of Research on Social Indicators and Dr. Charles Wolf of the Water Resources Institute, U.S. Army Corps of Engineers.

The U.S. Bureau of Outdoor Recreation and hundreds of Chambers of Commerce provided us the first-hand information on recreation, sports and cultural activities, and other agencies such as EPA and National Weather Records Center supplied essential pollution and meterological data.

It is impossible to name all individuals who have made important contributions to this study. Nevertheless, the author owes special gratitude to thousands of readers and reporters throughout the world who, for various purposes, used and commented on the state study which, in turn, resulted in the improvement of the metropolitan study.

Appreciation also goes to Dr. Harold Orel and especially to Mrs. Doris Nagel, who devoted their time to editing the manuscript and to Mrs. Sharon Wolverton and Mrs. Marsha Brown, who efficiently arranged the typing and reproduction of the report.

Finally, the author has to thank his wife, Jill, and their children, Tina, Roger and Milton for their endurance and patience, for lonely weekends and late dinners during the preparation of this study.

# CONTENTS

x

# TABLES

# Quality of Life Indicators in U.S. Metropolitan Areas

A century ago John Ruskin seriously criticized the political economists of his time for their preoccupation with material growth and neglect of human values. During the Great Depression, the most influential economist of this century, John Maynard Keynes, perceived the problems of economic motivation, suggested that some appropriate preparations for our destiny and for changes in our value system be made, and that the arts of life be encouraged and experimented with, wealth serving as a means rather than an end.[1] In his book The Affluent Society, John K. Galbraith warned us that "In large areas of economic affairs the march of events, above all the increase in our wealth and popular well-being, has again left the conventional wisdom sadly obsolete."[2] In a recent work on world dynamics, Jay Forrester suggests that we may just have passed through a golden age, and that our quality of life may decline from what it was in the 1960's for the next century or so.[3] In 1972, a team of systems analysts at M.I.T. concluded that if the present growth trends in world population, industrialization, pollution, food production, and resource depletion continue unchanged, the limits to growth on this planet will be reached within the next century.[4]

The U.S. society has certainly passed through an industrialization era and seems to be in a great transition period toward a postindustrial stage. Uncertainty and confusion have rolled across the U.S., and a discontent with the quality of life seems to have been growing

---

1/ See John Maynard Keynes, Essays in Persuasion (London: Macmillan and Co., 1933).

2/ John K. Galbraith, The Affluent Society (Boston: Houghton Mifflin Co., 1958).

3/ Jay Forrester, Urban Dynamics (Cambridge: The M.I.T. Press, 1969)

4/ D. H. Meadows, D. L. Meadows, J. Randers, and W. W. Behrens III, The Limits to Growth (New York: Universe Books, 1972).

faster than technological know-how and material wealth in this country. They have developed as a result of conflicting values: "operative values" in the industrial state and the "declared values" important in the founding of our nation. While the former is characterized by the competitive factor, the division of labor, indefinite economic persuasion, the use of the scientific method and technological advances the latter is highlighted by concerns with equality, justice, and natural rights such as life, liberty, and the pursuit of happiness.

In an industrial society, individuals struggle for survival with very limited time for leisure; hard work is a virtue, and wealth accumulation becomes the status symbol or the ultimate goal of the hard work. The great transition period--which leaves more time for thinking and leisure--makes it possible for people to move beyond their basic concerns of living to a humanistic concern for what living is all about. As John Rockefeller III pointed out in The Second American Revolution, the latter concern embodies a desire to create a human-centered society, and to harness the forces of economic and technological advancement in the service of humanistic values. In other words, people in the transitional period may be characterized by a devotion to human welfare, and an interest in all human beings.[5/] However, at the beginning of this period, people are puzzled about which path to follow as they search for a doctrine, set of attitudes, or a way of life centered upon human interests or values. The ultimate goal of the search is obviously to reach a society such as the Ta-Tong characterized by Confucius--a state of enduring wholeness and beauty in which an individual may identify himself and contribute his best to other men, to society, to nature, and to the land in exchange for a meaningful, happy, and satisfactory life.

In seeking ways to move our society from an industrial state toward a humanistic-oriented psychology that seeks to improve the quality of life of all Americans, the role of the government as a leader, as well as a servant, must be considered. In addition to the necessary duty of protecting international status and security and striving for economic growth and full employment with stable prices, the Federal Government is already beginning to manage social changes: civil rights legislation, income redistribution, environmental protection and problems involved with urbanization and population growth, etc. State and local governments are also increasingly concerned about the social problems of organized crime, urban renewal, mass transit, welfare

---

5/ John Rockefeller, III, The Second American Revolution (New York: Harper and Row, 1973).

provisions, community beautification, etc. To be specific, our Government is more aware of the change in social values than ever before and seeks to solve the problems in order to improve the national health and overall social well-being.

However, a problem is not likely to be solved until it has been perceived and identified as a problem. Although there exist thousands of decision makers within the private sector who are able, willing, and devoted to the enhancement of our overall quality of life, they are not certain about the direction that their philanthropical activities should take, just as many public decision makers are not always sure about the social, economic, political and environmental impacts of their actions.

In order to promote the general welfare, there is an urgent need in our transitional society to define the general welfare and to identify the factors that determine and influence our general welfare. In brief, it is essential to construct a mechanism which can distinguish better from worse. "For many of the important topics on which social critics blithely pass judgments, and on which policies are made," said Bauer, "there are not yardsticks by which to know if things are getting better or worse."[6] As it now stands, the United States has no comprehensive set of social statistics that reflect our changes in values and measure social progress or retrogression.[7] One of the most detrimental features of the social sciences to date has been the absence of any generally acceptable condensed set either of social welfare functions or of social conditions.

The search for quality of life indicators is an attempt to obtain new information that will be useful to evaluate the past, guide the action of the present, and plan for the future. The empirical measures of various levels of quality of life enjoyed by Americans are aimed at the identification of strengths and weaknesses of our national health so that decision makers, be they public or private, can be assisted as they seek to evaluate, guide, and plan for a better quality of life.

---

[6] Raymond Bauer (ed.), Social Indicators (Cambridge: The M.I.T. Press, 1966) p. 20.

[7] See National Goals Research Staff, Report to the President, Washington, D.C., 1970.

The study, The Quality of Life in the U.S., 1970, at the state level, and this study for all metropolitan areas, represent exploratory efforts to meet these needs.[8]

In the following text, we first review the state of the art of research efforts in the field of quality of life measurement. The relationship between welfare economics and the quality of life and a production model for quality of life are discussed in Chapter III. Chapter IV deals with the scope, methodology and data sources of the empirical quality of life study for all 243 standard metropolitan statistical areas. Empirical findings based primarily on 1970 data and policy implication are presented in Chapters V, VI, and VII, respectively, for the three groups of SMSA's--large, medium, and small. Finally, a summary and suggestions for future research are contained in the last chapter.

---

[8] Ben-Chieh Liu, Quality of Life in the U.S., 1970 (Kansas City: Midwest Research Institute, 1973).

# II

## QUALITY OF LIFE INDICATORS: A REVIEW OF THE STATE OF THE ART

This chapter presents an extensive review of the quality of life indicator development throughout the world. Discussion will first be on the conceptual development and, secondly, the specific models of social indicators. The last part of this chapter will focus on the general quality of life models. It is hoped that this review will provide useful information and guidance for future research in the field.

CONCEPTUAL DEVELOPMENT

Over the last decade, an era that does not coincide particularly with any specific political administration, this nation has witnessed an erosion of the consensus about our socioeconomic system. It has been a period in which real incomes grew unusually rapidly, yet the dissatisfaction with our social order and system was both overwhelming and unprecedented. Is economic growth really associated with some subtle forces which reduce social well-being in some dimensions, just as they improve it in others? Do the obvious manifestations of discontent in a rapid income-growing and highly affluent society simply misrepresent a general increase in contentment, or are there some people who have been made worse off as a consequence of economic growth? Why should new technology and a high rate of income growth fail to diminish social pathology and improve the overall quality of life?

Economic growth requires capital accumulation, technological change, and improvement in human skills. In modern times, it also often requires changes in institutional structure and resource location.[1] As a result, generally desirable economic growth may frequently be associated with undesirable social and environmental costs.

---

[1] For a variety of discussions on economic growth or no growth society, see Daedalus, Journal of the American Academy of Arts and Sciences (Fall, 1973).

Economic growth, no matter how measured or in which sector, tends to
increase the production of unwanted by-products--urban traffic conges-
tion and time spent on the roads; air, water and other types of pollution; social disorder and tension; housing problems and unequal distribution of incomes; loosening of family ties and friendships, etc.
When the costs of the by-products become greater than the economic
gains, societal discontent becomes unavoidable and the overall
quality of life degraded for most of the people.[2]

The effects of economic growth on our overall welfare or on the quality
of life are inextricably intertwined, but arguments for and against
economic growth are largely subjective.  As concern over the quality
of the environment and social welfare mounts, the conventional
measure of well-being, GNP, which has served for decades as a means of
establishing goals and measuring achievement of the goals at the
policy-making level, has been criticized--on the one hand--because it
is not an appropriate index of welfare, and--on the other--because it
does not include the important values of increased leisure, the
services of housewives, the hidden rent, farmer's consumption of
their own products, etc.  Governments, like private researchers, have
become more concerned with improving both the economic and social
performance of society.  Beyond providing for employment and price
stability, law and order, and national defense, governments are recog-
nizing that they must involve themselves with a wide variety of social
conditions which affect our quality of life such as the health of the
population; equal opportunity among individuals; the eradication of
poverty and discrimination; more security for the aged; more equal
distribution of incomes; urban housing; transportation; and pollution
problems, etc.[3]

The quality of life concept or the social indicator movement has been
a response to these needs for information on social conditions related

---

2/ Most notable arguments of these can be found in D. H. and D. L.
    Meadows, J. Randers and W. W. Behrens III, The Limits to Growth
    (New York:  Universe Books, 1972); E. J. Mishan, The Costs of
    Economic Growth (New York, 1967).

3/ For instance, see R. Cole, Errors in Provisional Estimates of Gross
    National Product (New York:  National Bureau of Economic Research,
    1969); N. Ruggles and R. Ruggles, The Design of Economic Accounts
    (New York, 1970); W. Nordhaus and J. Tobin, "Is Growth Obsolete,"
    in Economic Growth, 50th Anniversary Colloquium V (New York); and
    a section on "Social Indicators and a Framework for Social and
    Economic Accounts," 1974 Proceedings of the Social Statistics
    Section, American Statistical Association.

to a variety of dimensions of the national welfare beyond such economic measures as real income per capita. This movement is generally said to have begun in 1929, with President Hoover's Committee on Social Trends. That Committee's report, <u>Recent Social Trends in the United States</u> (1933), was an attempt to analyze social factors likely to have a bearing on public policy in the second third of the century. However, very little progress was made in regular social reporting until 1960. A variety of national goals on the social front were set up by President Eisenhower's Commission on National Goals in 1960. In 1962, the Social Science Advisory Committee (to President Kennedy) urged the establishment of a systematic collection of basic behavioral data for the U.S. The National Commission on Technology Automation and Economic Progress, in 1966, called for social accounting, annual social reports to the President, and a full opportunity and social accounting act.[4]

Methodological development of social indicators and interest in the quality of life concept development grew remarkably during the later years of the 1960's. Following the studies on social indicators by Bauer (1966), and Sheldon and Moore (1968), Wilbur Cohen, Secretary of HEW, proposed in 1968, establishment of a Council of Social Advisors to analyze the quality of life in the U.S.[5] The President's Commission on Federal Statistics also accepted the challenge to improve the quality of federal statistics in the 1970's, and new developments in labor statistics, such as employment safety and working conditions, are already underway at the Bureau of Labor Statistics.[6] The U.S. Environmental Protection Agency (EPA) also made an effort to improve the tools available to decision makers who are necessarily involved in the quality of life production and delivery systems. A large-scale

---

[4] See the Report of the President's Commission on National Goals, <u>Goals for Americans</u> (Englewood Cliffs, New Jersey: Prentice Hall, 1960), and for further information see Environmental Protection Agency, <u>The Quality of Life Concept</u> (Washington, D.C.: U.S. Government Printing Office, 1973), pp. 1-10.

[5] See Raymond B. Bauer (ed.) <u>Social Indicators</u> (Cambridge: M.I.T. Press, 1966), and Eleanor Sheldon and Wilbert Moore, <u>Indicators of Social Change: Concepts and Measurements</u> (New York: Russell Sage Foundation, 1968), and Wilbur Cohn, <u>Toward a Social Report</u> (Washington, D.C.: U.S. Government Printing Office, 1969) and <u>The Quality of Life and Social Indicators</u> (New York: National Bureau of Economic Research, 1972).

[6] See W. Moore and S. Maxine, "New Development in Labor Statistics," <u>Monthly Labor Review</u> (March 1972), pp. 3-13.

symposium on the subject, "The Quality of Life Concept--A Potential New Tool for Decision Makers," was sponsored by EPA in 1972, which set another significant milestone for quality of life research and the social indicator movement.[7] Two years later, the Office of Management and Budget published Social Indicators, 1973, a book of statistics selected and organized to describe social conditions and trends in the U.S. and the first of its kind to be published by the Federal Government.[8] Studies such as this present study have been recently supported by federal funds.

Although it is generally understood that the need for quality of life or other social indicators is urgent because they are essential to assessment of many aspects of social progress and social accounting, and are useful for national goal setting, project planning, priority ranking, program manipulation, and performance evaluation, there is no consensus as to what the quality of life is all about, and how the quality of life or other social indicators should be defined, for whom, and in what manner they should be constructed. This failure to reach a consensus can be substantially attributed to the absence of a commonly accepted social welfare function or value system.

The U.S. Department of Health, Education and Welfare, in Toward A Social Report, defines social indicators as follows:

> A social indicator--may be defined to be a statistic of direct normative interest which facilitates concise, comprehensive and balanced judgments about the condition of major aspects of a society. It is in all cases a direct measure of welfare and is subject to the interpretation that, if it changes in the "right" direction, while other things remain equal, things have gotten better or people are "better off."[9]

The key concepts here are "normative interest" which implies that social indicators must be those with which the majority of our people are directly concerned; their changes can normally be properly interpreted. Perloff notes that indicators are "normally used to describe the condition of a single element, factor, or the like, which is part

---

7/ The results of the symposium were published in Environmental Protection Agency, The Quality of Life Concept (Washington, D.C.: The Government Printing Office, 1973).

8/ Daniel B. Tunstall, Social Indicators, 1973 (Washington, D.C.: Office of Management and Budget, 1974).

9/ U.S. Department of Health, Education and Welfare, Toward a Social Report (Washington, D.C.: U.S. Government Printing Office, 1969), p. 97.

8

of a complex, interrelated system." Sheldon and Freedman state that
"social indicators are time series that allow comparisons over an
extended period which permit one to grasp long-term trends as well as
unusually sharp fluctuation rates."[10] The emphasis is thus changing
from the normative interest to positive, time series observation,
and predictions.

Land states that social indicators should be the constituent parts of
some social model or theory about how society operates. Olson views
them as part of a coherent system of socioeconomic measurement which
can facilitate comprehensive and balanced judgment about the condition
of major aspects of a society. Sawhill describes social indicators
as quantitative measures of social conditions designed to guide choices
at several levels of decision making. According to Smith, their
compilation and use should be related to public goals. For these
definitions social indicators are considered as strategical variables
included in a model which enables decision makers to make efficient
and effective policies concerning social well-being.[11]

"Quality of Life" is a new name for the older terms "general welfare"
or "social well-being." The preamble to the U.S. Constitution includes
as one statement of purpose, "to promote the general welfare." The
National Environmental Policy Act mandates the Federal Government to

_____

10/ Harvey Perloff, "A Framework for Dealing with Urban Environment:
      Introductory Statement," in Harvey Perloff (ed.), The Quality
      of the Urban Environment (Washington, D.C.: Resources for the
      Future, Inc., 1969); Eleanor Sheldon and Howard Freedman, "Notes
      on Social Indicators: Promises and Potential," Policy Sciences
      1 (1970), p. 97.

11/ See Kenneth C. Land, "Social Indicators," in R. B. Smith (ed.)
      Social Science Methods (New York: The Free Press, 1970); and
      "On the Definition of Social Indicators," American Sociology
      (November 1971), pp. 322-325; M. Olson, "Social Indicators and
      Social Accounts," Socioeconomic Planning Sciences, 2 (1969),
      pp. 335-346; I. V. Sawhill, "The Role of Social Indicators and
      Social Reporting in Public Expenditure Decisions," in The Analysis
      and Evaluation of Public Expenditures: The System, papers sub-
      mitted to the Joint Economic Committee of the U.S. Congress
      (Washington, D.C.: U.S. Government Printing Office, 1969);
      and David Smith, The Geography of Social Well-Being in the U.S.
      (New York: McGraw-Hill, 1973), p. 54.

take action "...in protecting and enhancing the quality of the Nation's environment to sustain and enrich human life." Most people approach quality of life with widely preconceived definitions which vary substantially with respect to time, place, and the individual. In the study, Pattern of Human Concerns, for example, Cantril found that most U.S. people in 1959 were first concerned about their own health and a decent standard of living; concerns about children, housing, happy family, and family health surpass other categories. With respect to the concerns people had for this country, almost one-half of the respondents wanted peace. Next to that were an improved standard of living (14 percent), employment (13 percent), economic stability (12 percent), and international cooperation (12 percent). Although a similar, personal preference picture of individual concerns was revealed in West Germany in 1957, the general categories of hopes for the nation were substantially different. That country's reunification ranked as first priority (44 percent), peace and economic stability stood high (37 percent and 24 percent, respectively), and next came standards of living and employment.[12]

In contrast, the national problems in the U.S. of greatest concern in 1973 were significantly different in nature and magnitude from those in 1959. Newsweek reported that inflation (64 percent) and lack of integrity in government (43 percent) became the most urgent concerns in the country in 1973. Next on the list were crime, welfare, federal spending, taxes, pollution, overpopulation, and energy shortage--each of them had more than 10 percent of the votes.[13] A recent survey revealed that although many Germans are puzzled by the expression, "Quality of Life," the majority of them still relate it to issues such as an improved standard of living, a pleasant, secure life, a demand for environmental protection, and some satisfactory love life.[14]

There are as many quality of life definitions as there are people. The following may serve as a sample of the variety. While Perloff considers quality of life as elements or accounts of comprehensive systems of data characterized by a balance between inputs and outputs or inflows and outflows, or providing the value of the total stock of various times in a total system, Whitman developed a complex quality

---

12/  See Hadley Cantril, The Pattern of Human Concerns (New Jersey: Rutgers University Press, 1965).
13/  See "What America Thinks of Itself," Newsweek (December 10, 1973).
14/  See U.S. Department of Housing and Urban Development, International Information Series, 26 (February 5, 1974), p. 6.

of life system--an environmental evaluation system, which is said to be replicable, analytical, and comprehensive, broad enough to include all relevant types of environmental measurements and indicators as determined through an interdisciplinary perspective. Hornback and Shaw define "Quality of Life" as a function of the objective conditions appropriate to a selected population and the subjective attitude toward those conditions held by persons in that population. Dalkey and Rourke think that by "Quality of Life" is meant a person's sense of well-being, his satisfaction or dissatisfaction with life, or happiness or unhappiness. Christakis and Terleckyz approach the quality of life definition through social goals and policy formulation, and they specify and examine a multidimensional entity of many quality of life components between the desired and the actual levels.[15]/

Wingo and Liu, in a microeconomic framework, suggest that quality of life may be reflected jointly in two dimensions: (1) the income or wealth which represents command over physical resources and is trans-ferable, and (2) the psychological inputs which are personal, non-transferable, and related to the intensity of private, subjective gratifications. However, while Wingo employs a utility maximization concept, Liu employs an individual production approach in which each individual is supposed to optimize his own level of quality of life.[16]/

---

15/ Harvey Perloff, op. cit.; Ira Whitman et al., Design of an Envi-ronmental Evaluation System (Columbus, Ohio: Battelle Columbus Laboratories, June 1971); Kenneth Hornback and Robert Shaw, Jr., "Toward a Quantitative Measure of the Quality of Life" in Environmental Protection Agency, The Quality of Life Concept, op. cit., Norman Dalkey and Daniel Rourke, "The Delphi Procedure and Rating Quality of Life Factors," in Experimental Assessment of Delphi Procedures with Group Value Judgments (California: Rand Corporation, 1971); Alexander Christakis, "Limits of Systems Analysis of Economic and Social Development Planning," Existics 200 (July 1972); and Nestor Terleckyz, "Measuring Progress Towards Social Goals: Some Possibilities at National and Local Levels," Management Science (Volume 16, Number 12, August 1970).

16/ Lowdon Wingo, "The Quality of Life: Toward a Microeconomic Definition," Urban Studies (October 1973); and Ben-Chieh Liu, "Variations in the Quality of Life in the U.S. by State, 1970," Review of Social Economy (Volume XXXII, Number 2, October 1974) and "Quality of Life: Concept, Measure and Results," The Ameri-can Journal of Economics and Sociology (Volume 34, Number 1, January 1975).

The quality of life concept has become a focal point of converging social, economic, political, and environmental considerations. Serious attempts are being made to develop the concept into a useful tool for decision makers in the public and private sectors. Although the concept of quality of life can be described in various forms, depending upon one's perspective, location, and time, it is no doubt a multi-dimensional interdisciplinary subject. The overall development of the quality of life concept may be generally summarized in the following models:

1. Precise definitions of what constitutes quality of life, e.g., happiness, satisfaction, wealth, life style, etc.

2. Definition through the employment of a specific type of subjective or objective social indicator, e.g., GNP, NEW, health or welfare indicator, educational indicator, environmental, etc.

3. Indirect definition by specification of variables or factors affecting the quality of life, e.g., a group of social, economic, political, and environmental indicators represented by different types of composite indexes.

In this study, quality of life is defined as the output of a certain production function of two different but often interdependent input categories--physical inputs which are objectively measurable and transferable, and the psychological inputs which are subjectively, ordinally differentiable but usually not interpersonally comparable. The basic assumption under this approach is that every rational individual always attempts to optimize the level of his life-quality subject to his capability constants in a given time and at a given place. To partially quantify quality of life, the aggregate over time, it is necessary and feasible at the present stage to measure the changes in the physical inputs over that period of time through some commonly agreed-on indexes.

SPECIFIC MODELS OF SOCIAL INDICATORS

Social indicators have been modeled by a number of major disciplines, including economics, sociology, psychology, political science, and environmental sciences. Each discipline has its own understanding of how values and ideas should be defined and quantified. As a result, the social indicator models cover a wide spectrum. A thorough review of these models becomes an endless task. Nevertheless, an understanding

of these various value perspectives will enable us to identify the
critical concerns regarding quality of life assessment.

## Economic Models

From an economic perspective, since the ages of Copernicus and Descartes,
people's thoughts in the Western Hemisphere have been directed at a
mechanical universe which can be experienced and measured scientifically.
The 19th century economists, W. S. Jevons, Leon Walras, and Alfred
Marshall, building theories based on these concepts developed the
economic principle of the greatest good for the greatest number by
assuming that interpersonal utility is measurable.  Individuals were
considered to possess cardinal utility, and it was assumed that human
nature is more complex than any simple summation of happiness and
dissatisfaction or pleasures and pains.  Although later economists in
the ordinal utility school deserted the assumption that interpersonal
utility is comparable, they still require that a rational individual's
preferences be consistent and transitive, i.e., the more you have and
the higher you move to the right and on to another indifference curve,
the better.  Consequently, economic growth in GNP or real income per
capita has been a dominating policy goal with near universal support
for the past 4 decades.  In fact, Simon Kuznets, developer of the GNP
measure or the national income accounting system which sums the earnings
of the labor and property which are used to produce final goods and
services for a given period, won the Nobel Prize in economics.[17]

The concept of economic indicators as instruments for predicting economic
fluctuations in the short run and for controlling business cycles in the
long run was nurtured by the Depression.  Methodologically, normative
models probably have been partially replaced by the positive approach
in that concerns with social goals have been distinguished from purely
scientific predictions.  The stress of positive economics has been on
technical analysis such as econometric simultaneous equation models,
input-output studies, linear (or mathematical) programming, game theory
and operation research (or simulation).[18]  Even the recently developed

---

[17]  For his studies, see Simon Kuznets, National Product Since 1869
     (New York:  National Bureau of Economic Research, 1946); "Pro-
     duction of Capital Formation to National Product," American
     Economic Review, Volume 42 (May 1952), pp. 507-526.
[18]  Incidently, Wisely Leontief, the inventor of input-output model,
     also won a Nobel Prize in Economics a couple of years ago.

Measure of Economic Welfare (MEW) by Nordhaus and Tobin, which attempts explicitly to take into account in the GNP measure the hitherto overlooked values of goods and services not traded on the market, such as leisure, and to exclude intermediate market traded items such as defense expenditures, still leaves the knotty problems of human action and behavior largely untouched.

Economic indicators have been the traditional principal measures of overall national prosperity and social well-being. Not until recently did the risks of economic growth and the social costs associated with such growth call sufficient attention to the need for reexamination of national goal setting and policy making.[19/] There are likely to be important changes in the existing national income accounting measures that will move the national income accounting series closer to a complete welfare measure. However, it seems ill-advised to change the national product measurement of GNP to a comprehensive social welfare measure. Efforts to do so, according to Denison, can only impair the usefulness of GNP or other economic measures of both long- and short-term economic analysis they now very well serve.[20/]

## Psychological Models

In the attempt to construct social indicators, psychologists usually approach them from a personal or individual perspective. Sir Isaiah Berlin observed that there are deep differences in the way in which people approach life. One approaches a problem in an integrative manner, trying to bring everything into a single, universal organizing principle that gives unity to the manifest diversities of life; another may pursue disparate problems with little concern for how they are related and fit into a larger framework. According to Norman Bradburn, the former group may be the pure theorists, and the latter, empiricists. The split in the field of mental health between the two groups, as pointed out by Bradburn, "has resulted in theories that dangerously approach explaining everything, and thus explaining nothing, or in disparate empirical findings that do not add up to anything."[21/]

---

19/  For interested readers, the controversial issues on growth are presented in Daedalus, Journal of the American Academy of Arts and Sciences (Fall 1973).

20/  See Edward Denison, "Welfare Measurement and the GNP," in Survey of Current Business (January 1971).

21/  See Norman Bradburn, The Structure of Psychological Well-Being (Chicago: Aldine Publishing Company), preface.

In a new theory of behavior, H. J. Campbell shows that human thinking
and behaving, human personality, and the human system of value may be
marked by five different classes when we search for pleasure or happiness, i.e., classes of the subhuman behavior, of the search for multiple pleasures, of the thinkers, of the human institutions and of the
human destiny.[22/] When measuring the quality of life or social health,
it is, therefore, essential to clearly identify the classes and individuals for whom the indicators are developed. Angus Campbell and
Philip Conversee discuss quality of life from the standpoint of personal experience, i.e., aspiration, satisfaction, disappointment, and
frustration. They assume that satisfaction or frustration are ex-
periences that most people can report with reasonable validity.[23/]

Abraham Maslow approaches the perspective of individual needs and values
with five levels of "needs hierarchy." They are, in ascending order,
physiological (or survival); safety; belongingness and love; esteem;
and self-actualization. According to Maslow, there will be no more
development after one has arrived at the level of "self-actualization."
A recent theory developed by Graves, Huntley, and Bier describes the
eight-level open-ended indicators which not only explain that current
social turmoil is due to the transition process of moving from one
"need" to another, but can be applied to both individuals and organizations as well. A person's or organization's level of satisfaction
can be discovered through the use of empirical survey.[24/] In
Sources of Satisfaction, Penelope and Maynard Shelly stressed that a
realistic study of the sources of man's satisfaction cannot ignore the
changes that are taking place during this great transition, and found
that the evolution of satisfaction shows progressive changes in three
components: genetic, personal, and social.[25/] The theoretical modeling
in the psychological field, thus, covers not only static and individual
well-being, but also dynamic, societal, and institutional elements.

---

22/  H. J. Campbell, The Pleasure Areas (New York: Delacorte Press, 1973).
23/  Angus Campbell and Philip Conversee, The Human Meaning of Social
     Change (New York: Russell Sage Foundation, 1972).
24/  Abraham Maslow, Motivation and Personality (New York: Harper and
     Row, 1970); and Clare Graves, W. Huntley and Douglas Bier,
     "Personality Structure and Perceptual Readings: An Investiga-
     tion of Their Relationship to Hypothesized Levels of Human
     Existence," mimeographed paper, 1965.
25/  Penelope and Maynard Shelly, Sources of Satisfaction (Lawrence,
     Kansas: The Key Press, 1973).

Empirical studies on the subject are numerous.  Scott utilized a three-dimensional interdependent model of the self, the other, and the community to measure happiness among children, high school students, university students, and normal adults for a given point in time.[26]

In the attempt to discover from the point of view of the individual participants in social and national life just what the dimensions and qualities of this reality world were, Cantril investigated the pattern of human concerns among countries, including indicators covering a broad spectrum ranging from individual and family health, job opportunity, and safety, to government and international peace.[27]  In measuring work satisfaction, Herzberg, Mansner, and Snyderman noted the existence of two groups of factors:  satisfiers and dissatisfiers.  Both played an important role in the work satisfaction level determination.[28]  Following them, Bradburn postulates a conceptual scheme that describes psychological well-being as a function of two independent dimensions--positive and negative effects--each of which is related to well-being by an independent set of variables.  When he translated those concepts into operational measures and collected systematic data for social, economic and demographic variables included in his model, he found not only that the two types of positive and negative factors are independent of one another, but also that "the more one has, the more one gets."  To those who have attributes that go with positions higher in social structure, such as higher education and income, also go the psychic rewards of greater happiness.[29]

In summary, psychological indicators are mostly subjective in nature, and the scope of their measurement is still focused on personal or individual well-being.  The empirical work in this field can be considered a part of, but far from complete, measurement of overall social well-being.

---

26/  Edward Scott, _An Arena for Happiness_ (Springfield, Illinois: Charles C. Thomas, 1971).

27/  See Hadley Cantril, _The Patterns of Human Concerns_ (New Brunswick, New Jersey:  The Rutgers University Press, 1965).

28/  F. Herzberg, B. Mansner and B. Snyderman, _The Motivation to Work_ (New York:  Wiley, 1959).

29/  See Norman Bradburn, _op. cit._, p. 226.

## Environmental Models

In the last few generations, mankind's propensity to change the environment has accelerated. The power to use and adapt the environment has become concomitantly the power to destroy it abruptly. We have been guided by the economic dogma that the common good emerges from the competitive struggle of private interests. The public interest has been neither expressed nor clarified and agreed upon. The national wealth of human and nonhuman resources, as observed by ecologists, has been converted into final products for consumption at a time when environmental conditions may have become so degraded as to render extravagant consumption wasteful and environmental problems incurable. As a result, The National Environmental Policy Act was enacted, and the Council on Environmental Quality was authorized to promote the development of indexes and monitory systems to determine the effectiveness of programs for protecting and enhancing environmental quality to sustain and enrich human life. A large number of environmental impact statements for highway construction and resource development projects have been produced.

Instruction and model specifications in measuring environmental quality and impacts were given in the interim guidelines for implementing NEPA in April 1970, by the Council on Environmental Quality. Subsequently, the U.S. Department of Transportation and the U.S. Army Corps of Engineers also issued guidelines for the preparation of environmental impact statements which include analyses of social and economic indicators in addition to the environmental indicators of possible project impacts. Various impacts under conditions with and without the project, plus differences among alternative projects, are required to be studied prior to the construction. Wolf and others have studied these environmental impacts in detail.[30]

One of the attempts to systematically relate project actions to environmental condition changes can be found in the U.S. Geological Survey

---

[30]    See C. P. Wolf, "Social Impact Assessment:  The State of the Art,"
        (Fort Belvoir, Virginia:  Institute for Water Resources, U.S.
        Army Corps, 1974); and John Kessler, "The Federal Highway Administration," and Donald Lawyer, "The U.S. Army Corps of
        Engineers," in Robert Ditton and Thomas Goodale (eds.), Environmental Impact Analysis:  Philosophy and Methods (Madison,
        Wisconsin:  University of Wisconsin Sea Grant Publication, 1972).

Circular 645 by Leopold and others, and in the "Information System for Environmental Planning" by Lyle and von Wodtke. They employed a matrix to show the relation of a project's action activities to a listing of environmental conditions that might be affected by the action activities.[31] This simple matrix model depicts the network of interrelationship between an action and its consequent environmental effects.

The National Wildlife Federation has constructed Environmental Quality Indexes since 1969. These indexes represent efforts designed to provide the concerned citizen with a comprehensive review of published information on factors affecting environmental quality. The principal variables considered in the model are soil, air, water, living space, minerals, wildlife and timber. Furthermore, the Environmental Protection Agency has been generating a variety of air, water and solid waste, and other environmental pollution indicators in the U.S., and the Federal Department of the Environment in Canada has also developed a National Environmental Quality Index for Canada.[32] In a description of an environmental evaluation system, Whitman and his associates simplify the environment into a relatively small number of measurements and indicators that can be used to determine the project's impact upon the environment. In the model, total environmental impacts are evaluated through four levels of generality, namely, environmental categories--ecology, pollution, aesthetics, and human interest; components within each category; and parameters and measurements within each component.[33] Thomas proposes to identify and classify the problems of environmental control for an animal farm on the basis of a mathematical structure and the type of utility or disutility pertaining

[31] Luna Leopold, Danke Frank, Bruce Hanshaw and James Balsley, A Procedure for Evaluating Environmental Impact (U.S. Department of the Interior, Geological Survey Circular 645, 1971); John Lyle and Mark von Wodtke, "Information System for Environmental Planning," in Journal of the American Institute of Planners, Volume 40, Number 6 (November 1974), pp. 394-413.

[32] Thomas Kimball, "Why Environmental Quality Indices," in Environmental Protection Agency, The Quality of Life Concept (Washington, D.C.: Government Printing Office, 1973); H. Inhaber, "Environmental Quality: Outline for a National Index for Canada," Science, Volume 186, Number 4166 (29 November 1974), pp. 798-804.

[33] Ira Whitman et al., "A Description of An Environmental Evaluation System," in EPA, op. cit.

to people, such as longevity, health, safety, aesthetics, etc.[34]
Lave and Seskin employed a multiple regression model to study air
pollution impacts on human health with varying pollution indicators
among metropolitan areas, while Leontief analyzed the environmental
repercussions and the economic structure with an input-output model.[35]

Taking into consideration the mental images that men have of geographic
space, Gould tried to model and map psychological preferences onto
the geographic locations.  Sonnenfeld, in another endeavor, attempted
to measure and account for variations in man's sensitivity to the
environment among cultural groups.[36]

Environmental models, in short, represent specific interests in natural
environments.  Although they differ from economic and psychological
models in the specification of variables included, the methodology for
constructing component indicators is similar among these different
economic, psychological, and environmental models.  Just as psychological well-being cannot represent the overall national health, environmental quality cannot fully reflect our life quality either.

## Political Models

Following Easton, the subjective political orientations may be directed
toward three distinctive levels of the political system:  the government,
the regime, and the political community.[37]  Each level may be regarded
as an object of orientation for elements of the political culture.
In a system form, Patterson developed a somewhat open-ended, multi-
faceted, sensitizing, political culture model to study the components

---

34/  Harold Thomas, Jr., "The Animal Farm:  A Mathematical Model for
     the Discussion of Social Standards for Control of the Environ-
     ment," Quarterly Journal Economics (February 1963).

35/  Lester Lave and Eugene Seskin, "Air Pollution and Human Health,"
     Science, Volume 169 (August 21, 1970); Wassily Leontief, "Envi-
     ronmental Repercussions and the Economic Structure:  An Input-
     Output Approach," The Review of Economics and Statistics, Volume
     52, Number 3 (August 1970).

36/  See Peter Gould, "On Mental Maps," and Joseph Sonnenfeld "Environ-
     mental Perception and Adaptation Level in the Arctic," in David
     Lowenthal  (ed.), Environmental Perception and Behavior (Chicago:
     Chicago University, Department of Geography, 1967).

37/  See David Easton, A System Analysis of Political Life (New York,
     1965).

of state political cultures which are often considered as determinants of policy processes and outputs. In the model, he considered three elements of political culture: empirical beliefs, expressive symbols, and values for the evaluation of political efficiency, citizen duty, etc.[38]

One of the most interesting works in the political models may be the Legislative Evaluation Study conducted by the Citizens Conference on State Legislatures (CCSL). The major tasks of the study are to develop specific criteria for the evaluation of the technical capabilities of the state legislatures and to collect data and, subsequently, rank state legislatures according to the specific criteria selected in the study. The primary objectives of the study are:

* To focus the attention and concerns of members of the public and legislators on many of the significant disabilities which limit the effective performance of some state legislatures;

* To furnish diagnostic indicators of particular deficiencies in particular states, and thus to give guidance to legislative efforts toward legislative improvement;

* To provide benchmark documentation as a yardstick for measuring progress over time in improving legislative capability.[39]

Five major strategic components are included in the model to evaluate the effectiveness of state legislatures:

* Functionality--including variables related to staff and facilities, structural characteristics related to manageability, organization and procedures, to expedite the flow of work and time allocation and utilization, etc.

* Accountability--including factors affecting the comprehensibility in principle, public accessibility to the adequate information, and internal accountability, etc.

---

[38] See Samuel Patterson, "The Political Cultures of the American States," _Journal of Politics_, Volume 30, Number 1 (February 1968), pp. 187-209.

[39] The Citizens Conference on State Legislature, _State Legislatures: An Evaluation of Their Effectiveness_ (New York: Prager Publishers, 1971), p. 3.

* Information-handling capability--including activities of standing committees, interim process, fiscal review and professional staffing, etc.

* Independence--including requirements of independence of the legislative autonomy, of the executive branch and its operation, plus that of interest groups, etc.

* Representativeness--including criteria of member and constitutents identification, diversity, and effectiveness of the members, etc.

The study collected data and statistics reflecting on each of the component variables by questionnaires mailed to legislators and legislative staff members in all 50 states. The 50 states were then ranked according to their indexes of effectiveness. Detailed recommendations for each state based on its weakness and strength were finally discussed and presented.

Francis developed some centralization indexes for state legislatures based on responses from a 1963 sample of 838 state legislators representing each house in all 50 states. Legislators were asked where they thought the most significant decisions were made in their legislature. Schlesinger employed tenure potential, appointive, budgetary and veto powers to measure the governor's formal powers. Grumm selected five variables in the model of legislative professionalism:

* Compensation of legislators (1964 to 1965);

* Total length of sessions during the 1963-64 biennium;

* Expenditures for legislative services and operations during the same biennium;

* Number of bills introduced in the 1963-64 session; and

* A legal services score.

Lockard constructed a party integration index to evaluate the output of the competitiveness and cohesion in state legislatures; Ranney, basing his work on average percentage figures for popular vote won by Democratic gubernatorial candidates, for percent of seats held by Democrats in state houses and senate, and for percent of all terms of governor, house, and senate in which Democrats control, developed some political partisanship indexes.[40]

All those studies cited above have been utilized as references and basic data sources in the CCSL model. Each of them defined a specific element in the political arena and then constructed a model to quantify the outputs and performance or effectiveness of the legislative actions or activities.

For criminal justice, the National Advisory Commission on Criminal Justice Standards and Goals set up a system in which criminal justice information systems were proposed. It recommends that each state create an organizational structure to prepare a master plan for the development of an integrated network of criminal justice information systems and to provide identical and consistent data for analytical purposes. The model includes systems for policy, courts and corrections, among others. In cross-sectional models, the Advisory Commission on Intergovernmental Relations has, for many years, made regular comparisons between revenues and expenditures among states and cities, and the Urban Institute has also launched programs to measure the effectiveness of government services.[41]

For governments, two types of models are conventionally used to reach public decision: normative versus positive. The normative approach

---

[40] See Wayne Francis, Legislative Issues in the Fifty States (Chicago: Rand McNally, 1967); Joseph Schlesinger, "The Politics of the Executive," in Politics in the American States, H. Jacob and K. Vines (eds.), (Boston: Little, Brown, and Company, 1965); John Grumm, "Structural Determinants of Legislative Output," Legislatures in Developmental Perspective, A. Kronberg and L. Musolf (eds.) (Durham, North Carolina: Duke University Press, 1970); Duane Lockard, "State Party Systems and Policy Output," in Political Research and Political Theory, Oliver Garceau (ed.), (Cambridge: Harvard University Press, 1968); and Austin Ranney "Parties in State Politics," op. cit., H. Jacob and K. Vines (eds.).

[41] For example, see National Advisory Commission on Criminal Justice Standards and Goals, A National Strategy to Reduce Crime (Washington, D.C., January 1973); Advisory Commission on Intergovernmental Relation, City Financial Emergencies (Washington, D.C.: U.S. Government Printing Office, 1973); and Urban Institute and International City Management Association, Measuring the Effectiveness of Basic Municipal Sciences (Washington, D.C.: The Urban Institute, 1974).

accepts well-defined objectives for governmental undertakings, and selects specific policies and actions for achieving them. The positive approach accepts the facts of reality and attempts to provide insight into what will happen under given circumstances.

Dorfman and Jacoby constructed a positive benefit-cost model with decision variables, costs, political and technology constraints to achieve the goal of pareto optimality or to accomplish pareto admissiblity decisions--a condition under which there exists no feasible alternative that some interested parties regard as superior and none regard as inferior. This type of benefit-cost model is expected to take into account social values of benefits and costs in addition to private market values when political decisions are to be made positively. They have been widely adopted in public investment projects.[42]

Rummel constructed a multidimensional model to analyze cross-national and international patterns. With indicators representing various patterns of national attributes and types of attributes--internal and external, as well as behavior indicators between nations--Rummel attempted to correlate international relations among the nations by a wide-angle mathematical lens that filtered out all but the distinct clusters of interrelated phenomena.[43]

In short, most political models deal primarily with some special subject within the political sciences, and are centered on issues of effectiveness, efficiency, performance, and party evaluation. The overall quality of life concerns must include the political elements, but the latter by no means fully reflect the essential ingredients of the former.

## Sociological Models

The growing interest in social problems is evidently derived from responses and reactions to the materialism that has traditionally

---

[42] Robert Dorfman and Henry Jacoby, "A Public Decision Model Applied to a Local Pollution Problem," Economics of the Environment, R. and N. Dorfman (eds.) (New York: W.W. Norton and Company, 1972); and Robert Dorfman, et al., Models for Water Quality Management (Cambridge: Harvard University Press, 1972).

[43] R. J. Rummel, "Indicators of Cross National and International Patterns," The American Political Science Review, Volume 63, Number 1 (March 1969), pp. 127-147.

pervaded the Western value system and ruled the capitalist society of the United States. Marginal utility or satisfaction derived from a higher level of consumption produced by great technological improvement in the past decades has diminished substantially. Social issues such as housing segregation, income distribution, discrimination and equal rights, education, health and social justice and fairness, and welfare are mounting concerns among the majority of Americans today. The marginal disutility of these social problems rises in an accelerated rate, surpassing the rate of marginal utility changes brought about by material wealth growth.

Hamilton, Johnson, and Stafford, among others, utilized regression models to measure wage or earnings differences between sexes. By isolating factors (other than sex) to which wage differentials might be attributed, they found that discrimination against females exists, and to a significant degree the differences in earnings are attributed to sex. In the same manner, regression models, varying in the specification of functional relationships constructed by Becker, Bergmann, Marshall, Welch, and others, also showed earnings differentials due to racial discrimination.[44]

Rokeach and Parker developed a value survey model in which 18 terminal values--desired end-states of existence (e.g., a comfortable life, a sense of accomplishment, a world at peace and of beauty, social recognition, self-respect, equality, security, freedom, happiness and mature love, etc.) and 18 instrumental values--preferred modes of behavior (e.g., ambitious, broadminded, capable, cheerful, clean, courageous, forgiving, helpful, honest, independent, imaginative, logical, polite, responsible, etc.) are employed for respondents to rank these values in terms of "their importance as guiding principles in your life."

---

[44] See Mary Hamilton, "Sex and Income Inequality Among the Employed," The Annals of the American Academy of Political and Social Science (September 1973), pp. 42-52; G. E. Johnson and F. P. Stafford, "The Economics and Promotion of Women Faculty," American Economic Review, pp. 888-903; G. Becker, The Economics of Discrimination (Chicago: University of Chicago Press, 1957), and The Economics of Human Capital (New York, 1963); B. Bergmann, "The Effects on White Incomes of Discrimination in Employment," Journal of Political Economy (August 1967), pp. 352-364; H. Marshall, Jr., "Black/White Economic Participation in Large U.S. Cities," The American Journal of Economics and Sociology, Volume 31, Number 4 (October 1972), pp. 361-372; and F. Welch, "Black/White Differences in Returns to Schooling," American Economic Review (December 1973), pp. 893-907.

The value survey has illustrated significant differences among people related to many different kinds of attitudes, actions, and occupational roles.[45/]

Most sociological models, even those whose theme does not focus on individuals, have to make assumptions about man. The assumptions may be implicit--as in Parsons: expectations, need dispositions, cognitive orientation and goal direction; or explicit and specific--as postulated by Lenski, in terms of self-interest, creatures' habit, etc. The "model of man" is said to be useful if it contains simple, testable and refutable propositions in the following areas of sociological concerns:

* The establishment of behavior;

* The maintenance of behavior;

* The extinction of behavior; and

* The modification of behavior (usually a combination of the first and third).

Such a model can be used to describe large-scale processes and small group phenomena. The behavioral models of man, best known in sociology, are those by Homans, McGinnies, Simon, Skinner, and Kunkel and Nagasawa.[46/]

---

45/  See M. Rokeach and S. Parker, "Values as Social Indicators of Poverty and Race Relations in America," The Annals of the American Academy of Political and Social Science, 388 (March 1970), pp. 97-111, and The Nature of Human Values (New York: Free Press, 1973); S. J. Ball and M. Rokeach, "Value and Violence: A Test of the Subculture of Violence Thesis," American Sociological Review, Volume 38, Number 6 (December 1973), pp. 736-749.

46/  See Talcott Parsons, The Social System (Glencoe: Free Press, 1951); Gerhard Lenski, Power and Privilege: A Theory of Stratification (New York: McGraw Hill, 1966); George Homans, Social Behavior: Its Elementary Forms (New York: Harcourt, Brace, 1961), and "Contemporary Theory in Sociology," Handbook of Modern Sociology, R. E. Faris (ed.) (Chicago: Rand McNally, 1964), pp. 951-977; Elliott McGinnies, Social Behavior: A Functional Analysis (Boston: Houghton Mifflin, 1970); Herbert Simon, Models of Man (New York: Wiley, 1957); B. F. Skinner, Beyond Freedom and Dignity (New York: Knopf, 1971); and John Kunkel and Richard Nagasawa, "A Behavioral Model of Man: Propositions and Implications," American Sociological Review, Volume 38, Number 5 (October 1973), pp. 530-542.

The application of multiple instruments for measuring structural characteristics of complex organizations was recommended by Pennings in order to determine their convergent and discriminant validity with respect to the degree of centralization and formalization, i.e., a combination of the institutional approach which relies on documents and informants, and the survey approach with questionnaires and interviews.[47]

The causes and consequences of variations in community power structure have been analyzed by Hawley. Reliable objective indicators of power concentration are classified as the group of managers, officials and proprietors in the labor force. The criticism has been made that the development of social system models has been hampered by the lack of the necessary methodology which takes into account the feedback effects. To meet this objection, Liu, Anderson, and others proposed a simultaneous causal-effect equation model linking sociodemographic characteristics of the population, socioeconomic, political, psychological, and other variables to study the migration patterns and health service provision, respectively. The structural equations and reduced form equations, of this type of models taken together, provide a means of predicting the impact of governmental policies on migration and medical care.[48]

To summarize, the sociological models, although covering a variety of sociological elements ranging from individual behavior to institutional organization, still are far from being able to take into account all tangible and intangible factors affecting our quality of life. There is an urgent need for a synthesized, fundamental framework in which the quality of life factors, be they social, economic, political, or environmental, can be systematically organized and structured in such

---

47/  Johannes Pennings, "Measures of Organizational Structure:  A
        Methodological Note," American Journal of Sociology, Volume 79,
        Number 3 (November 1973), pp. 686-704.

48/  Amos Hawley, "Community Power and Urban Renewal Success," American
        Journal of Sociology (January 1963), pp. 422-431; Ben-chieh Liu,
        "Impact of Local Government on Regional Growth," Proceedings of
        American Statistical Association, Business and Economics Section
        (1973); and James Anderson, "Causal Models and Social Indicators:
        Toward the Development of Social Systems Models," American
        Sociological Review, Volume 38, Number 3 (June 1973), pp. 285-301.

a form that the interwoven relationships among those complicated quality
of life ingredients can be clearly described, presented, evaluated, and
analyzed.  As a result of this need, several quality of life models have
been gradually developed in this country as well as in the rest of the
world.

QUALITY OF LIFE MODELS

In the preceding section, various models attempting to depict scientifically the behaviors and interactions of the human being--the social,
economic, political, psychological, and environmental areas have been
briefly described in terms of the nature of model structures and variations in methodological development.  One of the basic criticisms is
that the models, in general, focus on one of the quality of life elements,
but not all of them.  The following review discusses in brief the quality
of life models in the U.S. and abroad.

Quality of Life Models in the U.S.

Conceptual models of the quality of life in the U.S., as pointed out
previously, offically started at least as early as 1933, when the report
on Recent Social Trends in the U.S. was issued.  The report of the
President's Commission on National Goals, Goals for Americans, published
in 1960, significantly advanced the state of the art in modeling the
quality of life, and Social Indicators, 1973, produced by the Office of
Management and Budget, signifies the public interest in this kind of
research.

However, the combination of a theoretical model with empirical measurements of the quality of life in this country at the state level was
first attempted by Mencken as early as 1931, but was not so well-known
until the work by Wilson, The Quality of Life in America, was published
in 1967.[49]

---

49/  See John Berendt, "The Worst American State," Lifestyle Magazine
      (New York:  Lifestyle Magazine, Inc., November 1972), pp. 6-18.
      and John Wilson, The Quality of Life in America (Kansas City:
      Midwest Research Institute, 1967), and Quality of Life in the
      U.S. - An Excursion into the New Frontier of Socioeconomic
      Indicators (Kansas City:  Midwest Research Insitute, 1970).

Substantial efforts have been invested in the theoretical development
of quality of life models.  For example, based on Maslow's classification
of needs, Mitchell, Logothetti, and Kanton defined the quality of life
levels and developed five quality of life scales.  Garn, Flax, Springer
and Taylor, in the attempt to identify and classify the social indicators,
explored the indication relationship between consumption and productions to develop their interdependent models.  Terleckyz constructed a
goal accounting system for performance measurement through the input-
output approach.  The Ruggleses proposed the use of social and economic
accounts.  Wingo expressed the quality of life by a microeconomic
definition, and Castle suggested that an integration of the quality of
life and economic affluence be reviewed and studied.[50]

While Mencken selected variables in areas of wealth, welfare, health
and security, and crime affairs to measure the well-rounded picture of
the livable states, Wilson adopted as criteria the definition established by President Eisenhower's Commission on National Goals to develop
the quality of life indexes, and assessed the life quality for each
state through nine components--status of individual, equality, democratic process, education, economic growth, technology change, agriculture,
living conditions, and health and welfare.  Indexes for each of the
components were constructed either through the simple linear aggregation
method, or more sophisticated factor analyses, and the states were then
ranked accordingly.

States are not ideal territorial units for identifying regional variations in quality of life.  Neverthless, the use of states can be

---

50/  See A. Mitchell, T. Logothetti, and R. Kanton, "An Approach to
     Measuring Quality of Life," (Menlo Park, California:  Stanford
     Research Institue, 1971); H. Garn, M. Flax, M. Springer and
     J. Taylor, "Social Indicator Models for Urban Policy - Five
     Specific Applications," (Washington, D.C.:  The Urban Institute,
     1973); N. E. Terleckyz, "A Goals Accounting System," paper pre-
     sented in the annual meeting of the American Statistical Associ-
     ation (St. Louis, 1974); R. Ruggles and H. Ruggles, "Social In-
     dicator and a Framework for Social and Economic Accounts,"
     paper presented at the Annual Meeting of the  American Statistical
     Association (St. Louis, 1974); L. Wingo, "The Quality of Life:
     Toward a Microeconomic Definition," Urban Studies, Volume 10,
     (1973), pp. 3-18; E. N. Castle, "Economics and the Quality of
     Life," American Journal of Agricultural Economics  (December
     1972), pp. 723-735.

justified on the grounds that many state programs have an important
bearing on social well-being, and at the present time data compiled by
states provide the only practicable way of examining the weakness and
strength of quality of life among states at a broad regional level.
Recently, Smith selected a wide range of different variables to represent as closely as possible the general definitions of social well-being
for the states.  Seven components related to the variables are chosen
for empirical rating purposes:  income, wealth and employment, the
environment, health, education, social disorganization, alienation and
participation, and recreation.  Except for recreation, Smith collected
data and compiled the ratings of social well-being by components for
all the 50 states.  In the meantime, Berendt also updated the study
of Mencken (Liu developed a similar model) and revised Wilson's study
with quality of life rankings computed for the 50 states and the
District of Columbia.[51]

The study by Liu differs from the others in that it started with a two-
dimensional mode, fundamental but not rigorous, reflecting the psychological and the physiological attributes of the quality of life, and
that it measured the quality of life for a particular point in time by
taking variable data from 1970, or years very close, in recognition of
the changes in the quality of life over time.  In the model, data which
were not expected to be periodically published were not employed in
order to be consistent, so that future comparisons of the changes in
the quality of life among states can be made.  In addition, Liu also
made an effort to describe and compare the empirical findings among
these studies  and concluded that although income is a necessary condition for the basic quality of life, the quality of life in the states
is not essentially associated with the level of income when the state
income is beyond that of the national level.[52]

In an endeavor to measure the quality of life changes in the state, the
Office of Planning and Programming in the State of Iowa has consistently
published An Economic and Social Report to the Governor for the past
several years.  The quality of life components included in the report
range broadly from labor and personal income to lawful behavior and

_____

[51]  See David Smith, The Geography of Social Well-Being in the U.S.
      (New York:  McGraw Hill, 1973); John Berendt, op. cit., and Ben-
      chieh Liu, Quality of Life in the U.S., 1970 (Kansas City:
      Midwest Research Institute, 1973).

[52]  See Ben-chieh Liu, "Variations in the Quality of Life in the United
      States, 1970," Review of Social Economy, Volume 32, Number 2
      (October 1974), pp. 131-147, and "Quality of Life:  Concept,
      Measure and Results," American Journal of Economics and Sociology,
      Volume 34, Number 1 (January 1975).

minority population. In the 1974 Annual Report of the Economic Policy
Council and Office of Economic Policy, the State of New Jersey, a chapter
was wholly devoted to the statistical profile of the quality of life
in New Jersey.[53] In the report, issues on income, employment, health,
education, social well-being and security, and others were discussed.

In an attempt to describe and explain differences between cities in the
quality of life, Thorndike published two remarkable works, Your City
and 144 Smaller Cities, respectively, in 1939 and 1940. The quality of
life component studies for a special region, city or a group of the
regions or cities in this country have also proliferated. Among the
recent work, Bell and Stevenson constructed the economic health index
for Ontario counties and districts, Bullard and Stith presented urban
indicators and social disparity for community conditions in Charlotte,
Flaming and Ong, Jr., prepared a social report for Milwaukee, and Lowry
analyzed the race and social economic well-being, in Mississippi, while
Flax made comparisons over urban indicators for 18 large metropolitan
areas; Lineberry, Mandel and Shoemaker defined and measured Community
Activity Indicators for Little Rock, Arkansas; Monroe, Louisiana;
Shawnee and McAlester, Oklahoma; and San Marcos and Midland, Texas;
and Coughlin measured the attainment along goal dimensions in 101
metropolitan areas.[54]

---

[53] See Office for Planning and Programming, Iowa, The Quality of Life
In Iowa: An Economic and Social Report to the Governor for 1973
(Des Moines, Iowa, 1973); Department of Treasury of New Jersey,
Seventh Annual Report (Trenton, New Jersey, 1974).

[54] See E. L. Thorndike, Your City (New York: Harcourt, Brace, and Com-
pany, 1939), and 144 Smaller Cities (New York: Harcourt, Brace,
and Company, 1940); W. H. Bell and D. W. Stevenson, "An Index of
Economic Health for Ontario Counties and Districts," Ontario
Economic Review, 2 (1964), pp. 1-7; J. L. Bullard and R. Stith,
Community Conditions in Charlotte, 1970 (Charlotte, North Carolina:
The Charolotte-Mecklenburg Community Relations Committee, 1974);
K. H. Flaming and J. N. Ong, Jr., A Social Report for Milwaukee:
Trends and Indicators (Milwaukee, Wisconsin: Milwaukee Urban Ob-
servatory, 1973); M. Lowry, "Race and Socioeconomic Well-Being:
A Geographical Analysis of the Mississippi Case," Geographical
Review, 60 (1970), pp. 511-528; M. Flax, A Study in Comparative
Urban Indicators: Conditions on 18 Large Metropolitan Areas
(Washington, D.C.: The Urban Institute, 1972); R. Lineberry,
A. Mandel and P. Shoemaker, Community Indicators: Improving
Communities Management (Austin, Texas: Lyndon B. Johnson School
of Public Affairs, The University of Texas, 1974); R. Coughlin,
"Attainment Along Goal Dimensions in 101 Metropolitan Areas,"
Journal of the American Institute of Planners, Volume 39, Number
6 (November 1973), pp. 413-425.

Resources dedicated to quantification of the quality of life among urban
areas have tended to be increasing at an accelerated rate not only because people are more and more concerned about their life quality and
the associated causes and effects, but also because the task of
measuring the quality of life in itself is challenging and interesting.
For example, Torres tried to measure the quality of life in America's
major metropolitan areas by a very narrow definition, and Marlin attempted
to rank the performance of 31 cities by a few economic variables. After
Elgin found that the quality of life in the country goes down as city
size increases, Louis launched a project to see which are the worst
cities among the largest 50.[55] Currently, the Kettering Foundation
sponsors research in identifying the factors for urban success, the
Council on Municipal Performance is conducting evaluations among cities
in their respective performance on various quality of life components,
and Stanford Research Institute is engaged in modeling the minimum
acceptable level or standard of quality of life from the viewpoints of
social, economic, political, and environmental criteria, in conjunction
with the model and results presented in this study.[56]

## Quality of Life Models in the Rest of the World

There is now immense interest throughout the world in better social
measurement, in assessing the fruits of economic growth, and in measuring
needs and the distribution of benefits. Everywhere social statistics
and the measures of quality of life have increased priority.

---

[55] See Juan Torres, "The Quality of Life in America's Major Metropolitan Areas," The Conference Board Record, Volume 11, Number 2,
(1974), pp. 51-64; John Marlin, "Jobs and Well-Being:
Which Cities Perform the Best," Business and Society Review
(Summer 1974), pp. 43-54; Duane Elgin, City Size and the Quality
of Life (Menlo Park, California: Stanford Research Institute,
1974); Arthur Louis, "The Worst American City," Harper's Magazine
(January 1975), pp. 67-71.

[56] Geoff Ball is working on the research study sponsored by the Kettering Foundation, and O. W. Markley and Maryland Bagley are
working on the Stanford Research Institute's Project, funded
by the Environmental Protection Agency; for the Council on Municipal Performance projects, see for example, The Wealth of Cities,
Municipal Performance Reports, 1.3 (April 1974).

The Statistical Office of the United Nations has launched a significant project, "Towards a System of Social and Demographic Statistics," (SSDS) and a technical report was prepared by Stone in 1973.[57] In principle, the system should cover all areas of social life which are of interest or concern, and for which it is thought necessary to have a policy and to attempt remedial action. The aim of this project is to give a systematic account of the statistical information needed for the following subjects:

* The size and growth of the world's population

* Population density and urbanization

* High-level consumption and its growth

* National resources and the environment

* Learning activities

* Earning activities

* Family grouping

* Housing conditions and neighborhoods

* Leisure

* Social mobility

* The distribution of income, consumption and accommodation

* Social security and welfare service

* Health and medical care

* Public order and safety

_____

[57] See Richard Stone, Towards A System of Social and Demographic Statistics (New York: United Nations, ST/STAT. 68, July 1973).

SSDS represents one of the most comprehensive models formalizing current needs and developments in social indicators related to the world's quality of life. It began with a simple set of input-output matrices concerned basically with population, education and manpower, but has grown into other areas of leisure, health, housing, security, and social mobility.

The Organization for Economic Cooperation and Development (OECD), which comprises the more advanced industrial nations, has also recently approved the work designed to develop a set of social indicators which can jointly measure the social indicators of well-being in the member countries. The first stage of the work has consisted of identifying and agreeing upon what are the most important and conceivably measurable components of the quality of life from the viewpoint of present and potential government interest. The next step will be, logically, to find or to design the necessary method of measurement.[58] A total of 24 fundamental social concerns common to most OECD countries are listed in the model. They are described in the following categories:

* Health

* Individual development through learning

* Employment and quality of working life

* Time and leisure

* Command over goods and services

* Physical environment

* Personal safety and the administration of justice

* Social opportunity and participation

The overall project objectives under the OECD's social indicator program are to identify the social demands, aspirations, and problems which are or will become likely major concerns of social economic planning processes, to measure and report changes relative to these concerns,

---

58/  See David E. Christian, Social Indicators, the OECD Experience
     (Paris:  OECD, June 1974).

and to better focus and enlighten public discussion and public decision making. In conjunction with the efforts of OECD, a number of models have been developed for the member countries. Work for Germany can be found, for example, in Gehrmann and Koelle; and studies for Sweden, Finland, Japan and the United Kingdom have been completed in varying form by Elmhorn, Allardt and the Economic Planning Center, Hanayama and the Economic Planning Agency, and in Social Trends, respectively.[59]

Furthermore, Maruo has also briefly compared the welfare of Japanese people to that of the people in the U.S., Sweden, Germany, England, Italy, and France. Within his welfare category, he studied levels of needs-- basic (income, safety and health), amenity (natural, living and working environment), and higher needs (educational, leisure, and community participation). While Michalos employed aggregate indicators at the

[59] See Freidhelm Gehrmann, "Vorschläge zu Forschungsstrategien in Rahmen der Quantifizierung der städtischen Lebensqualität," (Paris: OECD Sector Group on the Urban Environment, Volume 25-26, July 1974); Überblick über den Stand der Forschung auf den Gebiet: Quantifizierungsversuche der (städtischen) Lebensqualität (Mono-graph, Universität Augsburg, Augsburg, July 1974); and "The Definition of Fundamental Indicators for Employment and Services" paper presented at the second meeting of the OECD Working Group on Environmental Indicators (Paris: October 3-4, 1974); and H. H. Koelle, "Entwurf eines zielorientierten, gesamtgesellschaft-lichen Simulations Models zur Unterstützung der Ziel-, Aufgaben- und Finanzplanung," (Monograph, Zentrum Berlin für Zukunftsforschung e.v., 1974); Kerstin Elmhorm, "Life Quality and Environmental Investigation" (Monograph, the Swedish National Board of Health and Social Welfare, July 1974); Economic Planning Center, "Quality of Life, Social Goals and Measurement" (Monograph, Division of the Economic Council of Finland, 1973); Erik Allardt, "About Dimensions of Welfare: An Exploratory Analysis of A Comparative Scandinavian Survey" (Monograph, University of Helsinki, 1973); Yuzuru Hanayama, "Development and Environment in Japan," Inter-nationales Asienforum, Volume 4 (1973), pp. 406-415; and Japanese Economic Planning Agency, White Paper on National Life: The Life and Its Quality in Japan (Minister of State, Japan, 1973); and Government Statistics Service, Social Trends, Number 4 (December 1974, London).

national level to compare the quality of life between U.S. and Canada, Macy and Foster used disaggregated city indicators to evaluate that in U.S. and Canadian cities.[60]

Almost all these models employed the objective social indicators or the physical approach with which secondary data on statistics were collected, organized, computed, and analyzed. Opinion surveys on the psychological approach, seeking for firsthand information to quantify subjectively quality of life, have just recently started. Among them, the University of Michigan's survey project in measuring the quality of employment and the job satisfaction among workers is a well-known one. In addition, pollsters from Gallup International Institute in Canada, Africa, and points between, are asking people all over the world a series of questions about happiness, personal satisfaction, and hopes and concerns for the future.[61] While the Center for Social Indicators, Social Science Research Council, has periodically reported through its Social Indicators Newsletter the quality of life projects in the U.S., the Social Indicators Research, an international and interdisciplinary journal for quality of life measurement, edited by Alex Michalos in Canada, has begun publication for all theoretical and empirical work related to the conceptual development and technical measurement of the quality of life throughout the world.

While this study was undertaken, Karl Fox published his book entitled Social Indicators and Social Theory. This book not only contains by far the richest references in social indicators but also brings the state of the art of social theory up to date.[62]

---

60/ See Naoni Maruo, "Measuring Welfare of the Japanese People--including International Comparison," Internationales Asienforum, Volume 4 (1973), pp. 550-554; Alex Michalos, "Methods of Developing Social Indicators," and Bruce Macy and Robert Foster, "A Tentative Comparison of Metropolitan Quality of Life, Canada and the U.S.," papers presented at the Conference on Growth Centers and Development Policy, Halifax, Nova Scotia, Canada, April 9-10, 1975.

61/ See Stanley Seashore, "Job Satisfaction as an Indicator of the Quality of Employment," Social Indicator Research, Volume 1, Number 2 (September 1974), pp. 135-169; and Robert Quinn and Linda Shepard, The 1972-73 Quality of Employment Survey (Ann Arbor, Michigan, University Institute for Social Research, 1974); and New Ways, quarterly report by the C. F. Kettering Foundation, Fall, 1974.

62/ See Karl A. Fox, Social Indicators and Social Theory: Elements of An Operational System (New York: John Wiley and Sons, 1974).

# CHAPTER

# III

## ECONOMICS IN CONTEMPORARY SOCIETY

WELFARE ECONOMICS AND THE QUALITY OF LIFE

Economics has long been defined as a scientific study that deals with the allocation of scarce resources among alternative uses to satisfy unlimited human wants.  It is fashionable for the modern positive economist to follow Robbins' argument that ethical value judgments have no place in scientific analysis, because ethical conclusions cannot be evaluated in the same way that scientific hypotheses are tested and verified.[1]  However, it is invalid on the basis of this observation to preclude economists from studying "welfare economics" or examining the consequences of various value judgments.  Just as the study of comparative ethics is itself a science, so in welfare economics a great many analyses do not require interpersonal comparisons of utility.  Besides, the welfare function need only be ordinally defined or technically transferable among the relationships of preferences:  e.g., better, worse, or indifferent.[2]  Furthermore, the complexity of our post-industrial society requires that economists step out from the orthodox framework of pure competition, guaranteed full employment, efficient production, and accelerated growth.  Externality, social costs, depleted natural resources, polluted environments, accelerated inflation, and a number of other social problems which adversely affect our quality of life, are waiting for solutions.

Much of the traditional academic teaching and research in economics has been criticized for its lack of empirical relevance, immediate

---

1/  For instance, see L. Robbins, <u>An Essay on the Nature and Significance of Economics Science</u> (London, 1932).

2/  For an equal argument, see Paul Samuelson, <u>Foundations of Economic Analysis</u> (New York:  Harvard University Press, 1965), Chapter 8.

practical impact, and adequate scientific means to meet the practical problems.<u>3</u>/  The decisive weaknesses in neoclassical and neo-Keynesian economics lie in the assumptions which tend to destroy its relation with the real world, especially in eliding "power" by making economics a non-political subject.  Thus, according to Galbraith, the neoclassical and neo-Keynesian economics are relegating their players to the social sidelines where they either call no plays or urge the wrong ones when the problems of our world are increasing, both in number and in the depth of their social affliction.<u>4</u>/  Kenneth Arrow has also admitted that inequality of economic development among groups and regions within a country, provides complicated difficulties for neoclassical theory.<u>5</u>/ Furthermore, there are new campaigns against the reigning fashion of the traditional political economy as we search for material growth and wealth.  Many economists are beginning to tackle the issues of human values.  Growth, it is charged, distorts national priorities, worsens the distribution of income, and irreparably damages the social and natural environments in which we all live.

The conventionally used national health indicator, the Gross National Product (GNP)--by which the growth in national production of goods and services per unit of time per capita has been measured, and national strength has been evaluated  for many decades--has also been under fire recently.  Nordhaus and Tobin characterize the GNP measure as an index of production, not of consumption, and much less of economic welfare.<u>6</u>/  The national income accounts largely ignore the many sources of utility or disutility that are not associated with market operation and measured by market values.  For example, Nordhaus and Tobin indicate that defense costs are intermediate rather than final demand, while educational services and leisure and environmental amenities are direct rather than indirect sources of consumer satisfaction.  They started with inadequacies of the conventional measure of national wealth--Gross National Product (GNP)--and developed some theoretical adjustments needed to convert GNP into a measure of Net Economic Welfare (NEW).

---

<u>3</u>/  See Wassily Leontief, "Theoretical Assumptions and Nonobserved Facts," <u>American Economic Review</u> (March 1971), pp. 1-7.

<u>4</u>/  John K. Galbraith, "Power and the Useful Economist," <u>American Economic Review</u>, (March 1973), pp. 1-11.

<u>5</u>/  Kenneth Arrow, "Limited Knowledge and Economic Analysis," <u>American Economic Review</u> (March 1974), pp. 1-10.

<u>6</u>/  For example, see William Nordhaus and James Tobin, "Is Growth Obsolete," <u>Economic Growth</u>, 50th Anniversary Colloquium V (New York).

Empirically, they estimated that the NEW grew at only two-thirds the
annual rate of per capita GNP over the period of 1929 to 1965. From
purely technical viewpoints, Cole and Ruggles also have criticized
the errors in the measurement of GNP.[7]

"Quality of Life" (QOL) is a new name for an old notion. It denotes
a set of wants, the satisfaction of which makes people happy. It reflects a combination of the subjective feelings and objective status
of the "well-being" of people and the environment in which they live
at a particular point in time. Dissatisfaction either with GNP as an
accurate measure of social welfare or with the growth of GNP as a
goal for national life, has led to a demand for some social indicators
which can be used to set policy priorities, and to measure the extent
to which we are satisfied with our human and environmental conditions.
In addition to the concern about efficient production with limited
resources to meet those unlimited human wants, new welfare economics
stresses even more an equitable system of distribution among groups
and regions as well. A robust GNP provides basic needs for an undefined
yet ever increasing level of subsistence, but a healthy economy enables
more people to pursue their aspirations and happiness beyond the level
of physical satisfaction, whether acquisitive or contemplative.

The quality of life indicators or social indicators represented by a
host of statistics on socioeconomic, political and environmental conditions may offer clues to human attitudes and behavior, and societal
performance over time. The statistical compilation of those social ab-
stractions, if their limitations are properly understood, would certainly
be useful to the extent they provide meaningful measurement of the
actual results of public and private programs designated to improve our
quality of life. The social turmoil of our age is reflected in everything from rising crime and inflation rates to the search for energy
resources and for psychic tranquility through exotic religions.
Yet happiness and inner harmony have never been directly, independently
achievable ends, but rather the by-products of philosophies, goals, and
values which are simultaneously determined by others in the society.
Social indicators, when properly constructed, interpreted, and used,
can shed light on many welfare issues involving value judgments and
ordinal utility comparisons among individuals. These, in turn, may
enable intelligent decision makers to devise timely, efficient policies
leading to a betterment of the quality of life for many individuals in
the community, without worsening it for others in the same community.

---

[7]  See R. Cole, Errors in Provisional Estimates of Gross National
     Product (New York: National Bureau of Economic Research, 1969);
     and N. Ruggles and R. Ruggles, The Design of Economic Accounts
     (Ibid, 1970).

Man does not live by bread alone, and economists are not all merely concerned with the income or GNP statistics. As Alfred Marshall stated, the economist, like everyone else, must concern himself with the ultimate aims of man. The issues of poverty within affluence, of discrimination within equality, of environment preservation within economic performance, etc., are controversial, and involve value judgment. Economic analysis can contribute a great deal to the elucidation of these issues. What do economists economize? It is "love," said Sir Dennis Robertson, for that is the scarcest commodity in the universe. Then what do economists attempt to optimize? The answer is, the quality of life or happiness, for that has been expressed often as a ratio of material to desire. As a society becomes more comfortably situated, the more it can afford to indulge its distaste for a purely pecuniary motivation based on self-desire.[8/] However, as quality of life is a function of both material wealth and psychological desire as illustrated in the subsequent section, the two input factors are normally interrelated. Thus, the objective is to maximize the ratio, rather than the numerator alone.

## A PRODUCTION APPROACH TO QUALITY OF LIFE

As the nation is rapidly approaching its 200th anniversary, the majority of Americans become more and more disturbed and feel less and less content with the quality of life in the U.S.[9/] In spite of our rapid growth in per capita income and the highest level of living standard among all nations in the world, dissatisfaction among our citizens grows at an increasing rate with our social, political, and environmental problems such as urban crimes and ghetto slums, political scandals, the generation of waste and pollution, inflation and the energy crises, etc. The integration of the quality of life concept into the general framework of production theory in the conventional microeconomic analyses becomes an important and as yet unexplored subject.

---

8/  For related material, see Paul Samuelson, _Economics_ (New York: McGraw-Hill, 8th Edition, 1970), Chapter 39, and Emery Castle, "Economics and the Quality of Life," _American Journal of Agricultural Economics_ (December 1972), pp. 723-735.

9/  For instance, see "What America Thinks of Itself," _Newsweek_ (December 10, 1973), pp. 40-48.

An attempt to accomplish this task will be outlined in this chapter.
To begin with, we feel that the structure of our systems not only influence the degree to which the members in the system can maximize
their quality of life at any given point in time, but also shape the
value concept as to what life is all about and how, in general,
an individual's achievement can be revealed and ranked when compared
with those of others. Therefore, the state of the quality of life
for any individual is interdependent via the following three mechanisms:
the intrapersonal capability of the individual, the interpersonal aspects
with other individuals, and the political system or society in which
they all live as members. Any exogeneous changes in one of these
components will result in changes in others and, as a result, there
will be feedback effects, too. In other words, the so-called "arena
of happiness" consists of three basic components, namely, the self,
the other, and the societal system.[10]

Man is a "wanting" creature. The nature of human activity consists of
his persistent effort and of his failure to reach a state of complete
satisfaction. No sooner is one want satisfied than another surfaces
to take its place. As Maslow clearly stated:

> The appearance of the drive or desire, the action that it
> arouses, and the satisfaction that comes from attaining
> the goal object, all taken together, give us only an arti-
> ficial, isolated, single instance taken out of the total
> complex of the motivational unit. This appearance practi-
> cally always depends on the state of satisfaction or dis-
> satisfaction of all other motivations that the total
> organism may have, i.e., on the fact that such other pre-
> potent desires have attained states of relative satis-
> faction. Wanting anything in itself implies already
> existing satisfactions of other wants.[11]

The essence of self is animation and ambition. The movements within
the happiness-seeking arena are incessant. There is no static ground
on which a motionless, tranquil arena will be sustained as long as the

---

10/   For some empirical work on the universally sought happiness in the
      arena, see Edward Scott and M. Erick Wright, An Arena of
      Happiness (Springfield, Illinois:  Charles C. Thomas, Publisher,
      1971).
11/   Abraham Maslow, Motivation and Personality (New York:  Harper and
      Row, Second Edition, 1970), p. 24.

"self" exists and activates. Consequently, the degrees of the quality
of life which an individual produces and enjoys, vary not only among
persons and places, but also in time.

In order to optimize an individual's life quality, which encompasses
matters of discovering one's true self, i.e., his "self" development
of latent potential and self-actualization, it is necessary, according
to Maslow, that needs on two levels be met--basic needs and growth
needs. The basic needs include the physiological needs, the safety
and security needs, the belongingness and love needs, and the esteem
needs. The growth needs consist of those which psychologically develop
and actualize one's fullest potentialities and capacities in relation
to others in the community. Thus, what constitutes one's quality of
life, in both a biological and psychological sense, must be related to
the extent of meaningfulness of, and satisfaction produced by, one's
existence in an organized human society. Each member of our society
owns certain amounts and varieties of private goods, and shares the
use of some public goods and services, such as schooling, housing,
medical care, police and fire protection. Concomitant with these
basic and primary desires and needs, an individual develops secondary
needs, among which the important ones are love, esteem, dignity, belongingness, lack of fear and anxiety, and an equal opportunity for self-
actualization and for enjoying the prosperity, accomplishment and
happiness of the entire society.

In defining the quality of life, Professor Wingo aptly states:

> While the quality of life is clearly a Good in the ethical
> sense, not everyone would agree immediately that it is a
> good in the economic sense yet, that people aspire to it,
> means that it is scarce and that people are willing to
> surrender other kinds of satisfaction for it. In this
> sense the quality of life is an economic good. Even if the
> quality of life were confined to such nonreproducible
> elements of nature as an appealing landscape, it must be
> somehow rationed, and the land market affords such a
> rationing process. If such benefits cannot be captured,
> contained, and withheld from others, so that many may
> enjoy it without paying for it, as is the case with
> common property resources, it enters into the production
> and consumption decisions of firms and individuals. If
> the quality of life consists mainly of reproducible goods

whose consumption cannot be restricted to particular consumers, then it fits the definition of a public good to which community resources will be allocated. If the quality of life fits any of these alternative formal characteristics, we have reason to think of it in economic terms.[12]

In addition, the very name of economics suggests economizing or maximizing and Marshall's Principles of Economics dealt much with maxima and minima with which most economists have been occupied.[13]

Thus, the quality of life (QOL) that each individual (i) attempts to maximize may be expressed as an output function with two factor inputs as arguments--the physical (PH) and the psychological (PS)--a portion of which he owns and a portion of which he shares with other people in the community at any given point of time (t):

$$QOL_{it} = F\ (PH_{it},\ PS_{it}) \tag{1}$$

It should be noted in passing that the input factors are not completely independent. In addition, they can be employed in varying proportion in the production of QOL. The physical inputs consist of the bundles of material goods and services which satisfy most of basic needs of human beings, while the psychological inputs are mostly self-actualized and developed. It is possible that the former inputs can be used as substitutes to a certain extent for the latter inputs, such as lack of fear, anxiety feelings of being loved and respected, and awareness of beauty. Although deprivations of one's ownership of physical goods and services below the subsistence level are most serious and physiological survival and/or psychological health is a hazard, depreciations in psychological inputs could also impoverish considerably the affluent society. That both PH and PS play an important role in determining the quality of life is vividly manifested by the growing discontent of today's Americans.

---

12/ Lowdon Wingo, "The Quality of Life: Toward a Microeconomic Definition," Urban Studies, Volume 10 (1973), p. 5.

13/ See Paul A. Samuelson, "Maximum Principles in Analytical Economics," Science, Volume 173 (September 10, 1972), pp. 991-997.

In a recent survey conducted by _Newsweek_, 45 percent of the respondents
believe that the quality of their lives has been growing worse since
1963, and only 35 percent felt it has improved.[14]  An explanation for
this paradox lies in the fact that wealth is only a necessary, but not
a sufficient condition, for the production of a normal level of quality
of life.  In terms of graphical illustrations, for a stipulated level
of QOL, only a portion of the "normal" iso-quality curve is relevant for
our analysis; that is the segment which is downward sloping and convex
to the origin as shown in Diagram 1, say, aa'.  An iso-quality curve
is the locus of points which are representations of combinations of
factor inputs (PH) and (PS) such that the level of QOL produced is the
same for all combinations of the two input factors.  Along this iso-
quality curve, varying proportions of physical and psychological inputs
can be employed to yield the same level of satisfaction derived from
the realized quality of life, and a person would feel equally happy
(or unhappy).  Analogous to an iso-quant curve in production theory,
the availability of additional input from one category while holding
the amount of the other input constant, beyond a certain level, will
not enable an individual to acquire a better quality of life.  For
instance, an input of oy' of (PS), and ox' of (PH) will produce the
same level of QOL, i.e., $Q_1$, as does the combination of oy and ox or
$oy_1$ and $ox_1$ of (PS) and (PH), respectively.  However, additional input
of PH in excess of ox' units, given (PS) input of oy', will not produce
a greater level of QOL than $Q_1$; neither will any additional PS in excess
of oy with given ox of PH contribute to enhance the happiness of an individual when compared with the situation that he is at a'.[15]  There is

Diagram 1

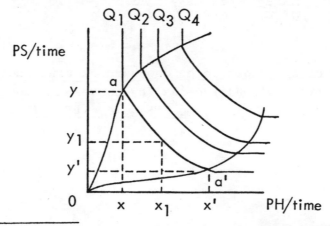

14/  See "What America Thinks of Itself," _Newsweek_  (December 10, 1973),
      p. 45.

15/  However, it is conceivable in reality that an individual may feel
      less and less happy with a substantial increase in PH input which
      induces some loss in PS input.  Typical examples are the broken
      marital relationships and suicide cases among the wealthy persons.
      For instance, see R.A. Easterlin, "Does Money Buy Happiness,"
      _The Public Interest_, 30 (Winter, 1973).

a saturation level with both the inputs beyond a or a'. Consider a higher level of satisfaction as represented by iso-quality curve $Q_2$ which lies uniformly above $Q_1$. Improvements in QOL can be achieved or produced by greater amounts of both inputs PS and PH, or by a greater amount of either input, with unchanged remaining input, or even by elimination of one input, but a sufficiently large increase in other input.

The segment aa' on iso-quality curve $Q_1$ is assumed to be twice differentiable, which implies that the curve is smooth. PH and PS are generally not grossly perfect substitutes. Convexity is assumed in the sense that the marginal rate of technical substitution between these two inputs is diminishing. The convexity property of the iso-quality curve implies that $d^2 (PS)/d (PH)^2 > 0$. The rate of technical substitution between (PH) and (PS) can be obtained by total differentiation of the QOL production function.

$$d(QOL) = \frac{\delta(QOL)}{\delta(PS)} d(PS) + \frac{\delta(QOL)}{\delta(PH)} d(PH)$$

For a given iso-quality curve, $d(QOL) = 0$, and thus (noticing that both marginal contributions are assumed to be nonnegative):

$$\frac{d(PS)}{d(PH)} = \frac{-\delta(QOL)}{\delta(PH)} \bigg/ \frac{\delta(QOL)}{\delta(PS)} < 0$$

The iso-quality curves are shown to be downward sloping and to the right. Further, these negatively sloped iso-quality curves are convex to the origin, as shown in Diagram 1, if $\frac{d^2(PS)}{d(PH)^2} = \frac{d[d(PS)/d(PH)]}{d(PH)} > 0$ or

$$\frac{d^2 \, (PS)}{d \, (PH)^2} = \frac{d}{d(PH)} \left[ \frac{-\delta(QOL)/\delta(PH)}{\delta(QOL)/\delta(PS)} \right] = \frac{d(-Z_h/Z_s)}{d(PH)} =$$

$$\frac{-1}{Z_h^3} \left[ Z_{ss} \, (Z_h)^2 - 2 \, Z_{sh} \, (Z_s) \, (Z_h) + Z_{hh} \, (Z_s)^2 \right] > 0$$

Where $Z_h = \delta(QOL)/\delta(PH)$

$Z_s = \delta(QOL)/\delta(PS)$

Normally, we expect $Z_{sh}$ to be nonnegative; therefore, $Z_{ss}$ and $Z_{hh}$ must be negative, or the rate of change of the marginal contributions of both factor inputs must be diminishing in order to assure the convexity property of the iso-quality curve. Since the rate of technical substitution (RTS) is defined as the negative of $\delta(PS)/\delta(PH)$, convexity also implies a decreasing RTS between these two factors, i.e.,

$$-\delta^2(PS)/\delta(PH)^2 < 0.$$

It is assumed that the QOL production function is homogeneous. However, the degree of homogeneity may be greater or less than one: i.e., the returns to scale may be increasing or diminishing. The case of increasing returns to scale is shown in Diagram 1 by the movement from $Q_1$ to $Q_3$. Note that $Q_2$ represents twice and $Q_3$ three times the intensity of satisfaction of $Q_1$ and the spacing between $Q_1$, $Q_2$, and $Q_3$ shrinks more than proportionately. The movement from $Q_3$ to $Q_4$, on the other hand, reveals the decreasing returns to scale portions of the QOL production function, i.e., to maintain an equal increase in happiness, more than proportional amounts of PS and PH are required. In addition, the iso-quality curves are assumed to be nonintersecting in the relevant range.

A rational individual attempts to maximize his overall QOL production, subject to certain capability constraints. Perceive a situation of no constraints of any form, or of limitless capability of a human being; each individual would move to the bliss point at which all his desires are fully satisfied. Unfortunately, that is not the case in reality. Each one has only 24 hours a day to spend in securing his PH and PS inputs for production of his QOL. Observe an individual's capability to exchange PH and PS inputs is limited by the social, economic, political conditions, and environments in which he lives.  In addition, the ability to acquire and to share with others the total PH goods and services available in a society depends strategically upon the individual's own economic wealth.  On the other hand, there are restrictions on each individual's effort to secure PS inputs.  For example, the amount of PS acquired is determined in part by one's degree of willingness to exchange resources and efforts for spiritual and psychological inputs, such as esteem, belovedness, belongingness, feeling of security, individual dignity and integrity, etc., that other people in the society are willing to render to him.  As expected, the esteem, security and dignity also depend, to some extent, on PH. Diagram 2 shows various forms of the capability constraints or iso-capability curves that an individual may possess at any particular point of time in his life span.

Diagram 2          PS/time

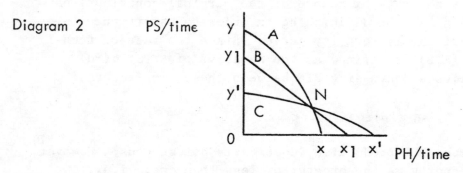

The points on the iso-capability curves indicate the maximum possible combinations of PS and PH that an individual is able to secure. Consider the case of the end points of the iso-capability curve, say for A.  Point y(x) indicates the maximum quantity of PS(PH) obtainable if the amount of PH(PS) is zero.  Similarly, for individual C, the maximum psychological intake, by foregoing all physical goods and services, he is able to secure is oy'.  The iso-capability curves for both A and C are concave to the origin, implying that the rates of capability transformation between (PS) and (PH) for these two persons are diminishing--more than proportionate PS must be sacrificed in order to secure additional PH inputs.  Consider the case of perfect substitutes between PH and PS, for individual B.  The iso-capability curve for B is a straight line, indicating that PH(PS) can be substituted for PS(PH) at a fixed ratio.  Although B's capability constraint lies between those of A and C, the three persons are capable of acquiring one common combination of PH and PS that is the intersection of the three iso-capability curves, as shown at N.  A special iso-capability curve for some special individual may even look like YNX', or $Y_1NX'$, i.e., a kinked one.

46

We stated earlier that rational individuals are usually maximizing
their quality of life production subject to their capability constraints.
Given the iso-quality map and the iso-capability curve (xy) of an
individual for any given point in time as shown in Diagram 3, the maximum level of QOL of that individual is attained when the iso-quality
curve is tangent to the iso-capability curve. To be specific, this
individual is most satisfied in his life at the level of $Q_3$ by
combining $O_a$ units of physical goods and services and $O_b$ units of
psychological inputs, given the limit of his capability by that time
is xy. Note that he is neither capable of producing $Q_4$, due to his
own capability constraint, nor would it be efficient by organizing
a combination of PS and PH other than at N, say, at M, in the sense
that he would end up with a lower iso-quality curve, $Q_1$. Thus, the
equilibrium position will be at the point where the slope of the iso-
quality and that of the iso-capability curve are identical.

Diagram 3   PS/time

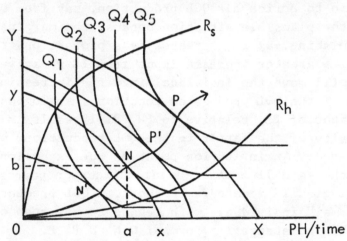

Undoubtedly, condition and environment in which an individual lives
changes from time to time. It is not unreasonable to assume that an
individual's ability and capability improve as one grows in age.
During a lifetime, although it has been observed that an individual's
iso-capability curve can switch, say from xy to x'y' or vice versa as
shown in Diagram 2, the iso-capability curve for a "normal" individual,
in general, is expected to shift onward in the east-north direction,
i.e., from xy to XY, as shown in Diagram 3. In the former case, the
individual's QOL may be improved, unchanged or worsened depending upon
the way that the iso-capability curve is being shifted. The individual
in the latter case, can be shown to be always better off than before.
Consequently, a "normal" person, experiencing outright shift of the
iso-capability curve over time would have a QOL expansion path, say
N'NP'P. The QOL expansion path is derived by connecting equilibrium
points N', N, P', P at each point of time.

The QOL expansion path generally exhibits a "staggering effect." That is, the path starting from the origin, initially may lean more toward the horizontal axis (PH) because of the greater importance in satisfying the basic needs or the Darwinian struggle for one's physical survival. Beyond a certain level of the basic needs being satisfied, the expansion path will lean more towards the vertical axis (PS). The basic needs are, in essence, the biological and physiological needs. As Maslow stated, "Frustration of basic needs creates psychopathological symptoms, and their satisfaction leads to healthy personalities."[16] A person who is lacking food, safety, love and esteem would probably hunger for food more strongly than for anything else.

The QOL expansion path may exhibit a point of inflection, say at N' at which some basic needs for survival are met and the individual begins to aspire for more inputs from the psychological arena relative to the physical domain to enrich his QOL production, say from $Q_1$ to $Q_2$ and to $Q_3$. This is the plausible situation because the marginal productivity of PH is diminishing, as PS increases less proportionately than does the PH input. A greater increase input from PS relative to that of PH beyond N' will move the individual into the increasing returns to scale portion of the QOL production function. Analogously, the greater increase in input of PS, relative to PH, will result in relatively high productivity of the latter in the QOL production, when the level of $Q_3$ is achieved. An inflection point on the expansion path is found at N. Along the same line of argument inflection points, such as P' and P, can be logically located. In short, a QOL production expansion path of a "normal" individual, with regard to his span of life time, may simply take the staggering form of O N' N P' P.

The range of the QOL expansion path is shown between $OR_s$ and $OR_h$. $OR_s$ and $OR_h$ are obtained by connecting the linked points on the iso-quality curves, or the points beyond which the curves become vertical and horizontal, respectively. The QOL expansion path, for a spiritualism-oriented person, will bend toward the $OR_s$ limit, whereas for a materialism-oriented person, the expansion path will be biased toward the $OR_h$ limit over his life horizon.

---

16/ Abraham Maslow, <u>Toward A Psychology of Being</u> (Second Edition, New York: Van Nostrand Reinhold, 1962), pp. 50-51; <u>Motivation and Personality</u> (Second Edition, New York: Harper and Row, 1970), pp. 36-37.

Consider a special case in which the second derivatives fail to exist for either the capability curve or the iso-quality curve, as shown in Diagram 4. In this case, PH and PS are perfect substitutes for each other in the production of QOL for a particular individual within the range of $R_s$ and $R_h$. The marginal rate of substitution between the two inputs is constant. Another special case involves the use of PH and PS, in fixed proportion, in producing any level of QOL, as shown in Diagram 5; the expansion path is, therefore, represented by a line radiating from the origin and passing through all the corner points of the QOL iso-quality curves. Additional inputs beyond the corner points, while holding the other input constant, will not produce a higher level of QOL for this individual.

Diagram 4

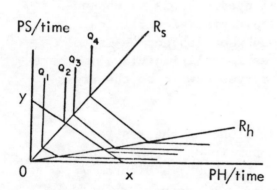

Diagram 5

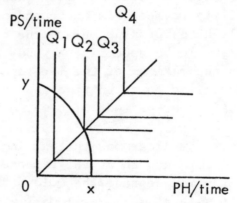

A pathology may emerge in a typical industrialized society that individuals who are capable of acquiring a substantial volume of physical inputs, experience a decrease in psychological inputs. As a result, the level of QOL they produce is declined, as indicated by the switch of the iso-quality curves from $Q_1$ to $Q_0$ in Diagram 6. Note that the expansion path $N^1N$, is downward-sloping in this case.

Diagram 6

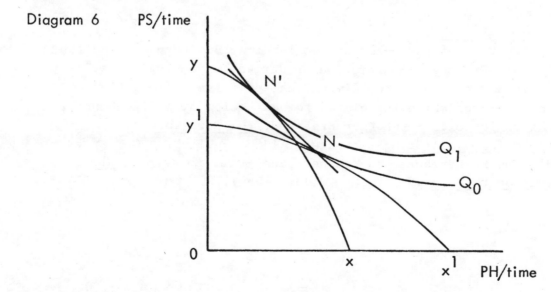

In summary, we have developed a micro quality of life production model on the assumption that rational individuals are always attempting to maximize their level of quality of life subject to their own capability constraints. As conceptualized and analyzed earlier, the quality of life is not only a function of material well-being, but also dependent on such nonmaterial or spiritual factors as psychological health, subjective feelings, etc. It has been illustrated that both physical and psychological inputs can, to a certain extent, substitute for each other and vary in proportion to produce a given level of QOL.[17] The assumptions employed under the normal situation are that the marginal technical rate of substitution is diminishing and that the marginal contribution of factor input is positive, but diminishing, given other things being equal. Thus, an increase in both inputs should yield a higher level of QOL. A "good" social system which enhances its member's capability to meet his basic and psychological needs is one which constantly helps pushing onward the capability constraints for all its members. To be specific, a good society is one whose objective is to ensure the maximum of the iso-capability curves for all individual members for any given point in time and to shift the curves upward to the right-hand side over periods of time.

It should be clear now that an increase in GNP alone or sheer stress on economic growth at the expense of some factor input in the psychological side may degrade the QOL in the country. As shown in Diagram 7, the shift in the iso-capability curve from xy to x'y' means a relatively smaller sacrifice in PS input but a considerable increase in the PH input. However, the overall QOL for the nation is adversely affected, and the level of social well-being is lessened from $Q_1$ to $Q_0$ (from equilibrium point N to N'). Unless the sacrifice is compensated for by a very substantial gain in PH input, say, from ox to OX, people will then feel indifferent and stay on the same iso-quality curve, $Q_1$.

---

17/  In the structure of psychological well-being, Bradburn assumed that following Herzberg, Mansner, and Snyderman, psychological well-being is a function of two dimensions--positive and negative effect, each of which is related to well-being by an independent set of variables. See Norman Bradburn, The Structure of Psychological Well-Being (Chicago: Aldine Publishing Company, 1969), and F. Herzberg, B. Mausner, and B. B. Snyderman, The Motivation to Work (New York: Wiley, 1959).

With the equilibrium point moved from N to P, the gain in economic well-being by an amount of xX, for an example, is just enough to cover the costs of the resulting environmental damage of, say, yY.[18]

This study outlines a framework to quantify the quality of life in U.S. metropolitan areas by measuring the QOL inputs, especially the PH inputs for which most data are available. Data on PS inputs are either not measurable or not existent for all SMSA's. As a proxy for quality inputs, indexes on some environmental input factors, nevertheless, were compiled in this study. Ultimately, it is hoped that future development in this type of analyses will enable us not only to measure and evaluate the shifts in the capability curves, but also to identify and predict the expansion path of the QOL over periods of time under different national goals and policies.

Diagram 7

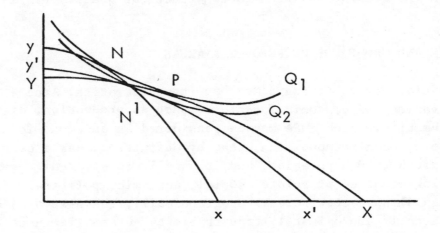

While many people would prefer the term "consumption" to "production" for the quality of life model under discussion, the latter term was chosen for two reasons; first, because of its collective characteristics in combining the three segments--individuals, the community, and the organizational institutes; and second, because people can only consume what they have already produced.

---

18/ It has been pointed out often enough that environmental pollution represents a long unpaid debt to nature. It is reasonable to attribute partially the economic growth in the U.S. since 1946, to the enlargement of that intangible debt. For this argument, see Barry Commoner, "The Environmental Costs of Economic Growth," in Robert and Nancy Dorfman (eds.), Economics of the Environment (New York: W.W. Norton and Company, 1972).

# CHAPTER

# IV

## MEASURING THE
## QUALITY OF LIFE IN
## METROPOLITAN AREAS

The purpose of this study is to develop measures or indicators of the quality of life in metropolitan areas. Basic concepts and theoretical issues have been discussed in the previous chapters. This chapter describes the methodology used to construct our quality of life indicators.

SELECTION AND GROUPS OF METROPOLITAN AREAS

Like a nation, every Standard Metropolitan Statistical Area (SMSA) performs a variety of economic functions, such as production, distribution, and consumption. Each SMSA may be considered as an economic entity. Furthermore, each metropolitan area, by definition, has a central city of at least 50,000 population, and it usually consists of several neighboring counties of related social, economic, political, and environmental characteristics. Geographically, the size of a metropolitan area is approximately traversable by automobile in much less than a day, i.e., a so-called "commuting distance." From the social science point of view, an SMSA is an urban area, and most of the people can complete their social life daily within the metropolitan area. In addition, all the SMSA's today account for about seven-tenths of the total United States population. However, social and economic conditions vary considerably among SMSA's within the country. Understanding how and why the quality of life differs among SMSA's seems to be one of the most important problems in our concerns with society and with urban pathology. That is to say, one of the substantive tasks in this quality of life study is to analyze theoretically and test empirically those variables which significantly determine the variations in the quality of life among regions.

There were 243 SMSA's in this country in 1970, according to the U.S. Department of Commerce definition. Although the number of SMSA's has increased since 1970, and more counties have been added to the definitions of some SMSA's, this study uses the 1970 definition in order to be consistent with other economic, political, and social data from the 1970 Population Census. These 243 SMSA's had 139.4 million residents or 68.6 percent of the total U.S. population in 1970. Their populations range from 56,000 in Meriden, Connecticut, to 11,529,000 in New York City, New York. From the analytical point of view, it seems to be desirable to compare the quality of life between SMSA's with comparable population sizes. Thus, in this study the 243 SMSA's are divided into three groups according to population: large, medium, and small. SMSA's with populations greater than 500,000 are in the first group; the small group includes all SMSA's with population less than 200,000; and the medium group has populations between 200,000 and 500,000. Although the total population within the three groups is overwhelmingly high for the large SMSA's, the numbers of SMSA's in each group are fairly even. There are 65 large SMSA's with a total population of 102.6 million; about 24.9 million and 11.9 million people live in the 83 medium and 95 small SMSA's, respectively. These three groups are referred to as Groups L, M, and S throughout this study.

THE QUALITY OF LIFE FACTORS AND DATA SOURCES

The physical inputs of the overall quality of life consist of five principal goal areas or QOL components. They are defined in broad terms, and cover most major concerns of all individuals:

1. Economic Component;

2. Political Component;

3. Environmental Component;

4. Health and Education Component; and

5. Social Component.

These concerns have been chosen with a view to developing as broad and common as possible a concept of well-being. Psychological inputs are not included because they are not amenable to quantification. The five goal areas encompass command over private goods and services being produced and consumed, and--in addition--the public counterparts not provided at "market prices" or consumed on an individual basis. The physical input factors selected in this study tend to possess the following characteristics:

*   They should be sufficiently universal so that the fundamental prin-
    ciples would generally be agreed upon by, and apply to, the majority
    of people in the metropolitan areas today; they should be of great
    present and potential interest to all levels of government as
    essential elements of well-being.

*   They should be commonly understood and have policy bearings which
    can be realistically and efficiently implemented.

*   They should be flexible enough to account for any lifestyle input
    variations over space and time, and easily adaptable to changes in
    social, economic, political, and environmental conditions in a
    dynamic society.

*   They should be open to verification according to recognized scientific
    approaches, and updative with new data so that intertemporal com-
    parisons can be made over time.

The number of variables selected under the five goal areas total more
than 120. Insofar as possible, they are formulated in a way as to
show both the concerns of the individual and the well-being of the
community. The interdependent relationship among variables is also
recognized; the same variable may appear simultaneously in two different
goal areas, and yet the independent objective among the five principal
goals is fundamentally unaffected.

The variables selected for the study in their respective order of sequence
are discussed below. As shown in Panel 1, page 57, the sign on the left
of each variable indicates the effect of the variable on the quality of
life--the positive or negative contribution to the input measurement.

Economic Component

The economic inputs to the quality of life are divided into two categories: individual economic well-being and community economic health.
Personal income and wealth status are considered to be the most sensitive
indicators of economic well-being of individuals. Personal income represents the flow variable; the wealth reflects the stock. On an individual
basis, a metropolitan area with a higher stock of wealth and a larger
flow of incomes tends to be healthier than those with lower wealth and
smaller incomes, ceteris paribus.

The wealth status of an individual can generally be measured by his
fixed assets, properties, and changes in income.  In this study, the
median value of owner-occupied single family housing, the percentage
of owner-occupied housing units, and the percent of households with
one or more automobiles are used to reflect wealth status.  Savings
per capita are employed to represent the variable assets and the ratio
of total property income to total personal income as an index of
property as cumulation and production.  They all are positive inputs
to the wealth category, and hence, become positive inputs to the
quality of life.

There are seven factor inputs to a community's economic health; these,
coupled with an individual's economic well-being, constitute the
economic component.  Affluency, employment, labor productivity, industrial diversification, availability of capital and the community's
economic development efforts are all essential inputs to strengthen
a community's economic health.  In addition, a more and more even distribution of economic resources among people is gradually expected for
a healthy economy.  For this, the inequality index between central city
and suburban income is also selected to measure the economic health of a
community.  Income inequality and unemployment rates are the negative
input factors, while the remaining five are positive attributes to the
metropolitan economy.

The inequality between central city and suburban income distribution
is one of two factors used in determining the income inequality index.
Urban blight has become one of the critical metropolitan issues.  The
distribution of population and income between the central city and the rest
of the SMSA is examined in a review of this factor, whereas the other
factor centers on the percentage of persons with either high or low
incomes within the SMSA as a whole.  The distribution of total income
between the persons in the central city and suburban part of the SMSA
identifies the inequalities which may exist.  The equation used in
calculating this factor is a reduced version of the Gini coefficient,
or is:

$$\left| 2(P_{cp} - P_{cy}) \right|$$

where $P_{cp}$ is the percentage of population living in the central city and
$P_{cy}$ is the percentage of total income that is distributed in the central
city.  The ideal situation would be a perfect equality, or for both of
these percentages to be equal; hence, the greater the deviation from
zero, the less favorable the distribution.

The degree of economic concentration is expressed by the percentage of persons employed in the manufacturing and services industries in the SMSA's as compared to the corresponding figures for the U.S. as a whole. "Services" is defined by the U.S. Department of Commerce as business, repair, and personal services. The equation used in calculating this factor is as follows:

$$\left| \sqrt{\frac{e_m \cdot e_s}{E_m \cdot E_s}} - 1 \right|$$

with $e_m$ and $e_s$ defined as the percent of total employed in manufacturing and services in the SMSA and $E_m$ and $E_s$ the corresponding totals for the U.S. Since a diversified regional economy is less vulnerable than a highly concentrated one when the national economy changes its structure or suffers from any unavoidable or uncontrollable conditions, the variable should be viewed like the inequality variable: i.e., the greater the deviation from zero, the less favorable the structure.

In summary, the economic component of the metropolitan quality of life is represented by 18 individual and community inputs ranging from income and wealth to economic concentration and income distribution. (See Panel 1). All selected variables are deemed as physical inputs that produce a certain level of quality of life under study regardless of their conventionally conceived input or output characteristics. In other words, they may jointly reflect a capability or command over goods and services of the metropolitan population that might have been differentiated otherwise. Moreover, all variables, be they individual or community concerns, depict not only the most essential fields of economic component in this country, but also the most critical area of today's political and welfare economy among metropolitan regions.

Statistics for those variables shown in Panel 1 are mainly collected from the Census of Population, 1970, (COP), County and City Data Book, 1972 (C and C), U.S. Statistical Abstract, 1972 (SA) Census of Government, 1967 (COG), etc. The Appendix contains raw data and data sources for all variables employed in this study.

## Panel 1. FACTORS IN ECONOMIC COMPONENT

| Factor Effect and Weight | Factors |
|---|---|

I. Individual Economic Well-Being

+ (.25)  A. Personal income per capita ($)

 B. Wealth

+ (.05)  1. Savings per capita ($)
+ (.05)  2. Ratio of total property income to total personal income
+ (.05)  3. Percent of owner-occupied housing units
+ (.05)  4. Percent of households with one or more automobiles
+ (.05)  5. Median value, owner-occupied, single family housing units ($1,000)

II. Community Economic Health

+ (.07)  A. Percent of families with income above poverty level

- (.07)  B. Degree of economic concentration, absolute value

 C. Productivity

+ (.014)  1. Value added per worker in manufacturing ($1,000)
+ (.014)  2. Value of construction per worker ($1,000)
+ (.014)  3. Sales per employee in retail trade ($1,000)
+ (.014)  4. Sales per employee in wholesale trade ($1,000)
+ (.014)  5. Sales per employee in selected services ($1,000)

+ (.07)  D. Total bank deposits per capita ($)

 E. Income inequality index

- (.035)  1. Central city and suburban income distribution
- (.035)  2. Percent of families with incomes below poverty level or greater than $15,000

- (.07)  F. Unemployment rate

+ (.07)  G. Number of full-time Chamber of Commerce employees per 100,000 population

The following two variables have special definitions and connotations:

The savings per capita variable includes only deposits in savings and loan associations, and excludes savings accounts in banks or other institutions. The amounts shown for the SMSA's are the totals for all savings and loan associations headquartered in that area, including their branches located elsewhere.

The number of full-time employees of the Chamber of Commerce was obtained by means of a questionnaire sent by MRI to the Chamber located in the central city of the SMSA. (The questionnaire form is contained in the Appendix.) Therefore, the information presented is only for the central city and is used as an approximation to the entire SMSA. Estimates were made for the Chambers that either did not return the questionnaire or did not fully complete it. Estimates for the large SMSA's were based on SMSA's of comparable population size. For the medium and small sized SMSA's, the minimum value of the SMSA's available in each group was used as a basis for estimation. As shown in the Appendix, all estimated figures are marked with a dot behind them.

## Political Component

While variables in the economic component are designed to measure either the command over goods and services or the capability to satisfy the basic needs for a decent standard of living of all the population within each metropolitan area, the political component is intended to describe the institutional factors and the functional operations of the democratic system which organize all individuals in a community to achieve some common goals and public objectives. The goals and objectives are determined collectively, and their products are characterized by the nature of nonmarketability, indivisibility, and relevant externalities.

Within the political arena, two types of factors are considered as vital inputs to the metropolitan quality of life. One is the professionalism and performance of the local governments and the other is individual activities. The most important input of any individual is undoubtedly his own active participation in political events. The ratio of presidential votes cast to voting age population is selected as the variable with available data that best represents individual participation. Individuals have to be well informed so that they can be well prepared and equipped for action or participation. Newspapers and radio and television broadcasts are most efficient communication media for the public in general and for governments in particular. Thus, they are selected to represent the informed citizenry and should have direct, positive effects upon the political quality of life of individuals.

The collective policies have to be implemented, and the public goods and services have to be provided for metropolitan residents by the governments. The quality of governments may be judged from the professionalism and number of employees, while efficiency or accomplishment may be reflected by the level of output or performance. The qualification and number of teachers, policemen, and firemen employed are by far the most conventional indicators of professionalism in state and local government. Eight variables are chosen for this category. Crime prevention is the most tangible and sensitive criterion when local governments are evaluated. The existence of high violent crime and property crime rates are indicators of poor government performance and detrimental to our quality of life. The willingness to finance production and to maintain the quality of these public goods and services is directly illustrated by the local government revenue per capita. The local governments are described as more efficient if they can secure more funds from the Federal Government.

In addition to the crime rate, community health and educational results are also good indicators of government performance, and constitute significant inputs to the quality of life. Therefore, although these two community indexes are computed under the health and education component, they also appear under the political component. This is one of the cases in which the interdependent relationship among variables manifests itself.

Public welfare payments and welfare assistance from the state and local governments are considered another important role of the political mechanism. With the Federal Government's emphasis on equal opportunity, the welfare assistance helps to assure a minimal level of living standard for all who are incapable or needy. As a result, the welfare variables are included to measure the degree to which the public provisions for the basic needs are generally extended.

The 21 variables shown in Panel 2 are by no means complete, and are not intended to be. However, they reflect the overall concerns of our political quality of life, and the yardsticks for them can be established. Consequently, related policies leading toward improvement can be designed and recommended. Except for the crime variables, they all are positive input factors in the model of quality of life production.

## Panel 2.  FACTORS IN POLITICAL COMPONENT

Factor Effect
and Weight                                          Factors

    I.  Individual Activites

        A.  Informed citizenry

+ (.083)        1.  Local Sunday newspaper circulation per 1,000 population

+ (.083)        2.  Percent of occupied housing units with TV available

+ (.083)        3.  Local radio stations per 1,000 population

+ (.25)      B.  Political activity participation-ratio of Presidential vote cast to voting age population

    II.  Local Government Factors

        A.  Professionalism

+ (.02)      1.  Average monthly earnings of full-time teachers ($)
+ (.02)      2.  Average monthly earnings of other full-time employees ($)
+ (.02)      3.  Entrance salary of patrolmen ($)
+ (.02)      4.  Entrance salary of firemen ($)
+ (.02)      5.  Total municipal employment per 1,000 population
+ (.02)      6.  Police protection employment per 1,000 population
+ (.02)      7.  Fire protection employment per 1,000 population
+ (.02)      8.  Insured unemployment rates under state, federal, and ex-servicemen's programs

        B.  Performance

− (.03)      1.  Violent crime rate per 100,000 population
− (.03)      2.  Property crime rate per 100,000 population
+ (.03)      3.  Local government revenue per capita
+ (.03)      4.  Percent of revenue from Federal Government
+ (.03)      5.  Community health index
+ (.03)      6.  Community education index

        C.  Welfare assistance

+ (.053)     1.  Per capita local government expenditures on public welfare ($)
+ (.053)     2.  Average monthly retiree benefits ($)
+ (.053)     3.  Average monthly payments to families with dependent children ($)

All data sources are detailed in the Appendix. Because of the paucity of comparable statistics for all metropolitan areas, however, many variables under this political component are substituted by close approximations. They are explained as follows.

Local Sunday newspaper circulation per 1,000 population measures the Sunday circulation of newspapers based in the central city of the SMSA. However, this figure may include areas outside the central city, and in some cases outside the SMSA itself. Local radio stations per 1,000 population include only the radio stations located in the central city of the SMSA. It therefore excludes stations which may be located either in the suburbs of the central city or perhaps in other SMSA's.

The 1973 Statistical Abstract contains the number of votes cast in the 1972 Presidential election for SMSA's with a population of more than 200,000. Information for the 1968 Presidential election was available for the smaller sized SMSA's in the County and City Data Book, 1972. The minimum voting age used to compute the ratio of Presidential vote to voting age population was 21 in all states except Georgia (18 years), Kentucky (18 years), Alaska (19 years), and Hawaii (20 years) for the 1968 election. In 1971, the voting age was lowered to 18 years in all states with the adoption of the 26th Amendment. Since voter registrations are kept by county, data for Standard Economic Areas (SEA) were substituted for the SMSA's in New England. In a few cases state data were also used for SMSA's.

The average monthly earnings of full-time teachers and other full-time employees were obtained from the Census of Government, Volume 5. However, where data were not available for an SMSA, state average data were used. The entrance salaries of patrolmen and firemen refer to that earned during the first 12 months on duty. The data shown are for the central city of the SMSA. The median entrance salary of all central cities was used if information was not available for the central city of the SMSA.

Since there are no comparable data on municipal employees for an entire metropolitan area, the total number of full-time municipal employees per 1,000 population in the central city of the SMSA is used as a substitute. The police and fire protection factors include full-time uniformed forces, administration, and clerical personnel.

The Manpower Report of the President contains unemployment data for
150 major labor areas as well as for states. The insured unemployment
rates under state, federal, and ex-servicemen's programs show the insured unemployment as a percent of the average covered employment for
the areas. State data were substituted if data for the major labor
area were not available for a particular SMSA. Because data for the
smaller sized SMSA's were very limited, this variable was omitted
from the study for the small SMSA's.

Violent crime is defined as offenses of murder, forcible rape, robbery,
and aggravated assault; property crime is offenses of burglary, larceny
of $50 and over, and auto theft. The FBI Uniform Crime Rates for the
United States contains these crime rates for SMSA's. County data were
gathered in place of these rates in the New England states, so SEA's are
shown instead of SMSA's. In other instances, state data were the only
available source of information.

Percent of revenue from Federal Government and local government revenue
per capita were taken from local government data as found in the
Census of Government. State data were used if SMSA data were not
available. Public assistance payments, recorded by county, were
aggregated to obtain SMSA figures. Information for the New England
SMSA's is actually SEA data. The state average was again substituted
if no county data were available.

Environmental Component

We are told frequently that human values and institutions have set
mankind on a collision course with the laws of nature. It is not yet
clear precisely when and in what form the collision between economic
growth, which can satisfy many human wants, and natural limits will
occur, but the recent energy shortage vividly signals the onrush
of crises and environmental problems. The environment is the unique
skin of soil, water, gaseous atmosphere, mineral nutrients, and
organisms which, powered by the energy of the sun, make Earth hospitable
to human life. We have long learned to modify and to exploit the environment to our advantage in numerous ways, yet we still cannot claim
either full understanding or control of the environmental systems that
support our growing population. Not until fairly recently did environmental protection and natural resource conservation become focal points
of public interest and national concern in this country.

The environmental component in this study ideally should take into
account factors other than pollution, climate, and recreational facilities

such as natural endowments and conservation, resource availability
and accessibility, etc. However, the scarcity of comparable data
for SMSA's prevents those representative variables from being selected
and included. Thus, the environmental variables affecting the metropolitan quality of life encompass only the air, visual, noise, solid
waste and water pollution, climatological and recreational factors.
All types of pollution are grouped under the individual and institutional environment because they are different by-products of various
human activities. Evidence suggests that the direct effects of
pollution on property, on human health, and on the quality of life are
varied. Their direct damages, however, may ultimately prove to be
even less critical for society as a whole than the latent effects of
pollution on the ecological systems that sustain human life.[1]

The natural environment component includes five climatological variables
and two recreational variables: sunshine days, inversion frequency,
thunderstorms, high and low temperatures, areas of parks and recreational areas, and miles of trails. Parks and recreational areas have
come to play an ever-increasing, important role in our city life.
As a result, this variable is used twice in the environmental component,
serving as a determinant of visual pollution and a factor of natural
environment as well (see Panel 3).

All variables, except the parks and recreational areas, miles of trails,
and sunshine days, in this section have adverse effects on our environmental
quality, and are negative inputs to our daily life. Thus 17 variables
shown in Panel 3 depict mostly our urban environmental "bads" rather
than "goods." They are chosen for the following reasons: making us
alert to our environmental problems, comparing the cleanliness of our
environment, and judging the efforts made to reduce and eliminate
the pollutants.

The air pollution index is comprised of two factors--total suspended
particulate levels and sulfur dioxide levels. The information provided
for total suspended particulates is the 1972 geometric mean level.

---

[1] For detailed discussion, see P. R. Ehrlich, A. H. Ehrlich, and
J. P. Holdren, Human Ecology (San Francisco: W. H. Feeman and
Company, 1973); Larry B. Barrett and Thomas E. Waddell, Cost of
Air Pollution Damage: A Status Report (Research Triangle Park,
North Carolina: National Environmental Research Center, 1973), and
Thomas E. Waddell, The Economic Damages of Air Pollution
(Washington, D.C.: EPA Washington Environmental Research Center,
May 1974).

Panel 3.   FACTORS IN ENVIRONMENTAL COMPONENT

Factor Effect
and Weight                              Factors

    I.   Individual and Institutional Environment

        A.  Air pollution index

-  (.05)          1.  Mean level for total suspended particulates ($\mu g/m^3$)
-  (.05)          2.  Mean level for sulfur dioxide ($\mu g/m^3$)

        B.  Visual pollution

-  (.033)         1.  Mean annual inversion frequency
-  (.033)         2.  Percent of housing units dilapidated
+  (.033)         3.  Acres of parks and recreational areas per
                      1,000 population

        C.  Noise

-  (.033)         1.  Population density in the central city of the
                      SMSA, persons per square mile
-  (.033)         2.  Motor vehicle registrations per 1,000 population
-  (.033)         3.  Motorcycle registrations per 1,000 population

-  (.10)      D.  Tons of solid waste generated by manufacturing per
                  million dollars value added

-  (.10)      E.  Water pollution index

   II.  Natural Environment

        A.  Climatological data

-  (.05)          1.  Mean annual inversion frequency
+  (.05)          2.  Possible annual sunshine days
-  (.05)          3.  Number of days with thunderstorms occurring
-  (.05)          4.  Number of days with temperature of 90° and above
-  (.05)          5.  Number of days with temperature of 32° and below

        B.  Recreation areas and facilities

+  (.125)         1.  Acres of parks and recreational areas per
                      1,000 population
+  (.125)         2.  Miles of trails per 100,000 population

The 1972 arithmetic mean level is shown for sulfur dioxide in the larger sized SMSA's, but due to data deficiencies the maximum observation is shown for the medium sized SMSA's. Estimates were made for some of the SMSA's where no Federal Air Monitoring Site was located, and hence no pollution concentrations were recorded. The air pollution information relates only to the central city of the SMSA, and where the data were not available, estimates were based on the central city of a neighboring SMSA. Information for the smaller sized SMSA's was extremely limited and therefore, omitted from the study for small SMSA's.

The frequency of low-level inversion (stable air) is an important factor of visual pollution. The data were obtained from the Air Quality and Emissions Trends Annual Report which includes a map showing the percent of total hours with inversions based 150 meters or less above the ground for the U.S. The map reflects the influences of mountains, lakes, and oceans on this factor.

Motor vehicle and motorcycle registrations are recorded by the Department of Transportation by county. Registration data for cities and towns were not available, so the data for SMSA's in the New England states are again SEA data. Where neither SMSA nor SEA data were available, estimates were made based on the average of the SMSA's in the state, census division, or census region, depending on the availability of data.

Solid waste generated in the manufacturing industry was obtained by multiplying a factor of 7.6 tons by the total number of employees in the manufacturing industry in the SMSA in the year 1970.[2/] This figure was then divided by the value added by manufacturing (in million dollars). For SMSA's where value added information was either not available or was withheld to avoid disclosure, the state average figures were substituted.

A water pollution index based on the prevalence, duration, and intensity of pollution has been developed for all SMSA's by the Mitre Corporation, and is called the PDI index. A lower PDI rank indicates a worse pollution problem. The figures shown for the water pollution index are the PDI rank for all Basic Data Units (BDU's) in the U.S. divided by the corresponding SMSA value. This was done so that the lower values reflect less of a water pollution problem. State values were substituted where SMSA values were not available.

---

2/  This is the waste multiplier used in J. L. Berry et al., Land Use, Urban Form and Environmental Quality (The University of Chicago, Department of Geography Research Paper, Number 155, 1974), p. 268.

The U.S. Department of Commerce presents climatological data for cities in an annual publication called Local Climatological Data. The figures for possible annual sunshine days represent the number of hours of sunshine as a percent of the number of hours between sunrise and sunset for each day of the year. The number of days with thunderstorms occurring and the maximum number of days with high (90° and above) or low (32° and below) temperatures are statistics for the weather stations. Data were not available for all of the central cities of the SMSA's, so observations for nearby stations having approximately the same climatic conditions were substituted in some cases.

The statistics for all parks and recreational areas, trails, etc., in this study were obtained from the 1972 Public Outdoor Recreation Areas and Facilities Inventory Survey conducted by the Bureau of Outdoor Recreation. Statistics are available at the county level, and the county data were aggregated to obtain SMSA information. Estimates based on the state totals were used for the SMSA's where no information was available.

## Health and Education Component

The quality of health and education is another principal concern. Three major health considerations have been identified as dominating factors, i.e., long life, life free of disability, and medical care availability and accessibility. Long life reflects the human desire to live out a natural life span, which means a low death probability at every age in the life cycle. It is conventionally measured by life expectancy at birth, or the average life expectancy. However, life expectancy at birth depends substantially on the infant mortality rate, and subsequently on the average death rate. For this reason, the infant mortality rate and the death rate are employed in the study to measure individual health condition.

While no specific variable was chosen for life free of disability, due to data deficiencies, the availability of and accessibility to medical care are employed to reflect the conditions of community health protection. Disability can be partly prevented if quality medical care services are provided when needed. The number of physicians and dentists per 100,000 population represent the availability of medical manpower, and the number of hospital beds indicates the facilities. The accessibility of medical care can probably be reflected by per capita local government expenditures on health. Although the hospital occupancy rate is undoubtedly an indicator of efficiency and utilization, it may possibly reflect accessibility--hospital occupancy rate can be higher in one area than another only if patients in the area have better access to the hospitals than those in the other, given that the demographic characteristics, health conditions, number of hospital beds, and everything else are the same in both areas.

The achievement of a basic level of education among residents and the opportunity for higher, better, and continuing education in a community are the primary concerns of today's intellectual health. Attaining a basic level of education implies that all persons, especially youth, have developed or been equipped with those essential skills required to participate and contribute in society independently, and to pursue their own interests and self-satisfaction intelligently. The existing opportunities and the willingness to invest in formal education or vocational training, whether for better employment opportunities, individual dignity and independence, or other general interest pursuits, are important community conditions for a healthy educational climate. Furthermore, personal relationships in a community are likely to be more harmonious and better communicated if educational backgrounds and the intellectual drives within the community are relatively homogeneous.

For individual educational attainment, the median school years completed by persons 25 years old and over, and the percentage among them with 4 years of high school or more, are selected as positive indicators. The percent of males between 16 and 21 years of age who are not high school graduates is considered as a negative indicator affecting educational homogeneity; the percent of population, ages 3 to 34, enrolled in schools is chosen as a positive indicator of individual willingness to invest in education. The willingness of a community to invest in education is shown by the variable of per capita local government expenditures on education, whereas a community's educational attainment and probably its homogeneity are illustrated by the percent of persons 25 years old and over who have completed 4 years of college or more.

The 13 factors described above are expected to portray, respectively, the individual and community conditions of health and education needed to evaluate the level of quality of life in the metropolitan areas. The policy implications of the health variables are that the overall social well-being is improved if life expectancy is lengthened,

Panel 4.  FACTORS IN HEALTH AND EDUCATION COMPONENT

Factor Effect
and Weight                              Factors

    I.   Individual Conditions

          A.  Health

- (.125)         1.  Infant mortality rate per 1,000 live births
- (.125)         2.  Death rate per 1,000 population

          B.  Education

+ (.063)        1.  Median school years completed by persons
                     25 years old and over
+ (.063)        2.  Percent of persons 25 years and over, who
                     completed 4 years of high school or more
- (.063)        3.  Percent of males ages 16 to 21 who are not
                     high school graduates
+ (.063)        4.  Percent of population ages 3 to 34 enrolled
                     in schools

    II.  Community Conditions

          A.  Medical care availability and accessibility

+ (.05)         1.  Number of dentists per 100,000 population
+ (.05)         2.  Number of hospital beds per 100,000 population
+ (.05)         3.  Hospital occupancy rates
+ (.05)         4.  Number of physicians per 100,000 population
+ (.05)         5.  Per capita local government expenditures on
                     health

          B.  Educational attainment

+ (.125)       1.  Per capita local government expenditures on
                     education
+ (.125)       2.  Percent of persons 25 years old and over who
                     completed 4 years of college or more

and more and better medical care services are made available and accessible. The policy implications of the educational variables are that quality of life can be enriched by increasing both public and private investment in education and stressing uniform educational attainment among individuals.

All educational variables contained in Panel 4 are found in the census. The infant mortality rate and death rate are based on information obtained from certificates filed in state or city Bureaus of Vital Statistics. Thus, this information is limited to registered occurrences only. Again, SEA data were used for the New England SMSA's; state data were substituted for SMSA in a few instances when no SMSA data were located.

Limitations of data existed for the five factors comprising medical care availability: the number of dentists and physicians was not available in the Statistical Abstract for SMSA's with populations of less than 200,000. As a result, these variables are not included for the small SMSA groups.

## Social Component

Insofar as the quality of life is conventionally defined as social well-being and measured by social indicators, the social component constitutes the most significant and important element of this study. Due to the wide range of social concerns, a relatively larger number of factors are included in the social component. These variables depict primarily three central social issues: individual concerns, individual equality, and community living conditions.

Among the individual concerns in the social component, the quality of life is identified with the opportunity for self-support, the promoting of maximum development of individual capability, and a widening opportunity for individual choice. The concern with self-support implies independence and self-reliance. The existing opportunity for self-support thus may be represented by the labor force participation rate, the percent of labor force employed, the mean level of income which reflects employment and income earning opportunity, the family status of the dependent children, and the independence of married couples. Education, as described previously, provides essential skills needed to acquire employment, and also more often than not education generates employment opportunities. Therefore, it is also included to identify the existing opportunity for self-support. For the development of individual capabilities in this country, no investment other than education can be formal, efficient, effective, and rewarding. For persons with less than 15 years of education, some vocational training apparently enhances their capabilities professionally. Physically, health is fundamental to any development of individual capability. Thus, the individual health index also becomes one of the essential determinants in this group; i.e., the index values, after they are computed, are included in this subcomponent.

Individuals are expected to be very much concerned with available choices and appreciative of chances to acquire better knowledge and information about selection among jobs, residences, friends, etc. In order to widen opportunity for individual choices, individuals have to be mobilized with better transportation, and information has to be broadly distributed and timingly expedited. To assure mobility and efficient communication, variables such as automobile registration, newspaper circulation, and television and radio stations are used as positive indicators. The mobility and spatial choices are limited for young and senior citizens in the central city, and these limitations are probably the more serious the higher the population density. In addition, individual equality seems to be one of the preconditions for widening individual choices which, in turn, are obviously affected by the individual and institutional environment delineated previously.

Individuals are born equal and are concerned about racial, sex, and other discriminations. Regardless of race, sex, religion, and location, people in this country are protected by the law to enjoy equally the educational and employment opportunities that exist. Discrimination, however, is still present in this country due to reasons other than education. To reveal the rate at which racial and sex discrimination are being gradually eliminated within the metropolitan areas, the income and employment differentials between nonwhite to total persons, between nonwhite males to total males, between nonwhite females to total females, and between males to females, are all adjusted by the level of education and presented under the individual equality criterion. The implication of these variables is that the higher the equality, and the less the discrimination not resulting from educational differences, the better the quality of life.

Four factors comprising racial differences identify the inequalities that may exist between Negroes and the total number of persons in the SMSA. The ratios of median family income, professional employment, and the male and female unemployment rates are adjusted for the different education levels of Negroes and total persons. The median family income and professional employment ratios are computed as follows:

$$\frac{\text{Negro data}}{\text{Total persons data}} \quad x \quad \frac{\text{Educational level of total persons}}{\text{Education level of Negroes}}$$

The education level is the median number of school years completed. The unemployment rate ratios are computed in basically the same manner, i.e.:

$$\left| \frac{\text{Negro data}}{\text{Total persons data}} \quad x \quad \frac{\text{Education level of total persons}}{\text{Education level of Negroes}} - 1 \right|$$

The ideal situation would be for no inequalities to exist, in which case the product of the two ratios would have a value of 1.0. For certain SMSA's the number of Negroes was so small that information was not available. In these cases a value of 1.0 was used.

Differences between male and female unemployment rates and numbers professionally employed are clearly evident. The method used to compute the male to female ratios is similar to the one described above for Negroes and total persons. The formula is as follows:

$$\left| \frac{\text{Male data}}{\text{Female data}} \quad x \quad \frac{\text{Education level of females}}{\text{Education level of males}} - 1 \right|$$

Again, the ideal product is a value of 1.0, while in most cases it is smaller. Three spatial variables are considered as negative attributes to the equality consideration. A high percentage of people working outside county of residence generally indicates that the surrounding counties benefit substantially from incomes earned in the central city, while the central city, after providing job opportunities and public services, is significantly suffering from property tax revenue losses. Moreover, the commuters are normally in high paying jobs in the central city of an SMSA. As a result, the income inequality problem between those in the central city and others in the rest of an SMSA tends to be aggravated over periods of time. The third concern is the housing segregation problem. A housing segregation index which measures the percentage of Negroes living in the central city, as compared to the SMSA as a whole, is constructed. The formula used in computing this index is as follows:

$$\dfrac{\text{Percent of Negroes living in central city}}{\text{Percent of Negroes living in SMSA}} - 1$$

Values closer to zero are considered to represent a good balance in the SMSA, and hence, the quality of life.

The last of the critical social concerns in this study is community living conditions. These conditions circumscribe our daily life, and everyone's quality of life is vitally affected by them. Among the conditions three major areas are studied and variables pertaining to these three are selected. They are general living conditions, facilities, and other social conditions.

Within the general living conditions category, factors of great concern are community poverty, decent housing and living space, adequate utility services, uses of public transportation, crime rate, and the cost of living. While most of the data for the preceding variables are available in the Census of Population, a special endeavor was made to construct the cost of living index. They are computed on the basis of the American Chamber of Commerce Researchers Association (ACCRA's) "Intercity Index Report" on the cost of living. The report, however, included indexes for only 105 central cities of the 243 SMSA's. The others were estimated according to the following formula:

$$I_n = I_a - 0.35\, I_a\, (1 - R_n/R_a)$$

where $I_n$ and $I_a$ are, respectively, the indexes for an SMSA where an ACCRA index is not available and for a neighboring SMSA with ACCRA data, and $R_n$ and $R_a$ are the median gross rents for the two SMSA's. The 0.35 represents the fact that rent was given a weight of 35 percent in the computation of the cost of living index by the ACCRA. The indexes are for the central cities in the SMSA's.

Under the facilities category, indicators representing public recreational facilities, financial institutions, service and trade establishments, hospitals and libraries are employed. As mentioned in the Environmental Component, data on recreation were surveyed by the United States Bureau of Outdoor Recreation and are incomplete as might be expected. The number of swimming pools, camping sites, tennis courts, and the miles of trails reported may, therefore, be much lower than is actually true for the SMSA's. Only public facilities are included, which may exclude a large number of private facilities in some SMSA's. Estimates based on the state totals, or based on the minimum value of the SMSA's available in each size group, were used for the SMSA for which no information was available.

The total number of banks and savings and loan associations located in each SMSA is given in the Statistical Abstract, Section 33. However, information was not provided for the SMSA's with population less than 200,000. The volumes of books in the main public library per 1,000 population includes only the volumes of books which are shelved in the main public library of the central city in each SMSA. Data for university or other libraries located in other parts of the SMSA are not included. Limitation of data was the only problem encountered in computing the number of trades and services establishments. Where information for the SMSA data was not available, the state figure was substituted.

All the facility variables are positive inputs of our urban life; their availability and the accessibility to those public facilities and commercial establishments are primary social concerns to every metropolitan resident.

In addition to the general living conditions in the community that persons in the community jointly participate in and collectively enjoy, there are special cultural, sports, and other social activities. While it is generally agreed that the more sports and cultural activities, the higher the community health, education and natural environment indexes, and the lower death rate, the better is the quality of social life, the negative contribution of birth rate may warrant some explanation. It is hypothesized in this study that the majority of the population in this country is in favor of family control, and that the zero rate of population growth is also a social goal. All birth and death rates are based on original certificates filed in state and city Bureaus of Vital Statistics, and therefore include only registered occurrence.

Information on both sports and cultural events was obtained through the questionnaire sent by MRI to the Chamber of Commerce in the central city.[3/] The sports category includes five major sports (football, baseball, basketball, hockey, and soccer). Each item is given points based on the class of team which played on a regular seasonal basis in the central city. Major league teams are given 3 points; minor league, 2 points; and college or university teams, 1 point. A maximum of 30 possible points is possible. The dance, drama, and music events factor includes the following 12 areas: ballet, modern

---

3/ The questionnaire forms are contained in the Appendix.

dance, folk/ethnic dance, plays, stage productions, opera, symphonic/
philharmonic, chamber music groups, choirs, country/western/bluegrass
rock concerts, and jazz. Again, SMSA's are given points depending upon
the type of event held regularly--professional, 3 points; semiprofes-
sional, 2 points; university, college or touring groups, 1 point.
The maximum here is 84 points. Cultural institutions include art,
science, history, and natural science museums located in the area.
The number and importance of fairs and festivals held are rated in the
following manner. Fairs or festivals of national importance are given
3 points; regional events, 2 points; and local, 1 point.

Of the total questionnaires sent to the 243 Chambers of Commerce in the
large (65), medium (83), and small (95) SMSA's, there were, respectively,
51, 69, and 77, or a total of 197 (81.1 percent) returned in time
for compilation. Some questionnaires were received too late to be
included. The minimum values of the returned questionnaires in the
medium and small groups were respectively assigned to those SMSA's whose
Chambers of Commerce failed to respond. For those which did not
respond, the values for the large SMSA's were estimated by taking the
average of other large SMSA's in the same state.

Thus, the Social Component, due to its broad nature and varying perceived
concerns with our social well-being, is comprised of 54 factors. They
are selected primarily according to our criteria set forth in the
beginning part of this section. They are assumed to reflect critical
social issues such as individual equality, individual concerns and
community living conditions, etc. While some variables are represented by published official sources, some are denoted by the firsthand
data collected and computed by MRI. (See Panel 5.)

In summary, about 125 variables have been selected and described in
connection with the current economic (EC), political (PO), environmental
(EN), health and education (HE), and social (SO) goal concerns. They
all have been considered as important determinants essential to measuring
the quality of life for today's urban population in the U.S. Jointly,
they are expected to represent the physical ingredients or objective
inputs which substantially contribute to the production of a certain
level of the quality of life among the metropolitan areas. The scope
of this study covers a wide spectrum. Under the five main components,
popular issues ranging from individual income and wealth, income inequality, political participation, pollution, educational attainment,
and individual equality, to economic structure, government performance,
environmental protection, community investment in education and health,

## Panel 5.  FACTORS IN SOCIAL COMPONENT

Factor Effect
and Weight                                    Factors

    I.  Individual Development

        A.  Existing opportunity for self-support

+ (.018)       1.  Labor force participation rate
+ (.018)       2.  Percent of labor force employed
+ (.018)       3.  Mean income per family member ($)
+ (.018)       4.  Percent of children under 18 years living with both parents
- (.018)       5.  Percent of married couples without own household
+ (.018)       6.  Individual education index

        B.  Promoting maximum development of individual capabilities

+ (.028)       1.  Per capita local government expenditures on education ($)
+ (.028)       2.  Percent of persons 25 years old and over who completed 4 years of high school or more
                  3.  Persons ages 16 to 64 with less than 15 years of school but with vocational training

+ (.014)          a.  Percent of males
+ (.014)          b.  Percent of females

+ (.028)       4.  Individual health index

        C.  Widening opportunity for individual choice

            1.  Mobility

+ (.007)          a.  Motor vehicle registrations per 1,000 population
+ (.007)          b.  Motorcycle registrations per 1,000 population
+ (.007)          c.  Percent of households with one or more automobiles

2. Information

+ (.007)         a. Local Sunday newspaper circulation per 1,000 population

+ (.007)         b. Percent of occupied housing units with TV available

+ (.007)         c. Local radio stations per 1,000 population

3. Spatial extension

- (.011)         a. Population density in SMSA, persons per square mile
- (.011)         b. Percent of population under 5 and 65+ living in central city

+ (.022)      4. Individual equality index

+ (.022)      5. Individual and institutional environment index

II. Individual Equality

     A. Race

+ (.028)      1. Ratio of Negro to total persons median family income adjusted for education
+ (.028)      2. Ratio of Negro to total persons in professional employment adjusted for education
- (.028)      3. Ratio of Negro males to total males unemployment rate adjusted for education, absolute value
- (.028)      4. Ratio of Negro females to total females unemployment rate adjusted for education, absolute value

     B. Sex

- (.055)      1. Ratio of male to female unemployment rate adjusted for education, absolute value
- (.055)      2. Ratio of male to female professional employment adjusted for education, absolute value

     C. Spatial

- (.037)      1. Percent working outside county of residence
- (.037)      2. Income inequality index--central city and suburban income distribution, absolute value
- (.037)      3. Housing segregation index, absolute value

III. Community Living Conditions

    A. General conditions

+ (.016)      1. Percent of families with income above poverty level

+ (.016)      2. Percent of occupied housing units with plumbing facilities

- (.016)      3. Percent of occupied housing units with 1.01 or more persons per room

+ (.016)      4. Percent of occupied housing units with a telephone available

+ (.016)      5. Percent of workers who use public transportation

- (.016)      6. Total crime rate per 100,000 population

- (.016)      7. Cost of living index

    B. Facilities

         1. Recreational facilities

+ (.005)      a. Number of swimming pools per 100,000 population

+ (.005)      b. Number of camping sites per 100,000 population

+ (.005)      c. Number of tennis courts per 100,000 population

+ (.005)      d. Miles of trails per 100,000 population

+ (.018)      2. Number of banks and savings and loan associations per 1,000 population

+ (.018)      3. Number of retail trade establishments per 1,000 population

+ (.018)      4. Number of selected service establishments per 1,000 population

+ (.018)      5. Number of hospital beds per 100,000 population

+ (.018)      6. Volumes of books in the main public library per 1,000 population

    C. Other social conditions

- (.018)      1. Death rate per 1,000 population

- (.018)      2. Birth rate per 1,000 population

+ (.018)      3. Sports events in the metropolitan area

         4. Cultural events in the metropolitan area

+ (.007)      a. Dance, drama, and music events

+ (.007)      b. Cultural institutions

+ (.007)      c. Fairs and festivals held

+ (.018)      5. Community health and education index

+ (.018)      6. Natural environment index

transportation, cultural and social activities and a host of urban problems such as housing segregation, population distribution, community crime, urban blight, etc., are recorded. The positive or negative effects of these attributes to our urban quality of life are specified, and the arena of happiness or satisfaction based on individuals, community, and activities are interwoven with the interdependent relationships among variables across the board.

The Quality of Life Model developed in the preceding chapter has been completely expressed by its physical inputs, and the entire model specification may look as follows:

$$QOL_{it} = F\ (PH_{it};\ PS_{it})$$

$$= F\ (EC_{it},\ PO_{it},\ EN_{it},\ HE_{it},\ SO_{it}\ \big|\ PS_{it})$$

and
$$EC_{it} = f\ (IEWB_{it}, CEH_{it})$$
$$PO_{it} = f\ (IA_{it}, LGF_{it})$$
$$EN_{it} = f\ (IIE_{it}, NE_{it})$$
$$HE_{it} = f\ (IC_{it}, CC_{it})$$
$$SO_{it} = f\ (ID_{it}, IE_{it}, CLC_{it})$$

The model states that the QOL at the ith SMSA in time t may be measured physically from the five goal components for a given level of psychological inputs, or by holding constant the psychological factors influencing the perceived level of quality of life among SMSA's. The economic component is in turn measured by the concerns with individual economic well-being (IEWB) and community economic health (CEH); the political component by the concerns of individual activities (IA) and local government factors (LGF); the environmental component by the individual and institutional environment (IIE) and the natural environment (NE); the health and educational component by the individual and community conditions (IC and CC) and finally, the social component by individual development (ID), individual equality (IE) and the community living conditions (CLC). These five goal components are theoretically assumed to be independent. In reality, however, their independent substance cannot be fully, practically realized, and the representative variables selected for each goal component have to capture empirically some interdependent relationships between events in this complex society to measure meaningfully the level of quality of life among SMSA's.

Representative QOL indicators are delineated with data being collected from both secondary sources as well as firsthand surveys. A detailed chart listing all data sources according to the order of sequence of variables appearing in this study is presented in the Appendix, together with all data for the 243 SMSA's under discussion. Most of the raw data have been transformed into forms with common units of measurement. They can be valuable inputs to scientific verifications, to other in-depth studies and extended research. Furthermore, it is the first of its kind, i.e., a QOL statistics handbook with complete coverage for all metropolitan areas in this country. A comparative static analysis across the statistical tables can provide substantial amounts of information for concurrent policy recommendations and various decision making.

It should be noted that all variables measured by dollars were deflated by the cost of living indexes prior to their employment and all estimated data were marked with dots as shown in the Appendix.

## INDICATOR CONSTRUCTION AND RATING SYSTEM DEVELOPMENT

The quality of life, as noted earlier, should be conceptually viewed as a stock variable. Theoretically, it reflects the status of human happiness and satisfaction at a particular point in time for the given physical and psychological conditions with which the individual in question is confronted. In Chapter III, a production model was developed in order to measure the level of quality of life perceived by any individual. In the model the level of quality of life is operationally assumed to be the output produced by both psychological and physical inputs. The output produced is generally referred to as though it is over a period of time and, hence, is a flow variable. Conceptually, social indicators designed to reflect the quality of life variations among metropolitan areas should be regarded as stock variables and constructed on the basis that they reflect a specific point in time. However, this presents an empirical problem since many statistics available today are in the form of flow variables. Furthermore, concerns with our social well-being have always been focused on issues related to both flow and stock variables; public interests are not likely to be dichotomized. As a result, the output production approach was employed for operational purposes, and both physical and psychological variables were selected as inputs to the model regardless of their flow or stock characteristics.

After the model has been specified and the variables included in the model have been identified, clearly the next requirement in measuring the variations in the level of quality of life among SMSA's is to collect empirically the statistics and data needed to construct the QOL indicators. Many technical problems arise relating to index construction and the development of the rating system. Generally, a model of measurement should include several attributes not always embodied in the model specification. Ideally, the index and weighting schemes designed to measure the quality of life should possess the following characteristics:

* They should distinguish between various levels of quality of life for different persons at different locations and different points in time.

* They should be embodied in an integrated model with their compilation and use clearly related to public policy goals and interpretations.

* They should be sufficiently universal that the underlying methodology is commonly understandable and generally acceptable for collecting quantitative information.

* They should be scientific so that the techniques can be repeated and verified.

* While they should be neutral and independent of variable units of measurement, an increase in the numerical value of the indexes should represent a better quality or a favorable trend.

The amount of effort that has been devoted to attaching quantitative values to the quality of life indicators discussed above is very limited, primarily because no consensus has emerged on what factors are important and what appropriate weights should be assigned to the important factors. In order to compare the measures associated with the factors, a common approach is to obtain individual weightings from the member of the sample population, i.e., through an opinion survey among the sample observations or the Delphi Procedure. This is one specific approach used by Dalkey and others.[4]

---

4/  See N. C. Dalkey, Studies in the Quality of Life - Delphi and Decision Making (Lexington, Massachusetts:  D.C. Heath Company, 1972).

It asks subjects to provide relative rankings of factors with some systematic procedure such as "Splitting 100." It is, however, very difficult in this approach to distinguish between the subjective measures and relative weights.

The National Wildlife Federation's Environmental Quality Index was constructed as the sum of the products of a subjectively rated numerical scale of 0 to 100 (with 0 for a disaster and 100 for the ideal condition) of the component measures (air, water, minerals, soil, etc.), and the relative importance of the components in relation to life (e.g., 30 points for soil, 20 for air and water, respectively, etc). The index in 1971 was 55.5.[5]

In the survey of Hopes and Fears of the American People, Cantril and Roll employed a 0 to 10 ladder-rating system on the "self-anchoring striving scale" to measure the individual and national accounts of hopes and fears by age, education, income, race and political affiliation strata. A shift of 0.6 in a rating from past to present and from present to future is considered statistically significant. In the survey covering 3 years (1959, 1964, and 1971), they found that Americans, on the personal level, express less concern than they did 5 or 10 years ago with the material elements that have traditionally comprised the "American Dream"; on the national level, people gave this country a present rating almost one step below that for the past, and a future rating that merely compensates for the ground lost in the last 5 years. "The American people clearly feel their nation is in trouble," noted Cantril and Roll.[6] The use of a matrix form for the quality of life measures followed by derivation of the weighting scheme according to the perceived importance for each real measure in the matrix by the participants has been another conventional technique.

Many attempts at developing social indicators without going through a personal survey have simply weighted all the basic measures equally in deriving an aggregate measure. This approach, while simple and easily understood, has frequently been criticized on the basis that many basic statistics are highly correlated; to weigh all these measures equally in deriving a simple measure of quality of life could be misleading. For this reason, Wilson and Smith have used factor

---

[5] See for instance, National Wildlife Federation, "1971 National Environmental Quality Index," National Wildlife (October-November 1971).

[6] A. H. Cantril and C. W. Roll, Jr., Hopes and Fears of the American People (New York: Universe Books, 1971), p. 15.

analysis to resolve the weighting problem. Factor analysis is one of
the techniques frequently used in multivariate studies. It not only
can reduce a large number of variables to a few components which
jointly explain most of the sum of the variances among the
variables but also can produce the loadings or weights for each
variable and, hence, the factor scores associated with each component.
Sample observations can then be rated or ranked according to the factor
scores and the standardized original statistics.[7]

The quality of numerical data available for the development of
national social well-being, such as the New Economic Welfare indicators,
leaves much to be desired, and the difficulties are apparently compounded at the regional level. Given the present state of social
statistics, not only does the model specification have to be limited
to its selection with representative variables, but also frequently
the numerical series that have to be used are close to social indicators
defined in the model. In other words, the social indicators are
empirically measured by indirect surrogates, like death rate, and
physicians per capita rather than the exact years of life expectancy
and the true availability and accessibility to medical care. Another
particularly knotty problem encountered by index construction and
rating development is that of variable weights; we will comment on
this later.

Despite the nature of true indicators or indirect surrogates, three
kinds of regional social indicators have been recognized. According
to Kamrany and Christakis, there are absolute indicators, relative
indicators, and autonomous indicators.[8] The absolute indicators are
those of scientifically established maximum or minimum levels for a
certain condition, such as the various pollution standards set by the
Environmental Protection Agency and the minimum wage rate enacted
by the U.S. Congress. The relative indicators are not bound by the
minimum or maximum levels, but rather measure the relative position
among regions, such as living cost and crime indexes, unemployment
and school attendance rates, etc. With a common denominator, the

---

[7] See J. O. Wilson, "Quality of Life in the U.S.--An Excursion into the
    New Frontier of Social Economic Indicators," (Kansas City: Midwest
    Research Institute, 1971), and D. M. Smith, The Geography of Social
    Well-Being (New York: McGraw Hill, 1973).

[8] For the three types of indicators, see N. M. Kamrany and A. N. Christakis,
    "Social Indicators in Perspective," Socioeconomic Planning
    Sciences, 4, (1970), pp. 207-216.

relative indicators serve very well as comparative statistics for interregional comparisions. The autonomous indicators are generally referred to as conditions unique or specific to particular areas, which are not common concerns over all regions. For instance, the number of movie stars to total professional people and the number of retired to working population may be very important social indicators for Los Angeles and Phoenix, respectively; however, they are not widespread social concerns.

In this study, both absolute and relative indicators were selected. As shown in the preceding section, a careful choice has been made between an absolute and a relative indicator when there are data which offer both alternatives. Relative indicators are chosen in favor of absolute indicators, mainly because this study is aimed at comparing the quality of life variations among SMSA's. Also for this reason, no autonomous indicator was included in this study.[9]

Three methods of indicator construction have been reviewed and considered in this study: (1) the standardized additive method; (2) the adjusted standardized additive method; and (3) the component and factor analyses.

Method 1: The standardized additive method involves the transformation of data on individual variables into standard scores, which in turn are added linearly to generate the quality of life indexes for each of the five components. The conventional method of standardization is to use the Z scores method. The Z score is a linear transformation of the original data, such that the mean of the Z score becomes "0" and its standard deviation becomes "1." In other words, two important parameters of the initial distribution of the original data set are normalized to show a uniform zero mean and unitary standard deviation. The basic reason for this standardization is to eliminate the units of measurement among different variables so that they can be neutral and further operated with addition or subtraction, depending only on the direction of those variables toward the explanation of the variations in the quality of life. For observation (i) on any variable (j), the standardized score ($Z_{ij}$) is measured by:

---

[9] A decision on the appropriate goal or desired state is a prerequisite to determining the required numerical indicator. The absolute indicators are of vital importance in judging the conditions as to what constitutes a reasonable or minimum acceptable standard for the QOL. A major effort in this area has been made by O. W. Markley and M. Bradley at Stanford Research Institute.

$$Z_{ij} = \frac{X_{ij} - \overline{X}_j}{S_j} \qquad (1)$$

where $X_{ij}$ is the original value that variable $j$ takes for observation $i$ ;

$\overline{X}_j$ represents the mean value of all observations for the variable $j$ ; and

$S_j$ denotes the standard deviation of variable $j$ .

One of the most significant characteristics of this transformation is that the Z scores are normally distributed with almost 99.8 percent of transformed observations falling between values of $(\overline{X}_j \pm 3S_j)$ or "$\pm 3$", 95.0 percent between $(\overline{X}_j \pm 2S_j)$ and 68.3 percent between $(\overline{X}_j \pm S_j)$ or "$\pm 2$" or "$\pm 1$", respectively, given that the original distribution is also normal.[10]

Since all variables take values independent of the unit of measurement after the transformation, the standardized additive method to obtain the quality of life indexes for all SMSA's is simply to add or subtract the weighted Z scores with weights being assigned to each of the variables separately. To be more specific, the method of constructing the QOL indicator "k" is given by

$$I_{ik} = \left( \sum_{j=1}^{n} W_j Z_{ij} \right)/n \longrightarrow I_{ik} = \left( \sum_{j=1}^{n} Z_{ij} \right)/n \text{ with } W_j = 1.0 \qquad (2)$$

where $I_{ik}$ stands for the magnitude or the indexes value for the kth component

$W_j$ is the weight assigned to variable $j$ .

$n$ indicates the number of variables measuring the criterion in question; or a subset of all variables used in the study.

If each variable in the subset is weighted equally, or with $W_j$ being equal to unity, the indicator takes on the mean value of the individual Z scores. In a like manner, the indexes for the five QOL components are also treated as weighted averages of the indicator values, as follows:

---

[10] For discussion on normal distribution, see P. G. Hoel and R. J. Jessen, Basic Statistics for Business and Economic (New York: John Wiley and Sons, 1971).

$$Q_{ip} = (\sum_{k=1}^{m} W_k I_{ik})/m \longrightarrow Q_{ip} = (\sum_{k=1}^{m} I_{ik})/m \qquad (3)$$

where $Q_{ip}$ represents the quality of life index value for component p for SMSA i and m the number of indicators included in the component.

The three steps described above illustrate the standardized additive method employed in this study with the weights being equal to unity for all variables in the same category (or indicator) and for all indicators in the same QOL component. The equal weighting scheme is used for the sake of simplification because there is even less theoretical guidance or consensus among social indicator researchers with respect to weighting schedule than for the representative variable selection. This lack of general agreement is entirely due to the absence of a social preference function among members within the society. The selection of generally agreed on variables in the social welfare function is a difficult task for any researcher, but the choice of a generally agreeable weighting scheme applicable to the variables is even more formidable.

Although the attitudinal survey seems to be the only way of deriving such weights theoretically, empirically it is not only costly but also difficult to conduct. For instance, the attempt to introduce the Dalkey and Rourke approach (described previously) to identify and weigh the quality of life factors at the Conference on the Quality of Life Concept sponsored by U.S. Environmental Protection Agency in 1972, was received with surprising hostility from a substantial percentage of the attendees. Despite the substantial spread in the weights that the conference attendees attached to the different variables, the three major components of the QOL were given relatively similar weights by them; on a "Splitting 100" scale, the economical component received 31.8 points, environmental component 31.2 points, and the political/social component 35.6 points.[11] This leads one to believe that the members tended to consider the major components almost equally important.

There are five components in this metropolitan QOL study, i.e., economic, political, environmental, health and education, and social.

---

11/   See U.S. Environmental Protection Agency, The Quality of Life Concept (Washington, D.C.: The U.S. Government Printing Office, 1973), PRI - 78-80.

Within each component, there are at least two category indicators--
generally one refers to individuals, another to the community. There
are also subcategories in these indicators, and many variables in each
subcategory. The equal weighting scheme employed in this study means
that variables in the same subcategory are weighted equally, and that
subcategory factors and component indicators at the same level are
weighted equally. Thus, the variables, factors, and indicators at
the same level among the five components are not necessarily weighted
equally; indeed, most of them carry different weights when intercom-
ponent comparisons are made.

For example, there are five variables in the wealth subcategory in the
economic component. The original values of these five variables were
first standardized or transformed to the Z scores as shown by equation
(1). The five Z scores were then weighted equally to derive the average
value for the wealth factor. According to equation (2), the wealth
and the standardized personal income per capita were weighted equally
to obtain the individual economic well-being indicator. In a similar
manner, the community economic health indicator was developed through
the standardized Z scores and the equal weighting process for the
variables such as the value added per work in manufacturing in the
productivity category, for the categories of economic diversification,
income inequality, unemployment rate, etc. Finally, the economic index
was derived by taking the average of these two indicators--an individual's
economic well-being and the community's economic health. As a result,
the variables in the wealth category were apparently weighted unequally
from those in the income inequality category as far as the construction
of the economic component index is concerned.

The equal weighting scheme applied to the variables at the same level--
subcategory, indicator category, and component--in this study has
another important aspect. Specifically, the weight attached to each
variable is determined implicitly after the model specification has
been completed as shown in the charts in the last section. For example,
the personal income per capita variable has a weight five times as high
as the variable of median values of owner-occupied single family
housing units in the wealth category. The income and wealth variables
in the individual economic well-being indicator carry with each a
weight that is 2.5 times higher than those at the same level in the
community health economic indicator, such as the degree of economic
concentration and productivity. The community economic health indicator
has seven categories, while there are only two in the individual
economic well-being indicator. Therefore, the specification of the
level at which each variable is used in this study, as it appears in

the five criteria charts, has been simultaneously assigned a variable
weight which, in essence, is based on the number of variables included
in each subcategory, the number of subcategories, and the number of
component indicators. This is the major reason for devoting a substantial amount of effort to a literature review and to the structure
development of the model.

Method 2: The adjusted standardized additive method differs slightly
from the standardized additive method in that the former approach, in
order to avoid extreme values, always converts the original standardized data into grade points prior to the use of the aggregating and
weighting technique as aforementioned. Specifically, all observations
are divided into five grades based on the percentile distribution of the
Z scores. SMSA's received grade points ranging from "1" to "5" depending upon their respective Z scores according to the following schedule:

$$Z > 0.83 \ (= \bar{X} + 0.83 \ S) \text{-------5 points}$$
$$0.83 \geq Z > 0.25 \ (= \bar{X} + 0.25 \ S) \text{-------4 points}$$
$$0.25 \geq Z > -0.25 \ (= \bar{X} - 0.25 \ S) \text{-------3 points}$$
$$-0.25 \geq Z > -0.83 \ (= \bar{X} - 0.83 \ S) \text{-------2 points}$$
$$-0.83 > Z \qquad\qquad\qquad \text{-------1 point}$$

In other words, every factor value for each SMSA has to be first converted into an ordinal grade point according to its group standing
among the SMSA's in the same population size group. The SMSA's with
a Z score greater than 0.83 are given 5 points, while SMSA's with
a Z score less than -0.83 are given 1 point. The critical values
are chosen such that about 20.0 percent of the SMSA's are in the same
group should the Z scores be normally distributed. The basic justi-
fication for this adjustment is that the overall index construction
is based on the additive which, as generally desired, should be
neither significantly pulled up by the extreme high values of the
Z scores on certain variables nor substantially pushed down by the
extreme low values of the Z scores on certain other variables. In
terms of the purpose--evaluating the QOL among SMSA's--this adjustment
seems to be warranted and more desirable than omitting the adjustment.
After all Z scores have been replaced by the point scores, the similar
weighting scheme and the steps involved for QOL component indexes
construction noted earlier are taken to compute the adjusted standardized scores for all observations.

Although the standardized additive method still retains the characteristic of having the zero mean value for all observations at the final stage when the component QOL indexes have been developed, this special mean value disappears in the adjusted standardized additive method. As expected, these two methods of index construction will produce somewhat different rankings among SMSA's being evaluated. For purposes of comparison, indexes derived from both methods will be reported for each of the five QOL components in the following chapters of empirical analyses. Nevertheless, more findings and results will be analyzed with reference to the adjusted standardized scores than those that are unadjusted.

The quality of life in the SMSA's is rated as Outstanding (A), Excellent (B), Good (C), Adequate (D), and Substandard (E) in accordance with their component indexes. The rating system used here is somewhat arbitrary. It is assumed that SMSA's with an index value of one standard deviation (S) beyond the mean level ($\overline{X}$) should be rated Outstanding (A), and SMSA's with an index value of one standard deviation below the mean should be rated Substandard (E). The other three fall in between ($\overline{X}$ + S) and are rated, respectively, Excellent ($\overline{X} + 0.28$ S $\leq$ B $< \overline{X}$ + S), Good ($\overline{X} - 0.28$ S $<$ C $< \overline{X} + 0.28$ S), and Adequate ($\overline{X}$ - S $<$ D $< \overline{X} - 0.28$ S). If the distributions of the QOL component indexes are normal, this rating system should give A's and E's to the top and bottom 16.0 percent of observations, respectively; and 23.0 percent would be in each of the B's and D's; and 22.0 percent in the C's.

Method 3: The third method considered in this study is the factor analysis. Factor analysis is a general name given to a class of techniques whose purpose often consists of data reduction and summarization. It does not entail partitioning the data into cause-effect or dependent-independent subsets, nor does it provide any hypothetical framework; rather, the analysis is primarily concerned with establishing the "strength" of the overall relationships among the whole set of variables selected in the study. In other words, this method attempts to account for the maximum variation, or to best reproduce the observed correlations in terms of a smaller set of linear combinations of the original variables. The major substantive purpose of the factor analysis is the search and test of structures or dimensions assumed to underlie manifest variables. Frequently, its stress is more on data reduction and description than hypothetical testing and statistical inference. However, it does provide one mathematical approach to resolution of the weighting problem: no assumption with respect to the weight of each variable is needed. For example, the standardized

88

additive method had to assume that the five variables under the wealth
category in the economic component were weighted equally to derive
the score on wealth which, in turn, was weighted equally with the
personal income per capita input variable to compute the score for
individual economic well-being.  Finally, the scores of the individual
economic well-being and the community economic health were averaged
to produce the QOL index for the economic component.

Two types of factor analyses have been widely applied to biological,
geographical, social, and economic studies:  one is intended to develop
a smaller set of uncorrelated variables, which jointly can extract
the maximum variance from the original set of variables (these may be
highly intercorrelated), and the other is an attempt to best reproduce the observed linear correlations in the original set of variables.
The former is conventionally referred to as the principal component
analysis, while the latter is usually called the factor analysis.

The mathematical operation for extracting the maximum variance from
the original  n  variables $(X_i, \ldots X_n)$ is shown as follows:

$$Z_1 = A_{11}F_1 + A_{12}F_2 + \ldots + A_{1n}F_n$$

$$Z_n = A_{n1}F_1 + A_{n2}F_2 + \ldots + A_{nn}F_n$$

where Z's are the standardized form (with zero mean and unit standard
deviation) of the observed variables, and are expressed as a linear
combination of n new components $F_1$, $F_2$ . . . . $F_n$ which are uncorrelated
among themselves but each of them, in order of importance, makes a
maximum contribution to the sum of the variances of the original n
variables.  The A's are factor weights or the correlation coefficients
between the original variables and the new factor component.  The sum
of the squared A's for any factor over all variables observed is
called the eigenvalue ($\lambda$) for that factor.  For component factor k,
the eigenvalue ($\lambda_k$) is also equal to the maximum amount of variance
among the original variables accounted by the factor, $V_k$, i.e.,

$$\lambda_k = V_k = \sum_{j=1}^{n} A^2_{j,k}$$

Once the factor loadings or weights for each variable are determined, a set of indicator or factor scores ($I_k$) associated with each component factor k can be derived from the set of the standardized, initial statistics $Z_j$. To be specific,

$$I_k = \sum_{j=1}^{n} (A_{jk}/\lambda_k) \cdot Z_j$$

In practice, a great portion of the total variance among the original set of variables can be explained by a few members or components. As a result, the component analysis provides an efficient summarization of the data.

The mathematical expression of the factor analysis which seeks to best reproduce the observed correlation among the original variables is slightly different from the component: the n original variables are expressed as a linear function of m ($m < n$) common factors (F) and one unique factor (U)--

$$Z_1 = b_{11}F_1 + b_{12}F_2 + \ldots + b_{1m}F_m + e_1U_1$$
$$Z_n = b_{n1}F_1 + b_{n2}F_2 + \ldots + b_{nm}F_m + e_nU_n$$

The common factors account for the correlations among the variables while the unique factor is used to account for the remaining variance on the residual of that variable. The factor scores for the factor analyses cannot be exactly determined as described above for the component analysis. The conventional least-squares regression technique has to be employed to estimate the factor scores in the factor analysis, and the b's and e's are factor loadings or weights from the regression study.

Both component and factor analyses can begin with a simple correlation matrix of dimensions (n x n) for a set of n original variables taking on standardized Z values. The solutions of a principal component analysis require the correlation matrix with values of unity in the principal diagonal and then performing an orthogonal transformation, transforming the n original variables into a new set of n components. The factor analysis allows less than unity values for the principal diagonal elements in the correlation matrix, or requires only the estimated values of communalities in the diagonal. The number of factors constructed as best uncorrelated representations of the original variables is less than that of the original variables because there is a unique variable in the model. Given a nonsingular matrix to begin with, the factor scores for the component analysis can be determined exactly as noted earlier and are unique. Nevertheless, the factor analysis involves both common and unique factors with the total number of factors exceeding the original number of variables. Thus, an inverse does not exist for such a singular correlation matrix, and the general approach to estimate the factor scores is to regress factor $(F_k)$ on the n variables. Further discussions of, and applications to, factor and component analyses can be found in Addman and Morris, Crew, Guertin and Bailey, and Harman.[12]

The application of the principal component method by bringing all variables up to the same level and pulling them together for statistical operation, however, violates our theoretical concept of quality of life input framework--such a procedure ruins the hierarchical structure based on the hypothesized importance of each variable towards explaining the total variations in the quality of life among regions. Many studies measuring the quality of life in the U.S. found little difference between ranking produced by the standardized additive methods, and by the complicated method of factor and component analyses.[12] For these reasons the results from the principal

---

11/ See Irma Addman and Cynthia T. Morris, "A Factor Analysis of the Interrelationship Between Social and Political Variables and Per Capita Gross National Product," Quarterly Journal of Economics (November 1965), pp. 555-578; Robert E. Crew, Jr., "Dimensions of Public Policy: A Factor Analysis of State Expenditures," Social Science Quarterly (September 1969), pp. 381-389; W. H. Guertin and J. P. Bailey, Introduction to Modern Factor Analysis (Ann Arbor, Michigan: Edwards Brothers, Inc., 1970); and H. H. Harman, Modern Factor Analysis (Chicago: Chicago University Press, 1966).

12/ In the quality of life study by John Wilson, state ranks computed from both factor analysis, using squared multiple correlation coefficients as estimates of existing communalities, and the principal component analysis were compared and showed a very highly significant spearman rank order correlation coefficient of about 0.96. In the interstate geography of social well-being, Smith found that the rank correlation coefficient between the general social well-being indicator derived from summing the unweighted Z scores and the indicators from the component analysis is 0.914. In other words, little difference is observed in state rankings so far as different weighting methods are concerned. See John Wilson, "Quality of Life in the U.S." (Kansas City: Midwest Research Institute, 1970), p. 22; and David Smith, The Geography of Social Well-Being (New York: McGraw-Hill, 1973), p. 101.

component analysis will not be completely presented for all QOL components in the following chapters. Nevertheless, the quality of life rankings for the economic component computed by this method will be employed and analyzed strictly for the purpose of methodological comparison.

In the following three chapters empirical findings on QOL variations and their policy implications will be discussed respectively for the large, medium, and small group of SMSA's. Again, only intragroup variation comparisons are legitimate. Intergroup comparisons are prohibited because the project is designed to measure the QOL variations among SMSA's within the same population size group. The original statistics are respectively normalized with their own group mean and standard deviation. Thus, SMSA's rated outstanding in one group may possibly be rated only excellent or good if they were in other groups, and vice versa.

# V

## QUALITY OF LIFE
## FINDINGS AND IMPLICATIONS:
## LARGE METROPOLITAN AREAS (L)

In 1970, there were 65 SMSA's in this country with a population of
more than 500,000 persons.  Geographically, most of these SMSA's are
located in the Middle Atlantic and the East North Central regions of
the U.S.  There are no large SMSA's in the States of Alaska, the Dakotas,
Delaware, Idaho, Maine, Mississippi, Montana, Nevada, New Hampshire,
New Mexico, South Carolina, Vermont, West Virginia, and Wyoming.  As a
result, the quality of life comparisons for the large SMSA's (L) mainly
refer to the most densely populated states in the U.S., especially in
the East.  (See Figure 1.)

According to the model development, the five components of the quality
of life measures, findings, and implications will be discussed in the
following order:  economic, political, environmental, health and education, and social.  A brief summary will be given in the last section.

ECONOMIC COMPONENT

The economic component constitutes one of the basic physical inputs to
our quality of life.  Material wealth satisfies our fundamental need
for survival, or meets the minimum requirement of freedom from hunger.
A decent standard of living was a most important concern, second only
to personal health, among all Americans surveyed by Cantril and Rolls
for the periods from 1959 to 1971.[1]  A broad concept of personal
command over goods and services--defined as the ability of individuals
and families to obtain and consume those goods and services available
through both the public and private sectors--has been used as the basis
for selecting the relevant variables for the study.

---

[1]  See Hadley Cantril, The Pattern of Human Concerns (New Brunswick,
New Jersey:  Rutgers University Press, 1965), p. 35; and A. H.
Cantril and C. W. Rolls, Jr., "Hopes and Fears of the American
People" in Environmental Protection Agency, The Quality of Life
Concept (Washington, D.C.: Governmental Printing Office, 1973),
p. 69.

Table 1 contains indexes and ratings of the economic component of all
65 large SMSA's. As of 1970, in terms of economic strength, the Dallas,
Texas, SMSA had the highest adjusted standardized score among the large
SMSA's, given the structure organization of the economic variables
proposed in this study. The index value for Dallas is 2.76, or about
1.9 standard deviations above the mean value (1.74) for all 65 SMSA's.
The Houston SMSA, with an index slightly below that of Dallas (2.70),
ranked second; and Portland, Oregon/Washington SMSA with an index
insignificantly different from Houston (2.68), ranked third. Cleveland,
Ohio; Indianapolis, Indiana; Fort Worth, Texas; Atlanta, Georgia;
Chicago, Illinois; Cincinnati, Ohio/Kentucky/Indiana; and Richmond,
Virginia, completed the top 10. The remaining two areas with index
values above the mean plus one standard deviation (0.55) are still rated
"A" or categorized as "outstanding"; they are Rochester, New York
Fort Lauderdale, Florida, and Hollywood, Florida. They are marked with
stars in Figure 1.

There are 16 SMSA's with an index valued between 1.89 ($\bar{x}$ + 0.28 S)
and 2.29 ($\bar{x}$ + S). They are rated "B" or excellent. Most industrialized
and manufacturing-oriented SMSA's, such as Seattle/Everett, Los Angeles,
Minneapolis/St. Paul, St. Louis, Grand Rapids, Detroit, Dayton, New York,
and others are in this group. They are marked with dots in Figure 1.

The outstanding (A) and excellent (B) SMSA's are distinguished from
the others by a combination of factors. They are outstanding or
excellent not only in the sense of individual economic well-being,
represented by personal income and wealth, but also have a very healthy
regional economy with higher labor productivity and lower unemployment
rate, more diversified economic structure and equal distribution of
income, a larger pool of available capital funds, and a greater local
effort in stimulating regional economic growth. In other words,
measures in the economic component are related to the individuals as
well as the community in which individuals conduct their economic life.
These measures cover the three vital functions of the economic per-
formance--production, distribution, and consumption.

In contrast, 13 SMSA's are rated "E" or substandard because of their
low index values--lower than the mean minus one standard deviation
(or 1.19). Jersey City, New Jersey, which received an adjusted
standardized score of 0.59, ranked last on the list. Reading from
Jersey City upwards are: San Antonio, Texas; New Orleans, Louisiana;
Norfolk/Portsmouth, Virginia; Jacksonville, Florida; Memphis, Tennessee/
Arkansas, Philadelphia, Pennsylvania/New Jersey, Birmingham, Alabama,
etc.

# TABLE 1

## INDEX AND RATING OF ECONOMIC COMPONENT (L)

| SMSA | Adjusted Standardized Scores | | | Standardized Scores | | |
|---|---|---|---|---|---|---|
| | Value | Rank | Rating | Value | Rank | Rating |
| 1. Akron, Ohio | 1.8786 | 29 | C | 0.0713 | 31 | C |
| 2. Albany-Schenectady-Troy, N.Y. | 1.3286 | 47 | D | -0.0939 | 42 | C |
| 3. Allentown-Bethlehem-Easton, Pa.-N.J. | 1.4286 | 43 | D | -0.1180 | 44 | D |
| 4. Anaheim-Santa Ana-Garden Grove, Ca. | 2.1786 | 15 | B | 0.4038 | 7 | A |
| 5. Atlanta, Ga. | 2.4714 | 7 | A | 0.5041 | 5 | A |
| 6. Baltimore, Md. | 1.3429 | 46 | D | -0.2146 | 48 | D |
| 7. Birmingham, Ala. | 1.0500 | 58 | E | -0.6756 | 62 | E |
| 8. Boston, Mass. | 1.1786 | 53 | E | -0.1819 | 47 | D |
| 9. Buffalo, N.Y. | 1.8357 | 32 | C | 0.0405 | 35 | C |
| 10. Chicago, Ill. | 2.3643 | 8 | A | 0.2824 | 18 | B |
| 11. Cincinnati, Ohio-Ky.-Ind. | 2.3429 | 9 | A | 0.3522 | 11 | B |
| 12. Cleveland, Ohio | 2.5143 | 4 | A | 0.3409 | 13 | B |
| 13. Columbus, Ohio | 1.7857 | 35 | C | -0.0127 | 38 | C |
| 14. Dallas, Texas | 2.7571 | 1 | A | 0.7489 | 2 | A |
| 15. Dayton, Ohio | 2.1214 | 18 | B | 0.2159 | 21 | B |
| 16. Denver, Colo. | 1.8357 | 33 | C | 0.1216 | 24 | B |
| 17. Detroit, Mich. | 1.8929 | 28 | B | 0.1044 | 27 | C |
| 18. Fort Lauderdale-Hollywood, Fla. | 2.3143 | 12 | A | 0.6708 | 3 | A |
| 19. Fort Worth, Texas | 2.4786 | 6 | A | 0.4829 | 6 | A |
| 20. Gary-Hammond-East Chicago, Ind. | 1.3929 | 44 | D | -0.1564 | 45 | D |
| 21. Grand Rapids, Mich. | 2.2643 | 14 | B | 0.3755 | 10 | B |
| 22. Greensboro-Winston-Salem-High Point, N.C. | 1.1571 | 54 | E | -0.2434 | 50 | D |
| 23. Hartford, Conn. | 2.0357 | 22 | B | 0.3958 | 8 | B |
| 24. Honolulu, Hawaii | 1.1357 | 55 | E | -0.4047 | 55 | E |
| 25. Houston, Texas | 2.7000 | 2 | A | 0.5379 | 4 | A |
| 26. Indianapolis, Ind. | 2.5143 | 5 | A | 0.3946 | 9 | B |
| 27. Jacksonville, Fla. | 0.8929 | 61 | E | -0.5800 | 59 | E |
| 28. Jersey City, N.J. | 0.5857 | 65 | E | -1.1323 | 65 | E |
| 29. Kansas City, Mo.-Ks. | 1.6857 | 38 | C | 0.0158 | 36 | C |
| 30. Los Angeles-Long Beach, Ca. | 2.0500 | 21 | B | 0.3507 | 12 | B |
| 31. Louisville, Ky.-Ind. | 1.9071 | 27 | B | 0.1031 | 28 | C |
| 32. Memphis, Tenn.-Ark. | 0.9429 | 60 | E | -0.5872 | 60 | E |
| 33. Miami, Fla. | 1.2857 | 48 | D | -0.1016 | 43 | C |
| 34. Milwaukee, Wis. | 2.1786 | 16 | B | 0.2858 | 17 | B |
| 35. Minneapolis-St. Paul, Minn. | 1.9357 | 25 | B | 0.0886 | 29 | C |
| 36. Nashville-Davidson, Tenn. | 1.7286 | 37 | C | 0.0025 | 37 | C |
| 37. New Orleans, La. | 0.7857 | 63 | E | -0.7046 | 63 | E |
| 38. New York, N.Y. | 1.9500 | 24 | B | 0.3003 | 16 | B |
| 39. Newark, N.J. | 1.2571 | 50 | D | -0.3293 | 53 | D |
| 40. Norfolk-Portsmouth, Va. | 0.8500 | 62 | E | -0.6368 | 61 | E |
| 41. Oklahoma City, Okla. | 2.1143 | 19 | B | 0.1935 | 22 | B |
| 42. Omaha, Nebraska-Iowa | 2.2786 | 13 | B | 0.2688 | 19 | B |
| 43. Paterson-Clifton-Passaic, N.J. | 1.9357 | 26 | B | 0.0597 | 33 | C |
| 44. Philadelphia, Pa.-N.J. | 0.9500 | 59 | E | -0.5513 | 58 | E |
| 45. Phoenix, Ariz. | 1.2786 | 49 | D | -0.1706 | 46 | D |
| 46. Pittsburg, Pa. | 1.5929 | 41 | C | -0.0636 | 41 | C |
| 47. Portland, Oreg.-Wash. | 2.6786 | 3 | A | 0.8879 | 1 | A |
| 48. Providence-Pawtucket-Warwick, R.I.-Mass. | 1.0786 | 57 | E | -0.3613 | 54 | D |
| 49. Richmond, Va. | 2.3357 | 10 | A | 0.3264 | 14 | B |
| 50. Rochester, N.Y. | 2.3214 | 11 | A | 0.3205 | 15 | B |
| 51. Sacramento, Ca. | 1.5929 | 40 | C | -0.2183 | 49 | D |
| 52. St. Louis, Mo.-Ill. | 2.0357 | 23 | B | 0.1120 | 26 | B |
| 53. Salt Lake City, Utah | 1.3714 | 45 | D | -0.2660 | 51 | D |
| 54. San Antonio, Texas | 0.7857 | 64 | E | -1.0204 | 64 | E |
| 55. San Bernadino-Riverside-Ontario, Ca. | 1.2000 | 52 | D | -0.4286 | 56 | E |
| 56. San Diego, Ca. | 1.8786 | 30 | C | 0.1471 | 23 | B |
| 57. San Francisco-Oakland, Ca. | 1.8357 | 34 | C | 0.0565 | 34 | C |
| 58. San Jose, Ca. | 1.7500 | 36 | C | 0.0814 | 30 | C |
| 59. Seattle-Everett, Wa. | 2.1071 | 20 | B | -0.0328 | 39 | C |
| 60. Springfield-Chicopee-Holyoke, Mass.-Conn. | 1.1357 | 56 | E | -0.4301 | 57 | E |
| 61. Syracuse, N.Y. | 1.2071 | 51 | D | -0.2962 | 52 | D |
| 62. Tampa-St. Petersburg, Fla. | 1.6214 | 39 | C | 0.0705 | 32 | C |
| 63. Toledo, Ohio-Mich. | 2.1714 | 17 | B | 0.2362 | 20 | B |
| 64. Washington, D.C.-Md.-Va. | 1.8571 | 31 | C | 0.1154 | 25 | B |
| 65. Youngstown-Warren, Ohio | 1.5857 | 42 | D | -0.0540 | 40 | C |

A = Outstanding ($\geq \bar{x} + s$)
B = Excellent ($\bar{x} + .28s \leq B < \bar{x} + s$)
C = Good ($\bar{x} - .28s < C < \bar{x} + .28s$)
D = Adequate ($\bar{x} - s < D \leq \bar{x} - .28s$)
E = Substandard ($\leq \bar{x} - s$)

Mean ($\bar{x}$) = 1.7390
Standard Deviation(s) = .5475

Mean ($\bar{x}$) = 0.0000
Standard Deviation(s) = 0.3997

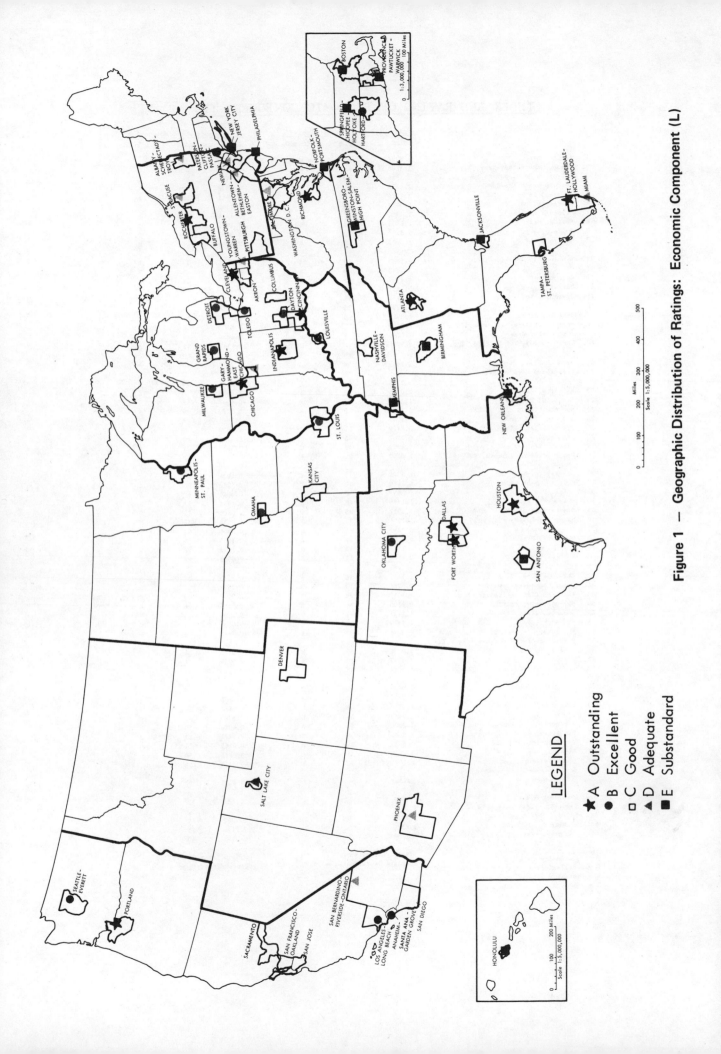

LEGEND

★ A Outstanding
● B Excellent
□ C Good
▲ D Adequate
■ E Substandard

**Figure 1 — Geographic Distribution of Ratings: Economic Component (L)**

As expected, the findings in this study differ from those which employ only one or several arbitrarily selected factors as economic measures, such as the studies by Louis and Flax. A vivid example is that in Louis' study, in the affluence component Honolulu was rated as one of the finest cities by the measures of median income per capita and the percentage of families below the poverty income level. However, in this study, Honolulu with an index value of 1.14 is rated "E" or substandard.

One of the reasons for this significant difference is, as correctly pointed out by Louis himself, that the Census Bureau statistics on individual and family income may be somewhat misleading since they are not adjusted for differences in the cost of living.[2] In this study the personal income variable and, in fact, all other variables with dollars as units of measurement, were deflated by the cost of living index before the other indexes were developed so that they become "relative indicators"--relative in terms of real purchasing power. Although the nominal income per capita in the Honolulu SMSA in 1969 was extremely high, $3,484, or about 11.0 percent higher than the national average of $3,139 (see Table A-1 in the Appendix), the cost of living index for the SMSA was even higher, 124.6 versus 100.0 (see Table A-5 in the Appendix). Consequently, the adjusted personal income per capita deflated by the cost of living was equivalent to $2,796 or only 89.1 percent of the U.S. average. Therefore, based on per capita income, the Honolulu SMSA is not rated high in this study.[3] Furthermore, income and the percentage of families with income below the poverty level are only two of 18 factors selected in this study. These two factors alone cannot reflect the overall affluence of the region because the stock of wealth and the viability of economic structure are not taken into account. In addition, the distribution of income would also have an effect upon regional quality of life. Considering all these factors jointly, the Honolulu SMSA was evaluated slightly below "adequate." Once again, readers should be alert that the ratings in this study are "relative" and not absolute terms. For example, Honolulu is relatively substandard only to the other 64 large SMSA's being studied.

---

[2] See Arthur Louis, "The Worst American City - A Scientific Study to Confirm or Deny Your Prejudices," Harper's Magazine (January 1975), pp. 67-71.

[3] For the same reason, Washington, D.C., SMSA and Paterson/Clifton/Passaic SMSA are ranked, respectively, 12th and 20th in adjusted personal income among the 65 SMSA's in this study rather than the first and second highest as shown by their unadjusted incomes.

Another example of contrast is the Dallas and Houston SMSA's. Flax observed that both Dallas and Houston SMSA's, among the 18 largest SMSA's in this country, were ranked, respectively, 7th and 11th in income and 16th and 17th in poverty.[4] These SMSA's are rated the best two in the economic component of our study of the 65 large SMSA's for these reasons: Dallas had very high rankings in productivity, available capital funds, and had a low unemployment rate; Houston had very high rankings in economic diversification and percentage of labor force employed. These favorable factors in balance made the two SMSA's outstanding.

Figure 1 provides information on geographical distribution of the 65 large SMSA's. A quick review of the map suggests that most of the SMSA's in the East North Central region had outstanding or excellent economic quality of life while the substandard ones (marked by squares) are found in the Middle Atlantic and in the South. All large SMSA's west of the Missouri River, except Honolulu, Hawaii and San Antonio, Texas, rated better than substandard in terms of the economic component. The picture revealed in this study for 1970 is similar to the concentration pattern of the so-called "industrial belt," and even more so to other factors in the 1950's, as presented by Ullman, such as the distribution of patents issued--a measure of innovation; of headquarters of the largest industries--a measure of decision making; and of Class One railroads in the U.S.--a measure of efficient transportation.[5]

The outstanding and the substandard SMSA's can exist concomitantly not only within one state, but also in a neighboring area: notable examples are Dallas, Houston, and Fort Worth versus San Antonio in Texas; and Richmond versus Norfolk/Portsmouth in Virginia.

In the light of regional economic growth theory which postulates "spread" and "backwash" effects, these are interesting observations. The spread effect refers to favorable impact of growth in the thriving center: the region around a center tends to gain from increasing demand by the center for agricultural products and raw materials and may feel the benefits of technical spillover. The East North Central region probably demonstrates the spread effect of economic growth. The backwash effect, as argued by Myrdal, implies that the beneficial effects of the growth center may be outweighed by the adverse effects: i.e.,

4/  See M. J. Flax, A Study in Comparative Urban Indicators: Condition in 18 Large Metropolitan Areas (Washington, D.C., Urban Institute, 1973).

5/  See Edward L. Ullman, "Regional Development and the Geography of Concentration," Papers and Proceeding of the Regional Science Association, Volume 4, (1958).

movements of labor, capital goods, and services generally favor the prosperous center at the expense of the poorer neighboring regions.[6] For example, migration may have harmful repercussions on the age distribution of the population in the originating region, and the capital market will deflect savings from poor regions where the effective demand for capital is low to the growing regions where returns on capital are high and less risky, etc. The cases in Texas (San Antonio) and Virginia (Norfolk/Portsmouth) may be attributed to the backwash effect.

To the decision makers the implication of this drastic contrast due to the backwash effect is whether or not in the future any state should consider a balanced growth policy or a concentrated growth policy. If balanced growth among regions is preferred, then various policies should be directed at examining the problems and seeking the means to improve the economic strength in the lagging regions. For instance, San Antonio and Norfolk/Portsmouth showed, respectively, an index of 0.79 and 0.85 in the economic component, and both are rated economically substandard. However, their individual problems are substantially different and thus require different corrective policies. Based on the static analysis on which this study is designed, it is appropriate to point out that what is needed by people in San Antonio is the know-how to enhance their productivity and economic diversity so that the income flow can be enlarged. These factors are relatively worse than others in the economic component. For Norfolk/Portsmouth, however, the flow of income in 1970, on a per capita basis, did not seem to be as serious a problem as the stock factors of wealth, or as the shortage of local capital funds measured by bank deposits per capita. While unemployment did not present a special problem in Norfolk/Portsmouth, there were a relatively significant large number of families with income below the poverty level--13.4 percent or 25 percent higher than the U.S. average (see Table A-1 in the Appendix). This implies either too many non-working dependents in each family or a large income gap among families or both prevailed in the SMSA. In a similar manner, diagnoses can be performed for all SMSA's rated substandard in the hope that their economic conditions will eventually be bettered.

---

[6] For these two countervailing sets of forces and arguments, see J. T. Romans, Capital Exports and Growth Among U.S. Regions (Middletown, Connecticut: Wesleyan University, 1965); G. H. Borts and J. L. Stein, Economic Growth in a Free Market (New York: Columbia University Press, 1964); and G. Myrdal, Economic Theory and Underdeveloped Regions (London: Duckworth, 1957).

Although all 12 SMSA's marked with stars are rated outstanding, the economic weakness and strength among them can also vary substantially. For instance, Fort Lauderdale/Hollywood SMSA ranked first in wealth as a result of having the highest property to personal income ratio (0.26 against 0.14 with U.S.), an extremely high percentage of owner-occupied housing units (72.8 percent versus 62.9 percent in the U.S.), and more than nine out of 10 households with one or more automobiles. In spite of relatively low productivity among workers in the area, the unemployment rate was only 3.4 percent in 1970, or 1 percentage point below the U.S. average. In addition, this SMSA is one of several regions with high equality in income distribution between the central city, the suburbs, and among all families. Chicago, on the contrary, was one of the regions with the highest adjusted personal income per capita but ranked only 12th in Individual Economic Well-Being because of a relatively low wealth level--especially in terms of housing and automobile ownership. Even though there was a very unequal distribution of income between city and suburban families (ranked 59th) and little effort to stimulate the local economy, Chicago benefited substantially from readily available capital funds, high employment, and productivity. On the whole, Chicago was rated outstanding and ranked eighth among the 65 SMSA's under consideration. It has been shown that any outstanding SMSA just as the substandard ones, may have weak spots in the economic component. This study provides useful information for detecting the total economic condition for each of the SMSA's.

In our earlier quality of life state study, the State of Georgia received a very low index for its economic status (0.67 or 67.0 percent of the U.S. average), and rated as substandard. Also, a number of other quality of life studies concur with our findings that the overall quality in Georgia rated lower than 40th among the 50 states.[7]
When interest is really in regional comparison, evaluations on the basis of the state average are not very meaningful, if not misleading. Although this is the reason for initiating a regional study, this study does generate promising results. The Atlanta SMSA in Georgia, for example, ranks outstanding in the economic component among the 65 large SMSA's. Neither the States of Texas nor of Florida showed better than the U.S. average economic status in the earlier study for states, but this study

---

[7] For comparisons see Ben-chieh Liu, The Quality of Life in the United States 1970 (Kansas City Midwest Research Institute, 1973), pp. 14 and 23; and "Quality of Life: Concept, Measured Results," The American Journal of Economics and Sociology (January 1975), pp. 1-13.

reveals that one-third of the SMSA's rated outstanding in the economic component are in Texas and Florida. These comparisons indicate the importance of a regional study and the preferability of the SMSA study over the state study.

The variation among the SMSA's in economic conditions can be measured by the "coefficient of variation," which is the ratio of the standard deviation divided by the mean. The higher the value, the greater the variation.[8/] The coefficient of variation for the 65 SMSA's is 0.32 (0.5475/1.7390). As noted in Chart 1, there are 25 SMSA's with adjusted standardized scores outside the range of mean plus and minus one standard deviation ($\bar{X} \pm S$), and the best and the worst SMSA differ in index value by as much as four standard deviations. The variation is smaller between scores for those SMSA's rated "good" than for those rated "adequate." Chart 1 is organized according to the order of ranks on the basis of the adjusted standardized scores contained in Table 1.

As noted in the preceding chapter, four methods of index construction were developed. The results from the standardized "Z" scores method differ only slightly from those adjusted standardized scores as expected--the rank order correlation coefficient between the two sets is highly significant and is equal to 0.96. However, the weighted index computed from the component analysis with the first three principal components which jointly explained more than 50 percent of the total variance, and those obtained from the factor analysis with the weights from the first four major factor scores produced considerably different rankings, especially for SMSA's rated "B," "C," and "D" by the other two methods. Consequently, the rank order correlation coefficients (r) between the results derived from the standard score methods and the component and factor analyses are very low: between the adjusted standardized scores and those of the principal component and the factor analysis, $r = 0.14$ and $r = 0.38$, respectively; between the standardized scores and those of the principal component and factor analyses, $r = 0.19$ and $r = 0.33$, respectively. Since a detailed technical investigation on factor or component analysis is beyond the scope of this work and the rankings are inconsistent, the empirical results from factor and component analysis will not be reported and discussed throughout the following chapters.

---

8/  For statistical presentation, reference to the coefficient can be found in most elementary statistics books. See A. Haber and R. P. Runyon, General Statistics (Reading, Massachusetts: Addison-Wesley Company, 1969), pp. 102-104.

## CHART 1

### REGIONAL VARIATIONS IN INDEXES:
### ECONOMIC COMPONENT (L)

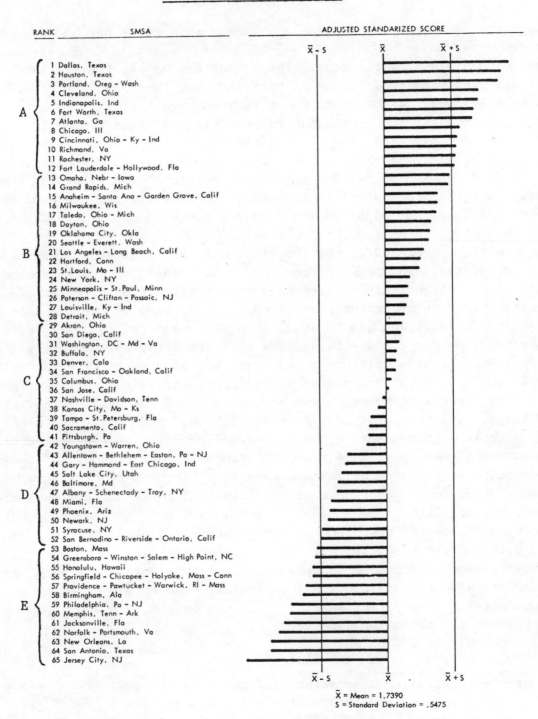

| RANK | SMSA |
|------|------|
| A | 1 Dallas, Texas |
| | 2 Houston, Texas |
| | 3 Portland, Oreg – Wash |
| | 4 Cleveland, Ohio |
| | 5 Indianapolis, Ind |
| | 6 Fort Worth, Texas |
| | 7 Atlanta, Ga |
| | 8 Chicago, Ill |
| | 9 Cincinnati, Ohio – Ky – Ind |
| | 10 Richmond, Va |
| | 11 Rochester, NY |
| | 12 Fort Lauderdale – Hollywood, Fla |
| B | 13 Omaha, Nebr – Iowa |
| | 14 Grand Rapids, Mich |
| | 15 Anaheim – Santa Ana – Garden Grove, Calif |
| | 16 Milwaukee, Wis |
| | 17 Toledo, Ohio – Mich |
| | 18 Dayton, Ohio |
| | 19 Oklahoma City, Okla |
| | 20 Seattle – Everett, Wash |
| | 21 Los Angeles – Long Beach, Calif |
| | 22 Hartford, Conn |
| | 23 St. Louis, Mo – Ill |
| | 24 New York, NY |
| | 25 Minneapolis – St. Paul, Minn |
| | 26 Paterson – Clifton – Passaic, NJ |
| | 27 Louisville, Ky – Ind |
| | 28 Detroit, Mich |
| C | 29 Akron, Ohio |
| | 30 San Diego, Calif |
| | 31 Washington, DC – Md – Va |
| | 32 Buffalo, NY |
| | 33 Denver, Colo |
| | 34 San Francisco – Oakland, Calif |
| | 35 Columbus, Ohio |
| | 36 San Jose, Calif |
| | 37 Nashville – Davidson, Tenn |
| | 38 Kansas City, Mo – Ks |
| | 39 Tampa – St. Petersburg, Fla |
| | 40 Sacramento, Calif |
| | 41 Pittsburgh, Pa |
| D | 42 Youngstown – Warren, Ohio |
| | 43 Allentown – Bethlehem – Easton, Pa – NJ |
| | 44 Gary – Hammond – East Chicago, Ind |
| | 45 Salt Lake City, Utah |
| | 46 Baltimore, Md |
| | 47 Albany – Schenectady – Troy, NY |
| | 48 Miami, Fla |
| | 49 Phoenix, Ariz |
| | 50 Newark, NJ |
| | 51 Syracuse, NY |
| | 52 San Bernadino – Riverside – Ontario, Calif |
| E | 53 Boston, Mass |
| | 54 Greensboro – Winston – Salem – High Point, NC |
| | 55 Honolulu, Hawaii |
| | 56 Springfield – Chicopee – Holyoke, Mass – Conn |
| | 57 Providence – Pawtucket – Warwick, RI – Mass |
| | 58 Birmingham, Ala |
| | 59 Philadelphia, Pa – NJ |
| | 60 Memphis, Tenn – Ark |
| | 61 Jacksonville, Fla |
| | 62 Norfolk – Portsmouth, Va |
| | 63 New Orleans, La |
| | 64 San Antonio, Texas |
| | 65 Jersey City, NJ |

$\bar{X}$ = Mean = 1.7390
S = Standard Deviation = .5475

POLITICAL COMPONENT

In evaluating the metropolitan quality of life the primary political
concerns may be differentiated according to those in which the individuals
participate directly and those that affect the individuals collectively.
In other words, political concerns may be evaluated through both
individual and institutional factors.  In this study, the criteria are
centered on how well people are informed and involved, how efficiently
the local governments perform, how qualified the employees in the public
sector are, and how much welfare assistance is provided for the needy.
Specifically, this section is concerned with the factors of input to the
political arena and output of public goods and services produced by
the local governments.  Metropolitan areas with better informed and
more involved citizenry, higher quality of public administration, and
greater collaboration and shared power among all levels of government
would be ranked above the others that lack such elements.

While the mass communication channels or the news media are used to
reflect the degree to which private citizens are informed, due to
lack of data, only one indicator was selected for political activity
participation or individual involvement--the ratio of presidential
votes cast to voting age population.  The professionalism of the local
governments can be evaluated both on the qualification of public
employees--a quality consideration, and the amount of public service
performed by the public employees--a quantity consideration.  The
entrance or average salaries of teachers, policemen, and firemen
are conventional indicators of their qualification.  Therefore, four
salary variables were included in this study.  As explained earlier,
throughout this study any variable measured by dollars and cents was
first deflated by the cost of living index to give a real term in the
sense of purchasing power.  Thus, the nominal values were deflated prior
to index development.  If the productivity of public employees does
not vary among regions, the services produced among regions may vary
because of the different numbers of people employed.  For this reason,
the number of public employees per 1,000 population was chosen as a
quantity criteria.

Safety and security are basic daily concerns, and the performance of
local governments is often judged by crime rates.  Violent crimes and
property crimes are substantially different in nature.  Hence, both
factors were chosen as criteria.  Community health and local educational
environment are equally important, but probably less sensitive criteria
than the crime rates.  These considerations, plus the power shared with
other levels of government in raising revenues, jointly determine the
performance of the local governments.  From the human welfare and the
equal rights points of view, the public is responsible for assisting the

handicapped and the needy. Therefore, the following rating and ranks among the metropolitan areas were derived from the more than 20 factors just mentioned.

Among the indexes and ratings shown in Table 2, the outstanding SMSA's in the political category are Buffalo, Albany/Schenectady/Troy, Rochester, and Syracuse in New York, Grand Rapids, Michigan; Hartford, Connecticut; Sacramento, California; Portland, Oregon/Washington; Minneapolis/St. Paul, Minnesota; Boston, Massachusetts; Salt Lake City, Utah; and Milwaukee, Wisconsin. Immediately after Milwaukee in Chart 2 are the 15 excellent SMSA's, starting with Detroit and Philadelphia and ending with Cincinnati and Oklahoma City. There are also 15 SMSA's with "E" ratings, referred to as "substandard"--a relative term meaningful only when they are compared to the other 50 large SMSA's in this country. In contrast to the four outstanding SMSA's in New York, all four SMSA's in Texas fall in this substandard category, with San Antonio at the bottom.

While Buffalo was disclosed to have an index as high as 3.88 for the political quality of life, the corresponding figure for San Antonio is only 1.34. Given the mean index value of 2.62 for all 65 SMSA's, these two indexes are, respectively, 48 percent above and 48 percent below the mean. Buffalo is shown to be one of the three best regions in providing public welfare assistance to the needy people in real terms rather than nominal dollar amount. The people in Buffalo may be considered best informed since it is one of the three SMSA's with the highest ratio of local radio stations and Sunday newspapers in circulation to population, and of television sets to occupied houses. According to adjusted salaries of teachers, policemen, and firemen, and the number of public employees per 1,000 population, Buffalo ranked high in local government professionalism. People in San Antonio, on the contrary, received a very small amount of real public welfare assistance, and the public employees in the area were paid low salaries that when deflated by the cost of living index were slightly higher than the U.S. average at 100.9. (See Table A-5 in the Appendix.) In fact, the average monthly earnings of teachers in San Antonio were $559 in 1970, the lowest among the 65 SMSA's without the cost of living adjustment, or equal to 82.0 percent of the U.S. average of $682. (See Table A-2 in the Appendix.) The professionalism of local governments in this area compared least favorably to its counterparts.

## TABLE 2

## INDEX AND RATING OF POLITICAL COMPONENT (L)

| SMSA | Adjusted Standardized Scores | | | Standardized Scores | | |
|------|------:|------:|:------:|------:|------:|:------:|
| | Value | Rank | Rating | Value | Rank | Rating |
| 1. Akron, Ohio | 2.6319 | 32 | C | 0.0431 | 33 | C |
| 2. Albany-Schenectady-Troy, N.Y. | 3.7431 | 2 | A | 0.7715 | 1 | A |
| 3. Allentown-Bethlehem-Easton, Pa.-N.J. | 2.4792 | 38 | C | -0.1195 | 41 | C |
| 4. Anaheim-Santa Ana-Garden Grove, Ca. | 3.0486 | 17 | B | -0.3419 | 49 | D |
| 5. Atlanta, Ga. | 1.8750 | 56 | E | -0.1198 | 42 | C |
| 6. Baltimore, Md. | 2.5278 | 36 | C | -0.1198 | 42 | C |
| 7. Birmingham, Ala. | 1.6944 | 62 | E | -0.5882 | 61 | E |
| 8. Boston, Mass. | 3.3889 | 10 | A | 0.4113 | 11 | B |
| 9. Buffalo, N.Y. | 3.8819 | 1 | A | 0.7226 | 3 | A |
| 10. Chicago, Ill. | 2.9653 | 23 | B | 0.1181 | 28 | C |
| 11. Cincinnati, Ohio-Ky.-Ind. | 2.8403 | 26 | B | 0.1454 | 24 | B |
| 12. Cleveland, Ohio | 2.7847 | 28 | C | 0.0334 | 34 | C |
| 13. Columbus, Ohio | 3.0208 | 21 | B | 0.1663 | 21 | B |
| 14. Dallas, Texas | 1.4653 | 64 | E | -0.5812 | 60 | E |
| 15. Dayton, Ohio | 2.5625 | 35 | C | -0.1077 | 40 | C |
| 16. Denver, Colo. | 3.0903 | 16 | B | 0.1286 | 26 | B |
| 17. Detroit, Mich. | 3.2222 | 13 | A | 0.2124 | 20 | B |
| 18. Fort Lauderdale-Hollywood, Fla. | 2.1319 | 47 | D | -0.2750 | 46 | D |
| 19. Fort Worth, Texas | 1.7986 | 60 | E | -0.4701 | 55 | E |
| 20. Gary-Hammond-East Chicago, Ind. | 2.2778 | 44 | D | -0.1602 | 44 | D |
| 21. Grand Rapids, Mich. | 3.6319 | 5 | A | 0.6428 | 8 | A |
| 22. Greensboro-Winston-Salem-High Point, N.C. | 1.8333 | 58 | E | -0.4707 | 56 | E |
| 23. Hartford, Conn. | 3.6181 | 6 | A | 0.6692 | 6 | A |
| 24. Honolulu, Hawaii | 2.1458 | 46 | D | -0.5277 | 59 | E |
| 25. Houston, Texas | 1.9167 | 53 | E | -0.4923 | 58 | E |
| 26. Indianapolis, Ind. | 2.4236 | 41 | D | -0.0388 | 37 | C |
| 27. Jacksonville, Fla. | 1.7569 | 61 | E | -0.4637 | 54 | E |
| 28. Jersey City, N.J. | 2.1250 | 48 | D | -0.4557 | 53 | E |
| 29. Kansas City, Mo.-Ks. | 2.0486 | 50 | D | -0.3581 | 51 | D |
| 30. Los Angeles-Long Beach, Ca. | 2.5278 | 37 | C | 0.0219 | 35 | C |
| 31. Louisville, Ky.-Ind. | 2.3403 | 42 | D | -0.1238 | 43 | D |
| 32. Memphis, Tenn.-Ark. | 1.8264 | 59 | E | -0.3737 | 52 | D |
| 33. Miami, Fla. | 1.9097 | 54 | E | -0.4887 | 57 | E |
| 34. Milwaukee, Wis. | 3.2708 | 12 | A | 0.3789 | 12 | B |
| 35. Minneapolis-St. Paul, Minn. | 3.4722 | 9 | A | 0.6543 | 7 | A |
| 36. Nashville-Davidson, Tenn. | 2.0833 | 49 | D | -0.2864 | 47 | D |
| 37. New Orleans, La. | 1.5625 | 63 | E | -0.6617 | 63 | E |
| 38. New York, N.Y. | 2.2014 | 45 | D | -0.2307 | 45 | D |
| 39. Newark, N.J. | 2.9931 | 22 | B | 0.3363 | 13 | B |
| 40. Norfolk-Portsmouth, Va. | 1.9306 | 52 | E | -0.6076 | 62 | E |
| 41. Oklahoma City, Okla. | 2.8056 | 27 | B | 0.1501 | 23 | B |
| 42. Omaha, Nebraska-Iowa | 2.5833 | 33 | C | 0.0110 | 36 | C |
| 43. Paterson-Clifton-Passaic, N.J. | 1.8542 | 57 | E | -1.2549 | 65 | E |
| 44. Philadelphia, Pa.-N.J. | 2.4306 | 40 | D | -0.0579 | 38 | C |
| 45. Phoenix, Ariz. | 1.9097 | 55 | E | -0.3235 | 48 | D |
| 46. Pittsburgh, Pa. | 3.1181 | 14 | B | 0.2883 | 17 | B |
| 47. Portland, Oreg.-Wash. | 3.5486 | 8 | A | 0.6050 | 9 | A |
| 48. Providence-Pawtucket-Warwick, R.I.-Mass. | 3.0347 | 18 | B | 0.3061 | 14 | B |
| 49. Richmond, Va. | 2.4722 | 39 | C | -0.0660 | 39 | C |
| 50. Rochester, N.Y. | 3.6667 | 3 | A | 0.6781 | 5 | A |
| 51. Sacramento, Ca. | 3.6181 | 7 | A | 0.6982 | 4 | A |
| 52. St. Louis, Mo.-Ill. | 2.5833 | 34 | C | 0.0707 | 29 | C |
| 53. Salt Lake City, Utah | 3.3542 | 11 | A | 0.7608 | 2 | A |
| 54. San Antonio, Texas | 1.3403 | 65 | E | -0.8781 | 64 | E |
| 55. San Bernadino-Riverside-Ontario, Ca. | 2.6944 | 30 | C | 0.0703 | 30 | C |
| 56. San Diego, Ca. | 3.1111 | 15 | B | 0.2885 | 16 | B |
| 57. San Francisco-Oakland, Ca. | 2.9444 | 24 | B | 0.0643 | 31 | C |
| 58. San Jose, Ca. | 2.9167 | 25 | B | 0.3029 | 15 | B |
| 59. Seattle-Everett, Wa. | 3.0347 | 19 | B | 0.2480 | 19 | B |
| 60. Springfield-Chicopee-Holyoke, Mass.-Conn. | 2.6667 | 31 | C | 0.0478 | 32 | C |
| 61. Syracuse, N.Y. | 3.6458 | 4 | A | 0.5524 | 10 | A |
| 62. Tampa-St. Petersburg, Fla. | 1.9514 | 51 | E | -0.3476 | 50 | D |
| 63. Toledo, Ohio-Mich. | 3.0278 | 20 | B | 0.1553 | 22 | B |
| 64. Washington, D.C.-Md.-Va. | 2.3403 | 43 | D | 0.1184 | 27 | C |
| 65. Youngstown-Warren, Ohio | 2.7222 | 29 | C | 0.1386 | 25 | B |

Mean ($\bar{x}$) = 2.6219          Mean ($\bar{x}$) = 0.0000
Standard Deviation(s) = 0.6466          Standard Deviation (s) = 0.4350

A = Outstanding ($\geq \bar{x} + s$)
B = Excellent ($\bar{x} + .28s \leq B < \bar{x} + s$)
C = Good ($\bar{x} - .28s < C < \bar{x} + .28s$)
D = Adequate ($\bar{x} - s < D \leq \bar{x} - .28s$)
E = Substandard ($\leq \bar{x} - s$)

# CHART 2

## REGIONAL VARIATIONS IN INDEXES:
### POLITICAL COMPONENT (L)

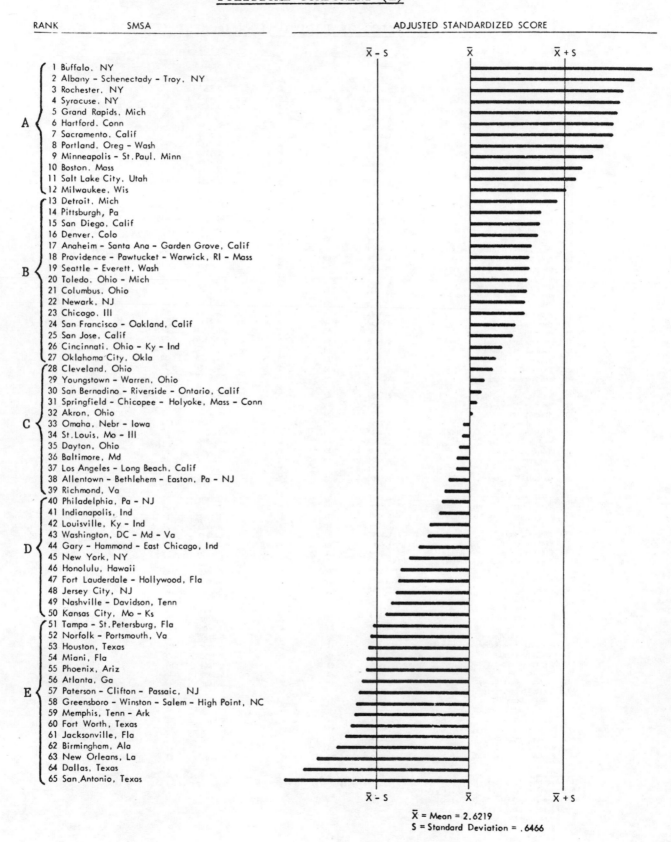

RANK      SMSA                                    ADJUSTED STANDARDIZED SCORE

**A**
1 Buffalo, NY
2 Albany – Schenectady – Troy, NY
3 Rochester, NY
4 Syracuse, NY
5 Grand Rapids, Mich
6 Hartford, Conn
7 Sacramento, Calif
8 Portland, Oreg – Wash
9 Minneapolis – St.Paul, Minn
10 Boston, Mass
11 Salt Lake City, Utah
12 Milwaukee, Wis

**B**
13 Detroit, Mich
14 Pittsburgh, Pa
15 San Diego, Calif
16 Denver, Colo
17 Anaheim – Santa Ana – Garden Grove, Calif
18 Providence – Pawtucket – Warwick, RI – Mass
19 Seattle – Everett, Wash
20 Toledo, Ohio – Mich
21 Columbus, Ohio
22 Newark, NJ
23 Chicago, Ill
24 San Francisco – Oakland, Calif
25 San Jose, Calif
26 Cincinnati, Ohio – Ky – Ind
27 Oklahoma City, Okla

**C**
28 Cleveland, Ohio
29 Youngstown – Warren, Ohio
30 San Bernadino – Riverside – Ontario, Calif
31 Springfield – Chicopee – Holyoke, Mass – Conn
32 Akron, Ohio
33 Omaha, Nebr – Iowa
34 St.Louis, Mo – Ill
35 Dayton, Ohio
36 Baltimore, Md
37 Los Angeles – Long Beach, Calif
38 Allentown – Bethlehem – Easton, Pa – NJ
39 Richmond, Va

**D**
40 Philadelphia, Pa – NJ
41 Indianapolis, Ind
42 Louisville, Ky – Ind
43 Washington, DC – Md – Va
44 Gary – Hammond – East Chicago, Ind
45 New York, NY
46 Honolulu, Hawaii
47 Fort Lauderdale – Hollywood, Fla
48 Jersey City, NJ
49 Nashville – Davidson, Tenn
50 Kansas City, Mo – Ks

**E**
51 Tampa – St.Petersburg, Fla
52 Norfolk – Portsmouth, Va
53 Houston, Texas
54 Miani, Fla
55 Phoenix, Ariz
56 Atlanta, Ga
57 Paterson – Clifton – Passaic, NJ
58 Greensboro – Winston – Salem – High Point, NC
59 Memphis, Tenn – Ark
60 Fort Worth, Texas
61 Jacksonville, Fla
62 Birmingham, Ala
63 New Orleans, La
64 Dallas, Texas
65 San Antonio, Texas

X̄ – S             X̄             X̄ + S

X̄ = Mean = 2.6219
S = Standard Deviation = .6466

In terms of funds from the Federal Government, local government in Buffalo did not show a strong position in sharing the power. Only 1.8 percent of all local government revenues came from the Federal Government, as compared to 2.7 percent in the U.S. and 8.3 percent in San Antonio. Grand Rapids, Michigan, another outstanding SMSA in the political component, showed the worst bargaining power with the Federal Government--revenues from the Federal Government consisted of only 0.5 percent.

Albany/Schenectady/Troy, New York, and Allentown/Bethlehem/Easton, Pennsylvania/New Jersey, were the safest SMSA's in 1970, with a violent crime rate as low as 133 cases per 100,000 population in that year or about nine and six times, respectively, better than the two worst areas: New York (1,357 cases per 100,000) and Baltimore (957 cases per 100,000). Other safe areas were Milwaukee, Syracuse, Honolulu, and Rochester. The high violent crime areas in 1970, as shown in Table A-2 in the Appendix, were Miami, Los Angeles, Detroit, Jacksonville, Chicago, and Washington, D.C. For property crime, Denver dominated all large SMSA's, with 4,611 cases per 100,000 population in that year. Following Denver are Los Angeles, San Francisco/Oakland, Miami, Phoenix, and Sacramento having property crime rates of over 4,000 cases. Areas with the lowest violent crime rate also have the lowest property crime rate.

Crime data are often considered suspect. One reason is that police officers see the usefulness of clerical work in terms of whether it can be used for later case documentation. "If there is no likelihood of finding a suspect, the police often consider filling out a report a waste of time."[9] Another reason for misleading crime data is that victims, because of personal reasons, do not always report crimes to the police. The above findings are very much the same as those found in other studies using different indexes and weighting schemes.[10]

Concerning crime prevention, suggestions have been made that the city or state in which the crime occurred should be held responsible for compensating the victim. Under present laws the private cost of crime

---

[9]   See Council of Municipal Performance, City Crime (Municipal Performance Report, 1:1, May-June 1973), p. 25.

[10]  For instance, see Council of Municipal Performance Ibid., and The Wealth of Cities (Municipal Performance Report, 1:3, April 1974), p. 42; and M. J. Flax, op. cit.

is borne by the individual and he has little hope of being compensated. Even if the attacker is caught and jailed, the victim ends up paying part of his own taxes for the prisoner's room and board. Presently five states--New York, California, Hawaii, Maryland, and Massachusetts-- provide some liability which is not in any form significant compensation. "Crime costs. So does crime prevention, but the latter also has benefits to society which can be weighted in the making of decisions about law enforcement methods and expenditures," stressed North and Miller.[11] After a crime occurs, the victim is all too often quickly forgotten. Our criminal justice system owes the crime victims far better treatment than they now receive in most cities. As a result of these criticisms, the Sacramento Police Department will create a position of Victims Advocate to work with the police and other law enforcement and medical agencies. The Portland, Oregon Rape Victim Advocate Project received a 2-year grant of $124,000 to assist the rape victim.[12]

The geographical distribution of the SMSA's with outstanding or "A" rating of political quality of life can be clearly visualized from Figure 2. Like the patterns revealed in the economic component, they are concentrated in the northern part of the Middle Atlantic and the East North Central Region. The most significant or critical finding in the South Atlantic and East South Central regions is that the sub- standard SMSA's are clustered there. Therefore, the political quality of life that each resident faces in these areas of the South may be completely different from the economic quality. Dallas, Houston, Fort Worth, and Atlanta received stars in the economic component but are all in black squares in the political component evaluation. In other words, while high positive correlation between economic and political quality are found in the Middle Atlantic and the East North Central regions, high negative correlation between the two components is also observed in the SMSA's in the South. The negative correlation implies that people in those SMSA's are economically healthy and able to enjoy a good quality of life, but politically their efforts to im- prove local government professionalism, to inform citizens for political involvement and participation, and to provide social welfare assistance to the needy tend to be relatively insufficient and substantially behind

---

11/   Douglas North and Roger Miller, The Economics of Public Issues
        (New York: Harper and Row, 1973), p. 124.
      See Patrice Horn (ed.), Behavior Today, Volume 61, Number 5,
      (February 3, 1975)

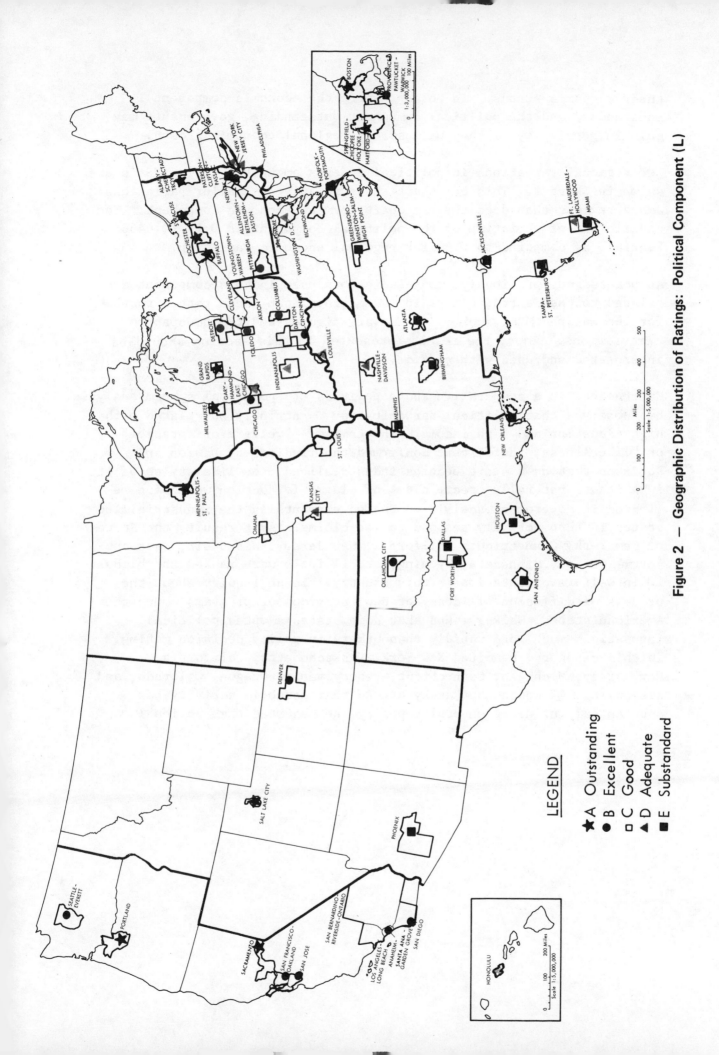

**Figure 2 — Geographic Distribution of Ratings: Political Component (L)**

LEGEND

★ A Outstanding
● B Excellent
□ C Good
▲ D Adequate
■ E Substandard

their economic status. In Boston, where the economic component is substandard and the political component outstanding, governments may gain in popularity if they will stress regional economic growth.

The regional variations in political indexes among the large SMSA's are shown in Chart 2. This bar chart shows relatively smaller variations among regions than does the bar chart for the economic component. The coefficient of variation of the political component is 0.25 (0.6466/ 2.6219), as compared to 0.32 for regional economic variation.

As pointed out previously, many indicators used in this component are related to the central cities in the metropolitan areas rather than for the entire SMSA, such as the salary figures and the newspaper circulations. Thus, the results presented in this section should be interpreted and used with caution.

Crittenden, in a comparative state politics and political system analysis, has observed that political participation is strongly correlated with high education and high income. In terms of "welfare orientation" or "liberalness," Hofferbert confirmed the findings by Dawson and Robinson that as a state becomes industrialized, the life styles of its inhabitants naturally create a set of claims for action which are reflected in government activity. The governments in the industrialized states in turn actively respond to the claims. As a result, the States of New York, Connecticut, California, New Jersey, Wisconsin, Massachusetts, Oregon, Minnesota, Wyoming, and Illinois were ranked the highest 10 in welfare orientation in this country. In an inquiry about the process of diffusion of ideas for new services or programs among the American states, Walker found that some states adopted political innovations much more rapidly than others in policy decision making. In this category, he cited New York, Massachusetts, California, New Jersey, Michigan, Connecticut, Pennsylvania, Oregon, Colorado, and Wisconsin. Although Sharkansky argued that economic activity has substantial influence on public policy, he asserted that regional phenomena make a significant contribution to the explanation of inter-state differences in policy. Regional affiliations of the states showed important relationships with most policy decisions.[13/]

The findings in this section tend to concur in a varying manner with those earlier studies relating state economy and regionalism to political divisions. However, a comparison between this metropolitan study and other earlier state studies by Liu, Wilson, and the Citizens Conference on State Legislatures leads one to reject quickly the hypothesis that states which rate low in political activities can have highly rated regions in the state. The states in the South were rated unfavorably in political quality in all three studies of varying definitions and measurements. The metropolitan areas in these southern states are no exception. This is in contrast to the findings in the preceding section on economic conditions.[14/]

## ENVIRONMENTAL COMPONENT

The concern over the dependence of the human community on the natural environment and the exchanges and flow of food, materials, energy, pollution, and the quality of life between man and nature has been our focal point and the central issue in the past several years. There is growing dissatisfaction over land use, natural resources extraction, and pollution damage to our natural environment by industrialization and urbanization. According to the estimate of the Council on Environmental Quality, a total of $200 billion will be spent on pollution

---

13/ See John Crittenden, "Dimensions of Modernization in the American States," _American Political Science Review_, Volume 61, Number 4, (1967), pp. 989-1,001; Richard Hofferbert, "The Relation Between Public Policy and Some Structural and Environmental Variables in the American States," _American Political Science Review_, Volume 60, Number 1 (1966), pp. 73-82; Jack Walker, "The Diffusion of Innovations Among the American States," _American Political Science Review_ (September 1969), pp. 880-899; and Ira Sharkansky, "Regionalism, Economic Status, and the Public Policies of American States," _The Social Science Quarterly_ (June 1968), pp. 9-25.

14/ See Ben-chieh Liu, _The Quality of Life in the U.S., 1970_, op.cit., p. 19; John Wilson, _The Quality of Life in America_ (Kansas City: Midwest Research Institute, 1967), pp. 10-11; and Citizens Conference on State Legislatures, _State Legislatures: An Evaluation of Their Effectiveness_ (New York: Praeger Publishers, 1971), p. 83.

control between now and 1980, in order to maintain present air and water quality standards.[15/] Since resources are finite and environmental protection or pollution control is costly, it is necessary to ascertain that the last unit of control bought imposes no additional costs greater than the additional benefits.

Kneese clearly stated that given the population, industrial production, and transport service in a regional economy, it is possible to visualize combinations of social policy which could lead to quite different relative burdens placed on the various residuals--receiving environmental media and tools need to be selected and developed which can be used to approximate optimal combinations of the environmental protection.[16/] The precondition for any effective and efficient policy combination in environmental protection, however, is a set of well-designed and meaningful environmental indicators which not only can directly reflect the well-being of the environment in which people live, but also can provide a yardstick for measuring the changes over time. Thus, the mandate by the National Environmental Protection Act of 1969, charged the Council on Environmental Quality with preparing a set of indicators to measure the state of the environment for the nation. As a result, the relative indicators have been published annually by the Council on Environmental Quality. Nevertheless, these indicators do not exist for all metropolitan areas in a comparable form, nor has a systematic framework been established to fulfill the requirement of developing a comparable set of indicators among regions. This section represents an exploratory effort devoted to such an establishment.

The environmental quality of life indicators in this study concern both individual and institutional environment and the natural environment. Air, visual, noise, water, and solid waste pollution are by-products of the postindustrialized society. Their existence and the attempts at eradication not only impose a heavy financial burden on our society, but they are also hazards to human health, animal fertility,

---

15/    See President's Council on Environmental Quality, Environmental
           Quality 1972:  Third Annual Report (Washington, D.C., 1972).
16/   Allen Kneese, "Analysis of Environmental Pollution," The Swedish
           Journal of Economics (March 1971).

crop production, etc.[17/]  Thus, relative indicators for these five categories were constructed based on the absolute indicators obtained from various public and private sources.  The individual and institutional environment among the metropolitan areas is evaluated jointly on 10 different factors.

The natural environment is evaluated from five climatological and two recreational factors.  The factors included in this component are fewer than desirable and are far from being complete because of the lack of empirical statistics.  Nevertheless, these factors provide basic information for a fairly accurate judgment on urban environment for all metropolitan areas.

All adjusted standardized scores in the environmental component have negative values because most factors used are "environmental bads" rather than "environmental goods."  Since most of the factors are hazardous to life, the quality of life would be the higher given smaller intakes of the environmental bads.  According to Table 3, Sacramento, California, had the best environment in 1970, with an index of -0.20; Seattle/Everett and Miami are rated, respectively, second and third.  The remaining "A" rated SMSA's are Honolulu, San Bernadino/ Riverside/Ontario, San Diego, San Jose, Phoenix, Allentown/Bethlehem/ Easton, Springfield/Chicopee/Holyoke, and Portland.

People in Sacramento have the longest trail mileage--or about 2 miles per 1,000 people--and the manufacturing industries in the area generated the least solid wastes--only 350 tons per million dollar value added. (See Table A-3 in the Appendix.)  The trail mileages were aggregated from the county data of the first survey of the U.S. Bureau of Outdoor Recreation, and the solid waste generation was computed from a regression model.  Both data are subject to the question of source reliability. Specifically, every aspect of urban life generates solid wastes, and the use of industrial solid wastes as an indicator for all household, commercial, municipal, and other solid wastes may be biased and misleading.

---

17/  For instance, L. D. Zeidberg, R. A. Prindle, and E. Landau pointed out that 25 to 50 percent of the total morbidity can be associated with air pollution.  Hence, Lave and Seskin estimated the cost of air pollution, because of health effects, would run between $14 and $29 billion per year in this country, and Liu estimated that for a 1.0 percent change in $SO_2$ level, the economic damage will change by 4.7 percent.  See Lester Lave and Eugene Seskin, "Air Pollution and Human Health," Science, Volume 169 (August 21, 1970), pp. 723-733, and Ben-chieh Liu, "Functions of Air Pollution Damage on Human Health." Air Pollution Control Association Proceedings (1975).

## TABLE 3

## INDEX AND RATING OF ENVIRONMENTAL COMPONENT (L)

| SMSA | Adjusted Standardized Scores | | | Standardized Scores | | |
|---|---|---|---|---|---|---|
| | Value | Rank | Rating | Value | Rank | Rating |
| 1. Akron, Ohio | -0.9667 | 23 | C | 0.0340 | 23 | C |
| 2. Albany-Schenectady-Troy, N.Y. | -1.2917 | 53 | D | -0.1209 | 49 | D |
| 3. Allentown-Bethlehem-Easton, Pa.-N.J. | -0.6167 | 9 | A | 0.1631 | 12 | B |
| 4. Anaheim-Santa Ana-Garden Grove, Ca. | -1.0500 | 33 | C | 0.1063 | 17 | B |
| 5. Atlanta, Ga. | -1.2833 | 52 | D | -0.0811 | 46 | C |
| 6. Baltimore, Md. | -1.2667 | 50 | D | -0.0787 | 45 | C |
| 7. Birmingham, Ala. | -1.4250 | 59 | E | -0.3185 | 60 | D |
| 8. Boston, Mass. | -1.2500 | 48 | D | -0.2825 | 58 | D |
| 9. Buffalo, N.Y. | -1.2000 | 45 | D | -0.0388 | 37 | C |
| 10. Chicago, Ill. | -1.8167 | 64 | E | -0.4576 | 62 | E |
| 11. Cincinnati, Ohio-Ky.-Ind. | -1.0333 | 30 | C | -0.0656 | 43 | C |
| 12. Cleveland, Ohio | -1.4250 | 60 | E | -0.4553 | 61 | E |
| 13. Columbus, Ohio | -1.0917 | 38 | C | -0.0184 | 33 | C |
| 14. Dallas, Texas | -0.9083 | 21 | B | 0.0258 | 24 | C |
| 15. Dayton, Ohio | -1.3167 | 56 | D | -0.1892 | 57 | D |
| 16. Denver, Colo. | -0.9917 | 24 | C | -0.0514 | 39 | C |
| 17. Detroit, Mich. | -1.7250 | 63 | E | -0.5801 | 63 | E |
| 18. Fort Lauderdale-Hollywood, Fla. | -1.0833 | 36 | C | 0.1103 | 16 | B |
| 19. Fort Worth, Texas | -0.8583 | 18 | B | -0.0031 | 28 | C |
| 20. Gary-Hammond-East Chicago, Ind. | -1.1750 | 43 | D | -0.0655 | 42 | C |
| 21. Grand Rapids, Mich. | -1.0333 | 31 | C | 0.0358 | 22 | C |
| 22. Greensboro-Winston-Salem-High Point, N.C. | -1.3000 | 54 | D | -0.1628 | 56 | D |
| 23. Hartford, Conn. | -1.1250 | 40 | C | -0.0647 | 41 | C |
| 24. Honolulu, Hawaii | -0.4583 | 4 | A | 0.1648 | 11 | B |
| 25. Houston, Texas | -1.0000 | 26 | C | -0.0114 | 31 | C |
| 26. Indianapolis, Ind. | -1.5250 | 61 | E | -1.0332 | 65 | E |
| 27. Jacksonville, Fla. | -1.2500 | 49 | D | -0.1441 | 53 | D |
| 28. Jersey City, N.J. | -1.0167 | 27 | C | -0.0482 | 38 | C |
| 29. Kansas City, Mo.-Ks. | -1.1250 | 39 | C | -0.0642 | 40 | C |
| 30. Los Angeles-Long Beach, Ca. | -1.0583 | 34 | C | 0.0957 | 19 | C |
| 31. Louisville, Ky.-Ind. | -1.4167 | 58 | E | -0.1389 | 52 | D |
| 32. Memphis, Tenn.-Ark. | -1.2083 | 47 | D | -0.0160 | 32 | C |
| 33. Miami, Fla. | -0.4167 | 3 | A | 1.5154 | 1 | A |
| 34. Milwaukee, Wis. | -1.0417 | 32 | C | -0.0245 | 35 | C |
| 35. Minneapolis-St. Paul, Minn. | -0.9000 | 20 | B | 0.0776 | 21 | C |
| 36. Nashville-Davidson, Tenn. | -1.0833 | 37 | C | -0.0244 | 34 | C |
| 37. New Orleans, La. | -1.2667 | 51 | D | -0.1624 | 55 | D |
| 38. New York, N.Y. | -1.3333 | 57 | D | -0.1289 | 51 | D |
| 39. Newark, N.J. | -1.2000 | 46 | D | -0.1504 | 54 | D |
| 40. Norfolk-Portsmouth, Va. | -0.8667 | 19 | B | 0.1278 | 14 | B |
| 41. Oklahoma City, Okla. | -0.8250 | 15 | B | 0.0009 | 27 | C |
| 42. Omaha, Nebraska-Iowa | -1.3083 | 55 | D | -0.1279 | 50 | D |
| 43. Paterson-Clifton-Passaic, N.J. | -1.0000 | 25 | C | 0.0070 | 26 | C |
| 44. Philadelphia, Pa.-N.J. | -1.0250 | 28 | C | -0.0050 | 29 | C |
| 45. Phoenix, Ariz. | -0.5917 | 8 | A | 0.1192 | 15 | B |
| 46. Pittsburgh, Pa. | -1.8667 | 65 | E | -0.8436 | 64 | E |
| 47. Portland, Oreg.-Wash. | -0.6500 | 11 | A | 0.2040 | 10 | B |
| 48. Providence-Pawtucket-Warwick, R.I.-Mass. | -0.7667 | 14 | B | 0.1308 | 13 | B |
| 49. Richmond, Va. | -1.1333 | 41 | D | -0.0072 | 30 | C |
| 50. Rochester, N.Y. | -0.7000 | 13 | B | 0.2366 | 8 | B |
| 51. Sacramento, Ca. | -0.2000 | 1 | A | 1.2102 | 2 | A |
| 52. St. Louis, Mo.-Ill. | -1.5833 | 62 | E | -0.2920 | 59 | D |
| 53. Salt Lake City, Utah | -1.0250 | 29 | C | -0.1141 | 48 | D |
| 54. San Antonio, Texas | -0.8333 | 17 | B | 0.0892 | 20 | C |
| 55. San Bernadino-Riverside-Ontario,Ca. | -0.4750 | 5 | A | 0.4583 | 3 | A |
| 56. San Diego, Ca. | -0.5333 | 6 | A | 0.2624 | 7 | B |
| 57. San Francisco-Oakland, Ca. | -0.7000 | 12 | B | 0.2163 | 9 | B |
| 58. San Jose, Ca. | -0.5333 | 7 | A | 0.3292 | 5 | B |
| 59. Seattle-Everett, Wa. | -0.2667 | 2 | A | 0.4327 | 4 | A |
| 60. Springfield-Chicopee-Holyoke, Mass.-Conn. | -0.6167 | 10 | A | 0.3035 | 6 | B |
| 61. Syracuse, N.Y. | -1.1500 | 42 | D | -0.0302 | 36 | C |
| 62. Tampa-St. Petersburg. Fla. | -1.0583 | 35 | C | -0.1041 | 47 | D |
| 63. Toledo, Ohio-Mich. | -1.1833 | 44 | D | -0.0712 | 44 | C |
| 64. Washington, D.C.-Md.-Va. | -0.8333 | 16 | B | 0.0991 | 18 | B |
| 65. Youngstown-Warren, Ohio | -0.9667 | 22 | C | 0.0203 | 25 | C |

Mean ($\bar{x}$) = -1.0342     Mean ($\bar{x}$) = 0.0000
Standard Deviation(s) = 0.3452     Standard Deviation(s) = 0.3491

A = Outstanding ($\geq \bar{x} + s$)
B = Excellent ($\bar{x} + 0.28s \leq B < \bar{x} + s$)
C = Good ($\bar{x} - 0.28s < C < \bar{x} + 0.28s$)
D = Adequate ($\bar{x} - s < D \leq \bar{x} - 0.28s$)
E = Substandard ($\leq \bar{x} - s$)

Furthermore, the waste multiplier of 7.6 tons per manufacturing employee per year is only an aggregate figure with no consideration whatsoever of different types of manufacturing industry. The solid waste indicator in this study only implies that for each million dollars worth of value added by manufacturing industries, the fewer workers employed, and hence, the fewer tons of solid wastes generated according to the formula, the better.

Although Sacramento ranked first in the environmental component, this does not mean that it has all the best in every environmental category. For instance, it had nearly the worst noise problem in that year because of its high motorcycle and vehicle registration per 1,000 population and high population density in the central city. Admittedly, these are only crude indicators of noise pollution, which in reality depends on the number of motorcycles and vehicles used per day, and their capacity of noise generation such as the age, size, etc. In comparison, Miami SMSA had the best natural environment and had virtually no visual pollution, but its water pollution and solid waste problems were considerably worse than most SMSA's under discussion. Seattle/ Everett SMSA had very little air, visual, and water pollution, but its noise pollution was worse than average.

Environmental problems were most serious in the East North Central region. Pittsburgh scored the lowest among the 65 SMSA's with an index value of -1.87. Chicago and Detroit followed closely with an index of -1.82 and -1.72, respectively. The other five SMSA's rated substandard are St. Louis (Missouri and Illinois), Indianapolis, Indiana; Cleveland, Ohio; Birmingham, Alabama; and Louisville (Kentucky and Indiana). While noise pollution did not seem to be a problem in Pittsburgh, the worst water pollution, plus very serious air and visual pollution, push the rating for Pittsburgh down to the bottom. For instance, the mean level for sulfur dioxide in Pittsburgh was 63.0 ppm, lower only than Cleveland (113.0 ppm) and Providence/Pawtucket/Warwick (64.0 ppm); the water pollution index was 48.0 for Pittsburgh, substantially higher than the second and the third worst SMSA's of Detroit (31.06) and Boston (24.00), and much higher than the majority of the SMSA's with indexes ranging from 0.68 (Anaheim/Santa Ana/Garden Grove) to 9.78 (Columbus). People in both Chicago and Detroit suffered seriously from the air and water pollution; however, people in Detroit enjoyed a relatively better natural environment and saw fewer dilapidated housing units than citizens in Chicago. St. Louis was observed to have little solid waste problem, but its very small park and recreational area (2.3 acres per 1,000 people) and bad climatological data forced its rating down.

Figure 3 contrasts vividly with Figure 1 in the East North Central
region:  the economic core of the industrial belt of this country has
the worst pollution and environmental problems.  This demonstrates
clearly the trade-off between industrial growth and environmental health.
Except in Birmingham, which was also troubled by air and visual pollution as well as climatological conditions, the environment in the
South has been kept in adequate or good condition probably because little
trading occurred between economic goods and environmental bads.  The
West Coast, on the other hand, is the only region in this country which
has enjoyed concurrently both a prosperous economy and beautiful
environment--probably due to public awareness of and proper planning
to protect the environment.

Regional variation in index values was high for 1970; the coefficient
of variation was 0.33.  This high coefficient of variation, however,
can be attributed largely to the extreme values in both the outstanding
and the substandard SMSA's.  As portrayed in Chart 3, very small
variations among environmental indexes exist for the majority of U.S.
urban areas.  This indicates that urban environmental problems have
not been significantly different among most of the SMSA's.  Even at the
bottom of the scale, the SMSA's rated "E" are fewer than in the economic
and the political components.  In fact, only the last five SMSA's in
the chart showed significant deviation from an adequate level and thus
require some special consideration.  The air pollution concentration
level has been, on the average, reduced by some 50 percent in the past
few years in this country because of the efforts of the Environmental
Protection Agency and the public awareness of environmental problems.
Continuing emphasis on cleaning and protecting the environment will
undoubtedly improve environmental quality and thus enrich future urban
life.  The rank-order correlation coefficient between the two sets of
rankings is also high, i.e., 0.93, meaning that the two methods differ
only slightly.

Plans for reduction of air pollution have centered on the improvement of
individual and institutional environments.  However, there is much to
be done in our natural environment.  Land use is the starting point
for most of man's polluting activites, and land dedicated to parks and
recreational areas makes a significant contribution to environmental
quality in at least two ways.  It is enjoyable both in and of itself,
and also for the relief it provides from surrounding and polluting land
uses.  The greatest contribution the cities could make to improve
their quality of life may be the acquisition of as much desirable land
as possible, as early as possible, before land prices soar out of
range, or development occurs causing permanent loss of open spaces

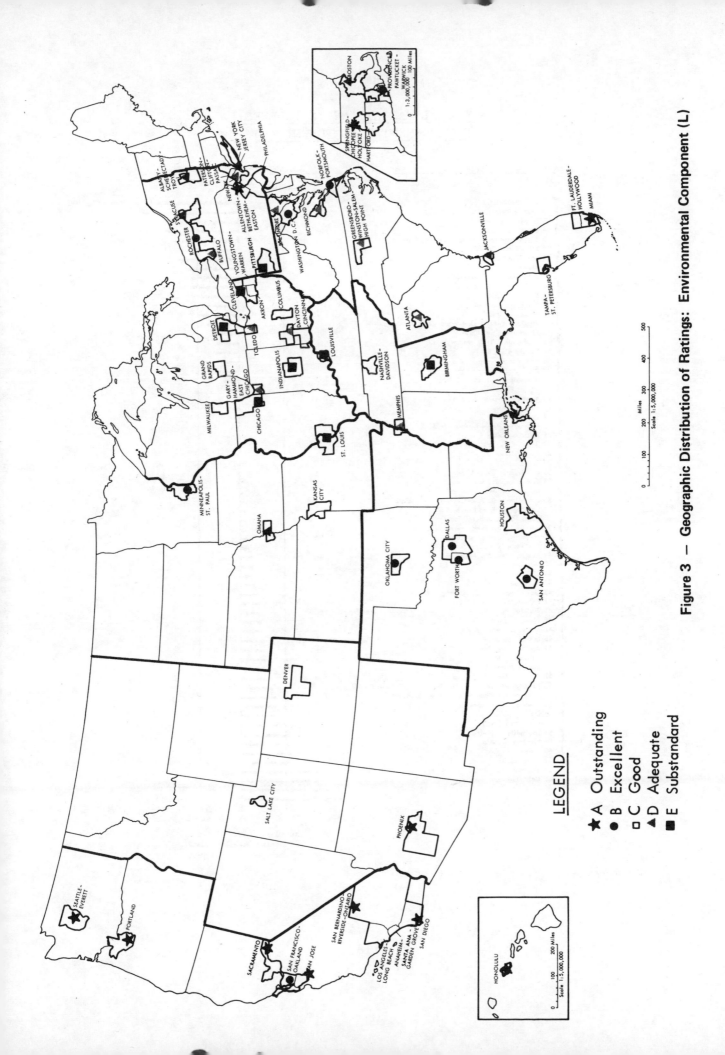

LEGEND

★ A Outstanding
● B Excellent
□ C Good
▲ D Adequate
■ E Substandard

Figure 3 — Geographic Distribution of Ratings: Environmental Component (L)

CHART 3

## REGIONAL VARIATIONS IN INDEXES:
## ENVIRONMENTAL COMPONENT (L)

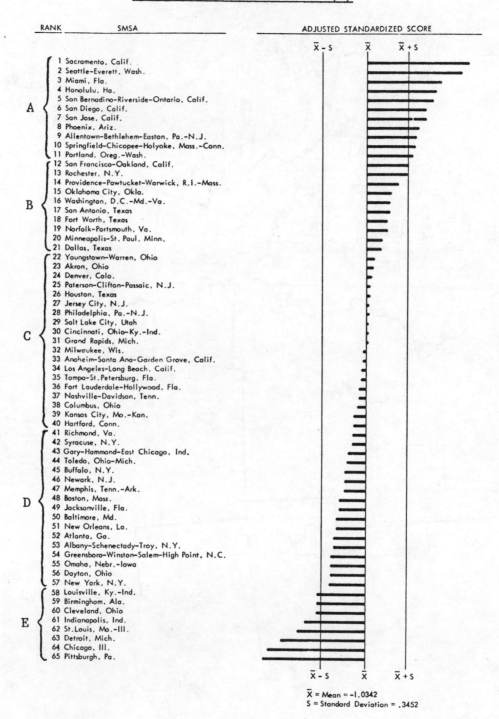

| RANK | SMSA | ADJUSTED STANDARDIZED SCORE |
|---|---|---|

A
1 Sacramento, Calif.
2 Seattle-Everett, Wash.
3 Miami, Fla.
4 Honolulu, Ha.
5 San Bernadino-Riverside-Ontario, Calif.
6 San Diego, Calif.
7 San Jose, Calif.
8 Phoenix, Ariz.
9 Allentown-Bethlehem-Easton, Pa.-N.J.
10 Springfield-Chicopee-Holyoke, Mass.-Conn.
11 Portland, Oreg.-Wash.

B
12 San Francisco-Oakland, Calif.
13 Rochester, N.Y.
14 Providence-Pawtucket-Warwick, R.I.-Mass.
15 Oklahoma City, Okla.
16 Washington, D.C.-Md.-Va.
17 San Antonio, Texas
18 Fort Worth, Texas
19 Norfolk-Portsmouth, Va.
20 Minneapolis-St. Paul, Minn.
21 Dallas, Texas

C
22 Youngstown-Warren, Ohio
23 Akron, Ohio
24 Denver, Colo.
25 Paterson-Clifton-Passaic, N.J.
26 Houston, Texas
27 Jersey City, N.J.
28 Philadelphia, Pa.-N.J.
29 Salt Lake City, Utah
30 Cincinnati, Ohio-Ky.-Ind.
31 Grand Rapids, Mich.
32 Milwaukee, Wis.
33 Anaheim-Santa Ana-Garden Grove, Calif.
34 Los Angeles-Long Beach, Calif.
35 Tampa-St. Petersburg, Fla.
36 Fort Lauderdale-Hollywood, Fla.
37 Nashville-Davidson, Tenn.
38 Columbus, Ohio
39 Kansas City, Mo.-Kan.
40 Hartford, Conn.

D
41 Richmond, Va.
42 Syracuse, N.Y.
43 Gary-Hammond-East Chicago, Ind.
44 Toledo, Ohio-Mich.
45 Buffalo, N.Y.
46 Newark, N.J.
47 Memphis, Tenn.-Ark.
48 Boston, Mass.
49 Jacksonville, Fla.
50 Baltimore, Md.
51 New Orleans, La.
52 Atlanta, Ga.
53 Albany-Schenectady-Troy, N.Y.
54 Greensboro-Winston-Salem-High Point, N.C.
55 Omaha, Nebr.-Iowa
56 Dayton, Ohio
57 New York, N.Y.

E
58 Louisville, Ky.-Ind.
59 Birmingham, Ala.
60 Cleveland, Ohio
61 Indianapolis, Ind.
62 St. Louis, Mo.-Ill.
63 Detroit, Mich.
64 Chicago, Ill.
65 Pittsburgh, Pa.

$\bar{X}$ = Mean = -1.0342
S = Standard Deviation = .3452

118

and green land.[18/]   The need for open space and green land in the metropolitan areas becomes more urgent as the percentage of American population in these areas continues to increase.

The availability of open space and green land as reflected by parks and
recreational areas varies significantly among large SMSA's.  The
statistics in Table A-3 in the Appendix reveal that people in Jersey
City had for small parks and recreational areas only 1 acre per 1,000
population in 1970 as compared to 447.2 acres per 1,000 in Miami, 130.1
acres per 1,000 in Sacramento, 116.3 acres per 1,000 in Phoenix, and
48.1 acres in Denver.  Almost one-half of the 65 large SMSA's had
fewer than 10 acres per 1,000 population.  The Citizen's Advisory
Committee on Environmental Quality has urged that land and water conservation funds be used for urban recreational programs, especially some
outreach programs and a substantial reordering of priorities on federal
aid to recreation.

One of the suggestions regarding our land use pattern and natural
environment conservation is the planned suburban community.  A study
by the Real Estate Research Corporation stated that planned suburban
communities with population densities slightly higher than those in
existing new towns can cut capital costs, energy consumption, and pollution by a significant amount.[19/]   In terms of environmental, economic,
and energy costs, planned development of all densities is less costly
to create and operate than is sprawl.  Nevertheless, higher density
communities will suffer from increased crime, noise, and diminished
privacy.  Therefore, the need for a land use plan which optimizes
our natural environment utilization and balances social benefits with
social costs is apparent in metropolitan and suburban expansion.

HEALTH AND EDUCATION COMPONENT

The term "quality of life" is something that everyone can talk about
but no one can define precisely.  Diffuse as the term becomes, few
can deny that health and education forms a significant part of it.  As

_____

18/   This suggestion was made clear by the Citizen's Advisory Com-
       mittee on Environmental Quality; see CACEQ, Annual Report to
       the President and to the Council on Environmental Quality 1972
       (Washington, D.C.:  Government Printing Office, 1972), pp. 20-27.
19/   See Real Estate Research Company, The Costs of Sprawl (Chicago:
       Real Estate Research Company, 1974).

mentioned earlier, Cantril and Rolls found that good health dominated all other concerns when they questioned individuals in this country in both the 1959 and 1971 surveys about their personal hopes. Similarly, good health was considered their number one hope by respondents in West Germany, Brazil, the Philippines, and Cuba. Ill health worried everyone most among respondents in Yugoslavia, Israel, Egypt, and Panama. [20] No wonder health was selected by the Organization on Economic Cooperation and Development to be the first in the list of fundamental social concerns common to most member countries.

Using cross-sectional sample observations from sixth grade pupils, teenagers, university students, alcoholic patients, mental patients, and other persons, Scott obtained a unanimous conclusion from the 880 respondents that death is the saddest event, despite the fact that these groups selected different occasions for the happiest event. [21] As a result, the individual health factor consists of mortality rates for the general population as well as for infants.

The community health conditions in the study are depicted by medical care availability--an input factor--in contrast to the mortality rates for the individual--an output factor. The five community health factors were chosen to represent, respectively, the medical care man- power, facility, the rate of utilization, and the public decision on health provision. The emphasis here is on preventing the occurrence of health disabilities and the avoidance of disease. The mortality rates were selected to reflect the level of health quality. Similar to the income and wealth factors employed in the economic component, both flow (mortality rate) and stock (medical care availability) variables are contained in this health component as input to our overall quality of life regardless of their conventional input-output characteristics.

Improvement in the quality of life necessitates improvement in the quality of human capital. While health constitutes physical quality of the human capital, the mental quality of human capital can be primarily enriched through education and experience. To evaluate the quality of human capital, the aggregate level of educational attainment of people in a community and the magnitude of similar educational background among them are deemed fundamental measurements for it. Although there is

---

20/ See Hadley Cantril, The Pattern of Human Concerns, op. cit.
21/ See Edward Scott, An Arena for Happiness (Springfield, Illinois: Charles C. Thomas Publishing, 1971), p. 107.

evidence that individuals can become less content and happy as their level of education increases, this individual observation is characterized over time and, hence, is of no concern in this static study of cross-sectional comparison. As a joint product in a collective sense, however, a community with many highly educated people is generally preferred to another without. In addition, a community consisting of residents of homogeneous cultural and educational background is normally assumed to be better than another comprising members of heterogeneous cultural and educational attainments. This hypothesis is analogous to that as postulated by some new welfare economists that total expected social welfare among individuals would be maximized if their incomes were equally distributed.

The index and ratings of the health and education component are shown in Table 4. Of the 13 outstanding SMSA's, the Pacific region accounted for six and the State of California contained four. San Jose SMSA had the highest quality of health and education. The composite index value for San Jose was 2.72 or 2.4 times as high as the metropolitan mean. The 12 other outstanding SMSA's are Salt Lake City, Denver, San Francisco/Oakland, Hartford, Seattle/Everett, Minneapolis/St. Paul, Sacramento, Portland, Washington, D.C.; Anaheim/Santa Ana/Garden Grove, Boston, and Rochester. From the other end of the scale are 11 substandard SMSA's led by Jersey City, Providence/Pawtucket/Warwick, Birmingham, Tampa, and Norfolk/Portsmouth.

San Jose surpassed other SMSA's in individual health and education conditions and ranked second in community educational attainment. Although the community health conditions in terms of medical care availability were outstanding for San Jose, it ranked only 12th in this category. In a like manner, Salt Lake City outstripped all large SMSA's except San Jose in individual health and education conditions, but fell behind in providing medical care services to the community, ranking only 38th in terms of available physicians, dentists, hospital beds, etc. New York was rated the best in community medical care availability with the highest number of physicians and dentists per 100,000 population (286 and 96, respectively, versus 154 and 59 in the U.S.) and the highest per capita local government expenditures on health ($8.82 against U.S. average of $2.96). Ironically, New York's death rate was also very high in 1970, 10.5 deaths per 1,000 population or one death more than the U.S. average. Among the 15 SMSA's with a death rate exceeding 10.0, New York ranked sixth. (See Table A-4 in the Appendix.)

## TABLE 4

## INDEX AND RATING OF HEALTH AND EDUCATION COMPONENT (L)

| | SMSA | Adjusted Standardized Scores | | | Standardized Scores | | |
|---|---|---|---|---|---|---|---|
| | | Value | Rank | Rating | Value | Rank | Rating |
| 1. | Akron, Ohio | 1.1250 | 30 | C | 0.0718 | 28 | C |
| 2. | Albany-Schenectady-Troy, N.Y. | 1.8625 | 14 | B | 0.3846 | 18 | B |
| 3. | Allentown-Bethlehem-Easton, Pa.-N.J. | 0.3875 | 52 | D | -0.3776 | 49 | D |
| 4. | Anaheim-Santa Ana-Garden Grove, Ca. | 2.0125 | 11 | A | 0.7431 | 7 | A |
| 5. | Atlanta, Ga. | 0.8375 | 37 | D | -0.0970 | 36 | C |
| 6. | Baltimore, Md. | 0.3625 | 53 | D | -0.4635 | 53 | D |
| 7. | Birmingham, Ala. | -0.0250 | 63 | E | -0.7143 | 62 | E |
| 8. | Boston, Mass. | 2.0125 | 12 | A | 0.6282 | 10 | A |
| 9. | Buffalo, N.Y. | 1.4250 | 25 | B | 0.1511 | 27 | C |
| 10. | Chicago, Ill. | 0.6625 | 42 | D | -0.3318 | 44 | D |
| 11. | Cincinnati, Ohio-Ky.-Ind. | 0.6250 | 46 | D | -0.3446 | 47 | D |
| 12. | Cleveland, Ohio | 1.0875 | 32 | C | -0.0458 | 33 | C |
| 13. | Columbus, Ohio | 1.4875 | 23 | B | 0.2651 | 22 | B |
| 14. | Dallas, Texas | 0.7625 | 39 | D | -0.2615 | 41 | D |
| 15. | Dayton, Ohio | 1.0625 | 34 | C | -0.0366 | 32 | C |
| 16. | Denver, Colo. | 2.5000 | 3 | A | 0.9190 | 4 | A |
| 17. | Detroit, Mich. | 0.9625 | 35 | C | -0.1208 | 37 | C |
| 18. | Fort Lauderdale-Hollywood, Fla. | 0.2000 | 58 | E | -0.5872 | 57 | E |
| 19. | Fort Worth, Texas | 0.3500 | 54 | D | -0.5269 | 55 | D |
| 20. | Gary-Hammond-East Chicago, Ind. | 0.7000 | 40 | D | -0.6149 | 59 | E |
| 21. | Grand Rapids, Mich. | 1.5375 | 21 | B | 0.1797 | 23 | B |
| 22. | Greensboro-Winston-Salem-High Point, N.C. | 0.1000 | 60 | E | -0.9202 | 63 | E |
| 23. | Hartford, Conn. | 2.2750 | 5 | A | 0.5289 | 13 | B |
| 24. | Honolulu, Hawaii | 1.5375 | 22 | B | 0.0121 | 30 | C |
| 25. | Houston, Texas | 1.0875 | 33 | C | -0.0824 | 35 | C |
| 26. | Indianapolis, Ind. | 0.6500 | 43 | D | -0.3626 | 48 | D |
| 27. | Jacksonville, Fla. | 0.1125 | 59 | E | -0.6149 | 58 | E |
| 28. | Jersey City, N.J. | -0.5250 | 65 | E | -1.6011 | 65 | E |
| 29. | Kansas City, Mo.-Ks. | 1.1125 | 31 | C | -0.0186 | 31 | C |
| 30. | Los Angeles-Long Beach, Ca. | 1.7375 | 18 | B | 0.4113 | 16 | B |
| 31. | Louisville, Ky.-Ind. | 0.3125 | 55 | E | -0.4356 | 51 | D |
| 32. | Memphis, Tenn.-Ark. | 0.6125 | 47 | D | -0.3393 | 46 | D |
| 33. | Miami, Fla. | 0.6000 | 48 | D | -0.2183 | 39 | D |
| 34. | Milwaukee, Wis. | 1.7000 | 19 | B | 0.4344 | 15 | B |
| 35. | Minneapolis-St. Paul, Minn. | 2.2375 | 7 | A | 0.7331 | 8 | A |
| 36. | Nashville-Davidson, Tenn. | 0.6375 | 45 | D | -0.2440 | 40 | D |
| 37. | New Orleans, La. | 0.4250 | 51 | D | -0.5696 | 56 | E |
| 38. | New York, N.Y. | 1.2125 | 29 | C | 0.2873 | 20 | B |
| 39. | Newark, N.J. | 1.2625 | 28 | C | 0.0144 | 29 | C |
| 40. | Norfolk-Portsmouth, Va. | 0.0625 | 61 | E | -0.6898 | 60 | E |
| 41. | Oklahoma City, Okla. | 1.3750 | 26 | B | 0.1734 | 25 | B |
| 42. | Omaha, Nebraska-Iowa | 1.7500 | 17 | B | 0.3847 | 17 | B |
| 43. | Paterson-Clifton-Passaic, N.J. | 1.4625 | 24 | B | 0.1735 | 24 | B |
| 44. | Philadelphia, Pa.-N.J. | 0.3000 | 56 | E | -0.4061 | 50 | D |
| 45. | Phoenix, Ariz. | 1.6000 | 20 | B | 0.2778 | 21 | B |
| 46. | Pittsburgh, Pa. | 0.7875 | 38 | D | -0.1372 | 38 | C |
| 47. | Portland, Oreg.-Wash. | 2.1375 | 9 | A | 0.6135 | 11 | A |
| 48. | Providence-Pawtucket-Warwick, R.I.-Mass. | -0.1750 | 64 | E | -0.6958 | 61 | E |
| 49. | Richmond, Va. | 0.4500 | 50 | D | -0.4548 | 52 | D |
| 50. | Rochester, N.Y. | 2.0000 | 13 | A | 0.5445 | 12 | B |
| 51. | Sacramento, Ca. | 2.1875 | 8 | A | 0.7818 | 6 | A |
| 52. | St. Louis, Mo.-Ill. | 0.5625 | 49 | D | -0.2646 | 42 | D |
| 53. | Salt Lake City, Utah | 2.5625 | 2 | A | 0.9570 | 3 | A |
| 54. | San Antonio, Texas | 0.2875 | 57 | E | -0.4715 | 54 | D |
| 55. | San Bernadino-Riverside-Ontario, Ca. | 1.3625 | 27 | B | 0.1585 | 26 | C |
| 56. | San Diego, Ca. | 1.8125 | 16 | B | 0.3203 | 19 | B |
| 57. | San Francisco-Oakland, Ca. | 2.3750 | 4 | A | 0.8512 | 5 | A |
| 58. | San Jose, Ca. | 2.7250 | 1 | A | 1.6010 | 1 | A |
| 59. | Seattle-Everett, Wa. | 2.2625 | 6 | A | 0.7010 | 9 | A |
| 60. | Springfield-Chicopee-Holyoke, Mass.-Conn. | 0.7000 | 41 | D | -0.2999 | 43 | D |
| 61. | Syracuse, N.Y. | 1.8500 | 15 | B | 0.4465 | 14 | B |
| 62. | Tampa-St. Petersburg, Fla. | 0.0000 | 62 | E | -0.9928 | 64 | E |
| 63. | Toledo, Ohio-Mich. | 0.9375 | 36 | C | -0.0821 | 34 | C |
| 64. | Washington, D.C.-Md.-Va. | 2.1000 | 10 | A | 1.0136 | 2 | A |
| 65. | Youngstown-Warren, Ohio | 0.6375 | 44 | D | -0.3387 | 45 | D |

A = Outstanding ($\geq \bar{x} + s$)
B = Excellent ($\bar{x} + .28s \leq B < \bar{x} + s$)
C = Good ($\bar{x} - .28s < C < \bar{x} + .28s$)
D = Adequate ($\bar{x} - s < D \leq \bar{x} - .28s$)
E = Substandard ($\leq \bar{x} - s$)

Mean ($\bar{x}$) = 1.1252
Standard Deviation(s) = 0.7868

Mean ($\bar{x}$) = 0.0000
Standard Deviation (s) = 0.5679

Other "A" rated SMSA's such as Seattle/Everett, Sacramento, and Anaheim/Santa Ana/Garden Grove also showed relatively incomparable positions in community medical care provision. The remaining "A" rated SMSA's in this component, however, showed a good balance among individual and community health and education factors.

Three SMSA's showed negative indexes in this component: Jersey City, Providence/Pawtucket/Warwick, and Birmingham. The negative indexes resulted from the fact that the scores of the negative input factors such as death rate, infant mortality rate, and the percentage of population 16 to 21 years of age not high school graduates in the individual conditions category were so low that they more than offset the positive input factors scores. Table A-4 in the Appendix reveals the death rate statistics for these three SMSA's, respectively, as 12.2, 10.5, and 10.3 per 1,000 population: the infant mortality rate as 23.5, 22.5, and 23.0 per 1,000 live births; and the percentage of males 16 to 21 not high school graduates as 18.0 percent, 17.2 percent, and 18.9 percent. However, these three SMSA's were relatively better as far as the community medical care availability is concerned. They ranked 48th, 37th, and 23rd, respectively, among the 65 large SMSA's.

The geographic distribution of various health and education ratings among SMSA's is presented in Figure 4. While the West Coast and the New England region had most "A" rated SMSA's, the "E" rated SMSA's were scattered in the South and along the East Coast. The State of California showed extremely well in health and education with no SMSA in the state rating below excellent or "B." In contrast, three of the four SMSA's in Florida received less than adequate or "substandard" ratings. The implication is that the precondition for a good quality of life in the South would be to invest in human resources by either expanding the educational programs, improving the health facilities and medical care availability, or both.

It is of interest that there exists a clear dividing line between states with outstanding and excellent ratings and those with substandard ratings. It is surprising to note that two neighboring SMSA's in the same state received completely opposite ratings. In Massachusetts, Boston was rated "A" yet Providence/Pawtucket/Warwick ranked 64th. Apparently, Boston showed better results than the national average in almost every factor, whereas Providence/Pawtucket/Warwick revealed the opposite. Given the reliability of the statistics one may question why, for instance, per capita local government health and educational expenditures in Boston amounted to $2.9 and $130.7, respectively, but

the corresponding figures in Providence/Pawtucket/Warwick were only
$0.9 and $118.4. In addition, one may attempt to seek causes of the
high death rates in the latter SMSA where more than two deaths per
1,000 were recorded in 1970, than in Boston SMSA in both infant and
general death category.

The index values computed for the health and education component for
the 65 SMSA's revealed a very high standard deviation, 0.79, which is
more than two-thirds of the mean, 1.13. The standard deviation reflects
dispersion of scores so that the variability of different distributions
may be compared in terms of the value of the standard deviation. With
a high value of standard deviation and low mean value, the coefficient
of variation thus becomes very large, 0.70, the highest among those
of the quality of life components analyzed so far. Chart 4 demonstrates
visually the wide dispersion of index scores. The implication of this
wide dispersion is, in short, that the health and education conditions
are significantly unequal among urban areas in this country.

The geographic variations in ratings in this section are very consistent
with those of the state studies by Liu and Wilson cited previously. To
be specific, the states that rated very high in health and education
quality are also found to have high ratings for the SMSA's in these
states, and vice versa. In this sense, the state indicators, though
aggregate, may still be good regional indicators for any purpose of
relative static comparison. Furthermore, the correlation coefficient
(r) between the rankings produced by the two methods is very high,
r = 0.98, indicating a great consistency between underlying methods
employed.

While health and educational manpower, facilities, and services are
lacking in some areas, they are in excess in others. There is also
functional as well as geographical maldistribution, causing regional
disparities and imbalanced results in the health and education quality
of life in this country. The market mechanism works imperfectly in
meeting needs for decent health care and adequate educational attainment.
As the Committee for Economic Development pointed out, faulty allocation
of resources is a major cause of inadequacies and inequalities in U.S.
health services, resulting in poor or substandard care for large segments
of the population.

Educational background is also a crucial determinant of the quality of
labor. Mounting evidence suggests that education and advances in
knowledge are critical factors contributing to national income growth
worldwide. For instance, Denison, in an extensively detailed empirical
study, found that about 15.0 percent and 23.0 percent of the U.S.
economic growth rate between 1950 and 1962, were accounted for by
increased education of the labor force and the advances of knowledge.

## CHART 4

### REGIONAL VARIATIONS IN INDEXES:
### HEALTH AND EDUCATION COMPONENT (L)

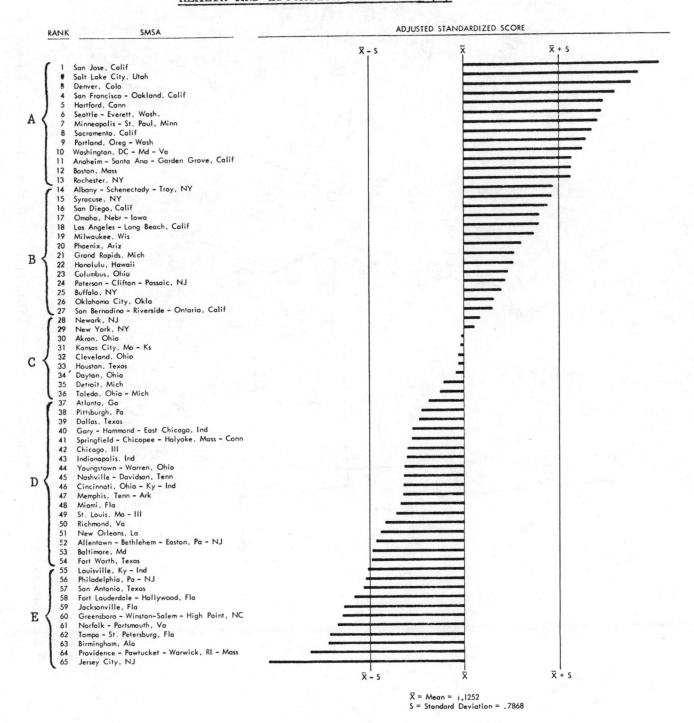

| RANK | SMSA | | ADJUSTED STANDARDIZED SCORE |
|------|------|---|------|

| | RANK | SMSA |
|---|---|---|
| A | 1 | San Jose, Calif |
| | 2 | Salt Lake City, Utah |
| | 3 | Denver, Colo |
| | 4 | San Francisco – Oakland, Calif |
| | 5 | Hartford, Conn |
| | 6 | Seattle – Everett, Wash. |
| | 7 | Minneapolis – St. Paul, Minn |
| | 8 | Sacramento, Calif |
| | 9 | Portland, Oreg – Wash |
| | 10 | Washington, DC – Md – Va |
| | 11 | Anaheim – Santa Ana – Garden Grove, Calif |
| | 12 | Boston, Mass |
| | 13 | Rochester, NY |
| B | 14 | Albany – Schenectady – Troy, NY |
| | 15 | Syracuse, NY |
| | 16 | San Diego, Calif |
| | 17 | Omaha, Nebr – Iowa |
| | 18 | Los Angeles – Long Beach, Calif |
| | 19 | Milwaukee, Wis |
| | 20 | Phoenix, Ariz |
| | 21 | Grand Rapids, Mich |
| | 22 | Honolulu, Hawaii |
| | 23 | Columbus, Ohio |
| | 24 | Paterson – Clifton – Passaic, NJ |
| | 25 | Buffalo, NY |
| | 26 | Oklahoma City, Okla |
| | 27 | San Bernadino – Riverside – Ontario, Calif |
| C | 28 | Newark, NJ |
| | 29 | New York, NY |
| | 30 | Akron, Ohio |
| | 31 | Kansas City, Mo – Ks |
| | 32 | Cleveland, Ohio |
| | 33 | Houston, Texas |
| | 34 | Dayton, Ohio |
| | 35 | Detroit, Mich |
| | 36 | Toledo, Ohio – Mich |
| D | 37 | Atlanta, Ga |
| | 38 | Pittsburgh, Pa |
| | 39 | Dallas, Texas |
| | 40 | Gary – Hammond – East Chicago, Ind |
| | 41 | Springfield – Chicopee – Holyoke, Mass – Conn |
| | 42 | Chicago, Ill |
| | 43 | Indianapolis, Ind |
| | 44 | Youngstown – Warren, Ohio |
| | 45 | Nashville – Davidson, Tenn |
| | 46 | Cincinnati, Ohio – Ky – Ind |
| | 47 | Memphis, Tenn – Ark |
| | 48 | Miami, Fla |
| | 49 | St. Louis, Mo – Ill |
| | 50 | Richmond, Va |
| | 51 | New Orleans, La |
| | 52 | Allentown – Bethlehem – Easton, Pa – NJ |
| | 53 | Baltimore, Md |
| | 54 | Fort Worth, Texas |
| E | 55 | Louisville, Ky – Ind |
| | 56 | Philadelphia, Pa – NJ |
| | 57 | San Antonio, Texas |
| | 58 | Fort Lauderdale – Hollywood, Fla |
| | 59 | Jacksonville, Fla |
| | 60 | Greensboro – Winston-Salem – High Point, NC |
| | 61 | Norfolk – Portsmouth, Va |
| | 62 | Tampa – St. Petersburg, Fla |
| | 63 | Birmingham, Ala |
| | 64 | Providence – Pawtucket – Warwick, RI – Mass |
| | 65 | Jersey City, NJ |

X̄ = Mean = 1.1252
S = Standard Deviation = .7868

125

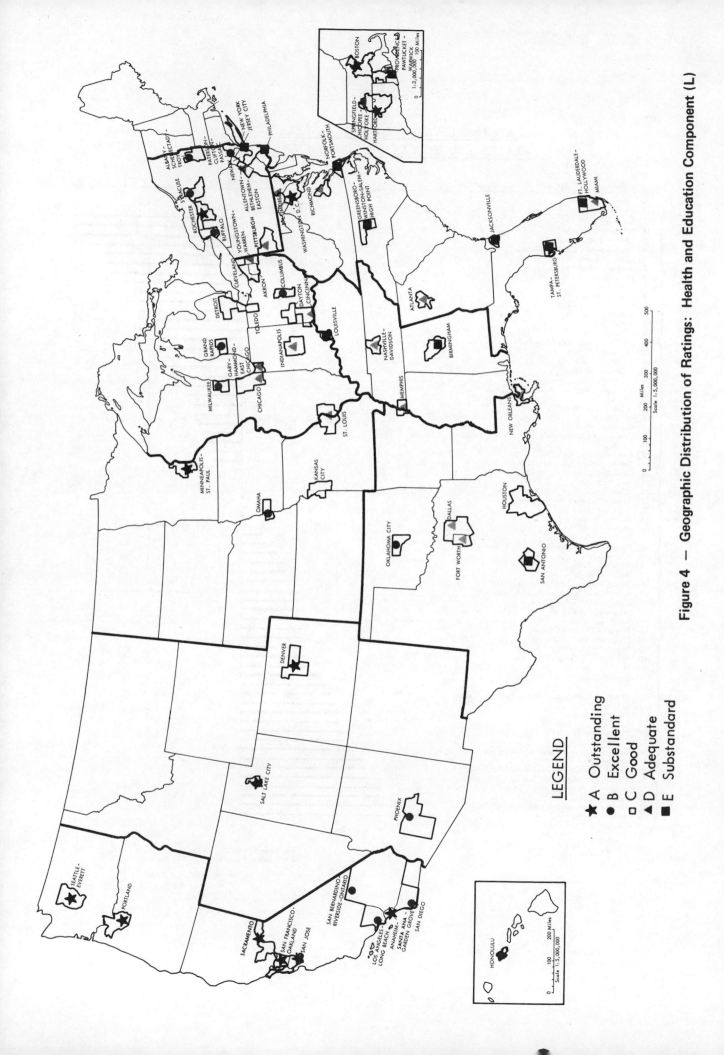

**Figure 4 — Geographic Distribution of Ratings: Health and Education Component (L)**

LEGEND

★ A Outstanding
● B Excellent
□ C Good
▲ D Adequate
■ E Substandard

In Belgium, the corresponding figures for the same period are 14.0 percent and 25.0 percent; in the United Kingdom, 12.0 percent and 32.0 percent; in Italy, 7.0 percent and 13.0 percent, etc.[22/] On an individual basis, Daniere and Mechling utilized data from the 1960 Census of Population and computed discounted lifetime earnings by occupation for people with 4 years of college and those with education beyond the graduate level. They found that on the average males with graduate education would earn 17.0 percent more income than those with college education--$187,818 against $160,992.[23/] In Greece, Psacharopoulos estimated the annual labor earnings difference between those with high school and those with college education was more than 49.0 percent in 1960.[24/]

In this country, the educational level of the population has been rising at a remarkable rate for several decades. The median school years completed among the population 25 years of age and over in 1940 was 8.6; the figure rose to 9.3, 10.5, and 12.1, respectively, in 1950, 1960, and 1970.[25/] Nevertheless, in 1970, the median school years completed was relatively lower in many SMSA's than the U.S. average. Examples are Greensboro/Winston-Salem/High Point, North Carolina--11.1; Baltimore, Maryland--11.3; and Birmingham--11.4, as compared to the U.S. average of 12.1 years completed. Improving the quality of education in the lagging regions will not only strengthen the skill level and earning potential but will also increase the mobility of individuals in these regions. Equal opportunity in education itself automatically will reduce the inequalities in employment and income distributions among people in this country. Eliminating the gap of educational attainment among regions will undoubtedly have other significant social benefits, tangible and intangible.

---

22/ Edward F. Denison, Why Growth Rates Differ (Washington, D.C.: The Brooking Institution, 1967).

23/ See Andre Daniere and Jerry Mechling, "Direct Marginal Productivity of College Education in Relation to College Aptitude of Students and Production Costs of Institutions," The Journal of Human Resources, Volume 5, Number 1 (Winter 1970), pp. 51-70.

24/ See George Psacharopoulos, "Estimating Shadow Rates of Return to Investment in Education," The Journal of Human Resources, Volume 5, Number 1 (Winter 1970), pp. 34-50.

25/ See U.S. Department of Commerce, Bureau of the Census, Statistical Abstract of the U.S., 1971 (Washington, D.C.: U.S. Government Printing Office, 1972), Table 164 on p. 109.

SOCIAL COMPONENT

The output of quality of life as perceived by people in any urban area
at a particular time is measured by the physical and psychological
inputs. This study focuses on the physical input measurements. In
the preceding sections measures, findings, and implications have been
discussed for four physical input components of the quality of life in
the large metropolitan areas: the economic component illustrates the
level and capacity of consumption and production of goods and services
to meet the basic human desire for a decent standard of living; the
political component measures the efficiency and performance of local
governments or institutions which provide goods and services for
satisfying basic public needs; the environmental component describes
the quality of both the man-made and the natural environment in which
we live; the health and education component depicts the quality of
human resources or human capital on which not only the existing but
also the future quality of life depends. This section presents the
empirical findings in the social component.

All economic, political, environmental, and health and education factors
are essential attributes to the production of quality of life for any
individual. However, no individual's quality of life can be completely
represented by the four components without the inputs from the social
component. As well demonstrated by Maslow, Scott, and others the arena
for human life is constituted of the self, other people, and the environment or community.[26] The human quality of life, therefore, has to be
reflected in the quality of self, other people, and the community. The
four components discussed previously cover these three elements in the
human life arena, but the linkage or the interflow relationships among
them has not yet been delineated. The interflow relationships are
considered in this study as the social component.

In the social component, major concerns center on the community living
conditions, the equality among individuals, and the independency of
each individual. In other words, the interflow relationships are
differentiated and reflected first, by factors measuring the level and
potentiality of the development and flourishing of individual independence and dignity; secondly, by factors describing the differences
between the actual and desired levels of equality or justice in seeking

---

26/  Abraham Maslow, Motivation and Personality (New York:  Harper and
     Row, 1970); and Edward Scott, An Arena for Happiness (Springfield,
     Illinois:  Charles C. Thomas, 1971).

employment and housing, in commanding goods and services, etc., as a result of race, sex, and spatial discrimination; and thirdly, by factors portraying desirable living conditions collectively enjoyed by individuals, such as high level of safety and security, good accessibility to basic health, commercial, and recreational facilities, and sufficient opportunities to participate in social, cultural, and sports activities.

Some of the factors chosen in this section may be conventionally regarded as input variables and some as output measures, but they are all physical inputs to our measure of social quality of life. There are two basic arguments for the exclusion of the conventionally defined input information from the social indicator approach with emphasis on output measurement. First, outputs are said to give a more accurate picture of actual social conditions than do inputs, e.g., educational attainment may be a better indicator than expenditure per capita. Second, our understanding about the technical relationships among inputs and outputs are sedimentary in particular and poor in general; e.g., the relationship between number of policemen per 100,000 population and the crime rate. For this reason this study attempts to balance empirically the two sets of factors, and, theoretically, they are all regarded as physical inputs to our quality of life.

The indexes and ratings for the social component are contained in Table 5. Portland ranks outstandingly as the finest metropolitan area with an index value of 1.03--1.86 standard deviations above the mean. Next are Seattle/Everett, Omaha, Denver, and Sacramento, all having very high index values. In addition, there are seven more outstanding SMSA's with index values higher than the mean (0.48) plus one standard deviation (0.29)--San Diego, Oklahoma City, Milwaukee, Minneapolis/ St. Paul, Los Angeles/Long Beach, San Francisco/Oakland, and Kansas City. Although the New England and Middle Atlantic regions showed unfavorably in the social component (no "A" rated SMSA) relative to preceding components, these regions had about one-half of the "B" or excellent SMSA's. As Figure 5 reveals, almost all large SMSA's west of the Mississippi River are rated either excellent or outstanding except those in the State of Texas. In fact, with the exception of Milwaukee, all 12 outstanding SMSA's are west of the Mississippi.

There are 13 SMSA's with substandard ratings; they all are located east of the Mississippi River and are clustered mainly in the Middle Atlantic and the East North Central regions. Jersey City and Detroit fall at the bottom of the list with index values substantially below the metropolitan average. In fact, they are the only two SMSA's with negative

# TABLE 5

## INDEX AND RATING OF SOCIAL COMPONENT (L)

| SMSA | Adjusted Standardized Scores | | | Standardized Scores | | |
|------|------|------|--------|------|------|--------|
| | Value | Rank | Rating | Value | Rank | Rating |
| 1. Akron, Ohio | 0.1835 | 53 | E | -0.1356 | 47 | D |
| 2. Albany-Schenectady-Troy, New York | 0.5836 | 25 | B | 0.0786 | 24 | B |
| 3. Allentown-Bethlehem-Easton, Pennsylvania-New Jersey | 0.2173 | 51 | D | -0.1060 | 42 | D |
| 4. Anaheim-Santa Ana-Garden Grove, California | 0.4762 | 33 | C | 0.0628 | 25 | B |
| 5. Atlanta, Georgia | 0.2806 | 44 | D | -0.1051 | 41 | D |
| 6. Baltimore, Maryland | 0.1392 | 57 | E | -0.2305 | 56 | E |
| 7. Birmingham, Alabama | 0.0931 | 62 | E | -0.2385 | 57 | E |
| 8. Boston, Massachusetts | 0.6036 | 22 | B | 0.0562 | 27 | C |
| 9. Buffalo, New York | 0.7019 | 18 | B | 0.1433 | 20 | B |
| 10. Chicago, Illinois | 0.3056 | 43 | D | -0.0930 | 40 | D |
| 11. Cincinnati, Ohio-Kentucky-Indiana | 0.0711 | 63 | E | -0.1189 | 44 | D |
| 12. Cleveland, Ohio | 0.5837 | 24 | B | -0.0252 | 35 | C |
| 13. Columbus, Ohio | 0.7621 | 14 | B | 0.1584 | 15 | B |
| 14. Dallas, Texas | 0.4585 | 35 | C | 0.0503 | 28 | C |
| 15. Dayton, Ohio | 0.3421 | 41 | D | -0.0591 | 38 | D |
| 16. Denver, Colorado | 0.9604 | 4 | A | 0.3241 | 4 | A |
| 17. Detroit, Michigan | -0.0248 | 64 | E | -0.3553 | 64 | E |
| 18. Fort Lauderdale-Hollywood, Florida | 0.5823 | 26 | B | 0.1572 | 16 | B |
| 19. Fort Worth, Texas | 0.4372 | 37 | C | -0.0323 | 37 | C |
| 20. Gary-Hammond-East Chicago, Indiana | 0.2106 | 52 | D | -0.1965 | 53 | D |
| 21. Grand Rapids, Michigan | 0.5527 | 30 | C | 0.0379 | 30 | C |
| 22. Greensboro-Winston-Salem-High Point, North Carolina | 0.2337 | 48 | D | -0.2608 | 59 | E |
| 23. Hartford, Connecticut | 0.5981 | 23 | B | 0.0352 | 32 | C |
| 24. Honolulu, Hawaii | 0.4496 | 36 | C | -0.2692 | 61 | E |
| 25. Houston, Texas | 0.5573 | 29 | C | 0.0374 | 31 | C |
| 26. Indianapolis, Indiana | 0.4303 | 38 | C | -0.1268 | 46 | D |
| 27. Jacksonville, Florida | 0.3169 | 42 | D | -0.0196 | 34 | C |
| 28. Jersey City, New Jersey | -0.1694 | 65 | E | -0.5717 | 65 | E |
| 29. Kansas City, Missouri-Kansas | 0.8089 | 12 | A | 0.2132 | 14 | A |
| 30. Los Angeles-Long Beach, California | 0.8315 | 10 | A | 0.2809 | 6 | A |
| 31. Louisville, Kentucky-Indiana | 0.2603 | 45 | D | -0.1199 | 45 | D |
| 32. Memphis, Tennessee-Arkansas | 0.1198 | 59 | E | -0.2219 | 55 | E |
| 33. Miami, Florida | 0.7634 | 13 | B | 0.2227 | 12 | A |
| 34. Milwaukee, Wisconsin | 0.8453 | 8 | A | 0.1496 | 18 | B |
| 35. Minneapolis-St. Paul, Minnesota | 0.8329 | 9 | A | 0.2530 | 9 | A |
| 36. Nashville-Davidson, Tennessee | 0.7218 | 17 | B | 0.2195 | 13 | A |
| 37. New Orleans, Louisiana | 0.1783 | 54 | E | -0.2756 | 62 | E |
| 38. New York, New York | 0.5179 | 32 | C | 0.0398 | 29 | C |
| 39. Newark, New Jersey | 0.1000 | 61 | E | -0.3204 | 63 | E |
| 40. Norfolk-Portsmouth, Virginia | 0.2507 | 46 | D | -0.1944 | 52 | D |
| 41. Oklahoma City, Oklahoma | 0.8852 | 7 | A | 0.3415 | 3 | A |
| 42. Omaha, Nebraska-Iowa | 0.9966 | 3 | A | 0.2747 | 7 | A |
| 43. Paterson-Clifton-Passaic, New Jersey | 0.1371 | 58 | E | -0.2677 | 60 | E |
| 44. Philadelphia, Pennsylvania-New Jersey | 0.2234 | 49 | D | -0.1554 | 50 | D |
| 45. Phoenix, Arizona | 0.7246 | 16 | B | 0.1476 | 19 | B |
| 46. Pittsburgh, Pennsylvania | 0.3510 | 40 | D | -0.0748 | 39 | D |
| 47. Portland, Oregon-Washington | 1.0273 | 1 | A | 0.3981 | 1 | A |
| 48. Providence-Pawtucket-Warwick, Rhode Island-Massachusetts | 0.1606 | 55 | E | -0.1508 | 49 | D |
| 49. Richmond, Virginia | 0.1123 | 60 | E | -0.2498 | 58 | E |
| 50. Rochester, New York | 0.2196 | 50 | D | -0.1409 | 48 | D |
| 51. Sacramento, California | 0.9576 | 5 | A | 0.3750 | 2 | A |
| 52. St. Louis, Missouri-Illinois | 0.1583 | 56 | E | -0.1709 | 51 | D |
| 53. Salt Lake City, Utah | 0.5728 | 27 | B | 0.0579 | 26 | C |
| 54. San Antonio, Texas | 0.2463 | 47 | D | -0.2018 | 54 | D |
| 55. San Bernadino-Riverside-Ontario, California | 0.6042 | 21 | B | 0.1034 | 22 | B |
| 56. San Diego, California | 0.9020 | 6 | A | 0.2661 | 8 | A |
| 57. San Francisco-Oakland, California | 0.8189 | 11 | A | 0.2300 | 11 | A |
| 58. San Jose, California | 0.7364 | 15 | B | 0.2354 | 10 | A |
| 59. Seattle-Everett, Washington | 1.0144 | 2 | A | 0.3063 | 5 | A |
| 60. Springfield-Chicopee-Holyoke, Massachusetts-Connecticut | 0.4634 | 34 | C | 0.0175 | 33 | C |
| 61. Syracuse, New York | 0.6157 | 20 | B | 0.1509 | 17 | B |
| 62. Tampa-St. Petersburg, Florida | 0.5526 | 31 | C | -0.0262 | 36 | C |
| 63. Toledo, Ohio-Michigan | 0.5617 | 28 | C | 0.0892 | 23 | B |
| 64. Washington, D.C.-Maryland-Virginia | 0.6848 | 19 | B | 0.1087 | 21 | B |
| 65. Youngstown-Warren, Ohio | 0.3634 | 39 | D | -0.1079 | 43 | D |

Mean ($\bar{x}$) = 0.4809          Mean ($\bar{x}$) = 0.0000
Standard Deviation (s) = 0.2928    Standard Deviation (s) = 0.2071

A = Outstanding ($\geq \bar{x} + s$)
B = Excellent ($\bar{x} + .28s \leq B < \bar{x} + s$)
C = Good ($\bar{x} - .28s < C < \bar{x} + .28s$)
D = Adequate ($\bar{x} - s < D \leq \bar{x} - .28s$)
E = Substandard ($\leq \bar{x} - s$)

adjusted standardized scores, -0.17 and -0.02, respectively. The negative scores indicate that these two SMSA's had extremely high negative input values that more than offset the positive input factors. As a result, the overall score is negative.

The remaining 11 substandard SMSA's, though still with index values below the mean minus one standard deviation ($\overline{X}$ - S), do not vary much from the adequate SMSA's. The remaining substandard SMSA's are Cincinnati, Birmingham, Newark, Richmond, Memphis, Paterson/Clifton/Passaic, Baltimore, St. Louis, Providence/Pawtucket/Warwick, New Orleans, and Akron. One finding in the social component is that the New York SMSA, while surrounded by three "E" rated SMSA's, still received an index of 0.52, slightly greater then the metropolitan mean value of 0.48. In the ranking, New York is the last SMSA with a value greater than the mean, ranked 32nd among the 65 SMSA's, and rated "good" in the social component. This is due primarily either to better opportunities for self-support and individual development, greater equality among individuals, better community living conditions, or a combination of the three. For example, the individual equality index for Newark is substantially below that for New York; while New York was ranked 17th in this category, Newark ranked 64th. Table A-5 in the Appendix gives the following information: Negro male to total male unemployment rate adjusted for educational differences in 1970, was 1.65 and 2.22, respectively; meaning that Negro males in New York had an unemployment rate 65 percent higher than the average for all males, but, in Newark the figure was 122 percent; the Negro females in both SMSA's had a 23 percent and 61 percent higher than average unemployment rate; the ratio of male to female unemployment rate adjusted for education in New York was 0.81, while in Newark it was 0.63.

As far as community living conditions are concerned, New York shows considerably higher indexes for many factors than does Jersey City. Jersey City, though showing an average birth rate, has the second highest death rate, next only to Tampa, with more than 12 deaths per 1,000 in 1970. Very few sports, dance, drama, or music events and virtually no cultural institutions and fairs and festivals were held in Jersey City in 1970. In addition, there were very few recreational facilities. The estimated cost of living index was 124, or 24 percent higher than the U.S. average.

131

# CHART 5

## REGIONAL VARIATIONS IN INDEXES:
## SOCIAL COMPONENT (L)

| RANK | SMSA | ADJUSTED STANDARIZED SCORE |
|------|------|----------------------------|

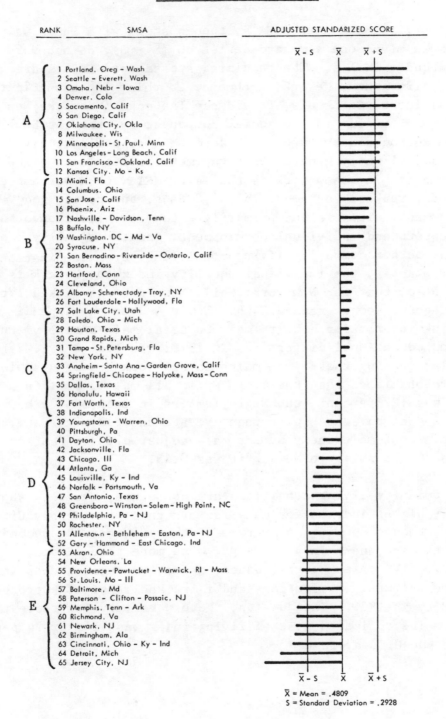

A
1 Portland, Oreg – Wash
2 Seattle – Everett, Wash
3 Omaha, Nebr – Iowa
4 Denver, Colo
5 Sacramento, Calif
6 San Diego, Calif
7 Oklahoma City, Okla
8 Milwaukee, Wis
9 Minneapolis – St. Paul, Minn
10 Los Angeles – Long Beach, Calif
11 San Francisco – Oakland, Calif
12 Kansas City, Mo – Ks

B
13 Miami, Fla
14 Columbus, Ohio
15 San Jose, Calif
16 Phoenix, Ariz
17 Nashville – Davidson, Tenn
18 Buffalo, NY
19 Washington, DC – Md – Va
20 Syracuse, NY
21 San Bernadino – Riverside – Ontario, Calif
22 Boston, Mass
23 Hartford, Conn
24 Cleveland, Ohio
25 Albany – Schenectady – Troy, NY
26 Fort Lauderdale – Hollywood, Fla
27 Salt Lake City, Utah

C
28 Toledo, Ohio – Mich
29 Houston, Texas
30 Grand Rapids, Mich
31 Tampa – St. Petersburg, Fla
32 New York, NY
33 Anaheim – Santa Ana – Garden Grove, Calif
34 Springfield – Chicopee – Holyoke, Mass – Conn
35 Dallas, Texas
36 Honolulu, Hawaii
37 Fort Worth, Texas
38 Indianapolis, Ind

D
39 Youngstown – Warren, Ohio
40 Pittsburgh, Pa
41 Dayton, Ohio
42 Jacksonville, Fla
43 Chicago, Ill
44 Atlanta, Ga
45 Louisville, Ky – Ind
46 Norfolk – Portsmouth, Va
47 San Antonio, Texas
48 Greensboro – Winston – Salem – High Point, NC
49 Philadelphia, Pa – NJ
50 Rochester, NY
51 Allentown – Bethlehem – Easton, Pa – NJ
52 Gary – Hammond – East Chicago, Ind

E
53 Akron, Ohio
54 New Orleans, La
55 Providence – Pawtucket – Warwick, RI – Mass
56 St. Louis, Mo – Ill
57 Baltimore, Md
58 Paterson – Clifton – Passaic, NJ
59 Memphis, Tenn – Ark
60 Richmond, Va
61 Newark, NJ
62 Birmingham, Ala
63 Cincinnati, Ohio – Ky – Ind
64 Detroit, Mich
65 Jersey City, NJ

$\overline{X}$ = Mean = .4809
S = Standard Deviation = .2928

The weakest factors in Jersey City are individual concerns.  People in
the city have very limited opportunities for development of individual
capabilities.  Individual choice is restricted by immobility, lack of
information, and spatial extension.  For instance, only 36.3 percent
of the population older than 25 have completed 4 years of high school or
more--some 16.0 percentage points below the U.S. level.  While 82.5
percent of the households in the U.S. have one or more automobiles, the
corresponding figure for Jersey City is only 59.1 percent.  Population
density in the city is extremely high, with 12,963 persons per square
mile--about 35 times the U.S. average of 360 persons.  It shows, on
the average, a fairly equal state between males and females, and whites
and nonwhites.  In fact, the city is one of the best in terms of racial
nondiscrimination as reflected by income and unemployment differences
adjusted for education.  The extremely low positive indexes in the
factors of individual concerns and community living conditions are more
than offset by the negative indexes in the category of individual
equality.  As a result, the overall index value for the city in the
social component becomes negative.

Detroit ranks low on all three counts in the social component--individual
concerns, individual equality, and community living conditions.
Nevertheless, Detroit received better than average ratings in several
social factors.  For instance, it ranks 29th in promoting maximum development of individual capabilities, 21st in racial equality, and 35th in
other social living conditions.  The low positive index values in
individual concerns and community living conditions, however, are not
enough to make up for the high negative index values in the individual
equality category.  For example, the SMSA had very high spatial inequalities as shown by housing segregation and income inequality indexes
between city and suburban residents--the central city's population share
was 10.0 percent higher than its income share, and the percentage of
nonwhites living in the central city was 2.42 times as many as those
living in the entire metropolitan area; comparing respectively to 6.0
percent and 1.3 times in the U.S.  The additive model employed in the
study, hence,derived a negative social component index for the SMSA
(-0.02).  This suggests that more local emphasis might be placed on
policies aimed at reducing individual inequalities between races, sexes,
central city, and suburban populations.

Portland, Seattle/Everett, Omaha, Denver, and the other "A" rated SMSA's
rated better than the U.S. average in almost all social factors.  However,
there are differences among them in terms of their strengths and
weaknesses.  Portland and Seattle/Everett are very close in the social
component with indexes of 1.03 and 1.01.  However, the living cost in

the former is much lower than in the latter SMSA. People in Portland have a lower birth rate and enjoy more recreational facilities on a per capita basis than in Seattle/Everett but have a higher unemployment rate and lower family income relative to Seattle/Everett.

Omaha has very good existing opportunity for self support and good community facilities. There is an excellent equality between sexes in the area; e.g., the male to female ratio of professional employment adjusted for education was 1.24, meaning that given equal educational background, males have only 24 percent more professional employment than females in employment distribution among occupations, while in the U.S. and Portland the corresponding figures are 49 percent and 48 percent, respectively. The higher male to female ratio in professional employment adjusted for education may be partly attributed to sex discrimination.

Another outstanding SMSA in the Midwest is Kansas City. It ranks fourth in terms of facilities for good community living and has excellent opportunities for self support and very little sex discrimination. Racial discrimination is evidently a problem for the area since it ranked 46th in terms of individual equality between white and nonwhite populations. By contrast, the St. Louis SMSA, which is also constituted of counties in two states, reveals a significantly lower social quality of life than Kansas City. The substandard rating for St. Louis is primarily due to its weak showing in the areas of individual concerns and individual equality. As far as living conditions are concerned St. Louis ranks 31st, or average. The weakest factors in St. Louis are considered to be spatial inequalities and the restricted opportunities for individual choice. The housing segregation index is 1.55 for St. Louis, for example; meaning that the central city has proportionally 1.55 times more nonwhite population than that of the metropolitan area as a whole. The U.S. figure was only 0.2. In the central city, the young (under five) and the old (over 65) age groups accounted for more than one-fifth of the total population (22.7 percent), the second highest among the large SMSA's next only to Fort Lauderdale/Hollywood. The number of motor vehicles registered in the area is 498 per 1,000 population, about 90 percent of the U.S. standard.

As noted earlier, the adjusted standardized scores for the larger SMSA's range from -0.17 to 1.03. In the social component widespread distribution among the indexes can be discerned from its coefficient of variation which is equal to 0.61 (0.29/0.48). This coefficient of variation is much greater than those obtained for the other components, implying that

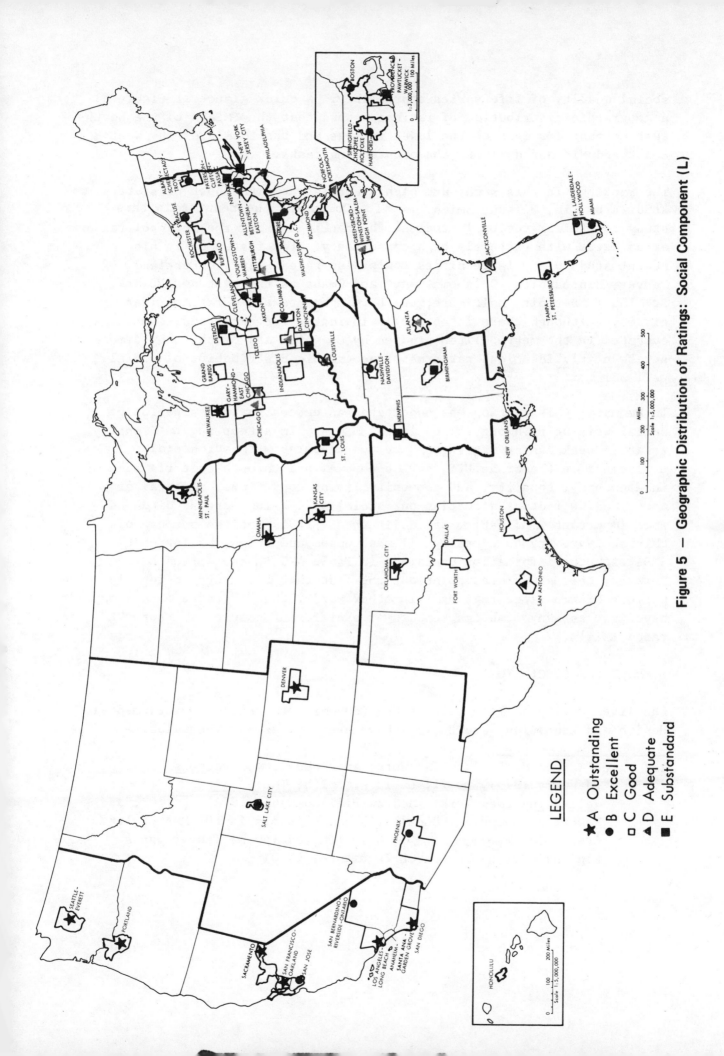

**Figure 5 — Geographic Distribution of Ratings: Social Component (L)**

LEGEND

★ A Outstanding
● B Excellent
□ C Good
▲ D Adequate
■ E Substandard

social quality of life varies appreciably. A quick glance at Figure 5, a geographic distribution of ratings, shows that the SMSA's of the Northeast account for most of the lower ratings and the SMSA's of the West Coast and Midwest dominate the outstanding ranks.

The rankings in this study are highly consistent with those of state studies by Liu, Wilson, Smith, et al. Comparing the results in this study to similar regional studies, the rankings among the metropolitan areas agree with extremely high consistency. For instance, in his recent study of 50 large cities Louis also rated Seattle, Portland Denver, Minneapolis, Oklahoma City, and Omaha as the best and Newark, St. Louis, Detroit, Baltimore, and Birmingham as the worst American cities. Although there is no single indicator for the social component computed in the metropolitan studies by Coughlin and Smith, they demonstrate nearly identical patterns of geographic distribution of social well-being.[27]

In summary, this section has undertaken an extensive investigation of social well-being among the 65 large SMSA's. In attempting to identify relative weakness and strength, numerous concerns with our social evolvement in the urban U.S. have been examined through criteria such as independency, equality, and community living conditions. A total of more than 50 factors affecting our social well-being were studied and some important implication are delineated. It is not the purpose of this study to try to identify all weaknesses and strengths for each SMSA with the information contained in Table A-5 in the Appendix. However, this study does point out the fact that there are no totally perfect or imperfect regions. In other words, the "A" rated SMSA's may have just as many problems, though of a different nature, as those "E" rated SMSA's.

SUMMARY AND CONCLUSION

The five quality of life components--Economic, Political, Environmental, Health and Education, and Social--have been analyzed. The relative

---

[27] See Arthur M. Louis, "The Worst American City," Harpers Magazine (January 1975), p. 71; David M. Smith, The Geography of Social Well-Being (New York: McGraw-Hill Company, 1973), p. 109; and Robert E. Coughlin, "Goal Attainment Levels in 101 Metropolitan Areas" (Mimeograph, Number 41) (Philadelphia, Pennsylvania: Regional Science Research Institute, 1970).

weaknesses and strengths of each of the 65 large SMSA's have been
studied with more than 100 factors.

For economic well-being, it is shown that the strongest areas in this
country are concentrated in the Northeast--the manufacturing belt--and
a few young metropolitan areas such as Dallas, Fort Worth, Houston, and
Portland.  The weak regions are in the South and in the New England
states.  The variation in economic factors among regions tends to be
relatively smaller than other quality of life components.  Different
methods of index construction have been used.  The standardized scores
differ only slightly from the adjusted standardized scores--the rank
order correlation coefficient between the two sets is highly significant
and is equal to 0.96.  However, the factor and component analyses produce
considerably different rankings, especially for SMSA's rated "B,"
"C," and "D" by the other two methods.  Since a detailed technical
investigation on factor or component analysis is beyond the scope of
this report, the results from factor and component analysis are not
included.

The local governments in the Northeast and the West Coast are found to
be more professional and efficient and people more active in politics
than in the southern states.  Although a clear visual differentiation
between the outstanding SMSA's and the substandard SMSA's was apparent
in Figure 2, the actual variations in this political component are not
appreciable.  In fact, the coefficient of variation computed from the
indexes for the political component is the smallest among the five being
discussed, i.e., 0.25.  This implies that the quality of political life
enjoyed by individuals among the large urban areas does not vary much.

The West Coast shows distinctly better environmental quality than the
manufacturing belt--particularly the East North Central region.  Industrialization and economic growth in the East North Central region have
apparently created a substandard environment in terms of air, water,
visual, noise, and solid waste pollution.  The land utilization pattern
in this region is such that relatively fewer green land and recreational
areas are made available for public use, as compared to the Pacific Coast
and other regions.  Variations in environmental deterioration among
regions are fairly high--the coefficient is 0.33.

The geographic distribution of the quality of health and education
varies from that of the other three components, although the Pacific Coast
region once again ranks as outstanding.  The position of southern states is
even more diminished--none of the large SMSA's in the South is rated
either excellent or outstanding.  The variations in health and education

quality in the areas are high with the coefficient being 0.70, highest among the five components under consideration. This implies that policies related to health and educational improvement or investment in human resources are essential and for the overall enrichment of urban quality of life.

Th evaluation of social well-being in this country tends to favor the Midwest and the Pacific Coast regions. The aging metropolitan areas in the Northeast and South are rated inferior when compared to others in social life quality as judged by individual concerns, equality, and community living conditions. A great dispersion in this social component was also observed geographically. The coefficient of variation for this component is 0.61, second highest among the five coefficients discussed. This indicates that social concerns are critical issues. The substandard regions must go a long way to catch up with the out-standing SMSA's, as shown by the social component. Conceivably, improvements in health and education will directly enhance the social quality of life. Policies to achieve these objectives for every American are essential.

# VI

## QUALITY OF LIFE
## FINDINGS AND IMPLICATIONS:
## MEDIUM METROPOLITAN AREAS (M)

The quality of life for the 83 medium sized SMSA's with a population between 200,000 and 500,000 was studied and the results will be discussed in this chapter. The geographic distribution of these SMSA's follows the same pattern as the large SMSA's, clustering mostly in the eastern regions, such as East, North and South Central, Middle and South Atlantic. Less than one-third of the 83 SMSA's are in the states west of the Mississippi River; of these about one-third are in the State of California. There is no medium SMSA in many states such as Missouri, the Dakota's, Nebraska, Montana, Wyoming, Idaho, Utah, or Maine.

Since the criteria employed to measure the quality of life in this chapter were identical to those discussed in the last chapter, only empirical results and their implications will be delineated.

The analyses in this chapter will follow the same format as those described in the preceding chapter. A short summary of the overall findings will be given in the last section after the five quality of life components have been described.

ECONOMIC COMPONENT

The index, rank, and rating for economic quality of life of the 83 medium sized SMSA's are contained in Table 6. There are 16 SMSA's with an economic quality of life index beyond 2.14, or the sum of mean plus one standard deviation ($\bar{x} + s$), and thus rated "A" or outstanding. This group of SMSA's is led by Fort Wayne and South Bend in Indiana, and Kalamazoo in Michigan, with indexes valued at 2.95, 2.70, and 2.54, respectively. Following them, most economic outstanding SMSA's are shown in the East North Central Region, especially surrounding the Great Lakes areas. West Palm Beach, Florida, is the only one in the South and Eugene, Oregon, the only other along the West Coast. Des Moines, Iowa, Wichita, Kansas, and Tulsa, Oklahoma, in the Midwest also scored "A." It is interesting to note that three "E" rated SMSA's appeared in the West Coast--Tacoma in Washington, Fresno and Salinas/Monterey in California. In contrast to the economic power of the

# TABLE 6

## INDEX AND RATING OF ECONOMIC COMPONENT (M)

| SMSA | Adjusted Standardized Scores | | | Standardized Scores | | |
|------|-------|------|--------|-------|------|--------|
|      | Value | Rank | Rating | Value | Rank | Rating |
| 66. Albuquerque, N. Mex. | 1.8571 | 26 | B | -0.0229 | 39 | C |
| 67. Ann Arbor, Mich. | 2.1429 | 15 | A | 0.2434 | 16 | B |
| 68. Appleton-Oshkosh, Wis. | 2.4214 | 7 | A | 0.4163 | 9 | A |
| 69. Augusta, Ga.-S.C. | 0.9571 | 80 | E | -0.4525 | 76 | E |
| 70. Austin, Texas | 1.7857 | 32 | C | -0.1103 | 53 | D |
| 71. Bakersfield, Calif. | 1.2643 | 68 | D | -0.4707 | 77 | E |
| 72. Baton Rouge, La. | 1.4143 | 57 | D | -0.0876 | 46 | C |
| 73. Beaumont-Port Arthur-Orange, Texas | 1.7214 | 33 | C | 0.0059 | 36 | C |
| 74. Binghamton, N.Y.-Pa. | 1.7071 | 35 | C | -0.0371 | 42 | C |
| 75. Bridgeport, Conn. | 1.8071 | 29 | B | 0.2115 | 18 | B |
| 76. Canton, Ohio | 2.1643 | 14 | A | 0.2695 | 15 | B |
| 77. Charleston, S.C. | 0.9643 | 78 | E | -0.5003 | 80 | E |
| 78. Charleston, W. Va. | 1.2714 | 67 | D | -0.3004 | 67 | D |
| 79. Charlotte, N.C. | 1.6643 | 40 | C | 0.0869 | 31 | C |
| 80. Chattanooga, Tenn.-Ga. | 1.3214 | 63 | D | -0.1591 | 58 | D |
| 81. Colorado Springs, Colo. | 1.5714 | 47 | C | -0.0924 | 47 | C |
| 82. Columbia, S.C. | 1.4286 | 56 | D | -0.1358 | 54 | D |
| 83. Columbus, Ga.-Ala. | 1.0786 | 76 | E | -0.5140 | 81 | E |
| 84. Corpus Christi, Texas | 1.9000 | 25 | B | 1.6571 | 1 | A |
| 85. Davenport-Rock Island-Moline, Iowa-Ill. | 2.0286 | 19 | B | 0.1872 | 20 | B |
| 86. Des Moines, Iowa | 2.2500 | 10 | A | 0.3633 | 12 | B |
| 87. Duluth-Superior, Minn.-Wis. | 1.4000 | 58 | D | -0.2761 | 66 | D |
| 88. El Paso, Texas | 0.9643 | 79 | E | -0.4831 | 78 | E |
| 89. Erie, Pa. | 1.6500 | 42 | C | -0.0240 | 40 | C |
| 90. Eugene, Oreg. | 2.2000 | 12 | A | 0.2416 | 17 | B |
| 91. Evansville, Ind.-Ky. | 1.9143 | 24 | B | 0.1100 | 26 | B |
| 92. Fayetteville, N.C. | 0.6643 | 83 | E | -0.7167 | 83 | E |
| 93. Flint, Mich. | 2.0000 | 21 | B | 0.1574 | 23 | B |
| 94. Fort Wayne, Ind. | 2.9500 | 1 | A | 0.6407 | 5 | A |
| 95. Fresno, Calif. | 1.0214 | 77 | E | -0.4896 | 79 | E |
| 96. Greenville, S.C. | 1.5643 | 48 | C | 0.0788 | 32 | C |
| 97. Hamilton-Middleton, Ohio | 2.0071 | 20 | B | 0.1766 | 21 | B |
| 98. Harrisburg, Pa. | 1.5643 | 49 | C | -0.1013 | 51 | C |
| 99. Huntington-Ashland, W. Va.-Ky.-Ohio | 1.1643 | 73 | E | -0.4157 | 75 | E |
| 100. Huntsville, Ala. | 1.6071 | 43 | C | -0.0160 | 38 | C |
| 101. Jackson, Miss. | 1.3929 | 60 | D | -0.2205 | 60 | D |
| 102. Johnstown, Pa. | 1.1786 | 72 | E | -0.3021 | 68 | D |
| 103. Kalamazoo, Mich. | 2.5429 | 3 | A | 0.4534 | 8 | A |
| 104. Knoxville, Tenn. | 1.7214 | 34 | C | -0.0628 | 44 | C |
| 105. Lancaster, Pa. | 1.8357 | 27 | B | 0.0879 | 30 | C |
| 106. Lansing, Mich. | 2.0929 | 17 | B | 0.1563 | 24 | B |
| 107. Las Vegas, Nev. | 1.6786 | 36 | C | 0.0706 | 33 | C |
| 108. Lawrence-Haverhill, Mass.-N.H. | 1.8000 | 30 | C | -0.0327 | 41 | C |
| 109. Little Rock-North Little Rock, Ark. | 1.4000 | 59 | D | -0.1527 | 56 | D |
| 110. Lorain-Elyria, Ohio | 1.9643 | 22 | B | 0.1077 | 27 | B |
| 111. Lowell, Mass. | 1.4571 | 53 | D | -0.2237 | 61 | D |
| 112. Macon, Ga. | 0.9357 | 81 | E | -0.3720 | 73 | E |
| 113. Madison, Wis. | 1.7857 | 31 | C | -0.0969 | 48 | C |
| 114. Mobile, Ala. | 1.1143 | 75 | E | -0.3779 | 74 | E |
| 115. Montgomery, Ala. | 0.7500 | 82 | E | -0.5886 | 82 | E |
| 116. New Haven, Conn. | 2.0429 | 18 | B | 0.1020 | 29 | C |
| 117. New London-Groton-Norwich, Conn. | 1.3357 | 62 | D | -0.2556 | 65 | D |
| 118. Newport News-Hampton, Va. | 1.3214 | 64 | D | -0.1545 | 57 | D |
| 119. Orlando, Fla. | 1.4500 | 54 | D | -0.1795 | 59 | D |
| 120. Oxnard-Ventura, Calif. | 1.3929 | 61 | D | -0.0576 | 43 | C |
| 121. Pensacola, Fla. | 1.1857 | 70 | E | -0.3716 | 72 | E |
| 122. Peoria, Ill. | 2.4071 | 8 | A | 0.3758 | 10 | A |
| 123. Raleigh, N.C. | 1.8214 | 28 | B | 0.1318 | 25 | B |
| 124. Reading, Pa. | 1.6714 | 39 | C | 0.1040 | 28 | B |
| 125. Rockford, Ill. | 2.2071 | 11 | A | 0.1677 | 22 | B |
| 126. Saginaw, Mich. | 2.4071 | 9 | A | 0.3682 | 11 | A |
| 127. Salinas-Monterey, Calif. | 1.1857 | 71 | E | -0.3076 | 69 | D |
| 128. Santa Barbara, Calif. | 1.6786 | 37 | C | 0.0527 | 34 | C |
| 129. Santa Rosa, Calif. | 1.6000 | 45 | C | -0.0991 | 49 | C |
| 130. Scranton, Pa. | 1.4786 | 52 | D | -0.1045 | 52 | D |
| 131. Shreveport, La. | 1.5071 | 51 | D | -0.1380 | 55 | D |
| 132. South Bend, Ind. | 2.7000 | 2 | A | 0.6627 | 4 | A |
| 133. Spokane, Wash. | 1.5214 | 50 | D | -0.0701 | 45 | C |
| 134. Stamford, Conn. | 2.4714 | 5 | A | 0.9151 | 2 | A |
| 135. Stockton, Calif. | 1.6071 | 44 | C | 0.8132 | 3 | A |
| 136. Tacoma, Wash. | 1.1500 | 74 | E | -0.3634 | 70 | D |
| 137. Trenton, N.J. | 1.3000 | 65 | D | -0.2524 | 63 | D |
| 138. Tucson, Ariz. | 1.2000 | 69 | D | -0.3673 | 71 | D |
| 139. Tulsa, Okla. | 2.4429 | 6 | A | 0.4586 | 7 | A |
| 140. Utica-Rome, N.Y. | 1.2786 | 66 | D | -0.2365 | 62 | D |
| 141. Vallejo-Napa, Calif. | 1.5786 | 46 | C | -0.0999 | 50 | C |
| 142. Waterbury, Conn. | 2.1429 | 16 | A | 0.2968 | 13 | B |
| 143. West Palm Beach, Fla. | 2.4786 | 4 | A | 0.4769 | 6 | A |
| 144. Wichita, Kansas | 2.1714 | 13 | A | 0.2748 | 14 | B |
| 145. Wilkes-Barre-Hazleton, Pa. | 1.4500 | 55 | D | -0.2535 | 64 | D |
| 146. Wilmington, Del.-N.J.-Md. | 1.6786 | 38 | C | 0.0160 | 35 | C |
| 147. Worcester, Mass. | 1.6643 | 41 | C | 0.0025 | 37 | C |
| 148. York, Pa. | 1.9643 | 23 | B | 0.2058 | 19 | B |

A = Outstanding ($\geq \bar{x} + s$)
B = Excellent ($\bar{x} + .28s \leq B < \bar{x} + s$)
C = Good ($\bar{x} - .28s < C < \bar{x} + .28s$)
D = Adequate ($\bar{x} - s < D \leq \bar{x} - .28s$)
E = Substandard ($\bar{x} - s$)

Mean ($\bar{x}$) = 1.6691
Standard Deviation(s) = 0.4695

Mean ($\bar{x}$) = 0.0000
Standard Deviation(s) = 0.3674

large SMSA's, the West Coast in general and California in particular
revealed a weaker economic status relative to other medium SMSA's in
the country.  Among the 14 SMSA's with index values lower than the
mean minus one standard deviation, Fayetteville, North Carolina;
Montgomery, Alabama; Macon, Georgia; Augusta, Georgia/South Carolina;
El Paso, Texas; and Charleston, South Carolina, received the lowest
economic indexes with values below 1.00 as compared to the metropolitan
average of 1.67.  Figure 6 depicts the geographic variations in economic
ratings among the 83 SMSA's.

For weakness and strength identification, Table B-1 in the Appendix
provides some useful information.  The results in the preceding
chapter have clearly indicated that there are neither perfect SMSA's
or SMSA's consistently ranked worse in all factors selected as criteria
in this study.  Conceivably, similar results can be observed through
careful study of Table B-1 in the Appendix.  For instance, Fort Wayne
rated only average in community income equality and the chamber's effort
in stimulating regional economic growth.  While there were 31.3 percent
of the families in the U.S. with income below the poverty level or
above $15,000 in 1970, this SMSA also had 28.6 percent, not very much
better than the U.S. average.  The Chamber of Commerce in the area
employed 4.3 persons per 100,000 population, ranking only 29th.  Nevertheless, this area is one of the few SMSA's with an extremely high
percentage of family income beyond the poverty level and many
owner-occupied housing units.

South Bend ranked second highest in terms of community economic health,
but when income distribution, productivity, economic concentration, etc.,
are all combined, its unemployment rate in 1970 was fairly high, 4.7
percent or 0.3 percentage points higher than the U.S. average.
Kalamazoo, as another example, ranked high in individual economic well-
being but only 16th in community economic health, and it had the same
high unemployment rate as South Bend.  Furthermore, the income distribution in Kalamazoo is more unequal than in South Bend; the percentage
of families with income below poverty level or greater than $15,000
was 31.4 percent in Kalamazoo versus 25.8 percent in South Bend.

The personal income per capita in Fayetteville amounted to $2,340 or
more than one quarter below the U.S. average of $3,139, and its total
bank deposits per capita showed $576, or just about 23.1 percent of the
U.S. average of $2,492.  These low values may be greatly attributed to
the low labor productivity and a high unemployment rate of 5.2 percent.
However, the inequality in income distribution in this SMSA tends to
be no problem at all.  Montgomery's best points are the rankings

141

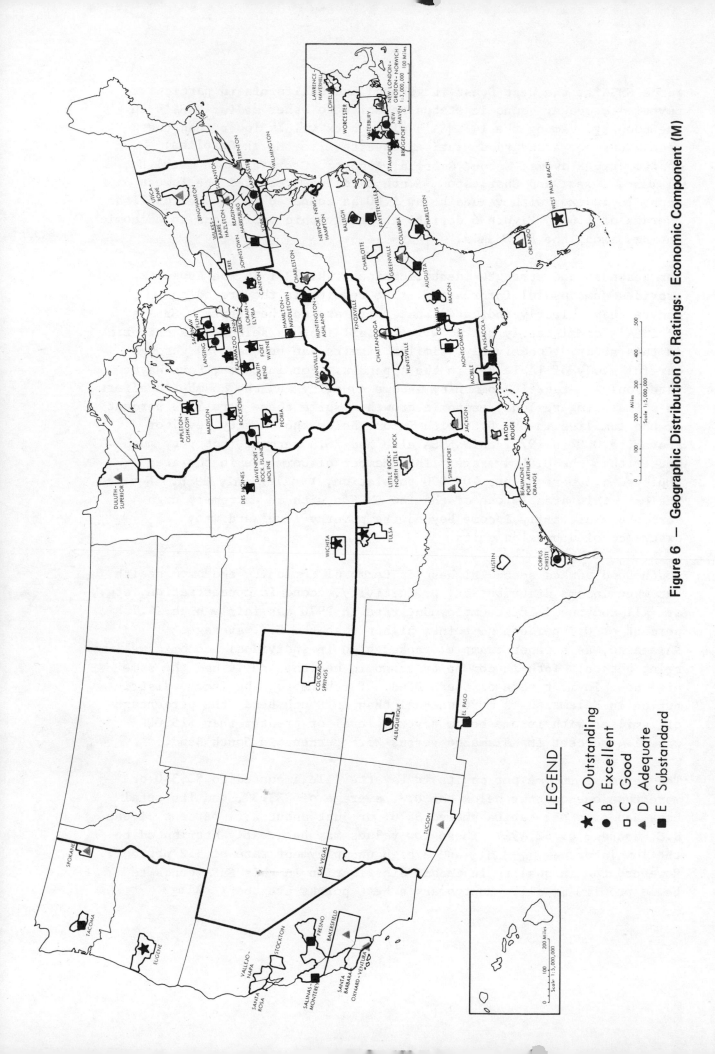

**Figure 6 — Geographic Distribution of Ratings: Economic Component (M)**

LEGEND

A Outstanding
B Excellent
C Good
D Adequate
E Substandard

of inequality and unemployment; for in these two factors, Montgomery ranked even above the average, 33rd and 28th, respectively. In Montgomery 96.2 percent of the total labor force in the SMSA were employed in 1969, as compared to only 95.6 percent in the U.S. as a whole.

Individual economic well-being in Macon, especially the average personal income per capita, was not as severe a problem as other community economic structures and viability, such as family poverty and capital funds available for investment. The undeflated income per capita in the SMSA was $2,733, or only 87.1 percent of the national level, but Macon ranked 50th among the 83 medium SMSA's. Partly due to unequal distribution of income, this area had only 84.6 percent of families with income above the poverty level or about 4.7 percentage points below the national counterpart. Probably because of the relatively low income per capita being partially ascribed to low labor productivity, total bank deposits per capita in the area were relatively lower than in other SMSA's and much lower than the national figure--only equal to 49.7 percent.

Two SMSA's in such opposite geographic locations as Tacoma and West Palm Beach were rated substandard and outstanding, respectively. Although West Palm Beach had almost the highest indicators in average income per capita and individual wealth, the income and wealth distribution among individuals and families in the area was fairly unequal. In contrast, the poverty and income distribution situation in Tacoma was about average, but the unemployment, the capital availability, and the specialized economic structure substantially impeded the area's community economic health. The closest SMSA to Tacoma, Eugene, with an unemployment rate as high as 8.1 percent in 1970, still obtained very high average income per capita and wealth status because of its higher labor productivity. A reasonably good distribution of income also helped advance the rating of this SMSA to the "A" category.

In passing, it should be noted that this study always evaluates the results deduced from the adjusted standardized rather than the unadjusted standardized scores because the extremely high value of one factor (or a few factors) may dominate the overall component rating if it is (they are) not adjusted. A good example was found with Stockton SMSA in California. Without adjusting the standardized "Z" scores of all factors, the area received an average economic index of 0.8132, or more than two standard deviations above the mean and hence, rated outstanding or "A." This could be the result of two extremely high "Z" scores computed for its savings and bank deposits per capita. These two "Z"

# CHART 6

## REGIONAL VARIATIONS IN INDEXES: ECONOMIC COMPONENT (M)

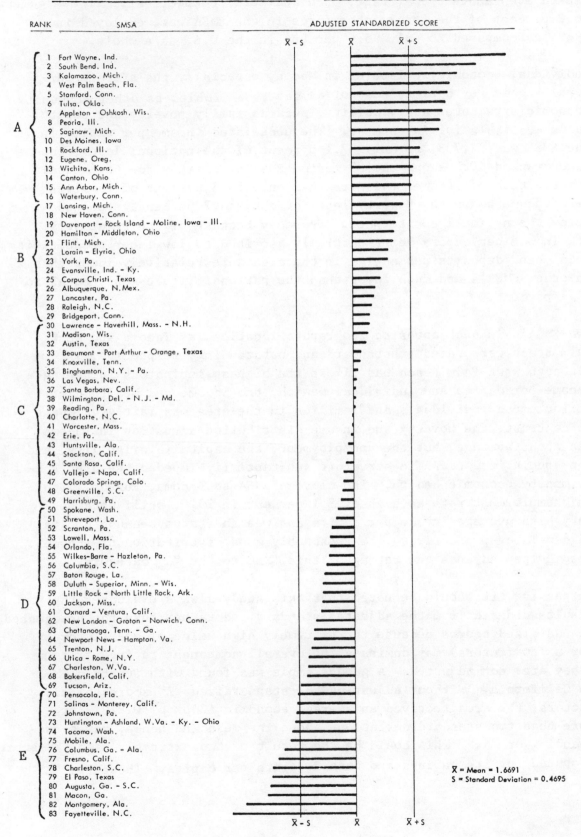

| RANK | SMSA |
|------|------|
| | ADJUSTED STANDARDIZED SCORE |
| 1 | Fort Wayne, Ind. |
| 2 | South Bend, Ind. |
| 3 | Kalamazoo, Mich. |
| 4 | West Palm Beach, Fla. |
| 5 | Stamford, Conn. |
| 6 | Tulsa, Okla. |
| 7 | Appleton – Oshkosh, Wis. |
| 8 | Peoria, Ill. |
| A 9 | Saginaw, Mich. |
| 10 | Des Moines, Iowa |
| 11 | Rockford, Ill. |
| 12 | Eugene, Oreg. |
| 13 | Wichita, Kans. |
| 14 | Canton, Ohio |
| 15 | Ann Arbor, Mich. |
| 16 | Waterbury, Conn. |
| 17 | Lansing, Mich. |
| 18 | New Haven, Conn. |
| 19 | Davenport – Rock Island – Moline, Iowa – Ill. |
| 20 | Hamilton – Middleton, Ohio |
| 21 | Flint, Mich. |
| 22 | Lorain – Elyria, Ohio |
| B 23 | York, Pa. |
| 24 | Evansville, Ind. – Ky. |
| 25 | Corpus Christi, Texas |
| 26 | Albuquerque, N. Mex. |
| 27 | Lancaster, Pa. |
| 28 | Raleigh, N.C. |
| 29 | Bridgeport, Conn. |
| 30 | Lawrence – Haverhill, Mass. – N.H. |
| 31 | Madison, Wis. |
| 32 | Austin, Texas |
| 33 | Beaumont – Port Arthur – Orange, Texas |
| 34 | Knoxville, Tenn. |
| 35 | Binghamton, N.Y. – Pa. |
| 36 | Las Vegas, Nev. |
| 37 | Santa Barbara, Calif. |
| 38 | Wilmington, Del. – N.J. – Md. |
| C 39 | Reading, Pa. |
| 40 | Charlotte, N.C. |
| 41 | Worcester, Mass. |
| 42 | Erie, Pa. |
| 43 | Huntsville, Ala. |
| 44 | Stockton, Calif. |
| 45 | Santa Rosa, Calif. |
| 46 | Vallejo – Napa, Calif. |
| 47 | Colorado Springs, Colo. |
| 48 | Greenville, S.C. |
| 49 | Harrisburg, Pa. |
| 50 | Spokane, Wash. |
| 51 | Shreveport, La. |
| 52 | Scranton, Pa. |
| 53 | Lowell, Mass. |
| 54 | Orlando, Fla. |
| 55 | Wilkes-Barre – Hazleton, Pa. |
| 56 | Columbia, S.C. |
| 57 | Baton Rouge, La. |
| 58 | Duluth – Superior, Minn. – Wis. |
| 59 | Little Rock – North Little Rock, Ark. |
| D 60 | Jackson, Miss. |
| 61 | Oxnard – Ventura, Calif. |
| 62 | New London – Groton – Norwich, Conn. |
| 63 | Chattanooga, Tenn. – Ga. |
| 64 | Newport News – Hampton, Va. |
| 65 | Trenton, N.J. |
| 66 | Utica – Rome, N.Y. |
| 67 | Charleston, W.Va. |
| 68 | Bakersfield, Calif. |
| 69 | Tucson, Ariz. |
| 70 | Pensacola, Fla. |
| 71 | Salinas – Monterey, Calif. |
| 72 | Johnstown, Pa. |
| 73 | Huntington – Ashland, W.Va. – Ky. – Ohio |
| 74 | Tacoma, Wash. |
| 75 | Mobile, Ala. |
| E 76 | Columbus, Ga. – Ala. |
| 77 | Fresno, Calif. |
| 78 | Charleston, S.C. |
| 79 | El Paso, Texas |
| 80 | Augusta, Ga. – S.C. |
| 81 | Macon, Ga. |
| 82 | Montgomery, Ala. |
| 83 | Fayetteville, N.C. |

$\bar{X}$ = Mean = 1.6691
S = Standard Deviation = 0.4695

144

scores jointly advanced the overall component rating significantly above those for other SMSA's in the same group. With the adjusted "Z" score method, the SMSA received the maximum grade of "5" points for these two factors which were weighted equally with other factors to derive the overall index. As a result of this adjustment, Stockton received an overall index value of only 1.61 or slightly below the group mean and hence, rated "good" rather than "outstanding."

The regional variations in indexes are shown in Chart 6. Although there are 30 SMSA's with indexes valued outside the range of the mean plus and minus one standard deviation, the overall variation in the indexes is small. The coefficient of variation is equal to 0.28 (0.47/1.67). In other words, the remaining 53 SMSA's in this group did not seem to have economic weaknesses and strengths significantly different from each other as far as the overall results are concerned. In addition, the distribution of the indexes for all SMSA's is very symmetrical and tends to approach normal.

POLITICAL COMPONENT

The East North Central Region has been quantitatively identified as the dominating region in economic viability and vitality when compared to other regions in the preceding section. In terms of political performance and government efficiency, the outstanding positions of the metropolitan areas in the region are once again retained. As shown in Table 7, the region accounts for more than one-half of the "A" rated SMSA's in the political component of the quality of life measures, i.e., 10 out of 19. Led by Duluth/Superior (Minnesota and Wisconsin) with an index as high as 3.73, Appleton/Oshkosh, Wisconsin--3.65, Kalamazoo, Michigan--3.51, and Madison, Wisconsin--3.51 in the East North Central, the remaining outstanding SMSA's are Eugene and Santa Barbara in the West Coast; Binghamton, New York/Pennsylvania; Waterbury, Connecticut; Fort Wayne, Indiana; Bridgeport, Connecticut; Des Moines, Iowa; South Bend, Indiana; Lansing, Michigan; Evansville, Indiana/Kentucky; Charleston, West Virginia; and Utica/Rome, New York.

On the other end of the scale, 15 SMSA's have been classified as substandard due to their low indexes relative to other medium sized SMSA's. Corpus Christi, Texas; Macon, Georgia; Columbia, South Carolina; Fayetteville, North Carolina; Columbus, Georgia/Alabama; and Charleston, South Carolina have index values substantially below the mean (2.62) minus one standard deviation (0.60). The remaining 11 SMSA's with index values lower than the threshhold level are also found in the southern states.

145

# TABLE 7
## INDEX AND RATING OF POLITICAL COMPONENT (M)

| SMSA | Adjusted Standardized Scores | | | Standardized Scores | | |
|------|-------|------|--------|-------|------|--------|
| | Value | Rank | Rating | Value | Rank | Rating |
| 66. Albuquerque, N. Mex. | 3.1111 | 22 | B | 0.2638 | 26 | B |
| 67. Ann Arbor, Mich. | 2.5764 | 45 | C | 0.1228 | 34 | B |
| 68. Appleton-Oshkosh, Wis. | 3.6528 | 2 | A | 0.7234 | 4 | A |
| 69. Augusta, Ga.-S.C. | 2.1111 | 63 | D | -0.4225 | 69 | D |
| 70. Austin, Texas | 2.3125 | 60 | D | -0.1483 | 53 | D |
| 71. Bakersfield, Calif. | 3.1667 | 20 | B | 0.5918 | 7 | A |
| 72. Baton Rouge, La. | 2.3958 | 52 | D | -0.2327 | 60 | D |
| 73. Beaumont-Port Arthur-Orange, Texas | 2.0833 | 66 | D | -0.3298 | 63 | D |
| 74. Binghamton, N.Y.-Pa. | 3.4375 | 7 | A | 0.3914 | 19 | B |
| 75. Bridgeport, Conn. | 3.3681 | 10 | A | 0.3952 | 16 | B |
| 76. Canton, Ohio | 2.7708 | 36 | C | 0.0703 | 37 | C |
| 77. Charleston, S.C. | 1.6458 | 78 | E | -0.6511 | 76 | E |
| 78. Charleston, W. Va. | 3.2431 | 18 | A | 0.4658 | 11 | A |
| 79. Charlotte, N.C. | 1.9028 | 72 | E | -0.4413 | 73 | E |
| 80. Chattanooga, Tenn.-Ga. | 2.3889 | 54 | D | -0.0622 | 48 | C |
| 81. Colorado Springs, Colo. | 2.3333 | 58 | D | 0.0520 | 39 | C |
| 82. Columbia, S.C. | 1.5764 | 81 | E | -0.7922 | 81 | E |
| 83. Columbus, Ga.-Ala. | 1.6319 | 79 | E | -0.9817 | 82 | E |
| 84. Corpus Christi, Texas | 1.5000 | 83 | E | -0.6822 | 78 | E |
| 85. Davenport-Rock Island-Moline, Iowa-Ill. | 2.6528 | 41 | C | 0.0300 | 43 | C |
| 86. Des Moines, Iowa | 3.3333 | 11 | A | 0.7497 | 3 | A |
| 87. Duluth-Superior, Minn.-Wis. | 3.7292 | 1 | A | 0.6525 | 5 | A |
| 88. El Paso, Texas | 1.6944 | 75 | E | -0.7156 | 79 | E |
| 89. Erie, Pa. | 2.8681 | 31 | B | 0.0646 | 38 | C |
| 90. Eugene, Oreg. | 3.5000 | 5 | A | 0.6345 | 6 | A |
| 91. Evansville, Ind.-Ky. | 3.2500 | 17 | A | 0.4985 | 9 | A |
| 92. Fayetteville, N.C. | 1.6042 | 80 | E | -1.1716 | 83 | E |
| 93. Flint, Mich. | 3.2917 | 16 | A | 0.4065 | 14 | B |
| 94. Fort Wayne, Ind. | 3.3750 | 9 | A | 0.8428 | 1 | A |
| 95. Fresno, Calif. | 3.0000 | 26 | B | 0.3926 | 18 | B |
| 96. Greenville, S.C. | 1.6944 | 76 | E | -0.7254 | 80 | E |
| 97. Hamilton-Middleton, Ohio | 2.3542 | 55 | D | -0.2152 | 58 | D |
| 98. Harrisburg, Pa. | 2.4514 | 49 | D | 0.1380 | 33 | B |
| 99. Huntington-Ashland, W. Va.-Ky.-Ohio | 2.4931 | 46 | C | -0.1040 | 50 | C |
| 100. Huntsville, Ala. | 2.1042 | 64 | D | -0.3161 | 62 | D |
| 101. Jackson, Miss. | 1.6944 | 77 | E | -0.6072 | 75 | E |
| 102. Johnstown, Pa. | 2.9375 | 29 | B | 0.1981 | 30 | B |
| 103. Kalamazoo, Mich. | 3.5069 | 3 | A | 0.4462 | 12 | A |
| 104. Knoxville, Tenn. | 2.4236 | 51 | D | -0.1924 | 56 | D |
| 105. Lancaster, Pa. | 2.1806 | 62 | D | -0.4401 | 72 | E |
| 106. Lansing, Mich. | 3.3194 | 13 | A | 0.4341 | 13 | A |
| 107. Las Vegas, Nev. | 2.3403 | 57 | D | -0.2344 | 61 | D |
| 108. Lawrence-Haverhill, Mass.-N.H. | 3.1319 | 21 | B | 0.3292 | 23 | B |
| 109. Little Rock-North Little Rock, Ark. | 1.7917 | 73 | E | -0.3820 | 67 | D |
| 110. Lorain-Elyria, Ohio | 2.4792 | 47 | C | -0.2189 | 59 | D |
| 111. Lowell, Mass. | 2.9653 | 28 | B | 0.2967 | 25 | B |
| 112. Macon, Ga. | 1.5417 | 82 | E | -0.5813 | 74 | E |
| 113. Madison, Wis. | 3.5069 | 4 | A | 0.5680 | 8 | A |
| 114. Mobile, Ala. | 1.7708 | 74 | E | -0.6627 | 77 | E |
| 115. Montgomery, Ala. | 1.9722 | 70 | E | -0.4259 | 70 | D |
| 116. New Haven, Conn. | 3.3056 | 15 | A | 0.3642 | 21 | B |
| 117. New London-Groton-Norwich, Conn. | 2.8264 | 35 | B | -0.0846 | 49 | C |
| 118. Newport News-Hampton, Va. | 2.0347 | 68 | D | -0.4127 | 68 | D |
| 119. Orlando, Fla. | 2.4722 | 48 | C | -0.0115 | 45 | C |
| 120. Oxnard-Ventura, Calif. | 2.8611 | 32 | B | 0.1108 | 36 | C |
| 121. Pensacola, Fla. | 2.0000 | 69 | E | -0.3618 | 66 | D |
| 122. Peoria, Ill. | 2.6528 | 42 | C | -0.0370 | 47 | C |
| 123. Raleigh, N.C. | 2.4306 | 50 | D | -0.1591 | 54 | D |
| 124. Reading, Pa. | 2.3958 | 53 | D | -0.1803 | 55 | D |
| 125. Rockford, Ill. | 2.5972 | 44 | C | 0.0113 | 44 | C |
| 126. Saginaw, Mich. | 2.7222 | 39 | C | 0.1657 | 32 | B |
| 127. Salinas-Monterey, Calif. | 2.0694 | 67 | D | -0.3327 | 64 | D |
| 128. Santa Barbara, Calif. | 3.4444 | 6 | A | 0.3996 | 15 | B |
| 129. Santa Rosa, Calif. | 3.3194 | 14 | A | 0.7994 | 2 | A |
| 130. Scranton, Pa. | 3.0625 | 25 | B | 0.2082 | 29 | B |
| 131. Shreveport, La. | 1.9514 | 71 | E | -0.4279 | 71 | D |
| 132. South Bend, Ind. | 3.3264 | 12 | A | 0.4805 | 10 | A |
| 133. Spokane, Wash. | 3.0694 | 24 | B | 0.3940 | 17 | B |
| 134. Stamford, Conn. | 2.9097 | 30 | B | 0.1175 | 35 | C |
| 135. Stockton, Calif. | 2.8542 | 33 | B | 0.3668 | 20 | B |
| 136. Tacoma, Wash. | 2.2014 | 61 | D | -0.1372 | 51 | D |
| 137. Trenton, N.J. | 2.7500 | 37 | C | 0.0463 | 41 | C |
| 138. Tucson, Ariz. | 2.3264 | 59 | D | -0.1961 | 57 | D |
| 139. Tulsa, Okla. | 2.6736 | 40 | C | 0.0362 | 42 | C |
| 140. Utica-Rome, N.Y. | 3.2222 | 19 | A | 0.3138 | 24 | B |
| 141. Vallejo-Napa, Calif. | 2.6111 | 43 | C | -0.0283 | 46 | C |
| 142. Waterbury, Conn. | 3.3889 | 8 | A | 0.3518 | 22 | B |
| 143. West Palm Beach, Fla. | 2.3542 | 56 | D | -0.1428 | 52 | D |
| 144. Wichita, Kansas | 3.0764 | 23 | B | 0.2199 | 28 | B |
| 145. Wilkes-Barre-Hazleton, Pa. | 2.7431 | 38 | C | 0.0469 | 40 | C |
| 146. Wilmington, Del.-N.J.-Md. | 2.8472 | 34 | B | 0.2218 | 27 | B |
| 147. Worcester, Mass. | 3.0000 | 27 | B | 0.1927 | 31 | B |
| 148. York, Pa. | 2.0903 | 65 | D | -0.3568 | 65 | D |

A = Outstanding ($\geq \bar{x} + s$)
B = Excellent ($\bar{x} + .28s \leq B < \bar{x} + s$)
C = Good ($\bar{x} - .28s < C < \bar{x} + .28s$)
D = Adequate ($\bar{x} - s < D \leq \bar{x} - .28s$)
E = Substandard ($\leq \bar{x} - s$)

Mean ($\bar{x}$) = 2.6236                     Mean ($\bar{x}$) = 0.0000
Standard Deviation (s) = 0.5970          Standard Deviation (s) = 0.4323

The geographic distribution of ratings in this component as portrayed by Figure 7 reveals a vivid, contrasting picture between the East North Central, the West Coast, and the southern states. The dividing line in this medium metropolitan area section is even clearer than that observed in the large metropolitan areas.

Studies tend to associate substantially affluence with governmental efficiency in that public expenditures are conventional measures of government performance, and a higher level of per capita expenditure has to come from a higher level of per capita revenue, which in turn depends on the affluence and wealth status of the community due to the characteristics of local tax structure. When comparing Figure 7 to Figure 6, this cause-effect relationship is upheld also for most metropolitan areas except those in the State of California. Economically speaking, none of the medium SMSA's in California was rated either outstanding(A) or excellent (B) as noted earlier, a surprising contrast to the large SMSA's in that state. However, almost all the medium SMSA's in the state were rated "A" or "B" in the quality of public administration and individual political participation.

Naturally, each SMSA has its weaknesses and strengths. SMSA's could not be rated either outstanding or substandard simply because of one or two typical factors since the standardized scores had been adjusted before the weighted component indexes were constructed. However, a combination of some of the 21 factors which made up the composite indexes for the political component would affect the rating. Duluth/Superior, though ranked first among the 83 SMSA's in the political component, did not have the best of all factors. In fact, the professionalism of its local governments in 1970 was only about average and Duluth/Superior ranked 34th in that category; nor did it have the best informed citizenry, and the rank for that category was about 20th in standardized "Z" scores. To be more specific, in terms of professionalism this SMSA showed lower than U.S. average monthly earnings for school teachers ($656 versus $682), and lower than average police protection services. The ratio of police protection employment per 1,000 population was 1.4 versus 2.5 in the U.S. Although by factors reflecting individual political activities, this SMSA had a much better than national average record. Its local Sunday newspaper circulation of 820 per 1,000 population and the percentage of occupied housing with television sets (96.0 percent), for example, was below that for some other SMSA's.

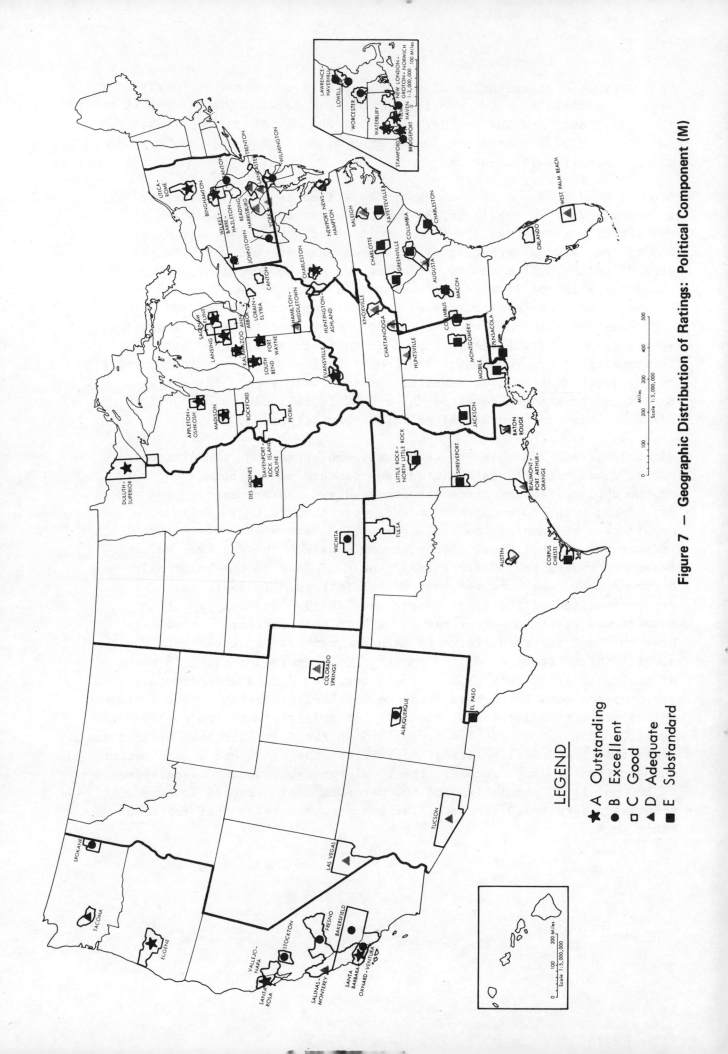

Figure 7 — Geographic Distribution of Ratings: Political Component (M)

LEGEND

★ A Outstanding
● B Excellent
□ C Good
▲ D Adequate
■ E Substandard

Appleton/Oshkosh demonstrated as one of the areas in which people received the best welfare assistance and the area with the best governmental performance, in that it had the lowest violent crime rate of 50.8 per 100,000 population (versus 397.7 per 100,000 in the U.S.) and a very low property crime rate. A high percentage of governmental revenues from the Federal Government (11.0 percent versus 2.7 percent for the entire U.S.) was observed in 1970. On the other hand, the people in Appleton/Oshkosh did not seem to be very interested in participating in political activities and were relatively less informed by local radio broadcasting; for instance, the percentage of presidential votes cast among the voting age population in 1968 was 63.4 percent, and the number of local radio stations per 1,000 population in 1970 was 0.72. Although these two figures are much higher than the U.S. counterparts, they are lower than those in many other SMSA's in the medium size group (see Table B-2 in the Appendix).

Although in terms of salaries paid to policemen and firemen, etc., local governments in the Kalamazoo SMSA employed staff members with outstanding professional quality; and in terms of numbers of governmental employees per 1,000 people as well as in salaries paid to teachers, the performance of the local governments judging by the observed crime rates, the community education, and health indicators did not conform to a high quality of professionalism. The violent crime rate in the area as released by the FBI records in 1970 was 567.9 per 100,000 and the property crime rate was 3,006.7 per 100,000. They were, respectively, 43.0 percent and 23.6 percent higher than the national average.

The aforementioned weaknesses of the three highest ranking SMSA's resulted from a rudimentary investigation among the 21 political factors selected for this study. In a like manner, the exercise can be carried out for the SMSA's whose political quality of life ratings are substandard.

For example, the most serious impediment for a good quality of political life component in Corpus Christi seems to be the lack of high quality and sufficient numbers of employees in local governments to provide essential public services, such as education, police and fire protection, etc. The average monthly earnings of teachers in Corpus Christi amounted to $562, equivalent to 82.4 percent of the U.S. standard. For every 1,000 people in Corpus Christi, there were only 1.3 policemen to protect safety and security. Probably due to this low level of protection--48.0 percent below the U.S. standard--the violent and property crime rates in the area were considerably higher than the U.S. average-- about 16.5 percent and 37.7 percent, respectively, in 1970.

# CHART 7

## REGIONAL VARIATIONS IN INDEXES:
## POLITICAL COMPONENT (M)

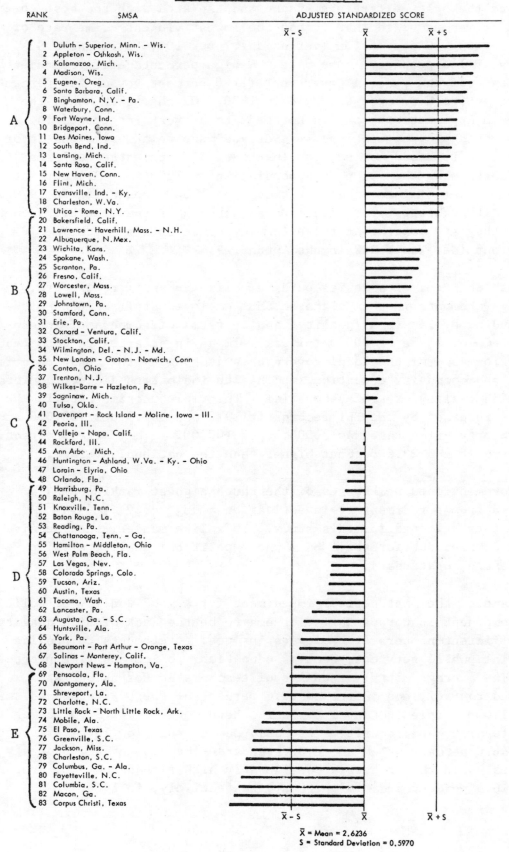

| RANK | SMSA | ADJUSTED STANDARDIZED SCORE |
|---|---|---|

A
- 1 Duluth – Superior, Minn. – Wis.
- 2 Appleton – Oshkosh, Wis.
- 3 Kalamazoo, Mich.
- 4 Madison, Wis.
- 5 Eugene, Oreg.
- 6 Santa Barbara, Calif.
- 7 Binghamton, N.Y. – Pa.
- 8 Waterbury, Conn.
- 9 Fort Wayne, Ind.
- 10 Bridgeport, Conn.
- 11 Des Moines, Iowa
- 12 South Bend, Ind.
- 13 Lansing, Mich.
- 14 Santa Rosa, Calif.
- 15 New Haven, Conn.
- 16 Flint, Mich.
- 17 Evansville, Ind. – Ky.
- 18 Charleston, W.Va.
- 19 Utica – Rome, N.Y.

B
- 20 Bakersfield, Calif.
- 21 Lawrence – Haverhill, Mass. – N.H.
- 22 Albuquerque, N.Mex.
- 23 Wichita, Kans.
- 24 Spokane, Wash.
- 25 Scranton, Pa.
- 26 Fresno, Calif.
- 27 Worcester, Mass.
- 28 Lowell, Mass.
- 29 Johnstown, Pa.
- 30 Stamford, Conn.
- 31 Erie, Pa.
- 32 Oxnard – Ventura, Calif.
- 33 Stockton, Calif.
- 34 Wilmington, Del. – N.J. – Md.
- 35 New London – Groton – Norwich, Conn

C
- 36 Canton, Ohio
- 37 Trenton, N.J.
- 38 Wilkes-Barre – Hazleton, Pa.
- 39 Saginaw, Mich.
- 40 Tulsa, Okla.
- 41 Davenport – Rock Island – Moline, Iowa – Ill.
- 42 Peoria, Ill.
- 43 Vallejo – Napa, Calif.
- 44 Rockford, Ill.
- 45 Ann Arbor, Mich.
- 46 Huntington – Ashland, W.Va. – Ky. – Ohio
- 47 Lorain – Elyria, Ohio
- 48 Orlando, Fla.

D
- 49 Harrisburg, Pa.
- 50 Raleigh, N.C.
- 51 Knoxville, Tenn.
- 52 Baton Rouge, La.
- 53 Reading, Pa.
- 54 Chattanooga, Tenn. – Ga.
- 55 Hamilton – Middleton, Ohio
- 56 West Palm Beach, Fla.
- 57 Las Vegas, Nev.
- 58 Colorado Springs, Colo.
- 59 Tucson, Ariz.
- 60 Austin, Texas
- 61 Tacoma, Wash.
- 62 Lancaster, Pa.
- 63 Augusta, Ga. – S.C.
- 64 Huntsville, Ala.
- 65 York, Pa.
- 66 Beaumont – Port Arthur – Orange, Texas
- 67 Salinas – Monterey, Calif.
- 68 Newport News – Hampton, Va.

E
- 69 Pensacola, Fla.
- 70 Montgomery, Ala.
- 71 Shreveport, La.
- 72 Charlotte, N.C.
- 73 Little Rock – North Little Rock, Ark.
- 74 Mobile, Ala.
- 75 El Paso, Texas
- 76 Greenville, S.C.
- 77 Jackson, Miss.
- 78 Charleston, S.C.
- 79 Columbus, Ga. – Ala.
- 80 Fayetteville, N.C.
- 81 Columbia, S.C.
- 82 Macon, Ga.
- 83 Corpus Christi, Texas

$\bar{X}$ = Mean = 2.6236
S = Standard Deviation = 0.5970

In view of the informed citizenry in 1970, Columbia, South Carolina, compared favorably to other SMSA's and ranked 30th in the group. Nevertheless, its low indicators of individual participation in political activities and local governmental factors in professionalism, performance, and welfare assistance significantly weakened its competitive situation. From the standpoint of local government performance, Columbus, Georgia/Alabama was rated much better than average with a rank of 32nd in the group. The weak spots in the area as seen through individual participation, welfare assistance, and professionalism are such that Columbus ranked last as compared to the other 82 SMSA's.

As Charts 7 and 8 display, although the composite indexes for the political quality of life among the 83 SMSA's give a relatively larger standard deviation, the political component shows thicker and more equal bars than the economic component. This is because the variations in the composite indexes in the former component are not as large as those in the latter. The coefficient of variation for the political component is 22.8 percent whereas the economic component is 28.1 percent. In other words, despite the relative ratings or ranks among the SMSA's the differences in political factors among regions are relatively smaller than those of economic factors and much smaller than environmental, health and education, and social factors to be discussed in the following sections. In addition, the variations in political quality of life indicators in the medium sized SMSA's are also smaller than those in the large sized SMSA's. All this implies that the degree of homogeneity from the viewpoint of political considerations is not only higher among medium SMSA's than among large SMSA's but also higher than other four quality of life components within the medium size SMSA group.

ENVIRONMENTAL COMPONENT

Pollution and environmental damages have been increasingly attacked by opponents to economic growth and industrialization. Economists have aptly used pollution as an illustration of externalities. "The discharge of pollutants into the atmosphere imposes, on some members of society, costs which are inadequately imputed to the sources of the pollution by free markets, resulting in more pollution than would be desirable from the point of view of society as a whole,"[1] explains Professor Mills

---

[1]   Edwin S. Mills, "Economic Incentives in Air Pollution Control," *Economics of Air Pollution*, Harold Wolzin (ed.), New York: W. W. Norton & Company, Inc. (1966).

regarding the failures of our free market mechanism when dealing with social benefits and social costs in production involving external diseconomies. The trade-off between economic activities and environmental deterioration, or the degradative changes in our ecosystems, have been thoroughly discussed by Commoner under the "Aquatic System" and the "productive activities" of human progress.[2] Quantitative measures of pollution and other environmental changes are made available by Tobin and others as previously described. This section presents some information as to where in the U.S. the trade-offs or damages have occurred.

This study of environmental quality in medium SMSA's supports the findings in the previous chapter that the Pacific region stands at the top of the listing. All the SMSA's in the Pacific region are rated either "outstanding" or "excellent." In fact, California has five outstanding SMSA's, or about 40.0 percent of the total of 13 rated "A." The five are Fresno, Salinas/Monterey, Santa Barbara, Oxnard/Ventura, and Bakersfield. However, the best of "A" rated SMSA's is Tacoma, which obtained an environmental quality index appreciably greater than others, i.e., -0.07 or about three standard deviations above the mean of -0.97. In short, this SMSA was found to have very few ecological damages or problems (see Table 8).

Las Vegas ranks fourth and Corpus Christi, the lowest ranked SMSA in the political component, ranks fifth in environmental quality evaluation. The other "A" rated SMSA's are Duluth/Superior, Davenport/Rock Island/ Moline, Newport News/Hampton, Trenton, and Eugene.

Tulsa, one of the best SMSA's in economic well-being, received the lowest environmental rating among the 83 SMSA's, with an index value of -1.62 or about 2.2 standard deviations below the mean. This resulted primarily from its extremely high level of total suspended particulates, high noise measures, and bad climatological data. Jointly, these factors deteriorated its environmental quality and more than offset the relatively good recreational areas and facilities, and the low volume of solid waste and visual pollution.

Huntington/Ashland, a metropolitan area comprised of counties in the States of West Virginia, Kentucky, and Ohio, has the second lowest index, -1.58.

---

[2] Barry Commoner, "The Environment Costs of Economic Growth," Economics of the Environment, Robert and Nancy Dorfman (eds.)(New York: W. W. Norton & Company, Inc., 1972).

# TABLE 8
## INDEX AND RATING OF ENVIRONMENTAL COMPONENT (M)

| SMSA | Adjusted Standardized Scores Value | Rank | Rating | Standardized Scores Value | Rank | Rating |
|---|---|---|---|---|---|---|
| 66. Albuquerque, N. Mex. | -1.2750 | 74 | E | -0.1555 | 63 | D |
| 67. Ann Arbor, Mich. | -0.9083 | 34 | C | 0.0132 | 36 | C |
| 68. Appleton-Oshkosh, Wis. | -0.9417 | 36 | C | 0.0084 | 38 | C |
| 69. Augusta, Ga.-S.C. | -1.0583 | 50 | D | -0.0526 | 48 | C |
| 70. Austin, Texas | -1.0583 | 53 | D | -0.1699 | 63 | D |
| 71. Bakersfield, Calif. | -0.6167 | 11 | A | 0.1790 | 11 | B |
| 72. Baton Rouge, La. | -1.0583 | 51 | D | -0.0693 | 51 | C |
| 73. Beaumont-Port Arthur-Orange, Texas | -0.9583 | 40 | C | 0.0475 | 27 | C |
| 74. Binghamton, N.Y.-Pa. | -1.0583 | 52 | D | -0.0468 | 46 | C |
| 75. Bridgeport, Conn. | -0.8083 | 20 | B | 0.0534 | 26 | C |
| 76. Canton, Ohio | -1.1917 | 63 | D | -0.1611 | 64 | D |
| 77. Charleston, S.C. | -1.2417 | 72 | D | -0.2596 | 73 | D |
| 78. Charleston, W. Va. | -1.3000 | 75 | E | -0.5169 | 82 | E |
| 79. Charlotte, N.C. | -1.3917 | 78 | E | -0.3757 | 78 | E |
| 80. Chattanooga, Tenn.-Ga. | -1.0917 | 56 | D | -0.0435 | 45 | C |
| 81. Colorado Springs, Colo. | -1.1333 | 58 | D | -0.1617 | 65 | D |
| 82. Columbia, S.C. | -1.4750 | 80 | E | -0.3548 | 77 | E |
| 83. Columbus, Ga.-Ala. | -1.2250 | 68 | D | -0.1422 | 62 | D |
| 84. Corpus Christi, Texas | -0.3917 | 5 | A | 0.3369 | 7 | A |
| 85. Davenport-Rock Island-Moline, Iowa-Ill. | -0.6000 | 9 | A | 0.1606 | 12 | B |
| 86. Des Moines, Iowa | -0.9583 | 41 | C | 0.0393 | 33 | C |
| 87. Duluth-Superior, Minn.-Wis. | -0.5333 | 6 | A | 0.1521 | 14 | B |
| 88. El Paso, Texas | -1.0417 | 47 | C | 0.0092 | 37 | C |
| 89. Erie, Pa. | -0.8917 | 31 | C | 0.0587 | 25 | C |
| 90. Eugene, Oreg. | -0.5833 | 8 | A | 0.5195 | 6 | A |
| 91. Evansville, Ind.-Ky. | -0.9750 | 42 | C | 0.0016 | 42 | C |
| 92. Fayetteville, N.C. | -1.0417 | 48 | C | -0.1100 | 54 | D |
| 93. Flint, Mich. | -1.0083 | 43 | C | 0.0049 | 40 | C |
| 94. Fort Wayne, Ind. | -0.9417 | 37 | C | 0.0362 | 34 | C |
| 95. Fresno, Calif. | -0.2833 | 2 | A | 1.3020 | 2 | A |
| 96. Greenville, S.C. | -1.1917 | 65 | D | -0.2653 | 75 | D |
| 97. Hamilton-Middleton, Ohio | -0.8500 | 21 | B | 0.0727 | 21 | C |
| 98. Harrisburg, Pa. | -0.8583 | 23 | B | 0.0473 | 28 | C |
| 99. Huntington-Ashland, W. Va.-Ky.-Ohio | -1.5750 | 82 | E | -0.4829 | 79 | E |
| 100. Huntsville, Ala. | -1.2000 | 66 | D | -0.1164 | 56 | D |
| 101. Jackson, Miss. | -1.0917 | 55 | D | -0.1084 | 53 | D |
| 102. Johnstown, Pa. | -1.2083 | 67 | D | -0.1983 | 69 | D |
| 103. Kalamazoo, Mich. | -0.8583 | 24 | B | 0.0702 | 22 | C |
| 104. Knoxville, Tenn. | -0.7583 | 17 | B | 0.1054 | 18 | B |
| 105. Lancaster, Pa. | -1.0250 | 45 | C | -0.0536 | 49 | C |
| 106. Lansing, Mich. | -0.9417 | 38 | C | 0.0400 | 31 | C |
| 107. Las Vegas, Nev. | -0.3417 | 4 | A | 1.3295 | 1 | A |
| 108. Lawrence-Haverhill, Mass.-N.H. | -0.6833 | 14 | B | 0.0394 | 32 | C |
| 109. Little Rock-North Little Rock, Ark. | -1.1917 | 64 | D | -0.1382 | 61 | D |
| 110. Lorain-Elyria, Ohio | -1.1750 | 60 | D | -0.0154 | 43 | C |
| 111. Lowell, Mass. | -0.8833 | 28 | B | -0.2078 | 70 | D |
| 112. Macon, Ga. | -1.2250 | 69 | D | -0.1347 | 60 | D |
| 113. Madison, Wis. | -0.9083 | 33 | C | 0.0697 | 23 | C |
| 114. Mobile, Ala. | -1.4917 | 81 | E | -0.5558 | 83 | E |
| 115. Montgomery, Ala. | -1.2500 | 73 | D | -0.2608 | 74 | D |
| 116. New Haven, Conn. | -0.8750 | 25 | B | 0.0867 | 20 | B |
| 117. New London-Groton-Norwich, Conn. | -0.8750 | 26 | B | 0.1098 | 17 | B |
| 118. Newport News-Hampton, Va. | -0.6417 | 12 | A | 0.3127 | 8 | A |
| 119. Orlando, Fla. | -1.1083 | 57 | D | -0.1824 | 67 | D |
| 120. Oxnard-Ventura, Calif. | -0.6000 | 10 | A | 0.2631 | 9 | B |
| 121. Pensacola, Fla. | -1.2250 | 70 | D | -0.1294 | 59 | D |
| 122. Peoria, Ill. | -1.0750 | 54 | D | 0.0077 | 39 | C |
| 123. Raleigh, N.C. | -1.1750 | 61 | D | -0.1111 | 55 | D |
| 124. Reading, Pa. | -1.1500 | 59 | D | -0.1195 | 57 | D |
| 125. Rockford, Ill. | -0.7000 | 15 | B | 0.1481 | 15 | B |
| 126. Saginaw, Mich. | -0.9250 | 35 | C | 0.0048 | 41 | C |
| 127. Salinas-Monterey, Calif. | -0.3000 | 3 | A | 0.5942 | 3 | A |
| 128. Santa Barbara, Calif. | -0.5667 | 7 | A | 0.5458 | 4 | A |
| 129. Santa Rosa, Calif. | -0.8833 | 29 | B | 0.0642 | 24 | C |
| 130. Scranton, Pa. | -1.3083 | 76 | E | -0.1868 | 68 | D |
| 131. Shreveport, La. | -1.4083 | 79 | E | -0.2529 | 72 | D |
| 132. South Bend, Ind. | -1.0417 | 49 | C | -0.0474 | 47 | C |
| 133. Spokane, Wash. | -1.0167 | 44 | C | -0.3464 | 76 | E |
| 134. Stamford, Conn. | -0.7083 | 16 | B | 0.2165 | 10 | B |
| 135. Stockton, Calif. | -0.8750 | 27 | B | 0.0943 | 19 | B |
| 136. Tacoma, Wash. | -0.0667 | 1 | A | 0.5236 | 5 | A |
| 137. Trenton, N.J. | -0.6583 | 13 | A | 0.0413 | 30 | C |
| 138. Tucson, Ariz. | -0.8833 | 30 | B | 0.1343 | 16 | B |
| 139. Tulsa, Okla. | -1.6250 | 83 | E | -0.5032 | 80 | E |
| 140. Utica-Rome, N.Y. | -0.9417 | 39 | C | 0.0466 | 29 | C |
| 141. Vallejo-Napa, Calif. | -0.8500 | 22 | B | -0.0413 | 44 | C |
| 142. Waterbury, Conn. | -0.7833 | 18 | B | 0.0291 | 35 | C |
| 143. West Palm Beach, Fla. | -1.3583 | 77 | E | -0.5097 | 81 | E |
| 144. Wichita, Kansas | -1.0250 | 46 | C | -0.0957 | 52 | D |
| 145. Wilkes-Barre-Hazleton, Pa. | -1.2333 | 71 | D | -0.2154 | 71 | D |
| 146. Wilmington, Del.-N.J.-Md. | -0.7917 | 19 | B | 0.1532 | 13 | B |
| 147. Worcester, Mass. | -0.9900 | 32 | C | -0.0541 | 50 | C |
| 148. York, Pa. | -1.1833 | 62 | D | -0.1206 | 58 | D |

A = Outstanding ($\geq \bar{x} + s$)
B = Excellent ($\bar{x} + .28s \leq B < \bar{x} + s$)
C = Good ($\bar{x} - .28s < C < \bar{x} + .28s$)
D = Adequate ($\bar{x} - s < D \leq \bar{x} - .28s$)
E = Substandard ($\leq \bar{x} - s$)

Mean ($\bar{x}$) = -0.9700          Mean ($\bar{x}$) = 0.0000
Standard Deviation (s) = 0.2963     Standard Deviation (s) = 0.3059

This SMSA had a very minor solid waste problem generated by the manufac-turing industry in 1970, but its water pollution was among the worst, with an index as high as 9.26. The water pollution index was developed on the basis of prevalence, duration, and intensity of pollution (PDI). The original PDI index was such that a higher rank number indicates a less urgent pollution problem. In order to be consistent with other pollution indicators used in this study, the original PDI rank was divided into the median PDI rank of all metropolitan areas and converted into another index, meaning the higher the value, the more urgent the problem of water pollution. While most medium SMSA's had water pollution indexes ranging from 0.59 (Bakersfield) to 2.71 (Evansville), Huntington/Ashland had an index of about 16 times as high as the best areas in California. In addition, this SMSA also suffered from bad climatological data. For example, it was among several SMSA's with very high mean annual inversion frequency (42.5 percent) and very low possible annual sunshine day (48 days).

Mobile, Alabama, and Columbia, South Carolina, are the next two SMSA's with indexes slightly higher than Tulsa and Huntington/Ashland. While water pollution and the lack of a relatively good natural environment are detrimental problems in Mobile, it compared favorably to others in noise pollution--virtually no indication of serious noise problems created by motorcycles or a densely populated central city, etc. Columbia had environ-mental problems quite similar to those of Mobile; in fact, the noise pollution in Columbia was slightly better than in Mobile, but the visual pollution and solid wastes are relatively worse.

Although Tacoma ranked first in environmental quality evaluation, this SMSA still had some air pollution and solid waste problems. Its mean level for total suspended particulates in 1970 was relatively high, 93.9 microgram per cubic meter, and its mean level for sulfur dioxide was 73.0 microgram per cubic meter, or 13.0 microgram per cubic meter higher than the secondary standard level specified by the U.S. Environmental Protection Agency. The solid waste generated in Tacoma by manufacturing industries totaled 645.4 tons per million dollars of value added, a relatively high figure compared to other SMSA's (see Table B-3 in the Appendix).

The most serious problem in Fresno was the noise pollution--it had a fairly high number of motorcycles and motor vehicles registered per 1,000 people and a relatively high population density in its central city. It should be noted that the three factors selected to measure noise pollu-tion need not be even the second best indicators at all since noise

# CHART 8

## REGIONAL VARIATIONS IN INDEXES: ENVIRONMENTAL COMPONENT (M)

| RANK | SMSA | ADJUSTED STANDARDIZED SCORE |
|---|---|---|

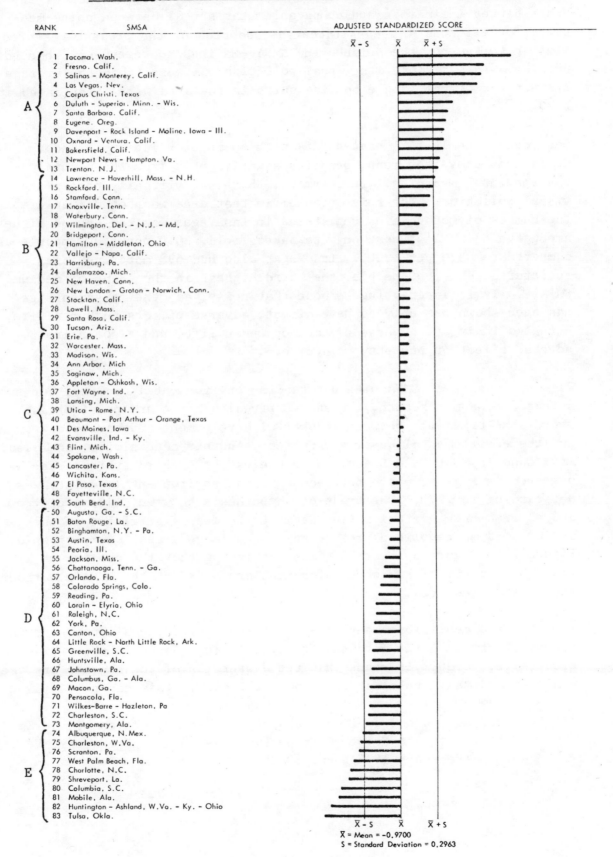

A
1 Tacoma, Wash.
2 Fresno, Calif.
3 Salinas – Monterey, Calif.
4 Las Vegas, Nev.
5 Corpus Christi, Texas
6 Duluth – Superior, Minn. – Wis.
7 Santa Barbara, Calif.
8 Eugene, Oreg.
9 Davenport – Rock Island – Moline, Iowa – Ill.
10 Oxnard – Ventura, Calif.
11 Bakersfield, Calif.
12 Newport News – Hampton, Va.
13 Trenton, N.J.

B
14 Lawrence – Haverhill, Mass. – N.H.
15 Rockford, Ill.
16 Stamford, Conn.
17 Knoxville, Tenn.
18 Waterbury, Conn.
19 Wilmington, Del. – N.J. – Md.
20 Bridgeport, Conn.
21 Hamilton – Middleton, Ohio
22 Vallejo – Napa, Calif.
23 Harrisburg, Pa.
24 Kalamazoo, Mich.
25 New Haven, Conn.
26 New London – Groton – Norwich, Conn.
27 Stockton, Calif.
28 Lowell, Mass.
29 Santa Rosa, Calif.
30 Tucson, Ariz.

C
31 Erie, Pa.
32 Worcester, Mass.
33 Madison, Wis.
34 Ann Arbor, Mich
35 Saginaw, Mich.
36 Appleton – Oshkosh, Wis.
37 Fort Wayne, Ind.
38 Lansing, Mich.
39 Utica – Rome, N.Y.
40 Beaumont – Port Arthur – Orange, Texas
41 Des Moines, Iowa
42 Evansville, Ind. – Ky.
43 Flint, Mich.
44 Spokane, Wash.
45 Lancaster, Pa.
46 Wichita, Kans.
47 El Paso, Texas
48 Fayetteville, N.C.
49 South Bend, Ind.

D
50 Augusta, Ga. – S.C.
51 Baton Rouge, La.
52 Binghamton, N.Y. – Pa.
53 Austin, Texas
54 Peoria, Ill.
55 Jackson, Miss.
56 Chattanooga, Tenn. – Ga.
57 Orlando, Fla.
58 Colorado Springs, Colo.
59 Reading, Pa.
60 Lorain – Elyria, Ohio
61 Raleigh, N.C.
62 York, Pa.
63 Canton, Ohio
64 Little Rock – North Little Rock, Ark.
65 Greenville, S.C.
66 Huntsville, Ala.
67 Johnstown, Pa.
68 Columbus, Ga. – Ala.
69 Macon, Ga.
70 Pensacola, Fla.
71 Wilkes-Barre – Hazleton, Pa
72 Charleston, S.C.
73 Montgomery, Ala.

E
74 Albuquerque, N. Mex.
75 Charleston, W.Va.
76 Scranton, Pa.
77 West Palm Beach, Fla.
78 Charlotte, N.C.
79 Shreveport, La.
80 Columbia, S.C.
81 Mobile, Ala.
82 Huntington – Ashland, W.Va. – Ky. – Ohio
83 Tulsa, Okla.

$\bar{X} - S$     $\bar{X}$     $\bar{X} + S$

$\bar{X}$ = Mean = -0.9700
S = Standard Deviation = 0.2963

created is a function of the age and the frequency of vehicle use, not necessarily the number that are registered. However, the lack of any other better indicators and comparable statistical data on noise measures for all SMSA's necessitates the adoption of the present measures. Similar to Fresno, the neighboring SMSA--Salinas/Monterey--had some noise problem. In addition, its visual pollution was worse than the average-- 2.9 percent of the single housing units in the area were dilapidated in 1970.

Las Vegas, the last "A" rated SMSA with an index value two standard deviations above the mean, benefits significantly from the natural environmental measures. Furthermore, there was virtually no air and visual pollution. The noise problem in that area was found intolerable. The number of motorcycles registered in Las Vegas was the second highest among the 83 SMSA's, next only to Bakersfield, 36.0 per 1,000 people as compared to 43.0 per 1,000. Las Vegas also had 698 motor vehicles registered per 1,000 people, the third highest in the group of medium SMSA's. It is interesting to note that noise, as other disamenities, has been shown not only to have direct, adverse effects on human life, but also indirect, adverse effects on human life, and also indirect, adverse effect on property values, etc.[3]

Tacoma ranks as an SMSA with outstanding environmental quality, but substandard economic health. Tulsa was revealed to be an opposite case, where some trade-off between industrial development and economic growth and the environmental quality occurred. Another case similar to Tulsa was found in West Palm Beach. Nevertheless, the third typical case was observed in Eugene, where both economic and environmental quality was outstanding in 1970. The trade-off hypothesis between industrial growth and environmental deterioration seems to be less significant in the medium size metropolitan areas than in the large areas. Comparison of Figure 7 to Figure 8 is still quite convincing that the hypothesis is plausible, particularly when references are made for the SMSA's surrounding the Great Lakes area.

The standard deviation among indexes in the environmental component is the smallest among the five quality of life components in this size group, i.e., 0.30. It means that the dispersion of the indexes are the smallest and they are clustered around the mean. This can be easily

---

[3] For instance, see Jean-Francois Gautrin, "An Evaluation of the Impact of Aircraft Noise on Property Values," Land Economics, Vol. 51, No. 1 (February 1975), pp. 80-85.

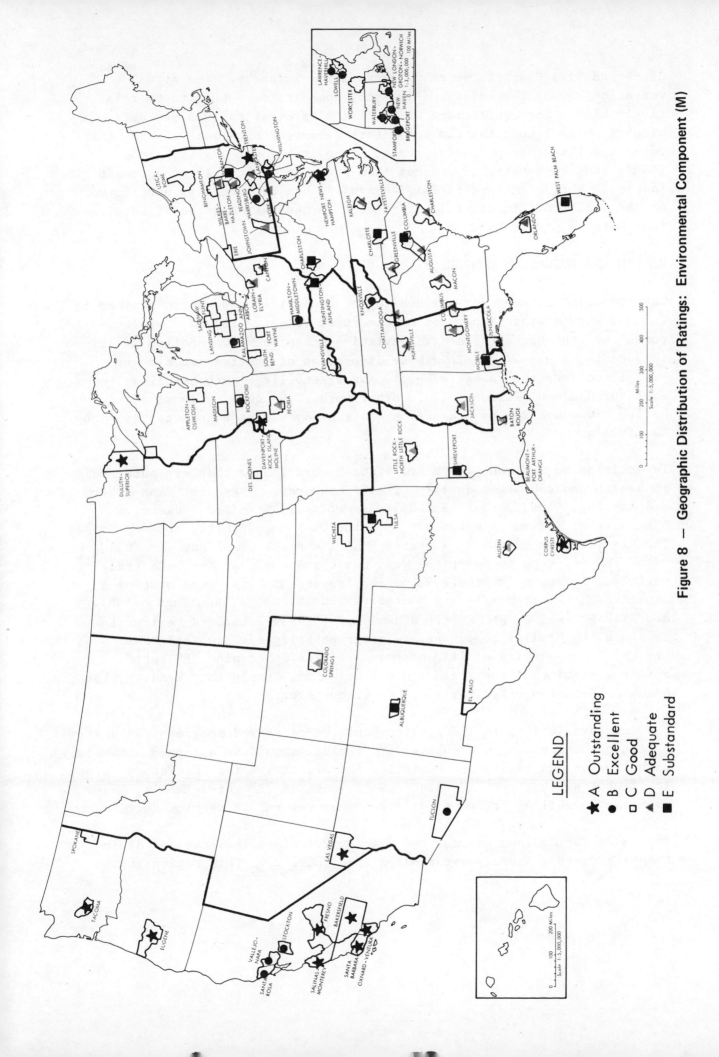

**Figure 8 — Geographic Distribution of Ratings: Environmental Component (M)**

LEGEND

★ A  Outstanding
● B  Excellent
□ C  Good
◀ D  Adequate
■ E  Substandard

discerned from Chart 8, which is very narrow in shape. The actual variations among the values of indexes, however, does tend to be relatively high. The coefficient of variation is equal to 30.5 percent, slightly higher than the two components discussed previously. What this means is, the geographic differences in environmental quality among SMSA's tend to be slightly higher than those in political and economic factors. This higher variation, obviously, can be partially attributed to the variations in natural environment in general, and the climatological data in particular.

HEALTH AND EDUCATION COMPONENT

The composite indexes for the health and education component contained in Table 9 show a wide dispersion of the index values. Indeed, this component has the highest standard deviation among the five quality of life components, i.e., 0.67. This wide dispersion of indexes can also be visualized from the lowest of -0.19 for Greenville, South Carolina, to 2.92 for Madison, Wisconsin. In other words, the quality level of health and education as measured by this study varies significantly among the SMSA's.

In addition to Madison, there are a dozen more SMSA's that are outstanding in health and education quality of life measures. They are: Ann Arbor and Lansing, Santa Barbara and Salinas/Monterey, Stamford, Eugene, Albuquerque, Tucson, Binghamton, Appleton/Oshkosh, Wichita, and Des Moines. The distribution of these "A" rated SMSA's and the excellent, or "B" rated SMSA's, tend to favor the West Coast and the East North Central regions. As shown in Figure 9, no substandard SMSA is found west of a line drawn through Mobile and Montgomery, Chattanooga, Huntington/Ashland, and Wilkes-Barre/Hazelton. In other words, the substandard regions in this quality of life component are geographically more typical than are the other quality of life components. The other nine "E" rated SMSA's east of the line are Macon and Columbus, Charleston, Reading, York, Augusta, Scranton, Fayetteville, and Greenville.

The large variations in index values and the clustered geographical distribution of outstanding and substandard ratings should be analyzed separately with the various health and education factors chosen for this study, since it is obvious that the "A" rated SMSA's, just as "E" rated SMSA's, have problems as well as prides of different natures and in varying degrees.

The index for Madison exceeds the mean by 2.7 times the standard deviation and ranks extremely outstanding (see Chart 9). This region shows

158

# TABLE 9

## INDEX AND RATING OF HEALTH AND EDUCATION COMPONENT (M)

| SMSA | Adjusted Standardized Scores | | | Standardized Scores | | |
|---|---|---|---|---|---|---|
| | Value | Rank | Rating | Value | Rank | Rating |
| 66. Albuquerque, N. Mex. | 2.2000 | 7 | A | 0.7270 | 8 | A |
| 67. Ann Arbor, Mich. | 2.4250 | 2 | A | 1.7834 | 1 | A |
| 68. Appleton-Oshkosh, Wis. | 1.8625 | 11 | A | 0.7346 | 7 | A |
| 69. Augusta, Ga.-S.C. | 0.3250 | 72 | E | -0.5948 | 72 | E |
| 70. Austin, Texas | 1.7250 | 14 | B | 0.5820 | 9 | A |
| 71. Bakersfield, Calif. | 0.9250 | 44 | C | 0.1912 | 26 | B |
| 72. Baton Rouge, La. | 1.7250 | 15 | B | 0.3598 | 17 | B |
| 73. Beaumont-Port Arthur-Orange, Texas | 0.9000 | 46 | C | -0.1707 | 49 | D |
| 74. Binghamton, N.Y.-Pa. | 1.9375 | 10 | A | 0.5664 | 10 | A |
| 75. Bridgeport, Conn. | 1.4625 | 21 | B | 0.2134 | 25 | B |
| 76. Canton, Ohio | 0.6500 | 61 | D | -0.2771 | 62 | D |
| 77. Charleston, S.C. | 0.0875 | 78 | E | -0.6201 | 74 | E |
| 78. Charleston, W. Va. | 0.6500 | 62 | D | -0.2364 | 60 | D |
| 79. Charlotte, N.C. | 1.1125 | 38 | C | -0.0124 | 38 | C |
| 80. Chattanooga, Tenn.-Ga. | 0.1750 | 76 | E | -0.5614 | 70 | E |
| 81. Colorado Springs, Colo. | 1.4750 | 20 | B | 0.2375 | 23 | B |
| 82. Columbia, S.C. | 0.5875 | 63 | D | -0.3255 | 65 | D |
| 83. Columbus, Ga.-Ala. | 0.1000 | 77 | E | -0.7272 | 80 | E |
| 84. Corpus Christi, Texas | 0.8000 | 52 | D | -0.1791 | 52 | D |
| 85. Davenport-Rock Island-Moline, Iowa-Ill. | 0.5000 | 69 | D | -0.4070 | 67 | D |
| 86. Des Moines, Iowa | 1.7750 | 13 | A | 0.4405 | 14 | B |
| 87. Duluth-Superior, Minn.-Wis. | 1.5375 | 19 | B | 0.2950 | 21 | B |
| 88. El Paso, Texas | 1.2875 | 30 | B | 0.1266 | 32 | C |
| 89. Erie, Pa. | 1.0125 | 40 | C | -0.0711 | 41 | C |
| 90. Eugene, Oreg. | 2.2875 | 6 | A | 0.9609 | 4 | A |
| 91. Evansville, Ind.-Ky. | 0.7375 | 57 | D | -0.2224 | 57 | D |
| 92. Fayetteville, N.C. | 0.3625 | 70 | E | -0.6854 | 77 | E |
| 93. Flint, Mich. | 1.1250 | 37 | C | 0.1683 | 28 | B |
| 94. Fort Wayne, Ind. | 1.3000 | 29 | B | 0.0689 | 34 | C |
| 95. Fresno, Calif. | 1.4500 | 23 | B | 0.2980 | 20 | B |
| 96. Greenville, S.C. | -0.1875 | 83 | E | -0.8821 | 82 | E |
| 97. Hamilton-Middleton, Ohio | 1.1500 | 35 | C | 0.0028 | 36 | C |
| 98. Harrisburg, Pa. | 0.9875 | 41 | C | -0.0832 | 42 | C |
| 99. Huntington-Ashland, W. Va.-Ky.-Ohio | 0.0750 | 79 | E | -0.5970 | 73 | E |
| 100. Huntsville, Ala. | 1.2500 | 34 | C | 0.1349 | 30 | C |
| 101. Jackson, Miss. | 0.8500 | 48 | D | -0.2080 | 54 | D |
| 102. Johnstown, Pa. | 0.5125 | 68 | D | -0.6673 | 76 | E |
| 103. Kalamazoo, Mich. | 1.6375 | 17 | B | 0.4193 | 15 | B |
| 104. Knoxville, Tenn. | 0.9750 | 42 | C | -0.1180 | 45 | C |
| 105. Lancaster, Pa. | 0.5875 | 64 | D | -0.4906 | 68 | D |
| 106. Lansing, Mich. | 2.4250 | 3 | A | 0.7987 | 6 | A |
| 107. Las Vegas, Nev. | 0.8250 | 49 | D | -0.2330 | 59 | D |
| 108. Lawrence-Haverhill, Mass.-N.H. | 1.3750 | 26 | B | 0.1578 | 29 | B |
| 109. Little Rock-North Little Rock, Ark. | 0.7750 | 54 | D | -0.1790 | 51 | D |
| 110. Lorain-Elyria, Ohio | 0.7000 | 59 | D | -0.2156 | 56 | D |
| 111. Lowell, Mass. | 1.3750 | 27 | B | 0.1334 | 31 | C |
| 112. Macon, Ga. | 0.0625 | 80 | E | -0.6359 | 75 | E |
| 113. Madison, Wis. | 2.9250 | 1 | A | 1.5937 | 2 | A |
| 114. Mobile, Ala. | 0.0250 | 81 | E | -0.7247 | 79 | E |
| 115. Montgomery, Ala. | -0.0250 | 82 | E | -0.9653 | 83 | E |
| 116. New Haven, Conn. | 1.4625 | 22 | B | 0.2660 | 22 | B |
| 117. New London-Groton-Norwich, Conn. | 0.8250 | 50 | D | -0.2598 | 61 | D |
| 118. Newport News-Hampton, Va. | 0.5625 | 65 | D | -0.2261 | 58 | D |
| 119. Orlando, Fla. | 0.5375 | 67 | D | -0.3040 | 64 | D |
| 120. Oxnard-Ventura, Calif. | 1.7125 | 16 | B | 0.4873 | 13 | B |
| 121. Pensacola, Fla. | 0.5500 | 66 | D | -0.2885 | 63 | D |
| 122. Peoria, Ill. | 0.7500 | 56 | D | -0.1558 | 47 | D |
| 123. Raleigh, N.C. | 1.4375 | 24 | B | 0.2234 | 24 | B |
| 124. Reading, Pa. | 0.2750 | 74 | E | -0.5928 | 71 | E |
| 125. Rockford, Ill. | 0.8125 | 51 | D | -0.2111 | 55 | D |
| 126. Saginaw, Mich. | 0.7750 | 55 | D | -0.1744 | 50 | D |
| 127. Salinas-Monterey, Calif. | 2.0750 | 9 | A | 0.5359 | 12 | A |
| 128. Santa Barbara, Calif. | 2.3750 | 4 | A | 0.8828 | 5 | A |
| 129. Santa Rosa, Calif. | 1.4000 | 25 | B | 0.1771 | 27 | B |
| 130. Scranton, Pa. | 0.3250 | 71 | E | -0.7011 | 78 | E |
| 131. Shreveport, La. | 0.8625 | 47 | D | -0.1442 | 46 | C |
| 132. South Bend, Ind. | 1.1375 | 36 | C | -0.0078 | 37 | C |
| 133. Spokane, Wash. | 1.5875 | 18 | B | 0.3045 | 18 | B |
| 134. Stamford, Conn. | 2.3500 | 5 | A | 1.1208 | 3 | A |
| 135. Stockton, Calif. | 1.2625 | 32 | C | 0.2983 | 19 | B |
| 136. Tacoma, Wash. | 0.8000 | 53 | D | -0.1839 | 53 | D |
| 137. Trenton, N.J. | 0.9375 | 43 | C | -0.0845 | 43 | C |
| 138. Tucson, Ariz. | 2.1750 | 8 | A | 0.5653 | 11 | A |
| 139. Tulsa, Okla. | 1.2750 | 31 | B | 0.0387 | 35 | C |
| 140. Utica-Rome, N.Y. | 1.2625 | 33 | C | -0.0214 | 40 | C |
| 141. Vallejo-Napa, Calif. | 1.3750 | 28 | B | 0.1164 | 33 | C |
| 142. Waterbury, Conn. | 0.7125 | 58 | D | -0.1649 | 48 | D |
| 143. West Palm Beach, Fla. | 0.6875 | 60 | D | -0.3617 | 66 | D |
| 144. Wichita, Kans. | 1.8250 | 12 | A | 0.3958 | 16 | B |
| 145. Wilkes-Barre-Hazleton, Pa. | 0.2125 | 75 | E | -0.7857 | 81 | E |
| 146. Wilmington, Del.-N.J.-Md. | 1.1000 | 39 | C | -0.0133 | 39 | C |
| 147. Worcester, Mass. | 0.9125 | 45 | C | -0.0849 | 44 | C |
| 148. York, Pa. | 0.3125 | 73 | E | -0.5498 | 69 | E |

Mean ($\bar{x}$) = 1.0779    (Mean ($\bar{x}$) = 0.0000

Standard Deviation (s) = 0.6727    Standard Deviation (s) = 0.5198

A = Outstanding ($\geq \bar{x} + s$)
B = Excellent ($\bar{x} + .28s \leq B < \bar{x} + s$)
C = Good ($\bar{x} - .28s < C < \bar{x} + .28s$)
D = Adequate ($\bar{x} - s < D \leq \bar{x} - .28s$)
E = Substandard ($\leq \bar{x} - s$)

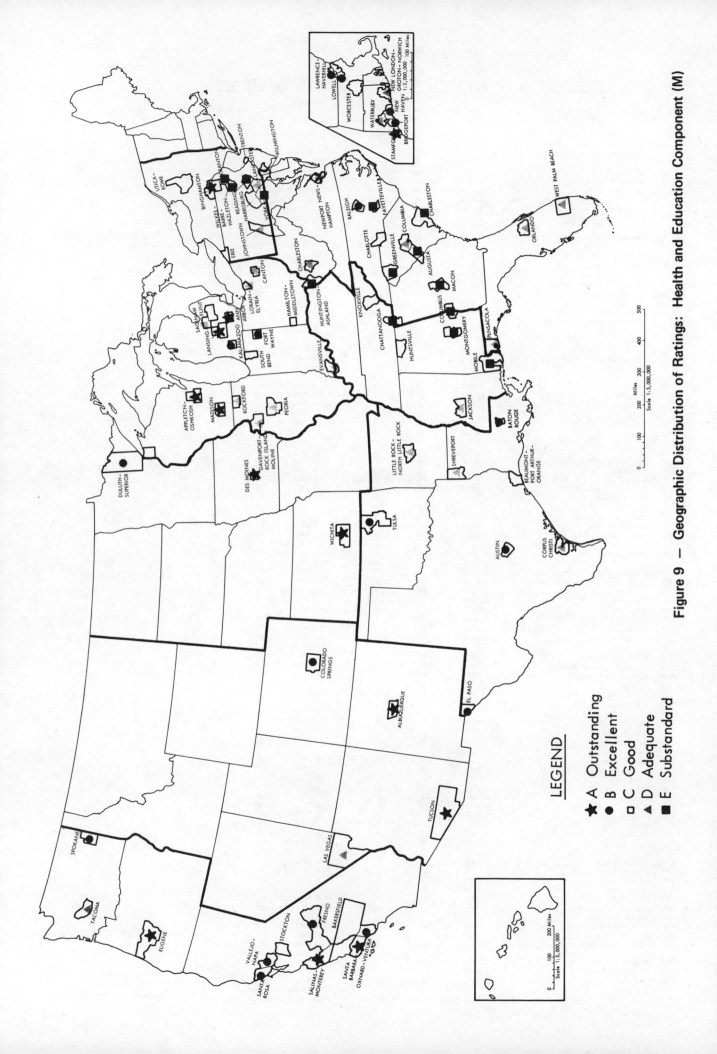

Figure 9 — Geographic Distribution of Ratings:  Health and Education Component (M)

LEGEND

A  Outstanding
B  Excellent
C  Good
D  Adequate
E  Substandard

## CHART 9

## REGIONAL VARIATIONS IN INDEXES: HEALTH AND EDUCATION COMPONENT (M)

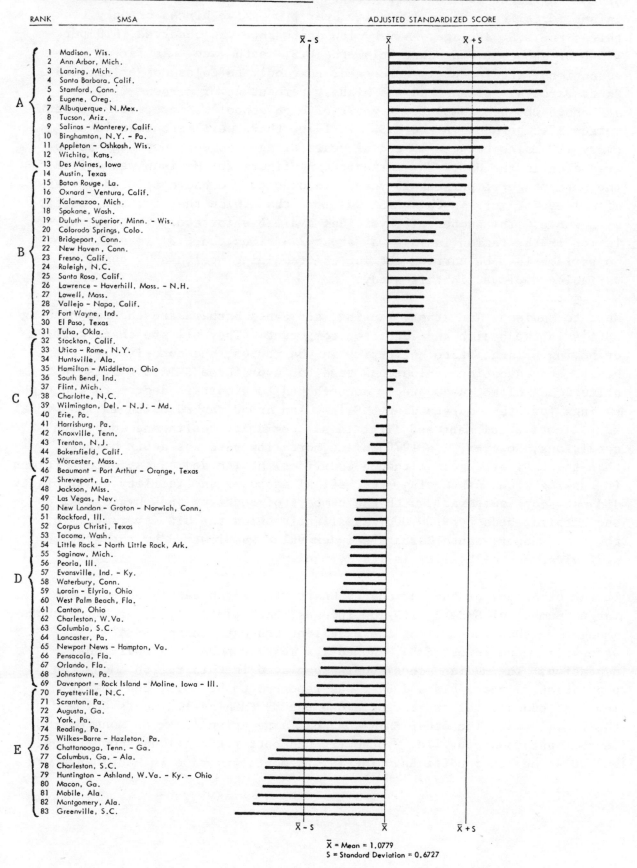

| RANK | SMSA |
|------|------|
| 1 | Madison, Wis. |
| 2 | Ann Arbor, Mich. |
| 3 | Lansing, Mich. |
| 4 | Santa Barbara, Calif. |
| 5 | Stamford, Conn. |
| 6 | Eugene, Oreg. |
| 7 | Albuquerque, N.Mex. |
| 8 | Tucson, Ariz. |
| 9 | Salinas – Monterey, Calif. |
| 10 | Binghamton, N.Y. – Pa. |
| 11 | Appleton – Oshkosh, Wis. |
| 12 | Wichita, Kans. |
| 13 | Des Moines, Iowa |
| 14 | Austin, Texas |
| 15 | Baton Rouge, La. |
| 16 | Oxnard – Ventura, Calif. |
| 17 | Kalamazoo, Mich. |
| 18 | Spokane, Wash. |
| 19 | Duluth – Superior, Minn. – Wis. |
| 20 | Colorado Springs, Colo. |
| 21 | Bridgeport, Conn. |
| 22 | New Haven, Conn. |
| 23 | Fresno, Calif. |
| 24 | Raleigh, N.C. |
| 25 | Santa Rosa, Calif. |
| 26 | Lawrence – Haverhill, Mass. – N.H. |
| 27 | Lowell, Mass. |
| 28 | Vallejo – Napa, Calif. |
| 29 | Fort Wayne, Ind. |
| 30 | El Paso, Texas |
| 31 | Tulsa, Okla. |
| 32 | Stockton, Calif. |
| 33 | Utica – Rome, N.Y. |
| 34 | Huntsville, Ala. |
| 35 | Hamilton – Middleton, Ohio |
| 36 | South Bend, Ind. |
| 37 | Flint, Mich. |
| 38 | Charlotte, N.C. |
| 39 | Wilmington, Del. – N.J. – Md. |
| 40 | Erie, Pa. |
| 41 | Harrisburg, Pa. |
| 42 | Knoxville, Tenn. |
| 43 | Trenton, N.J. |
| 44 | Bakersfield, Calif. |
| 45 | Worcester, Mass. |
| 46 | Beaumont – Port Arthur – Orange, Texas |
| 47 | Shreveport, La. |
| 48 | Jackson, Miss. |
| 49 | Las Vegas, Nev. |
| 50 | New London – Groton – Norwich, Conn. |
| 51 | Rockford, Ill. |
| 52 | Corpus Christi, Texas |
| 53 | Tacoma, Wash. |
| 54 | Little Rock – North Little Rock, Ark. |
| 55 | Saginaw, Mich. |
| 56 | Peoria, Ill. |
| 57 | Evansville, Ind. – Ky. |
| 58 | Waterbury, Conn. |
| 59 | Lorain – Elyria, Ohio |
| 60 | West Palm Beach, Fla. |
| 61 | Canton, Ohio |
| 62 | Charleston, W.Va. |
| 63 | Columbia, S.C. |
| 64 | Lancaster, Pa. |
| 65 | Newport News – Hampton, Va. |
| 66 | Pensacola, Fla. |
| 67 | Orlando, Fla. |
| 68 | Johnstown, Pa. |
| 69 | Davenport – Rock Island – Moline, Iowa – Ill. |
| 70 | Fayetteville, N.C. |
| 71 | Scranton, Pa. |
| 72 | Augusta, Ga. |
| 73 | York, Pa. |
| 74 | Reading, Pa. |
| 75 | Wilkes-Barre – Hazleton, Pa. |
| 76 | Chattanooga, Tenn. – Ga. |
| 77 | Columbus, Ga. – Ala. |
| 78 | Charleston, S.C. |
| 79 | Huntington – Ashland, W.Va. – Ky. – Ohio |
| 80 | Macon, Ga. |
| 81 | Mobile, Ala. |
| 82 | Montgomery, Ala. |
| 83 | Greenville, S.C. |

ADJUSTED STANDARDIZED SCORE

$\bar{X} - S$    $\bar{X}$    $\bar{X} + S$

$\bar{X}$ = Mean = 1.0779
S = Standard Deviation = 0.6727

the best factors of health and education as compared to the rest of the 82 SMSA's in the medium sized group. For example, Madison had the lowest infant mortality rate in 1970, 14.2 per 1,000 live births or only two-thirds the U.S. average. A very low death rate was observed, 6.9 per 1,000 or about 30.0 percent below the U.S. death rate. As far as educational attainment is concerned, next only to Colorado Springs and Santa Barbara, Madison had the highest percentage of persons 25 years and above who had completed 4 years of high school or more, 71.2 percent versus 52.3 percent in the U.S. In 1970, there were more than 15 of every 100 males between 16 and 21 years of age who were not high school graduates in the U.S. The corresponding figure for Madison was only 5. The percentage of persons 25 years old or over who had completed 4 years of college or more in this SMSA was more than twice that for the country as a whole. The number of physicians available for every 100,000 population in the region in 1970 was about 2.4 times the U.S. level. Such comparisons can be carried out for the remaining health and education variables employed in this study.

Next to Madison, Ann Arbor, Lansing, and Santa Barbara are the top ranking SMSA's in the health and education component. They all are characterized by having a large state university in the region, and conceivably, the health and education evaluations tend to favor these SMSA's. This institutional effect undoubtedly contributed to a certain degree to the high ratings for other outstanding SMSA's. Ann Arbor ranked third in individual educational attainment and first in all community health and education conditions; however, its 1970 infant mortality rate was a bit higher than the U.S. average. Although individual health and education conditions in Lansing were outstanding, its medical manpower and facility availability did not score comparably with the numbers of dentists and physicians, and the hospital beds per 100,000 was slightly below the U.S. average. In the same manner, Santa Barbara's index value was lowered by the average medical care availability in its community.

At the other end of the bar chart, Chart 9, one can easily observe a larger number of SMSA's with low indexes, but relatively fewer differences among them than those among the excellent and outstanding SMSA's. Greenville, the lowest SMSA, showed its weakest points in individual education. The median school years completed in this region among the population 25 years old and over was reported to be 10.9, the lowest level of educational attainment among the 83 SMSA's--1.2 years below the U.S. level. The other SMSA that has a negative index is Montgomery. In contrast to Greenville, Montgomery had better educational conditions, but worse health conditions. The infant mortality rate in Montgomery was

162

the highest. It was the only SMSA with more than 30 deaths per 1,000
live births in 1970, a record of 10 deaths more than the U.S. average.

Mobile is one of the few SMSA's consistently rated substandard in the
quality of life components. It ranks 81st in this component with a
positive index, meaning that its negative factors were at the aggregate
level still more than offset by positive factors. Its index is 0.03,
or about 1.6 standard deviations below the mean. The weakest point of
this region was in its education; individual as well as community efforts
in human investment tend to be far behind the national standard. In
1970, for every 100 persons 25 years of age or over, about 42 persons had
completed 4 years of high school and seven persons had finished college, 10
and 3 persons fewer than the U.S. counterparts, respectively. The health
situation and the medical care provision in the region were not much
better than educational attainment. The infant mortality rate in the
area outnumbered the U.S. by 1.6 deaths more per 1,000 live births. For
every 100,000 population, the region was served only by about 103
physicians, 50 physicians short of the U.S. level. Its per capita local
government expenditure on health in 1970 was more than one-third below
the national average.

The health and education indexes for the medium SMSA's displayed not only
a large standard deviation but also a very high coefficient of variation,
i.e., the r = 0.62. In comparison, the indexes for this medium size
group are ultimately less heterogeneous than those for the large SMSA's
in which the coefficient of variation was computed at 0.70. If the large
variation in indexes is interpreted to denote the differential health and
education quality among U.S. urban areas, the coefficient of variation
indicates that the problem of health and education inequality in the
medium SMSA's was relatively less serious than in the large SMSA's.

SOCIAL COMPONENT

The social quality of life among the medium SMSA's as measured by this
study tends to confirm the findings from the study for the large SMSA's
in that most outstanding SMSA's are in the regions west of the Mississippi
River. While most of the substandard large SMSA's are scattered throughout the Middle Atlantic, East, North and South Central, the substandard
medium SMSA's are clustered in the South Atlantic and East South Central
regions. In addition, this study found that the social quality of life
measures are even more highly associated with the health and education
quality of life measures in the medium than in the large group of SMSA's.

Table 10 shows that Des Moines, one of the outstanding regions in economic, political, and health and education components, scores first in the social component with an index of 1.32, or about 2.4 standard deviations above the mean score of 0.49. With indexes slightly below Des Moines, Eugene ranked second and Madison third. The list of outstanding medium SMSA's in social quality of life includes 10 more SMSA's--Wichita, Spokane, Appleton/Oshkosh, Duluth/Superior, Ann Arbor, Santa Barbara, Worcester, Tacoma, Colorado Springs, and Fort Wayne.

Among individual concerns that people in Des Moines tend to enjoy most are widening opportunity for individual choice with high mobility, better information, and spatial extension. As far as community living conditions are concerned, Des Moines is one of the best SMSA's. The residents' social quality of life is enriched outstandingly by the availability of various facilities such as banking, shopping, recreational, etc. However, the area is by no means the perfect place for providing all types of social quality of life. As revealed by this study, it has a critical problem in racial inequality. It ranked 72nd among the 83 SMSA's when income, unemployment rate, and professional employment ratios between nonwhite and total population adjusted for educational attainment were compared to other areas. As an example, the ratio of Negro to total population median family income adjusted for education in 1970 was 0.71, meaning that Negro median family income was only 71.0 percent of the average median family income in Des Moines. This ratio was seven percentage points below the U.S. level. The ratio of professional employment in Des Moines between the populations, adjusted for educational difference, was only 43 percent of the U.S. average.

Eugene is one of the few SMSA's whose ratings have been consistently outstanding in all quality of life components as disclosed by this study. This fact, however, does not imply that Eugene had all the best ratings either. On a relative basis, Eugene, though ranked high in many sub-component categories, showed only average rankings in community general living conditions and the facilities category. For instance, only 91 percent of occupied housing had telephones available; its cost of living is about the same as the U.S. average; its number of selected service establishments per 1,000 people was slightly below the corresponding national figure.

Except for the economic component, Madison stands exceptionally high in all the quality of life components. The strong points of this region in the social component categories are demonstrated by the highest over-all rating in the individual concerns such as the existing opportunities for self-support, for individual capability development, and for

TABLE 10

## INDEX AND RATING OF SOCIAL COMPONENT (M)

| SMSA | Adjusted Standardized Scores Value | Rank | Rating | Standardized Scores Value | Rank | Rating |
|---|---|---|---|---|---|---|
| 66. Albuquerque, New Mexico | 0.4704 | 45 | C | -0.0181 | 41 | C |
| 67. Ann Arbor, Michigan | 1.0205 | 8 | A | 0.5311 | 4 | A |
| 68. Appleton-Oshkosh, Wisconsin | 1.1075 | 6 | A | 0.7624 | 1 | A |
| 69. Augusta, Georgia-South Carolina | 0.0539 | 74 | E | -0.2847 | 73 | E |
| 70. Austin, Texas | 0.7041 | 20 | B | 0.1916 | 17 | B |
| 71. Bakersfield, California | 0.2502 | 64 | D | -0.0600 | 50 | C |
| 72. Baton Rouge, Louisiana | 0.5199 | 36 | C | 0.0323 | 34 | C |
| 73. Beaumont-Port Arthur-Orange, Texas | 0.4404 | 49 | C | -0.0226 | 43 | C |
| 74. Binghamton, New York-Pennsylvania | 0.6848 | 21 | B | 0.1510 | 22 | B |
| 75. Bridgeport, Connecticut | 0.5826 | 31 | C | 0.0525 | 31 | C |
| 76. Canton, Ohio | 0.3160 | 59 | D | -0.0701 | 55 | C |
| 77. Charleston, South Carolina | -0.1268 | 82 | E | -0.4419 | 79 | E |
| 78. Charleston, West Virginia | 0.3726 | 52 | D | -0.0659 | 53 | C |
| 79. Charlotte, North Carolina | 0.5993 | 29 | B | 0.0868 | 26 | B |
| 80. Chattanooga, Tennessee-Georgia | 0.0014 | 78 | E | -0.2815 | 72 | E |
| 81. Colorado Springs, Colorado | 0.8953 | 12 | A | 0.2563 | 15 | B |
| 82. Columbia, South Carolina | 0.0657 | 73 | E | -0.2128 | 64 | D |
| 83. Columbus, Georgia-Alabama | -0.0701 | 79 | E | -0.4957 | 82 | E |
| 84. Corpus Christi, Texas | 0.4818 | 43 | C | -0.0659 | 52 | C |
| 85. Davenport-Rock Island-Moline, Iowa-Illinois | 0.5864 | 30 | C | 0.0692 | 29 | C |
| 86. Des Moines, Iowa | 1.3197 | 1 | A | 0.5766 | 3 | A |
| 87. Duluth-Superior, Minnesota-Wisconsin | 1.0333 | 7 | A | 0.3995 | 6 | A |
| 88. El Paso, Texas | 0.4601 | 46 | C | -0.1044 | 59 | D |
| 89. Erie, Pennsylvania | 0.5385 | 34 | C | -0.0119 | 40 | C |
| 90. Eugene, Oregon | 1.2617 | 2 | A | 0.4985 | 5 | A |
| 91. Evansville, Indiana-Kentucky | 0.4387 | 50 | C | -0.0405 | 48 | C |
| 92. Fayetteville, North Carolina | 0.0068 | 77 | E | -0.4507 | 80 | E |
| 93. Flint, Michigan | 0.5172 | 38 | C | 0.0783 | 27 | B |
| 94. Fort Wayne, Indiana | 0.8673 | 13 | A | 0.3737 | 9 | A |
| 95. Fresno, California | 0.6579 | 24 | B | 0.1576 | 21 | B |
| 96. Greenville, South Carolina | 0.1535 | 66 | D | -0.2711 | 71 | D |
| 97. Hamilton-Middleton, Ohio | 0.2516 | 63 | D | -0.1148 | 60 | D |
| 98. Harrisburg, Pennsylvania | 0.4825 | 42 | C | -0.1000 | 57 | D |
| 99. Huntington-Ashland, West Virginia-Kentucky-Ohio | 0.0780 | 71 | E | -0.2647 | 68 | D |
| 100. Huntsville, Alabama | -0.1253 | 81 | E | -0.5550 | 83 | E |
| 101. Jackson, Mississippi | 0.0691 | 72 | E | -0.3256 | 74 | E |
| 102. Johnstown, Pennsylvania | 0.3667 | 54 | D | -0.2445 | 66 | D |
| 103. Kalamazoo, Michigan | 0.8011 | 16 | B | 0.1704 | 19 | B |
| 104. Knoxville, Tennessee | 0.2258 | 65 | D | -0.1041 | 58 | D |
| 105. Lancaster, Pennsylvania | 0.1355 | 68 | E | -0.4222 | 76 | E |
| 106. Lansing, Michigan | 0.7408 | 17 | B | 0.2114 | 16 | B |
| 107. Las Vegas, Nevada | 0.8404 | 14 | B | 0.3666 | 10 | A |
| 108. Lawrence-Haverhill, Massachusetts-New Hampshire | 0.6545 | 25 | B | 0.1185 | 24 | B |
| 109. Little Rock-North Little Rock, Arkansas | 0.3733 | 51 | D | -0.0310 | 45 | C |
| 110. Lorain-Elyria, Ohio | 0.3523 | 57 | D | -0.0581 | 49 | C |
| 111. Lowell, Massachusetts | 0.5119 | 40 | C | -0.0644 | 51 | C |
| 112. Macon, Georgia | 0.0200 | 76 | E | -0.2693 | 70 | D |
| 113. Madison, Wisconsin | 1.2014 | 3 | A | 0.6336 | 2 | A |
| 114. Mobile, Alabama | -0.2661 | 83 | E | -0.4815 | 81 | E |
| 115. Montgomery, Alabama | -0.1114 | 80 | E | -0.4270 | 77 | E |
| 116. New Haven, Connecticut | 0.6692 | 22 | B | 0.1780 | 18 | B |
| 117. New London-Groton-Norwich, Connecticut | 0.5058 | 41 | C | 0.0436 | 32 | C |
| 118. Newport News-Hampton, Virginia | 0.3679 | 53 | D | -0.1581 | 61 | D |
| 119. Orlando, Florida | 0.3552 | 55 | D | -0.0858 | 56 | D |
| 120. Oxnard-Ventura, California | 0.4437 | 48 | C | 0.0194 | 38 | C |
| 121. Pensacola, Florida | 0.0217 | 75 | E | -0.2663 | 69 | D |
| 122. Peoria, Illinois | 0.5174 | 37 | C | 0.0153 | 39 | C |
| 123. Raleigh, North Carolina | 0.3074 | 61 | D | -0.0683 | 54 | C |
| 124. Reading, Pennsylvania | 0.2705 | 62 | D | -0.1838 | 63 | D |
| 125. Rockford, Illinois | 0.5126 | 39 | C | 0.0270 | 35 | C |
| 126. Saginaw, Michigan | 0.3535 | 56 | D | -0.0340 | 46 | C |
| 127. Salinas-Monterey, California | 0.6651 | 23 | B | 0.1692 | 20 | B |
| 128. Santa Barbara, California | 0.9701 | 9 | A | 0.3355 | 11 | A |
| 129. Santa Rosa, California | 0.7239 | 18 | B | 0.1435 | 23 | B |
| 130. Scranton, Pennsylvania | 0.5358 | 35 | C | 0.0253 | 37 | C |
| 131. Shreveport, Louisiana | 0.1250 | 69 | E | -0.4327 | 78 | E |
| 132. South Bend, Indiana | 0.6098 | 28 | B | 0.0656 | 30 | C |
| 133. Spokane, Washington | 1.1078 | 5 | A | 0.3848 | 8 | A |
| 134. Stamford, Connecticut | 0.8212 | 15 | B | 0.2928 | 14 | A |
| 135. Stockton, California | 0.6136 | 27 | B | 0.0326 | 33 | C |
| 136. Tacoma, Washington | 0.9543 | 11 | A | 0.3254 | 13 | A |
| 137. Trenton, New Jersey | 0.3168 | 58 | D | -0.1745 | 62 | D |
| 138. Tucson, Arizona | 0.5731 | 32 | C | 0.0990 | 25 | B |
| 139. Tulsa, Oklahoma | 0.5416 | 33 | C | -0.0237 | 44 | C |
| 140. Utica-Rome, New York | 0.4485 | 47 | C | -0.0186 | 42 | C |
| 141. Vallejo-Napa, California | 0.6496 | 26 | B | 0.0741 | 28 | C |
| 142. Waterbury, Connecticut | 0.4734 | 44 | C | -0.0343 | 47 | C |
| 143. West Palm Beach, Florida | 0.7189 | 19 | B | 0.0259 | 36 | C |
| 144. Wichita, Kansas | 1.1741 | 4 | A | 0.3856 | 7 | A |
| 145. Wilkes-Barre-Hazelton, Pennsylvania | 0.1482 | 67 | D | -0.2575 | 67 | D |
| 146. Wilmington, Delaware-New Jersey-Maryland | 0.3135 | 60 | D | -0.2145 | 65 | D |
| 147. Worcester, Massachusetts | 0.9578 | 10 | A | 0.3264 | 12 | A |
| 148. York, Pennsylvania | 0.1015 | 70 | E | -0.3749 | 75 | E |

A = Outstanding ($\geq \bar{x} + s$)
B = Excellent ($\bar{x} + .28s \leq B < \bar{x} + s$)
C = Good ($\bar{x} - .28s < C < \bar{x} + .28s$)
D = Adequate ($\bar{x} - s < D \leq \bar{x} - .28s$)
E = Substandard ($\leq \bar{x} - s$)

Mean ($\bar{x}$) = 0.4901          Mean ($\bar{x}$) = 0.0000
Standard Deviation (s) = 0.3515          Standard Deviation (s) = 0.2744

individual choices. It also displayed very good community living
conditions with a very low percentage of people working outside the
county of residence (3.4 percent versus 17.8 for the U.S.); very little
problem in housing segregation and central city-suburban sprawl; lots
of sports, cultural and recreational activities. The weaker points in
the region are some racial discrimination and some unpleasant factors
in general living conditions, such as the national equivalent crime rate
and living costs.

After assessing more than 50 factors which influence our social quality
of life, this study derived a lowest social component index of -0.27
for Mobile. This means that the combined positive factors affecting
social quality of life in that region are outweighed by the negative
factors. In contrast to Eugene, Mobile is one of the few regions whose
quality of life ratings have consistently fallen into the substandard
category. The low index for Mobile in the social component resulted
from its low ratings in individual concerns, especially in promoting
maximum development of individual capability such as investment efforts
in education and vocational training by individuals and government,
and the lack of opportunities for self-support or for becoming independent. For example, the labor force participation rate was very
low, 61.8 percent. And among those a high percentage was unemployed.
A relatively high percentage of married couples was found without
their own households, and yet a very high percentage of children under
18 were not living with both of their parents (22.8 percent in Mobile
versus 17.3 percent in the U.S.). Per capita local government expenditure for education was $94, or $52 short of the U.S. norm in 1970.
Only a small percentage of both males and females in the area between
16 and 64 who completed less than 15 years of school had vocational
training. The negative sign for Mobile's index was derived from the
high value of negative factors in individual inequality between races,
sexes, and central city and suburban. Other negative factors such as
percent of occupied housing with one or more persons per room (12.0
percent against 8.2 percent in the U.S.) and a high birth rate also
partly contributed to the negative index.

A negative index is also found in Charleston, Huntsville, Montgomery,
and Columbus (Georgia/Alabama). Except for Huntsville, all of these
low ranking SMSA's have been mentioned at least three times as being
substandard. Although they have average or good environmental quality,
they compared unfavorably to other medium SMSA's economically, politically, and socially. The most critical reason for their consistent low
rating is probably due to the relatively low educational attainment

166

# CHART 10

## REGIONAL VARIATIONS IN INDEXES: SOCIAL COMPONENT (M)

| RANK | SMSA | ADJUSTED STANDARIZED SCORE |

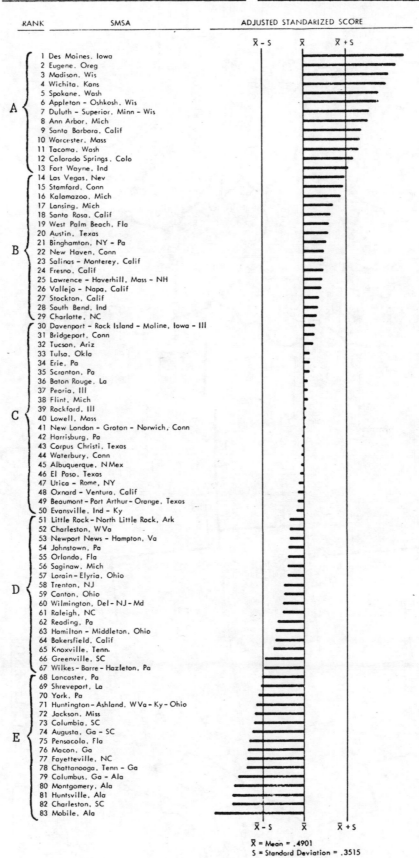

**A**
1 Des Moines, Iowa
2 Eugene, Oreg
3 Madison, Wis
4 Wichita, Kans
5 Spokane, Wash
6 Appleton – Oshkosh, Wis
7 Duluth – Superior, Minn – Wis
8 Ann Arbor, Mich
9 Santa Barbara, Calif
10 Worcester, Mass
11 Tacoma, Wash
12 Colorado Springs, Colo
13 Fort Wayne, Ind

**B**
14 Las Vegas, Nev
15 Stamford, Conn
16 Kalamazoo, Mich
17 Lansing, Mich
18 Santa Rosa, Calif
19 West Palm Beach, Fla
20 Austin, Texas
21 Binghamton, NY – Pa
22 New Haven, Conn
23 Salinas – Monterey, Calif
24 Fresno, Calif
25 Lawrence – Haverhill, Mass – NH
26 Vallejo – Napa, Calif
27 Stockton, Calif
28 South Bend, Ind
29 Charlotte, NC

**C**
30 Davenport – Rock Island – Moline, Iowa – Ill
31 Bridgeport, Conn
32 Tucson, Ariz
33 Tulsa, Okla
34 Erie, Pa
35 Scranton, Pa
36 Baton Rouge, La
37 Peoria, Ill
38 Flint, Mich
39 Rockford, Ill
40 Lowell, Mass
41 New London – Groton – Norwich, Conn
42 Harrisburg, Pa
43 Corpus Christi, Texas
44 Waterbury, Conn
45 Albuquerque, N Mex
46 El Paso, Texas
47 Utica – Rome, NY
48 Oxnard – Ventura, Calif
49 Beaumont – Port Arthur – Orange, Texas
50 Evansville, Ind – Ky

**D**
51 Little Rock – North Little Rock, Ark
52 Charleston, W Va
53 Newport News – Hampton, Va
54 Johnstown, Pa
55 Orlando, Fla
56 Saginaw, Mich
57 Lorain – Elyria, Ohio
58 Trenton, NJ
59 Canton, Ohio
60 Wilmington, Del – NJ – Md
61 Raleigh, NC
62 Reading, Pa
63 Hamilton – Middleton, Ohio
64 Bakersfield, Calif
65 Knoxville, Tenn.
66 Greenville, SC
67 Wilkes – Barre – Hazleton, Pa

**E**
68 Lancaster, Pa
69 Shreveport, La
70 York, Pa
71 Huntington – Ashland, W Va – Ky – Ohio
72 Jackson, Miss
73 Columbia, SC
74 Augusta, Ga – SC
75 Pensacola, Fla
76 Macon, Ga
77 Fayetteville, NC
78 Chattanooga, Tenn – Ga
79 Columbus, Ga – Ala
80 Montgomery, Ala
81 Huntsville, Ala
82 Charleston, SC
83 Mobile, Ala

X̄ = Mean = .4901
S = Standard Deviation = .3515

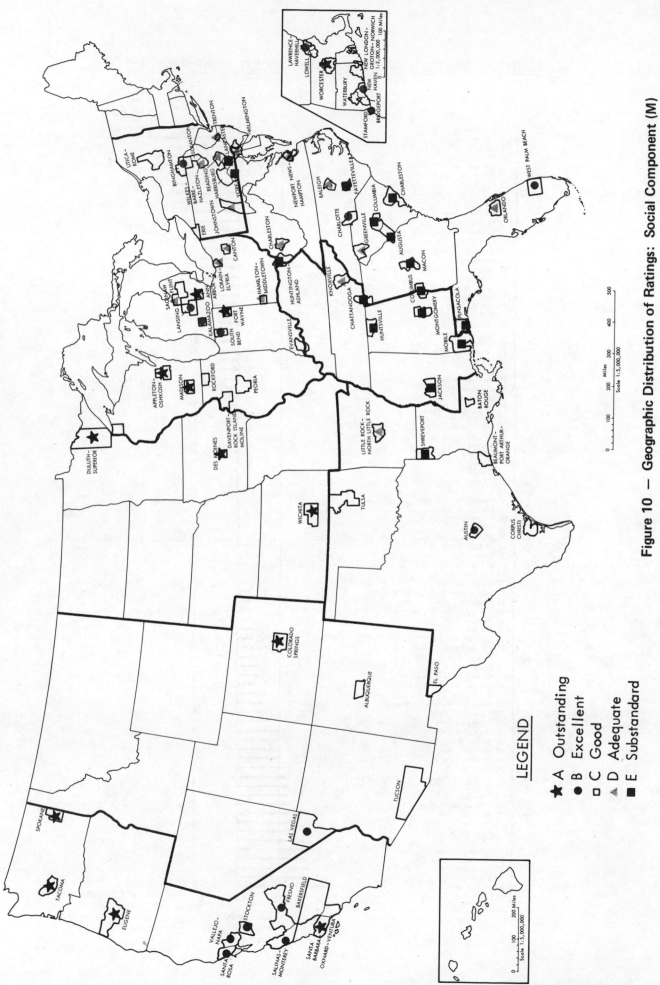

**Figure 10 — Geographic Distribution of Ratings: Social Component (M)**

LEGEND

A Outstanding
B Excellent
C Good
D Adequate
E Substandard

and lower quality of physical health among the residents. The educational and health policies directed at solving these areas' problems would seem to be not only desirable but also more efficient than other policies.

The number of SMSA's identified by this study to have substandard social quality of life totaled 16. In addition to the five SMSA's with negative indexes, the remaining 11 are Chattanooga, Fayetteville, Macon, Pensacola, Augusta, Columbia, Jackson, Huntington/Ashland, York, Shreveport, and Lancaster. As Charts 9 and 10 illustrate, there exists an extremely strong correlation between SMSA's rated substandard in both the health and education component and the social component. For the East South Central and the South Atlantic regions, this strong correlation is observed even for the four quality of life components except environmental. As pointed out previously, economic, political, health and education, and social quality of life are interdependent. Neither the education and health nor the political factors can fully explain the low ratings of the social component in the South. However, economic weakness in the South can be considered as the probable basic cause for the strong correlations among the low quality of life ratings for the SMSA's.

The standard deviation which has been used to show the range of index values is found to be relatively small for the social component, equal only to 0.35, because many negative quality of life factors were included in the component. As a result, the bar chart, Chart 10, looks much narrower than the others, such as health and education for example. In terms of variation among index values, it is the coefficient of variation that matters. The coefficient of variation for the social component for medium SMSA's is extremely high, i.e., 0.71. Specifically, this high coefficient indicates that people in the medium SMSA's had substantially differing levels of quality of life in 1970. Indeed, the varying quality of life experienced by them is less equal in social concerns than in any others.

SUMMARY AND CONCLUSIONS

Among the medium SMSA's, the preceding sections have illustrated different quality of life patterns as compared to those measured for the large SMSA's. Economically, the most viable and wealthy SMSA's are concentrated in the East North Central Region. The Pacific region is found to be relatively weaker than the Midwest and the Middle Atlantic regions. This is in contrast to the economic powers that the large SMSA's displayed in the Pacific region. However, the only SMSA in the State of Oregon, Eugene, was still rated outstanding. The South Atlantic Region showed little economic strength; the only exception being West Palm Beach, the only outstandingly wealthy SMSA in the South. The quality variation of economic well-being over regions is not appreciably large, however; the coefficient of variation among the composite economic indexes is 0.28 percent, even smaller than that for the large SMSA's.

The highest political quality of life is found in the States of Michigan, Indiana, Wisconsin, Connecticut, California, and New York, while the local governments in the South tend to be incompetent and less efficient in the provision of public goods and services. Despite the fact that the SMSA's in this group are geographically drastically differentiated by political component ratings, the actual index variations within the 83 SMSA's are the smallest among the five quality of life components, with a coefficient of 0.24 percent. This is similar to the findings in the large SMSA group. In short, political quality of life in the country tends to be closer than in the other components.

The Pacific region once again is identified as enjoying the best environmental quality. Except for a few SMSA's, the East North Central Region reveals some support for the trade-off hypothesis between economic growth and environmental damages since most SMSA's in the region were rated only "adequate." The coastal SMSA's in New England and Middle Atlantic regions are classified as excellent. There are only about 10 substandard SMSA's scattered through the East and South of the United States. The environmental deterioration and the quality variation in the medium sized SMSA's as measured do not seem to be appreciable since the coefficient of variation of the indexes is only about 0.30.

The health and education component measures indicate the best quality areas are in the Pacific and the East North Central regions, though they are mixed with "good" and "adequate" SMSA's. The SMSA's in the Midwest are also recognized as outstanding and excellent. The "E" rated SMSA's are found in Pennsylvania, South Carolina, Georgia, and Alabama. The variation in index values for this component is very high, next only to the social component. This implies that a great deal of improvement in the health and education fields can be made among the SMSA's so that regional differentials in health and education quality may be eliminated.

The social component received the highest coefficient of variation, 0.71, indicating that a wide range of social factors are found in varying levels of quality over all medium SMSA's in this country. The East North Central Region and the Pacific region had the most "A" and "B" ranking SMSA's, while those in the four southern states rated markedly below average.

In comparison, the medium SMSA's jointly display clearer geographic patterns in terms of quality of life ratings than the large SMSA's. The variations in the composite indexes are high for the health and education component and the social component and relatively low for the other quality of life components in both size groups. However, the trade-off hypothesis of quality of life components between the results of industrialization and environmental quality is much more discernible in the large SMSA's than in the medium SMSA's. The two methods employed to compute the ratings and rankings also demonstrated significant consistency between rankings for the medium group SMSA's as they were for the large SMSA's. The rank-order correlation co-efficients for the five quality of life components are, respectively, 0.94, 0.96, 0.92, 0.98, and 0.97.

# CHAPTER
# VII

## QUALITY OF LIFE
## FINDINGS AND IMPLICATIONS:
## SMALL METROPOLITAN AREAS (S)

By definition of the U.S. Department of Commerce, there were 95 SMSA's in this country with a population smaller than 200,000 in 1970. Most of these SMSA's are geographically concentrated in the East North Central and the West South Central regions, especially in the State of Texas. There are only two SMSA's on the West Coast and seven in the Mountain area. The remaining are scattered through New England, the West North Central, and the South. Although the quality of life factors selected to assess the level of quality inputs in the small SMSA's are identical to those employed in the large and medium SMSA's, some factors have been excluded either because of incomplete data or because data were not available at all. Sometimes estimated data were used in order to complete the overall evaluation. Those estimated data are marked with dots as shown in the tables in the Appendix.

The five quality of life components will be presented in this chapter in a like manner to the preceding two chapters. In passing, it should be noted again that only the relative ratings for the SMSA, not the indexes themselves, can be compared with those in the preceding two chapters, since the factor means used to compute the indexes are different. Specifically with respect to the index values of SMSA's no comparison should be made other than with those SMSA's in the same group.

### ECONOMIC COMPONENT

Out of the 95 small SMSA's, 13 outstanding were identified. More than 30 SMSA's in the group were classified as excellent. In other words, the economic component composite indexes for the small SMSA's tend to be more clustered in the "B" category than in any others. With 21 substandard SMSA's, the number remaining for "adequate" and "good" is apparently small. What this amounts to is that economically this group of small SMSA's is either relatively rich, affluent, and viable for growth or substandard, unhealthy and impeded by obstacles to industrial development.

172

# TABLE 11

## INDEX AND RATING OF ECONOMIC COMPONENT (S)

| | Adjusted Standardized Scores | | | Standardized Scores | | |
|---|---|---|---|---|---|---|
| SMSA | Value | Rank | Rating | Value | Rank | Rating |
| 149. Abilene, Texas | 1.9214 | 45 | B | 0.2116 | 33 | B |
| 150. Albany, Ga. | 0.4643 | 93 | E | -0.8210 | 91 | E |
| 151. Altoona, Pa. | 1.2143 | 70 | D | -0.2996 | 71 | D |
| 152. Amarillo, Texas | 2.7500 | 3 | A | 0.6064 | 8 | A |
| 153. Anderson, Ind. | 2.3429 | 16 | B | 0.6297 | 7 | A |
| 154. Asheville, N.C. | 1.9000 | 47 | C | 0.0663 | 51 | C |
| 155. Atlantic City, N.J. | 0.7643 | 86 | E | -0.5729 | 85 | E |
| 156. Bay City, Mich. | 2.3071 | 20 | B | 0.3176 | 27 | B |
| 157. Billings, Mont. | 1.8429 | 50 | C | 0.0776 | 50 | C |
| 158. Biloxi-Gulfport, Miss. | 0.5857 | 91 | E | -0.6833 | 89 | E |
| 159. Bloomington-Normal, Ill. | 1.9000 | 46 | C | 0.1957 | 38 | B |
| 160. Boise City, Idaho | 2.3857 | 14 | B | 0.3665 | 20 | B |
| 161. Bristol, Conn. | 2.2571 | 24 | B | 0.2040 | 36 | B |
| 162. Brockton, Mass. | 1.1786 | 71 | D | -0.2854 | 70 | D |
| 163. Brownsville-Harlingen-San Benito, Texas | 0.2714 | 94 | E | -1.5980 | 94 | E |
| 164. Bryan-College Station, Texas | 1.6643 | 63 | C | -0.0463 | 62 | C |
| 165. Cedar Rapids, Iowa | 2.3214 | 19 | B | 0.3454 | 22 | B |
| 166. Champaign-Urbana, Ill. | 1.4786 | 69 | D | -0.2260 | 69 | D |
| 167. Columbia, Mo. | 1.5214 | 68 | D | -0.1695 | 68 | D |
| 168. Danbury, Conn. | 2.1429 | 28 | B | 0.3264 | 26 | B |
| 169. Decatur, Ill. | 2.5929 | 7 | A | 0.4347 | 14 | B |
| 170. Dubuque, Iowa | 1.9857 | 38 | B | 0.1982 | 37 | B |
| 171. Durham, N.C. | 1.8786 | 49 | C | -0.0056 | 58 | C |
| 172. Fall River, Mass.-R.I. | 1.1214 | 74 | D | -0.4919 | 80 | D |
| 173. Fargo-Moorhead, N. Dak.-Minn. | 1.7929 | 52 | C | -0.0604 | 63 | C |
| 174. Fitchburg-Leominster, Mass. | 1.6929 | 60 | C | 0.0059 | 56 | C |
| 175. Fort Smith, Ark.-Okla. | 0.9929 | 77 | E | -0.4156 | 75 | D |
| 176. Gadsden, Alabama | 0.8429 | 85 | E | -0.6246 | 86 | E |
| 177. Gainesville, Fla. | 0.9214 | 81 | E | -0.5426 | 82 | E |
| 178. Galveston-Texas City, Texas | 2.1357 | 30 | B | 0.3669 | 19 | B |
| 179. Great Falls, Mont. | 0.8643 | 83 | E | -0.4649 | 77 | D |
| 180. Green Bay, Wis. | 2.3429 | 17 | B | 0.3922 | 17 | B |
| 181. Jackson, Mich. | 2.2143 | 26 | B | 0.3901 | 18 | B |
| 182. Kenosha, Wis. | 1.9643 | 40 | B | 0.2116 | 34 | B |
| 183. La Crosse, Wis. | 2.1000 | 31 | B | 0.2496 | 31 | B |
| 184. Lafayette, La. | 0.8500 | 84 | E | -0.4808 | 79 | D |
| 185. Lafayette-West Lafayette, Ind. | 2.1429 | 29 | B | 0.2106 | 35 | B |
| 186. Lake Charles, La. | 1.1500 | 73 | D | -0.3171 | 72 | D |
| 187. Laredo, Texas | 0.0571 | 95 | E | -1.8953 | 95 | E |
| 188. Lawton, Okla. | 0.6000 | 90 | E | -0.8447 | 92 | E |
| 189. Lewiston-Auburn, Maine | 0.9571 | 78 | E | -0.4968 | 81 | D |
| 190. Lexington, Ky. | 1.9357 | 44 | B | 0.1674 | 40 | B |
| 191. Lima, Ohio | 1.7071 | 57 | C | 0.1152 | 46 | C |
| 192. Lincoln, Nebraska | 2.7571 | 2 | A | 0.6347 | 6 | A |
| 193. Lubbock, Texas | 2.0214 | 34 | B | 0.1591 | 41 | B |
| 194. Lynchburg, Va. | 2.0429 | 33 | B | 0.1097 | 47 | C |
| 195. Manchester, N.H. | 2.0571 | 32 | B | 0.2830 | 28 | B |
| 196. Mansfield, Ohio | 2.0214 | 35 | B | 0.1192 | 45 | C |
| 197. McAllen-Pharr-Edinburg, Texas | 0.5071 | 92 | E | -1.5788 | 93 | E |
| 198. Meriden, Conn. | 1.9429 | 41 | B | 0.2211 | 32 | B |

173

# TABLE 11 (Concluded)

| SMSA | Adjusted Standardized Scores | | | Standardized Scores | | |
|---|---|---|---|---|---|---|
| | Value | Rank | Rating | Value | Rank | Rating |
| 199. Midland, Texas | 2.7143 | 4 | A | 1.1825 | 1 | A |
| 200. Modesto, Calif. | 1.7929 | 53 | C | -0.1692 | 67 | D |
| 201. Monroe, La. | 1.1571 | 72 | D | -0.4373 | 76 | D |
| 202. Muncie, Ind. | 2.3286 | 18 | B | 0.4815 | 12 | B |
| 203. Muskegon-Muskegon Heights, Mich. | 1.7857 | 54 | C | 0.0835 | 48 | C |
| 204. Nashua, N.H. | 1.6857 | 61 | C | -0.0286 | 59 | C |
| 205. New Bedford, Mass. | 1.0500 | 76 | E | -0.5561 | 84 | E |
| 206. New Britain, Conn. | 1.7786 | 55 | C | -0.0056 | 57 | C |
| 207. Norwalk, Conn. | 2.6214 | 6 | A | 0.9004 | 3 | A |
| 208. Odessa, Texas | 2.3714 | 15 | B | 0.5761 | 9 | A |
| 209. Ogden, Utah | 1.6143 | 65 | C | -0.0938 | 65 | C |
| 210. Owensboro, Ky. | 1.7000 | 58 | C | -0.0384 | 60 | C |
| 211. Petersburg-Colonial Heights, Va. | 1.0571 | 75 | E | -0.4115 | 73 | D |
| 212. Pine Bluff, Ark. | 0.6929 | 89 | E | -0.6492 | 87 | E |
| 213. Pittsfield, Mass. | 1.8429 | 51 | C | 0.1332 | 42 | C |
| 214. Portland, Maine | 1.7786 | 56 | C | 0.0433 | 53 | C |
| 215. Provo-Orem, Utah | 0.7071 | 88 | E | -0.6624 | 88 | E |
| 216. Pueblo, Colo. | 1.6429 | 64 | C | -0.0445 | 61 | C |
| 217. Racine, Wis. | 2.4214 | 13 | A | 0.4329 | 15 | B |
| 218. Reno, Nev. | 2.5071 | 9 | A | 1.0243 | 2 | A |
| 219. Roanoke, Va. | 2.5143 | 8 | A | 0.4695 | 13 | B |
| 220. Rochester, Minn. | 1.5571 | 66 | C | 0.0074 | 55 | C |
| 221. St. Joseph, Mo. | 2.2500 | 25 | B | 0.3381 | 24 | B |
| 222. Salem, Oreg. | 2.2786 | 22 | B | 0.2546 | 30 | B |
| 223. San Angelo, Texas | 2.4214 | 12 | A | 0.5206 | 10 | A |
| 224. Savannah, Ga. | 0.9214 | 80 | E | -0.4688 | 78 | D |
| 225. Sherman-Denison, Texas | 2.2714 | 23 | B | 0.3437 | 23 | B |
| 226. Sioux City, Iowa-Nebraska | 1.7000 | 59 | C | 0.1259 | 44 | C |
| 227. Sioux Falls, S. Dak. | 1.8857 | 48 | C | 0.0585 | 52 | C |
| 228. Springfield, Ill. | 2.4643 | 11 | A | 0.4075 | 16 | B |
| 229. Springfield, Mo. | 2.4857 | 10 | A | 0.4866 | 11 | B |
| 230. Springfield, Ohio | 2.0143 | 36 | B | 0.0820 | 49 | C |
| 231. Steubenville-Weirton, Ohio-W. Va. | 2.0143 | 37 | B | 0.3663 | 21 | B |
| 232. Tallahassee, Fla. | 1.5286 | 67 | D | -0.1376 | 66 | C |
| 233. Terre Haute, Ind. | 2.2000 | 27 | B | 0.2619 | 29 | B |
| 234. Texarkana, Texas-Ark. | 1.9429 | 42 | B | 0.0399 | 54 | C |
| 235. Topeka, Kans. | 2.6857 | 5 | A | 0.8234 | 4 | A |
| 236. Tuscaloosa, Alabama | 0.7286 | 87 | E | -0.7510 | 90 | E |
| 237. Tyler, Texas | 2.7643 | 1 | A | 0.7159 | 5 | A |
| 238. Vineland-Millville-Bridgeton, N.J. | 0.8929 | 82 | E | -0.5485 | 83 | E |
| 239. Waco, Texas | 1.9786 | 39 | B | 0.1698 | 39 | B |
| 240. Waterloo, Iowa | 1.9357 | 43 | B | 0.1302 | 43 | C |
| 241. Wheeling, W. Va.-Ohio | 1.6786 | 62 | C | -0.0709 | 64 | C |
| 242. Wichita Falls, Texas | 2.3071 | 21 | B | 0.3322 | 25 | B |
| 243. Wilmington, N.C. | 0.9571 | 79 | E | -0.4136 | 74 | D |

A = Outstanding ($\geq \bar{x} + s$)
B = Excellent ($\bar{x} + .28s \leq B < \bar{x} + s$)
C = Good ($\bar{x} - .28s < C < \bar{x} + .28s$)
D = Adequate ($\bar{x} - s < D \leq \bar{x} - .28s$)
E = Substandard ($\leq \bar{x} - s$)

Mean ($\bar{x}$) = 1.7372
Standard Deviation (s) = 0.6491

Mean ($\bar{x}$) = 0.0000
Standard Deviation (s) = 0.5202

Among the 13 outstanding SMSA's four are in Texas; with an index of 2.76, or about 1.57 standard deviations above the mean of 1.74, Tyler is one of three which scored the highest. The other three in the state are Amarillo, Midland, and San Angelo; they ranked, respectively, third, fourth, and 12th. These four SMSA's are characterized by high ratings of the individual economic well-being index in terms of average income and wealth, and low ratings in the degree of economic concentration and unequal income distribution. Therefore, the economic structure in the SMSA's is concentrated; however, the relatively unequal distribution of income and wealth among residents in the SMSA's does have important political implication and is worth noting. For instance, despite the fact that Midland had the highest income per capita adjusted for living cost among the 95 SMSA's in 1970, it still had a very high percentage of families with income below the poverty level-- one of every 10 families had income below the poverty level. The corresponding figures were 12.9 percent, 9.1 percent, and 14.6 percent respectively in Tyler, Amarillo, and San Angelo.

The remaining outstanding SMSA's are Lincoln (Nebraska), Topeka (Kansas), Norwalk (Connecticut), Decatur (Illinois), Roanoke (Virginia), Reno (Nevada), Springfield (Missouri), Springfield (Illinois), and Racine (Wisconsin). For these SMSA's, the impact of their state governments and the governments' employment on the regional economy would seem to be significant.

Three SMSA's in southern Texas along with those SMSA's in the southern states are rated substandard economically. In vivid contrast to the SMSA's in the northern part of the State of Texas, Laredo and Brownsville/Harlingen/San Benito ranked at the bottom of the list. McAllen/Pharr/Edinburg, with an index slightly higher than that for Albany (Georgia), came up as the fourth-lowest rated SMSA in the group. The index for Laredo is 0.06 or 2.6 standard deviations below the group mean. For McAllen/Pharr/Edinburg, it is 0.51 or 1.9 standard deviations lower than the mean. Apparently the extremely low personal income per capita and the weak economy in these SMSA's are generally expected. As shown in Table C-1 in the Appendix, the average personal income per capita in 1970 was $1,573, $1,580, and $1,523, respectively, for Laredo, Brownsville/Harlingen/San Benito and McAllen/Pharr/Edinburg; this was just about 50 percent of the average personal income in the United States in 1970. The high unemployment rates, low labor productivity, and housing values, etc., worsen the quality of economic life in these SMSA's. The dichotomized economic situation unveiled in the State of Texas was also observed for the entire eastern half of the United States. As shown in Figure 11, there are no excellent or outstanding SMSA's found in the southern states east of the Mississippi River, and almost all of the SMSA's in the Great Lakes area are rated better than "good." While industrialization achieved the high economic

175

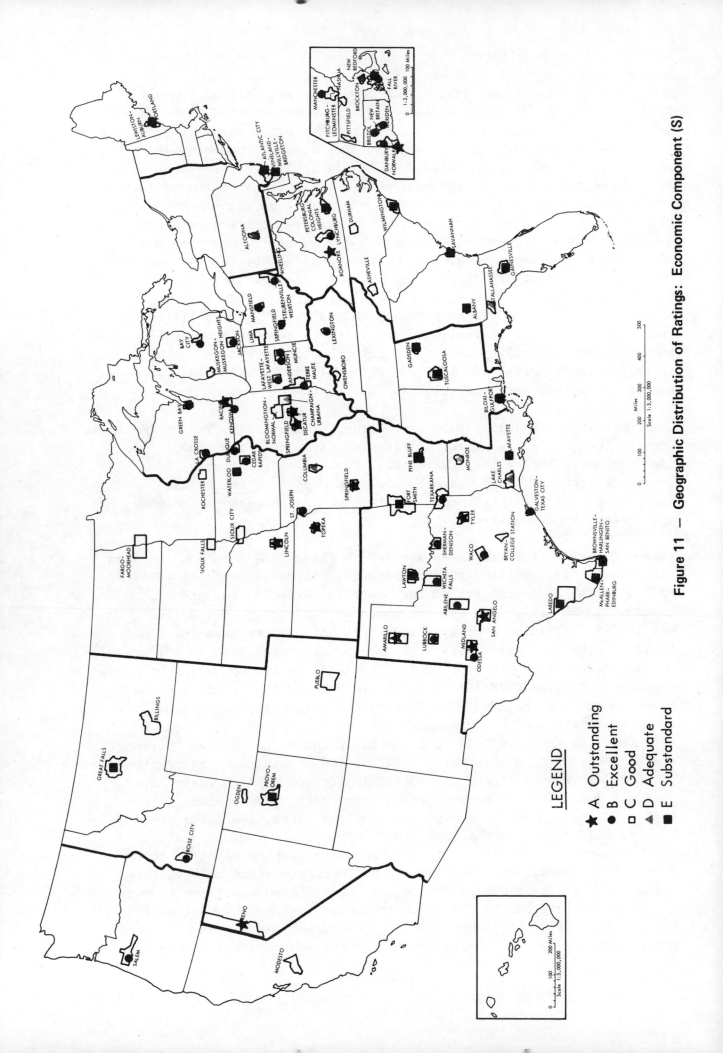

**Figure 11 — Geographic Distribution of Ratings: Economic Component (S)**

LEGEND

A  Outstanding
B  Excellent
C  Good
D  Adequate
E  Substandard

# CHART 11
## REGIONAL VARIATIONS IN INDEXES:   ECONOMIC COMPONENT (S)

RANK          SMSA                                    ADJUSTED STANDARDIZED SCORE

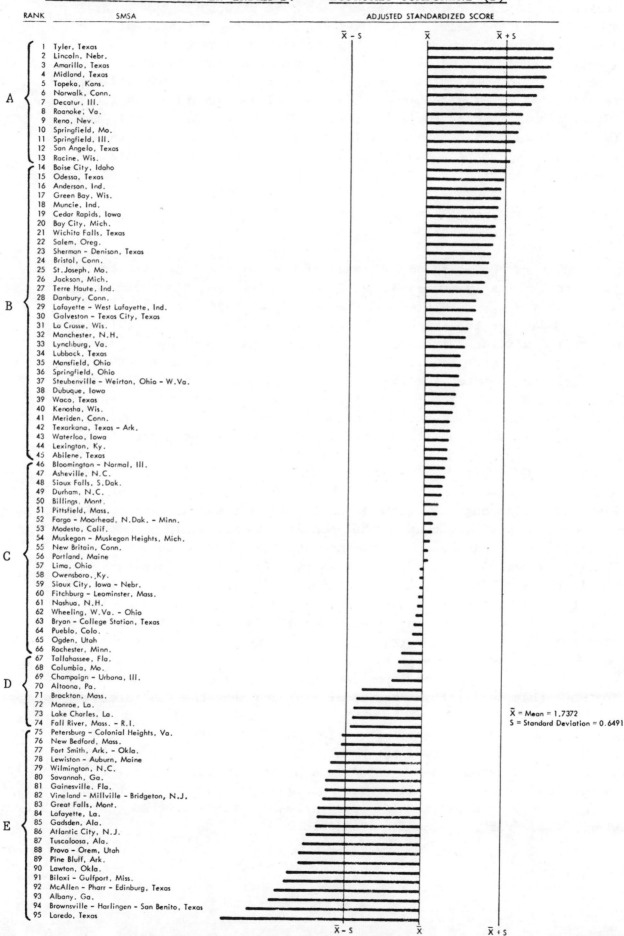

| Rank | SMSA |
|------|------|
| 1 | Tyler, Texas |
| 2 | Lincoln, Nebr. |
| 3 | Amarillo, Texas |
| 4 | Midland, Texas |
| 5 | Topeka, Kans. |
| 6 | Norwalk, Conn. |
| 7 | Decatur, Ill. |
| 8 | Roanoke, Va. |
| 9 | Reno, Nev. |
| 10 | Springfield, Mo. |
| 11 | Springfield, Ill. |
| 12 | San Angelo, Texas |
| 13 | Racine, Wis. |
| 14 | Boise City, Idaho |
| 15 | Odessa, Texas |
| 16 | Anderson, Ind. |
| 17 | Green Bay, Wis. |
| 18 | Muncie, Ind. |
| 19 | Cedar Rapids, Iowa |
| 20 | Bay City, Mich. |
| 21 | Wichita Falls, Texas |
| 22 | Salem, Oreg. |
| 23 | Sherman – Denison, Texas |
| 24 | Bristol, Conn. |
| 25 | St. Joseph, Mo. |
| 26 | Jackson, Mich. |
| 27 | Terre Haute, Ind. |
| 28 | Danbury, Conn. |
| 29 | Lafayette – West Lafayette, Ind. |
| 30 | Galveston – Texas City, Texas |
| 31 | La Crosse, Wis. |
| 32 | Manchester, N.H. |
| 33 | Lynchburg, Va. |
| 34 | Lubbock, Texas |
| 35 | Mansfield, Ohio |
| 36 | Springfield, Ohio |
| 37 | Steubenville – Weirton, Ohio – W.Va. |
| 38 | Dubuque, Iowa |
| 39 | Waco, Texas |
| 40 | Kenosha, Wis. |
| 41 | Meriden, Conn. |
| 42 | Texarkana, Texas – Ark. |
| 43 | Waterloo, Iowa |
| 44 | Lexington, Ky. |
| 45 | Abilene, Texas |
| 46 | Bloomington – Normal, Ill. |
| 47 | Asheville, N.C. |
| 48 | Sioux Falls, S.Dak. |
| 49 | Durham, N.C. |
| 50 | Billings, Mont. |
| 51 | Pittsfield, Mass. |
| 52 | Fargo – Moorhead, N.Dak. – Minn. |
| 53 | Modesto, Calif. |
| 54 | Muskegon – Muskegon Heights, Mich. |
| 55 | New Britain, Conn. |
| 56 | Portland, Maine |
| 57 | Lima, Ohio |
| 58 | Owensboro, Ky. |
| 59 | Sioux City, Iowa – Nebr. |
| 60 | Fitchburg – Leominster, Mass. |
| 61 | Nashua, N.H. |
| 62 | Wheeling, W.Va. – Ohio |
| 63 | Bryan – College Station, Texas |
| 64 | Pueblo, Colo. |
| 65 | Ogden, Utah |
| 66 | Rochester, Minn. |
| 67 | Tallahassee, Fla. |
| 68 | Columbia, Mo. |
| 69 | Champaign – Urbana, Ill. |
| 70 | Altoona, Pa. |
| 71 | Brockton, Mass. |
| 72 | Monroe, La. |
| 73 | Lake Charles, La. |
| 74 | Fall River, Mass. – R.I. |
| 75 | Petersburg – Colonial Heights, Va. |
| 76 | New Bedford, Mass. |
| 77 | Fort Smith, Ark. – Okla. |
| 78 | Lewiston – Auburn, Maine |
| 79 | Wilmington, N.C. |
| 80 | Savannah, Ga. |
| 81 | Gainesville, Fla. |
| 82 | Vineland – Millville – Bridgeton, N.J. |
| 83 | Great Falls, Mont. |
| 84 | Lafayette, La. |
| 85 | Gadsden, Ala. |
| 86 | Atlantic City, N.J. |
| 87 | Tuscaloosa, Ala. |
| 88 | Provo – Orem, Utah |
| 89 | Pine Bluff, Ark. |
| 90 | Lawton, Okla. |
| 91 | Biloxi – Gulfport, Miss. |
| 92 | McAllen – Pharr – Edinburg, Texas |
| 93 | Albany, Ga. |
| 94 | Brownsville – Harlingen – San Benito, Texas |
| 95 | Laredo, Texas |

Groups: A (1–13), B (14–45), C (46–66), D (67–74), E (75–95)

X̄ = Mean = 1.7372
S = Standard Deviation = 0.6491

status in the latter area, the weak economic structure, low labor productivity, and scarcity of investments are common causes of poverty in the former region. This striking difference between regional economic strengths in the U.S. is more distinguished for small SMSA's than for medium and large SMSA's, when they are compared on a relative basis. The remaining "E" rated SMSA's are Biloxi/Gulfport (Mississippi), Lawton (Oklahoma), Pine Bluff (Arkansas), Provo/Orem (Utah), Tuscaloosa (Alabama), Atlantic City (New Jersey), Gadsden (Alabama), Lafayette (Louisiana), Great Falls (Montana), Vineland/ Millville/Bridgeton (New Jersey), Gainesville (Florida), Savannah (Georgia), Wilmington (North Carolina), Lewiston/Auburn (Maine), Fort Smith (Arkansas/Oklahoma), New Bedford (Massachusetts), and Petersburg/Colonial Heights (Virginia).

The long bars centering on both ends of the bar chart as illustrated in Chart 11 clearly indicate the strong, healthy positions of the SMSA's in the upper portion and the much more desperate conditions of the SMSA's at the lower part. Not only is the standard deviation of the index values high, but also the coefficient of the variation of indexes is large, i.e., 37.4 percent which is much larger than the coefficients computed for the economic component for the medium and large size SMSA's. The implication of this is that the economic quality of life experienced by the people in the small SMSA's is relatively more unequal than that by the people in the larger SMSA's.

POLITICAL COMPONENT

Regional variations in political quality of life in the small SMSA's are even more striking than in the economic quality of life comparison. A dividing line can be drawn from Modesto (California) through Pueblo (Colorado), Springfield (Missouri), Terre Haute (Indiana), Wheeling (West Virginia/Ohio) to Atlantic City (New Jersey). There is not a single "E" rated SMSA north of the line, but south of the line, no SMSA has been classified as either "excellent" or "outstanding," except Midland (Texas). In the preceding discussion on economic well-being, one notes that there are more "E" than "A" rated SMSA's. In this political section, "A" rated SMSA's account for more than one-fifth of the total and outnumber the "E" rated.

As shown in Table 12, the indexes for the SMSA's are such that 43 SMSA's, or 46.2 percent of the total, have index figures exceeding the mean plus 0.28 standard deviation, and hence, are rated either excellent or outstanding. This implies that, based on the political considerations, many more small SMSA's are relatively better off than they were when judged from the economic standpoint.

TABLE 12

## INDEX AND RATING OF POLITICAL COMPONENT (S)

| | Adjusted Standardized Scores | | | Standardized Scores | | |
|---|---|---|---|---|---|---|
| SMSA | Value | Rank | Rating | Value | Rank | Rating |
| 149. Abilene, Texas | 1.8929 | 82 | E | -0.5093 | 83 | E |
| 150. Albany, Ga. | 1.4008 | 89 | E | -1.0381 | 92 | E |
| 151. Altoona, Pa. | 2.5476 | 56 | C | -0.0699 | 60 | C |
| 152. Amarillo, Texas | 2.2857 | 64 | D | -0.2076 | 67 | D |
| 153. Anderson, Ind. | 3.1905 | 21 | B | 0.3449 | 22 | B |
| 154. Asheville, N.C. | 2.4683 | 58 | C | -0.0437 | 55 | C |
| 155. Atlantic City, N.J. | 3.3214 | 17 | A | 0.6483 | 4 | A |
| 156. Bay City, Mich. | 3.6151 | 4 | A | 0.5908 | 6 | A |
| 157. Billings, Mont. | 3.3095 | 18 | A | 0.3823 | 20 | B |
| 158. Biloxi-Gulfport, Miss. | 1.9087 | 81 | E | -0.6434 | 85 | E |
| | | | | | | |
| 159. Bloomington-Normal, Ill. | 2.9246 | 39 | B | 0.0928 | 44 | C |
| 160. Boise City, Idaho | 3.2817 | 19 | A | 0.4193 | 16 | B |
| 161. Bristol, Conn. | 3.1349 | 24 | B | 0.3947 | 18 | B |
| 162. Brockton, Mass. | 2.8333 | 43 | B | 0.1661 | 42 | B |
| 163. Brownsville-Harlingen-San Benito, Texas | 1.2222 | 95 | E | -1.1802 | 94 | E |
| 164. Bryan-College Station, Texas | 2.0714 | 77 | D | -0.2116 | 68 | D |
| 165. Cedar Rapids, Iowa | 3.1508 | 23 | B | 0.2951 | 30 | B |
| 166. Champaign-Urbana, Ill. | 2.0873 | 75 | D | -0.1567 | 64 | D |
| 167. Columbia, Mo. | 2.5873 | 55 | C | 0.0655 | 47 | C |
| 168. Danbury, Conn. | 3.6190 | 3 | A | 0.5003 | 11 | A |
| | | | | | | |
| 169. Decatur, Ill. | 2.6151 | 51 | C | 0.0433 | 52 | C |
| 170. Dubuque, Iowa | 3.3651 | 11 | A | 0.4273 | 15 | B |
| 171. Durham, N.C. | 2.0317 | 80 | D | -0.3463 | 76 | D |
| 172. Fall River, Mass.-R.I. | 2.8016 | 44 | C | 0.2755 | 34 | B |
| 173. Fargo-Moorhead, N. Dak.-Minn. | 3.3651 | 12 | A | 0.4166 | 17 | B |
| 174. Fitchburg-Leominster, Mass. | 3.3333 | 16 | A | 0.3091 | 28 | B |
| 175. Fort Smith, Ark.-Okla. | 1.5159 | 88 | E | -0.6980 | 87 | E |
| 176. Gadsden, Alabama | 2.0873 | 76 | D | -0.4026 | 79 | D |
| 177. Gainesville, Fla. | 1.7619 | 85 | E | -0.6729 | 86 | E |
| 178. Galveston-Texas City, Texas | 2.1706 | 72 | D | -0.3022 | 75 | D |
| | | | | | | |
| 179. Great Falls, Mont. | 2.4643 | 59 | C | -0.0445 | 56 | C |
| 180. Green Bay, Wis. | 3.3849 | 9 | A | 0.5004 | 10 | A |
| 181. Jackson, Mich. | 2.8373 | 42 | B | 0.2792 | 33 | B |
| 182. Kenosha, Wis. | 2.9643 | 35 | B | 0.3429 | 23 | B |
| 183. La Crosse, Wis. | 3.8016 | 1 | A | 0.7718 | 2 | A |
| 184. Lafayette, La. | 1.6190 | 87 | E | -0.5899 | 84 | E |
| 185. Lafayette-West Lafayette, Ind. | 3.0675 | 28 | B | 0.2700 | 35 | B |
| 186. Lake Charles, La. | 1.7976 | 84 | E | -0.5020 | 82 | E |
| 187. Laredo, Texas | 1.3690 | 91 | E | -1.2235 | 95 | E |
| 188. Lawton, Okla. | 1.3730 | 90 | E | -0.9506 | 90 | E |
| | | | | | | |
| 189. Lewiston-Auburn, Maine | 2.8810 | 40 | B | 0.0562 | 50 | C |
| 190. Lexington, Ky. | 2.0516 | 78 | D | -0.4619 | 81 | E |
| 191. Lima, Ohio | 2.7579 | 46 | C | 0.0887 | 46 | C |
| 192. Lincoln, Nebraska | 2.8016 | 45 | C | 0.0600 | 48 | C |
| 193. Lubbock, Texas | 2.2857 | 65 | D | -0.2250 | 71 | D |
| 194. Lynchburg, Va. | 2.1548 | 74 | D | -0.2042 | 66 | D |
| 195. Manchester, N.H. | 3.3532 | 14 | A | 0.3248 | 25 | B |
| 196. Mansfield, Ohio | 2.6071 | 53 | C | -0.1137 | 63 | C |
| 197. McAllen-Pharr-Edinburg, Texas | 1.3413 | 92 | E | -1.0807 | 93 | E |
| 198. Meriden, Conn. | 3.3532 | 15 | A | 0.2970 | 29 | B |

TABLE 12 (Concluded)

| SMSA | Adjusted Standardized Scores | | | Standardized Scores | | |
|------|-------|------|--------|-------|------|--------|
|      | Value | Rank | Rating | Value | Rank | Rating |
| 199. Midland, Texas | 2.9484 | 37 | B | 0.1586 | 43 | B |
| 200. Modesto, Calif. | 2.8690 | 41 | B | 0.5974 | 5 | A |
| 201. Monroe, La. | 1.8333 | 83 | E | -0.3931 | 78 | D |
| 202. Muncie, Ind. | 3.1706 | 22 | B | 0.2882 | 31 | B |
| 203. Muskegon-Muskegon Heights, Mich. | 3.4127 | 7 | A | 0.6626 | 3 | A |
| 204. Nashua, N.H. | 3.0833 | 27 | B | 0.3191 | 26 | B |
| 205. New Bedford, Mass. | 2.9563 | 36 | B | 0.3600 | 21 | B |
| 206. New Britain, Conn. | 2.6190 | 50 | C | 0.0448 | 51 | C |
| 207. Norwalk, Conn. | 3.0476 | 30 | B | 0.2069 | 39 | B |
| 208. Odessa, Texas | 2.2143 | 69 | D | -0.2540 | 72 | D |
| | | | | | | |
| 209. Ogden, Utah | 3.4960 | 6 | A | 0.4369 | 14 | B |
| 210. Owensboro, Ky. | 2.2302 | 68 | D | -0.0002 | 53 | C |
| 211. Petersburg-Colonial Heights, Va. | 2.3333 | 63 | D | -0.2172 | 69 | D |
| 212. Pine Bluff, Ark. | 1.3214 | 93 | E | -0.7065 | 88 | E |
| 213. Pittsfield, Mass. | 3.6627 | 2 | A | 0.8415 | 1 | A |
| 214. Portland, Maine | 3.0079 | 32 | B | 0.4945 | 12 | A |
| 215. Provo-Orem, Utah | 2.5913 | 54 | C | -0.0597 | 58 | C |
| 216. Pueblo, Colo. | 3.3770 | 10 | A | 0.4822 | 13 | A |
| 217. Racine, Wis. | 3.0278 | 31 | B | 0.3109 | 27 | B |
| 218. Reno, Nev. | 2.6111 | 52 | C | -0.0561 | 57 | C |
| | | | | | | |
| 219. Roanoke, Va. | 2.4365 | 62 | D | -0.0675 | 59 | C |
| 220. Rochester, Minn. | 3.0675 | 29 | B | 0.3872 | 19 | B |
| 221. St. Joseph, Mo. | 2.6865 | 49 | C | -0.0273 | 54 | C |
| 222. Salem, Oreg. | 2.6905 | 48 | C | 0.0897 | 45 | C |
| 223. San Angelo, Texas | 2.1865 | 70 | D | -0.2198 | 70 | D |
| 224. Savannah, Ga. | 1.6429 | 86 | E | -0.7386 | 89 | E |
| 225. Sherman-Denison, Texas | 2.4643 | 60 | C | -0.1901 | 65 | D |
| 226. Sioux City, Iowa-Nebraska | 3.0913 | 25 | B | 0.2409 | 37 | B |
| 227. Sioux Falls, S. Dak. | 3.3889 | 8 | A | 0.5857 | 7 | A |
| 228. Springfield, Ill. | 3.0040 | 33 | B | 0.2521 | 36 | B |
| | | | | | | |
| 229. Springfield, Mo. | 2.9444 | 38 | B | 0.0569 | 49 | C |
| 230. Springfield, Ohio | 2.4643 | 61 | C | -0.0716 | 61 | C |
| 231. Steubenville-Weirton, Ohio-W. Va. | 3.0873 | 26 | B | 0.2216 | 38 | B |
| 232. Tallahassee, Fla. | 2.7302 | 47 | C | 0.1721 | 41 | B |
| 233. Terre Haute, Ind. | 3.6111 | 5 | A | 0.5044 | 9 | A |
| 234. Texarkana, Texas-Ark. | 2.1825 | 71 | D | 0.2020 | 40 | B |
| 235. Topeka, Kans. | 3.2579 | 20 | B | 0.3273 | 24 | B |
| 236. Tuscaloosa, Alabama | 1.3214 | 94 | E | -1.0331 | 91 | E |
| 237. Tyler, Texas | 2.2540 | 66 | D | -0.2920 | 74 | D |
| 238. Vineland-Millville-Bridgeton, N.J. | 2.4881 | 57 | C | -0.1091 | 62 | C |
| | | | | | | |
| 239. Waco, Texas | 2.1627 | 73 | D | -0.3866 | 77 | D |
| 240. Waterloo, Iowa | 3.0000 | 34 | B | 0.2819 | 32 | B |
| 241. Wheeling, W. Va.-Ohio | 3.3571 | 13 | A | 0.5116 | 8 | A |
| 242. Wichita Falls, Texas | 2.0357 | 79 | D | -0.4149 | 80 | D |
| 243. Wilmington, N.C. | 2.2500 | 67 | D | -0.2842 | 73 | D |

| | Mean ($\bar{x}$) = 2.6293 | Mean ($\bar{x}$) = 0.0000 |
|---|---|---|
| | Standard Deviation (s) = 0.6464 | Standard Deviation (s) = 0.4583 |

A = Outstanding ($\geq \bar{x} + s$)
B = Excellent ($\bar{x} + .28s \leq B < \bar{x} + s$)
C = Good ($\bar{x} - .28s < C < \bar{x} + .28s$)
D = Adequate ($\bar{x} - s < D \leq \bar{x} - .28s$)
E = Substandard ($\leq \bar{x} - s$)

La Crosse (Wisconsin) received the highest political component index of 3.80, or about 1.8 standard deviations above the mean. Next are Pittsfield (Massachusetts), Danbury (Connecticut), Bay City (Michigan), Terre Haute (Indiana), Ogden (Utah), Muskegon/Muskegon Heights (Michigan), Sioux Falls (South Dakota), Green Bay (Wisconsin), and Pueblo (Colorado), which make up the top 10 SMSA's. It is very surprising to note that none of these 10 SMSA's was mentioned as outstanding in the economic component, though some were rated as excellent. In fact, Ogden, Sioux Falls, and Pueblo were shown to be only adequate or "good" economically. The per capita income in La Crosse in 1970 was 47th when compared to others. In this case, the usual assertion that the quality of political life must be tied to the strength of economic achievements seems to lose ground.

It is aptly evident from the earlier discussions that there exist various problems, even in the outstanding SMSA's, although they are not as serious as those found in the lower rated SMSA's. In other words, even in the outstanding or excellent SMSA's, courses of action can be taken to improve the quality of life or to reduce the relatively less desirable conditions influencing quality of life. For instance, people in La Crosse could be better informed through public and private information channels and be more active in participating in political activities, etc.; residents in Pittsfield would enjoy even better political quality of life if the professionalism and performance of the local governments can be enhanced; Danbury would score much higher if its ranking in local government professionalism were higher than 64th, e.g., the property crime rate in the SMSA might be lowered from 2,762.8 per 100,000 population in 1970 (the corresponding rate in the U.S. was 2,431.8) if it had better quality or better paid patrolmen. (The entrance salary of patrolmen in this SMSA was about $300 below the U.S. average.)

Brownsville/Harlingen/San Benito, McAllen/Pharr/Edinburg, and Laredo in Texas, showing the least favorable indexes in economic well-being in the last section, were no exception in the political component evaluation. In addition to these three SMSA's, many with substandard economic ratings are shown in Table 12 as substandard, such as Pine Bluff, Lawton, Fort Smith, Lafayette, Savannah, Gainesville, and Biloxi/Gulfport. Nevertheless, the number of SMSA's in this group is smaller than that in the economic component. The lowest 10 indexes in this component do not differ significantly from each other, meaning that the composite evaluation on political backwardness for the 10 SMSA's is about equal. However, their individual weaknesses, to a certain degree, are still varying among the SMSA's.

While people in Lawton tended to be less active in political activities than those in Pine Bluff, the local governments in the former SMSA compared even less effectively than in the latter SMSA as far as the performance of the governments is concerned. The lower crime rates and more efficient fire protection services in Pine Bluff would probably be ascribed to the relatively high paying jobs of patrolmen and firemen. In terms of the welfare system and the associated payments, welfare recipients in Lawton were treated relatively better than recipients in Pine Bluff.

Although Biloxi/Gulfport (Mississippi) had low rankings in almost all political considerations, it ranked incredibly high among the 95 SMSA's from the viewpoint of local government performance. Its very low income rates and the very low entrance salary of patrolmen suggest that crime rates are not necessarily related to the high salaries of policemen. It is one of the SMSA's which received from the Federal Government the highest percentage of revenues, i.e., more than one-fifth of its total local revenues in 1970 were federal funds. Despite the low salaries for teachers (the average monthly earnings of teachers in the area was $442, only 64.9 percent of the U.S. average), its percentage of persons 25 years old and over who have completed 4 years high school education or more was higher than the U.S. average, 54.7 percent versus 52.3 percent. There were fewer males ages 16 to 21 who were not high school graduates. Economically this area was not wealthy, but its unadjusted expenditures on health amounted to $3.88 per capita, or about one-third above the national level. As a result of these factors, the local government performance in Biloxi/Gulfport was rated outstanding when compared to the other 94 small SMSA's.

The variation in index values, smaller in this component than in the economic component, is clearly illustrated in Chart 12. The standard deviation for the component was computed at 0.65, just about the size for the economic component, but the coefficient of variation was 24.7 percent, almost 13 percentage points below that for the economic component since the mean value for this component was more than 51.1 percent higher than that for the economic component. This implies a smaller variation within the SMSA's when political factors are compared than when economic factors are compared.

When intergroup comparison between the large, medium, and small groups of SMSA's are made on a geographic basis, Figures 2, 7, and 12 show that the political component is the only quality of life component which does not have a higher than "excellent" rating for any SMSA in the southern states.

## CHART 12
## REGIONAL VARIATION IN INDEXES:   POLITICAL COMPONENT (S)

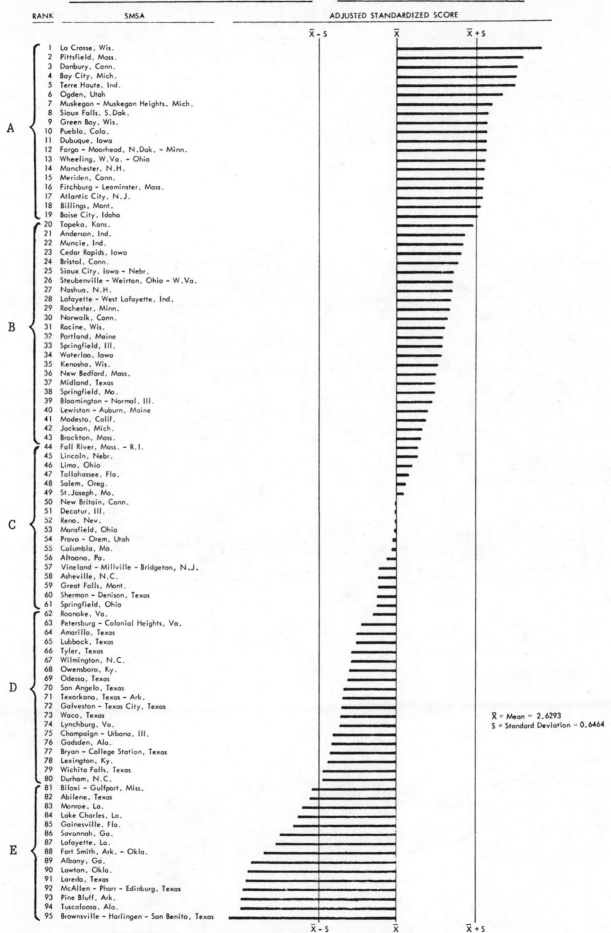

| RANK | SMSA | ADJUSTED STANDARDIZED SCORE |
|------|------|------|

A
1 La Crosse, Wis.
2 Pittsfield, Mass.
3 Danbury, Conn.
4 Bay City, Mich.
5 Terre Haute, Ind.
6 Ogden, Utah
7 Muskegon – Muskegon Heights, Mich.
8 Sioux Falls, S.Dak.
9 Green Bay, Wis.
10 Pueblo, Colo.
11 Dubuque, Iowa
12 Fargo – Moorhead, N.Dak. – Minn.
13 Wheeling, W.Va. – Ohio
14 Manchester, N.H.
15 Meriden, Conn.
16 Fitchburg – Leominster, Mass.
17 Atlantic City, N.J.
18 Billings, Mont.
19 Boise City, Idaho

B
20 Topeka, Kans.
21 Anderson, Ind.
22 Muncie, Ind.
23 Cedar Rapids, Iowa
24 Bristol, Conn.
25 Sioux City, Iowa – Nebr.
26 Steubenville – Weirton, Ohio – W.Va.
27 Nashua, N.H.
28 Lafayette – West Lafayette, Ind.
29 Rochester, Minn.
30 Norwalk, Conn.
31 Racine, Wis.
32 Portland, Maine
33 Springfield, Ill.
34 Waterloo, Iowa
35 Kenosha, Wis.
36 New Bedford, Mass.
37 Midland, Texas
38 Springfield, Mo.
39 Bloomington – Normal, Ill.
40 Lewiston – Auburn, Maine
41 Modesto, Calif.
42 Jackson, Mich.
43 Brockton, Mass.

C
44 Fall River, Mass. – R.I.
45 Lincoln, Nebr.
46 Lima, Ohio
47 Tallahassee, Fla.
48 Salem, Oreg.
49 St.Joseph, Mo.
50 New Britain, Conn.
51 Decatur, Ill.
52 Reno, Nev.
53 Mansfield, Ohio
54 Provo – Orem, Utah
55 Columbia, Mo.
56 Altoona, Pa.
57 Vineland – Millville – Bridgeton, N.J.
58 Asheville, N.C.
59 Great Falls, Mont.
60 Sherman – Denison, Texas
61 Springfield, Ohio

D
62 Roanoke, Va.
63 Petersburg – Colonial Heights, Va.
64 Amarillo, Texas
65 Lubbock, Texas
66 Tyler, Texas
67 Wilmington, N.C.
68 Owensboro, Ky.
69 Odessa, Texas
70 San Angelo, Texas
71 Texarkana, Texas – Ark.
72 Galveston – Texas City, Texas
73 Waco, Texas
74 Lynchburg, Va.
75 Champaign – Urbana, Ill.
76 Gadsden, Ala.
77 Bryan – College Station, Texas
78 Lexington, Ky.
79 Wichita Falls, Texas
80 Durham, N.C.

E
81 Biloxi – Gulfport, Miss.
82 Abilene, Texas
83 Monroe, La.
84 Lake Charles, La.
85 Gainesville, Fla.
86 Savannah, Ga.
87 Lafayette, La.
88 Fort Smith, Ark. – Okla.
89 Albany, Ga.
90 Lawton, Okla.
91 Laredo, Texas
92 McAllen – Pharr – Edinburg, Texas
93 Pine Bluff, Ark.
94 Tuscaloosa, Ala.
95 Brownsville – Harlingen – San Benito, Texas

$\bar{X}$ = Mean = 2.6293
S = Standard Deviation = 0.6464

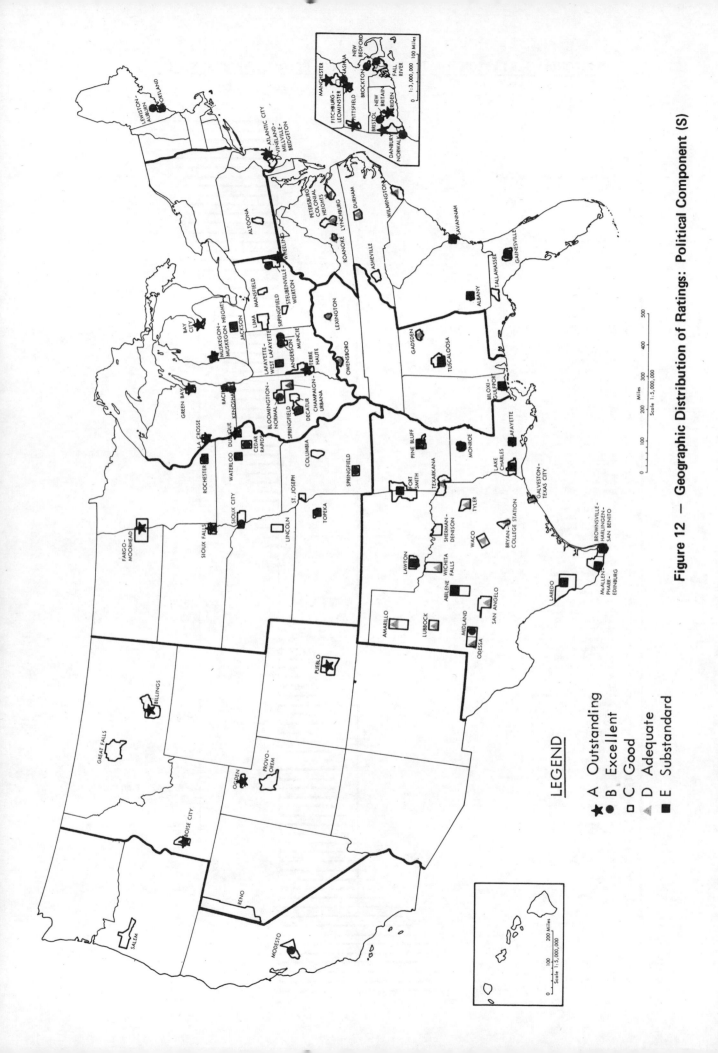

**Figure 12 — Geographic Distribution of Ratings: Political Component (S)**

LEGEND

A Outstanding
B Excellent
C Good
D Adequate
E Substandard

ENVIRONMENTAL COMPONENT

Environmental quality evaluation for the large and medium groups of
SMSA's was shown to be favorable to the Pacific region. The trade-
off between industrialization and environmental deterioration was
described to be very obvious among the large SMSA's in the Great Lakes
area, and this relationship was also evident from the medium sized
SMSA's, though to a lesser degree. When the small SMSA's are compared,
the trade-off pattern, if it exists at all, does not seem to be very
significant. This is due mainly to either of the following two
reasons. First, this finding may be in fact true, i.e., there is
little trade-off associated between growth and ecology in the small
SMSA's. Second, the finding may be misleading because many environmental factors employed in the preceding evaluations are not included
in this chapter, due to the nonavailability of data. For example,
there is no readily available information on air pollution and climate
for many small sized SMSA's. Consequently these factors are not
shown in the concerns with individual and institutional environment
and natural environment.

Based on available information on various levels of pollution other
than air, and the recreational areas and facilities, the 95 small
SMSA's were evaluated according to the original formula in which
natural environment was weighted equally with the individual and
institutional environment. As a result, the evaluation was in favor
of SMSA's with greater areas and facilities for recreation, and less
emphasis was placed on each type of pollution. Bearing in mind these
precautions about limited information, Table 13 represents the overall evaluation of environmental quality among the small SMSA's.

Jackson in Michigan and San Angelo in Texas, ranked at the top of
the outstanding group, followed by four SMSA's in the New England
region--Fitchburg/Leominster and Pittsfield in Massachusetts, and
Meriden and Bristol in Connecticut. Jackson, San Angelo, Fitchburg/
Leominster, and Meriden each had an index greater than the group
mean plus 2.0 standard deviations. While Jackson had very low
visual pollution and very high recreational areas and large facilities,
San Angelo had even better ratings in those categories. However, the
latter had the worst water pollution problem. Although noise pollution was probably not in existence at all in Fitchburg/Leominster, the
SMSA had above average problems in visual pollution and solid waste
generation. Pittsfield SMSA also suffered from greater than average
problems of visual and water pollution. While people in Meriden and

TABLE 13

## INDEX AND RATING OF ENVIRONMENTAL COMPONENT (S)

| | Adjusted Standardized Scores | | | Standardized Scores | | |
|---|---|---|---|---|---|---|
| SMSA | Value | Rank | Rating | Value | Rank | Rating |
| 149. Abilene, Texas | -0.0417 | 60 | D | -0.1095 | 55 | C |
| 150. Albany, Ga. | 0.1250 | 41 | C | -0.0810 | 49 | C |
| 151. Altoona, Pa. | -0.0833 | 68 | D | -0.1818 | 64 | D |
| 152. Amarillo, Texas | 0.0833 | 45 | C | 0.8161 | 6 | A |
| 153. Anderson, Ind. | -0.0417 | 61 | D | -0.0993 | 54 | C |
| 154. Asheville, N. C. | 0.4583 | 20 | B | 0.0688 | 25 | C |
| 155. Atlantic City, N.J. | -0.0417 | 62 | D | -0.0560 | 44 | C |
| 156. Bay City, Mich. | -0.3333 | 87 | E | -0.2148 | 73 | D |
| 157. Billings, Mont. | -0.2917 | 82 | E | -0.2745 | 80 | D |
| 158. Biloxi-Gulfport, Miss. | -0.2917 | 83 | E | -0.2011 | 70 | D |
| 159. Bloomington-Normal, Ill. | 0.5833 | 13 | A | 0.0572 | 28 | C |
| 160. Boise City, Idaho | -0.2917 | 84 | E | -0.3183 | 85 | D |
| 161. Bristol, Conn. | 0.9167 | 5 | A | 0.3250 | 13 | B |
| 162. Brockton, Mass. | 0.0000 | 55 | D | -0.2255 | 74 | D |
| 163. Brownsville-Harlingen-San Benito, Texas | 0.4583 | 21 | B | 0.0761 | 24 | C |
| 164. Bryan-College Station, Texas | -0.2083 | 76 | D | -0.2342 | 75 | D |
| 165. Cedar Rapids, Iowa | 0.0000 | 56 | D | -0.0350 | 42 | C |
| 166. Champaign-Urbana, Ill. | -0.2500 | 81 | E | -0.2511 | 77 | D |
| 167. Columbia, Mo. | -0.2500 | 80 | E | -0.1550 | 60 | D |
| 168. Danbury, Conn. | 0.4167 | 27 | B | 0.0560 | 29 | C |
| 169. Decatur, Ill. | 0.5833 | 14 | A | 0.1945 | 16 | B |
| 170. Dubuque, Iowa | 0.3750 | 29 | B | 0.0204 | 35 | C |
| 171. Durham, N.C. | 0.0833 | 46 | C | -0.0569 | 45 | C |
| 172. Fall River, Mass.-R.I. | -0.0833 | 69 | D | -0.4163 | 91 | E |
| 173. Fargo-Moorhead, N. Dak.-Minn. | 0.0000 | 54 | D | -0.4012 | 90 | E |
| 174. Fitchburg-Leominster, Mass. | 1.1250 | 3 | A | 0.5361 | 8 | A |
| 175. Fort Smith, Ark.-Okla. | 0.6250 | 12 | A | 0.7342 | 7 | A |
| 176. Gadsden, Alabama | 0.5833 | 15 | A | 0.0876 | 23 | C |
| 177. Gainesville, Fla. | -0.2083 | 77 | D | -0.1920 | 67 | D |
| 178. Galveston-Texas City, Texas | 0.1250 | 42 | C | -0.8224 | 95 | E |
| 179. Great Falls, Mont. | 0.4583 | 22 | B | 0.3976 | 11 | A |
| 180. Green Bay, Wis. | 0.4583 | 23 | B | 0.1118 | 21 | B |
| 181. Jackson, Mich. | 1.3333 | 1 | A | 0.5164 | 10 | A |
| 182. Kenosha, Wis. | -0.0417 | 63 | D | -0.1197 | 57 | D |
| 183. La Crosse, Wis. | 0.0000 | 57 | D | -0.0074 | 38 | C |
| 184. Lafayette, La. | -0.3750 | 91 | E | -0.3128 | 84 | D |
| 185. Lafayette-West Lafayette, Ind. | 0.0000 | 58 | D | -0.0790 | 48 | C |
| 186. Lake Charles, La. | -0.2917 | 85 | E | -0.3112 | 83 | D |
| 187. Laredo, Texas | -0.3333 | 88 | E | -0.6500 | 93 | E |
| 188. Lawton, Okla. | -0.6667 | 95 | E | -0.3965 | 89 | E |
| 189. Lewiston-Auburn, Maine | -0.3333 | 89 | E | -0.1874 | 65 | D |
| 190. Lexington, Ky. | 0.0833 | 47 | C | 0.0312 | 32 | C |
| 191. Lima, Ohio | -0.3750 | 92 | E | -0.3799 | 88 | D |
| 192. Lincoln, Nebraska | 0.3750 | 28 | B | 0.0914 | 22 | C |
| 193. Lubbock, Texas | -0.3333 | 90 | E | -0.2783 | 81 | D |
| 194. Lynchburg, Va. | 0.1667 | 37 | C | 0.0127 | 36 | C |
| 195. Manchester, N.H. | 0.7083 | 10 | A | 0.3240 | 14 | B |
| 196. Mansfield, Ohio | -0.0417 | 64 | D | -0.0684 | 47 | C |
| 197. McAllen-Pharr-Edinburg, Texas | 0.0417 | 51 | D | -0.3386 | 86 | D |
| 198. Meriden, Conn. | 1.0417 | 4 | A | 0.3020 | 15 | B |

TABLE 13 (Concluded)

| SMSA | Adjusted Standardized Scores | | | Standardized Scores | | |
|---|---|---|---|---|---|---|
| | Value | Rank | Rating | Value | Rank | Rating |
| 199. Midland, Texas | -0.4583 | 94 | E | -0.7514 | 94 | E |
| 200. Modesto, Calif. | 0.3333 | 31 | B | -0.1161 | 56 | D |
| 201. Monroe, La. | -0.1667 | 75 | D | -0.2680 | 79 | D |
| 202. Muncie, Ind. | 0.4167 | 25 | B | -0.0340 | 41 | C |
| 203. Muskegon-Muskegon Heights, Mich. | 0.5000 | 18 | B | 0.0281 | 33 | C |
| 204. Nashua, N.H. | -0.2083 | 78 | D | -0.1917 | 66 | D |
| 205. New Bedford, Mass. | -0.0833 | 70 | D | -0.2583 | 78 | D |
| 206. New Britain, Conn. | -0.0833 | 71 | D | -0.1354 | 59 | D |
| 207. Norwalk, Conn. | 0.0000 | 59 | D | 0.0063 | 37 | C |
| 208. Odessa, Texas | -0.0833 | 72 | D | -0.1600 | 61 | D |
| 209. Ogden, Utah | 0.4167 | 26 | B | -0.0864 | 51 | C |
| 210. Owensboro, Ky. | -0.0833 | 73 | D | -0.2102 | 72 | D |
| 211. Petersburg-Colonial Heights, Va. | 0.0833 | 48 | C | 0.0583 | 27 | C |
| 212. Pine Bluff, Ark. | 0.2917 | 32 | B | -0.0109 | 39 | C |
| 213. Pittsfield, Mass. | 0.9167 | 6 | A | 1.0792 | 3 | A |
| 214. Portland, Maine | -0.0417 | 65 | D | 0.0206 | 34 | C |
| 215. Provo-Orem, Utah | 0.5000 | 17 | B | 1.7216 | 1 | A |
| 216. Pueblo, Colo. | 0.0417 | 52 | D | -0.1610 | 63 | D |
| 217. Racine, Wis. | 0.0833 | 49 | C | -0.0904 | 53 | C |
| 218. Reno, Nev. | 0.2083 | 33 | C | -0.1603 | 62 | D |
| 219. Roanoke, Va. | 0.1250 | 43 | C | -0.0887 | 52 | C |
| 220. Rochester, Minn. | 0.7500 | 9 | A | 0.1615 | 17 | B |
| 221. St. Joseph, Mo. | 0.6667 | 11 | A | 1.0561 | 4 | A |
| 222. Salem, Oreg. | 0.8750 | 7 | A | 0.5307 | 9 | A |
| 223. San Angelo, Texas | 1.1667 | 2 | A | 0.9168 | 5 | A |
| 224. Savannah, Ga. | 0.2083 | 34 | C | -0.0214 | 40 | C |
| 225. Sherman-Denison, Texas | 0.1250 | 39 | C | 1.2377 | 2 | A |
| 226. Sioux City, Iowa-Nebraska | 0.5000 | 19 | B | 0.1452 | 19 | B |
| 227. Sioux Falls, S. Dak. | -0.1250 | 74 | D | -0.1992 | 69 | D |
| 228. Springfield, Ill. | 0.2083 | 35 | C | 0.0337 | 30 | C |
| 229. Springfield, Mo. | 0.1250 | 40 | C | -0.0847 | 50 | C |
| 230. Springfield, Ohio | -0.2083 | 79 | D | -0.2484 | 76 | D |
| 231. Steubenville-Weirton, Ohio-W. Va. | 0.1250 | 44 | C | 0.0333 | 31 | C |
| 232. Tallahassee, Fla. | 0.4583 | 24 | B | -0.2021 | 71 | D |
| 233. Terre Haute, Ind. | 0.0417 | 53 | D | -0.3412 | 87 | D |
| 234. Texarkana, Texas-Ark. | -0.4167 | 93 | E | -0.4774 | 92 | E |
| 235. Topeka, Kans. | -0.0417 | 66 | D | -0.1261 | 58 | D |
| 236. Tuscaloosa, Alabama | 0.1667 | 38 | C | -0.0578 | 46 | C |
| 237. Tyler, Texas | 0.8750 | 8 | A | 0.3402 | 12 | B |
| 238. Vineland-Millville-Bridgeton, N.J. | 0.0833 | 50 | C | 0.1372 | 20 | B |
| 239. Waco, Texas | 0.3750 | 30 | B | -0.0454 | 43 | C |
| 240. Waterloo, Iowa | 0.5833 | 16 | A | 0.1476 | 18 | B |
| 241. Wheeling, W. Va.-Ohio | -0.2917 | 86 | E | -0.1988 | 68 | D |
| 242. Wichita Falls, Texas | -0.0417 | 67 | D | -0.2981 | 82 | D |
| 243. Wilmington, N.C. | 0.2083 | 36 | C | 0.0656 | 26 | C |

Mean ($\bar{x}$) = 0.1592     Standard Deviation (s) = 0.4026

Mean ($\bar{x}$) = 0.0000     Standard Deviation (s) = 0.3958

A = Outstanding ($\geq \bar{x} + s$)
B = Excellent ($\bar{x} + .28s \leq B < \bar{x} + s$)
C = Good ($\bar{x} - .28s < C < \bar{x} + .28s$)
D = Adequate ($\bar{x} - s < D \leq \bar{x} - .28s$)
E = Substandard ($\leq \bar{x} - s$)

Bristol benefited from larger recreational areas and facilities per capita, the solid wastes generated in these two SMSA's for every $1 million of value added was substantially higher than the rest of the SMSA's. As contained in Table C-3 in the Appendix, the solid waste generated in these two areas for every $8 million of value added totaled 710.5 and 868.1 tons, respectively.

Similarly, the remaining 12 outstanding ranked SMSA's are geographically scattered among the lower ranking SMSA's, and each of them has its own outstanding quality factors as well as less desirable environmental problems. Salem in Oregon, for example, the only western outstanding SMSA in the environmental component--largely because of its recreational facilities--suffered from above average problems of noise pollution, with very high motor vehicle and motorcycle registrations per 1,000 population. Manchester in New Hampshire, as another example, had no problem at all with noise pollution but in visual pollution, the area ranked 82nd in the list, 40 percent of its housing units in the central city being dilapidated, and for every 1,000 people there were only 5.9 acres of parks and recreational areas.

The substandard SMSA's in this component, though equal to the outstanding group in number--16, are even more scattered throughout the U.S. The State of Texas had one-quarter of the 16 substandard SMSA's. Together with Lawton (Oklahoma), Lake Charles (Louisiana), Lafayette (Louisiana), and Biloxi/Gulfport (Mississippi), they made up one-half of the total in the South.

Lawton was found economically to be the most backward SMSA in the group and again appears to be the one with the lowest environmental quality. Its index of -0.67 is about 2.1 standard deviations below the mean and is significantly lower than Midland, Texarkana, Lima (Ohio), and Lafayette (Louisiana)--the five lowest ranking SMSA's. Because of less vehicle and motorcycle registration per 1,000 population, which is probably due to the area's poverty status, noise pollution was rated better than average in Lawton. The water pollution index for the area was 5.13 times as high as the U.S. average, one of the worst SMSA's in the list.

Midland was the second worst SMSA in the environmental component. It is located close to the outstanding SMSA San Angelo in Texas. Midland generated the most solid waste tonnages per million dollars of value added and had very few parks and recreational areas. In 1970, the area generated 1,648.6 tons of solid waste per million dollars worth of value added by manufacturing industries, and each 1,000 residents in the region collectively had only 1.5 acres of green areas for

# CHART 13
## REGIONAL VARIATIONS IN INDEXES: ENVIRONMENTAL COMPONENT (S)

RANK      SMSA      ADJUSTED STANDARDIZED SCORE

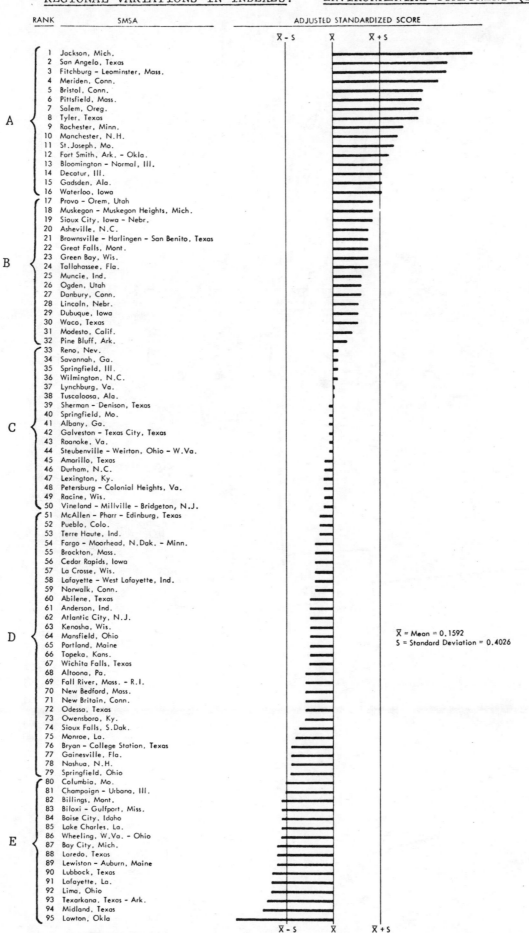

| Rank | SMSA |
|------|------|
| 1 | Jackson, Mich. |
| 2 | San Angelo, Texas |
| 3 | Fitchburg – Leominster, Mass. |
| 4 | Meriden, Conn. |
| 5 | Bristol, Conn. |
| 6 | Pittsfield, Mass. |
| 7 | Salem, Oreg. |
| 8 | Tyler, Texas |
| 9 | Rochester, Minn. |
| 10 | Manchester, N.H. |
| 11 | St. Joseph, Mo. |
| 12 | Fort Smith, Ark. – Okla. |
| 13 | Bloomington – Normal, Ill. |
| 14 | Decatur, Ill. |
| 15 | Gadsden, Ala. |
| 16 | Waterloo, Iowa |
| 17 | Provo – Orem, Utah |
| 18 | Muskegon – Muskegon Heights, Mich. |
| 19 | Sioux City, Iowa – Nebr. |
| 20 | Asheville, N.C. |
| 21 | Brownsville – Harlingen – San Benito, Texas |
| 22 | Great Falls, Mont. |
| 23 | Green Bay, Wis. |
| 24 | Tallahassee, Fla. |
| 25 | Muncie, Ind. |
| 26 | Ogden, Utah |
| 27 | Danbury, Conn. |
| 28 | Lincoln, Nebr. |
| 29 | Dubuque, Iowa |
| 30 | Waco, Texas |
| 31 | Modesto, Calif. |
| 32 | Pine Bluff, Ark. |
| 33 | Reno, Nev. |
| 34 | Savannah, Ga. |
| 35 | Springfield, Ill. |
| 36 | Wilmington, N.C. |
| 37 | Lynchburg, Va. |
| 38 | Tuscaloosa, Ala. |
| 39 | Sherman – Denison, Texas |
| 40 | Springfield, Mo. |
| 41 | Albany, Ga. |
| 42 | Galveston – Texas City, Texas |
| 43 | Roanoke, Va. |
| 44 | Steubenville – Weirton, Ohio – W.Va. |
| 45 | Amarillo, Texas |
| 46 | Durham, N.C. |
| 47 | Lexington, Ky. |
| 48 | Petersburg – Colonial Heights, Va. |
| 49 | Racine, Wis. |
| 50 | Vineland – Millville – Bridgeton, N.J. |
| 51 | McAllen – Pharr – Edinburg, Texas |
| 52 | Pueblo, Colo. |
| 53 | Terre Haute, Ind. |
| 54 | Fargo – Moorhead, N.Dak. – Minn. |
| 55 | Brockton, Mass. |
| 56 | Cedar Rapids, Iowa |
| 57 | La Crosse, Wis. |
| 58 | Lafayette – West Lafayette, Ind. |
| 59 | Norwalk, Conn. |
| 60 | Abilene, Texas |
| 61 | Anderson, Ind. |
| 62 | Atlantic City, N.J. |
| 63 | Kenosha, Wis. |
| 64 | Mansfield, Ohio |
| 65 | Portland, Maine |
| 66 | Topeka, Kans. |
| 67 | Wichita Falls, Texas |
| 68 | Altoona, Pa. |
| 69 | Fall River, Mass. – R.I. |
| 70 | New Bedford, Mass. |
| 71 | New Britain, Conn. |
| 72 | Odessa, Texas |
| 73 | Owensboro, Ky. |
| 74 | Sioux Falls, S.Dak. |
| 75 | Monroe, La. |
| 76 | Bryan – College Station, Texas |
| 77 | Gainesville, Fla. |
| 78 | Nashua, N.H. |
| 79 | Springfield, Ohio |
| 80 | Columbia, Mo. |
| 81 | Champaign – Urbana, Ill. |
| 82 | Billings, Mont. |
| 83 | Biloxi – Gulfport, Miss. |
| 84 | Boise City, Idaho |
| 85 | Lake Charles, La. |
| 86 | Wheeling, W.Va. – Ohio |
| 87 | Bay City, Mich. |
| 88 | Laredo, Texas |
| 89 | Lewiston – Auburn, Maine |
| 90 | Lubbock, Texas |
| 91 | Lafayette, La. |
| 92 | Lima, Ohio |
| 93 | Texarkana, Texas – Ark. |
| 94 | Midland, Texas |
| 95 | Lawton, Okla |

Groups: A (1–16), B (17–32), C (33–50), D (51–79), E (80–95)

X̄ = Mean = 0.1592
S = Standard Deviation = 0.4026

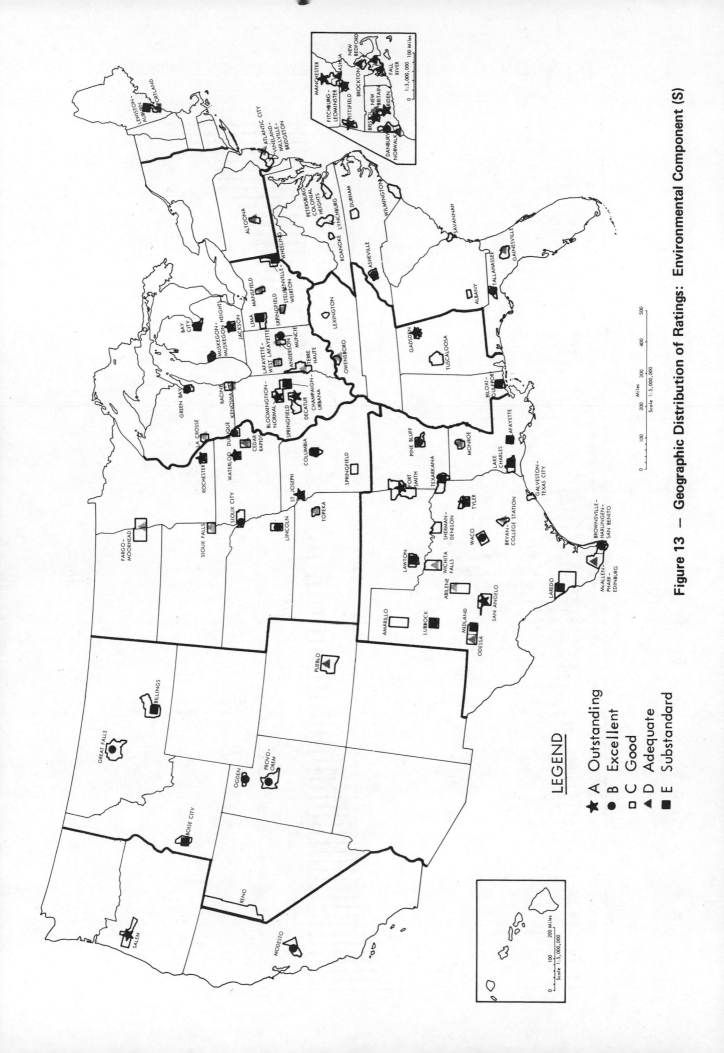

**LEGEND**

A Outstanding ★
B Excellent ●
C Good ▢
D Adequate ◀
E Substandard ■

**Figure 13 — Geographic Distribution of Ratings: Environmental Component (S)**

recreational activities. Texarkana, the SMSA consisting of counties in both Texas and Arkansas, had the same kind of problem as did Midland but ranked much better in noise pollution.

Boise City (Idaho) and Billings (Montana) are two "E" rated SMSA's in the Mountain Region. Boise City ranked eighth in water quality and Billings third in least solid waste generated per million dollars worth of manufacturing value added. Their low rankings are thus attributed to environmental criteria other than water and solid waste pollution. Lewiston/Auburn is the only substandard area in the entire New England region which has five outstanding SMSA's. This SMSA had the least noise pollution as measured by population density in the central city and the volume of vehicle and motorcycle registration. Like Boise City and Billings, the component rating of Lewiston/Auburn was significantly degraded by other factors such as visual, water, and solid waste pollution. The lack of recreational areas and facilities aggravates the overall evaluation.

Variation in the index values in this component as shown by Chart 13 is relatively larger than the indexes previously discussed in this chapter since the mean index value approaches zero. This variation is more striking at the upper portion of the bar chart than at the bottom half. Since incomplete factors of environmental consideration were used, no reference is made to compare the indexes in this section to the environmental indexes derived for the large and medium group. In general, it may be summarized that the New England and the West North Central regions tend to demonstrate better environmental quality than do other regions. However, the substandard SMSA's do not seem to have any special pattern of geographic concentration. In other words environmental quality protection for small SMSA's tends to be more of a local than a regional problem.

HEALTH AND EDUCATION COMPONENT

The criteria used to evaluate the small SMSA's are similar to those in the last two chapters. Due to data deficiency, the community health conditions were, however, evaluated without two manpower factors--the numbers of physicians and dentists per 100,000 population.

Geographically, the quality of health and education in 1970 among the small SMSA's was found to be outstanding in most areas west of the Mississippi River in the West North Central Region. The States of Florida, Texas, and Utah also had two outstanding SMSA's in each. Except Norwalk (Connecticut), there is no "A" rated SMSA east of

Lafayette/West Lafayette (Indiana). In total, there are 17 "A" rated SMSA's led by Columbia (Missouri) and followed by Rochester (Minnesota) and Gainesville (Florida). Respectively, the quality of health and education indexes for the three SMSA's are 2.79, 2.69, and 2.65; they all exceed the mean (1.09) plus two standard deviations (0.74).

Columbia ranked outstanding in almost all health and education categories except for health facilities which ranked 13th among the 95 SMSA's. The infant mortality rate in Columbia was 12.2 deaths per 1,000 live births, or nine deaths lower than the comparable U.S. rate. The median school years completed in the area was 12.7, and 68.2 percent of the persons 25 years old or over in Columbia completed 4 years of high school or more--15.9 percentage points beyond the U.S. norm. The hospital beds per 100,000 population in Columbia numbered 971, or about twice as many as the U.S. average; consequently, the hospital occupancy rate in the SMSA was 73.5 percent, or about six percentage points lower than the U.S. average occupancy rate. Rochester ranked second to Columbia primarily because of its lower individual educational attainment. Rochester had 5.8 percent of males 16 to 21 years of age who were not high school graduates; the corresponding figure for Columbia was only 4.9 percent. The percentage of population 3 to 34 years of age enrolled in school was much higher in Columbia (64.9 percent) than in the U.S., which was 54.3 percent. This figure, in turn, exceeded the percentage for Rochester, which was 52.2 percent.

Comparing the two outstanding areas in Florida, Gainesville and Tallahassee, Gainesville is observed with top rankings in all subcomponents, be they health or education. Tallahassee ranked only 24th in community medical health considerations; the ratio of hospital beds per 100,000 population was even lower than the U.S. standard. This is the basic reason for Tallahassee's index falling to that of Gainesville's, and it may explain, at least in part, why infant mortality rates were higher in the former than in the latter SMSA.

The aforementioned SMSA's plus Topeka (Kansas), Lincoln (Nebraska), Sioux Falls (South Dakota), Fargo/Moorehead (North Dakota), and other "A" rated SMSA's in this group tend to uphold the assertion that the health and education quality of an area is significantly influenced by institutional effects, particularly those of state universities or colleges.

# TABLE 14

## INDEX AND RATING OF HEALTH AND EDUCATION COMPONENT (S)

| | SMSA | Adjusted Standardized Scores | | | Standardized Scores | | |
|---|---|---|---|---|---|---|---|
| | | Value | Rank | Rating | Value | Rank | Rating |
| 149. | Abilene, Texas | 0.9167 | 48 | C | -0.0956 | 49 | C |
| 150. | Albany, Ga. | 0.7292 | 65 | D | -0.1903 | 58 | D |
| 151. | Altoona, Pa. | 0.2917 | 84 | E | -0.5787 | 83 | E |
| 152. | Amarillo, Texas | 1.7292 | 19 | B | 0.2447 | 26 | B |
| 153. | Anderson, Ind. | 0.7292 | 66 | D | -0.2214 | 60 | D |
| 154. | Asheville, N.C. | 0.8125 | 57 | D | -0.2027 | 59 | D |
| 155. | Atlantic City, N.J. | -0.0417 | 92 | E | -0.9749 | 95 | E |
| 156. | Bay City, Mich. | 1.2083 | 38 | C | 0.0312 | 43 | C |
| 157. | Billings, Mont. | 2.0000 | 15 | A | 0.4991 | 17 | B |
| 158. | Biloxi-Gulfport, Miss. | 1.3125 | 34 | B | 0.2282 | 27 | B |
| 159. | Bloomington-Normal, Ill. | 1.7083 | 20 | B | 0.4226 | 19 | B |
| 160. | Boise City, Idaho | 1.2500 | 36 | C | 0.1620 | 33 | B |
| 161. | Bristol, Conn. | 1.2917 | 35 | C | 0.0826 | 36 | C |
| 162. | Brockton, Mass. | 0.8333 | 54 | D | -0.2214 | 61 | D |
| 163. | Brownsville-Harlingen-San Benito, Texas | 0.6667 | 70 | D | -0.5934 | 84 | E |
| 164. | Bryan-College Station, Texas | 2.3542 | 6 | A | 0.9632 | 5 | A |
| 165. | Cedar Rapids, Iowa | 1.3333 | 31 | B | 0.0818 | 38 | C |
| 166. | Champaign-Urbana, Ill. | 2.0000 | 16 | A | 0.8191 | 10 | A |
| 167. | Columbia, Mo. | 2.7917 | 1 | A | 1.4331 | 2 | A |
| 168. | Danbury, Conn. | 1.3333 | 32 | B | 0.2043 | 30 | B |
| 169. | Decatur, Ill. | 0.7292 | 67 | D | -0.4144 | 73 | D |
| 170. | Dubuque, Iowa | 0.7917 | 59 | D | -0.3087 | 68 | D |
| 171. | Durham, N.C. | 1.5417 | 25 | B | 0.4992 | 16 | B |
| 172. | Fall River, Mass.-R.I. | 0.1458 | 87 | E | -0.8463 | 90 | E |
| 173. | Fargo-Moorhead, N. Dak.-Minn. | 2.2708 | 9 | A | 0.7081 | 13 | A |
| 174. | Fitchburg-Leominster, Mass. | 0.5833 | 73 | D | -0.2681 | 65 | D |
| 175. | Fort Smith, Ark.-Okla. | -0.4167 | 95 | E | -0.9202 | 92 | E |
| 176. | Gadsden, Alabama | -0.2500 | 93 | E | -0.9310 | 93 | E |
| 177. | Gainesville, Fla. | 2.6458 | 3 | A | 1.2575 | 3 | A |
| 178. | Galveston-Texas City, Texas | 1.3333 | 33 | B | 0.1908 | 31 | B |
| 179. | Great Falls, Mont. | 1.6667 | 22 | B | 0.3254 | 24 | B |
| 180. | Green Bay, Wis. | 1.4583 | 27 | B | 0.1428 | 35 | C |
| 181. | Jackson, Mich. | 0.8125 | 58 | D | -0.2804 | 66 | D |
| 182. | Kenosha, Wis. | 0.7917 | 60 | D | -0.1459 | 53 | C |
| 183. | La Crosse, Wis. | 2.1667 | 11 | A | 0.9199 | 7 | A |
| 184. | Lafayette, La. | 1.5833 | 23 | B | 0.3960 | 21 | B |
| 185. | Lafayette-West Lafayette, Ind. | 2.2292 | 10 | A | 0.8930 | 8 | A |
| 186. | Lake Charles, La. | 0.7708 | 62 | D | -0.1868 | 57 | D |
| 187. | Laredo, Texas | 0.6458 | 71 | D | -0.6227 | 87 | E |
| 188. | Lawton, Okla. | 0.9792 | 47 | C | -0.2287 | 64 | D |
| 189. | Lewiston-Auburn, Maine | -0.3750 | 94 | E | -0.9320 | 94 | E |
| 190. | Lexington, Ky. | 1.4167 | 29 | B | 0.2140 | 29 | B |
| 191. | Lima, Ohio | 0.3750 | 80 | D | -0.4508 | 75 | D |
| 192. | Lincoln, Nebraska | 2.1667 | 12 | A | 0.7475 | 11 | A |
| 193. | Lubbock, Texas | 1.4583 | 28 | B | 0.1708 | 32 | B |
| 194. | Lynchburg, Va. | 0.0625 | 89 | E | -0.7167 | 89 | E |
| 195. | Manchester, N.H. | 0.4583 | 75 | D | -0.3420 | 70 | D |
| 196. | Mansfield, Ohio | 0.4375 | 76 | D | -0.3897 | 71 | D |
| 197. | McAllen-Pharr-Edinburg, Texas | 0.5208 | 74 | D | -0.6938 | 88 | E |
| 198. | Meriden, Conn. | 0.4167 | 78 | D | -0.5088 | 80 | D |

## TABLE 14 (Concluded)

| SMSA | Adjusted Standardized Scores | | | Standardized Scores | | |
|---|---|---|---|---|---|---|
| | Value | Rank | Rating | Value | Rank | Rating |
| 199. Midland, Texas | 1.9583 | 17 | A | 0.4370 | 18 | B |
| 200. Modesto, Calif. | 0.8750 | 51 | D | 0.0380 | 42 | C |
| 201. Monroe, La. | 0.7500 | 64 | D | -0.2812 | 67 | D |
| 202. Muncie, Ind. | 1.1042 | 42 | C | -0.0564 | 46 | C |
| 203. Muskegon-Muskegon Heights, Mich. | 1.0417 | 44 | C | 0.0794 | 39 | C |
| 204. Nashua, N.H. | 1.1458 | 41 | C | 0.0821 | 37 | C |
| 205. New Bedford, Mass. | 0.0417 | 90 | E | -0.8494 | 91 | E |
| 206. New Britain, Conn. | 0.8542 | 52 | D | -0.1755 | 55 | D |
| 207. Norwalk, Conn. | 2.0417 | 14 | A | 0.7106 | 12 | A |
| 208. Odessa, Texas | 1.0208 | 46 | C | -0.1045 | 50 | C |
| 209. Ogden, Utah | 2.4167 | 5 | A | 0.8276 | 9 | A |
| 210. Owensboro, Ky. | 1.5625 | 24 | B | 0.4042 | 20 | B |
| 211. Petersburg-Colonial Heights, Va. | 0.6875 | 69 | D | -0.4894 | 76 | D |
| 212. Pine Bluff, Ark. | 0.0208 | 91 | E | -0.5767 | 82 | E |
| 213. Pittsfield, Mass. | 0.7708 | 63 | D | -0.0799 | 47 | C |
| 214. Portland, Maine | 0.7917 | 61 | D | -0.1682 | 54 | D |
| 215. Provo-Orem, Utah | 2.2917 | 7 | A | 0.9631 | 6 | A |
| 216. Pueblo, Colo. | 1.2083 | 39 | C | -0.0173 | 44 | C |
| 217. Racine, Wis. | 1.0417 | 45 | C | -0.0503 | 45 | C |
| 218. Reno, Nev. | 1.7500 | 18 | B | 0.3884 | 23 | B |
| 219. Roanoke, Va. | 1.0625 | 43 | C | 0.0481 | 41 | C |
| 220. Rochester, Minn. | 2.6875 | 2 | A | 1.4524 | 1 | A |
| 221. St. Joseph, Mo. | 0.3958 | 79 | D | -0.6175 | 86 | E |
| 222. Salem, Oreg. | 1.7083 | 21 | B | 0.3889 | 22 | B |
| 223. San Angelo, Texas | 1.2292 | 37 | C | 0.1487 | 34 | C |
| 224. Savannah, Ga. | 0.3125 | 82 | E | -0.3340 | 69 | D |
| 225. Sherman-Denison, Texas | 1.3958 | 30 | B | 0.2901 | 25 | B |
| 226. Sioux City, Iowa-Nebraska | 0.8333 | 55 | D | -0.0931 | 48 | C |
| 227. Sioux Falls, S. Dak. | 2.2917 | 8 | A | 0.6962 | 14 | A |
| 228. Springfield, Ill. | 0.9167 | 49 | C | -0.1802 | 56 | D |
| 229. Springfield, Mo. | 1.2083 | 40 | C | 0.0791 | 40 | C |
| 230. Springfield, Ohio | 0.8542 | 53 | D | -0.1178 | 52 | C |
| 231. Steubenville-Weirton, Ohio-W. Va. | 0.2292 | 86 | E | -0.3944 | 72 | D |
| 232. Tallahassee, Fla. | 2.4583 | 4 | A | 0.9930 | 4 | A |
| 233. Terre Haute, Ind. | 0.7083 | 68 | D | -0.4289 | 74 | D |
| 234. Texarkana, Texas-Ark. | 0.2917 | 85 | E | -0.5015 | 78 | D |
| 235. Topeka, Kans. | 2.0625 | 13 | A | 0.5847 | 15 | A |
| 236. Tuscaloosa, Alabama | 0.8333 | 56 | D | -0.2258 | 63 | D |
| 237. Tyler, Texas | 0.9167 | 50 | C | -0.1066 | 51 | C |
| 238. Vineland-Millville-Bridgeton, N.J. | 0.3125 | 83 | E | -0.4937 | 77 | D |
| 239. Waco, Texas | 0.4375 | 77 | D | -0.5024 | 79 | D |
| 240. Waterloo, Iowa | 1.5417 | 26 | B | 0.2163 | 28 | B |
| 241. Wheeling, W. Va.-Ohio | 0.3750 | 81 | D | -0.5209 | 81 | D |
| 242. Wichita Falls, Texas | 0.6250 | 72 | D | -0.2221 | 62 | D |
| 243. Wilmington, N.C. | 0.1250 | 88 | E | -0.6076 | 85 | E |

---

A = Outstanding ($\geq \bar{x} + s$)
B = Excellent ($\bar{x} + .28s \leq B < \bar{x} + s$)
C = Good ($\bar{x} - .28s < C < \bar{x} + .28s$)
D = Adequate ($\bar{x} - s < D \leq \bar{x} - .28s$)
E = Substandard ($\leq \bar{x} - s$)

Mean ($\bar{x}$) = 1.0932
Standard Deviation (s) = 0.7368

Mean ($\bar{x}$) = 0.0000
Standard Deviation (s) = 0.5426

In contrast to the "A" rated SMSA's, there are also 17 "B" rated "excellent" SMSA's with respect to health and education quality of life. They are much more randomly distributed than the "outstanding" ones. However, only 14 substandard SMSA's were revealed by Table 14. The New England, Middle Atlantic and West South Central regions each had three or four substandard SMSA's. Fort Smith (Arkansas-Oklahoma) led other "E" rated SMSA's with an index as low as -0.42, or just about 2.0 standard deviations below the mean. The index for Lewiston/ Auburn was the second lowest and Gadsden (Alabama) the third. Other substandard SMSA's are Atlantic City, Pine Bluff, Texarkana, Altoona, Vineland/Millville/Bridgeton, and Savannah. Except for the part of Texarkana in Texas, this component is the only one that this state showed "A" rated without being accompanied by "E" rated SMSA's.

It is expected that we identify those substandard SMSA's with inferior figures in health and education comparisons with the U.S. average. The degrees to which the figures are below the U.S. level are important measures for decision makers to set up policy priority toward quality of life improvements. However, it may be even more important here to describe the good part of the quality of life among those low rating SMSA's. For instance, Fort Smith ranked 76th in community medical facilities; Lewiston/Auburn's best was found in individual health, ranked 89th; Gadsden and Atlantic City even showed relative strength in medical facilities with a ranking of 38th and 26th, respectively; etc. Furthermore, it is extremely important to recall that this study is motivated to make only relative comparisons rather than absolute differentiations.

The great variation in the index values is shown in Chart 14, in which not only the standard deviation is large (0.74), the largest deviation among the five components, but the coefficient of variation is 0.68 percent, substantially higher than that for economic and political components. The implication of this is that the health and education needs in the small sized SMSA's vary appreciably in quality. This quality variation is even more pronounced for the excellent and the outstanding SMSA's than for the substandard SMSA's. Moreover, although the variation in health and education indexes for the small and large SMSA's is about the same, it is much greater than that for the medium SMSA. This finding means that the need for bridging the health and education quality gap among either the large or the small SMSA's is likely to be more urgent than that among the medium SMSA's.

# CHART 14

## HEALTH AND EDUCATION COMPONENT (S)    REGIONAL VARIATIONS IN INDEXES:

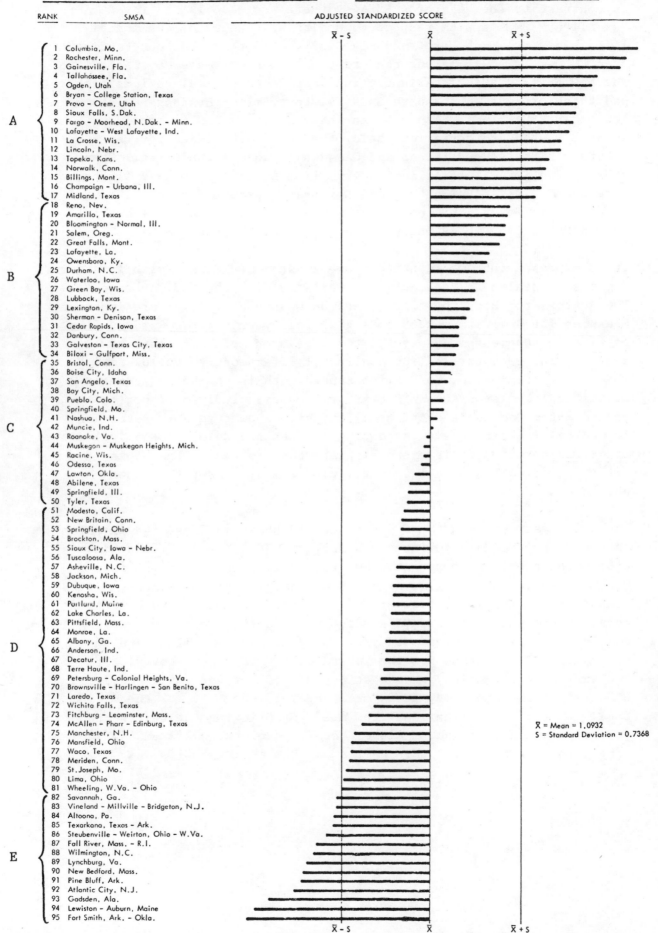

| RANK | SMSA |
|------|------|
| | ADJUSTED STANDARDIZED SCORE |

**A**
1 Columbia, Mo.
2 Rochester, Minn.
3 Gainesville, Fla.
4 Tallahassee, Fla.
5 Ogden, Utah
6 Bryan – College Station, Texas
7 Provo – Orem, Utah
8 Sioux Falls, S.Dak.
9 Fargo – Moorhead, N.Dak. – Minn.
10 Lafayette – West Lafayette, Ind.
11 La Crosse, Wis.
12 Lincoln, Nebr.
13 Topeka, Kans.
14 Norwalk, Conn.
15 Billings, Mont.
16 Champaign – Urbana, Ill.
17 Midland, Texas

**B**
18 Reno, Nev.
19 Amarillo, Texas
20 Bloomington – Normal, Ill.
21 Salem, Oreg.
22 Great Falls, Mont.
23 Lafayette, La.
24 Owensboro, Ky.
25 Durham, N.C.
26 Waterloo, Iowa
27 Green Bay, Wis.
28 Lubbock, Texas
29 Lexington, Ky.
30 Sherman – Denison, Texas
31 Cedar Rapids, Iowa
32 Danbury, Conn.
33 Galveston – Texas City, Texas
34 Biloxi – Gulfport, Miss.

**C**
35 Bristol, Conn.
36 Boise City, Idaho
37 San Angelo, Texas
38 Bay City, Mich.
39 Pueblo, Colo.
40 Springfield, Mo.
41 Nashua, N.H.
42 Muncie, Ind.
43 Roanoke, Va.
44 Muskegon – Muskegon Heights, Mich.
45 Racine, Wis.
46 Odessa, Texas
47 Lawton, Okla.
48 Abilene, Texas
49 Springfield, Ill.
50 Tyler, Texas

**D**
51 Modesto, Calif.
52 New Britain, Conn.
53 Springfield, Ohio
54 Brockton, Mass.
55 Sioux City, Iowa – Nebr.
56 Tuscaloosa, Ala.
57 Asheville, N.C.
58 Jackson, Mich.
59 Dubuque, Iowa
60 Kenosha, Wis.
61 Portland, Maine
62 Lake Charles, La.
63 Pittsfield, Mass.
64 Monroe, La.
65 Albany, Ga.
66 Anderson, Ind.
67 Decatur, Ill.
68 Terre Haute, Ind.
69 Petersburg – Colonial Heights, Va.
70 Brownsville – Harlingen – San Benito, Texas
71 Laredo, Texas
72 Wichita Falls, Texas
73 Fitchburg – Leominster, Mass.
74 McAllen – Pharr – Edinburg, Texas
75 Manchester, N.H.
76 Mansfield, Ohio
77 Waco, Texas
78 Meriden, Conn.
79 St.Joseph, Mo.
80 Lima, Ohio
81 Wheeling, W.Va. – Ohio

**E**
82 Savannah, Ga.
83 Vineland – Millville – Bridgeton, N.J.
84 Altoona, Pa.
85 Texarkana, Texas – Ark.
86 Steubenville – Weirton, Ohio – W.Va.
87 Fall River, Mass. – R.I.
88 Wilmington, N.C.
89 Lynchburg, Va.
90 New Bedford, Mass.
91 Pine Bluff, Ark.
92 Atlantic City, N.J.
93 Gadsden, Ala.
94 Lewiston – Auburn, Maine
95 Fort Smith, Ark. – Okla.

$\bar{X}$ = Mean = 1.0932
S = Standard Deviation = 0.7368

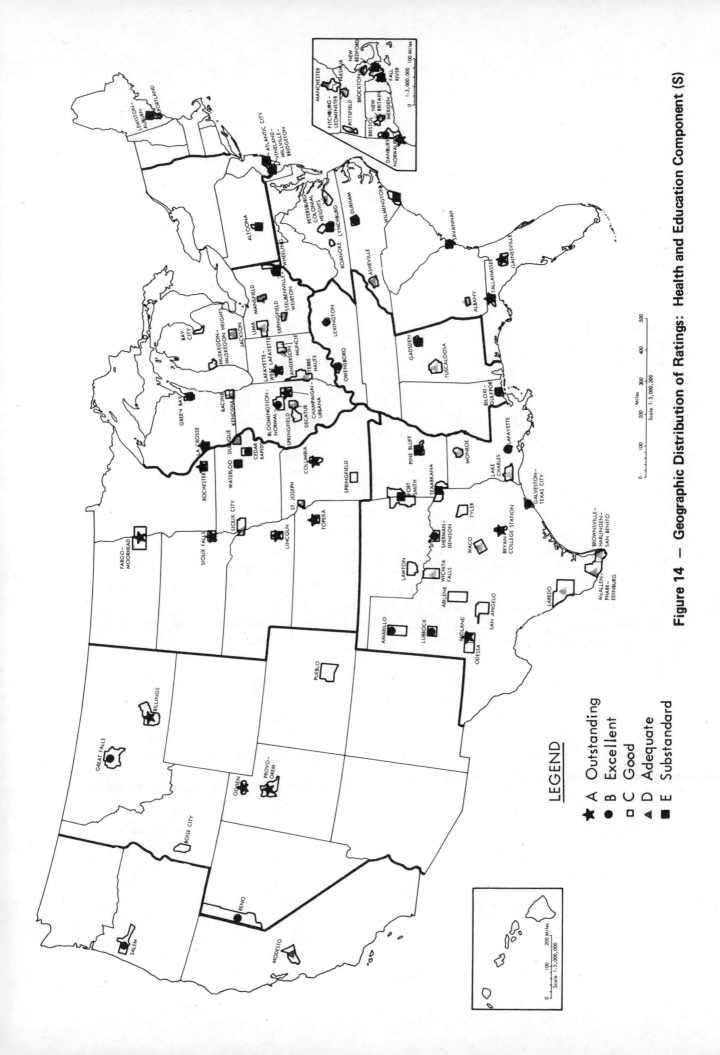

**Figure 14 — Geographic Distribution of Ratings:  Health and Education Component (S)**

LEGEND

- A  Outstanding  ★
- B  Excellent  ●
- C  Good  ▢
- D  Adequate  ▲
- E  Substandard  ■

SOCIAL COMPONENT

Except for one factor in the community living conditions--the number
of banks and savings and loan associations per 1,000 population, for
which statistical data were not available--all factors used to assess
the social quality of life in the large and medium SMSA's were retained in the measurement of the social component for the small SMSA's.
Since more than 50 variable factors are included, one missing factor
should not make a significant change in the overall evaluation.
Thus, the resulting findings in this section are comparable on a relative basis to those for the social component in the preceding chapters.

The number of small SMSA's with outstanding social quality of life is
relatively smaller than is the case with the other components such as
political, environmental, and health and education.  Only 13 SMSA's
had index values exceeding the mean (0.50) plus one standard deviation
(0.35), and hence, denoted as "A" or "outstanding."  La Crosse, the
small SMSA which led other outstanding SMSA's in political quality,
also leads in the social component.  It received an index of value
1.47 or about 2.8 standard deviations above the mean.  As shown in
Table 15, the index for La Crosse appreciably exceeds that for
Rochester, the second highest in the group.  The second runner-up
is Lincoln which also scored "A" in the economic and health and education component.   Slightly behind Lincoln in score are Green Bay and
Topeka, both with excellent or outstanding records in other quality
of life components under discussion.  The remaining "A" regions are
Billings, Sioux Falls, Reno, Fargo/Moorhead, Manchester, St. Joseph
(Missouri), Provo/Orem (Utah), and Lewiston/Auburn.  It is significant
to note from Figure 15 that with the exception of two in New England,
no SMSA south of Topeka and east of Green Bay was rated outstanding
in the social component.

Of special interest is that the northern part of the State of Texas,
which was strong in the economic and health comparisons, was considerably lower in the political and social quality assessments.  Two
southern SMSA's in the state, McAllen/Pharr/Edinburg and Brownsville/
Harlingen/San Benito, which had been rated substandard in both the
economic and political components, again rated as "substandard" in the
social quality of life evaluation.  Those two SMSA's showed very good
ratings in the individual quality category, especially in the area
of racial discrimination.  Nevertheless, the areas were substantially
inadequate in providing good community living conditions, in general,
and social conditions in particular.  Due primarily to the weak

# TABLE 15

## INDEX AND RATING OF SOCIAL COMPONENT (S)

| SMSA | Adjusted Standardized Scores | | | Standardized Scores | | |
|------|-------|------|--------|-------|------|--------|
|      | Value | Rank | Rating | Value | Rank | Rating |
| 149. Abilene, Texas | 0.5198 | 47 | C | 0.0866 | 37 | B |
| 150. Albany, Georgia | 0.1927 | 77 | D | -0.2301 | 77 | D |
| 151. Altoona, Pennsylvania | 0.4158 | 55 | C | -0.0222 | 47 | C |
| 152. Amarillo, Texas | 0.7387 | 25 | B | 0.0372 | 43 | C |
| 153. Anderson, Indiana | 0.2506 | 68 | D | -0.1215 | 65 | D |
| 154. Asheville, North Carolina | 0.2266 | 72 | D | -0.1369 | 69 | D |
| 155. Atlantic City, New Jersey | 0.0448 | 87 | E | -0.3424 | 85 | E |
| 156. Bay City, Michigan | 0.3497 | 62 | D | -0.1663 | 74 | D |
| 157. Billings, Montana | 1.0761 | 6 | A | 0.3768 | 9 | A |
| 158. Biloxi-Gulfport, Mississippi | 0.2225 | 75 | D | -0.1384 | 70 | D |
| 159. Bloomington-Normal, Illinois | 0.8250 | 14 | B | 0.2796 | 15 | A |
| 160. Boise City, Idaho | 0.7689 | 22 | B | 0.0785 | 38 | B |
| 161. Bristol, Connecticut | 0.7228 | 28 | B | 0.2509 | 17 | B |
| 162. Brockton, Massachusetts | 0.4370 | 50 | C | -0.1029 | 61 | D |
| 163. Brownsville-Harlingen-San Benito, Texas | 0.1202 | 84 | E | -0.4890 | 91 | E |
| 164. Bryan-College Station, Texas | 0.2265 | 73 | D | -0.1823 | 75 | D |
| 165. Cedar Rapids, Iowa | 0.5359 | 43 | C | 0.0753 | 39 | C |
| 166. Champaign-Urbana, Illinois | 0.5211 | 46 | C | 0.0020 | 44 | C |
| 167. Columbia, Missouri | 0.7782 | 20 | B | 0.3279 | 12 | A |
| 168. Danbury, Connecticut | 0.7511 | 24 | B | 0.2495 | 18 | B |
| 169. Decatur, Illinois | 0.6225 | 36 | B | 0.0961 | 35 | B |
| 170. Dubuque, Iowa | 0.7862 | 19 | B | 0.1927 | 22 | B |
| 171. Durham, North Carolina | 0.5900 | 38 | C | 0.1095 | 34 | B |
| 172. Fall River, Massachusetts-Rhode Island | 0.1497 | 79 | E | -0.2950 | 83 | E |
| 173. Fargo-Moorhead, North Dakota-Massachusetts | 1.0028 | 9 | A | 0.4659 | 3 | A |
| 174. Fitchburg-Leominster, Massachusetts | 0.6858 | 30 | B | 0.1247 | 31 | B |
| 175. Fort Smith, Arkansas-Oklahoma | -0.2266 | 95 | E | -0.5033 | 92 | E |
| 176. Gadsden, Alabama | 0.0363 | 88 | E | -0.2621 | 80 | D |
| 177. Gainesville, Florida | 0.5839 | 39 | C | 0.1241 | 32 | B |
| 178. Galveston-Texas City, Texas | 0.3493 | 63 | D | -0.1182 | 64 | D |
| 179. Great Falls, Montana | 0.7300 | 27 | B | 0.1589 | 28 | B |
| 180. Green Bay, Wisconsin | 1.1032 | 4 | A | 0.4518 | 5 | A |
| 181. Jackson, Michigan | 0.4329 | 52 | C | -0.0702 | 55 | C |
| 182. Kenosha, Wisconsin | 0.3637 | 59 | D | -0.0613 | 53 | C |
| 183. La Crosse, Wisconsin | 1.4668 | 1 | A | 0.7014 | 1 | A |
| 184. Lafayette, Louisiana | 0.2263 | 74 | D | -0.1228 | 66 | D |
| 185. Lafayette-West Lafayette, Indiana | 0.6378 | 34 | B | 0.1765 | 26 | B |
| 186. Lake Charles, Louisiana | 0.3063 | 65 | D | -0.0322 | 48 | C |
| 187. Laredo, Texas | 0.2451 | 69 | D | -0.5677 | 93 | E |
| 188. Lawton, Oklahoma | 0.4396 | 49 | C | -0.0820 | 58 | D |
| 189. Lewiston-Auburn, Maine | 0.8716 | 13 | A | 0.2592 | 16 | B |
| 190. Lexington, Kentucky | 0.3373 | 64 | D | -0.0564 | 52 | C |
| 191. Lima, Ohio | 0.2131 | 76 | D | -0.2676 | 81 | D |
| 192. Lincoln, Nebraska | 1.1356 | 3 | A | 0.4160 | 8 | A |
| 193. Lubbock, Texas | 0.5378 | 42 | C | 0.0412 | 42 | C |
| 194. Lynchburg, Virginia | -0.0461 | 91 | E | -0.4206 | 90 | E |
| 195. Manchester, New Hampshire | 0.9797 | 10 | A | 0.3530 | 11 | A |
| 196. Mansfield, Ohio | 0.3511 | 61 | D | -0.1057 | 62 | D |
| 197. McAllen-Pharr-Edinburg, Texas | 0.0489 | 86 | E | -0.6721 | 95 | E |
| 198. Meriden, Connecticut | 0.4795 | 48 | C | -0.0748 | 56 | C |

199

# TABLE 15 (Concluded)

| SMSA | Adjusted Standardized Scores Value | Rank | Rating | Standardized Scores Value | Rank | Rating |
|------|-------|------|--------|-------|------|--------|
| 199. Midland, Texas | 0.6024 | 37 | B | -0.0443 | 51 | C |
| 200. Modesto, California | 0.1461 | 80 | E | -0.2565 | 79 | D |
| 201. Monroe, Louisiana | 0.2938 | 66 | D | -0.0906 | 59 | D |
| 202. Muncie, Indiana | 0.2443 | 70 | D | -0.1333 | 68 | D |
| 203. Muskegon-Muskegon Heights, Michigan | 0.4360 | 51 | C | -0.0388 | 49 | C |
| 204. Nashua, New Hampshire | 0.5257 | 45 | C | -0.0671 | 54 | C |
| 205. New Bedford, Massachusetts | 0.0599 | 85 | E | -0.3070 | 84 | E |
| 206. New Britain, Connecticut | 0.6735 | 31 | B | 0.0653 | 40 | C |
| 207. Norwalk, Connecticut | 0.8007 | 18 | B | 0.1664 | 27 | B |
| 208. Odessa, Texas | 0.7754 | 21 | B | 0.2837 | 14 | A |
| 209. Ogden, Utah | 0.6713 | 32 | B | 0.1255 | 30 | B |
| 210. Owensboro, Kentucky | 0.2863 | 67 | D | -0.1311 | 67 | D |
| 211. Petersburgh-Colonial Heights, Virginia | 0.1233 | 83 | E | -0.3797 | 87 | E |
| 212. Pine Bluff, Arkansas | -0.1229 | 92 | E | -0.4031 | 88 | E |
| 213. Pittsfield, Massachusetts | 0.8211 | 15 | B | 0.2926 | 13 | A |
| 214. Portland, Maine | 0.6884 | 29 | B | -0.0815 | 57 | D |
| 215. Provo-Orem, Utah | 0.8749 | 12 | A | 0.4529 | 4 | A |
| 216. Pueblo, Colorado | 0.5784 | 40 | C | 0.1159 | 33 | B |
| 217. Racine, Wisconsin | 0.3585 | 60 | D | -0.0395 | 50 | C |
| 218. Reno, Nevada | 1.0046 | 8 | A | 0.4311 | 7 | A |
| 219. Roanoke, Virginia | 0.4196 | 54 | C | -0.1116 | 63 | D |
| 220. Rochester, Minnesota | 1.2354 | 2 | A | 0.6810 | 2 | A |
| 221. St. Joseph, Missouri | 0.8899 | 11 | A | 0.1905 | 25 | B |
| 222. Salem, Oregon | 0.4244 | 53 | C | -0.0214 | 46 | C |
| 223. San Angelo, Texas | 0.8204 | 16 | B | 0.2406 | 20 | B |
| 224. Savannah, Georgia | 0.1233 | 82 | E | -0.2358 | 78 | D |
| 225. Sherman-Denison, Texas | 0.5271 | 44 | C | 0.0539 | 41 | C |
| 226. Sioux City, Iowa-Nebraska | 0.6545 | 33 | B | 0.1280 | 29 | B |
| 227. Sioux Falls, South Dakota | 1.0083 | 7 | A | 0.3563 | 10 | A |
| 228. Springfield, Illinois | 0.7625 | 23 | B | 0.1913 | 24 | B |
| 229. Springfield, Missouri | 0.7363 | 26 | B | 0.1924 | 23 | B |
| 230. Springfield, Ohio | 0.1460 | 81 | E | -0.1877 | 76 | D |
| 231. Steubenville-Weirton, Ohio-West Virginia | 0.0194 | 89 | E | -0.2949 | 82 | E |
| 232. Tallahassee, Florida | 0.5683 | 41 | C | 0.0898 | 36 | B |
| 233. Terre Haute, Indiana | 0.3948 | 57 | D | -0.1014 | 60 | D |
| 234. Texarkana, Texas-Arkansas | -0.2097 | 94 | E | -0.4037 | 89 | E |
| 235. Topeka, Kansas | 1.1026 | 5 | A | 0.4422 | 6 | A |
| 236. Tuscaloosa, Alabama | -0.0177 | 90 | E | -0.3521 | 86 | E |
| 237. Tyler, Texas | 0.4105 | 56 | C | -0.1559 | 73 | D |
| 238. Vineland-Millville-Bridgeton, New Jersey | 0.2427 | 71 | D | -0.1449 | 71 | D |
| 239. Waco, Texas | 0.3823 | 58 | D | -0.0001 | 45 | C |
| 240. Waterloo, Iowa | 0.8065 | 17 | B | 0.2455 | 19 | B |
| 241. Wheeling, West Virginia-Ohio | 0.1664 | 78 | D | -0.1530 | 72 | D |
| 242. Wichita Falls, Texas | 0.6269 | 35 | B | 0.1968 | 21 | B |
| 243. Wilmington, North Carolina | -0.1506 | 93 | E | -0.5979 | 94 | E |

Mean $(\bar{x})$ = 0.4957          Mean $(\bar{x})$ = 0.0000
Standard Deviation (s) = 0.3451    Standard Deviation (s) = 0.2742

A = Outstanding ($\geq \bar{x} + s$)
B = Excellent ($\bar{x} + .28s \leq B < \bar{x} + s$)
C = Good ($\bar{x} - .28s < C < \bar{x} + .28s$)
D = Adequate ($\bar{x} - s < D \leq \bar{x} - .28s$)
E = Substandard ($\leq \bar{x} - s$)

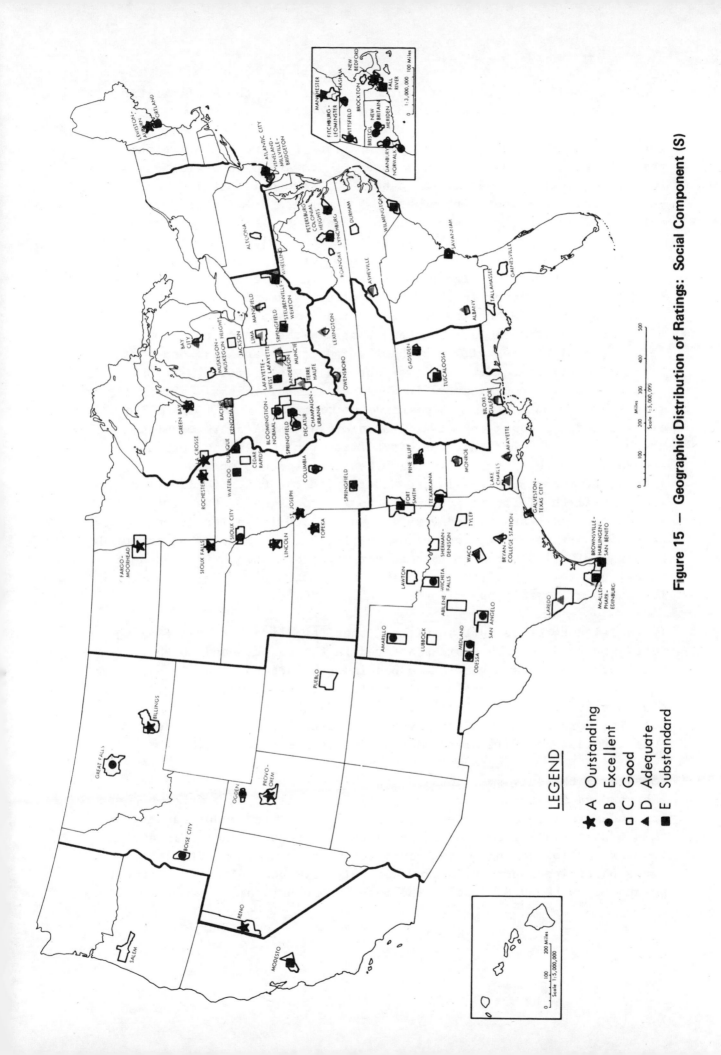

Figure 15 – Geographic Distribution of Ratings: Social Component (S)

LEGEND

A Outstanding
B Excellent
C Good
D Adequate
E Substandard

economic conditions, residents in these areas were short of existing
opportunities for self-support and for independence.

The lowest city in social quality comparison is Fort Smith, which obtained a negative index of -0.23 or about 2.1 standard deviations below
the mean.  Texarkana was found to have the second lowest index of
-0.21.  The other four with negative indexes are Wilmington (North
Carolina), Pine Bluff, Lynchburg, and Tuscaloosa.  The negative indexes
resulted from extremely high values of factors which have adverse
effects upon the social quality of life.  For instance, the high population density and the high percentage of population under 5 and over
65 years of age living in the central city are considered negative
inputs in spatial extention related to individuals' choice; all kinds
of discrimination--racial, sex, and spatial--the crowdedness in living
space, the high rates of death, birth, and crimes are also undesirable
social factors which tend to lower our quality of life.  Therefore,
if the negative input factors in any area are sufficiently strong to
more than compensate for the positive factors, the area's overall quality
of life index becomes negative.  The aforesaid SMSA's are examples
of the extremes.  For instance, Fort Smith ranked last in spatial
inequality in that it had very high housing segregation and income
inequality indexes; they all are three times the U.S. average, and more
than one-fifth of its residents had to work outside of the county of
residence; Texarkana ranked very low in the provision for decent
community living conditions because of its high percentage of occupied
housing, with 1.01 or more persons per room, and high crime and death
rates; the sex inequality in Wilmington and the crowded living space
in Pine Bluff were problem areas in those SMSA's.

In addition to those just mentioned, there are 11 additional SMSA's
rated substandard.  They are scattered in the eastern and southern
regions.  Among them, six SMSA's had index values only barely exceeding
the threshold of the mean minus one standard deviation.  In order of
rankings, they are Brownsville/Harlingen/San Benito, Petersburg/
Colonial Heights (Virginia), Savannah, Springfield (Ohio), Modesto
(California), and Fall River (Massachusetts-Rhode Island).

Modesto is the only small SMSA along the West Coast where only one
substandard rating was given among all five quality of life components.
Its index is 0.15 and ranked 80th in the group.  The major causes for
this SMSA to fall into the "E" category are its high racial inequality
indexes and low rating of self-supporting opportunities--its labor
force participation rate in 1969 was only 63.2 percent or 2.8 percentage
points below the U.S. level.  The mean income per family member

# CHART 15
## REGIONAL VARIATIONS IN INDEXES: SOCIAL COMPONENT (S)

RANK          SMSA                    ADJUSTED STANDARIZED SCORE

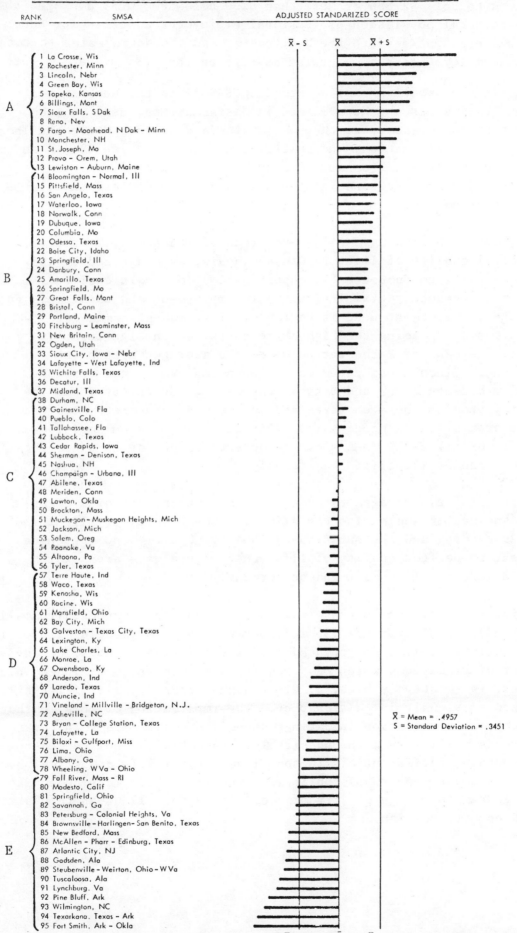

A
{
1 La Crosse, Wis
2 Rochester, Minn
3 Lincoln, Nebr
4 Green Bay, Wis
5 Topeka, Kansas
6 Billings, Mont
7 Sioux Falls, S Dak
8 Reno, Nev
9 Fargo – Moorhead, N Dak – Minn
10 Monchester, NH
11 St. Joseph, Mo
12 Provo – Orem, Utah
13 Lewiston – Auburn, Maine

B
{
14 Bloomington – Normal, Ill
15 Pittsfield, Mass
16 San Angelo, Texas
17 Waterloo, Iowa
18 Norwalk, Conn
19 Dubuque, Iowa
20 Columbia, Mo
21 Odessa, Texas
22 Boise City, Idaho
23 Springfield, Ill
24 Danbury, Conn
25 Amarillo, Texas
26 Springfield, Mo
27 Great Falls, Mont
28 Bristol, Conn
29 Portland, Maine
30 Fitchburg – Leominster, Mass
31 New Britain, Conn
32 Ogden, Utah
33 Sioux City, Iowa – Nebr
34 Lafayette – West Lafayette, Ind
35 Wichita Falls, Texas
36 Decatur, Ill
37 Midland, Texas

C
{
38 Durham, NC
39 Gainesville, Fla
40 Pueblo, Colo
41 Tallahassee, Fla
42 Lubbock, Texas
43 Cedar Rapids, Iowa
44 Sherman – Denison, Texas
45 Nashua, NH
46 Champaign – Urbana, Ill
47 Abilene, Texas
48 Meriden, Conn
49 Lawton, Okla
50 Brockton, Mass
51 Muckegon – Muskegon Heights, Mich
52 Jackson, Mich
53 Salem, Oreg
54 Roanoke, Va
55 Altoona, Pa
56 Tyler, Texas

D
{
57 Terre Haute, Ind
58 Waco, Texas
59 Kenosha, Wis
60 Racine, Wis
61 Mansfield, Ohio
62 Bay City, Mich
63 Galveston – Texas City, Texas
64 Lexington, Ky
65 Lake Charles, La
66 Monroe, La
67 Owensboro, Ky
68 Anderson, Ind
69 Laredo, Texas
70 Muncie, Ind
71 Vineland – Millville – Bridgeton, N.J.
72 Asheville, NC
73 Bryan – College Station, Texas
74 Lafayette, La
75 Biloxi – Gulfport, Miss
76 Lima, Ohio
77 Albany, Ga
78 Wheeling, W Va – Ohio

E
{
79 Fall River, Mass – RI
80 Modesto, Calif
81 Springfield, Ohio
82 Savannah, Ga
83 Petersburg – Colonial Heights, Va
84 Brownsville – Harlingen – San Benito, Texas
85 New Bedford, Mass
86 McAllen – Pharr – Edinburg, Texas
87 Atlantic City, NJ
88 Gadsden, Ala
89 Steubenville – Weirton, Ohio – W Va
90 Tuscaloosa, Ala
91 Lynchburg, Va
92 Pine Bluff, Ark
93 Wilmington, NC
94 Texarkana, Texas – Ark
95 Fort Smith, Ark – Okla

X̄ = Mean = .4957
S = Standard Deviation = .3451

X̄ – S          X̄          X̄ + S

amounted to only $2,886 or more than $200 below the U.S. average; the Negro to total population professional employment adjusted for education was only one-seventh the U.S. ratio, and the Negro males to total males unemployment rate was twice as high as the U.S. situation, etc.

Among all the excellent and outstanding SMSA's in the New England region, Fall River and New Bedford in Massachusetts, next to each other near the coast, were the two substandard areas. While the lack of mobility, information, and spatial extention were identified as the serious individual concerns in both areas, Fall River experienced very little racial inequality and New Bedford had little sex discrimination.

Again, the high ranking SMSA's have areas of weakness. To perfect its social quality of life, La Crosse should, as diagnosed by this study, attempt to increase its opportunities for individual self-support and reduce racial inequality in employment and earnings. For Rochester, the urgent need is to improve its general community living conditions by reducing the high crime rates, which significantly dragged the rank of Rochester to below the average in this sub-component. Lincoln was rated very low in employment and earning equality between races and between the sexes. Green Bay faces inequality problems between sexes, and Topeka was unfavorably evaluated in the area of racial inequality. Similar diagnoses on social quality of life for all small SMSA's can be undertaken and areas of potential weakness can be identified accordingly.

The preceding two paragraphs once again attempt to pinpoint examples of weaknesses in social factors affecting the quality of life in both the outstanding and the substandard SMSA's. Clearly, no region has the best or perfect quality of life--there are always areas which deserve further enrichment and betterment.

The dispersion of the indexes in this component is unexpectedly small; the standard deviation of 0.35 is lower than any comparable figures in other quality of life components in this small size group. The coefficient of variation, which measures the differences among index values, however, is relatively high, 0.70, or higher than any coefficients obtained previously in this chapter. The implication of this is that the geographic variation in ratings among the small SMSA's in this country is still very much undesirable. Essentially, how to reduce the geographic differentials in social quality of life among regions becomes a major concern of public agencies if an ultimate objective is to guarantee a high quality of social life for all urban population regardless of location.

SUMMARY AND CONCLUSIONS

Generally, the quality of life assessments for the small SMSA's reveal
no stronger pattern of regional concentration of the various quality
of life ratings than those observed in the preceding two chapters for
the large and medium SMSA's. However, most discussions in this chapter
have centered around the East North Central and New England regions
and the State of Texas because these areas contain a large number of
small SMSA's.

Relatively excellent and outstanding ratings for the economic component
were observed in the East North Central region and the northern part
of the State of Texas. The three southern SMSA's in Texas and the
southeastern states include a large proportion of the substandard
SMSA's. The dispersion of the economic component indexes for the
small SMSA's is larger than those for the large and medium SMSA's, as
is the coefficient of variation. This indicates that the disparity in
terms of economic quality of life among small SMSA's is larger than
that among the large or the medium SMSA's. In other words, should
there be regional inequality between economic well-being among people
in the U.S., it is more so among the small than among the large or
medium metropolitan areas.

The strong geographic concentration pattern of political ratings disclosed for the large and medium SMSA's was repeated here for the small
SMSA's. The quality of life in terms of political concerns was found
to be superior in the northern part of this country to those in the
southern part of the U.S. The small SMSA's in the New England region
and the Mountain states were outstanding with respect to political
quality. In spite of regional differentials in political ratings, the
index values in this group result in a small variation with the coefficient of variation being 0.25. The small coefficient indicates
that, as far as political considerations are concerned, people among
the small SMSA's do not experience significant deviations in quality
of life even though the relative patterns between north and south
prevailed and were persistent for the three size groups.

Due to the lack of air quality and climatological data, the environmental component in this chapter was evaluated only with the remaining
pollution factors and the parks and recreational data. Thus, geographic comparisons on patterns of environmental rating distribution
between the large, medium, and small group of SMSA's are not appropriate. Probably because of this data limitation, the environmental

quality evaluation for the small SMSA's indicates in general very little
regional pattern in the ratings.  The SMSA's in the New England region
nevertheless, did show off outstandingly.  The environmental ratings
for the two small SMSA's on the West Coast did support the pattern of
high environmental quality found in the large and medium SMSA's on
the West Coast.

The quality of health and education among the populations in various small
SMSA's tended to depict more or less a random regional distribution,
although the West North Central, the Mountain regions, and the Pacific region
seem to be differentiated from the rest.  A large standard deviation
and high coefficient of variation for the health and education component indicates that regional differences in health and educational
quality are appreciable.  In addition, the influence of institutions,
especially the leading state universities and colleges, on regional
quality of health and education was strikingly evident in the small
SMSA's.

Among quality of life components in both the large and medium groups,
the clearest patterns of regional distribution among quality ratings
were found in the social concerns.  The social component ratings in the
small group tend to confirm the existence of this regional differentiation.  Almost all SMSA's in the Pacific region plus those to the north
of Wichita (Kansas) and west of Ann Arbor (Michigan) were rated outstanding.  Except a few in New England and one in Florida, none of the
remaining SMSA's received the "A" rating.  In contrast, almost all "E"
rated medium and small SMSA's were found in the southeastern states.
Among the small SMSA's, the quality ratings for the social component
are highly correlated geographically to those for health and education
and to a lesser degree to those for the economic component.  The coefficient of variation among index values for the social component is
0.70, or the highest among the five quality of life components in the
small SMSA's.  This indicates wide variations in the social quality of
life enjoyed by people in different urban areas in the U.S.  Specifically, it reflects a need for both public and private efforts to provide an acceptable level of social quality of life for the substandard
regions.  There is clearly a need for further investigation into the
regional inequalities in social concerns and the courses of action that
can be launched to remove the deep-rooted factors adversely affecting
our social quality of life in the concentrated substandard regions.

Except for the environmental component, the rankings produced by the two methods are also very consistent for the small group of SMSA's, with the rank-order correlation coefficient being greater than 0.95 for the four quality of life components.  For the environmental component, the coefficient is 0.82.

CHAPTER

# VIII

**SUMMARY AND
CONCLUSIONS**

The practical importance of social indicators has been recognized since
the publication of the first census, conducted for purposes of taxation
or to determine potential military strength.  In fact, many people
in this country would admit that the leading role played by the
U.S. in the world economy after the Depression can be partially attributed to the establishment of a system of economic indicators which
have been constantly relied on to evaluate our economic performance
and to help guide our economy.[1/]  The ideal to be sought in this
country is not a planned society but a continuously planning society
in which integration and equilibrium are produced by groups and individuals undergoing a continual process of reviewing the past,
adjusting the present and planning for the future.  Our ability to
evaluate what we have done, and to plan ahead, is dependent on our
ability to assess how we are relative to how we were.  To enhance
the ability, the President's Science Advisory Committee in 1962, called
for the systematic collection of basic behavioral data for the United
States--the data that are comparable, systematic and periodically
gathered, organized, and analyzed.[2/]

Last year, Social Indicators 1973 was published.  It is "a book of
statistics, the first of its kind to be published by the Federal
Government.  It contains a collection of statistics selected and organized to describe social conditions and trends in the United
States."[3/]  The major criticisms of this book of statistics are the
lack of interpretative text, the concentration on output measures,

---

1/  For instance, see Raymond Bauer, "Social Indicators and Sample
    Surveys," in Public Opinion Quarterly, Vol. 30, No. 3 (Fall 1966,
    pp. 339-352).
2/  President's Science Advisory Committee, Strengthening the Behavioral
    Sciences:  Statement by the Behavioral Science Subpanel (Washing-
    ton D.C., April 20, 1962).
3/  Daniel Tunstall, Social Indicators 1973 (Washington, D.C.: Office
    of Management and Budget, 1974).

and the ambiguity among objectives--whether for goal setting or for policy implementation, for government or for general public information.[4]

This present study provides not only a set of comprehensive economic, political, environmental, health and education, and social quality of life indicators for all 243 SMSA's in the U.S., but also a theoretical framework in which the interwoven relationships among individuals and the institutions in the community can be objectively measured, evaluated and analyzed. The ultimate objective of this study is, naturally, to stimulate actions toward the improvement of the overall quality of life for all people. The report represents a first step by identifying potential weaknesses and strengths for all the metropolitan areas in this country.

An economic production model has been developed in this study. The quality of life for any individual is conceptually viewed in the model as an output produced by variable combinations of both psychological and physical inputs that the individual can normally exchange with, or acquire from, others in his community. Therefore, the quality of life that each individual perceives is assumed to be directly dependent on his capability constraints to exchange and to acquire, which vary from place to place and from time to time. For policy decision makers who attempt to maximize the quality of life output for all constituents collectively, however, the major concern is how to improve an individual's capability by shifting the constraint curve outward to the right.

To measure objectively the output level of quality of life as subjectively perceived by an individual, we may start with the input measures, since the optimum level of quality of life is produced only by combining both the physical and psychological inputs in such forms as to locate the tangency point between the iso-quality and the capability constraint curves. Without an extensive survey of attitudes among the individuals under study, it is very difficult for anyone even to attempt to quantify, much less to actually measure, the number of psychological inputs employed in the quality of life production.

---

[4] For various critics, see Roxann Van Dusen, "Problems of Measurement in Areas of Social Concerns," Monthly Labor Review (September 1974), pp. 7 and 8; and Richard Taeuber, "Social Indicators and Policy Making," Proceedings of the American Statistical Association, Social Statistics Section (1974).

Nevertheless, it is much less difficult to attempt to measure the physical inputs used in the quality of life production if we assume that the psychological inputs are constant over time. Although it is more complicated to measure the physical input for a community than for a person at a particular point in time, the quality of life output measured for a community by this particular approach tends to be more informative and reliable than for any individual because of the collective nature and the common law of large numbers. In addition, the assumption of constant psychological input for a community on the whole is more realistic and less rejectable than for any individual.

In social statistics, as in economic and political statistics, attention has been traditionally focused on the state of the nation as a whole. Although it is very important to have the aggregate national statistics such as the Gross National Product for national policy and decision making, the aggregate statistics and national averages fail to reveal the regional and local situations, and hence, overlook the extremes. Yet regional variations in social, economic, political, and environmental conditions are critical issues of our national problems today. For instance, regional migration has been found to be more responsive to the quality of life indicators than to the conventionally assumed determinant--income or employment.[5]

Based on the preceding rationale and in full awareness of the mounting needs for the social indicators with which to determine priority, define targets, and assess performance, this metropolitan quality of life comparison study was originated. The quality of life indexes that this study developed for the Standard Statistical Metropolitan Areas (SMSA's) actually represent physical input indicators in these areas. The variations among the indexes so constructed may reflect the quality of life variations only by assuming a constant level of psychological inputs throughout the SMSA's in the country. Interpretations of the results shown in the study have to be given with care, and the users of this study are urged to be fully aware of the weakness and limitations of this type of descriptive analysis, and the definitions, methodology, and data sources used.

---

[5] See Ben-Chieh Liu, "Net Migration Rate and the Quality of Life," Review of Economics and Statistics, Vol. 57, No.3 (August 1975).

Incorporating some 123 factors and variables which are of substantial
influence upon the objective quality of life or can most represent
the physical inputs to the production of the basic quality of life,
the level of quality of life in the 243 SMSA's in this country in 1970
was measured through the five different quality of life components--
economic, political, environmental, health and education, and social.
The economic component consists of factors representing individual
economic well-being as well as community economic health.  The political component consists of variables relating to individual political activities, local government professionalism and performance, and
welfare assistance.  The environmental component comprises quality
measures of all types of pollution (air, water, noise, visual, and
solid waste) and natural environment (climatological data and parks,
trails, and recreational areas).  The health and education component
includes indicators of individual health and education attainment, and
community educational investment and medical care provision.  The social
component encompasses the ratings of individual equality and individual
concerns plus the level of community living conditions.

The 243 SMSA's were divided into three groups--large, medium, and small.
According to the 1970 population, there are 65 large SMSA's with a population over 500,000, 83 medium SMSA's (200,000 to 500,000), and 95 small
SMSA's with population less than 200,000.  Based on 1970 data, the
composite indexes were developed and constructed for the five quality of
life components for each of the 243 SMSA's individually.

The composite indexes were constructed on the basis of the group means,
and hence, are in relative terms.  The value of the composite indexes
for any special component is of importance only relative to its group
mean value.  The relative composite indexes are meaningful only when
comparisons are made among members within the same group.  Intergroup
comparisons should be interpreted with caution.  Bearing in mind those
characteristics of the composite indexes, the indexes themselves are
then considered as cardinal rather than ordinal.  In other words, if an
SMSA has an index two times as large as that for another SMSA in the
same group for the same component, the quality of life in the former
SMSA may be interpreted as twice as good as that in the latter SMSA.
However, since the index value depends entirely upon the structure of
the model and the factor weights expressed in the model, it is safe to
consider the composite indexes as ordinal.  Given the indexes and the
means $(\bar{x})$ and standard deviations (s) of the indexes in the same group,
the quality of life of the SMSA's were then identified to be either outstanding (A), excellent (B), good (C), adequate (D), or substandard (E).
The empirical findings of the quality of life enjoyed by residents in
different SMSA's by the quality of life component are summarized in the
following tables.

211

# TABLE 16

## QUALITY OF LIFE INDEXES AND RATINGS IN LARGE SMSA'S

| SMSA | Economic Value | Economic Rating | Political Value | Political Rating | Environmental Value | Environmental Rating | Health and Education Value | Health and Education Rating | Social Value | Social Rating | Overall Value | Overall Rating |
|------|------|------|------|------|------|------|------|------|------|------|------|------|
| 1. Akron, Ohio | 1.8786 | C | 2.6319 | C | -0.9667 | C | 1.1250 | C | 0.1835 | E | 0.9705 | C |
| 2. Albany-Schenectady-Troy, N.Y. | 1.3286 | D | 3.7431 | A | -1.2917 | D | 1.8625 | B | 0.5836 | B | 1.2452 | B |
| 3. Allentown-Bethlehem-Easton, Pa.-N.J. | 1.4286 | D | 2.4792 | C | -0.6167 | A | 0.3875 | D | 0.2173 | D | .7792 | D |
| 4. Anaheim-Santa Ana-Garden Grove, Ca. | 2.1786 | B | 3.0486 | B | -1.0500 | C | 2.0125 | A | 0.4762 | C | 1.3332 | B |
| 5. Atlanta, Ga. | 2.4714 | A | 1.8750 | E | -1.2833 | D | 0.8375 | D | 0.2806 | D | .8362 | D |
| 6. Baltimore, Md. | 1.3429 | D | 2.5278 | C | -1.2667 | D | 0.3625 | D | 0.1392 | E | .6211 | D |
| 7. Birmingham, Ala. | 1.0500 | E | 1.6944 | E | -1.4250 | E | -0.0250 | E | 0.0931 | E | .2775 | E |
| 8. Boston, Mass. | 1.1786 | E | 3.3889 | A | -1.2500 | D | 2.0125 | A | 0.6036 | B | 1.1867 | B |
| 9. Buffalo, N.Y. | 1.8357 | C | 3.8819 | A | -1.2000 | D | 1.4250 | B | 0.7019 | B | 1.3289 | B |
| 10. Chicago, Ill. | 2.3643 | A | 2.9653 | B | -1.8167 | E | 0.6625 | D | 0.3056 | D | .8962 | C |
| 11. Cincinnati, Ohio-Ky.-Ind. | 2.3429 | A | 2.8403 | B | -1.0333 | C | 0.6250 | D | 0.0711 | E | .9692 | C |
| 12. Cleveland, Ohio | 2.5143 | A | 2.7847 | C | -1.4250 | E | 1.0875 | C | 0.5837 | B | 1.1090 | B |
| 13. Columbus, Ohio | 1.7857 | C | 3.0208 | B | -1.0917 | C | 1.4875 | B | 0.7621 | B | 1.1929 | B |
| 14. Dallas, Texas | 2.7571 | A | 1.4653 | E | -0.9083 | B | 0.7625 | D | 0.4585 | C | .9070 | C |
| 15. Dayton, Ohio | 2.1214 | B | 2.5625 | C | -1.3167 | D | 1.0625 | C | 0.3421 | D | .9544 | C |
| 16. Denver, Colo. | 1.8357 | C | 3.0903 | B | -0.9917 | C | 2.5000 | A | 0.9604 | A | 1.4789 | A |
| 17. Detroit, Mich. | 1.8929 | B | 3.2222 | B | -1.7250 | E | 0.9625 | C | -0.0248 | E | .8656 | D |
| 18. Fort Lauderdale-Hollywood, Fla. | 2.3143 | A | 2.1319 | D | -1.0833 | C | 0.2000 | E | 0.5823 | B | .8290 | D |
| 19. Fort Worth, Texas | 2.4786 | A | 1.7986 | E | -0.8583 | B | 0.3500 | D | 0.4372 | C | .8412 | D |
| 20. Gary-Hammond-East Chicago, Ind. | 1.3929 | D | 2.2778 | C | -1.1750 | D | 0.7000 | D | 0.2106 | D | .6813 | D |
| 21. Grand Rapids, Mich. | 2.2643 | B | 3.6319 | A | -1.0333 | C | 1.5375 | B | 0.5527 | C | 1.3906 | A |
| 22. Greensboro-Winston-Salem-High Point, N.C. | 1.1571 | E | 1.8333 | E | -1.3000 | D | 0.1000 | E | 0.2337 | D | .4048 | E |
| 23. Hartford, Conn. | 2.0357 | B | 3.6181 | A | -1.1250 | C | 2.2750 | A | 0.5981 | B | 1.4804 | A |
| 24. Honolulu, Hawaii | 1.1357 | E | 2.1458 | D | -0.4583 | A | 1.5375 | B | 0.4496 | C | .9621 | C |
| 25. Houston, Texas | 2.7000 | A | 1.9167 | E | -1.0000 | C | 1.0875 | C | 0.5573 | C | 1.0523 | C |
| 26. Indianapolis, Ind. | 2.5143 | A | 2.4236 | D | -1.5250 | E | 0.6500 | D | 0.4303 | C | .8986 | C |
| 27. Jacksonville, Fla. | 0.8929 | E | 1.7569 | E | -1.2500 | D | 0.1125 | E | 0.3169 | D | .3658 | E |
| 28. Jersey City, N.J. | 0.5857 | E | 2.1250 | D | -1.0167 | C | -0.5250 | E | -0.1694 | E | .1999 | E |
| 29. Kansas City, Mo.-Ks. | 1.6857 | C | 2.0486 | D | -1.1250 | C | 1.1125 | C | 0.8089 | A | .9061 | C |
| 30. Los Angeles-Long Beach, Ca. | 2.0500 | B | 2.5278 | C | -1.0583 | C | 1.7375 | B | 0.8315 | A | 1.2177 | B |
| 31. Louisville, Ky.-Ind. | 1.9071 | B | 2.3403 | D | -1.4167 | E | 0.3125 | E | 0.2603 | D | .6807 | D |
| 32. Memphis, Tenn.-Ark. | 0.9429 | E | 1.8264 | E | -1.2083 | D | 0.6125 | D | 0.1198 | E | .4587 | E |
| 33. Miami, Fla. | 1.2857 | D | 1.9097 | E | -0.4167 | A | 0.6000 | D | 0.7634 | B | .8284 | D |
| 34. Milwaukee, Wis. | 2.1786 | B | 3.2708 | A | -1.0417 | C | 1.7000 | B | 0.8453 | A | 1.3906 | A |
| 35. Minneapolis-St. Paul, Minn. | 1.9357 | B | 3.4722 | A | -0.9000 | B | 2.2375 | A | 0.8329 | A | 1.5157 | A |
| 36. Nashville-Davidson, Tenn. | 1.7286 | C | 2.0833 | D | -1.0833 | C | 0.6375 | D | 0.7218 | B | .8176 | D |
| 37. New Orleans, La. | 0.7857 | E | 1.5625 | E | -1.2667 | D | 0.4250 | D | 0.1783 | E | .3370 | E |
| 38. New York, N.Y. | 1.9500 | B | 2.2014 | D | -1.3333 | D | 1.2125 | C | 0.5179 | C | .9097 | C |
| 39. Newark, N.J. | 1.2571 | D | 2.9931 | B | -1.2000 | D | 1.2625 | C | 0.1000 | E | .8825 | D |
| 40. Norfolk-Portsmouth, Va. | 0.8500 | E | 1.9306 | E | -0.8667 | B | 0.0625 | E | 0.2507 | D | .4454 | E |

TABLE 16 (Concluded)

## QUALITY OF LIFE INDEXES AND RATINGS IN LARGE SMSA'S

| SMSA | Economic Value | Rating | Political Value | Rating | Environmental Value | Rating | Health and Education Value | Rating | Social Value | Rating | Overall Value | Rating |
|---|---|---|---|---|---|---|---|---|---|---|---|---|
| 41. Oklahoma City, Okla. | 2.1143 | B | 2.8056 | B | -0.8250 | B | 1.3750 | B | 0.8852 | A | 1.2710 | B |
| 42. Omaha, Nebraska-Iowa | 2.2786 | B | 2.5833 | C | -1.3083 | D | 1.7500 | B | 0.9966 | A | 1.2600 | B |
| 43. Paterson-Clifton-Passaic, N.J. | 1.9357 | B | 1.8542 | E | -1.0000 | C | 1.4625 | B | 0.1371 | E | .8779 | D |
| 44. Philadelphia, Pa.-N.J. | 0.9500 | E | 2.4306 | D | -1.0250 | C | 0.3000 | E | 0.2234 | D | .5758 | E |
| 45. Phoenix, Ariz. | 1.2786 | D | 1.9097 | E | -0.5917 | A | 1.6000 | B | 0.7246 | B | .9842 | C |
| 46. Pittsburgh, Pa. | 1.5929 | C | 3.1181 | B | -1.8667 | E | 0.7875 | D | 0.3510 | D | .7966 | D |
| 47. Portland, Oreg.-Wash. | 2.6786 | A | 3.5486 | A | -0.6500 | A | 2.1375 | A | 1.0273 | A | 1.7484 | A |
| 48. Providence-Pawtucket-Warwick, R.I.-Mass. | 1.0786 | E | 3.0347 | B | -0.7667 | B | -0.1750 | E | 0.1606 | E | .6664 | D |
| 49. Richmond, Va. | 2.3357 | A | 2.4722 | C | -1.1333 | D | 0.4500 | D | 0.1123 | E | .8474 | D |
| 50. Rochester, N.Y. | 2.3214 | A | 3.6667 | A | -0.7000 | B | 2.0000 | A | 0.2196 | D | 1.5015 | A |
| 51. Sacramento, Ca. | 1.5929 | C | 3.6181 | A | -0.2000 | A | 2.1875 | A | 0.9576 | A | 1.6312 | A |
| 52. St. Louis, Mo.-Ill. | 2.0357 | B | 2.5833 | C | -1.5833 | E | 0.5625 | D | 0.1583 | E | .7513 | D |
| 53. Salt Lake City, Utah | 1.3714 | D | 3.3542 | A | -1.0250 | C | 2.5625 | A | 0.5728 | B | 1.3672 | A |
| 54. San Antonio, Texas | 0.7857 | E | 1.3403 | E | -0.8333 | B | 0.2875 | E | 0.2463 | D | .3653 | E |
| 55. San Bernadino-Riverside-Ontario, Ca. | 1.2000 | D | 2.6944 | C | -0.4750 | A | 1.3625 | B | 0.6042 | B | 1.0772 | C |
| 56. San Diego, Ca. | 1.8786 | C | 3.1111 | B | -0.5333 | A | 1.8125 | B | 0.9020 | A | 1.4342 | A |
| 57. San Francisco-Oakland, Ca. | 1.8357 | C | 2.9444 | B | -0.7000 | B | 2.3750 | A | 0.8189 | A | 1.4548 | A |
| 58. San Jose, Ca. | 1.7500 | C | 2.9167 | B | -0.5333 | A | 2.7250 | A | 0.7364 | B | 1.5190 | A |
| 59. Seattle-Everett, Wa. | 2.1071 | B | 3.0347 | B | -0.2667 | A | 2.2625 | A | 1.0144 | A | 1.6304 | A |
| 60. Springfield-Chicopee-Holyoke, Mass.-Conn. | 1.1357 | E | 2.6667 | C | -0.6167 | A | 0.7000 | D | 0.4634 | C | .8698 | D |
| 61. Syracuse, N.Y. | 1.2071 | D | 3.6458 | A | -1.1500 | D | 1.8500 | B | 0.6157 | B | 1.2337 | B |
| 62. Tampa-St. Petersburg, Fla. | 1.6214 | C | 1.9514 | E | -1.0583 | C | 0.0000 | E | 0.5526 | C | .6134 | E |
| 63. Toledo, Ohio-Mich. | 2.1714 | B | 3.0278 | B | -1.1833 | D | 0.9375 | C | 0.5617 | C | 1.1030 | B |
| 64. Washington, D.C.-Md.-Va. | 1.8571 | C | 2.3403 | D | -0.8333 | B | 2.1000 | A | 0.6848 | B | 1.2298 | B |
| 65. Youngstown-Warren, Ohio | 1.5857 | D | 2.7222 | C | -0.9667 | C | 0.6375 | D | 0.3634 | D | .8684 | D |
| Mean ($\bar{x}$) = | 1.7390 | | 2.6219 | | -1.0342 | | 1.1252 | | 0.4809 | | .9865 | |
| Standard Deviation (s) = | .5475 | | 0.6466 | | 0.3452 | | 0.7868 | | 0.2928 | | .3688 | |

A = Outstanding ($\geq \bar{x} + s$)
B - Excellent ($\bar{x} + .28s \leq B < \bar{x} + s$)
C = Good ($\bar{x} - .28s < C < \bar{x} + .28s$)
D = Adequate ($\bar{x} - s < D \leq \bar{x} - .28s$)
E = Substandard ($\leq \bar{x} - s$)

## TABLE 17

## QUALITY OF LIFE INDEXES AND RATINGS IN MEDIUM SMSA'S

| | SMSA | Economic Value | Economic Rating | Political Value | Political Rating | Environmental Value | Environmental Rating | Health and Education Value | Health and Education Rating | Social Value | Social Rating | Overall Value | Overall Rating |
|---|---|---|---|---|---|---|---|---|---|---|---|---|---|
| 66. | Albuquerque, N.M. | 1.8571 | B | 3.1111 | B | -1.2750 | E | 2.2000 | A | 0.4704 | C | 1.2727 | B |
| 67. | Ann Arbor, Mich. | 2.1429 | A | 2.5764 | C | -0.9083 | C | 2.4250 | A | 1.0205 | A | 1.4513 | A |
| 68. | Appleton-Oshkosh, Wis. | 2.4214 | A | 3.6528 | A | -0.9417 | C | 1.8625 | A | 1.1075 | A | 1.6205 | A |
| 69. | Augusta, Ga.-S.C. | 0.9571 | E | 2.1111 | D | -1.0583 | D | 0.3250 | E | 0.0539 | E | .4778 | E |
| 70. | Austin, Texas | 1.7857 | C | 2.3125 | D | -1.0583 | D | 1.7250 | B | 0.7041 | B | 1.0938 | B |
| 71. | Bakersfield, Ca. | 1.2643 | D | 3.1667 | B | -0.6167 | A | 0.9250 | C | 0.2502 | D | .9979 | C |
| 72. | Baton Rouge, La. | 1.4143 | D | 2.3958 | D | -1.0583 | D | 1.7250 | B | 0.5199 | C | .9993 | C |
| 73. | Beaumont-Port Arthur-Orange, Texas | 1.7214 | C | 2.0833 | D | -0.9583 | C | 0.9000 | C | 0.4404 | C | .8374 | D |
| 74. | Binghamton, N.Y.-Pa. | 1.7071 | C | 3.4375 | A | -1.0583 | D | 1.9375 | A | 0.6848 | B | 1.3417 | B |
| 75. | Bridgeport, Conn. | 1.8071 | B | 3.3681 | A | -0.8083 | B | 1.4625 | B | 0.5826 | C | 1.2824 | B |
| 76. | Canton, Ohio | 2.1643 | A | 2.7708 | C | -1.1917 | D | 0.6500 | D | 0.3160 | D | .9419 | C |
| 77. | Charleston, S.C. | 0.9643 | E | 1.6458 | E | -1.2417 | D | 0.0875 | E | -0.1268 | E | .2658 | E |
| 78. | Charleston, W. Va. | 1.2714 | D | 3.2431 | A | -1.3000 | E | 0.6500 | D | 0.3726 | D | .8474 | D |
| 79. | Charlotte, N.C. | 1.6643 | C | 1.9028 | E | -1.3917 | E | 1.1125 | C | 0.5993 | B | .7774 | D |
| 80. | Chattanooga, Tenn.-Ga. | 1.3214 | D | 2.3889 | D | -1.0917 | D | 0.1750 | E | 0.0014 | E | .5590 | E |
| 81. | Colorado Springs, Colo. | 1.5714 | C | 2.3333 | D | -1.1333 | D | 1.4750 | B | 0.8953 | A | 1.0283 | C |
| 82. | Columbia, S.C. | 1.4286 | D | 1.5764 | E | -1.4750 | E | 0.5875 | D | 0.0657 | E | .4366 | E |
| 83. | Columbus, Ga.-Ala. | 1.0786 | E | 1.6319 | E | -1.2250 | D | 0.1000 | E | -0.0701 | E | .3031 | E |
| 84. | Corpus Christi, Texas | 1.9000 | B | 1.5000 | E | -0.3917 | A | 0.8000 | D | 0.4818 | C | .8580 | D |
| 85. | Davenport-Rock Island-Moline, Iowa-Ill. | 2.0286 | B | 2.6528 | C | -0.6000 | A | 0.5000 | D | 0.5864 | C | 1.0336 | C |
| 86. | Des Moines, Iowa | 2.2500 | A | 3.3333 | A | -0.9583 | C | 1.7750 | A | 1.3197 | A | 1.5439 | A |
| 87. | Duluth-Superior, Minn.-Wis. | 1.4000 | D | 3.7292 | A | -0.5333 | A | 1.5375 | B | 1.0333 | A | 1.4333 | A |
| 88. | El Paso, Texas | 0.9643 | E | 1.6944 | E | -1.0417 | C | 1.2875 | B | 0.4601 | C | .6729 | D |
| 89. | Erie, Pa. | 1.6500 | C | 2.8681 | B | -0.8917 | C | 1.0125 | C | 0.5385 | C | 1.0355 | C |
| 90. | Eugene, Oregon | 2.2000 | A | 3.5000 | A | -0.5833 | A | 2.2875 | A | 1.2617 | A | 1.7332 | A |
| 91. | Evansville, Ind.-Ky. | 1.9143 | B | 3.2500 | A | -0.9750 | C | 0.7375 | D | 0.4387 | C | 1.0731 | C |
| 92. | Fayetteville, N.C. | 0.6643 | E | 1.6042 | E | -1.0417 | C | 0.3625 | E | 0.0068 | E | .3192 | E |
| 93. | Flint, Mich. | 2.0000 | B | 3.2917 | A | -1.0083 | C | 1.1250 | C | 0.5172 | C | 1.1851 | B |
| 94. | Fort Wayne, Ind. | 2.9500 | A | 3.3750 | A | -0.9417 | C | 1.3000 | B | 0.8673 | A | 1.5101 | A |
| 95. | Fresno, Ca. | 1.0214 | E | 3.0000 | B | -0.2833 | A | 1.4500 | B | 0.6579 | B | 1.1692 | B |
| 96. | Greenville, S.C. | 1.5643 | C | 1.6944 | E | -1.1917 | D | -0.1875 | E | 0.1535 | D | .4066 | E |
| 97. | Hamilton-Middleton, Ohio | 2.0071 | B | 2.3542 | D | -0.8500 | B | 1.1500 | C | 0.2516 | D | .9826 | C |
| 98. | Harrisburg, Pa. | 1.5643 | C | 2.4514 | D | -0.8583 | B | 0.9875 | C | 0.4825 | C | .9255 | C |
| 99. | Huntington-Ashland, W. Va.-Ky.-Ohio | 1.1643 | E | 2.4931 | C | -1.5750 | E | 0.0750 | E | 0.0780 | E | .4471 | E |
| 100. | Huntsville, Ala. | 1.6071 | C | 2.1042 | D | -1.2000 | D | 1.2500 | C | -0.1253 | E | .7272 | D |
| 101. | Jackson, Miss. | 1.3929 | D | 1.6944 | E | -1.0917 | D | 0.8500 | D | 0.0691 | E | .5829 | E |
| 102. | Johnstown, Pa. | 1.1786 | E | 2.9375 | B | -1.2083 | D | 0.5125 | D | 0.3667 | D | .7574 | D |
| 103. | Kalamazoo, Mich. | 2.5429 | A | 3.5069 | A | -0.8583 | B | 1.6375 | B | 0.8011 | B | 1.5260 | A |
| 104. | Knoxville, Tenn. | 1.7214 | C | 2.4236 | D | -0.7583 | B | 0.9750 | C | 0.2258 | D | .9175 | C |
| 105. | Lancaster, Pa. | 1.8357 | B | 2.1806 | D | -1.0250 | C | 0.5875 | D | 0.1355 | E | .7429 | D |

214

TABLE 17 (Concluded)

## QUALITY OF LIFE INDEXES AND RATINGS IN MEDIUM SMSA'S

| SMSA | Economic Value | Rating | Political Value | Rating | Environmental Value | Rating | Health and Education Value | Rating | Social Value | Rating | Overall Value | Rating |
|---|---|---|---|---|---|---|---|---|---|---|---|---|
| 106. Lansing, Mich. | 2.0929 | B | 3.3194 | A | -0.9417 | C | 2.4250 | A | 0.7408 | B | 1.5273 | A |
| 107. Las Vegas, Nev. | 1.6786 | C | 2.3403 | D | -0.3417 | A | 0.8250 | D | 0.8404 | B | 1.0685 | C |
| 108. Lawrence-Haverhill, Mass.-N.H. | 1.8000 | C | 3.1319 | B | -0.6833 | B | 1.3750 | B | 0.6545 | B | 1.2556 | B |
| 109. Little Rock-North Little Rock, Ark. | 1.4000 | D | 1.7917 | E | -1.1917 | D | 0.7750 | D | 0.3733 | D | .6297 | D |
| 110. Lorain-Elyria, Ohio | 1.9643 | B | 2.4792 | C | -1.1750 | D | 0.7000 | D | 0.3523 | D | .8642 | D |
| 111. Lowell, Mass. | 1.4571 | D | 2.9653 | B | -0.8833 | B | 1.3750 | B | 0.5119 | C | 1.0852 | B |
| 112. Macon, Ga. | 0.9357 | E | 1.5417 | E | -1.2250 | D | 0.0625 | E | 0.0200 | E | .2670 | E |
| 113. Madison, Wis. | 1.7857 | C | 3.5069 | A | -0.9083 | C | 2.9250 | A | 1.2014 | A | 1.7021 | A |
| 114. Mobile, Ala. | 1.1143 | E | 1.7708 | E | -1.4917 | E | 0.0250 | E | -0.2661 | E | .2305 | E |
| 115. Montgomery, Ala. | 0.7500 | E | 1.9722 | E | -1.2500 | D | -0.0250 | E | -0.1114 | E | .2672 | E |
| 116. New Haven, Conn. | 2.0429 | B | 3.3056 | A | -0.8750 | B | 1.4625 | B | 0.6692 | B | 1.3210 | B |
| 117. New London-Groton-Norwich, Conn. | 1.3357 | D | 2.8264 | B | -0.8750 | B | 0.8250 | D | 0.5058 | C | .9236 | C |
| 118. Newport News-Hampton, Va. | 1.3214 | D | 2.0347 | D | -0.6417 | A | 0.5625 | D | 0.3679 | D | .7290 | D |
| 119. Orlando, Fla. | 1.4500 | D | 2.4722 | C | -1.1083 | D | 0.5375 | D | 0.3552 | D | .7413 | D |
| 120. Oxnard-Ventura, Ca. | 1.3929 | D | 2.8611 | B | -0.6000 | A | 1.7125 | B | 0.4437 | C | 1.1620 | B |
| 121. Pensacola, Fla. | 1.1857 | E | 2.0000 | E | -1.2250 | D | 0.5500 | D | 0.0217 | E | .5065 | E |
| 122. Peoria, Ill. | 2.4071 | A | 2.6528 | C | -1.0750 | D | 0.7500 | D | 0.5174 | C | 1.0505 | C |
| 123. Raleigh, N.C. | 1.8214 | B | 2.4306 | D | -1.1750 | D | 1.4375 | B | 0.3074 | D | .9644 | C |
| 124. Reading, Pa. | 1.6714 | C | 2.3958 | D | -1.1500 | D | 0.2750 | E | 0.2705 | D | .6925 | D |
| 125. Rockford, Ill. | 2.2071 | A | 2.5972 | C | -0.7000 | B | 0.8125 | D | 0.5126 | C | 1.0859 | B |
| 126. Saginaw, Mich. | 2.4071 | A | 2.7222 | C | -0.9250 | C | 0.7750 | D | 0.3535 | D | 1.0666 | C |
| 127. Salinas-Monterey, Ca. | 1.1857 | E | 2.0694 | D | -0.3000 | A | 2.0750 | A | 0.6651 | B | 1.1390 | B |
| 128. Santa Barbara, Ca. | 1.6786 | C | 3.4444 | A | -0.5667 | A | 2.3750 | A | 0.9701 | A | 1.5803 | A |
| 129. Santa Rosa, Ca. | 1.6000 | C | 3.3194 | A | -0.8833 | B | 1.4000 | B | 0.7239 | B | 1.2320 | B |
| 130. Scranton, Pa. | 1.4786 | D | 3.0625 | B | -1.3083 | E | 0.3250 | E | 0.5358 | C | .8187 | D |
| 131. Shreveport, La. | 1.5071 | D | 1.9514 | E | -1.4083 | E | 0.8625 | D | 0.1250 | E | .6075 | E |
| 132. South Bend, Ind. | 2.7000 | A | 3.3264 | A | -1.0417 | C | 1.1375 | C | 0.6098 | B | 1.3464 | A |
| 133. Spokane, Wash. | 1.5214 | D | 3.0694 | B | -1.0167 | C | 1.5875 | B | 1.1078 | A | 1.2539 | B |
| 134. Stamford, Conn. | 2.4714 | A | 2.9097 | B | -0.7083 | B | 2.3500 | A | 0.8212 | B | 1.5688 | A |
| 135. Stockton, Ca. | 1.6071 | C | 2.8542 | B | -0.8750 | B | 1.2625 | C | 0.6136 | B | 1.0925 | B |
| 136. Tacoma, Wash. | 1.1500 | E | 2.2014 | D | -0.0667 | A | 0.8000 | D | 0.9543 | A | 1.0078 | C |
| 137. Trenton, N.J. | 1.3000 | D | 2.7500 | C | -0.6583 | A | 0.9375 | C | 0.3168 | D | .9292 | C |
| 138. Tucson, Ariz. | 1.2000 | D | 2.3264 | D | -0.8833 | B | 2.1750 | A | 0.5731 | C | 1.0782 | C |
| 139. Tulsa, Okla. | 2.4429 | A | 2.6736 | C | -1.6250 | E | 1.2750 | B | 0.5416 | C | 1.0616 | C |
| 140. Utica-Rome, N.Y. | 1.2786 | D | 3.2222 | A | -0.9417 | C | 1.2625 | C | 0.4485 | C | 1.0540 | C |
| 141. Vallejo-Napa, Ca. | 1.5786 | C | 2.6111 | C | -0.8500 | C | 1.3750 | B | 0.6496 | B | 1.0729 | C |
| 142. Waterbury, Conn. | 2.1429 | A | 3.3889 | A | -0.7833 | B | 0.7125 | D | 0.4734 | C | 1.1869 | B |
| 143. West Palm Beach, Fla. | 2.4786 | A | 2.3542 | D | -1.3583 | E | 0.6875 | D | 0.7189 | B | .9762 | C |
| 144. Wichita, Kansas | 2.1714 | A | 3.0764 | B | -1.0250 | C | 1.8250 | A | 1.1741 | A | 1.4444 | A |
| 145. Wilkes-Barre-Hazelton, Pa. | 1.4500 | D | 2.7431 | C | -1.2333 | D | 0.2125 | E | 0.1482 | D | .6641 | D |
| 146. Wilmington, Del.-N.J.-Md. | 1.6786 | C | 2.8472 | B | -0.7917 | B | 1.1000 | C | 0.3135 | D | 1.0295 | C |
| 147. Worcester, Mass. | 1.6643 | C | 3.0000 | B | -0.9000 | C | 0.9125 | C | 0.9578 | A | 1.1269 | B |
| 148. York, Pa. | 1.9643 | B | 2.0903 | D | -1.1833 | D | 0.3125 | E | 0.1015 | E | .6571 | D |
| Mean ($\bar{x}$) = | 1.6691 | | 2.6236 | | -0.9700 | | 1.0799 | | 0.4901 | | 0.9781 | |
| Standard Deviation (s) = | 0.4695 | | 0.5970 | | 0.2963 | | 0.6727 | | 0.3515 | | 0.3649 | |

A = Outstanding ($\geq \bar{x} + s$)
B = Excellent ($\bar{x} + .28s \leq B < \bar{x} + s$)
C = Good ($\bar{x} - .28s \leq C < \bar{x} + .28s$)
D = Adequate ($\bar{x} - s < D \leq \bar{x} - .28s$)
E = Substandard ($\bar{x} - s$)

TABLE 18

## QUALITY OF LIFE INDEXES AND RATINGS IN SMALL SMSA'S

| SMSA | Economic Value | Rating | Political Value | Rating | Environmental Value | Rating | Health and Education Value | Rating | Social Value | Rating | Overall Value | Rating |
|---|---|---|---|---|---|---|---|---|---|---|---|---|
| 149. Abilene, Texas | 1.9214 | B | 1.8929 | E | -0.0417 | D | 0.9167 | C | 0.5198 | C | 1.0418 | D |
| 150. Albany, Ga. | 0.4643 | E | 1.4008 | E | 0.1250 | C | 0.7292 | D | 0.1927 | D | .5824 | E |
| 151. Altoona, Pa. | 1.2143 | D | 2.5476 | C | -0.0833 | D | 0.2917 | E | 0.4158 | C | .8772 | D |
| 152. Amarillo, Texas | 2.7500 | A | 2.2857 | D | 0.0833 | C | 1.7292 | B | 0.7387 | B | 1.5174 | B |
| 153. Anderson, Ind. | 2.3429 | B | 3.1905 | B | -0.0417 | D | 0.7292 | D | 0.2506 | D | 1.2943 | C |
| 154. Asheville, N. C. | 1.9000 | C | 2.4683 | C | 0.4583 | B | 0.8125 | D | 0.2266 | D | 1.1731 | C |
| 155. Atlantic City, N. J. | 0.7643 | E | 3.3214 | A | -0.0417 | D | -0.0417 | E | 0.0448 | E | .8094 | E |
| 156. Bay City, Mich. | 2.3071 | B | 3.6151 | A | -0.3333 | E | 1.2083 | C | 0.3497 | D | 1.4294 | B |
| 157. Billings, Mont. | 1.8429 | C | 3.3095 | A | -0.2917 | E | 2.0000 | A | 1.0761 | A | 1.5874 | B |
| 158. Biloxi-Gulfport, Miss. | 0.5857 | E | 1.9087 | E | -0.2917 | E | 1.3125 | B | 0.2225 | D | .7475 | E |
| 159. Bloomington-Normal, Ill. | 1.9000 | C | 2.9246 | B | 0.5833 | A | 1.7083 | B | 0.8250 | B | 1.5882 | B |
| 160. Boise City, Idaho | 2.3857 | B | 3.2817 | A | -0.2917 | E | 1.2500 | C | 0.7689 | B | 1.4789 | B |
| 161. Bristol, Conn. | 2.2571 | B | 3.1349 | B | 0.9167 | A | 1.2917 | C | 0.7228 | B | 1.6646 | A |
| 162. Brockton, Mass. | 1.1786 | D | 2.8333 | B | 0.0000 | D | 0.8333 | D | 0.4370 | C | 1.0564 | D |
| 163. Brownsville-Harlingen-San Benito, Texas | 0.2714 | E | 1.2222 | E | 0.4583 | B | 0.6667 | D | 0.1202 | E | .5478 | E |
| 164. Bryan-College Station, Texas | 1.6643 | C | 2.0714 | D | -0.2083 | D | 2.3542 | A | 0.2265 | D | 1.2216 | C |
| 165. Cedar Rapids, Iowa | 2.3214 | B | 3.1508 | B | 0.0000 | D | 1.3333 | B | 0.5359 | C | 1.4683 | B |
| 166. Champaign-Urbana, Ill. | 1.4786 | D | 2.0873 | D | -0.2500 | E | 2.0000 | A | 0.5211 | C | 1.1674 | C |
| 167. Columbia, Mo. | 1.5214 | D | 2.5873 | C | -0.2500 | E | 2.7917 | A | 0.7782 | B | 1.4857 | B |
| 168. Danbury, Conn. | 2.1429 | B | 3.6190 | A | 0.4167 | B | 1.3333 | B | 0.7511 | B | 1.6526 | A |
| 169. Decatur, Ill. | 2.5929 | A | 2.6151 | C | 0.5833 | A | 0.7292 | D | 0.6225 | B | 1.4286 | B |
| 170. Dubuque, Iowa | 1.9857 | B | 3.3651 | A | 0.3750 | B | 0.7917 | D | 0.7862 | B | 1.4607 | B |
| 171. Durham, N. C. | 1.8786 | C | 2.0317 | D | 0.0833 | C | 1.5417 | B | 0.5900 | C | 1.2251 | C |
| 172. Fall River, Mass.-R. I. | 1.1214 | D | 2.8016 | C | -0.0833 | D | 0.1458 | E | 0.1497 | E | .6830 | E |
| 173. Fargo-Moorhead, N. Dak.-Minn. | 1.7929 | C | 3.3651 | A | 0.0000 | D | 2.2708 | A | 1.0028 | A | 1.6863 | A |
| 174. Fitchburg-Leominster, Mass. | 1.6929 | C | 3.3333 | A | 1.1250 | A | 0.5833 | D | 0.6858 | B | 1.4841 | B |
| 175. Fort Smith, Ark.-Okla. | 0.9929 | E | 1.5159 | E | 0.6250 | A | -0.4167 | E | -0.2266 | E | .4981 | E |
| 176. Gadsden, Ala. | 0.8429 | E | 2.0873 | D | 0.5833 | A | -0.2500 | E | 0.0363 | E | .6600 | E |
| 177. Gainesville, Fla. | 0.9214 | E | 1.7619 | E | -0.2083 | D | 2.6458 | A | 0.5839 | C | 1.1409 | C |
| 178. Galveston-Texas City, Texas | 2.1357 | B | 2.1706 | D | 0.1250 | C | 1.3333 | B | 0.3493 | D | 1.2228 | C |
| 179. Great Falls, Mont. | 0.8643 | E | 2.4643 | C | 0.4583 | B | 1.6667 | B | 0.7300 | B | 1.2367 | C |
| 180. Green Bay, Wis. | 2.3429 | B | 3.3849 | A | 0.4583 | B | 1.4583 | B | 1.1032 | A | 1.7495 | A |
| 181. Jackson, Mich. | 2.2143 | B | 2.8373 | B | 1.3333 | A | 0.8125 | D | 0.4329 | C | 1.5261 | B |
| 182. Kenosha, Wis. | 1.9643 | B | 2.9643 | B | -0.0417 | D | 0.7917 | D | 0.3637 | D | 1.2085 | C |
| 183. La Crosse, Wis. | 2.1000 | B | 3.8016 | A | 0.0000 | D | 2.1667 | A | 1.4668 | A | 1.9070 | A |
| 184. Lafayette, La. | 0.8500 | E | 1.6190 | E | -0.3750 | E | 1.5833 | B | 0.2263 | D | .7807 | E |
| 185. Lafayette-West Lafayette, Ind. | 2.1429 | B | 3.0675 | B | 0.0000 | D | 2.2292 | A | 0.6378 | B | 1.6155 | A |
| 186. Lake Charles, La. | 1.1500 | D | 1.7976 | E | -0.2917 | E | 0.7708 | D | 0.3063 | D | .7466 | E |
| 187. Laredo, Texas | 0.0571 | E | 1.3690 | E | -0.3333 | E | 0.6458 | D | 0.2451 | D | .3967 | E |
| 188. Lawton, Okla. | 0.6000 | E | 1.3730 | E | -0.6667 | E | 0.9792 | C | 0.4396 | C | .5450 | E |
| 189. Lewiston-Auburn, Maine | 0.9571 | E | 2.8810 | B | -0.3333 | E | -0.3750 | E | 0.8716 | A | .8003 | E |
| 190. Lexington, Ky. | 1.9357 | B | 2.0516 | D | 0.0833 | C | 1.4167 | B | 0.3373 | D | 1.1649 | C |
| 191. Lima, Ohio | 1.7071 | C | 2.7579 | C | -0.3750 | E | 0.3750 | D | 0.2131 | D | .9356 | D |
| 192. Lincoln, Neb. | 2.7571 | A | 2.8016 | C | 0.3750 | B | 2.1667 | A | 1.1356 | A | 1.8472 | A |
| 193. Lubbock, Texas | 2.0214 | B | 2.2857 | D | -0.3333 | E | 1.4583 | B | 0.5378 | C | 1.1940 | C |
| 194. Lynchburg, Va. | 2.0429 | B | 2.1548 | D | 0.1667 | C | 0.0625 | E | -0.0461 | E | .8762 | D |
| 195. Manchester, N. H. | 2.0571 | B | 3.3532 | A | 0.7083 | A | 0.4583 | D | 0.9797 | A | 1.5113 | B |
| 196. Mansfield, Ohio | 2.0214 | B | 2.6071 | C | -0.0417 | D | 0.4375 | D | 0.3511 | D | 1.0751 | D |
| 197. McAllen-Pharr-Edinburg, Texas | 0.5071 | E | 1.3413 | E | 0.0417 | D | 0.5208 | D | 0.0489 | E | .4920 | E |
| 198. Meriden, Conn. | 1.9429 | B | 3.3532 | A | 1.0417 | A | 0.5167 | D | 0.4795 | C | 1.4468 | B |

# TABLE 18 (Concluded)

## QUALITY OF LIFE INDEXES AND RATINGS IN SMALL SMSA'S

| SMSA | Economic Value | Economic Rating | Political Value | Political Rating | Environmental Value | Environmental Rating | Health and Education Value | Health and Education Rating | Social Value | Social Rating | Overall Value | Overall Rating |
|---|---|---|---|---|---|---|---|---|---|---|---|---|
| 199. Midland, Texas | 2.7143 | A | 2.9484 | B | -0.4583 | E | 1.9583 | A | 0.6024 | B | 1.5530 | B |
| 200. Modesto, Calif. | 1.7929 | C | 2.8690 | B | 0.3333 | B | 0.8750 | D | 0.1461 | E | 1.2033 | C |
| 201. Monroe, La. | 1.1571 | D | 1.8333 | E | -0.1667 | D | 0.7500 | D | 0.2938 | D | .7735 | E |
| 202. Muncie, Ind. | 2.3286 | B | 3.1706 | B | 0.4167 | B | 1.1042 | C | 0.2443 | D | 1.4529 | B |
| 203. Muskegon-Muskegon Heights, Mich. | 1.7857 | C | 3.4127 | A | 0.5000 | B | 1.0417 | C | 0.4360 | C | 1.4352 | B |
| 204. Nashua, N. H. | 1.6857 | C | 3.0833 | B | -0.2083 | D | 1.1458 | C | 0.5257 | C | 1.2464 | C |
| 205. New Bedford, Mass. | 1.0500 | E | 2.9563 | B | -0.0833 | D | 0.0417 | E | 0.0599 | E | .8049 | E |
| 206. New Britain, Conn. | 1.7786 | C | 2.6190 | C | -0.0833 | D | 0.8542 | D | 0.6735 | B | 1.1684 | C |
| 207. Norwalk, Conn. | 2.6214 | A | 3.0476 | B | 0.0000 | D | 2.0417 | A | 0.8007 | B | 1.7023 | A |
| 208. Odessa, Texas | 2.3714 | B | 2.2143 | D | -0.0833 | D | 1.0208 | C | 0.7754 | B | 1.2597 | C |
| 209. Ogden, Utah | 1.6143 | C | 2.4960 | A | 0.4167 | B | 2.4167 | A | 0.6713 | B | 1.7230 | A |
| 210. Owensboro, Ky. | 1.7000 | C | 2.2302 | D | -0.0833 | D | 1.5625 | B | 0.2863 | D | 1.1391 | C |
| 211. Petersburg-Colonial Heights, Va. | 1.0571 | E | 2.3333 | D | 0.0833 | C | 0.6875 | D | 0.1233 | E | .8569 | D |
| 212. Pine Bluff, Ark. | 0.6929 | E | 1.3214 | E | 0.2917 | B | 0.0208 | E | -0.1229 | E | .4408 | E |
| 213. Pittsfield, Mass. | 1.8429 | C | 3.6627 | A | 0.9167 | A | 0.7708 | D | 0.8211 | B | 1.6028 | A |
| 214. Portland, Maine | 1.7786 | C | 3.0079 | B | -0.0417 | D | 0.7917 | D | 0.6884 | B | 1.2450 | C |
| 215. Provo-Orem, Utah | 0.7071 | E | 2.5913 | C | 0.5000 | B | 2.2917 | A | 0.8749 | A | 1.3930 | B |
| 216. Pueblo, Colo. | 1.6429 | C | 3.3770 | A | 0.0417 | D | 1.2083 | C | 0.5784 | C | 1.3697 | B |
| 217. Racine, Wis. | 2.4214 | A | 3.0278 | B | 0.0833 | C | 1.0417 | C | 0.3585 | D | 1.3865 | B |
| 218. Reno, Nevada | 2.5071 | A | 2.6111 | C | 0.2083 | C | 1.7500 | B | 1.0046 | A | 1.6162 | A |
| 219. Roanoke, Va. | 2.5143 | A | 2.4365 | D | 0.1250 | C | 1.0625 | C | 0.4196 | C | 1.3116 | C |
| 220. Rochester, Minn. | 1.5571 | C | 3.0675 | B | 0.7500 | A | 2.6875 | A | 1.2354 | A | 1.8595 | A |
| 221. St. Joseph, Mo. | 2.2500 | B | 2.6865 | C | 0.6667 | A | 0.3958 | D | 0.8899 | A | 1.3778 | B |
| 222. Salem, Oregon | 2.2786 | B | 2.6905 | C | 0.8750 | A | 1.7083 | B | 0.4244 | C | 1.5954 | B |
| 223. San Angelo, Texas | 2.4214 | A | 2.1865 | D | 1.1667 | A | 1.2292 | C | 0.8204 | B | 1.5648 | B |
| 224. Savannah, Ga. | 0.9214 | E | 1.6429 | E | 0.2083 | C | 0.3125 | E | 0.1233 | E | .6417 | E |
| 225. Sherman-Denison, Texas | 2.2714 | B | 2.4643 | C | 0.1250 | C | 1.3958 | B | 0.5271 | C | 1.3567 | B |
| 226. Sioux City, Iowa-Nebr. | 1.7000 | C | 3.0913 | B | 0.5000 | B | 0.8333 | D | 0.6545 | B | 1.3558 | B |
| 227. Sioux Falls, S. Dak. | 1.8857 | C | 3.3889 | A | -0.1250 | D | 2.2917 | A | 1.0083 | A | 1.6899 | A |
| 228. Springfield, Ill. | 2.4643 | A | 3.0040 | B | 0.2083 | C | 0.9167 | C | 0.7625 | B | 1.4712 | B |
| 229. Springfield, Mo. | 2.4857 | A | 2.9444 | B | 0.1250 | C | 1.2083 | C | 0.7363 | B | 1.4999 | B |
| 230. Springfield, Ohio | 2.0143 | B | 2.4643 | C | -0.2083 | D | 0.8542 | D | 0.1460 | E | 1.0541 | D |
| 231. Steubenville-Weirton, Ohio-W. Va. | 2.0143 | B | 3.0873 | B | 0.1250 | C | 0.2292 | E | 0.0194 | E | 1.0950 | D |
| 232. Tallahassee, Fla. | 1.5286 | D | 2.7302 | C | 0.4583 | B | 2.4583 | A | 0.5683 | C | 1.5487 | B |
| 233. Terre Haute, Ind. | 2.2000 | B | 3.6111 | A | 0.0417 | D | 0.7083 | D | 0.3948 | D | 1.3912 | B |
| 234. Texarkana, Texas-Ark. | 1.9429 | B | 2.1825 | D | -0.4167 | E | 0.2917 | E | -0.2097 | E | .7581 | E |
| 235. Topeka, Kansas | 2.6857 | A | 3.2579 | B | -0.0417 | D | 2.0625 | A | 1.1026 | A | 1.8134 | A |
| 236. Tuscaloosa, Ala. | 0.7286 | E | 1.3214 | E | 0.1667 | C | 0.8333 | D | -0.0177 | E | .6065 | E |
| 237. Tyler, Texas | 2.7643 | A | 2.2540 | D | 0.8750 | A | 0.9167 | C | 0.4105 | C | 1.4441 | B |
| 238. Vineland-Millville-Bridgeton, N. J. | 0.8929 | E | 2.4881 | C | 0.0833 | C | 0.3125 | E | 0.2427 | D | .8039 | E |
| 239. Waco, Texas | 1.9786 | B | 2.1627 | D | 0.3750 | B | 0.4375 | D | 0.3823 | D | 1.0672 | D |
| 240. Waterloo, Iowa | 1.9357 | B | 3.0000 | B | 0.5833 | A | 1.5417 | B | 0.8065 | B | 1.5734 | B |
| 241. Wheeling, W. Va.-Ohio | 1.6786 | C | 3.3571 | A | -0.2917 | E | 0.3750 | D | 0.1664 | D | 1.0571 | D |
| 242. Wichita Falls, Texas | 2.3071 | B | 2.0357 | D | -0.0417 | D | 0.6250 | D | 0.6269 | B | 1.1106 | D |
| 243. Wilmington, N.C. | 0.9571 | E | 2.2500 | D | 0.2083 | C | 0.1250 | E | -0.1506 | E | .6780 | E |
| Mean ($\bar{x}$) = | 1.7372 | | 2.6293 | | 0.1592 | | 1.0932 | | 0.4957 | | 1.2214 | |
| Standard Deviation (s) = | 0.6491 | | 0.6464 | | 0.4026 | | 0.7368 | | 0.3451 | | .3778 | |

A = Outstanding ($\geq \bar{x} + s$)
B = Excellent ($\bar{x} + .28s \leq B < \bar{x} + s$)
C = Good ($\bar{x} - .28s < C < \bar{x} + .28s$)
D = Adequate ($\bar{x} - s < D \leq \bar{x} = .28s$)
E = Substandard ($\leq \bar{x} - s$)

Since both methods of the standardized and the adjusted standardized scores produced highly consistent rankings with the rank-order correlation coefficients higher than 0.95 in all but environmental quality of life components, only the adjusted standardized results are presented.

It should be noted that the summary tables include an overall quality of life rating. This composite index is simply the weighted average of the five individual components. The overall indexes are presented with a certain degree of hesitancy since any effort to describe the quality of life by a single measure may not be particularly informative and may, in fact, be misleading. Economists may employ the GNP to measure the flow of goods and services produced in any year; however, the quality of life is a stock concept which may only be approximated by a set of component indicators. It is our belief that only by looking below the surface--by analyzing the individual components and subcomponents-- is it possible to determine why a metropolitan area performed the way it did and what the particular areas of strength and weakness are.

The most important findings in this study and their implications are broadly delineated as follows:

1. Although it is normally expected that the levels of objectively measured quality of life vary from region to region and from component to component, it is very interesting to note that only five of the 243 SMSA's--three in the large group and two in the medium sized group-- showed exactly the same ratings for each of the five quality of life components. In other words, this finding implies that in this country there is neither a perfect region offering the best of all quality of life nor a worst region suffering substandard quality of life in all components. Some SMSA's rated high in one or more components but not in others; the reverse is also true. Two important implications are deduced from this observation. First, for policy decision makers, it indicates that there is (are) always an area (or areas) requiring special attention and extra effort in order to balance the overall satisfaction in our quality of life. This study identifies the relative weaknesses for each SMSA in terms of quality of life components or factors. Secondly, for social indicator students, it points out the difficulty of constructing a single index to reflect the overall quality of life or the social well-being for a specific region at a specific point in time. Quality of life is a notion for multidimensional concepts. Thus, at the present time it is not only theoretically controversial to consider a sole indicator for the overall social welfare, but it is also empirically difficult to single out an index for the multi- dimensional quality of life measurements, due to the lack of consensus in weighting among the quality of life components.

218

2.  This study covering all metropolitan areas found that although the Pacific, the East North Central, the Mountain, and the New England regions had relatively more SMSA's with outstanding and excellent ratings than the other regions, they also had substandard areas, though relatively fewer in number.  In contrast, the southern states did show relatively larger numbers of low rated SMSA's, but they also include some SMSA's with quality of life measures beyond the "adequate" or "good" category, e.g., West South Central and South Atlantic regions showed up fairly strong in the economic component.  In other words, the hypothesis is inconclusive with respect to this test of regional differential, and much less significant in this metropolitan study than in an earlier state study.  The implication of this is that, for urban policy to be efficient and effective, each SMSA must be examined independently and its priorities set individually.  The state data are usually insufficient, if not misleading for providing basic policy guidance for SMSA action programs.

3.  It has been frequently asserted that money cannot always buy happiness.[6]  In a like manner, many previous studies have argued that quality of life is not necessarily a direct function of income and material wealth, at least beyond a certain level of subsistence.  In the quality of life study for all states, for instance, we found that some states ranked fairly high in terms of quality of life ratings, but had relatively low personal income per capita.[7]  The findings of this metropolitan study tend to validate that conclusion in that SMSA's which had outstanding ratings in the economic component did not simultaneously have outstanding ratings in social, political, environmental, and health and education components.  Indeed, there are just as many, if not more, SMSA's with relatively high ratings in the other quality of life components but relatively low ratings in the economic components as the reversed combination.  The association between economic component ratings and other quality of life component ratings is also weaker among the large SMSA's than that among the medium and the small SMSA's.  The implication is that policies focusing on economic growth alone do not concomitantly guarantee the betterment of quality of life concerns, especially in the large SMSA's.

---

6/  For instance, see R. A. Easterlin, "Does Money Buy Happiness?" The Public Interest, 30 (Winter 1973).

7/  See Ben-chieh Liu, "Quality of Life:  Concept, Measure and Results," The American Journal of Economics and Sociology, Vol. 34, No. 1 (January 1975), pp. 1-13.

4.  Despite the generally weak relationship between the economic component and other quality of life components, the trade-off or inverse relationship, between economic development and environmental quality was highlighted in the large metropolitan areas, especially in the East North Central Region. This inverse relationship was not as evident in the medium and small SMSA's. To avoid the adverse impacts of economic growth on environment, or to alleviate the degree to which the trade-offs may occur, appropriate environmental protection policies and careful planning for the future seem to be timely for the medium and small SMSA's. The large SMSA's in the Pacific, the Mountain and the West South Central regions showed significantly better environmental quality than those in other regions.

5.  The conventional statement that political quality and economic attributes are bound hand in hand is not strongly supported by this study. There is a general, positive correlation between the two on a geographical basis if the country is divided into two parts, north and south. Politically, the SMSA's in the North rated relatively more favorable than those in the South. Proportionately more of the SMSA's surrounding the Great Lakes, in the Middle Atlantic, East North Central, and many in New England and the Pacific region are found to have outstanding political quality of life. Even though there is a general dividing line, the extent of quality variation among SMSA's, as measured by this study, is the smallest among the five quality of life components for all three SMSA size groups. The smallest quality variation implies that people in this democratic country enjoy on the whole, a relatively similar quality of public goods and services, regardless of their regional location.

6.  Most of the large and medium SMSA's in the Pacific region and many of the medium and small SMSA's in the West and East North Central regions showed either excellent or outstanding quality of life in health and education. Although there are only a dozen SMSA's in the Mountain states, more than one-half of them were ranked outstanding in the health and education component. The South Atlantic, Middle Atlantic and East South Central regions, on the other hand, lagged significantly in health and education quality as compared to other regions. This regional phenomenon is much more evident in the medium SMSA's than in the large and the small SMSA's.

This regional inequality pattern in terms of health and educational quality distribution deserves further attention. The coefficient of variation among the health and education indexes was more than twice as large as those among the economic, political and environmental indexes. The health and educational quality coefficient of variation among the large SMSA's (70.0 percent) is the highest among the three groups of cities. The coefficients for the medium and small sized groups are, respectively, 62.0 percent and 68.0 percent.

The high coefficient of variation implies that there exists an appreciable quality variation among the SMSA's as far as the health and education factors are concerned. This high variation in quality, compounded with the pattern of geographic concentration, suggests that there are serious problems of human resource development in certain sections of this country. Investments in human capital which bring about greater mobility, better health, and higher technological learning capability among individuals are therefore necessary if a national objective is to equalize the health and educational differentials both geographically and among individuals.

7. The regional inequality pattern observed for the health and education component is also prevalent in the social component. Figures 5 and 10 show an intensive concentration of high ratings in social quality of life in the West Coast and in the East and West North Central regions. For the small SMSA's, most of "A" and "B" ratings were displayed in the West North Central and the Mountain regions, except for a couple of SMSA's in New England which also demonstrated excellent or outstanding quality of life in social considerations. The concentration of substandard medium SMSA's in the South Atlantic and the East South Central regions is most striking, as shown in Figure 10.

In addition to the regional concentration phenomenon, the quality of life indexes in the social component also exhibited as significant variations as did those in the health and education component. The highest coefficient of variation of the indexes was found for the medium size SMSA's (71.0 percent); the small SMSA's were next with the coefficient being 70.0 percent, and for the large SMSA's the coefficient was relatively smaller (61.0 percent). As discussed earlier, the significant variations in quality and the unequal geographical distribution inevitably suggest the need for appropriate policies, both national and regional, to cope with those factors adversely affecting our social quality of life in the lagging areas.

In short, the findings in this study tend to indicate that the major disparities in quality of life are neither in the economic nor in the political component; rather, they are in social, health and education and to a lesser degree, in environmental concerns. The geographic differentials and apparent concentrations of adverse quality of life conditions present special problems which warrant targeted policies and actions.

8.   As noted earlier, the overall QOL indexes which were simply taken as the average of the component indexes are presented only for the satisfaction of general curiosity since it is well understood that the overall QOL production perceived by any individual is not necessarily a simple, linear-additive from the five components. Nevertheless, scientific knowledge so far is still unable to derive a social welfare or utility function on which a general consensus with respect to the variable definition, measurement and weighting scheme can be deduced. As a result, the overall indexes so developed serve as no more than a rough QOL comparison over regions in this country, and hopefully it may stimulate more profound, useful research in the area of social welfare measurements.

Given those words of caution, it may be of interest to note that most of the large outstanding SMSA's are in the North and the Pacific--Denver, Grand Rapids, Hartford, Milwaukee, Minneapolis/St. Paul, Portland, Rochester, Sacramento, Salt Lake City, San Diego, San Francisco/Oakland, San Jose, and Seattle/Everett, while most of the large substandard SMSA's are in the South--Birmingham, Greensboro/Winston-Salem/High Point, Jacksonville, Jersey City, Memphis, New Orleans, Norfolk/Portsmouth, Philadelphia, San Antonio, and Tampa/St. Petersburg.

For the medium SMSA's, the concentration pattern differs slightly from the large SMSA's with most of the outstanding SMSA's in the East North Central region--Ann Arbor (Michigan), Appleton/Oshkosh (Wisconsin), Des Moines (Iowa), Duluth/Superior, Eugene (Oregon), Fort Wayne (Indiana), Kalamazoo (Michigan),Lansing (Michigan), Madison (Wisconsin), Santa Barbara (California), South Bend (Indiana), Stamford (Connecticut), and Wichita (Kansas), and most of the substandard ones fall again in the South--Augusta (Georgia/South Carolina), Charleston (South Carolina), Chattanooga (Tennessee/Georgia), Columbia (South Carolina), Columbus (Georgia/Alabama), Fayetteville (North Carolina), Greenville (South Carolina), Huntington/Ashland (West Virginia/Kentucky/Ohio), Jackson (Mississippi), Macon (Georgia), Mobile (Alabama), Montogomery (Alabama), Pensacola (Florida), and Shreveport (Louisiana).

As far as the small SMSA's are concerned, the geographic distribution of the ratings tend to be less concentrated relative to the medium and the large SMSA's. However, there are more outstanding SMSA's in the East North Central than other regions and the substandard SMSA's are scattered in the country. The 14 outstanding SMSA's are Bristol (Connecticut), Danbury (Connecticut), Fargo/Moorhead (North Dakota/Minnesota), Green Bay (Wisconsin), La Crosse (Wisconsin), Lafayette/West Lafayette (Indiana), Lincoln (Nebraska), Norwalk (Connecticut), Ogden (Utah), Pittsfield (Massachusetts), Reno (Nevada), Rochester (Minnesota), Sioux Falls (South Dakota), and Topeka (Kansas), and the 13 substandard SMSA's are Albany (Georgia), Atlantic City (New Jersey), Biloxi/Gulfport (Mississippi), Brownsville/Harlingen/San Benito (Texas), Fall River (Massachusetts/Rhode Island), Fort Smith (Arkansas/Oklahoma), Gadsden (Alabama), Lafayette (Louisiana), Lake Charles (Louisiana), Laredo (Texas), Lawton (Oklahoma), Lewiston/Auburn (Maine), and McAllen/Pharr/Edinburg (Texas).

Figures 16, 17, and 18 show the geographical distributions of various ratings for the three groups of SMSA's.

This study represents a step forward in the social welfare arena because it theoretically developed a conceptual model for coping with the arguments in quality of life determination, and empirically employed the model to systematically quantify the varying elements of urban quality of life in the U.S. It also represents a monumental statistical task in collecting, organizing, analyzing and presenting the latest quality of life factors for all of the nation's metropolitan areas. The comprehensive data presented in the Appendix should be very useful to researchers and students interested in a variety of cross-metropolitan studies.

It is our hope that by describing the apparent weaknesses and strengths among the metropolitan areas, the findings will stimulate and aid decision makers at all levels in their efforts to improve the overall quality of life for all people in this country.

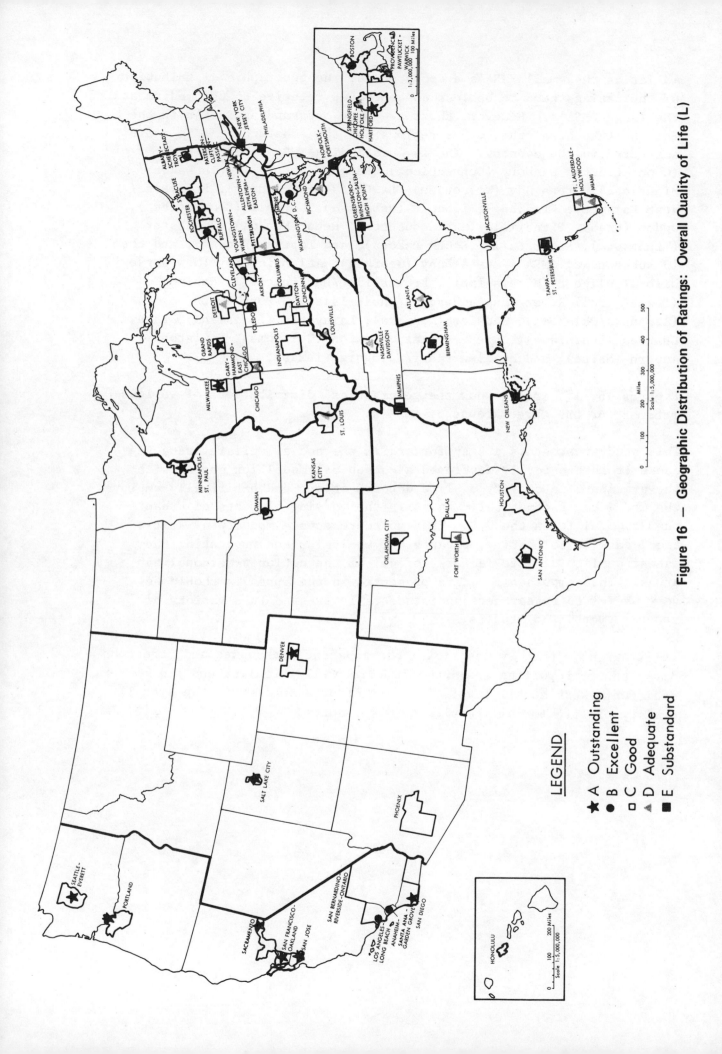

**Figure 16 — Geographic Distribution of Ratings: Overall Quality of Life (L)**

LEGEND

★ A Outstanding
● B Excellent
□ C Good
◀ D Adequate
■ E Substandard

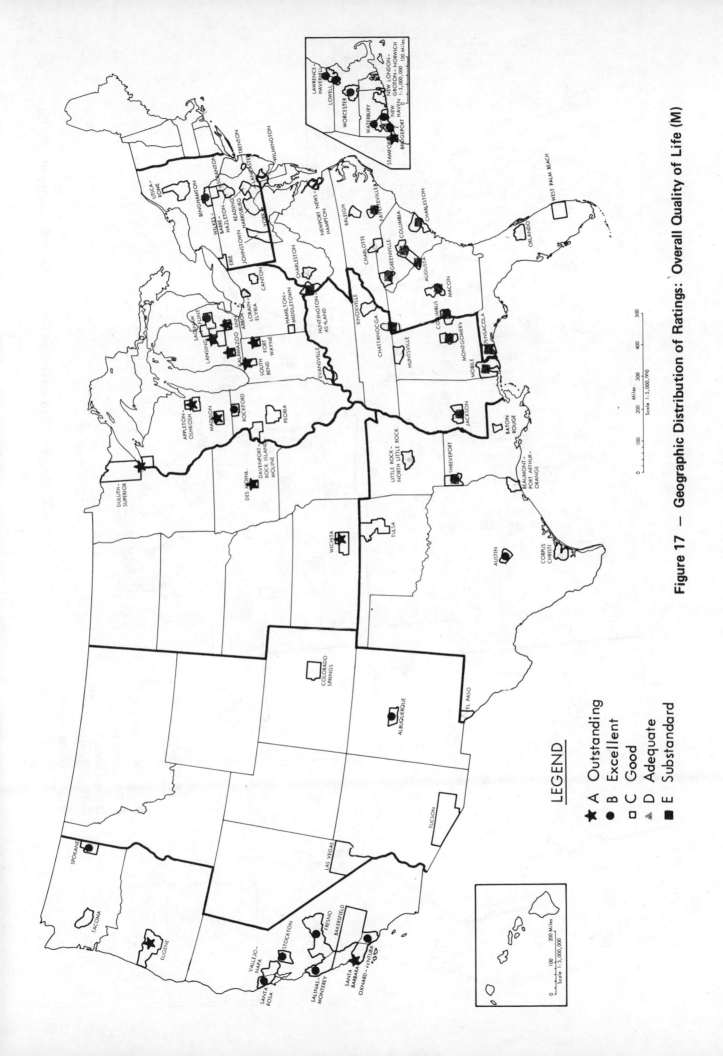

**Figure 17 — Geographic Distribution of Ratings: Overall Quality of Life (M)**

LEGEND

★ A Outstanding
● B Excellent
□ C Good
▲ D Adequate
■ E Substandard

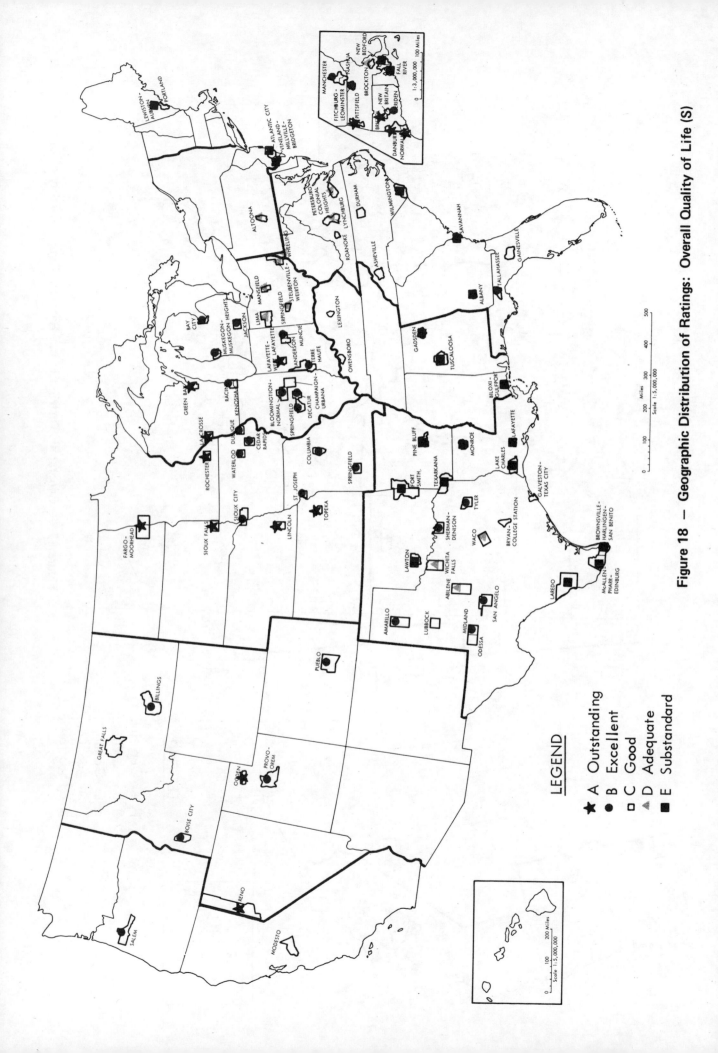

**Figure 18 — Geographic Distribution of Ratings: Overall Quality of Life (S)**

LEGEND

A Outstanding
B Excellent
C Good
D Adequate
E Substandard

There is certainly no guarantee at the present early stage in this type of social indicator research that decision makers, public or private, will pay much attention to this kind of information. As Professor Campbell commented about our earlier state study, "The kinds of data considered in this monograph do not tell us directly how society's problems are to be solved, but they may serve a useful purpose in showing where the problems exist."[8]

Other limitations of this study hinge upon the model development and methodology. Undoubtedly, the model can be further refined, and the quality of life components can be modified and quantified in finer detail. For instance, actual levels of noise pollution and solid waste generation should be used rather than employing approximate indicators in the environmental component. The weakest point of this study, needless to say, is its failure to account for the psychological aspects of the individual regarding his perceptions of quality of life. Attitudinal surveys on a variety of aspects of quality of life evaluation for the metropolitan areas should strengthen the reliability and enrich the substance of this type of study.

The indexes developed in this study are of use only when the SMSA's in the same size group are compared; intergroup comparisons among SMSA's with respect to their absolute index values are precluded and inferences can only be made on a relative basis. In order to be able to make intergroup comparisons between large and small, large and medium, and medium and small SMSA's, a similar study based on the U.S. means should probably be the next task. In order to complete the series of quality of life study for the U.S., another similar study for the rural counties is highly recommended.

The model used in this study was confined in its process of development to the requirements that it can be employed universally, and the study can be updated periodically. In other words, all factors selected in the model are expected to have consistent empirical data available in the future so that the quality of life status among metropolitan areas can be studied intertemporally and some comparative static analyses can be performed. As soon as new statistical data become available, the study should be repeated to shed light on changes in quality of life among regions and to evaluate the impacts of various policies on the level of quality of life over periods of time.

---

[8] See A. Campbell, "Measuring the Quality of Life," _Michigan Business Review_, 261 (January 1974), pp. 8-10.

Since there are definite regional concentration patterns and in-equalities in the quality of life, a more thorough investigation of input factors in the average or substandard regions should reveal the cause-effect relationships and suggest policy alternatives and feasible remedies.

Within a complicated society such as we have in the United States, the multidimensional quality of life indicators approach seems to be the desirable approach. As demonstrated in this study, the direct social, economic, political, and environmental impacts as well as the cross-impacts from various quality of life factors are taken into account. This multidimensional analysis tends to be the fundamental background for contemplating, evaluating, and creating relatively large investment projects or making critical policy decisions.

Specifically, at any stage of operation, it is the net change in the quality of life indicators which should be borne in mind, rather than the economic benefits and costs or other similar considerations alone. The externalities or social welfare elements cannot be accurately measured by the free market system or the price mechanism but are probably largely reflected in the social accounts through interaction of the social indicators.

Precisely what quality of life is, no one person can interpret for another; but the one who lives only for himself definitely could not enjoy the best. The best quality of life seems to grow out of harmonious relationships with others, based on attitudes of goodwill, tolerance, understanding and love. The joy of living may temporarily rest on present or past glory, but it is the immersion in planning for the future--the living ahead of one's time--which ensures permanently the flourising of the joy of life. In a commonwealth society, happiness does not come from doing what we like to do, but from liking what we have to do!

This appendix contains the data from which the five component ratings were made. Most of the statistics used in this study are combinations of two or more sets of data and are thus not readily available elsewhere. The original raw data, however, were based on a number of government documents. In addition, a Midwest Research Institute questionnaire was sent to each SMSA to gather certain cultural and sports information not found in published documents. A copy of this questionnaire is included at the end of the Appendix.

Tables showing all the factors used in the study constitute the major portion of the Appendix. Preceding the tables for each of the three sizes of SMSA's is a list of the three letter codes used for the SMSA's (e.g., AKR is the abbrevation for Akron, Ohio).

Collection of data for the SMSA's was limited in several instances, particularly for the smaller sized SMSA's and the SMSA's of the New England states. Since the SMSA's in New England are composed of towns rather than counties, whenever statistics were based upon county data the Standard Economic Areas (SEA's), which are composed of counties, were used if possible. Data for the smaller sized SMSA's (SMSA's with population of less than 200,000) were also limited, so certain factors were either eliminated, or similar, but not identical, information was used instead. Finally, estimations had to be made based on either state or neighboring SMSA data if no other data could be found. Any estimated data are marked in the tables by a black dot behind the figure.

Five charts show the data sources for each factor of the five components. Each factor is listed by its corresponding code in the variable charts in the text (e.g., the economic factor "personal income per capita" is listed as IA). In addition to the source, the year to which the data apply is also shown. To avoid numerous repetitions however, the source for the population figures used in calculating all "per capita" factors was omitted. The County and City Data Book, 1972, provides this information in Item 3. The four most frequently used sources for this study are publications of the Bureau of the Census:

1. <u>County and City Data Book, 1972</u>, hereafter referred to as C&C.

2. <u>Census of Population, 1970</u>, either referred to as COP or COP, US depending upon whether the state parts (COP) or the U.S. Summary (COP, US) was used.

3. <u>Census of Government</u>, 1967 (COG).

4. <u>Statistical Abstract of the United States</u> (SA).

# LIST A

## SMSA'S WITH POPULATION OVER 500,000 (L)

| | Code | SMSA | Population, 1970 (in 1,000) |
|---|---|---|---|
| 1 | AKR | Akron, Ohio | 679 |
| 2 | ALB | Albany-Schenectady-Troy, N.Y. | 721 |
| 3 | ALL | Allentown-Bethlehem-Easton, Pa.-N.J. | 544 |
| 4 | ANA | Anaheim-Santa Ana-Garden Grove, Calif. | 1,420 |
| 5 | ATL | Atlanta, Ga. | 1,390 |
| 6 | BAL | Baltimore, Md. | 2,071 |
| 7 | BIR | Birmingham, Ala. | 739 |
| 8 | BOS | Boston, Mass. | 2,754 |
| 9 | BUF | Buffalo, N.Y. | 1,349 |
| 10 | CHI | Chicago, Ill. | 6,979 |
| 11 | CIN | Cincinnati, Ohio-Ky.-Ind. | 1,385 |
| 12 | CLE | Cleveland, Ohio | 2,064 |
| 13 | COL | Columbus, Ohio | 916 |
| 14 | DAL | Dallas, Texas | 1,556 |
| 15 | DAY | Dayton, Ohio | 850 |
| 16 | DEN | Denver, Colo. | 1,228 |
| 17 | DET | Detroit, Mich. | 4,200 |
| 18 | FOR | Fort Lauderdale-Hollywood, Fla. | 620 |
| 19 | FOR | Fort Worth, Texas | 762 |
| 20 | GAR | Gary-Hammond-East Chicago, Ind. | 633 |
| 21 | GRA | Grand Rapids, Mich. | 539 |
| 22 | GRE | Greensboro-Winston-Salem-High Point, N.C. | 604 |
| 23 | HAR | Hartford, Conn. | 664 |
| 24 | HON | Honolulu, Hawaii | 629 |
| 25 | HOU | Houston, Texas | 1,985 |
| 26 | IND | Indianapolis, Ind. | 1,110 |
| 27 | JAC | Jacksonville, Fla. | 529 |
| 28 | JER | Jersey City, N.J. | 609 |
| 29 | KAN | Kansas City, Mo.-Kans. | 1,254 |
| 30 | LOS | Los Angeles-Long Beach, Calif. | 7,032 |

| | Code | SMSA | Population, 1970 (in 1,000) |
|---|---|---|---|
| 31 | LOU | Louisville, Ky.-Ind. | 827 |
| 32 | MEM | Memphis, Tenn.-Ark. | 770 |
| 33 | MIA | Miami, Fla. | 1,268 |
| 34 | MIL | Milwaukee, Wis. | 1,404 |
| 35 | MIN | Minneapolis-St. Paul, Minn. | 1,814 |
| 36 | NAS | Nashville-Davidson, Tenn. | 541 |
| 37 | NEW | New Orleans, La. | 1,046 |
| 38 | NEW | New York, N.Y. | 11,529 |
| 39 | NEW | Newark, N.J. | 1,857 |
| 40 | NOR | Norfolk-Portsmouth, Va. | 681 |
| 41 | OKL | Oklahoma City, Okla. | 641 |
| 42 | OMA | Omaha, Nebraska-Iowa | 540 |
| 43 | PAT | Paterson-Clifton-Passaic, N.J. | 1,359 |
| 44 | PHI | Philadelphia, Pa.-N.J. | 4,818 |
| 45 | PHO | Phoenix, Ariz. | 968 |
| 46 | PIT | Pittsburgh, Pa. | 2,401 |
| 47 | POR | Portland, Oreg.-Wash. | 1,009 |
| 48 | PRO | Providence-Pawtucket-Warwick, R.I.-Mass. | 911 |
| 49 | RIC | Richmond, Va. | 518 |
| 50 | ROC | Rochester, N.Y. | 883 |
| 51 | SAC | Sacramento, Calif. | 801 |
| 52 | STL | St. Louis, Mo.-Ill. | 2,363 |
| 53 | SAL | Salt Lake City, Utah | 558 |
| 54 | SAN | San Antonio, Texas | 864 |
| 55 | SAN | San Bernadino-Riverside-Ontario, Calif. | 1,143 |
| 56 | SAN | San Diego, Calif. | 1,358 |
| 57 | SAN | San Francisco-Oakland, Calif. | 3,110 |
| 58 | SAN | San Jose, Calif. | 1,065 |
| 59 | SEA | Seattle-Everett, Wash. | 1,422 |
| 60 | SPR | Springfield-Chicopee-Holyoke, Mass.-Conn. | 530 |
| 61 | SYR | Syracuse, N.Y. | 636 |
| 62 | TAM | Tampa-St. Petersburg, Fla. | 1,013 |
| 63 | TOL | Toledo, Ohio-Mich. | 693 |
| 64 | WAS | Washington, D.C.-Md.-Va. | 2,861 |
| 65 | YOU | Youngstown-Warren, Ohio | 536 |

# TABLE A-1

## BASIC STATISTICS OF ECONOMIC COMPONENT (L)

| | | Personal Income Per Capita IA | Savings Per Capita IB1 | Property Income/ Personal Income IB2 | % Owner-Occupied Housing Units IB3 | % Households With one or More Automobiles IB4 | Median Value, Owner Occupied Single Family Housing (in $1,000) IB5 | % of Families With Income Above Poverty Level IIA | Degree of Economic Concentration IIB |
|---|---|---|---|---|---|---|---|---|---|
| | US | 3139.00 | 702.00 | .14 | 62.90 | 82.50 | 17.10 | 89.30 | .00 |
| 1 | AKR | 3377.00 | 792.00 | .12 | 71.50 | 88.80 | 18.10 | 93.90 | .08 |
| 2 | ALB | 3429.00 | 302.00 | .13 | 63.60 | 82.00 | 18.80 | 93.90 | .15 |
| 3 | ALL | 3352.00 | 188.00 | .12 | 70.70 | 85.50 | 14.60 | 94.80 | .09 |
| 4 | ANA | 3899.00 | 290.00 | .14 | 64.70 | 94.50 | 27.30 | 94.80 | .04 |
| 5 | ATL | 3495.00 | 900.00 | .12 | 57.50 | 85.70 | 19.90 | 90.90 | .04 |
| 6 | BAL | 3332.00 | 865.00 | .11 | 58.20 | 76.70 | 15.20 | 91.50 | .06 |
| 7 | BIR | 2756.00 | 583.00 | .13 | 66.40 | 80.80 | 13.20 | 84.50 | .07 |
| 8 | BOS | 3713.00 | 375.00 | .15 | 52.60 | 76.00 | 23.80 | 93.90 | .11 |
| 9 | BUF | 3363.00 | 226.00 | .13 | 62.90 | 81.00 | 18.00 | 93.20 | .02 |
| 10 | CHI | 3827.00 | 1263.00 | .14 | 52.90 | 75.60 | 24.40 | 93.20 | .08 |
| 11 | CIN | 3215.00 | 1343.00 | .15 | 60.90 | 81.50 | 17.80 | 91.90 | .08 |
| 12 | CLE | 3675.00 | 1376.00 | .15 | 62.40 | 82.90 | 22.90 | 93.10 | .09 |
| 13 | COL | 3328.00 | 1002.00 | .12 | 59.10 | 85.70 | 18.60 | 92.40 | .11 |
| 14 | DAL | 3554.00 | 716.00 | .15 | 60.00 | 89.00 | 16.80 | 91.40 | .06 |
| 15 | DAY | 3522.00 | 990.00 | .12 | 66.40 | 88.80 | 18.60 | 94.00 | .11 |
| 16 | DEN | 3497.00 | 1142.00 | .13 | 61.50 | 88.70 | 19.10 | 93.20 | .16 |
| 17 | DET | 3739.00 | 524.00 | .11 | 72.10 | 85.20 | 19.60 | 93.50 | .11 |
| 18 | FOR | 3930.00 | 1782.00 | .26 | 72.80 | 91.60 | 20.00 | 92.10 | .12 |
| 19 | FOR | 3299.00 | 376.00 | .15 | 66.70 | 90.80 | 13.40 | 92.00 | .10 |
| 20 | GAR | 3185.00 | 777.00 | .10 | 68.10 | 84.70 | 17.30 | 93.00 | .07 |
| 21 | GRA | 3208.00 | 352.00 | .14 | 77.20 | 89.40 | 16.20 | 93.90 | .04 |
| 22 | GRE | 3065.00 | 890.00 | .12 | 66.20 | 85.10 | 15.40 | 89.70 | .15 |
| 23 | HAR | 3926.00 | 540.00 | .15 | 59.10 | 85.30 | 25.10 | 95.10 | .08 |
| 24 | HON | 3484.00 | 713.00 | .12 | 45.00 | 89.20 | 38.40 | 92.80 | .30 |
| 25 | HOU | 3314.00 | 580.00 | .14 | 60.10 | 88.40 | 14.70 | 90.20 | .01 |
| 26 | IND | 3425.00 | 610.00 | .12 | 65.40 | 86.00 | 14.90 | 93.50 | .02 |
| 27 | JAC | 2861.00 | 452.00 | .08 | 67.60 | 83.30 | 12.20 | 85.90 | .20 |
| 28 | JER | 3203.00 | 893.00 | .10 | 29.60 | 59.10 | 20.00 | 90.90 | .10 |
| 29 | KAN | 3477.00 | 653.00 | .12 | 65.70 | 85.50 | 16.00 | 93.10 | .09 |
| 30 | LOS | 3884.00 | 2097.00 | .13 | 48.50 | 84.90 | 24.30 | 91.80 | .11 |
| 31 | LOU | 3177.00 | 834.00 | .13 | 66.20 | 83.30 | 15.00 | 91.40 | .10 |
| 32 | MEM | 2710.00 | 453.00 | .11 | 57.30 | 78.70 | 14.30 | 83.20 | .06 |
| 33 | MIA | 3467.00 | 1948.00 | .17 | 54.10 | 80.40 | 19.10 | 89.10 | .01 |
| 34 | MIL | 3508.00 | 1329.00 | .14 | 59.80 | 82.20 | 21.50 | 94.30 | .01 |
| 35 | MIN | 3631.00 | 1160.00 | .14 | 65.20 | 85.80 | 21.60 | 95.40 | .02 |
| 36 | NAS | 3068.00 | 667.00 | .13 | 62.30 | 84.70 | 15.80 | 88.80 | .01 |
| 37 | NEW | 2814.00 | 849.00 | .10 | 51.40 | 73.60 | 20.10 | 83.60 | .15 |
| 38 | NEW | 3922.00 | 630.00 | .17 | 36.80 | 55.10 | 28.40 | 90.80 | .02 |
| 39 | NEW | 3962.00 | 1243.00 | .16 | 53.40 | 78.40 | 28.20 | 93.20 | .14 |
| 40 | NOR | 2820.00 | 509.00 | .10 | 54.90 | 81.40 | 17.00 | 86.60 | .18 |
| 41 | OKL | 3202.00 | 685.00 | .13 | 67.70 | 89.80 | 13.40 | 90.60 | .24 |
| 42 | OMA | 3178.00 | 745.00 | .12 | 63.30 | 84.80 | 15.00 | 93.20 | .20 |
| 43 | PAT | 4214.00 | 1159.00 | .13 | 62.70 | 86.10 | 30.50 | 95.70 | .10 |
| 44 | PHI | 3419.00 | 621.00 | .14 | 67.10 | 76.70 | 14.90 | 92.70 | .05 |
| 45 | PHO | 3226.00 | 647.00 | .13 | 66.30 | 91.20 | 17.60 | 91.10 | .10 |
| 46 | PIT | 3195.00 | 837.00 | .14 | 67.70 | 79.50 | 15.40 | 92.80 | .04 |
| 47 | POR | 3512.00 | 959.00 | .14 | 65.00 | 86.20 | 16.90 | 93.10 | .10 |
| 48 | PRO | 3161.00 | 396.00 | .13 | 59.00 | 84.00 | 18.20 | 92.20 | .01 |
| 49 | RIC | 3328.00 | 1108.00 | .14 | 61.40 | 80.10 | 17.50 | 91.10 | .09 |
| 50 | ROC | 3674.00 | 1839.00 | .14 | 66.80 | 85.70 | 20.80 | 94.80 | .01 |
| 51 | SAC | 3340.00 | 1051.00 | .11 | 61.60 | 89.40 | 18.20 | 91.40 | .41 |
| 52 | STL | 3331.00 | 1028.00 | .14 | 64.60 | 82.00 | 16.50 | 91.90 | .01 |
| 53 | SAL | 2922.00 | 738.00 | .13 | 67.40 | 90.00 | 18.30 | 92.50 | .28 |
| 54 | SAN | 2566.00 | 565.00 | .13 | 63.90 | 85.80 | 12.60 | 84.00 | .25 |
| 55 | SAN | 3046.00 | 634.00 | .15 | 63.90 | 90.50 | 17.80 | 89.70 | .12 |
| 56 | SAN | 3392.00 | 679.00 | .15 | 56.50 | 89.00 | 22.30 | 91.40 | .09 |
| 57 | SAN | 4122.00 | 1818.00 | .15 | 51.70 | 80.70 | 26.90 | 92.80 | .13 |
| 58 | SAN | 3855.00 | 891.00 | .11 | 61.70 | 93.10 | 27.30 | 94.40 | .11 |
| 59 | SEA | 3858.00 | 1373.00 | .14 | 64.90 | 86.60 | 21.60 | 94.80 | .07 |
| 60 | SPR | 3229.00 | 11.00 | .14 | 59.30 | 82.20 | 18.00 | 93.30 | .03 |
| 61 | SYR | 3246.00 | 222.00 | .12 | 65.80 | 84.40 | 17.50 | 92.90 | .06 |
| 62 | TAM | 3054.00 | 1452.00 | .19 | 74.50 | 85.00 | 13.50 | 89.30 | .09 |
| 63 | TOL | 3408.00 | 932.00 | .13 | 70.60 | 87.60 | 17.30 | 93.40 | .03 |
| 64 | WAS | 4273.00 | 997.00 | .11 | 46.00 | 81.50 | 28.20 | 93.90 | .45 |
| 65 | YOU | 3174.00 | 852.00 | .11 | 75.30 | 88.30 | 16.30 | 93.50 | .06 |

| | Value Added/ Worker in Manufacturing (in $1,000) IIC1 | Value of Construction/ Worker (in $1,000) IIC2 | Sales/ Employee in Retail Trade (in $1,000) IIC3 | Sales/ Employee in Wholesale Trade (in $1,000) IIC4 | Sales/ Employee in Selected Services (in $1,000) IIC5 | Total Bank Deposits Per Capita IID | Central City and Suburban Income Distribution IIE1 | Percent of Families With Income Below Pov. Level or Greater Than $15,000 IIE2 | Unemployment Rate IIF | Chamber of Commerce Employees/ 100,000 Pop. IIG |
|---|---|---|---|---|---|---|---|---|---|---|
| US | 13.50 | 4.30 | 33.00 | 130.60 | 15.80 | 2492.00 | .06 | 31.30 | 4.40 | NA |
| 1 AKR | 13.80 | 5.58 | 30.90 | 171.70 | 14.60 | 1861.00 | .04 | 30.60 | 4.40 | 2.10 |
| 2 ALB | 13.70 | 3.40 | 32.60 | 116.30 | 17.30 | 4413.00 | .04 | 29.80 | 3.30 | .80 |
| 3 ALL | 10.60 | 4.73 | 31.90 | 85.70 | 13.80 | 2284.00 | .02 | 24.10 | 2.30 | 1.30 |
| 4 ANA | 15.60 | 11.03 | 34.90 | 120.30 | 15.20 | 1281.00 | .06 | 38.90 | 5.40 | .60 |
| 5 ATL | 13.70 | 9.22 | 31.10 | 162.10 | 13.90 | 2189.00 | .08 | 35.20 | 3.00 | 3.70 |
| 6 BAL | 13.60 | 4.59 | 29.30 | 120.70 | 15.90 | 1711.00 | .12 | 32.90 | 3.50 | 1.50 |
| 7 BIR | 13.30 | 4.98 | 30.70 | 122.70 | 12.40 | 1668.00 | .06 | 29.80 | 4.20 | 4.30 |
| 8 BOS | 13.10 | 4.30 | 28.60 | 143.30 | 15.10 | 4803.00 | .08 | 36.20 | 3.50 | 1.30 |
| 9 BUF | 15.10 | 4.46 | 30.20 | 130.60 | 14.20 | 3356.00 | .08 | 28.20 | 4.80 | 2.70 |
| 10 CHI | 13.90 | 4.92 | 32.00 | 166.10 | 19.10 | 3398.00 | .10 | 38.80 | 3.50 | 1.40• |
| 11 CIN | 16.20 | 4.10 | 32.20 | 173.30 | 15.30 | 1625.00 | .02 | 30.00 | 3.80 | 3.60 |
| 12 CLE | 14.00 | 3.92 | 31.90 | 153.60 | 15.10 | 2936.00 | .16 | 35.10 | 3.50 | 1.60• |
| 13 COL | 14.00 | 6.66 | 32.60 | 114.90 | 12.50 | 1824.00 | .06 | 30.60 | 3.40 | 3.30 |
| 14 DAL | 12.20 | 6.72 | 30.90 | 155.20 | 14.30 | 3162.00 | -.06 | 32.90 | 3.00 | 2.10• |
| 15 DAY | 15.10 | 7.39 | 32.70 | 117.60 | 14.60 | 1260.00 | .08 | 32.90 | 3.80 | 3.40 |
| 16 DEN | 15.10 | 8.15 | 30.20 | 122.00 | 13.80 | 2006.00 | -.02 | 31.60 | 3.70 | 3.10 |
| 17 DET | 14.50 | 5.50 | 35.80 | 172.20 | 18.70 | 2610.00 | .10 | 39.50 | 5.70 | .90• |
| 18 FOR | 12.40 | 12.19 | 30.30 | 88.50 | 11.40 | 1886.00 | -.06 | 29.90 | 3.40 | 2.30 |
| 19 FOR | 15.30 | 4.94 | 31.60 | 111.00 | 14.90 | 1974.00 | .02 | 29.30 | 3.50 | 4.20• |
| 20 GAR | 17.20 | 4.38 | 33.70 | 110.70 | 13.80 | 1331.00 | .06 | 30.90 | 4.00 | 2.70• |
| 21 GRA | 14.40 | 4.79 | 32.60 | 103.70 | 14.50 | 2321.00 | .02 | 28.00 | 5.70 | 3.50 |
| 22 GRE | 14.10 | 5.00 | 31.10 | 106.50 | 12.60 | 1724.00 | -.06 | 27.40 | 2.80 | 3.00 |
| 23 HAR | 12.90 | 3.33 | 32.00 | 101.10 | 14.60 | 4084.00 | .10 | 38.00 | 2.90 | 9.00 |
| 24 HON | 12.90 | 7.83 | 25.60 | 84.90 | 13.90 | 2162.00 | -.14 | 42.20 | 3.00 | 3.70 |
| 25 HOU | 20.80 | 2.94 | 33.10 | 138.90 | 14.20 | 2681.00 | -.04 | 32.40 | 3.00 | 3.70 |
| 26 IND | 13.80 | 3.86 | 31.30 | 136.60 | 14.20 | 2829.00 | -.04 | 30.40 | 3.90 | 2.30 |
| 27 JAC | 14.30 | 4.46 | 29.50 | 175.20 | 13.60 | 2081.00 | .00 | 30.40 | 3.30 | 5.50 |
| 28 JER | 14.80 | 1.18 | 36.90 | 96.80 | 12.40 | 2611.00 | .04 | 28.50 | 4.70 | 2.30 |
| 29 KAN | 16.00 | 5.15 | 31.20 | 170.70 | 13.80 | 2491.00 | .02 | 29.90 | 3.30 | 2.20 |
| 30 LOS | 14.10 | 5.87 | 34.80 | 128.90 | 17.10 | 2198.00 | -.02 | 36.60 | 6.20 | 1.40 |
| 31 LOU | 18.90 | 5.69 | 30.70 | 122.60 | 12.90 | 2081.00 | .06 | 27.80 | 4.00 | 5.40 |
| 32 MEM | 13.90 | 5.96 | 31.20 | 181.60 | 12.70 | 2075.00 | -.06 | 33.00 | 4.80 | 5.80• |
| 33 MIA | 10.10 | 8.93 | 30.10 | 89.60 | 12.60 | 2228.00 | .08 | 32.40 | 3.70 | 1.50 |
| 34 MIL | 13.80 | 4.29 | 29.00 | 136.30 | 14.40 | 2316.00 | .08 | 31.80 | 3.50 | 3.70• |
| 35 MIN | 13.80 | 6.98 | 28.50 | 167.40 | 15.50 | 2591.00 | .04 | 33.20 | 3.20 | 1.90 |
| 36 NAS | 11.90 | 3.59 | 31.90 | 99.90 | 14.10 | 2681.00 | -.06 | 28.90 | 3.30 | 5.40• |
| 37 NEW | 15.50 | 5.02 | 29.40 | 129.20 | 11.40 | 2080.00 | .04 | 33.80 | 5.00 | 5.70 |
| 38 NEW | 12.00 | 3.89 | 32.40 | 183.80 | 24.20 | 8813.00 | .06 | 38.40 | 3.80 | .90• |
| 39 NEW | 15.40 | 2.45 | 34.00 | 142.30 | 12.80 | 3218.00 | .16 | 39.80 | 3.70 | 1.90• |
| 40 NOR | 12.10 | 4.81 | 28.10 | 91.80 | 11.80 | 1127.00 | .04 | 29.50 | 3.80 | 2.50 |
| 41 OKL | 11.00 | 8.07 | 31.10 | 120.70 | 13.10 | 2372.00 | -.02 | 28.40 | 3.20 | 4.70 |
| 42 OMA | 16.50 | 3.66 | 29.60 | 192.10 | 14.20 | 2014.00 | -.04 | 28.00 | 3.00 | 5.40 |
| 43 PAT | 13.10 | 3.02 | 35.90 | 150.90 | 15.90 | 2324.00 | .08 | 40.90 | 3.70 | .40 |
| 44 PHI | 13.90 | 2.91 | 32.20 | 135.50 | 15.30 | 2842.00 | .08 | 32.70 | 3.70 | .90 |
| 45 PHO | 13.00 | 9.52 | 32.50 | 96.50 | 11.60 | 2104.00 | -.02 | 30.20 | 3.90 | 4.60 |
| 46 PIT | 12.80 | 2.72 | 31.70 | 140.40 | 15.60 | 2807.00 | .02 | 26.00 | 4.30 | .80 |
| 47 POR | 13.90 | 7.55 | 33.20 | 164.20 | 15.00 | 2033.00 | .00 | 29.10 | 6.10 | 3.50• |
| 48 PRO | 11.10 | 2.89 | 31.20 | 91.80 | 14.20 | 2676.00 | .00 | 27.10 | 3.90 | 2.10 |
| 49 RIC | 15.10 | 3.32 | 31.00 | 150.20 | 11.70 | 2583.00 | .04 | 30.10 | 2.20 | 5.60• |
| 50 ROC | 20.00 | 4.14 | 33.30 | 114.40 | 17.10 | 2975.00 | .08 | 36.70 | 3.50 | 4.00 |
| 51 SAC | 21.50 | 9.00 | 34.90 | 96.40 | 14.10 | 2039.00 | -.02 | 32.60 | 7.20 | 5.60• |
| 52 STL | 14.10 | 3.94 | 32.20 | 157.50 | 15.90 | 2353.00 | .08 | 31.00 | 4.90 | 1.50 |
| 53 SAL | 17.50 | 7.19 | 28.90 | 100.00 | 13.50 | 1686.00 | -.06 | 27.10 | 4.60 | 1.30• |
| 54 SAN | 10.50 | 2.99 | 28.40 | 89.90 | 10.90 | 1592.00 | .08 | 30.90 | 4.20 | 4.40 |
| 55 SAN | 14.60 | 5.70 | 34.30 | 85.20 | 13.60 | 1225.00 | -.02 | 29.40 | 5.90 | .50 |
| 56 SAN | 12.70 | 11.52 | 34.30 | 90.00 | 14.40 | 1420.00 | -.06 | 31.80 | 6.30 | 2.70• |
| 57 SAN | 15.90 | 5.94 | 35.30 | 159.20 | 16.70 | 4258.00 | .02 | 39.30 | 5.80 | 1.20 |
| 58 SAN | 15.80 | 10.95 | 37.80 | 123.00 | 15.10 | 1650.00 | .10 | 40.50 | 5.80 | 1.80 |
| 59 SEA | 12.50 | 5.24 | 35.10 | 133.00 | 15.10 | 2350.00 | -.04 | 35.00 | 8.20 | 2.30 |
| 60 SPR | 12.90 | 3.79 | 28.90 | 88.40 | 12.40 | 3065.00 | .06 | 27.70 | 4.20 | 2.80 |
| 61 SYR | 13.70 | 2.11 | 32.70 | 140.20 | 14.20 | 2934.00 | .00 | 29.60 | 4.50 | 2.70 |
| 62 TAM | 11.90 | 7.63 | 29.70 | 93.20 | 13.00 | 2028.00 | .04 | 24.90 | 3.60 | 3.50 |
| 63 TOL | 15.50 | 4.24 | 32.90 | 109.40 | 12.70 | 1711.00 | .02 | 31.10 | 4.20 | 2.60 |
| 64 WAS | 13.10 | 5.96 | 31.80 | 131.70 | 13.60 | 1823.00 | .04 | 45.70 | 2.70 | .70 |
| 65 YOU | 15.20 | 4.72 | 31.10 | 110.60 | 14.00 | 1473.00 | .04 | 27.40 | 5.60 | 2.40 |

## TABLE A-2

## BASIC STATISTICS OF POLITICAL COMPONENT (L)

| | Local Sun. newspaper circ./ 1,000 pop. IA1 | % occupied housing with TV IA2 | Local radio stations/ 100,000 pop. IA3 | Pres. vote cast/voting age pop. IB | Avg. monthly earnings of teachers IIA1 | Avg. monthly earnings of other employees IIA2 | Entrance salary of patrolmen IIA3 | Entrance salary of firemen IIA4 | Total municipal employment/ 1,000 pop. IIA5 | Police protection employment/ 1,000 pop. IIA6 |
|---|---|---|---|---|---|---|---|---|---|---|
| US | 243.00 | 95.50 | .03 | 54.90 | 682.00 | 515.00 | 6848.00 | 6569.00 | 15.80 | 2.50 |
| 001 AKR | 752.00 | 97.40 | .88 | 61.20 | 747.00 | 487.00 | 8278.00 | 8278.00 | 9.50 | 1.70 |
| 002 ALB | 1248.00 | 97.20 | 1.10 | 79.70 | 763.00 | 392.00 | 6800.00 | 7055.00 | 25.30 | 2.40 |
| 003 ALL | 1185.00 | 97.00 | .91 | 58.00 | 637.00 | 434.00 | 6830.00 | 6839.00 | 9.00 | 1.70 |
| 004 ANA | 108.00 | 97.10 | .21 | 73.30 | 881.00 | 671.00 | 9162.00 | 8940.00 | 8.50 | 1.80 |
| 005 ATL | 1135.00 | 96.50 | 1.36 | 50.40 | 632.00 | 421.00 | 6760.00 | 6760.00 | 13.90 | 2.10 |
| 006 BAL | 687.00 | 97.00 | .77 | 51.80 | 741.00 | 474.00 | 7452.00 | 7824.00 | 42.80 | 5.00 |
| 007 BIR | 736.00 | 95.60 | 1.89 | 49.00 | 569.00 | 383.00 | 6900.00 • | 6758.00 • | 11.70 | 2.10 |
| 008 BOS | 1341.00 | 96.70 | .72 | 64.10 • | 700.00 | 558.00 | 8030.00 | 7718.00 | 35.70 | 4.40 |
| 009 BUF | 1338.00 | 97.60 | 1.33 | 64.60 | 850.00 | 516.00 | 7400.00 | 7400.00 | 26.20 | 3.50 |
| 010 CHI | 781.00 | 96.10 | .45 | 64.00 | 758.00 | 589.00 | 9840.00 | 9840.00 | 12.40 | 4.00 |
| 011 CIN | 664.00 | 97.00 | .93 | 58.50 | 703.00 | 457.00 | 8636.00 | 8636.00 | 27.90 | 2.50 |
| 012 CLE | 722.00 | 97.20 | .82 | 58.10 | 702.00 | 515.00 | 8432.00 | 8430.00 | 18.70 | 3.50 |
| 013 COL | 615.00 | 97.60 | 1.20 | 69.50 | 584.00 | 473.00 | 7436.00 | 7436.00 | 9.40 | 1.80 |
| 014 DAL | 669.00 | 95.90 | .96 | 50.10 | 561.00 | 424.00 | 6900.00 | 6900.00 | 11.80 | 2.30 |
| 015 DAY | 908.00 | 97.70 | 1.05 | 53.10 | 677.00 | 506.00 | 7748.00 | 7748.00 | 12.50 | 2.10 |
| 016 DEN | 1122.00 | 95.00 | 1.46 | 69.40 | 615.00 | 492.00 | 6600.00 | 6600.00 | 17.80 | 2.20 |
| 017 DET | 1000.00 | 97.30 | .52 | 62.60 | 887.00 | 602.00 | 8000.00 | 8000.00 | 17.90 | 3.60 |
| 018 FOR | 842.00 | 97.50 | .96 | 60.60 | 717.00 | 446.00 | 7816.00 | 7442.00 | 13.50 | 2.70 |
| 019 FOR | 708.00 | 96.40 | 1.04 | 50.10 | 580.00 | 407.00 | 7590.00 | 7032.00 | 9.30 | 1.80 |
| 020 GAR | 421.00 | 96.40 | .31 | 61.60 | 824.00 | 477.00 | 8620.00 | 7939.00 | 8.00 | 2.20 |
| 021 GRA | 680.00 | 96.70 | 2.22 | 70.10 | 630.00 | 542.00 | 8133.00 | 8083.00 | 9.10 | 1.80 |
| 022 GRE | 729.00 | 95.30 | .82 | 58.60 | 619.00 | 407.00 | 6612.00 | 5712.00 | 10.50 | 1.90 |
| 023 HAR | 2077.00 | 96.90 | 1.35 | 68.80 • | 786.00 | 568.00 | 7865.00 | 7865.00 | 34.30 | 2.90 |
| 024 HON | 544.00 | 94.40 | 2.86 | 52.00 | 0.00 | 612.00 | 6660.00 | 6660.00 | 20.10 | 3.70 |
| 025 HOU | 561.00 | 94.70 | 1.15 | 53.30 | 599.00 | 437.00 | 7800.00 | 7800.00 | 8.00 | 1.60 |
| 026 IND | 501.00 | 96.60 | 1.26 | 62.10 | 713.00 | 393.00 | 7000.00 | 6800.00 | 5.70 | 1.70 |
| 027 JAC | 335.00 | 95.80 | 2.83 | 59.10 | 578.00 | 462.00 | 6564.00 | 6252.00 | 11.60 | 1.40 |
| 028 JER | 325.00 | 96.40 | 0.00 | 52.90 | 672.00 | 441.00 | 10112.00 | 10045.00 | 15.50 | 3.70 |
| 029 KAN | 785.00 | 95.90 | .87 | 57.90 | 589.00 | 466.00 | 7218.00 | 7044.00 | 10.80 | 2.50 |
| 030 LOS | 631.00 | 95.00 | .36 | 59.40 | 965.00 | 694.00 | 9564.00 | 9564.00 | 14.70 | 2.90 |
| 031 LOU | 977.00 | 96.40 | 1.33 | 56.10 | 724.00 | 380.00 | 6900.00 • | 6548.00 | 17.30 | 2.40 |
| 032 MEM | 435.00 | 95.30 | 1.68 | 56.90 | 673.00 | 390.00 | 6740.00 | 6765.00 | 37.80 | 2.00 |
| 033 MIA | 1532.00 | 94.90 | 1.26 | 48.70 | 910.00 | 506.00 | 7836.00 | 7836.00 | 12.00 | 2.40 |
| 034 MIL | 748.00 | 97.30 | .99 | 62.50 | 766.00 | 575.00 | 7950.00 | 7950.00 | 13.40 | 3.10 |
| 035 MIN | 1461.00 | 96.80 | 1.15 | 76.90 | 783.00 | 572.00 | 9000.00 | 8580.00 | 11.80 | 2.00 |
| 036 NAS | 527.00 | 96.10 | 2.21 | 56.90 | 695.00 | 469.00 | 5970.00 | 5970.00 | 32.00 | 1.70 |
| 037 NEW | 509.00 | 95.90 | 1.62 | 46.00 | 711.00 | 398.00 | 6360.00 | 6360.00 | 16.20 | 2.70 |
| 038 NEW | 645.00 | 95.20 | .28 | 45.10 | 791.00 | 659.00 | 9499.00 | 9499.00 | 45.50 | 4.80 |
| 039 NEW | 2046.00 | 97.00 | .16 | 66.90 | 803.00 | 545.00 | 6900.00 • | 6758.00 • | 37.20 | 4.60 |
| 040 NOR | 674.00 | 95.90 | 1.61 | 39.70 | 650.00 | 360.00 | 6144.00 | 6144.00 | 28.90 | 2.10 |
| 041 OKL | 863.00 | 96.40 | 2.02 | 67.30 | 595.00 | 394.00 | 6450.00 | 6450.00 | 8.90 | 1.50 |
| 042 OMA | 845.00 | 96.00 | 1.29 | 57.20 | 644.00 | 568.00 | 7452.00 | 7452.00 | 6.20 | 1.70 |
| 043 PAT | 319.00 | 97.90 | 0.00 | 18.90 | 817.00 | 512.00 | 8350.00 | 8350.00 | 20.00 | 2.80 |
| 044 PHI | 814.00 | 97.00 | .51 | 61.70 | 824.00 | 526.00 | 8478.00 | 8478.00 | 17.40 | 4.10 |
| 045 PHO | 438.00 | 95.70 | 2.68 | 56.80 | 761.00 | 359.00 | 7224.00 | 6612.00 | 9.10 | 1.80 |
| 046 PIT | 1421.00 | 97.30 | .66 | 59.30 | 643.00 | 448.00 | 8463.00 | 8463.00 | 14.60 | 3.20 |
| 047 POR | 1069.00 | 94.70 | 2.08 | 68.90 | 687.00 | 577.00 | 8955.00 | 8091.00 | 11.30 | 2.40 |
| 048 PRO | 1174.00 | 97.70 | 1.20 | 67.10 • | 696.00 | 448.00 | 6932.00 | 7436.00 | 26.20 | 2.80 |
| 049 RIC | 788.00 | 95.50 | 2.31 | 55.60 | 673.00 | 451.00 | 7020.00 | 6396.00 | 32.60 | 2.30 |
| 050 ROC | 744.00 | 97.50 | 1.47 | 73.30 | 840.00 | 503.00 | 6864.00 | 6864.00 | 33.40 | 2.70 |
| 051 SAC | 1123.00 | 95.60 | 1.37 | 70.90 | 766.00 | 620.00 | 9306.00 | 9210.00 | 11.50 | 2.20 |
| 052 ST | 1396.00 | 95.60 | .97 | 61.10 | 704.00 | 469.00 | 7657.00 | 7463.00 | 20.30 | 4.50 |
| 053 SAL | 1059.00 | 96.30 | 2.68 | 81.40 | 611.00 | 466.00 | 6168.00 | 6168.00 | 9.70 | 2.40 |
| 054 SAN | 434.00 | 93.90 | 1.85 | 46.70 | 559.00 | 409.00 | 6708.00 | 6295.00 | 10.70 | 1.50 |
| 055 SAN | 760.00 | 95.10 | .43 | 57.90 | 900.00 | 596.00 | 8472.00 | 8700.00 | 10.80 | 2.30 |
| 056 SAN | 383.00 | 95.00 | 1.10 | 65.10 | 930.00 | 644.00 | 8988.00 | 8664.00 | 7.30 | 1.60 |
| 057 SAN | 920.00 | 93.00 | .80 | 64.30 | 840.00 | 681.00 | 10476.00 | 11196.00 | 27.90 | 3.10 |
| 058 SAN | 460.00 | 95.60 | .93 | 67.80 | 954.00 | 668.00 | 9546.00 | 9324.00 | 5.50 | 1.30 |
| 059 SEA | 1070.00 | 94.60 | 1.89 | 67.80 | 713.00 | 580.00 | 8856.00 | 8850.00 | 18.30 | 2.40 |
| 060 SPR | 734.00 | 96.70 | 1.50 | 60.10 • | 741.00 | 492.00 | 7100.00 | 7072.00 | 28.10 | 2.20 |
| 061 SYR | 1245.00 | 97.30 | 1.57 | 65.40 | 764.00 | 438.00 | 7030.00 | 7030.00 | 26.00 | 3.00 |
| 062 TAM | 664.00 | 95.80 | .88 | 61.90 | 725.00 | 388.00 | 7043.00 | 6321.00 | 14.90 | 2.50 |
| 063 TOL | 528.00 | 97.40 | 1.15 | 64.70 | 696.00 | 519.00 | 8070.00 | 8070.00 | 9.50 | 2.10 |
| 064 WAS | 1336.00 | 96.30 | .69 | 50.10 | 732.00 | 536.00 | 8000.00 | 8000.00 | 57.20 | 6.50 |
| 065 YOU | 1129.00 | 97.40 | .93 | 61.30 | 661.00 | 470.00 | 7186.00 | 7186.00 | 10.30 | 2.40 |

234

| | Fire protection employment/ 1,000 pop. IIA7 | Insured unemployment rates IIA8 | Violent Crime rate/ 100,000 pop. IIB1 | Property Crime rate/ 100,000 pop. IIB2 | Local govt. revenue per capita IIB3 | % of revenue from federal govt. IIB4 | Per capita local govt. expend. on public welfare IIC1 | Avg. monthly retiree benefits IIC2 | Avg. monthly payments to families w/dependent children IIC3 |
|---|---|---|---|---|---|---|---|---|---|
| US | 1.40 | 3.40 | 397.70 | 2431.80 | 329.86 | 2.70 | 11.88 | 132.00 | 190.00 |
| 001 AKR | 1.30 | 1.90 | 275.00 | 2434.20 | 288.02 | 1.20 | 18.03 | 148.00 | 156.00 |
| 002 ALB | 2.20 | 2.40 | 133.70 | 1518.20 | 344.60 | 2.80 | 30.57 | 141.00 | 211.00 |
| 003 ALL | 1.50 | 1.40 | 133.00 | 1457.10 | 240.99 | 2.10 | 9.81 | 142.00 | 215.00 |
| 004 ANA | 1.10 | 4.20 | 261.60 | 3678.70 | 425.18 | .90 | 20.54 | 139.00 | 203.00 |
| 005 ATL | 1.80 | 1.30 | 553.90 | 3470.70 | 301.42 | 2.10 | 3.88 | 126.00 | 102.00 |
| 006 BAL | 2.40 | 2.50 | 956.60 | 3095.10 | 352.05 | 2.00 | 33.25 | 136.00 | 162.00 |
| 007 BIR | 1.90 | 3.10 | 448.80 | 2421.70 | 228.04 | 2.30 | 1.99 | 130.00 | 59.00 |
| 008 BOS | 3.20 | 3.50 | 350.40 • | 3053.60• | 426.30 | 2.90 | 54.77 | 140.00• | 257.00• |
| 009 BUF | 2.70 | 3.70 | 300.80 | 2375.80 | 395.73 | 1.80 | 40.48 | 145.00 | 231.00 |
| 010 CHI | 1.50 | 1.80 | 671.70 | 2241.80 | 340.32 | 3.20 | 9.09 | 146.00 | 241.00 |
| 011 CIN | 2.00 | 1.70 | 297.60 | 2346.20 | 309.19 | 6.00 | 15.58 | 138.00 | 147.00 |
| 012 CLE | 1.80 | 2.00 | 483.00 | 2459.90 | 321.97 | 2.00 | 17.07 | 145.00 | 180.00 |
| 013 COL | 1.40 | 1.40 | 336.10 | 2912.80 | 259.97 | 2.70 | 18.82 | 133.00 | 159.00 |
| 014 DAL | 1.50 | .90 | 563.20 | 3117.10 | 262.27 | .90 | 1.37 | 127.00 | 117.00 |
| 015 DAY | 2.00 | 1.80 | 299.40 • | 2061.70• | 282.10 | 3.50 | 14.01 | 138.00 | 152.00 |
| 016 DEN | 1.50 | .80 | 493.60 | 4610.60 | 350.79 | 2.50 | 35.60 | 133.00 | 179.00 |
| 017 DET | 1.30 | 4.40 | 821.10 | 3997.10 | 378.83 | 2.50 | 10.35 | 150.00 | 244.00 |
| 018 FOR | 1.70 | 2.10 • | 465.10 | 3869.20 | 245.47 | 1.30 | 2.91 | 143.00 | 94.00 |
| 019 FOR | 1.40 | 2.00 | 272.00 | 2520.50 | 241.48 | 1.90 | 1.09 | 125.00 | 117.00 |
| 020 GAR | 1.60 | 1.50 | 516.70 | 3689.30 | 336.20 | 3.10 | 26.20 | 151.00 | 152.00 |
| 021 GRA | 1.50 | 4.40 | 231.80 | 2080.30 | 298.12 | .50 | 11.85 | 143.00 | 231.00 |
| 022 GRE | 1.50 | 1.40 | 602.00 | 2216.90 | 303.94 | 3.80 | 21.72 | 124.00 | 124.00 |
| 023 HAR | 3.10 | 3.00 | 238.20• | 2015.30• | 354.90 | 2.50 | 6.12 | 149.00• | 264.00• |
| 024 HON | 2.40 | 2.80 | 148.50 | 2978.00 | 188.45 | 5.40 | 0.00 | 131.00 | 298.00 |
| 025 HOU | 1.50 | .50 | 459.90 | 3109.70 | 256.75 | 1.20 | 1.16 | 132.00 | 123.00 |
| 026 IND | 1.20 | 1.90 | 292.80 | 2367.80 | 325.96 | .50 | 13.00 | 140.00 | 153.00 |
| 027 JAC | 1.10 | .90 | 799.10 | 3522.00 | 330.59 | 1.50 | .30 | 121.00 | 87.00 |
| 028 JER | 3.00 | 5.70 | 440.50 | 2696.00 | 318.70 | 2.60 | 20.03 | 143.00 | 267.00 |
| 029 KAN | 1.80 | 2.20 | 530.30 | 2889.10 | 303.61 | 3.70 | 5.92 | 137.00 | 134.00 |
| 030 LOS | 1.20 | 4.60 | 853.00 | 4578.70 | 514.00 | .70 | 59.78 | 136.00 | 222.00 |
| 031 LOU | 1.60 | 1.80 | 340.00 | 2703.10 | 275.36 | 8.00 | 6.05 | 133.00 | 128.00 |
| 032 MEM | 2.20 | 1.50 | 512.80 | 3538.60 | 389.79 | 1.40 | .69 | 118.00 | 107.00 |
| 033 MIA | 2.10 | 2.90 | 869.30 | 4282.10 | 344.55 | 5.20 | 3.11 | 135.00 | 104.00 |
| 034 MIL | 1.50 | 2.20 | 138.60 | 2111.80 | 407.36 | 1.00 | 25.09 | 146.00 | 272.00 |
| 035 MIN | 1.30 | 1.70 | 325.30 | 3172.30 | 385.46 | 1.80 | 48.03 | 140.00 | 259.00 |
| 036 NAS | 1.30 | 1.30 | 557.20 | 2735.40 | 321.94 | 5.40 | 1.86 | 121.00 | 106.00 |
| 037 NEW | 1.60 | 2.50 | 658.90 | 3275.10 | 245.74 | 5.50 | .66 | 127.00 | 96.00 |
| 038 NEW | 1.80 | 3.20 | 1357.10 | 3737.10 | 633.53 | 2.10 | 70.87 | 146.00 | 248.00 |
| 039 NEW | 2.80 | 3.60 | 638.90 | 3064.20 | 343.85 | 3.00 | 31.90 | 147.00 | 275.00 |
| 040 NOR | 1.40 | 1.20 | 544.80 | 2809.30 | 273.78 | 6.80 | 18.32 | 120.00 | 193.00 |
| 041 OKL | 1.70 | 1.50 | 319.90 | 2766.50 | 273.70 | 5.80 | 1.05 | 127.00 | 144.00 |
| 042 OMA | 1.30 | 1.30 | 372.20 | 2751.50 | 407.66 | 2.90 | 15.10 | 135.00 | 164.00 |
| 043 PAT | 2.30 | 4.40 | 282.90 | 2240.90 | 280.81 | 1.10 | 12.43 | 147.00 | 264.00 |
| 044 PHI | 1.60 | 2.60 | 441.10 | 2146.90 | 273.35 | 4.60 | 9.16 | 142.00 | 255.00 |
| 045 PHO | .90 | 4.10 | 550.90 | 4101.10 | 394.02 | 2.80 | .05 | 137.00 | 129.00 |
| 046 PIT | 2.20 | 2.40 | 284.40 | 1603.70 | 279.69 | 4.80 | 2.57 | 148.00 | 237.00 |
| 047 POR | 1.90 | 4.20 | 427.20 | 3931.80 | 331.16 | 1.80 | 1.39 | 136.00 | 176.00 |
| 048 PRO | 2.60 | 4.70 | 264.70 • | 3133.50 • | 251.76 | 4.40 | 9.92 | 136.00• | 230.00• |
| 049 RIC | 2.10 | .40 | 565.20 | 3019.40 | 271.85 | 1.60 | 25.16 | 133.00 | 189.00 |
| 050 ROC | 2.40 | 2.60 | 145.00 | 1905.00 | 426.09 | 2.00 | 32.50 | 146.00 | 269.00 |
| 051 SAC | 1.70 | 6.20 | 366.70 | 4048.90 | 527.17 | 2.40 | 66.33 | 129.00 | 226.00 |
| 052 ST | 1.90 | 3.30 | 559.50 | 3027.60 | 278.49 | 2.40 | 2.26 | 139.00 | 152.00 |
| 053 SAL | 1.50 | 2.50 | 243.80 | 3197.00 | 280.83 | 3.60 | .10 | 139.00 | 181.00 |
| 054 SAN | 1.00 | 1.40 | 419.40 | 3141.80 | 262.24 | 8.30 | .45 | 115.00 | 122.00 |
| 055 SAN | 1.80 | 4.80 | 421.20 | 3967.10 | 479.00 | 2.20 | 67.37 | 132.00 | 226.00 |
| 056 SAN | .90 | 4.70 | 266.20 | 3083.80 | 425.37 | 4.80 | 42.41 | 133.00 | 222.00 |
| 057 SAN | 2.50 | 3.90 | 643.00 | 4362.80 | 554.82 | 2.20 | 62.29 | 141.00 | 226.00 |
| 058 SAN | 1.10 | 4.50 | 271.50 | 3464.70 | 484.95 | 2.20 | 50.85 | 136.00 | 227.00 |
| 059 SEA | 1.90 | 8.40 | 317.30 | 3554.60 | 408.41 | 2.80 | .08 | 142.00 | 230.00 |
| 060 SPR | 2.80 | 4.60 | 281.80 • | 3418.00 • | 340.23 | 2.40 | 40.16 | 138.00 • | 228.00• |
| 061 SYR | 2.50 | 3.40 | 146.40 | 1529.50 | 395.19 | 2.50 | 40.86 | 143.00 | 231.00 |
| 062 TAM | 2.20 | 1.60 | 566.50 | 3415.50 | 293.39 | 2.60 | 3.96 | 133.00 | 89.00 |
| 063 TOL | 1.50 | 2.60 | 323.30 | 2587.20 | 279.19 | 1.90 | 15.83 | 148.00 | 161.00 |
| 064 WAS | 2.00 | .90 | 669.30 | 2811.00 | 396.46 | 17.40 | 19.52 | 126.00 | 191.00 |
| 065 YOU | 1.90 | 3.30 | 277.70 | 1788.10 | 239.55 | 1.50 | 11.96 | 148.00 | 156.00 |

## TABLE A-3

## BASIC STATISTICS OF ENVIRONMENTAL COMPONENT (L)

| | Mean Level for Total Suspended Particulates IA1 | Mean Level for Sulfur Dioxide IA2 | Mean Annual Inversion Frequency IB1 | % of Housing Units Dilapidated IB2 | Park and Recreation Acres/ 1,000 pop. IB3 | Pop. Density in Central City IC1 | Motor Vehicle Registrations/ 1,000 Pop. IC2 | Motorcycle Registrations/ 1,000 Pop. IC3 | Solid Waste Generated by Manufacturing ID | Water Pollution Index IE |
|---|---|---|---|---|---|---|---|---|---|---|
| 1 AKR | 79.85 | 48.00 | 27.50 | 1.50 | 34.80 | 5082.00 | 563.00 | 15.00 | 554.50 | 5.23 |
| 2 ALB | 117.85 | 51.00 | 32.50 | 3.60 | 16.00 | 6212.00 | 458.00 | 5.00 | 539.80 | 1.70 |
| 3 ALL | 86.93 | 13.00 | 27.50 | 3.10 | 19.80 | 5083.00 | 481.00• | 12.00• | 720.90 | .87 |
| 4 ANA | 103.34 | 13.00 | 37.50 | 1.60 | 5.90 | 5738.00 | 627.00 | 35.00 | 606.40 | .68 |
| 5 ATL | 81.63 | 14.00 | 37.50 | 2.20 | 5.60 | 3779.00 | 621.00 | 16.00 | 549.10 | 3.54 |
| 6 BAL | 147.39 | 48.00 | 22.50 | 1.80 | 4.80 | 11568.00 | 462.00 | 7.00 | 542.00 | 7.14 |
| 7 BIR | 182.44 | 8.00 | 37.50 | 3.10 | 16.20 | 3785.00 | 588.00 | 15.00 | 553.30 | 3.52 |
| 8 HOS | 107.83 | 67.00 | 27.50 | 1.80 | 3.90 | 13936.00 | 481.00• | 10.00• | 465.50 | 24.00 |
| 9 BUF | 125.71 | 6.00 | 22.50 | 2.30 | 5.10 | 11205.00 | 427.00 | 6.00 | 488.00 | 12.57 |
| 10 CHI | 154.77 | 58.00 | 32.50 | 1.80 | 4.70 | 15126.00 | 437.00 | 10.00 | 499.10 | 17.60 |
| 11 CIN | 105.76 | 19.00 | 32.50 | 2.00 | 11.90 | 5794.00 | 521.00 | 13.00 | 481.20 | 3.24 |
| 12 CLE | 200.86 | 113.00 | 22.50 | 2.20 | 6.50 | 9893.00 | 527.00 | 10.00 | 518.20 | 14.67 |
| 13 COL | 79.50 | 29.00 | 27.50 | 2.00 | 30.90 | 4009.00 | 533.00 | 14.00 | 561.70 | 9.78 |
| 14 DAL | 102.37 | 5.00 | 27.50 | 2.30 | 17.70 | 3179.00 | 631.00 | 19.00 | 653.90 | 2.15 |
| 15 DAY | 113.91 | 32.00 | 27.50 | 1.90 | 12.90 | 6360.00 | 580.00 | 16.00 | 494.60 | 14.27 |
| 16 DEN | 152.47 | 8.00 | 37.50 | 1.40 | 48.10 | 5406.00 | 681.00 | 24.00 | 567.90 | 1.47 |
| 17 DET | 152.85 | 59.00 | 32.50 | 1.10 | 13.10 | 10953.00 | 510.00 | 17.00 | 525.90 | 31.06 |
| 18 FOR | 61.80• | 15.00• | 12.50 | 2.20 | 3.80 | 4506.00 | 747.00 | 22.00 | 1049.90 | 13.20 |
| 19 FOR | 90.36 | 4.00 | 27.50 | 2.40 | 11.70 | 1919.00 | 655.00 | 24.00 | 610.80 | 3.30 |
| 20 GAR | 105.13 | 38.00 | 32.50 | 2.20 | 21.40 | 4212.00 | 482.00 | 13.00 | 436.20 | 2.81 |
| 21 GRA | 74.54 | 13.00 | 32.50 | 1.50 | 9.10 | 4402.00 | 542.00 | 26.00 | 473.50 | .80 |
| 22 GRE | 86.58 | 8.00 | 42.50 | 2.20 | 3.20 | 2401.00 | 652.00 | 16.00• | 491.30 | 2.92 |
| 23 HAR | 73.97 | 26.00• | 27.50 | 3.80 | 11.00 | 9081.00 | 566.00• | 10.00• | 439.90 | 5.56 |
| 24 HON | 74.82 | 13.00 | 27.50 | 7.70 | 9.30 | 3872.00 | 520.00 | 13.00 | 711.30 | 3.72 |
| 25 HOU | 88.73 | 4.00 | 22.50 | 3.40 | 6.10 | 3102.00 | 601.00 | 17.00 | 432.00 | 2.78 |
| 26 IND | 75.41• | 18.00 | 32.50 | 2.20 | 9.00 | 2113.00 | 544.00 | 17.00 | 531.10 | 22.00 |
| 27 JAC | 72.76 | 5.00 | 32.50 | 3.10 | 5.30 | 1505.00 | 603.00 | 21.00 | 543.80 | 2.13 |
| 28 JER | 83.37 | 48.00• | 22.50 | 5.20 | 1.00 | 17255.00 | 481.00• | 10.00• | 423.90 | .92 |
| 29 KAN | 86.25 | 28.00• | 37.50 | 1.90 | 11.60 | 2101.00 | 549.00 | 21.00• | 434.50 | .98 |
| 30 LOS | 118.49 | 24.00 | 37.50 | 3.30 | 4.80 | 6196.00 | 588.00 | 28.00 | 484.70 | .91 |
| 31 LOU | 146.71 | 41.00• | 32.50 | 1.80 | 7.10 | 6025.00 | 550.00 | 9.00 | 394.10 | 1.94 |
| 32 MEM | 93.28 | 11.00 | 37.50 | 2.70 | 27.10 | 3513.00 | 459.00 | 12.00 | 546.90 | 5.07 |
| 33 MIA | 61.80 | 15.00• | 7.50 | .90 | 447.20 | 9763.00 | 644.00 | 14.00 | 977.40 | 13.54 |
| 34 MIL | 91.63 | 22.00 | 32.50 | 1.70 | 11.10 | 7548.00 | 457.00 | 10.00 | 513.00 | 6.86 |
| 35 MIN | 75.78 | 6.00 | 32.50 | 1.20 | 14.20 | 6937.00 | 544.00 | 20.00 | 506.50 | 2.53 |
| 36 NAS | 123.87 | 11.00 | 37.50 | 1.70 | 20.20 | 1305.00 | 540.00 | 13.00 | 614.60 | 3.11 |
| 37 NEW | 79.82 | 15.00 | 27.50 | 3.80 | 1.10 | 6846.00 | 620.00• | 20.00• | 458.60 | 2.56 |
| 38 NEW | 94.78 | 48.00 | 22.50 | 3.10 | 7.60 | 26343.00 | 313.00 | 3.00 | 524.20 | 16.00 |
| 39 NEW | 133.85 | 48.00• | 27.50 | 4.50 | 5.00 | 16273.00 | 481.00• | 10.00• | 466.00 | 3.00 |
| 40 NOR | 113.46 | 30.00 | 22.50 | 2.40 | 8.70 | 5134.00 | 436.00 | 16.00• | 984.90 | .82 |
| 41 OKL | 66.66 | 4.00 | 37.50 | 1.90 | 9.40 | 1658.00 | 693.00 | 29.00 | 848.70 | 1.58 |
| 42 OMA | 140.65 | 9.00 | 37.50 | 1.70 | 15.20 | 4534.00 | 562.00 | 22.00 | 444.30 | 1.38 |
| 43 PAT | 55.60 | 48.00• | 27.50 | 3.50 | 5.40 | 12068.00 | 481.00• | 10.00• | 579.10 | 1.80 |
| 44 PHI | 77.55 | 45.00 | 27.50 | 3.50 | 6.80 | 15164.00 | 481.00• | 9.00 | 553.00 | 2.16 |
| 45 PHO | 188.32 | 8.00 | 42.50 | 2.30 | 116.30 | 2346.00 | 682.00 | 25.00 | 722.40 | 1.22 |
| 46 PIT | 134.66 | 63.00 | 32.50 | 3.90 | 8.30 | 9422.00 | 481.00• | 12.00 | 546.50 | 48.00 |
| 47 POR | 85.52 | 28.00 | 37.50 | 1.80 | 11.60 | 4294.00 | 588.00• | 28.00 | 572.40 | 1.42 |
| 48 PRO | 77.23 | 64.00 | 22.50 | 3.70 | 25.00 | 5430.00 | 538.00• | 13.00• | 695.60 | 2.13 |
| 49 RIC | 113.46• | 30.00• | 27.50 | 2.00 | 6.50 | 4140.00 | 534.00 | 16.00• | 452.70 | 2.35 |
| 50 ROC | 89.99 | 13.00 | 22.50 | 3.50 | 29.00 | 8072.00 | 468.00 | 7.00 | 362.40 | 3.18 |
| 51 SAC | 61.45 | 7.00• | 42.50 | 2.30 | 130.10 | 2712.00 | 622.00 | 35.00 | 349.90 | 1.33 |
| 52 STL | 119.50 | 28.00 | 37.50 | 2.70 | 2.30 | 10167.00 | 498.00 | 21.00• | 473.10 | 3.35 |
| 53 SAL | 94.76 | 10.00 | 42.50 | 1.50 | 10.40 | 2966.00 | 648.00 | 35.00 | 480.90 | 3.59 |
| 54 SAN | 53.66 | 4.00 | 27.50 | 2.80 | 3.20 | 3555.00 | 522.00 | 13.00 | 859.70 | 2.11 |
| 55 SAN | 135.19 | 6.00 | 42.50 | 2.80 | 45.10 | 2230.00 | 598.00 | 36.00 | 745.80 | 4.55 |
| 56 SAN | 58.60 | 6.00 | 37.50 | 2.30 | 18.90 | 3261.00 | 582.00 | 33.00 | 713.90 | .72 |
| 57 SAN | 59.83 | 7.00 | 37.50 | 2.20 | 23.10 | 10903.00 | 564.00 | 25.00 | 508.20 | 7.33 |
| 58 SAN | 59.83• | 5.00 | 37.50 | 1.70 | 25.50 | 3817.00 | 615.00 | 29.00 | 498.50 | 1.10 |
| 59 SEA | 57.47 | 30.00 | 27.50 | 1.80 | 9.20 | 5177.00 | 574.00 | 20.00 | 502.60 | 1.75 |
| 60 SPR | 64.29 | 32.00 | 27.50 | 4.00 | 15.90 | 3679.00 | 481.00• | 10.00• | 571.80 | 4.26 |
| 61 SYR | 110.76 | 17.00• | 27.50 | 3.30 | 7.40 | 7644.00 | 455.00 | 7.00 | 534.60 | 3.43 |
| 62 TAM | 75.40 | 15.00 | 27.50 | .40 | 14.00 | 3531.00 | 665.00 | 15.00 | 738.90 | 8.95 |
| 63 TOL | 123.95 | 15.00 | 27.50 | 2.00 | 5.50 | 4727.00 | 560.00 | 16.00 | 567.10 | 1.35 |
| 64 WAS | 89.75 | 40.00 | 27.50 | .70 | 30.00 | 12321.00 | 498.00 | 16.00• | 795.20 | 1.33 |
| 65 YOU | 110.37 | 38.00 | 27.50 | 1.60 | 41.50 | 4458.00 | 577.00 | 13.00 | 515.50 | 4.03 |

| | | Mean Annual Inversion Frequency IIA1 | Possible Annual Sunshine Days IIA2 | No. of Days With Thunder-Storms IIA3 | No. of Days With Temp. 90° or Above IIA4 | No. of Days With Temp. 32° or Below IIA5 | Park and Recreation Acres/1,000 Pop. IIB1 | Miles of Trails/ 100,000 Pop. IIB2 |
|---|---|---|---|---|---|---|---|---|
| 1 | AKR | 27.50 | 52.00 • | 40.00 | 10.00 | 105.00 | 34.80 | 148.70 |
| 2 | ALB | 32.50 | 54.00 | 24.00 | 17.00 | 127.00 | 16.00 | 22.10 |
| 3 | ALL | 27.50 | 57.00 • | 32.00 | 17.00 | 101.00 | 19.80 | 165.40 |
| 4 | ANA | 37.50 | 73.00 | 1.00 • | 21.00 • | 0.00 • | 5.90 | 51.40 |
| 5 | ATL | 37.50 | 61.00 | 58.00 | 16.00 | 55.00 | 5.60 | 56.80 |
| 6 | BAL | 22.50 | 58.00 | 24.00 | 27.00 | 84.00 | 4.80 | 11.50 |
| 7 | BIR | 37.50 | 58.00 | 84.00 | 30.00 | 58.00 | 16.20 | 18.90 |
| 8 | BOS | 27.50 | 60.00 | 17.00 | 19.00 | 76.00 | 3.90 | 89.60 |
| 9 | BUF | 22.50 | 53.00 | 36.00 | 2.00 | 111.00 | 5.10 | 42.20 |
| 10 | CHI | 32.50 | 57.00 | 47.00 | 29.00 | 100.00 | 4.70 | 34.10 |
| 11 | CIN | 32.50 | 54.00 | 58.00 | 18.00 | 94.00 | 11.90 | 119.80 |
| 12 | CLE | 22.50 | 52.00 | 40.00 | 11.00 | 94.00 | 6.50 | 112.40 |
| 13 | COL | 27.50 | 55.00 | 46.00 | 17.00 | 99.00 | 30.90 | 51.30 |
| 14 | DAL | 27.50 | 65.00 | 48.00 | 86.00 | 27.00 | 17.70 | 70.60 |
| 15 | DAY | 27.50 | 57.00 | 48.00 | 21.00 | 101.00 | 12.90 | 123.50 |
| 16 | DEN | 37.50 | 70.00 | 38.00 | 33.00 | 158.00 | 48.10 | 205.20 |
| 17 | DET | 32.50 | 54.00 | 33.00 | 14.00 | 113.00 | 13.10 | 51.10 |
| 18 | FOR | 12.50 | 73.00 • | 71.00 • | 13.00 • | 0.00 • | 3.80 | 9.60 |
| 19 | FOR | 27.50 | 65.00 | 52.00 | 82.00 | 20.00 | 11.70 | 68.20 |
| 20 | GAR | 32.50 | 57.00 | 47.00 • | 29.00 • | 100.00 • | 21.40 | 47.30 |
| 21 | GRA | 32.50 | 51.00 | 36.00 | 14.00 | 124.00 | 9.10 | 243.00 |
| 22 | GRE | 42.50 | 62.00 | 45.00 | 21.00 | 92.00 | 3.20 | 19.90 |
| 23 | HAR | 27.50 | 57.00 | 28.00 | 30.00 | 113.00 | 11.00 | 63.30 |
| 24 | HON | 27.50 | 69.00 | 8.00 | 10.00 | 0.00 | 9.30 | 9.50 |
| 25 | HOU | 22.50 | 59.00 | 72.00 | 68.00 | 24.00 | 6.10 | 27.70 |
| 26 | IND | 32.50 | 59.00 | 49.00 | 17.00 | 100.00 | 9.00 | 93.70 |
| 27 | JAC | 32.50 | 61.00 | 85.00 | 81.00 | 15.00 | 5.30 | 5.70 |
| 28 | JER | 22.50 | 59.00 • | 33.00 • | 18.00 • | 60.00 • | 1.00 | 3.30 |
| 29 | KAN | 37.50 | 64.00 | 54.00 | 26.00 | 90.00 | 11.60 | 56.60 |
| 30 | LOS | 37.50 | 73.00 | 1.00 | 21.00 | 0.00 | 4.80 | 156.30 |
| 31 | LOU | 32.50 | 58.00 | 52.00 | 27.00 | 77.00 | 7.10 | 72.60 |
| 32 | MEM | 37.50 | 65.00 | 62.00 | 57.00 | 51.00 | 27.10 | 80.50 |
| 33 | MIA | 7.50 | 73.00 • | 71.00 | 13.00 | 0.00 | 447.20 | 128.50 |
| 34 | MIL | 32.50 | 56.00 | 29.00 | 15.00 | 117.00 | 11.10 | 74.10 |
| 35 | MIN | 32.50 | 58.00 | 40.00 | 13.00 | 138.00 | 14.20 | 236.50 |
| 36 | NAS | 37.50 | 58.00 | 58.00 | 37.00 | 59.00 | 20.20 | 175.60 |
| 37 | NEW | 27.50 | 60.00 • | 75.00 | 70.00 | 18.00 | 1.10 | 3.80 |
| 38 | NEW | 22.50 | 59.00 | 33.00 | 18.00 | 60.00 | 7.60 | 30.00 |
| 39 | NEW | 27.50 | 59.00 • | 30.00 | 31.00 | 57.00 | 5.00 | 80.20 |
| 40 | NOR | 22.50 | 63.00 | 36.00 | 29.00 | 48.00 | 8.70 | 13.20 |
| 41 | OKL | 37.50 | 67.00 | 64.00 | 53.00 | 68.00 | 9.40 | 352.60 |
| 42 | OMA | 37.50 | 62.00 | 36.00 | 38.00 | 119.00 | 15.20 | 88.90 |
| 43 | PAT | 27.50 | 59.00 • | 30.00 • | 31.00 • | 57.00 • | 5.40 | 14.70 |
| 44 | PHI | 27.50 | 58.00 | 25.00 | 28.00 | 76.00 | 6.80 | 112.30 |
| 45 | PHO | 42.50 | 86.00 | 20.00 | 172.00 | 3.00 | 116.30 | 263.40 |
| 46 | PIT | 32.50 | 52.00 | 38.00 | 17.00 | 101.00 | 8.30 | 41.20 |
| 47 | POR | 37.50 | 47.00 | 7.00 | 18.00 | 27.00 | 11.60 | 659.10 |
| 48 | PRO | 22.50 | 57.00 | 14.00 | 17.00 | 95.00 | 25.00 | 199.80 |
| 49 | RIC | 27.50 | 60.00 | 40.00 | 32.00 | 80.00 | 6.50 | 54.10 |
| 50 | ROC | 22.50 | 55.00 | 25.00 | 25.00 | 106.00 | 29.00 | 231.00 |
| 51 | SAC | 42.50 | 79.00 | 8.00 | 78.00 | 14.00 | 130.10 | 1968.80 |
| 52 | STL | 37.50 | 59.00 | 52.00 | 42.00 | 88.00 | 2.30 | 37.70 |
| 53 | SAL | 42.50 | 69.00 | 41.00 | 58.00 | 116.00 | 10.40 | 363.80 |
| 54 | SAN | 27.50 | 62.00 | 37.00 | 96.00 | 29.00 | 3.20 | 67.10 |
| 55 | SAN | 42.50 | 73.00 • | 1.00 • | 21.00 • | 0.00 • | 45.10 | 955.40 |
| 56 | SAN | 37.50 | 67.00 | 3.00 | 5.00 | 0.00 | 18.90 | 134.80 |
| 57 | SAN | 37.50 | 67.00 • | 2.00 • | 6.00 • | 2.00 • | 23.10 | 206.10 |
| 58 | SAN | 37.50 | 67.00 | 2.00 | 6.00 | 2.00 | 25.50 | 200.00 |
| 59 | SEA | 27.50 | 48.00 | 4.00 | 1.00 | 17.00 | 9.20 | 643.50 |
| 60 | SPR | 27.50 | 57.00 • | 28.00 • | 30.00 • | 113.00 • | 15.90 | 701.90 |
| 61 | SYR | 27.50 | 51.00 | 33.00 | 15.00 | 111.00 | 7.40 | 51.90 |
| 62 | TAM | 27.50 | 66.00 | 91.00 | 96.00 | 6.00 | 14.00 | 28.60 |
| 63 | TOL | 27.50 | 57.00 | 47.00 | 16.00 | 122.00 | 5.50 | 14.40 |
| 64 | WAS | 27.50 | 57.00 | 26.00 | 37.00 | 103.00 | 30.00 | 197.10 |
| 65 | YOU | 27.50 | 52.00 • | 30.00 | 6.00 | 115.00 | 41.50 | 33.60 |

## TABLE A-4

## BASIC STATISTICS OF HEALTH AND EDUCATION COMPONENT (L)

| | Infant Mortality Rate/1,000 Live Births IA1 | Death Rate/ 1,000 pop. IA2 | Median Schools Years Completed IB1 | % of Persons, 25+, Completed 4 yrs, High Scool or more IB2 | % of Males 16-21, not High School Graduates IB3 | % of pop., 3-34 Enrolled in Schools IB4 |
|---|---|---|---|---|---|---|
| US | 21.20 | 9.50 | 12.10 | 52.30 | 15.20 | 54.30 |
| 1 AKR | 20.60 | 8.50 | 12.20 | 55.60 | 10.20 | 56.90 |
| 2 ALB | 19.90 | 10.90 | 12.20 | 56.10 | 8.90 | 58.10 |
| 3 ALL | 18.00 | 10.40 | 11.70 | 47.80 | 10.10 | 55.60 |
| 4 ANA | 20.60 | 6.00 | 12.60 | 70.50 | 12.10 | 57.70 |
| 5 ATL | 22.20 | 7.80 | 12.10 | 53.40 | 18.40 | 50.40 |
| 6 BAL | 23.00 | 9.40 | 11.30 | 44.60 | 19.60 | 53.80 |
| 7 BIR | 23.00 | 10.30 | 11.40 | 45.40 | 18.90 | 54.20 |
| 8 BOS | 20.10 • | 8.10 • | 12.40 | 64.40 | 9.90 | 57.60 |
| 9 BUF | 22.20 | 10.10 | 12.00 | 50.40 | 11.20 | 58.50 |
| 10 CHI | 24.40 | 9.70 | 12.10 | 53.90 | 16.10 | 54.60 |
| 11 CIN | 20.30 | 10.00 | 11.80 | 48.40 | 16.60 | 55.10 |
| 12 CLE | 21.40 | 9.60 | 12.10 | 54.60 | 12.70 | 55.30 |
| 13 COL | 20.60 | 8.20 | 12.30 | 60.70 | 11.20 | 54.40 |
| 14 DAL | 22.10 | 7.70 | 12.20 | 54.80 | 20.30 | 49.40 |
| 15 DAY | 19.80 | 7.80 | 12.20 | 56.20 | 12.00 | 53.90 |
| 16 DEN | 18.00 | 7.40 | 12.50 | 67.40 | 11.70 | 55.50 |
| 17 DET | 22.20 | 8.60 | 12.10 | 52.10 | 16.40 | 56.20 |
| 18 FOR | 23.00 | 11.10 | 12.20 | 55.40 | 18.00 | 54.00 |
| 19 FOR | 24.20 | 7.90 | 12.10 | 52.00 | 16.00 | 51.60 |
| 20 GAR | 26.80 | 8.20 | 12.00 | 50.00 | 13.90 | 56.40 |
| 21 GRA | 18.90 | 8.20 | 12.10 | 54.00 | 11.00 | 58.20 |
| 22 GRE | 28.20 | 8.40 | 11.10 | 42.40 | 18.20 | 52.30 |
| 23 HAR | 19.00 • | 8.50 • | 12.30 | 59.10 | 11.40 | 56.90 |
| 24 HON | 18.40 | 4.80 | 12.40 | 66.00 | 13.60 | 51.30 |
| 25 HOU | 23.10 | 7.00 | 12.10 | 51.70 | 19.90 | 51.80 |
| 26 IND. | 24.60 | 9.10 | 12.20 | 56.00 | 19.50 | 52.90 |
| 27 JAC | 22.10 | 9.00 | 12.00 | 51.60 | 17.70 | 50.00 |
| 28 JER | 23.50 | 12.20 | 10.20 | 36.30 | 18.00 | 50.70 |
| 29 KAN | 21.20 | 9.20 | 12.30 | 60.10 | 13.60 | 53.80 |
| 30 LOS | 18.90 | 9.00 | 12.40 | 62.00 | 13.30 | 54.80 |
| 31 LOU | 21.40 | 9.50 | 11.60 | 46.90 | 18.40 | 53.10 |
| 32 MEM | 23.40 | 9.10 | 11.90 | 49.20 | 17.80 | 52.60 |
| 33 MIA | 21.60 | 10.50 | 12.10 | 51.90 | 15.30 | 55.40 |
| 34 MIL | 19.20 | 8.90 | 12.20 | 56.80 | 10.70 | 56.80 |
| 35 MIN | 18.50 | 7.70 | 12.40 | 66.10 | 7.40 | 55.00 |
| 36 NAS | 21.60 | 9.10 | 11.90 | 49.00 | 19.30 | 52.30 |
| 37 NEW | 22.80 | 9.70 | 11.40 | 45.80 | 21.90 | 54.70 |
| 38 NEW | 21.60 | 10.50 | 12.10 | 51.80 | 15.60 | 53.10 |
| 39 NEW | 23.00 | 9.80 | 12.20 | 55.10 | 13.00 | 56.10 |
| 40 NOR | 22.90 | 7.70 | 11.80 | 48.30 | 18.40 | 45.30 |
| 41 OKL | 20.10 | 8.00 | 12.30 | 61.00 | 11.30 | 55.80 |
| 42 OMA | 20.10 | 8.30 | 12.30 | 62.70 | 10.50 | 55.60 |
| 43 PAT | 18.10 | 9.00 | 12.20 | 54.80 | 10.40 | 57.10 |
| 44 PHI | 23.40 | 10.10 | 12.00 | 50.60 | 15.10 | 55.20 |
| 45 PHO | 19.30 | 7.90 | 12.30 | 60.10 | 15.50 | 56.00 |
| 46 PIT | 22.00 | 10.70 | 12.10 | 53.40 | 8.10 | 57.60 |
| 47 POR | 19.00 | 9.90 | 12.40 | 62.90 | 10.30 | 55.30 |
| 48 PRO | 22.50 • | 10.50 • | 11.50 | 45.90 | 17.20 | 55.10 |
| 49 RIC | 25.50 | 9.80 | 11.70 | 47.10 | 16.70 | 53.50 |
| 50 ROC | 20.40 | 9.00 | 12.20 | 56.10 | 12.00 | 55.40 |
| 51 SAC | 20.30 | 7.80 | 12.40 | 65.10 | 7.10 | 59.40 |
| 52 STL | 21.80 | 10.00 | 11.70 | 48.00 | 14.30 | 56.20 |
| 53 SAL | 18.00 | 6.20 | 12.50 | 68.50 | 11.10 | 59.10 |
| 54 SAN | 23.00 | 7.50 | 11.50 | 46.80 | 15.40 | 52.30 |
| 55 SAN | 19.50 | 8.90 | 12.20 | 57.40 | 14.90 | 56.20 |
| 56 SAN | 19.90 | 7.50 | 12.40 | 65.30 | 19.60 | 50.80 |
| 57 SAN | 18.90 | 9.10 | 12.50 | 66.10 | 10.30 | 54.60 |
| 58 SAN | 15.50 | 5.70 | 12.60 | 69.00 | 8.50 | 58.10 |
| 59 SEA | 17.80 | 8.50 | 12.50 | 67.80 | 9.50 | 55.50 |
| 60 SPR | 21.20 • | 10.00 • | 12.10 | 53.50 | 13.60 | 57.50 |
| 61 SYR | 17.90 | 9.30 | 12.20 | 57.80 | 10.60 | 58.60 |
| 62 TAM | 24.50 | 13.70 | 12.00 | 51.40 | 17.00 | 55.10 |
| 63 TOL | 20.90 | 9.80 | 12.00 | 51.70 | 10.60 | 57.10 |
| 64 WAS | 19.90 | 7.00 | 12.60 | 68.50 | 14.20 | 51.50 |
| 65 YOU | 19.80 | 9.90 | 12.10 | 52.10 | 9.50 | 57.30 |

| | Dentists/ 100,000 pop. IIA1 | Hospital Beds/ 100,000 pop. IIA2 | Hospital Occupancy Rates IIA3 | Physicians/ 100,000 pop. IIA4 | Per Capita Local Gov't Expend. on Health IIA5 | Per Capita Local Gov't Expend. on Educ. IIB1 | % of Persons, 25+, Completed 4 yrs. College or more IIB2 |
|---|---|---|---|---|---|---|---|
| US | 59.50 | 414.90 | 79.80 | 153.80 | 2.96 | 145.69 | 10.70 |
| 1 AKR | 48.30 | 329.60 | 87.70 | 127.10 | 2.62 | 153.62 | 10.80 |
| 2 ALB | 58.50 | 447.60 | 87.30 | 213.10 | 4.96 | 188.46 | 12.60 |
| 3 ALL | 55.60 | 363.90 | 82.30 | 127.70 | 1.05 | 131.74 | 8.20 |
| 4 ANA | 62.20 | 258.80 | 71.00 | 164.80 | 2.30 | 213.39 | 15.80 |
| 5 ATL | 51.90 | 321.00 | 83.60 | 174.00 | 2.94 | 141.30 | 14.30 |
| 6 BAL | 47.10 | 377.70 | 79.60 | 243.40 | 5.45 | 147.36 | 10.30 |
| 7 BIR | 58.20 | 493.30 | 82.70 | 176.30 | 3.07 | 102.60 | 8.90 |
| 8 BOS | 82.50 • | 466.80 • | 80.00 • | 274.00 • | 2.92 | 130.66 | 15.80 |
| 9 BUF | 69.40 | 493.80 | 85.20 | 185.10 | 5.66 | 178.37 | 9.60 |
| 10 CHI | 67.50 | 436.90 | 84.10 | 176.60 | 2.51 | 127.76 | 11.70 |
| 11 CIN | 43.20 | 370.70 | 79.10 | 169.00 | 2.34 | 141.78 | 10.60 |
| 12 CLE | 66.90 | 418.30 | 83.70 | 209.40 | 2.22 | 139.72 | 10.90 |
| 13 COL | 69.40 | 352.00 | 88.80 | 174.60 | 2.06 | 127.60 | 14.00 |
| 14 DAL | 57.00 | 346.50 | 78.70 | 161.40 | 1.39 | 123.59 | 13.90 |
| 15 DAY | 43.50 | 332.40 | 84.20 | 107.60 | 2.19 | 141.51 | 11.00 |
| 16 DEN | 69.20 | 448.00 | 83.20 | 242.60 | 4.20 | 151.94 | 17.30 |
| 17 DET | 57.40 | 339.50 | 84.70 | 146.00 | 2.76 | 178.38 | 9.50 |
| 18 FOR | 80.10 | 341.90 | 82.30 | 185.60 | .69 | 119.33 | 9.70 |
| 19 FOR | 41.20 | 365.20 | 74.80 | 99.20 | 1.74 | 128.53 | 11.40 |
| 20 GAR | 41.20 | 336.10 | 81.50 | 83.80 | 1.77 | 175.52 | 6.90 |
| 21 GRA | 57.50 | 309.50 | 87.00 | 125.60 | 2.49 | 145.55 | 9.70 |
| 22 GRE | 41.60 | 415.10 | 81.30 | 145.10 | 3.23 | 130.77 | 11.00 |
| 23 HAR | 65.00 • | 383.50 • | 84.20 • | 221.10 • | 2.89 | 182.77 | 14.80 |
| 24 HON | 69.50 | 230.60 | 82.00 | 169.00 | 0.00 | 0.00 | 15.50 |
| 25 HOU | 52.40 | 431.20 | 78.80 | 159.50 | 2.76 | 142.56 | 13.90 |
| 26 IND | 63.00 | 412.70 | 83.70 | 166.20 | .18 | 156.00 | 10.40 |
| 27 JAC | 39.10 | 365.70 | 83.80 | 131.20 | 3.29 | 120.12 | 8.90 |
| 28 JER | 56.80 | 393.30 | 81.70 | 133.90 | 3.48 | 90.35 | 5.60 |
| 29 KAN | 64.50 | 470.00 | 83.70 | 158.00 | 2.13 | 135.28 | 11.60 |
| 30 LOS | 66.00 | 368.50 | 78.00 | 207.00 | 5.70 | 171.50 | 12.70 |
| 31 LOU | 53.20 | 418.80 | 84.50 | 152.30 | 3.18 | 144.58 | 9.00 |
| 32 MEM | 65.70 | 472.00 | 88.90 | 185.90 | 3.46 | 117.64 | 9.60 |
| 33 MIA | 66.50 | 458.90 | 81.70 | 266.40 | .49 | 135.42 | 10.80 |
| 34 MIL | 71.10 | 444.40 | 99.00 | 156.30 | 4.51 | 142.39 | 11.20 |
| 35 MIN | 79.60 | 547.20 | 77.00 | 176.80 | 2.47 | 174.67 | 14.80 |
| 36 NAS | 58.40 | 539.60 | 81.70 | 223.40 | 3.27 | 122.62 | 11.10 |
| 37 NEW | 55.70 | 507.20 | 76.40 | 223.00 | 2.61 | 111.71 | 11.30 |
| 38 NEW | 96.00 | 462.50 | 83.80 | 286.20 | 8.82 | 180.20 | 12.40 |
| 39 NEW | 78.90 | 436.90 | 84.30 | 198.10 | 3.27 | 148.95 | 14.20 |
| 40 NOR | 41.00 | 281.40 | 92.50 | 105.60 | 2.10 | 121.02 | 9.30 |
| 41 OKL | 47.60 | 405.80 | 78.70 | 183.50 | 1.31 | 119.36 | 13.60 |
| 42 OMA | 64.20 | 694.60 | 73.60 | 184.00 | 2.78 | 133.53 | 11.80 |
| 43 PAT | 74.40 | 336.50 | 79.40 | 163.00 | 2.74 | 139.42 | 13.20 |
| 44 PHI | 62.30 | 429.80 | 83.20 | 208.80 | 2.20 | 133.69 | 10.70 |
| 45 PHO | 57.20 | 351.20 | 78.70 | 183.70 | 3.53 | 168.15 | 12.80 |
| 46 PIT | 62.10 | 494.00 | 87.40 | 154.10 | 1.91 | 129.16 | 9.60 |
| 47 POR | 93.50 | 415.20 | 78.90 | 196.70 | 4.42 | 162.61 | 12.80 |
| 48 PRO | 55.20 • | 408.00 • | 86.40 • | 190.70 • | .88 | 118.37 | 8.80 |
| 49 RIC | 66.00 | 506.30 | 84.00 | 232.10 | .66 | 122.21 | 12.50 |
| 50 ROC | 68.90 | 290.60 | 86.80 | 216.40 | 8.23 | 225.75 | 13.30 |
| 51 SAC | 58.80 | 414.30 | 78.10 | 178.50 | 4.73 | 205.37 | 13.30 |
| 52 STL | 54.20 | 496.40 | 82.90 | 160.40 | 2.86 | 142.28 | 10.10 |
| 53 SAL | 65.10 | 334.10 | 80.20 | 197.60 | 2.58 | 173.95 | 15.00 |
| 54 SAN | 41.60 | 332.30 | 93.90 | 149.40 | 2.03 | 107.14 | 10.20 |
| 55 SAN | 55.40 | 364.40 | 71.10 | 155.90 | 3.72 | 214.28 | 9.80 |
| 56 SAN | 68.60 | 266.70 | 79.20 | 202.90 | 4.42 | 169.29 | 14.00 |
| 57 SAN | 89.90 | 444.30 | 76.50 | 272.40 | 7.83 | 187.01 | 16.80 |
| 58 SAN | 72.80 | 312.30 | 77.70 | 233.10 | 7.90 | 224.00 | 19.50 |
| 59 SEA | 84.70 | 318.70 | 77.20 | 206.10 | 3.01 | 179.35 | 15.90 |
| 60 SPR | 59.30 • | 437.50 • | 84.40 • | 131.70 • | 2.41 | 118.91 | 9.70 |
| 61 SYR | 54.60 | 291.40 | 76.10 | 186.00 | 6.13 | 196.85 | 13.20 |
| 62 TAM | 54.60 | 394.50 | 81.00 | 139.40 | 1.67 | 114.25 | 9.40 |
| 63 TOL | 46.20 | 464.80 | 88.80 | 139.90 | 3.87 | 142.99 | 8.90 |
| 64 WAS | 66.40 | 306.90 | 81.30 | 212.50 | 8.20 | 176.02 | 23.40 |
| 65 YOU | 47.00 | 366.80 | 84.60 | 125.40 | 1.14 | 121.40 | 6.90 |

239

## BASIC STATISTICS OF SOCIAL COMPONENT (L)

| | Labor Force Participation Rate (%) IA1 | % of Labor Force Employed IA2 | Mean Income Per Family Member IA3 | % of Children Under 18 Living With Both Parents IA4 | % of Married Couples Without Own Household IA5 | Per Capita Local Gov't Expend. on Education IB1 | % of Persons 25+, Completed 4 yrs High School or More IB2 | % of Males,16-64 Less Than 15 yrs School But Vocational Training IB3a | % of Females 16-64 Less Than 15 yrs School But Vocational Training IB3b | Motor Vehicle Registrations/ 1,000 pop. IC1a |
|---|---|---|---|---|---|---|---|---|---|---|
| US | 66.00 | 95.60 | 3092.00 | 82.70 | 1.30 | 145.69 | 52.30 | 28.70 | 21.90 | 551.00 |
| 1 AKR | 66.50 | 95.60 | 3361.00 | 86.00 | 1.20 | 153.62 | 55.60 | 30.70 | 22.70 | 563.00 |
| 2 ALB | 68.80 | 96.70 | 3402.00 | 86.90 | 1.10 | 188.46 | 56.10 | 30.30 | 24.60 | 455.00 |
| 3 ALL | 70.60 | 97.70 | 3357.00 | 88.40 | 1.70 | 131.74 | 47.80 | 29.50 | 19.30 | 481.00 • |
| 4 ANA | 87.40 | 94.60 | 3796.00 | 86.00 | 1.00 | 213.39 | 70.50 | 37.30 | 27.70 | 627.00 |
| 5 ATL | 70.40 | 97.00 | 3415.00 | 80.50 | 1.40 | 141.30 | 53.40 | 29.50 | 24.90 | 621.00 |
| 6 BAL | 66.70 | 96.50 | 3284.00 | 77.50 | 1.90 | 147.36 | 44.60 | 30.10 | 23.10 | 462.00 |
| 7 BIR | 63.90 | 95.80 | 2728.00 | 77.40 | 1.70 | 102.60 | 45.40 | 26.10 | 20.80 | 588.00 |
| 8 BOS | 70.90 | 96.50 | 3665.00 | 85.60 | 1.30 | 130.66 | 64.40 | 33.60 | 26.00 | 481.00 • |
| 9 BUF | 66.90 | 95.20 | 3315.00 | 85.30 | 1.10 | 178.37 | 50.40 | 31.60 | 25.20 | 427.00 |
| 10 CHI | 70.20 | 96.50 | 3730.00 | 82.00 | 1.30 | 127.76 | 53.90 | 31.90 | 24.90 | 437.00 |
| 11 CIN | 67.40 | 96.20 | 3174.00 | 84.20 | 1.00 | 141.78 | 48.40 | 27.90 | 23.00 | 521.00 |
| 12 CLE | 68.90 | 96.50 | 3609.00 | 83.80 | 1.20 | 139.72 | 54.60 | 31.70 | 25.20 | 527.00 |
| 13 COL | 67.40 | 96.60 | 3334.00 | 82.40 | 1.00 | 127.60 | 60.70 | 30.20 | 23.20 | 533.00 |
| 14 DAL | 72.60 | 97.00 | 3478.00 | 81.80 | 1.20 | 123.59 | 54.80 | 31.70 | 24.80 | 631.00 |
| 15 DAY | 66.90 | 96.20 | 3473.00 | 84.90 | .90 | 141.51 | 56.20 | 31.10 | 23.20 | 580.00 |
| 16 DEN | 60.10 | 96.30 | 3427.00 | 85.00 | 1.00 | 151.94 | 67.40 | 36.50 | 28.30 | 681.00 |
| 17 DET | 46.70 | 94.30 | 3657.00 | 83.10 | 1.50 | 178.38 | 52.10 | 30.80 | 22.90 | 510.00 |
| 18 FOR | 67.10 | 96.60 | 3855.00 | 81.60 | 1.50 | 119.33 | 55.40 | 35.30 | 24.40 | 747.00 |
| 19 FOR | 69.50 | 96.50 | 3252.00 | 84.00 | 1.10 | 128.53 | 52.00 | 34.60 | 25.20 | 655.00 |
| 20 GAR | 65.20 | 96.00 | 3118.00 | 84.60 | 1.30 | 175.52 | 50.00 | 27.40 | 20.90 | 482.00 |
| 21 GRA | 69.90 | 94.30 | 3184.00 | 87.50 | .60 | 145.55 | 54.00 | 26.10 | 19.50 | 542.00 |
| 22 GRE | 71.90 | 97.20 | 3071.00 | 81.00 | 1.60 | 130.77 | 42.40 | 24.90 | 20.00 | 652.00 |
| 23 HAR | 60.20 | 97.10 | 3860.00 | 85.90 | 1.00 | 182.77 | 59.10 | 35.10 | 26.40 | 566.00 • |
| 24 HON | 59.70 | 97.00 | 3391.00 | 83.70 | 4.70 | 0.00 | 66.00 | 35.50 | 27.80 | 520.00 |
| 25 HOU | 68.20 | 97.00 | 3218.00 | 82.80 | 1.20 | 142.56 | 51.70 | 30.60 | 25.80 | 601.00 |
| 26 IND | 70.50 | 96.10 | 3353.00 | 83.50 | .90 | 156.00 | 56.00 | 28.90 | 22.10 | 544.00 |
| 27 JAC | 61.60 | 96.70 | 2792.00 | 75.00 | 1.60 | 120.12 | 51.60 | 35.20 | 24.30 | 603.00 |
| 28 JER | 70.10 | 95.30 | 3094.00 | 79.40 | 1.40 | 90.35 | 36.30 | 28.90 | 22.40 | 481.00 • |
| 29 KAN | 72.30 | 96.70 | 3413.00 | 83.70 | .90 | 135.28 | 60.10 | 33.80 | 25.60 | 549.00 |
| 30 LOS | 69.00 | 93.80 | 3727.00 | 78.60 | 1.10 | 171.50 | 62.00 | 34.80 | 29.00 | 588.00 |
| 31 LOU | 68.40 | 96.00 | 3126.00 | 82.30 | 1.30 | 144.58 | 46.90 | 27.20 | 21.40 | 550.00 |
| 32 MEM | 64.50 | 95.20 | 2664.00 | 73.10 | 1.80 | 117.64 | 49.20 | 29.60 | 22.00 | 459.00 |
| 33 MIA | 69.60 | 96.30 | 3385.00 | 78.50 | 3.00 | 135.42 | 51.90 | 34.00 | 28.40 | 644.00 |
| 34 MIL | 72.00 | 96.50 | 3450.00 | 86.30 | .70 | 142.39 | 56.80 | 34.70 | 24.90 | 457.00 |
| 35 MIN | 73.80 | 96.80 | 3568.00 | 88.80 | .70 | 174.67 | 66.10 | 34.80 | 24.90 | 544.00 |
| 36 NAS | 68.70 | 96.70 | 3075.00 | 79.70 | 1.50 | 122.62 | 49.00 | 27.60 | 21.10 | 540.00 |
| 37 NEW | 63.00 | 95.00 | 2736.00 | 76.10 | 1.90 | 111.71 | 45.80 | 31.70 | 25.40 | 620.00 • |
| 38 NEW | 67.00 | 94.20 | 3788.00 | 78.80 | 1.50 | 180.20 | 51.80 | 30.10 | 26.40 | 313.00 |
| 39 NEW | 69.90 | 96.30 | 3900.00 | 81.50 | 1.50 | 148.95 | 55.10 | 30.80 | 25.80 | 481.00 • |
| 40 NOR | 49.70 | 96.20 | 2732.00 | 75.90 | 1.40 | 121.02 | 48.30 | 37.50 | 23.90 | 436.00 |
| 41 OKL | 69.10 | 96.80 | 3187.00 | 81.80 | .70 | 119.36 | 61.00 | 32.40 | 24.80 | 693.00 |
| 42 OMA | 68.50 | 97.00 | 3117.00 | 85.60 | .80 | 133.53 | 62.70 | 32.30 | 25.40 | 562.00 |
| 43 PAT | 71.10 | 96.30 | 4172.00 | 88.30 | 1.60 | 139.42 | 54.80 | 33.00 | 26.30 | 481.00 • |
| 44 PHI | 67.10 | 96.30 | 3380.00 | 81.50 | 1.80 | 133.69 | 50.60 | 33.50 | 25.70 | 481.00 • |
| 45 PHO | 66.10 | 96.10 | 3156.00 | 83.40 | 1.20 | 168.15 | 60.10 | 35.70 | 25.80 | 682.00 |
| 46 PIT | 62.20 | 95.70 | 3168.00 | 86.50 | 1.40 | 129.16 | 53.40 | 30.10 | 21.60 | 481.00 • |
| 47 POR | 70.30 | 93.90 | 3472.00 | 84.90 | .70 | 162.61 | 62.90 | 35.90 | 27.00 | 588.00 • |
| 48 PRO | 71.10 | 96.10 | 3149.00 | 86.10 | 1.20 | 118.37 | 45.90 | 29.00 | 20.90 | 538.00 • |
| 49 RIC | 70.10 | 97.80 | 3294.00 | 78.50 | 1.90 | 122.21 | 47.10 | 26.30 | 23.10 | 534.00 |
| 50 ROC | 70.70 | 96.50 | 3651.00 | 86.50 | 1.30 | 225.75 | 56.10 | 31.60 | 25.60 | 468.00 |
| 51 SAC | 62.90 | 92.80 | 3276.00 | 82.10 | .80 | 205.37 | 65.10 | 36.80 | 26.20 | 622.00 |
| 52 STL | 68.30 | 95.10 | 3285.00 | 82.10 | 1.00 | 142.28 | 48.00 | 30.90 | 23.40 | 498.00 |
| 53 SAL | 67.70 | 95.40 | 2887.00 | 87.90 | .80 | 173.95 | 68.50 | 34.00 | 24.90 | 648.00 |
| 54 SAN | 56.80 | 95.80 | 2484.00 | 80.30 | 2.00 | 107.14 | 46.80 | 31.30 | 22.90 | 522.00 |
| 55 SAN | 60.40 | 94.10 | 3006.00 | 81.60 | .90 | 214.28 | 57.40 | 34.90 | 25.20 | 598.00 |
| 56 SAN | 53.70 | 93.70 | 3330.00 | 79.40 | .90 | 169.29 | 65.30 | 39.70 | 28.60 | 582.00 |
| 57 SAN | 68.00 | 94.20 | 3969.00 | 80.40 | 1.00 | 187.01 | 66.10 | 36.50 | 29.90 | 564.00 |
| 58 SAN | 66.70 | 94.20 | 3750.00 | 85.80 | 1.10 | 224.00 | 69.00 | 37.00 | 26.80 | 615.60 |
| 59 SEA | 69.70 | 91.80 | 3759.00 | 85.60 | .80 | 179.35 | 67.80 | 38.80 | 28.90 | 574.00 |
| 60 SPR | 69.00 | 95.80 | 3241.00 | 85.10 | 1.00 | 118.91 | 53.50 | 34.50 | 25.70 | 481.00 • |
| 61 SYR | 67.20 | 95.50 | 3216.00 | 85.70 | 1.20 | 196.85 | 57.80 | 30.20 | 25.90 | 455.00 |
| 62 TAM | 64.70 | 96.40 | 3018.00 | 79.20 | 1.30 | 114.25 | 51.40 | 35.30 | 27.70 | 665.00 |
| 63 TOL | 68.10 | 95.80 | 3394.00 | 85.30 | 1.10 | 142.99 | 51.70 | 29.60 | 23.90 | 560.00 |
| 64 WAS | 67.10 | 97.30 | 4089.00 | 81.70 | 1.20 | 176.02 | 68.50 | 36.30 | 29.70 | 498.00 |
| 65 YOU | 65.70 | 94.60 | 3144.00 | 86.70 | 1.70 | 121.40 | 52.10 | 25.40 | 19.00 | 577.00 |

| | Motorcycle Registrations/ 1,000 pop. IC1b | % of Households With One or More Automobiles IC1c | Local Sunday Newspaper Circ./ 1,000 pop. IC2a | % Occupied Housing With TV IC2b | Local Radio Stations/ 100,000 pop. IC2c | Population Density In SMSA IC3a | % Pop. under 5 and 65+ in Central City IC3b | Negro to Total Pop. Median Family Income Adj. For Education IIA1 | Negro to Total Pop. Professional Emp. Adj. For Education IIA2 | Negro Males To Total Males Unemployment Rate Adj. For Education IIA3 |
|---|---|---|---|---|---|---|---|---|---|---|
| US | 16.00 | 82.50 | 243.00 | 95.50 | .03 | 360.00 | 18.30 | .78 | .07 | 2.08 |
| 1 AKR | 15.00 | 88.80 | 752.00 | 97.40 | .88 | 752.00 | 20.00 | .83 | .04 | 3.07 |
| 2 ALB | 5.00 | 82.00 | 1248.00 | 97.20 | 1.10 | 326.00 | 21.90 | .78 | .02 | 3.08 |
| 3 ALL | 12.00 | 85.50 | 1185.00 | 97.00 | .91 | 501.00 | 20.60 | .76 | .01 | 3.60 |
| 4 ANA | 35.00 | 94.50 | 108.00 | 97.10 | .21 | 1816.00 | 14.50 | .68 | .01 | 1.48 |
| 5 ATL | 16.00 | 85.70 | 1135.00 | 96.50 | 1.36 | 804.00 | 17.90 | .74 | .13 | 2.01 |
| 6 BAL | 7.00 | 76.70 | 687.00 | 97.00 | .77 | 917.00 | 19.00 | .83 | .15 | 2.21 |
| 7 BIR | 15.00 | 80.80 | 736.00 | 95.60 | 1.89 | 272.00 | 19.40 | .79 | .19 | 2.03 |
| 8 BOS | 10.00 | 76.00 | 1341.00 | 96.70 | .72 | 2791.00 | 20.60 | .63 | .02 | 1.99 |
| 9 BUF | 6.00 | 81.00 | 1338.00 | 97.60 | 1.33 | 849.00 | 21.30 | .81 | .04 | 2.63 |
| 10 CHI | 10.00 | 75.60 | 781.00 | 96.10 | .45 | 1877.00 | 19.00 | .75 | .09 | 2.39 |
| 11 CIN | 13.00 | 81.50 | 664.00 | 97.00 | .93 | 644.00 | 21.50 | .78 | .06 | 2.68 |
| 12 CLE | 10.00 | 82.90 | 722.00 | 97.20 | .82 | 1359.00 | 19.50 | .79 | .09 | 2.59 |
| 13 COL | 14.00 | 85.70 | 615.00 | 97.60 | 1.20 | 614.00 | 17.60 | .81 | .06 | 2.00 |
| 14 DAL | 19.00 | 89.00 | 669.00 | 95.90 | .96 | 345.00 | 17.10 | .69 | .07 | 2.19 |
| 15 DAY | 16.00 | 88.80 | 908.00 | 97.70 | 1.05 | 498.00 | 19.00 | .86 | .08 | 2.32 |
| 16 DEN | 24.00 | 88.70 | 1122.00 | 95.00 | 1.46 | 335.00 | 19.60 | .70 | .02 | 1.85 |
| 17 DET | 17.00 | 85.20 | 1000.00 | 97.30 | .52 | 2152.00 | 20.30 | .81 | .10 | 2.19 |
| 18 FOR | 22.00 | 91.60 | 842.00 | 97.50 | .96 | 509.00 | 24.60 | .91 | .09 | 2.11 |
| 19 FOR | 24.00 | 90.80 | 708.00 | 96.40 | 1.04 | 476.00 | 18.70 | .73 | .05 | 2.02 |
| 20 GAR | 13.00 | 84.70 | 421.00 | 96.40 | .31 | 675.00 | 16.80 | .88 | .13 | 1.72 |
| 21 GRA | 26.00 | 89.40 | 680.00 | 96.70 | 2.22 | 380.00 | 20.90 | .77 | .02 | 3.30 |
| 22 GRE | 16.00 | 85.10 | 729.00 | 95.30 | .82 | 274.00 | 15.70 | .74 | .13 | 2.12 |
| 23 HAR | 10.00 | 85.30 | 2077.00 | 96.90 | 1.35 | 988.00 | 20.30 | .72 | .04 | 2.29 |
| 24 HON | 13.00 | 89.20 | 544.00 | 94.40 | 2.86 | 1056.00 | 15.00 | .55 | .01 | 1.12 |
| 25 HOU | 17.00 | 88.40 | 561.00 | 94.70 | 1.15 | 316.00 | 15.90 | .73 | .10 | 2.03 |
| 26 IND | 17.00 | 86.00 | 501.00 | 96.60 | 1.26 | 361.00 | 17.70 | .84 | .07 | 3.10 |
| 27 JAC | 21.00 | 83.30 | 335.00 | 95.80 | 2.83 | 690.00 | 16.10 | .76 | .15 | 2.29 |
| 28 JER | 10.00 | 59.10 | 325.00 | 96.40 | 0.00 | 12963.00 | 19.60 | .76 | .05 | 1.30 |
| 29 KAN | 21.00 | 85.50 | 785.00 | 95.90 | .87 | 453.00 | 19.90 | .77 | .07 | 2.62 |
| 30 LOS | 28.00 | 84.90 | 631.00 | 95.00 | .36 | 1728.00 | 18.20 | .70 | .06 | 1.75 |
| 31 LOU | 9.00 | 83.30 | 977.00 | 96.40 | 1.33 | 910.00 | 20.10 | .75 | .07 | 2.23 |
| 32 MEM | 12.00 | 78.70 | 435.00 | 95.30 | 1.68 | 565.00 | 17.40 | .79 | .24 | 2.63 |
| 33 MIA | 14.00 | 80.40 | 1532.00 | 94.90 | 1.26 | 621.00 | 20.80 | .84 | .09 | 1.73 |
| 34 MIL | 10.00 | 82.20 | 748.00 | 97.30 | .99 | 964.00 | 19.70 | .78 | .03 | 3.13 |
| 35 MIN | 20.00 | 85.80 | 1461.00 | 96.80 | 1.15 | 860.00 | 22.40 | .68 | .01 | 2.13 |
| 36 NAS | 13.00 | 84.70 | 527.00 | 96.10 | 2.21 | 336.00 | 16.60 | .77 | .15 | 1.81 |
| 37 NEW | 20.00 | 73.60 | 509.00 | 95.90 | 1.62 | 532.00 | 19.10 | .64 | .15 | 2.24 |
| 38 NEW | 3.00 | 55.10 | 645.00 | 95.20 | .28 | 5415.00 | 19.80 | .75 | .10 | 1.65 |
| 39 NEW | 10.00 | 78.40 | 2046.00 | 97.00 | .16 | 2648.00 | 18.70 | .74 | .09 | 2.22 |
| 40 NOR | 16.00 | 81.40 | 674.00 | 95.90 | 1.61 | 998.00 | 15.20 | .85 | .18 | 2.11 |
| 41 OKL | 29.00 | 89.80 | 863.00 | 96.40 | 2.02 | 302.00 | 19.20 | .82 | .06 | 2.46 |
| 42 OMA | 22.00 | 84.80 | 845.00 | 96.00 | 1.29 | 351.00 | 19.00 | .68 | .04 | 2.99 |
| 43 PAT | 10.00 | 86.10 | 319.00 | 97.90 | 0.00 | 3190.00 | 21.40 | .71 | .03 | 2.38 |
| 44 PHI | 9.00 | 76.70 | 814.00 | 97.00 | .51 | 1356.00 | 19.80 | .78 | .09 | 2.27 |
| 45 PHO | 25.00 | 91.20 | 438.00 | 95.70 | 2.68 | 106.00 | 17.40 | .68 | .02 | 2.30 |
| 46 PIT | 12.00 | 79.50 | 1421.00 | 97.30 | .66 | 788.00 | 20.20 | .76 | .04 | 2.48 |
| 47 POR | 28.00 | 86.20 | 1069.00 | 94.70 | 2.08 | 276.00 | 21.80 | .74 | .01 | 2.08 |
| 48 PRO | 13.00 | 84.00 | 1174.00 | 97.70 | 1.20 | 1340.00 | 22.30 | .64 | .02 | 1.40 |
| 49 RIC | 16.00 | 80.10 | 788.00 | 95.50 | 2.31 | 433.00 | 18.90 | .80 | .14 | 2.58 |
| 50 ROC | 7.00 | 85.70 | 744.00 | 97.50 | 1.47 | 381.00 | 23.10 | .77 | .03 | 3.61 |
| 51 SAC | 35.00 | 89.40 | 1123.00 | 95.60 | 1.37 | 233.00 | 19.10 | .70 | .03 | 2.04 |
| 52 STL | 21.00 | 82.00 | 1396.00 | 95.60 | .97 | 574.00 | 22.70 | .76 | .10 | 2.72 |
| 53 SAL | 35.00 | 90.00 | 1059.00 | 96.30 | 2.68 | 526.00 | 22.10 | .67 | .01 | 2.01 |
| 54 SAN | 13.00 | 85.80 | 434.00 | 93.90 | 1.85 | 441.00 | 18.10 | .71 | .05 | 1.50 |
| 55 SAN | 36.00 | 90.50 | 760.00 | 95.10 | .43 | 42.00 | 16.40 | .72 | .03 | 1.87 |
| 56 SAN | 33.00 | 89.00 | 383.00 | 95.00 | 1.10 | 319.00 | 16.60 | .75 | .02 | 1.72 |
| 57 SAN | 25.00 | 80.70 | 920.00 | 93.00 | .80 | 1254.00 | 20.00 | .72 | .05 | 2.18 |
| 58 SAN | 29.00 | 93.10 | 460.00 | 95.60 | .93 | 819.00 | 16.00 | .87 | .01 | 1.41 |
| 59 SEA | 20.00 | 86.60 | 1070.00 | 94.60 | 1.89 | 336.00 | 19.70 | .80 | .02 | 1.65 |
| 60 SPR | 10.00 | 82.20 | 734.00 | 96.70 | 1.50 | 991.00 | 21.00 | .70 | .02 | 2.28 |
| 61 SYR | 7.00 | 84.40 | 1245.00 | 97.30 | 1.57 | 263.00 | 21.30 | .74 | .02 | 2.30 |
| 62 TAM | 15.00 | 85.00 | 664.00 | 95.80 | .88 | 777.00 | 20.00 | .86 | .06 | 2.07 |
| 63 TUL | 16.00 | 87.60 | 528.00 | 97.40 | 1.15 | 456.00 | 19.90 | .83 | .06 | 2.68 |
| 64 WAS | 16.00 | 81.50 | 1336.00 | 96.30 | .69 | 1216.00 | 17.30 | .74 | .14 | 1.85 |
| 65 YOU | 13.00 | 88.30 | 1129.00 | 97.40 | .93 | 524.00 | 20.20 | .88 | .04 | 2.75 |

| | Negro Females To Total Females Unemployment Rate Adj. For Education IIA4 | Male to Female Unemployment Rate Adj For Education IIB1 | Male to Female Professional Emp. Adj. For Education IIB2 | % Working Outside County of Residence IIC1 | Central City & Suburban Income Dist. IIC2 | Housing Segregation Index IIC3 | % Families With Income Above Poverty Level IIIA1 | % Occupied Housing With Plumbing IIIA2 | % Occupied Housing With 1.01 or More Persons Per Room IIIA3 | % Occupied Housing With Telephone IIIA4 |
|---|---|---|---|---|---|---|---|---|---|---|
| US | 1.79 | .75 | 1.49 | 17.80 | .06 | .27 | 89.30 | 94.50 | 8.00 | 87.30 |
| 1 AKR | 2.09 | .66 | 1.76 | 21.00 | .04 | 1.20 | 93.90 | 97.10 | 5.70 | 93.80 |
| 2 ALB | 1.30 | .94 | 1.67 | 26.90 | .04 | 1.32 | 93.90 | 96.60 | 4.20 | 92.80 |
| 3 ALL | 1.05 | .62 | 1.76 | 25.10 | .02 | .82 | 94.80 | 95.80 | 3.70 | 94.10 |
| 4 ANA | 1.52 | .66 | 2.16 | 25.00 | .06 | 1.37 | 94.80 | 99.50 | 5.90 | 93.30 |
| 5 ATL | 1.78 | .60 | 1.43 | 36.00 | .08 | 1.29 | 90.90 | 97.50 | 7.30 | 89.30 |
| 6 BAL | 1.67 | .70 | 1.62 | 34.90 | .12 | .96 | 91.50 | 97.70 | 6.70 | 87.80 |
| 7 BIR | 2.14 | .62 | 1.02 | 5.50 | .06 | .43 | 84.50 | 91.30 | 9.20 | 86.90 |
| 8 BOS | 1.67 | 1.00 | 1.56 | 31.00 | .08 | 2.58 | 93.90 | 97.30 | 5.40 | 92.50 |
| 9 BUF | 2.32 | .82 | 1.46 | 6.60 | .08 | 1.51 | 93.20 | 98.30 | 5.20 | 93.00 |
| 10 CHI | 1.99 | .73 | 1.63 | 10.80 | .10 | .85 | 93.20 | 97.60 | 8.00 | 82.40 |
| 11 CIN | 1.88 | .63 | 1.62 | 23.30 | .02 | 1.52 | 91.90 | 95.70 | 9.10 | 90.40 |
| 12 CLE | 1.82 | .80 | 1.67 | 11.10 | .16 | 1.38 | 93.10 | 98.50 | 5.30 | 92.80 |
| 13 COL | 1.58 | .86 | 1.55 | 5.60 | .06 | .60 | 92.40 | 97.50 | 5.80 | 92.30 |
| 14 DAL | 1.69 | .74 | 1.73 | 8.30 | -.06 | .57 | 91.40 | 97.80 | 8.40 | 86.40 |
| 15 DAY | 1.75 | .65 | 1.75 | 16.70 | .08 | 1.76 | 94.00 | 97.20 | 6.00 | 91.90 |
| 16 DEN | 1.56 | .92 | 1.67 | 35.80 | -.02 | 1.24 | 93.20 | 97.70 | 5.20 | 91.60 |
| 17 DET | 1.86 | .83 | 1.87 | 22.80 | .10 | 1.42 | 93.50 | 98.30 | 7.60 | 92.20 |
| 18 FOR | 1.87 | .84 | 1.44 | 15.90 | -.06 | .22 | 92.10 | 98.40 | 6.70 | 86.90 |
| 19 FOR | 1.93 | .66 | 1.91 | 12.50 | .02 | .84 | 92.00 | 98.40 | 8.10 | 88.50 |
| 20 GAR | 2.09 | .46 | 1.37 | 18.00 | .06 | .90 | 93.00 | 97.00 | 11.80 | 89.90 |
| 21 GRA | 1.90 | .77 | 1.44 | 9.90 | .02 | 1.62 | 93.90 | 97.90 | 6.00 | 93.70 |
| 22 GRE | 1.73 | .48 | 1.27 | 13.80 | -.06 | .50 | 89.70 | 93.60 | 7.50 | 85.40 |
| 23 HAR | 2.28 | .90 | 1.67 | 10.70 | .10 | 2.63 | 95.10 | 98.00 | 5.60 | 92.90 |
| 24 HON | 1.93 | .74 | 1.28 | .90 | -.14 | .44 | 92.80 | 97.10 | 19.10 | 92.40 |
| 25 HOU | 1.80 | .59 | 1.81 | 4.90 | -.04 | .34 | 90.20 | 97.30 | 9.90 | 86.20 |
| 26 IND | 1.90 | .66 | 1.57 | 16.90 | -.04 | .46 | 93.50 | 96.50 | 7.70 | 89.40 |
| 27 JAC | 2.18 | .64 | 1.18 | 2.60 | 0.00 | .01 | 85.90 | 95.50 | 8.10 | 82.90 |
| 28 JER | 1.17 | .63 | 1.38 | 33.00 | .04 | 1.10 | 90.90 | 95.10 | 9.40 | 80.90 |
| 29 KAN | 1.90 | .74 | 1.33 | 28.60 | .02 | .84 | 91.10 | 97.40 | 5.90 | 91.10 |
| 30 LOS | 1.49 | .91 | 1.77 | 2.90 | -.02 | .52 | 91.80 | 98.80 | 8.20 | 89.10 |
| 31 LOU | 1.66 | .59 | 1.29 | 12.60 | .06 | .95 | 91.40 | 96.60 | 8.70 | 89.10 |
| 32 MEM | 2.13 | .70 | 1.17 | 4.20 | -.06 | .14 | 83.20 | 94.50 | 12.30 | 85.90 |
| 33 MIA | 1.33 | .74 | 1.49 | 3.50 | .08 | .52 | 89.10 | 97.30 | 13.30 | 85.40 |
| 34 MIL | 2.37 | .82 | 1.61 | 14.60 | .08 | .94 | 94.30 | 97.40 | 6.50 | 93.60 |
| 35 MIN | 1.48 | .90 | 1.73 | 23.10 | .04 | 1.29 | 95.40 | 97.10 | 6.40 | 95.80 |
| 36 NAS | 1.81 | .94 | 1.31 | 8.60 | -.06 | .12 | 88.80 | 94.30 | 7.30 | 86.90 |
| 37 NEW | 1.97 | .79 | 1.43 | 26.60 | .04 | .46 | 83.60 | 97.00 | 13.10 | 86.90 |
| 38 NEW | 1.23 | .81 | 1.53 | 42.20 | .06 | .29 | 90.80 | 97.90 | 8.60 | 85.80 |
| 39 NEW | 1.61 | .63 | 1.75 | 31.40 | .16 | 1.89 | 93.20 | 97.90 | 6.30 | 89.30 |
| 40 NOR | 1.72 | .47 | 1.06 | 27.20 | .04 | .27 | 86.60 | 97.10 | 7.70 | 84.00 |
| 41 OKL | 1.57 | .71 | 1.64 | 8.50 | -.02 | .58 | 90.60 | 98.10 | 6.40 | 89.60 |
| 42 OMA | 2.45 | .82 | 1.24 | 16.30 | -.04 | .43 | 93.20 | 97.00 | 7.70 | 93.20 |
| 43 PAT | 1.41 | .58 | 1.76 | 38.20 | .08 | 2.16 | 95.70 | 98.60 | 5.00 | 93.60 |
| 44 PHI | 1.66 | .77 | 1.70 | 28.40 | .08 | .92 | 92.70 | 98.40 | 5.20 | 90.70 |
| 45 PHO | 1.29 | .80 | 1.65 | 1.50 | -.02 | .40 | 91.10 | 97.90 | 9.60 | 83.60 |
| 46 PIT | 1.77 | .76 | 1.75 | 11.80 | .02 | 1.85 | 92.80 | 96.00 | 5.90 | 94.40 |
| 47 POR | 1.45 | 1.03 | 1.48 | 24.40 | 0.00 | 1.53 | 93.10 | 97.40 | 4.20 | 91.90 |
| 48 PRO | 1.37 | .76 | 1.48 | 24.70 | 0.00 | 1.18 | 92.20 | 97.50 | 6.10 | 91.70 |
| 49 RIC | 2.06 | .62 | 1.35 | 44.00 | .04 | .68 | 91.10 | 95.90 | 5.90 | 87.20 |
| 50 ROC | 2.15 | .70 | 1.85 | 8.30 | .08 | 1.61 | 94.80 | 97.30 | 4.50 | 91.90 |
| 51 SAC | 1.55 | .89 | 1.64 | 10.80 | -.02 | 1.22 | 91.40 | 99.10 | 6.90 | 91.10 |
| 52 STL | 1.87 | .78 | 1.47 | 34.20 | .08 | 1.55 | 91.90 | 96.40 | 9.80 | 90.00 |
| 53 SAL | 2.04 | .75 | 1.86 | 11.70 | -.06 | .58 | 92.50 | 98.60 | 9.30 | 92.90 |
| 54 SAN | 1.31 | .70 | 1.19 | 3.00 | .08 | .12 | 84.00 | 94.30 | 14.90 | 85.80 |
| 55 SAN | 1.51 | .77 | 1.48 | 16.20 | -.02 | .70 | 89.70 | 98.80 | 8.80 | 87.20 |
| 56 SAN | 1.29 | .80 | 1.48 | 1.50 | -.06 | .66 | 91.40 | 98.50 | 7.20 | 91.60 |
| 57 SAN | 1.82 | .92 | 1.59 | 24.10 | .02 | .93 | 92.80 | 97.30 | 5.90 | 91.20 |
| 58 SAN | 1.40 | .68 | 2.18 | 12.20 | .10 | .46 | 94.40 | 99.20 | 6.40 | 94.00 |
| 59 SEA | 1.27 | .92 | 1.84 | 10.70 | -.04 | 1.28 | 94.80 | 97.80 | 4.10 | 91.70 |
| 60 SPR | 2.24 | .71 | 1.22 | 15.20 | .06 | .81 | 93.30 | 97.80 | 6.20 | 91.90 |
| 61 SYR | 2.46 | 1.00 | 1.57 | 9.80 | 0.00 | 1.94 | 92.90 | 96.90 | 5.00 | 92.80 |
| 62 TAM | 1.72 | .67 | 1.28 | 7.10 | .04 | .64 | 89.30 | 96.90 | 5.60 | 82.70 |
| 63 TOL | 2.27 | .71 | 1.44 | 18.10 | .02 | .68 | 93.40 | 97.00 | 6.00 | 92.80 |
| 64 WAS | 1.46 | .76 | 1.74 | 43.50 | .04 | 1.89 | 93.90 | 98.50 | 6.70 | 92.70 |
| 65 YOU | 2.31 | .75 | 1.41 | 19.00 | .04 | 1.27 | 93.50 | 96.60 | 6.70 | 93.00 |

| | % Workers Who Use Public Transport To Work IIIA5 | Total Crime Rate/ 100,000 pop. IIIA6 | Cost of Living Index IIIA7 | Public Swimming Pools/ 100,000 pop. IIIB1a | Public Camping Sites/ 100,000 pop. IIIB1b | Public Tennis Courts/ 100,000 pop. IIIB1c | Miles of Trails/ 1,000 pop. IIIB1d | Banks and S&L Assoc./ 1,000 pop. IIIB2 | Retail Trade Establishments/ 1,000 pop. IIIB3 | Selected Service Establishments 1,000 pop. IIIB4 |
|---|---|---|---|---|---|---|---|---|---|---|
| US | 8.90 | 2829.50 | 100.00 | N.A. | N.A. | N.A. | N.A. | .09 | 8.68 | 5.85 |
| 1 AKR | 2.10 | 2709.20 | 105.60• | 8.80 | 0.00 | 101.60 | 148.70 | .04 | 6.52 | 4.94 |
| 2 ALB | 7.60 | 1651.90 | 112.10 | 15.20 | 542.00 | 99.90 | 22.10 | .05 | 8.65 | 5.20 |
| 3 ALL | 3.20 | 1590.10 | 111.00 | 1.80 | 121.30 | 165.40 | 165.40 | .09 | 8.92 | 5.61 |
| 4 ANA | .40 | 3940.20 | 106.50• | 14.70 | 1102.10 | 181.60 | 51.40 | .03 | 7.11 | 5.39 |
| 5 ATL | 9.40 | 4024.50 | 97.10• | 41.70 | 0.00 | 189.20 | 56.80 | .06 | 6.73 | 5.31 |
| 6 BAL | 13.80 | 4051.70 | 102.90• | 28.90 | 182.50 | 90.70 | 11.50 | .05 | 6.99 | 4.42 |
| 7 BIR | 6.20 | 2870.40 | 102.40 | 32.40 | 200.20 | 136.60 | 18.90 | .04 | 7.45 | 4.42 |
| 8 BOS | 20.00 | 3404.00• | 120.80• | 5.40 | 143.00 | 63.90 | 89.60 | .07 | 7.71 | 6.08 |
| 9 BUF | 10.40 | 2676.90 | 104.80 | 10.30 | 252.70 | 252.70 | 42.20 | .02 | 8.40 | 5.44 |
| 10 CHI | 23.20 | 2913.50 | 109.80 | 25.30 | 132.90 | 188.80 | 34.10 | .08 | 6.97 | 5.41 |
| 11 CIN | 8.30 | 2643.80 | 96.20 | 19.40 | 237.50 | 33.90 | 119.80 | .15 | 7.39 | 5.06 |
| 12 CLE | 13.30 | 2942.80 | 106.30• | 33.40 | 202.50 | 130.80 | 112.40 | .03 | 7.01 | 5.31 |
| 13 COL | 8.10 | 3251.00 | 105.30 | 9.80 | 478.10 | 29.40 | 51.30 | .04 | 6.66 | 5.07 |
| 14 DAL | 6.30 | 3680.30 | 95.30• | 86.10 | 496.10 | 152.30 | 70.60 | .09 | 6.49 | 6.52 |
| 15 DAY | 5.40 | 2361.10• | 104.30• | 17.60 | 1023.50 | 172.90 | 123.50 | .06 | 6.41 | 5.16 |
| 16 DEN | 4.40 | 5014.20 | 108.30 | 34.20 | 666.10 | 151.40 | 205.20 | .09 | 7.66 | 6.52 |
| 17 DET | 8.20 | 4818.10 | 106.50• | 8.50 | 292.30 | 112.10 | 51.10 | .02 | 6.32 | 4.66 |
| 18 FOR | 2.10 | 4334.30 | 114.60 | 19.30 | 72.50 | 196.70 | 9.60 | .07 | 8.02 | 7.30 |
| 19 FOR | 2.70 | 2792.50 | 93.30 | 32.80 | 212.50 | 108.90 | 68.20 | .06 | 8.20 | 6.29 |
| 20 GAR | 7.70 | 4206.00 | 103.90• | 22.10 | 252.70 | 175.30 | 47.30 | .06 | 6.61 | 4.25 |
| 21 GRA | 2.20 | 2312.10 | 94.80 | 13.00 | 1044.50 | 254.20 | 243.00 | .04 | 6.96 | 4.42 |
| 22 GRE | 3.50 | 2818.90 | 105.30 | 5.00 | 132.40 | 43.00 | 19.90 | .05 | 8.39 | 5.88 |
| 23 HAR | 9.90 | 2253.50• | 122.20• | 16.60 | 70.80 | 79.80 | 63.30 | .06 | 7.12 | 4.98 |
| 24 HON | 7.40 | 3126.50 | 124.60• | 1.00 | 0.00 | 4.90 | 9.50 | .03 | 6.10 | 5.10 |
| 25 HOU | 5.40 | 3569.60 | 95.00 | 7.60 | 222.20 | 14.10 | 27.70 | .08 | 8.17 | 6.11 |
| 26 IND | 5.80 | 2660.50 | 99.10 | 17.10 | 90.10 | 86.50 | 93.70 | .06 | 6.80 | 5.47 |
| 27 JAC | 6.70 | 4321.20 | 102.80 | 15.10 | 113.40 | 64.30 | 5.70 | .07 | 8.12 | 5.90 |
| 28 JER | 35.60 | 3136.50 | 124.10 | 9.90 | 0.00 | 4.90 | 3.30 | .05 | 10.04 | 5.04 |
| 29 KAN | 5.50 | 3419.40 | 109.90 | 13.60 | 177.80 | 69.40 | 56.60 | .12 | 7.79 | 6.47 |
| 30 LOS | 5.60 | 5431.70 | 106.30• | 14.40 | 271.80 | 44.90 | 156.30 | .02 | 8.15 | 7.53 |
| 31 LOU | 6.70 | 3043.10 | 100.40 | 20.60 | 1293.80 | 183.80 | 72.60 | .04 | 7.19 | 5.37 |
| 32 MEM | 9.90 | 4051.40 | 98.60• | 19.50 | 39.00 | 77.90 | 80.50 | .02 | 6.78 | 4.51 |
| 33 MIA | 9.10 | 5151.40 | 112.10• | 23.70 | 195.60 | 123.80 | 128.50 | .07 | 8.14 | 7.54 |
| 34 MIL | 12.00 | 2250.30 | 107.70• | 17.10 | 194.40 | 145.30 | 74.10 | .10 | 7.98 | 4.77 |
| 35 MIN | 9.10 | 3497.60 | 119.00 | 9.40 | 343.40 | 251.40 | 236.50 | .07 | 6.08 | 4.72 |
| 36 NAS | 6.60 | 3292.60 | 103.40• | 46.20 | 1730.10 | 166.40 | 175.60 | .05 | 7.73 | 6.22 |
| 37 NEW | 20.40 | 3934.00 | 100.30 | 1.00 | 0.00 | 17.20 | 3.80 | .06 | 7.44 | 5.54 |
| 38 NEW | 48.00 | 5094.20 | 115.60• | 10.00 | 150.40 | 33.10 | 30.00 | .02 | 8.77 | 6.75 |
| 39 NEW | 18.50 | 3703.10 | 131.50• | 17.20 | 8.10 | 130.90 | 80.20 | .06 | 8.44 | 5.69 |
| 40 NOR | 9.70 | 3354.10 | 95.40 | 2.90 | 0.00 | 208.50 | 13.20 | .03 | 5.55 | 4.11 |
| 41 OKL | 1.60 | 3086.40 | 96.90• | 99.80 | 29.60 | 140.40 | 352.60 | .10 | 9.11 | 7.44 |
| 42 OMA | 7.20 | 3123.70 | 97.30 | 38.90 | 533.30 | 164.80 | 88.90 | .08 | 7.14 | 6.23 |
| 43 PAT | 14.40 | 2523.70 | 127.20• | 9.60 | 1.50 | 77.30 | 14.70 | .06 | 8.54 | 5.61 |
| 44 PHI | 20.60 | 2587.90 | 123.30• | 14.10 | 47.30 | 89.90 | 112.30 | .06 | 8.18 | 5.21 |
| 45 PHO | 1.30 | 4652.00 | 111.70• | 38.20 | 665.30 | 74.40 | 263.40 | .01 | 7.52 | 5.97 |
| 46 PIT | 14.50 | 1888.50 | 104.30• | 5.40 | 113.30 | 30.80 | 41.20 | .06 | 8.07 | 5.50 |
| 47 POR | 6.00 | 4358.90 | 88.10 | 16.80 | 1388.50 | 126.90 | 659.10 | .04 | 7.57 | 5.89 |
| 48 PRO | 5.30 | 3398.20• | 112.90 | 9.90 | 1191.00 | 108.70 | 199.80 | .04 | 8.71 | 5.72 |
| 49 RIC | 13.00 | 3584.60 | 102.00 | 11.60 | 139.00 | 142.90 | 54.10 | .04 | 6.33 | 4.70 |
| 50 ROC | 8.00 | 2100.00 | 116.70• | 18.10 | 997.70 | 103.10 | 231.00 | .04 | 7.22 | 5.10 |
| 51 SAC | 2.30 | 4415.60 | 103.90• | 38.70 | 997.50 | 88.60 | 1968.80 | .03 | 7.83 | 5.95 |
| 52 STL | 5.10 | 3587.10 | 101.00 | 10.20 | 157.00 | 42.30 | 37.70 | .09 | 7.67 | 5.74 |
| 53 SAL | 2.30 | 3440.80 | 99.10 | 12.50 | 795.70 | 86.00 | 363.80 | .05 | 6.57 | 5.65 |
| 54 SAN | 5.80 | 3561.30 | 100.90 | 24.30 | 170.10 | 60.20 | 67.10 | .05 | 7.91 | 4.90 |
| 55 SAN | .90 | 4388.30 | 103.10 | 35.00 | 3628.20 | 72.60 | 955.40 | .03 | 8.11 | 5.95 |
| 56 SAN | 4.30 | 3350.00 | 100.40 | 25.00 | 11001.50 | 188.50 | 134.80 | .02 | 6.78 | 5.26 |
| 57 SAN | 15.40 | 5005.90 | 124.30 | 17.70 | 191.00 | 128.60 | 206.10 | .02 | 8.14 | 7.06 |
| 58 SAN | 2.30 | 3736.20 | 113.00 | 29.10 | 272.30 | 105.20 | 200.00 | .02 | 6.42 | 5.39 |
| 59 SEA | 7.10 | 3872.00 | 118.30• | 7.70 | 846.00 | 139.90 | 643.50 | .04 | 7.24 | 5.44 |
| 60 SPR | 5.00 | 3899.80• | 115.90• | 71.70 | 160.40 | 113.20 | 701.90 | .07 | 8.10 | 5.93 |
| 61 SYR | 6.80 | 1675.90 | 112.60• | 40.90 | 930.80 | 117.90 | 51.90 | .04 | 8.50 | 5.76 |
| 62 TAM | 3.10 | 3982.00 | 102.10 | 5.90 | 536.00 | 73.00 | 28.60 | .08 | 8.42 | 7.05 |
| 63 TOL | 3.80 | 2910.50 | 102.70• | 37.50 | 277.10 | 138.50 | 14.40 | .04 | 7.25 | 5.52 |
| 64 WAS | 16.50 | 3480.30 | 110.40• | 28.70 | 127.20 | 168.50 | 197.10 | .04 | 4.62 | 4.53 |
| 65 YOU | 2.30 | 2065.80 | 101.40• | 18.70 | 910.40 | 69.00 | 33.60 | .04 | 7.58 | 5.41 |

TABLE A-5 (Concluded)

| | | Hospital Beds/ 100,000 pop. IIIB5 | Vols. of Books in Main Public Library/ 1,000 pop. IIIB6 | Death Rate/ 1,000 pop. IIIC1 | Birth Rate/ 1,000 pop. IIIC2 | Sports Events IIIC3 | Dance Drama and Music Events IIIC4a | Cultural Institutions IIIC4b | Fairs and Festivals Held IIIC4c |
|---|---|---|---|---|---|---|---|---|---|
| | US | 414.90 | 1568.40 | 9.50 | 17.50 | N.A. | N.A. | N.A. | N.A. |
| 1 | AKR | 329.60 | 1040.50 | 8.50 | 17.40 | 9.00 | 61.00 | 7.00 | 15.00 |
| 2 | ALB | 447.60 | 316.10 | 10.90 | 16.80 | 7.00 | 51.00 | 3.00 | 2.00 |
| 3 | ALL | 363.90 | 253.70 | 10.40 | 14.60 | 7.00 | 34.00 | 2.00 | 7.00 |
| 4 | ANA | 258.80 | 155.40 | 6.00 | 18.20 | 6.00 | 28.00 | 0.00 | 4.00 |
| 5 | ATL | 321.00 | 480.10 | 7.80 | 19.90 | 17.00 | 66.00 | 10.00 | 9.00 |
| 6 | BAL | 377.70 | 913.90 | 9.40 | 17.10 | 26.00 | 71.00 | 11.00 | 14.00 |
| 7 | BIR | 493.30 | 1070.30 | 10.30 | 17.10 | 5.00 | 40.00 | 4.00 | 12.00 |
| 8 | BOS | 466.80 | 957.70 | 8.10 | 16.70 | 20.00 | 67.00 | 4.00 | 6.00 |
| 9 | BUF | 493.80 | 1836.90 | 10.10 | 16.80 | 22.00 | 66.00 | 13.00 | 7.00 |
| 10 | CHI | 436.90 | 599.60 | 9.70 | 18.30 | 22.00 | 84.00 | 7.00 | 21.00 |
| 11 | CIN | 370.70 | 1888.00 | 10.00 | 18.30 | 13.00 | 39.00 | 4.00 | 5.00 |
| 12 | CLE | 418.30 | 1558.50 | 9.60 | 17.20 | 26.00 | 71.00 | 11.00 | 14.00 |
| 13 | COL | 352.00 | 1025.40 | 8.20 | 19.40 | 7.00 | 6.00 | 4.00 | 7.00 |
| 14 | BAL | 346.50 | 672.90 | 7.70 | 19.70 | 15.00 | 31.00 | 4.00 | 2.00 |
| 15 | DAY | 332.40 | 1344.20 | 7.80 | 18.30 | 6.00 | 49.00 | 8.00 | 6.00 |
| 16 | DEN | 448.00 | 953.90 | 7.40 | 17.50 | 15.00 | 81.00 | 15.00 | 12.00 |
| 17 | DET | 339.50 | 503.80 | 8.60 | 18.20 | 12.00 | 35.00 | 23.00 | 0.00 |
| 18 | FOR | 341.90 | 273.00 | 11.10 | 13.60 | 5.00 | 35.00 | 1.00 | 0.00 |
| 19 | FOR | 365.20 | 815.40 | 7.90 | 18.90 | 5.00 | 40.00 | 4.00 | 12.00 |
| 20 | GAR | 336.10 | 632.40 | 8.20 | 18.30 | 12.00 | 52.00 | 15.00 | 9.00 |
| 21 | GRA | 309.50 | 1027.50 | 8.20 | 18.20 | 11.00 | 29.00 | 2.00 | 4.00 |
| 22 | GRE | 415.10 | 455.30 | 8.40 | 17.70 | 6.00 | 68.00 | 3.00 | 6.00 |
| 23 | HAR | 383.50 | 691.20 | 8.50 | 16.60 | 15.00 | 81.00 | 6.00 | 9.00 |
| 24 | HON | 230.60 | 1777.90 | 4.80 | 20.00 | 4.00 | 12.00 | 13.00 | 8.00 |
| 25 | HOU | 431.20 | 580.70 | 7.00 | 19.10 | 15.00 | 81.00 | 7.00 | 4.00 |
| 26 | IND | 412.70 | 788.00 | 9.10 | 18.40 | 11.00 | 76.00 | 5.00 | 14.00 |
| 27 | JAC | 365.70 | 1133.10 | 9.00 | 19.10 | 6.00 | 48.00 | 4.00 | 2.00 |
| 28 | JER | 393.30 | 863.40 | 12.20 | 17.10 | 4.00 | 10.00 | 0.00 | 0.00 |
| 29 | KAN | 470.00 | 922.30 | 9.20 | 17.40 | 15.00 | 61.00 | 15.00 | 15.00 |
| 30 | LOS | 368.50 | 437.90 | 9.00 | 18.10 | 22.00 | 84.00 | 7.00 | 21.00 |
| 31 | LOU | 418.80 | 1018.20 | 9.50 | 17.90 | 11.00 | 74.00 | 3.00 | 13.00 |
| 32 | MEM | 472.00 | 1097.60 | 9.10 | 19.50 | 4.00 | 33.00 | 2.00 | 5.00 |
| 33 | MIA | 458.90 | 572.30 | 10.50 | 14.40 | 16.00 | 59.00 | 9.00 | 17.00 |
| 34 | MIL | 444.40 | 1452.60 | 8.90 | 17.80 | 17.00 | 66.00 | 10.00 | 9.00 |
| 35 | MIN | 547.20 | 612.60 | 7.70 | 19.00 | 14.00 | 70.00 | 9.00 | 8.00 |
| 36 | NAS | 539.60 | 620.50 | 9.10 | 16.70 | 9.00 | 59.00 | 7.00 | 19.00 |
| 37 | NEW | 507.20 | 603.10 | 9.70 | 19.30 | 12.00 | 74.00 | 11.00 | 5.00 |
| 38 | NEW | 462.50 | 622.70 | 10.50 | 16.40 | 22.00 | 84.00 | 7.00 | 21.00 |
| 39 | NEW | 436.90 | 552.00 | 9.80 | 16.30 | 14.00 | 70.00 | 9.00 | 8.00 |
| 40 | NOR | 281.40 | 560.00 | 7.70 | 19.60 | 13.00 | 57.00 | 15.00 | 7.00 |
| 41 | OKL | 405.80 | 873.30 | 8.00 | 17.80 | 10.00 | 63.00 | 9.00 | 8.00 |
| 42 | OMA | 694.60 | 776.90 | 8.30 | 19.00 | 9.00 | 59.00 | 7.00 | 19.00 |
| 43 | PAT | 336.50 | 191.10 | 9.00 | 14.90 | 5.00 | 18.00 | 4.00 | 2.00 |
| 44 | PHI | 429.80 | 526.20 | 10.10 | 16.90 | 17.00 | 23.00 | 0.00 | 2.00 |
| 45 | PHO | 351.20 | 678.60 | 7.90 | 18.10 | 14.00 | 84.00 | 6.00 | 11.00 |
| 46 | PIT | 494.00 | 863.90 | 10.70 | 14.80 | 17.00 | 84.00 | 34.00 | 21.00 |
| 47 | POR | 415.20 | 970.80 | 9.90 | 16.10 | 12.00 | 54.00 | 4.00 | 8.00 |
| 48 | PRO | 408.00 | 644.00 | 10.50 | 20.80 | 6.00 | 19.00 | 7.00 | 5.00 |
| 49 | RIC | 506.30 | 819.20 | 9.80 | 17.50 | 6.00 | 48.00 | 4.00 | 2.00 |
| 50 | ROC | 290.60 | 853.00 | 9.00 | 18.80 | 8.00 | 30.00 | 5.00 | 6.00 |
| 51 | SAC | 414.30 | 964.10 | 7.80 | 16.30 | 4.00 | 33.00 | 2.00 | 5.00 |
| 52 | STL | 496.40 | 560.90 | 10.00 | 17.60 | 19.00 | 55.00 | 8.00 | 22.00 |
| 53 | SAL | 334.10 | 748.60 | 6.20 | 22.70 | 7.00 | 39.00 | 2.00 | 7.00 |
| 54 | SAN | 332.30 | 753.20 | 7.50 | 21.30 | 15.00 | 24.00 | 10.00 | 16.00 |
| 55 | SAN | 364.40 | 501.30 | 8.90 | 17.50 | 0.00 | 14.00 | 1.00 | 5.00 |
| 56 | SAN | 266.70 | 716.60 | 7.50 | 17.10 | 22.00 | 66.00 | 13.00 | 7.00 |
| 57 | SAN | 444.30 | 405.70 | 9.10 | 16.10 | 12.00 | 35.00 | 23.00 | 0.00 |
| 58 | SAN | 312.30 | 653.10 | 5.70 | 18.50 | 9.00 | 20.00 | 3.00 | 2.00 |
| 59 | SEA | 318.70 | 935.60 | 8.50 | 17.80 | 9.00 | 52.00 | 11.00 | 4.00 |
| 60 | SPR | 437.50 | 1082.50 | 10.00 | 15.80 | 7.00 | 6.00 | 8.00 | 13.00 |
| 61 | SYR | 291.40 | 557.00 | 9.30 | 18.70 | 12.00 | 52.00 | 15.00 | 9.00 |
| 62 | TAM | 394.50 | 369.70 | 13.70 | 13.70 | 12.00 | 54.00 | 4.00 | 8.00 |
| 63 | TOL | 464.80 | 1938.30 | 9.80 | 17.80 | 9.00 | 50.00 | 3.00 | 7.00 |
| 64 | WAS | 306.90 | 677.90 | 7.00 | 19.50 | 3.00 | 27.00 | 15.00 | 15.00 |
| 65 | YOU | 366.80 | 1096.70 | 9.90 | 16.20 | 5.00 | 31.00 | 4.00 | 14.00 |

## SMSA'S WITH POPULATION 200,000--500,000 (M)

| | SMSA | Code | Population, 1970 (in 1,000) |
|---|---|---|---|
| 66 | Albuquerque, N. Mex. | ALB | 316 |
| 67 | Ann Arbor, Mich. | ANN | 234 |
| 68 | Appleton-Oshkosh, Wis. | APP | 277 |
| 69 | Augusta, Ga.-S.C. | AUG | 253 |
| 70 | Austin, Texas | AUS | 296 |
| 71 | Bakersfield, Calif. | BAK | 329 |
| 72 | Baton Rouge, La. | BAT | 285 |
| 73 | Beaumont-Port Authur-Orange, Texas | BEA | 316 |
| 74 | Binghamton, N.Y.-Pa. | BIN | 303 |
| 75 | Bridgeport, Conn. | BRI | 389 |
| 76 | Canton, Ohio | CAN | 372 |
| 77 | Charleston, S.C. | CHA | 304 |
| 78 | Charleston, W. Va. | CHA | 230 |
| 79 | Charlotte, N.C. | CHA | 409 |
| 80 | Chattanooga, Tenn.-Ga. | CHA | 305 |
| 81 | Colorado Springs, Colo. | COL | 236 |
| 82 | Columbia, S.C. | COL | 323 |
| 83 | Columbus, Ga.-Ala. | COL | 239 |
| 84 | Corpus Christi, Texas | COR | 285 |
| 85 | Davenport-Rock Island-Moline, Iowa-Ill. | DAV | 363 |
| 86 | Des Moines, Iowa | DES | 286 |
| 87 | Duluth-Superior, Minn.-Wis. | DUL | 265 |
| 88 | El Paso, Tex. | ELP | 359 |
| 89 | Erie, Pa. | ERI | 264 |
| 90 | Eugene, Oreg. | EUG | 213 |
| 91 | Evansville, Ind.-Ky. | EVA | 233 |
| 92 | Fayetteville, N.C. | FAY | 212 |
| 93 | Flint, Mich. | FLI | 497 |
| 94 | Fort Wayne, Ind. | FOR | 280 |
| 95 | Fresno, Calif. | FRE | 413 |
| 96 | Greenville, S.C. | GRE | 300 |
| 97 | Hamilton-Middleton, Ohio | HAM | 226 |
| 98 | Harrisburg, Pa. | HAR | 411 |
| 99 | Huntington-Ashland, W. Va.-Ky.-Ohio | HUN | 254 |
| 100 | Huntsville, Ala. | HUN | 228 |
| 101 | Jackson, Miss. | JAC | 259 |
| 102 | Johnstown, Pa. | JOH | 263 |
| 103 | Kalamazoo, Mich. | KAL | 202 |
| 104 | Knoxville, Tenn. | KNO | 400 |
| 105 | Lancaster, Pa. | LAN | 320 |

| | SMSA | Code | Population, 1970 (in 1,000) |
|---|---|---|---|
| 106 | Lansing, Mich. | LAN | 378 |
| 107 | Las Vegas, Nev. | LAS | 273 |
| 108 | Lawrence-Haverhill, Mass.-N.H. | LAW | 232 |
| 109 | Little Rock-North Little Rock, Ark. | LIT | 323 |
| 110 | Lorain-Elyria, Ohio | LOR | 257 |
| 111 | Lowell, Mass. | LOW | 213 |
| 112 | Macon, Ga. | MAC | 206 |
| 113 | Madison, Wis. | MAD | 290 |
| 114 | Mobile, Ala. | MOB | 377 |
| 115 | Montgomery, Ala. | MON | 201 |
| 116 | New Haven, Conn. | NEW | 356 |
| 117 | New London-Groton-Norwich, Conn. | NEW | 208 |
| 118 | Newport News-Hampton, Va. | NEW | 292 |
| 119 | Orlando, Fla. | ORL | 428 |
| 120 | Oxnard-Ventura, Calif. | OXN | 376 |
| 121 | Pensacola, Fla. | PEN | 243 |
| 122 | Peoria, Ill. | PED | 342 |
| 123 | Raleigh, N.C. | RAL | 228 |
| 124 | Reading, Pa. | REA | 296 |
| 125 | Rockford, Ill. | ROC | 272 |
| 126 | Saginaw, Mich. | SAG | 220 |
| 127 | Salinas-Monterey, Calif. | SAL | 250 |
| 128 | Santa Barbara, Calif. | SAN | 264 |
| 129 | Santa Rosa, Calif. | SAN | 205 |
| 130 | Scranton, Pa. | SCR | 234 |
| 131 | Shreveport, La. | SHR | 295 |
| 132 | South Bend, Ind. | SOU | 280 |
| 133 | Spokane, Wash. | SPO | 287 |
| 134 | Stamford, Conn. | STA | 206 |
| 135 | Stockton, Calif. | STO | 290 |
| 136 | Tacoma, Wash. | TAC | 411 |
| 137 | Trenton, N.J. | TRE | 304 |
| 138 | Tucson, Ariz. | TUC | 352 |
| 139 | Tulsa, Okla. | TUL | 477 |
| 140 | Utica-Rome, N.Y. | UTI | 340 |
| 141 | Vallejo-Napa, Calif. | VAL | 249 |
| 142 | Waterbury, Conn. | WAT | 209 |
| 143 | West Palm Beach, Fla. | WES | 349 |
| 144 | Wichita, Kans. | WIC | 389 |
| 145 | Wilkes-Barre-Hazleton, Pa. | WIL | 342 |
| 146 | Wilmington, Del.-N.J.-Md. | WIL | 499 |
| 147 | Worcester, Mass. | NOR | 344 |
| 148 | York, Pa. | YOR | 330 |

# TABLE B-1

## BASIC STATISTICS OF ECONOMIC COMPONENT (M)

| | Personal Income Per Capita IA | Savings Per Capita IB1 | Property Income/ Personal Income IB2 | % Owner-Occupied Housing Units IB3 | % Households With One Or More Automobiles IB4 | Median Value, Owner Occupied Single Family Housing (in $1,000) IB5 | Percent of Families With Income Above Poverty Level IIA | Degree of Economic Concentration IIB |
|---|---|---|---|---|---|---|---|---|
| US | 3139.00 | 702.00 | .14 | 62.90 | 82.50 | 17.10 | 89.30 | .00 |
| 66 ALH | 2872.00 | 625.00 | .14 | 65.30 | 89.70 | 15.70 | 87.00 | .25 |
| 67 ANN | 3767.00 | 517.00 | .14 | 57.10 | 91.20 | 23.30 | 94.90 | .20 |
| 68 APP | 3004.00 | 562.00 | .14 | 75.00 | 89.70 | 17.00 | 94.50 | .03 |
| 69 AUG | 2573.00 | 640.00 | .10 | 64.50 | 82.30 | 14.00 | 84.60 | .20 |
| 70 AUS | 3014.00 | 745.00 | .15 | 54.90 | 90.40 | 16.60 | 89.20 | .34 |
| 71 BAK | 2823.00 | 435.00 | .10 | 59.50 | 89.20 | 14.40 | 87.40 | .46 |
| 72 BAT | 2854.00 | 639.00 | .09 | 66.40 | 88.10 | 17.90 | 86.40 | .06 |
| 73 BEA | 2897.00 | 726.00 | .12 | 69.60 | 88.10 | 11.50 | 88.40 | .14 |
| 74 BIN | 3036.00 | 80.00 | .12 | 69.30 | 85.40 | 17.70 | 92.70 | .06 |
| 75 BRI | 3748.00 | 114.00 | .22 | 63.00 | 85.20 | 28.60 | 94.80 | .05 |
| 76 CAN | 3167.00 | 1351.00 | .13 | 73.50 | 88.00 | 16.10 | 94.20 | .08 |
| 77 CHA | 2440.00 | 532.00 | .09 | 60.10 | 80.10 | 16.20 | 79.40 | .02 |
| 78 CHA | 2829.00 | 246.00 | .12 | 64.50 | 80.30 | 15.40 | 87.00 | .16 |
| 79 CHA | 3207.00 | 430.00 | .11 | 61.60 | 84.90 | 17.10 | 90.10 | .02 |
| 80 CHA | 2811.00 | 596.00 | .11 | 65.90 | 82.70 | 12.70 | 86.70 | .20 |
| 81 COL | 2928.00 | 224.00 | .12 | 58.80 | 92.80 | 18.50 | 90.80 | .24 |
| 82 COL | 2628.00 | 859.00 | .09 | 67.30 | 85.20 | 17.80 | 85.70 | .10 |
| 83 COL | 2496.00 | 400.00 | .11 | 52.70 | 82.10 | 15.10 | 81.30 | .16 |
| 84 COR | 8141.00 | 579.00 | .14 | 64.40 | 88.50 | 11.50 | 81.60 | .25 |
| 85 DAV | 3298.00 | 747.00 | .16 | 69.80 | 87.80 | 18.00 | 93.30 | .01 |
| 86 DES | 3446.00 | 1733.00 | .11 | 69.60 | 86.90 | 16.20 | 93.90 | .14 |
| 87 DUL | 2735.00 | 562.00 | .13 | 73.30 | 81.40 | 12.80 | 91.70 | .32 |
| 88 ELP | 2359.00 | 323.00 | .10 | 58.70 | 84.20 | 13.60 | 82.60 | .17 |
| 89 ERI | 2829.00 | 584.00 | .12 | 71.60 | 86.10 | 14.60 | 93.20 | .07 |
| 90 EUG | 3045.00 | 83.00 | .13 | 64.10 | 91.10 | 16.50 | 92.10 | .06 |
| 91 EVA | 2832.00 | 1138.00 | .14 | 69.70 | 84.40 | 12.60 | 90.90 | .07 |
| 92 FAY | 2340.00 | 347.00 | .06 | 55.20 | 87.40 | 16.50 | 82.90 | .09 |
| 93 FLI | 3261.00 | 128.00 | .10 | 77.70 | 91.00 | 16.40 | 93.10 | .06 |
| 94 FOR | 3355.00 | 555.00 | .14 | 73.20 | 88.90 | 15.50 | 94.90 | .02 |
| 95 FRE | 2761.00 | 883.00 | .12 | 60.10 | 88.20 | 15.40 | 85.80 | .29 |
| 96 GRE | 2706.00 | 859.00 | .11 | 68.10 | 85.80 | 14.50 | 88.20 | .21 |
| 97 HAM | 3111.00 | 1048.00 | .13 | 69.40 | 88.70 | 17.20 | 93.00 | .09 |
| 98 HAR | 3254.00 | 822.00 | .04 | 68.30 | 85.00 | 15.30 | 93.40 | .20 |
| 99 HUN | 2584.00 | 650.00 | .11 | 68.00 | 79.00 | 14.00 | 85.20 | .00 |
| 100 HUN | 2961.00 | 309.00 | .10 | 68.00 | 89.40 | 17.40 | 86.50 | .06 |
| 101 JAC | 2548.00 | 715.00 | .12 | 66.40 | 83.80 | 13.80 | 81.40 | .10 |
| 102 JOH | 2540.00 | 340.00 | .10 | 71.10 | 82.20 | 10.00 | 90.30 | .10 |
| 103 KAL | 3342.00 | 885.00 | .15 | 71.50 | 90.90 | 16.70 | 94.20 | .02 |
| 104 KNO | 2719.00 | 589.00 | .12 | 68.20 | 84.90 | 12.80 | 85.70 | .05 |
| 105 LAN | 3097.00 | 224.00 | .13 | 68.90 | 84.70 | 16.20 | 93.50 | .11 |
| 106 LAN | 3371.00 | 496.00 | .11 | 69.80 | 91.40 | 17.80 | 93.90 | .16 |
| 107 LAS | 3546.00 | 933.00 | .09 | 58.00 | 92.80 | 23.10 | 93.00 | .16 |
| 108 LAW | 3397.00 | 99.00 | .15 | 56.60 | 81.10 | 19.50 | 94.20 | .01 |
| 109 LIT | 2764.00 | 756.00 | .12 | 64.60 | 84.60 | 14.50 | 86.60 | .07 |
| 110 LOR | 3170.00 | 486.00 | .11 | 73.20 | 91.20 | 18.30 | 94.30 | .07 |
| 111 LOW | 3011.00 | 365.00 | .15 | 64.20 | 82.50 | 19.40 | 93.90 | .03 |
| 112 MAC | 2733.00 | 736.00 | .12 | 58.40 | 81.90 | 14.20 | 84.90 | .07 |
| 113 MAD | 3453.00 | 924.00 | .13 | 56.40 | 85.90 | 21.70 | 84.60 | .36 |
| 114 MOB | 2401.00 | 456.00 | .14 | 68.30 | 83.10 | 13.10 | 81.40 | .05 |
| 115 MON | 2565.00 | 253.00 | .14 | 61.50 | 79.70 | 16.40 | 80.80 | .10 |
| 116 NEW | 3656.00 | 726.00 | .16 | 56.90 | 81.90 | 24.80 | 92.70 | .08 |
| 117 NEW | 3286.00 | 320.00 | .13 | 62.10 | 89.00 | 20.20 | 91.70 | .06 |
| 118 NEW | 3102.00 | 187.00 | .08 | 60.30 | 85.50 | 18.00 | 89.90 | .05 |
| 119 ORL | 3018.00 | 1006.00 | .11 | 69.70 | 88.40 | 15.50 | 88.70 | .16 |
| 120 OXN | 3252.00 | 363.00 | .12 | 65.70 | 93.80 | 23.20 | 92.60 | .22 |
| 121 PEN | 2567.00 | 336.00 | .07 | 70.80 | 86.40 | 12.40 | 84.50 | .06 |
| 122 PEO | 3370.00 | 1446.00 | .13 | 71.60 | 88.50 | 15.90 | 94.30 | .03 |
| 123 PAL | 3007.00 | 595.00 | .13 | 58.80 | 87.10 | 18.80 | 88.80 | .18 |
| 124 REA | 3250.00 | 338.00 | .11 | 72.00 | 82.80 | 12.80 | 95.00 | .10 |
| 125 ROC | 3429.00 | 693.00 | .13 | 67.20 | 88.90 | 18.70 | 93.60 | .14 |
| 126 SAG | 3152.00 | 1033.00 | .13 | 77.80 | 89.30 | 16.40 | 92.30 | .02 |
| 127 SAL | 3140.00 | 470.00 | .15 | 52.50 | 90.40 | 23.00 | 90.40 | .29 |
| 128 SAN | 3369.00 | 1680.00 | .21 | 53.80 | 90.40 | 23.40 | 92.40 | .16 |
| 129 SAN | 3177.00 | 311.00 | .18 | 64.40 | 89.40 | 21.10 | 89.60 | .28 |
| 130 SCR | 2735.00 | 212.00 | .08 | 63.40 | 78.90 | 12.30 | 92.20 | .01 |
| 131 SHR | 2552.00 | 310.00 | .12 | 64.80 | 81.90 | 13.60 | 81.80 | .03 |
| 132 SOU | 3194.00 | 685.00 | .14 | 77.30 | 87.80 | 12.70 | 94.10 | .03 |
| 133 SPO | 3018.00 | 768.00 | .16 | 69.20 | 85.30 | 14.10 | 91.40 | .24 |
| 134 STA | 6360.00 | 401.00 | .22 | 61.70 | 89.50 | 50.20 | 96.00 | .26 |
| 135 STO | 3061.00 | 8925.00 | .12 | 61.40 | 85.80 | 16.70 | 88.80 | .23 |
| 136 TAC | 3178.00 | 1487.00 | .11 | 66.00 | 88.40 | 17.50 | 92.00 | .19 |
| 137 THE | 3631.00 | 576.00 | .15 | 65.30 | 82.60 | 17.40 | 93.60 | .09 |
| 138 TUC | 2988.00 | 763.00 | .15 | 65.40 | 90.00 | 16.70 | 89.20 | .35 |
| 139 TUL | 3234.00 | 674.00 | .15 | 68.30 | 88.40 | 13.40 | 90.20 | .06 |
| 140 UTI | 2928.00 | 290.00 | .13 | 66.30 | 83.80 | 16.10 | 92.60 | .04 |
| 141 VAL | 3153.00 | 265.00 | .11 | 60.50 | 90.70 | 19.40 | 91.20 | .14 |
| 142 WAT | 3486.00 | 737.00 | .16 | 61.80 | 84.40 | 20.70 | 94.50 | .00 |
| 143 WES | 3893.00 | 1527.00 | .24 | 67.60 | 87.50 | 17.70 | 89.80 | .01 |
| 144 WIC | 3159.00 | 644.00 | .13 | 64.70 | 90.80 | 13.50 | 92.00 | .05 |
| 145 WIL | 2674.00 | 528.00 | .08 | 66.60 | 79.80 | 11.10 | 91.10 | .01 |
| 146 WIL | 3426.00 | 218.00 | .16 | 68.30 | 87.20 | 17.10 | 92.90 | .13 |
| 147 WOR | 3276.00 | 875.00 | .13 | 59.90 | 82.30 | 18.80 | 94.60 | .08 |
| 148 YOR | 3259.00 | 304.00 | .12 | 72.60 | 87.90 | 14.90 | 94.10 | .04 |

| | Value Added/ Worker in Manufacturing (in $1,000) IIC1 | Value of Construction/ Worker (in $1,000) IIC2 | Sales/ Employee in Retail Trade (in $1,000) IIC3 | Sales/ Employee in Wholesale Trade (in $1,000) IIC4 | Sales/ Employee in Selected Services (in $1,000) IIC5 | Total Bank Deposits Per Capita IID | Central City and Suburban Income Distribution IIE1 | Percent of Families With Income Below Pov. Level or Greater Than $15,000 IIE2 | Unemployment Rate IIF | Chamber of Commerce Employees/ 100,000 Pop. IIG |
|---|---|---|---|---|---|---|---|---|---|---|
| US | 13.50 | 4.30 | 33.00 | 130.60 | 15.80 | 2492.00 | .06 | 31.30 | 4.40 | NA |
| 66 ALB | 12.10 | 8.01 | 30.20 | 80.40 | 14.80 | 1795.00 | -.12 | 32.90 | 5.50 | .60 • |
| 67 ANN | 16.20 | 11.84 | 34.20 | 89.40 | 14.30 | 1756.00 | -.08 | 39.90 | 5.00 | 3.80 |
| 68 APP | 13.20 | 3.61 • | 28.40 | 102.20 | 14.60 • | 1844.00 | -.04 | 25.10 | 3.30 | 2.50 |
| 69 AUG | 14.90 | 6.05 | 33.60 | 76.90 | 10.50 | 1286.00 | .04 | 29.40 | 3.90 | 2.40 |
| 70 AUS | 9.40 | 7.10 | 29.10 | 77.70 | 11.20 | 2281.00 | .00 | 31.20 | 3.10 | 6.80 |
| 71 BAK | 16.00 | 5.30 | 34.50 | 114.60 | 14.10 | 1502.00 | -.06 | 30.10 | 6.70 | .60 • |
| 72 BAT | 28.30 | 3.97 | 33.40 | 97.00 | 12.00 | 2550.00 | -.08 | 34.50 | 4.50 | 4.60 |
| 73 BEA | 35.10 | 1.16 | 33.40 | 101.80 | 12.20 | 1594.00 | .00 | 27.60 | 4.40 | 3.20 |
| 74 BIN | 11.60 | 2.06 | 35.60 | 79.90 | 12.30 | 2250.00 | -.02 | 27.30 | 3.70 | 5.30 |
| 75 BRI | 14.50 | 3.53 | 33.00 | 89.30 | 12.50 | 3542.00 | .10 | 35.60 | 3.80 | 2.60 |
| 76 CAN | 14.30 | 6.45 | 32.00 | 85.50 | 13.30 | 1671.00 | .04 | 24.80 | 4.30 | 3.50 |
| 77 CHA | 11.90 | 2.40 | 31.50 | 89.70 | 11.70 | 765.00 | -.06 | 34.20 | 4.10 | 7.20 |
| 78 CHA | 26.80 | 1.18 | 33.10 | 76.80 | 12.00 | 2186.00 | -.12 | 28.30 | 4.10 | 3.00 |
| 79 CHA | 10.50 | 6.84 | 32.70 | 185.20 | 13.80 | 2605.00 | -.02 | 30.90 | 2.70 | .50 • |
| 80 CHA | 11.80 | 4.98 | 31.10 | 114.80 | 11.10 | 1882.00 | .08 | 27.90 | 3.00 | 6.90 |
| 81 COL | 12.00 | 9.44 | 33.60 | 62.60 | 13.10 | 1268.00 | -.04 | 26.40 | 5.50 | 4.70 |
| 82 COL | 9.50 | 3.78 | 31.70 | 97.60 | 10.50 | 1077.00 | .00 | 30.50 | 3.00 | 6.20 |
| 83 COL | 10.70 | 7.65 | 30.80 | 84.30 | 10.20 | 1020.00 | -.10 | 30.00 | 4.70 | 5.40 |
| 84 COR | 24.20 | 1.50 | 30.50 | 88.50 | 11.50 | 1382.00 | -.06 | 33.00 | 4.30 | 4.60 |
| 85 DAV | 15.60 | 2.70 | 32.70 | 143.00 | 12.40 | 2120.00 | -.04 | 28.30 | 4.50 | .60 • |
| 86 DES | 15.40 | 5.67 | 28.30 | 145.80 | 13.30 | 2848.00 | .00 | 29.60 | 2.80 | 7.70 |
| 87 DUL | 11.50 | 2.12 | 31.80 | 131.10 | 13.90 | 2010.00 | -.06 | 20.90 | 7.30 | 5.30 |
| 88 ELP | 10.40 | 6.94 | 28.70 | 94.90 | 11.00 | 1287.00 | -.04 | 31.60 | 5.20 | 5.80 |
| 89 FHI | 13.60 | 3.03 | 31.10 | 76.40 | 13.60 | 1825.00 | .02 | 22.40 | 4.10 | 2.70 |
| 90 EUG | 11.40 | 6.30 | 34.20 | 91.40 | 13.10 | 1220.00 | -.06 | 24.60 | 8.10 | 3.80 |
| 91 EVA | 15.50 | 2.39 | 29.30 | 88.20 | 13.90 | 1997.00 | -.02 | 24.40 | 4.40 | 5.20 |
| 92 FAY | 8.40 | 2.88 | 32.70 | 63.50 | 10.90 | 576.00 | -.08 | 26.40 | 5.20 | .90 • |
| 93 FLI | 15.20 • | 7.77 | 34.40 | 61.50 | 13.10 | 1928.00 | .00 | 33.40 | 5.30 | 1.20 |
| 94 FOR | 14.40 | 4.29 | 29.20 | 101.50 | 14.60 | 2370.00 | .04 | 28.60 | 3.10 | 4.30 |
| 95 FRE | 14.60 | 7.28 | 36.10 | 100.30 | 13.70 | 1624.00 | -.04 | 31.50 | 8.00 | 2.90 |
| 96 GRE | 9.60 | 4.28 | 34.10 | 101.20 | 16.90 | 1088.00 | -.04 | 25.40 | 2.60 | 7.30 |
| 97 HAM | 14.80 | 5.31 | 32.20 | 79.70 | 13.00 | 1112.00 | -.02 | 28.10 | 3.70 | 1.80 |
| 98 HAR | 12.80 | 3.20 | 31.20 | 98.00 | 11.90 | 1906.00 | .04 | 26.20 | 2.20 | 2.40 |
| 99 HUN | 15.50 | .94 | 31.80 | 102.30 | 10.70 | 1552.00 | -.10 | 26.30 | 5.10 | 1.60 |
| 100 HUN | 12.20 | 2.41 | 32.00 | 77.40 | 16.30 | 880.00 | -.18 | 38.00 | 4.40 | 1.80 |
| 101 JAC | 12.50 | 3.94 | 33.80 | 95.30 | 12.30 | 2538.00 | -.14 | 34.70 | 3.40 | 4.60 |
| 102 JOH | 10.60 | 1.03 | 31.80 | 75.30 | 14.70 | 1721.00 | .00 | 20.90 | 4.90 | 2.30 |
| 103 KAL | 16.90 | 6.70 | 32.30 | 74.90 | 13.60 | 1435.00 | .04 | 31.40 | 4.70 | 4.50 |
| 104 KNO | 13.30 | 3.59 | 31.20 | 87.60 | 11.40 | 1625.00 | .00 | 24.40 | 3.90 | 5.00 |
| 105 LAN | 13.30 | 2.11 | 32.60 | 93.70 | 14.30 | 2004.00 | .04 | 24.60 | 2.10 | 2.80 |
| 106 LAN | 20.10 | 5.24 | 34.20 | 118.70 | 13.60 | 1989.00 | .00 | 33.10 | 5.10 | 1.90 |
| 107 LAS | 20.30 | 11.52 | 36.60 | 105.10 | 15.80 | 1898.00 | -.02 | 33.20 | 5.20 | 3.30 |
| 108 LAW | 10.90 | 3.61 | 29.00 | 85.60 | 14.50 | 2974.00 | .04 | 28.60 | 4.10 | 2.60 |
| 109 LIT | 11.00 | 5.56 | 32.50 | 94.10 | 11.30 | 1867.00 | -.14 | 27.60 | 3.30 | .60 • |
| 110 LOR | 15.80 | 6.95 | 33.90 | 68.00 | 11.80 | 1672.00 | .02 | 27.40 | 3.70 | .80 |
| 111 LOW | 12.70 | 5.08 | 30.40 | 84.90 | 12.40 | 1794.00 | .04 | 29.20 | 4.10 | .90 • |
| 112 MAC | 11.40 | 4.84 | 31.50 | 72.50 | 11.30 | 1238.00 | .00 | 31.60 | 3.90 | 1.00 • |
| 113 MAD | 12.00 | 5.26 | 28.40 | 79.30 | 12.40 | 1766.00 | -.02 | 32.60 | 2.90 | 4.10 |
| 114 MOB | 14.90 | 2.15 | 29.90 | 81.70 | 10.80 | 1372.00 | -.12 | 30.60 | 5.30 | .50 • |
| 115 MON | 9.80 | 2.89 | 32.90 | 83.20 | 11.90 | 1888.00 | -.12 | 34.30 | 3.80 | 1.00 • |
| 116 NEW | 13.10 | 3.46 | 32.50 | 112.90 | 11.20 | 3472.00 | .10 | 24.80 | 3.40 | 7.00 |
| 117 NEW | 11.80 | 6.39 | 33.20 | 72.30 | 14.00 | 2320.00 | .00 | 30.90 | 3.90 | 1.00 • |
| 118 NEW | 9.40 | 6.88 | 30.50 | 58.80 | 11.40 | 1031.00 | .06 | 29.50 | 3.60 | 1.70 |
| 119 ORL | 12.50 | 6.86 | 31.70 | 74.20 | 11.80 | 1754.00 | .00 | 29.50 | 4.80 | .50 • |
| 120 OXN | 14.90 | 9.73 | 35.00 | 78.40 | 13.50 | 1058.00 | -.02 | 34.40 | 5.90 | 1.10 |
| 121 PEN | 17.30 | 5.25 | 32.40 | 73.40 | 12.20 | 877.00 | -.04 | 27.70 | 5.00 | 2.90 |
| 122 PEO | 16.40 | 5.20 | 34.00 | 150.50 | 13.40 | 1818.00 | -.04 | 28.00 | 3.20 | 3.20 |
| 123 RAL | 10.40 | 7.01 | 30.20 | 127.60 | 16.30 | 2122.00 | -.10 | 31.90 | 2.50 | 3.10 |
| 124 REA | 10.60 | 2.56 | 31.20 | 87.20 | 14.20 | 2540.00 | .06 | 22.40 | 2.40 | 1.70 |
| 125 ROC | 14.40 | 3.58 | 31.00 | 90.00 | 14.30 | 1923.00 | -.04 | 29.60 | 4.00 | .70 • |
| 126 SAG | 17.50 | 7.02 | 32.30 | 98.20 | 13.60 | 1690.00 | .04 | 31.70 | 4.90 | 4.50 |
| 127 SAL | 18.60 | 7.83 | 34.50 | 73.50 | 14.20 | 1628.00 | -.06 | 30.50 | 7.00 | 2.00 |
| 128 SAN | 12.80 | 7.29 | 32.40 | 63.50 | 16.00 | 1744.00 | -.06 | 33.90 | 6.40 | .80 • |
| 129 SAN | 12.90 | 7.19 • | 39.70 | 78.00 | 15.80 | 2147.00 | -.08 | 29.90 | 7.30 | 1.00 • |
| 130 SCR | 8.70 | 1.14 | 35.60 | 71.60 | 14.80 | 2584.00 | -.02 | 20.00 | 5.20 | 6.40 |
| 131 SHR | 12.70 | 4.20 | 32.60 | 88.50 | 11.90 | 2072.00 | -.12 | 22.20 | 5.00 | 6.80 |
| 132 SOU | 24.60 | 3.36 | 32.00 | 89.70 | 13.40 | 2172.00 | -.04 | 25.80 | 4.70 | 7.50 |
| 133 SPO | 16.00 | 7.62 | 32.80 | 98.50 | 13.20 | 2257.00 | -.02 | 26.60 | 6.90 | 6.60 |
| 134 STA | 19.00 | 3.80 | 38.40 | 115.90 | 14.90 | 4188.00 | .26 | 56.30 | 2.30 | 4.90 |
| 135 STO | 19.60 | 5.62 | 35.40 | 112.00 | 14.50 | 20024.00 | -.02 | 30.20 | 8.20 | 2.40 |
| 136 TAC | 14.30 | 6.01 | 34.80 | 109.70 | 14.90 | 1512.00 | .00 | 30.00 | 8.40 | 2.20 |
| 137 TRE | 13.70 | 6.25 | 33.60 | 97.30 | 13.20 | 3136.00 | .18 | 33.80 | 3.50 | 2.60 |
| 138 TUC | 11.30 | 10.08 | 30.00 | 78.10 | 11.70 | 1557.00 | .09 | 29.00 | 4.00 | .60 • |
| 139 TUL | 12.30 | 5.40 | 32.60 | 120.70 | 14.30 | 2452.00 | -.12 | 27.90 | 4.60 | 8.00 |
| 140 UTI | 14.60 | 4.85 | 37.20 | 87.10 | 14.70 | 2554.00 | .02 | 22.60 | 5.70 | .60 • |
| 141 VAL | 16.70 | 8.92 | 35.40 | 77.60 | 14.90 | 1459.00 | -.08 | 30.10 | 6.70 | 2.00 |
| 142 WAT | 11.80 | 6.29 | 36.40 | 104.70 | 11.40 | 2974.00 | .06 | 32.00 | 4.80 | 8.60 |
| 143 WES | 15.30 | 11.65 | 30.10 | 74.00 | 10.70 | 2125.00 | .04 | 32.20 | 3.00 | 4.60 • |
| 144 WIC | 12.70 | 2.23 | 29.50 | 113.60 | 12.90 | 2056.00 | -.06 | 25.70 | 7.10 | 4.60 |
| 145 WIL | 9.30 | 1.87 | 34.40 | 84.50 | 15.70 | 2193.00 | .00 | 29.80 | 4.00 | 2.90 |
| 146 WIL | 12.40 | 3.49 | 33.30 | 142.30 | 14.10 | 2596.00 | .04 | 31.50 | 3.80 | 1.40 |
| 147 WOR | 11.80 | 5.47 | 31.50 | 86.50 | 14.30 | 3345.00 | .00 | 28.60 | 3.60 | 7.30 |
| 148 YOR | 11.60 | 3.04 | 32.60 | 89.90 | 13.70 | 2265.00 | .04 | 33.10 | 2.30 | 2.40 |

## BASIC STATISTICS OF POLITICAL COMPONENT (M)

| | Local Sun. newspaper circ./ 1,000 pop. IA1 | % occupied housing with TV IA2 | Local radio stations/ 100,000 pop. IA3 | Pres. vote cast/voting age pop. IB | Avg. monthly earnings of teachers IIA1 | Avg. monthly earnings of other employees IIA2 | Entrance salary of patrolmen IIA3 | Entrance salary of firemen IIA4 | Total municipal employment/ 1,000 pop. IIA5 | Police protection employment/ 1,000 pop. IIA6 |
|---|---|---|---|---|---|---|---|---|---|---|
| US | 243.00 | 95.50 | .03 | 54.90 | 682.00 | 515.00 | 6848.00 | 6569.00 | 15.80 | 2.40 |
| 66 ALB | 376.00 | 95.00 | 4.43 | 71.60 | 629.00 | 454.00 | 6046.00 | 5640.00 | 8.10 | 1.90 |
| 67 ANN | 363.00 | 95.00 | 1.28 | 65.90 | 759.00 | 543.00 | 6900.00• | 6758.00• | 7.80 | 1.60 |
| 68 APP | 844.00 | 98.50 | .72 | 63.40 | 658.00• | 497.00• | 7254.00 | 7002.00 | 22.20 | 1.70 |
| 69 AUG | 1133.00 | 94.60 | 3.95 | 41.10 | 554.00 | 329.00• | 6900.00• | 6758.00• | 14.90 | 2.50 |
| 70 AUS | 341.00 | 94.30 | 3.71 | 67.20 | 558.00 | 436.00 | 6447.00 | 5922.00 | 15.60 | 1.70 |
| 71 BAK | 703.00 | 94.90 | 3.34 | 57.80 | 751.00 | 592.00 | 8826.00 | 8406.00 | 8.70 | 2.80 |
| 72 BAT | 540.00 | 96.50 | 3.15 | 58.70 | 702.00 | 427.00 | 6000.00 | 6000.00 | 16.40 | 4.40 |
| 73 BEA | 666.00 | 95.90 | 1.58 | 51.70 | 588.00 | 412.00 | 6600.00 | 6600.00 | 9.10 | 1.70 |
| 74 BIN | 1266.00 | 96.60 | 1.32 | 64.30 | 715.00 | 444.00 | 6540.00 | 6610.00 | 27.50 | 2.70 |
| 75 BRI | 565.00 | 97.50 | 1.54 | 69.70• | 783.00 | 550.00 | 7676.00 | 7310.00 | 27.40 | 3.20 |
| 76 CAN | 778.00 | 97.10 | .80 | 64.50 | 627.00 | 458.00 | 7950.00 | 7950.00 | 9.90 | 2.10 |
| 77 CHA | 1323.00 | 94.80 | 1.97 | 44.90 | 540.00 | 318.00 | 5876.00 | 5590.00 | 15.10 | 2.80 |
| 78 CHA | 1488.00 | 95.40 | 3.47 | 75.80 | 609.00 | 356.00 | 6402.00 | 6402.00 | 13.10 | 2.30 |
| 79 CHA | 852.00 | 95.90 | 2.20 | 45.70 | 638.00 | 430.00 | 7052.00 | 6427.00 | 11.50 | 2.00 |
| 80 CHA | 1021.00 | 96.10 | 2.95 | 54.50 | 626.00 | 396.00 | 6900.00• | 5791.00 | 41.60 | 2.20 |
| 81 COL | 602.00 | 95.50 | 5.43 | 52.30 | 597.00 | 443.00 | 6612.00 | 6612.00 | 14.00 | 1.50 |
| 82 COL | 1067.00 | 95.40 | 2.47 | 42.10 | 524.00 | 341.00 | 5460.00 | 5200.00 | 9.90 | 1.90 |
| 83 COL | 390.00 | 95.30 | 3.34 | 29.70 | 603.00 | 338.00 | 5545.00 | 5536.00 | 16.60 | 1.60 |
| 84 COR | 425.00 | 44.30 | 2.10 | 51.50 | 562.00 | 397.00 | 6270.00 | 6000.00 | 10.00 | 1.30 |
| 85 DAV | 835.00 | 97.00 | 1.37 | 65.70 | 660.00 | 453.00 | 6672.00 | 6672.00 | 6.80 | 1.40 |
| 86 DES | 2421.00 | 96.70 | 2.44 | 77.10 | 695.00 | 495.00 | 7507.00 | 6858.00 | 10.60 | 1.60 |
| 87 DUL | 820.00 | 96.00 | 3.01 | 71.30 | 656.00 | 465.00 | 7869.00 | 7869.00 | 13.40 | 1.40 |
| 88 ELP | 267.00 | 95.60 | 2.78 | 39.00 | 651.00 | 358.00 | 6900.00• | 6758.00• | 8.20 | 1.50 |
| 89 ERI | 752.00 | 97.50 | 1.13 | 62.40 | 635.00 | 419.00 | 7011.00 | 7011.00 | 8.80 | 1.90 |
| 90 EUG | 713.00 | 93.70 | 4.69 | 70.00 | 672.00 | 523.00 | 7122.00 | 7122.00 | 12.30 | 1.70 |
| 91 EVA | 811.00 | 97.50 | 1.71 | 77.90 | 687.00 | 403.00 | 6900.00• | 6758.00• | 10.10 | 2.10 |
| 92 FAY | 789.00 | 95.90 | 1.41 | 25.70 | 623.00 | 375.00 | 5364.00 | 5100.00 | 13.80 | 2.50 |
| 93 FLI | 583.00 | 97.50 | 1.20 | 63.10 | 777.00 | 566.00 | 8743.00 | 8619.00 | 20.30 | 2.20 |
| 94 FOR | 604.00 | 96.60 | 2.50 | 85.30 | 788.00 | 461.00 | 6900.00• | 8113.00 | 10.00 | 1.70 |
| 95 FRE | 856.00 | 95.00 | 2.90 | 56.70 | 765.00 | 582.00 | 9222.00 | 9222.00 | 9.80 | 2.10 |
| 96 GRE | 1631.00 | 95.90 | 2.33 | 36.70 | 512.00 | 358.00 | 5432.00 | 5432.00 | 14.90 | 2.50 |
| 97 HAM | 453.00 | 97.20 | 1.32 | 50.70 | 669.00 | 461.00 | 8424.00 | 8424.00 | 10.10 | 1.50 |
| 98 HAR | 2487.00 | 96.50 | 1.45 | 53.10 | 602.00 | 382.00 | 6200.00 | 6200.00 | 12.30 | 3.30 |
| 99 HUN | 762.00 | 95.40 | 1.96 | 66.10 | 564.00 | 362.00 | 5844.00 | 5844.00 | 7.80 | 1.60 |
| 100 HUN | 395.00 | 96.80 | 2.63 | 55.70 | 480.00 | 374.00 | 5999.00 | 5160.00 | 16.70 | 1.90 |
| 101 JAC | 722.00 | 95.00 | 1.93 | 48.10 | 520.00 | 335.00 | 6546.00 | 6408.00 | 13.20 | 2.40 |
| 102 JOH | 1377.00 | 96.70 | 1.52 | 58.60 | 624.00 | 355.00 | 6900.00• | 6758.00• | 10.10 | 1.80 |
| 103 KAL | 723.00 | 97.30 | 2.97 | 64.50 | 679.00 | 518.00 | 7911.00 | 7440.00 | 14.60 | 2.70 |
| 104 KNO | 936.00 | 95.80 | 2.75 | 50.00 | 567.00 | 381.00 | 4800.00 | 5010.00 | 33.60 | 2.00 |
| 105 LAN | 2043.00 | 89.30 | 1.56 | 51.00 | 618.00 | 400.00 | 6413.00 | 6413.00 | 9.90 | 2.20 |
| 106 LAN | 611.00 | 96.50 | 2.11 | 67.50 | 778.00 | 506.00 | 8064.00 | 7843.00 | 15.60 | 2.10 |
| 107 LAS | 802.00 | 96.10 | 3.29 | 51.40 | 756.00 | 582.00 | 8358.00 | 8358.00 | 9.50 | 3.10 |
| 108 LAW | 712.00 | 97.30 | .86 | 64.10• | 686.00 | 492.00 | 7345.00 | 7345.00 | 21.70 | 2.20 |
| 109 LIT | 1705.00 | 95.90 | 2.16 | 49.30 | 548.00 | 354.00 | 6456.00 | 5838.00 | 9.40 | 1.70 |
| 110 LOR | 501.00 | 97.70 | .38 | 57.60 | 625.00 | 499.00 | 7618.00 | 7618.00 | 6.80 | .90 |
| 111 LOW | 454.00 | 97.90 | 1.87 | 64.10• | 622.00 | 504.00 | 7010.00 | 6984.00 | 20.80 | 2.10 |
| 112 MAC | 604.00 | 95.50 | 2.42 | 46.50 | 647.00 | 348.00 | 5352.00 | 5352.00 | 21.70 | 2.10 |
| 113 MAD | 642.00 | 95.00 | 2.41 | 71.40 | 598.00 | 539.00 | 7470.00 | 7686.00 | 25.00 | 2.10 |
| 114 MOB | 501.00 | 94.20 | 2.65 | 44.60 | 603.00 | 381.00 | 5364.00 | 5364.00 | 10.60 | 2.10 |
| 115 MON | 595.00 | 95.20 | 4.47 | 52.80 | 629.00 | 344.00 | 5520.00 | 5520.00 | 14.10 | 2.50 |
| 116 NEW | 940.00 | 96.70 | 1.12 | 68.30• | 702.00 | 516.00 | 8696.00 | 7190.00 | 28.10 | 3.40 |
| 117 NEW | 1228.00 | 96.40 | .48 | 61.70• | 684.00 | 506.00 | 6816.00 | 7058.00 | 24.20 | 2.80 |
| 118 NEW | 584.00 | 95.90 | .34 | 52.70 | 606.00 | 332.00 | 5880.00 | 5880.00 | 30.80 | 1.50 |
| 119 ORL | 1655.00 | 95.60 | 2.33 | 59.40 | 648.00 | 389.00 | 7280.00 | 6508.00 | 21.30 | 2.80 |
| 120 OXN | 311.00 | 96.60 | .53 | 66.20 | 804.00 | 596.00 | 8340.00 | 8340.00 | 6.80 | 1.50 |
| 121 PEN | 1075.00 | 94.70 | 3.29 | 54.80 | 675.00 | 359.00 | 6214.00 | 5928.00 | 13.40 | 2.10 |
| 122 PEO | 898.00 | 96.00 | 1.16 | 62.60 | 690.00 | 470.00 | 8372.00 | 8372.00 | 6.70 | 2.10 |
| 123 RAL | 1268.00 | 95.80 | 3.07 | 51.60 | 634.00 | 369.00 | 6432.00 | 5568.00 | 9.10 | 2.20 |
| 124 REA | 1048.00 | 96.50 | 1.68 | 51.70 | 535.00 | 417.00 | 6350.00 | 6400.00 | 10.40 | 2.30 |
| 125 ROC | 567.00 | 96.50 | 1.83 | 60.50 | 708.00 | 496.00 | 7560.00 | 7381.00 | 6.00 | 1.60 |
| 126 SAG | 664.00 | 97.90 | 1.81 | 59.80 | 739.00 | 466.00 | 8042.00 | 7705.00 | 8.60 | 1.90 |
| 127 SAL | 372.00 | 93.80 | 1.60 | 48.80 | 792.00 | 582.00 | 7854.00 | 7476.00 | 6.20 | 1.70 |
| 128 SAN | 639.00 | 93.30 | 3.40 | 68.90 | 878.00 | 581.00 | 8772.00 | 8664.00 | 10.70 | 2.00 |
| 129 SAN | 1049.00 | 93.70 | 1.46 | 76.60 | 880.00• | 650.00• | 7140.00 | 7500.00 | 8.30 | 1.20 |
| 130 SCR | 944.00 | 96.10 | 2.13 | 58.40 | 580.00 | 387.00 | 6363.00 | 6363.00 | 9.10 | 2.20 |
| 131 SHR | 648.00 | 95.20 | 3.05 | 51.60 | 568.00 | 377.00 | 5040.00 | 5040.00 | 10.30 | 2.10 |
| 132 SOU | 1014.00 | 97.30 | 1.78 | 66.80 | 672.00 | 400.00 | 6500.00 | 6500.00 | 9.70 | 2.10 |
| 133 SPO | 752.00 | 95.50 | 5.57 | 65.80 | 722.00 | 538.00 | 6900.00• | 7005.00 | 9.70 | 1.70 |
| 134 STA | 292.00 | 98.00 | .48 | 69.70• | 833.00 | 558.00 | 7525.00 | 6758.00• | 25.90 | 2.20 |
| 135 STO | 464.00 | 94.00 | 2.41 | 58.10 | 862.00 | 610.00 | 9060.00 | 8844.00 | 8.70 | 2.00 |
| 136 TAC | 663.00 | 95.40 | 2.18 | 54.00 | 706.00 | 563.00 | 9416.00 | 8760.00 | 17.70 | 1.90 |
| 137 TRE | 1046.00 | 97.00 | .98 | 63.60 | 841.00 | 519.00 | 7600.00 | 7200.00 | 29.90 | 3.40 |
| 138 TUC | 333.00 | 94.60 | 3.69 | 56.90 | 871.00 | 487.00 | 8240.00 | 7940.00 | 8.70 | 1.40 |
| 139 TUL | 541.00 | 95.70 | 1.67 | 71.20 | 558.00 | 438.00 | 6144.00 | 6504.00 | 7.80 | 1.50 |
| 140 UTI | 634.00 | 97.20 | 2.05 | 63.70 | 784.00 | 411.00 | 6400.00 | 6400.00 | 12.80 | 2.80 |
| 141 VAL | 412.00 | 95.80 | 0.00 | 59.10 | 777.00 | 576.00 | 8694.00 | 8694.00 | 5.80 | 1.60 |
| 142 WAT | 539.00 | 97.60 | 1.43 | 68.30• | 715.00 | 491.00 | 7485.00 | 7320.00 | 23.70 | 2.90 |
| 143 WES | 1294.00 | 95.10 | .85 | 61.20 | 712.00 | 412.00 | 7050.00 | 7200.00 | 14.60 | 3.10 |
| 144 WIC | 643.00 | 95.80 | 2.82 | 57.40 | 604.00 | 459.00 | 6120.00 | 6120.00 | 8.90 | 1.70 |
| 145 WIL | 947.00 | 97.60 | 1.75 | 58.40 | 623.00 | 387.00 | 6850.00 | 6450.00 | 7.70 | 1.80 |
| 146 WIL | 1156.00 | 97.40 | 1.20 | 66.60 | 731.00 | 442.00 | 7000.00 | 7000.00 | 31.10 | 4.30 |
| 147 WOR | 610.00 | 97.80 | 2.03 | 64.10• | 671.00 | 526.00 | 7012.00 | 7012.00 | 31.30 | 2.60 |
| 148 YOR | 901.00 | 96.00 | 1.21 | 51.80 | 627.00 | 375.00 | 6900.00 | 6900.00 | 6.80 | 2.00 |

| | Fire protection employment/ 1,000 pop. IIA7 | Insured unemployment rates IIA8 | Violent Crime rate/ 100,000 pop. IIB1 | Property Crime rate/ 100,000 pop. IIB2 | Local govt. revenue per capita IIB3 | % of revenue from federal govt. IIB4 | Per capita local govt. Expend. on public welfare IIC1 | Avg. monthly retiree benefits IIC2 | Avg. monthly payments to families w/dependent children IIC3 |
|---|---|---|---|---|---|---|---|---|---|
| US | 1.40 | 3.40 | 397.70 | 2431.80 | 329.86 | 2.70 | 11.88 | 132.00 | 190.00 |
| 66 ALB | 1.50 | 4.00 | 785.40 | 5124.90 | 287.17 | 6.10 | .01 | 129.00 | 120.00 |
| 67 ANN | 1.10 | 4.80• | 437.90 | 4552.10 | 286.58 | .10 | 6.97 | 148.00 | 267.00 |
| 68 APP | 1.90 | 3.20• | 50.80 | 1410.20 | 544.23• | 11.00• | 40.00• | 140.00 | 226.00 |
| 69 AUG | 2.10 | 2.10 | 350.40 | 1469.70 | 214.34 | 6.50 | 1.49 | 116.00 | 96.00 |
| 70 AUS | 1.40 | .70 | 540.60 | 2575.60 | 360.06 | 2.40 | 2.90 | 125.00 | 104.00 |
| 71 BAK | 2.20 | 5.10• | 370.10 | 3852.90 | 512.92 | 2.40 | 40.64 | 129.00 | 252.00 |
| 72 BAT | 2.10 | 3.00 | 774.50 | 4454.70 | 250.32 | .60 | .06 | 128.00 | 86.00 |
| 73 BEA | 1.70 | 2.30 | 471.60 | 2057.30 | 358.42 | 1.60 | 2.02 | 139.00 | 113.00 |
| 74 BIN | 2.90 | 2.90 | 69.10 | 1252.90 | 432.91 | 4.10 | 27.32 | 138.00 | 212.00 |
| 75 BRI | 3.00 | 5.40 | 201.70• | 2762.80• | 288.91 | 4.50 | 1.98 | 150.00• | 259.00• |
| 76 CAN | 1.70 | 2.50 | 299.00 | 1875.10 | 218.24 | .50 | 8.83 | 144.00 | 154.00 |
| 77 CHA | 2.30 | 2.20 | 497.10 | 2582.70 | 158.88 | 8.40 | .83 | 116.00 | 77.00 |
| 78 CHA | 2.40 | 2.40 | 173.00 | 1689.30 | 209.17 | 3.40 | 1.94 | 138.00 | 110.00 |
| 79 CHA | 1.90 | 1.10 | 574.90 | 2535.00 | 309.42 | 3.40 | 18.94 | 127.00 | 122.00 |
| 80 CHA | 2.40 | 1.80 | 470.00 | 2973.00 | 361.62 | 3.70 | 1.40 | 125.00 | 104.00 |
| 81 COL | 1.20 | 1.40• | 328.60 | 3125.50 | 415.79 | 5.70 | 31.28 | 127.00 | 179.00 |
| 82 COL | 1.60 | 2.70• | 703.80 | 2946.80 | 166.49 | 2.10 | .50 | 119.00 | 77.00 |
| 83 COL | 1.30 | 2.00 | 271.20 | 1632.90 | 225.91 | 5.80 | 1.24 | 114.00 | 98.00 |
| 84 COR | 1.30 | 1.40 | 463.20 | 3349.60 | 300.78 | 3.80 | 2.51 | 121.00 | 113.00 |
| 85 DAV | 1.30 | 2.30• | 251.80 | 1787.90 | 278.29 | 2.30 | 6.18 | 139.00 | 209.00 |
| 86 DES | 1.20 | 1.10 | 196.40 | 2368.20 | 314.12 | 2.20 | 5.64 | 140.00 | 202.00 |
| 87 DUL | 1.50 | 3.90 | 79.70 | 1916.70 | 435.77 | 1.50 | 59.24 | 134.00 | 207.00 |
| 88 ELP | 1.30 | 2.00 | 360.40 | 2739.70 | 223.05 | 2.30 | .88 | 121.00 | 120.00 |
| 89 ERI | 1.70 | 2.20 | 223.70 | 1748.50 | 228.31 | 1.10 | 7.97 | 140.00 | 229.00 |
| 90 EUG | 1.70 | 5.20• | 161.70 | 3682.60 | 365.67 | 8.80 | .24 | 136.00 | 165.00 |
| 91 EVA | 1.90 | 2.40 | 437.70 | 2114.60 | 262.22 | 4.50 | 15.87 | 131.00 | 136.00 |
| 92 FAY | 1.80 | 2.40 | 553.80 | 2973.70 | 217.39 | 7.80 | 16.08 | 108.00 | 123.00 |
| 93 FLI | 1.60 | 6.00 | 543.90 | 2878.10 | 370.89 | 1.30 | 12.47 | 149.00 | 240.00 |
| 94 FOR | 1.50 | 1.60 | 208.50 | 2867.80 | 275.99 | 1.30 | 15.01 | 144.00 | 151.00 |
| 95 FRE | 1.50 | 6.70 | 330.80 | 4988.00 | 502.43 | 2.10 | 99.87 | 125.00 | 237.00 |
| 96 GRE | 2.20 | 1.60 | 452.10 | 3168.50 | 177.33 | .50 | 2.48 | 121.00 | 76.00 |
| 97 HAM | 1.60 | 2.70 | 299.40• | 2061.70• | 305.29 | 2.00 | 11.22 | 141.00 | 147.00 |
| 98 HAR | 1.50 | 1.30 | 204.40 | 1305.00 | 251.02 | 3.40 | 10.33 | 134.00 | 225.00 |
| 99 HUN | 2.00 | 3.70 | 248.00 | 1548.00 | 189.41 | 3.20 | 7.39 | 127.00 | 122.00 |
| 100 HUN | 1.60 | 3.10• | 182.60 | 1729.60 | 308.44 | 7.60 | .37 | 109.00 | 60.00 |
| 101 JAC | 2.10 | 1.40 | 227.90 | 2059.90 | 238.70 | 1.20 | .71 | 115.00 | 56.00 |
| 102 JOH | 2.40 | 4.00 | 63.30 | 646.50 | 206.96 | 2.00 | 6.79 | 137.00 | 207.00 |
| 103 KAL | 2.30 | 3.50 | 567.90 | 3006.70 | 285.04 | .70 | 10.61 | 147.00 | 228.00 |
| 104 KNO | 2.10 | 1.50 | 203.40 | 1676.30 | 304.13 | 5.30 | 3.31 | 126.00 | 102.00 |
| 105 LAN | 2.00 | 1.10 | 73.70 | 869.50 | 220.94 | 3.10 | 5.64 | 138.00 | 222.00 |
| 106 LAN | 2.00 | 4.90 | 307.80 | 3660.10 | 382.69 | 2.60 | 10.74 | 145.00 | 248.00 |
| 107 LAS | 2.00 | 4.00 | 506.90 | 4225.40 | 399.78 | 4.60 | 4.18 | 134.00 | 118.00 |
| 108 LAW | 3.00 | 6.00 | 350.40• | 3053.60• | 329.09 | 4.40 | 54.73 | 140.00• | 257.00• |
| 109 LIT | 1.70 | 1.00 | 548.90 | 3070.20 | 216.10 | 6.80 | .51 | 119.00 | 96.00 |
| 110 LOR | 1.20 | 2.60 | 208.40 | 1754.30 | 267.70 | 1.50 | 11.21 | 145.00 | 163.00 |
| 111 LOW | 2.50 | 6.50 | 350.40• | 3053.60• | 322.97 | 2.70 | 62.45 | 140.00• | 257.00• |
| 112 MAC | 1.60 | 1.80 | 318.40 | 3005.70 | 268.76 | 6.50 | 4.84 | 111.00 | 105.00 |
| 113 MAD | 1.60 | 1.40 | 116.60 | 2769.30 | 337.93 | 1.50 | 27.36 | 142.00 | 260.00 |
| 114 MOB | 2.00 | 2.80 | 338.70 | 2303.50 | 217.69 | 5.40 | .04 | 120.00 | 61.00 |
| 115 MON | 2.50 | 3.10• | 313.20 | 1529.00• | 191.46 | 3.30 | .44 | 114.00 | 56.00 |
| 116 NEW | 2.90 | 4.00 | 178.80• | 2662.50• | 298.21 | 7.80 | 4.53 | 148.00• | 269.00• |
| 117 NEW | 1.40 | 4.30• | 189.50• | 2048.60• | 306.90 | 7.10 | 3.16 | 141.00• | 247.00• |
| 118 NEW | 1.10 | 2.00 | 363.10 | 2029.10 | 215.10 | 7.10 | 10.20 | 129.00 | 178.00 |
| 119 ORL | 2.10 | 2.10• | 422.70 | 3175.40 | 290.69 | 1.70 | 4.93 | 127.00 | 90.00 |
| 120 OXN | .90 | 5.10• | 249.90 | 3551.00 | 412.90 | 2.20 | 33.09 | 135.00 | 200.00 |
| 121 PEN | 1.90 | 2.10• | 447.20 | 3207.60 | 262.83 | 2.90 | 1.19 | 113.00 | 80.00 |
| 122 PEO | 1.30 | 1.70 | 486.50 | 2132.70 | 264.18 | .80 | 4.21 | 142.00 | 210.00 |
| 123 RAL | 1.60 | 2.40• | 413.60 | 2218.50 | 267.46 | 1.70 | 18.70 | 121.00 | 122.00 |
| 124 REA | 1.10 | 1.60 | 116.60 | 884.30 | 236.64 | 2.70 | 7.33 | 137.00 | 209.00 |
| 125 ROC | 1.30 | 2.90 | 192.10 | 1798.00 | 259.23 | .20 | 4.26 | 147.00 | 228.00 |
| 126 SAG | 1.60 | 3.20 | 700.80 | 3177.60 | 297.25 | 1.20 | 6.46 | 144.00 | 234.00 |
| 127 SAL | 1.10 | 5.10• | 306.80 | 3257.50 | 392.57 | 3.50 | 39.50 | 132.00 | 240.00 |
| 128 SAN | 1.40 | 5.10• | 204.20 | 3087.40 | 402.53 | 3.90 | 35.76 | 135.00 | 231.00 |
| 129 SAN | 1.30 | 5.10• | 260.00 | 3970.40 | 758.58• | 15.70• | 86.25• | 133.00 | 219.00 |
| 130 SCR | 2.40 | 4.70 | 110.40 | 943.00 | 183.06 | 6.40 | 6.74 | 131.00 | 216.00 |
| 131 SHR | 1.60 | 2.70 | 327.70 | 1992.40 | 230.68 | 2.30 | .02 | 118.00 | 87.00 |
| 132 SOU | 2.30 | 3.20 | 297.40 | 2565.10 | 287.26 | 2.40 | 19.67 | 146.00 | 154.00 |
| 133 SPO | 1.80 | 6.00 | 170.60 | 2700.20 | 269.21 | 2.70 | .32 | 133.00 | 209.00 |
| 134 STA | 1.80 | 2.60 | 201.70• | 2762.80• | 386.76 | 1.40 | 7.95 | 150.00• | 259.00• |
| 135 STO | 1.80 | 8.90 | 512.60 | 4957.50 | 542.18 | 5.20 | 80.94 | 127.00 | 253.00 |
| 136 TAC | 2.10 | 8.40 | 324.70 | 2910.00 | 365.95 | 3.80 | .13 | 137.00 | 220.00 |
| 137 TRE | 2.70 | 2.70 | 570.00 | 3284.80 | 306.69 | 1.40 | 22.77 | 144.00 | 249.00 |
| 138 TUC | 1.00 | 4.20• | 351.10 | 2940.50 | 313.27 | 3.50 | .16 | 135.00 | 117.00 |
| 139 TUL | 1.50 | 2.30 | 331.10 | 2960.20 | 255.12 | 2.90 | .61 | 134.00 | 144.00 |
| 140 UTI | 2.70 | 4.50 | 66.70 | 988.10 | 346.74 | 4.10 | 38.07 | 137.00 | 229.00 |
| 141 VAL | 1.30 | 5.10• | 300.30 | 3449.80 | 384.61 | 5.90 | 49.54 | 126.00 | 246.00 |
| 142 WAT | 2.30 | 7.50 | 178.80• | 2662.50• | 248.67 | 2.00 | 3.08 | 148.00• | 269.00• |
| 143 WES | 1.90 | 2.10• | 655.10 | 3773.40 | 402.19 | 1.00 | 6.85 | 139.00 | 94.00 |
| 144 WIC | 1.50 | 5.70 | 247.00 | 2886.20 | 327.72 | 4.20 | 31.16 | 138.00 | 172.00 |
| 145 WIL | 1.80 | 4.30 | 50.10 | 935.80 | 156.75 | .60 | 5.33 | 134.00 | 206.00 |
| 146 WIL | 2.60 | 2.70 | 359.50 | 2788.70 | 297.81 | 1.90 | 6.79 | 141.00 | 137.00 |
| 147 WOR | 2.70 | 3.60 | 209.70• | 3408.90• | 342.90 | 1.10 | 49.84 | 139.00• | 219.00• |
| 148 YOR | 1.30 - | 1.40 | 132.40 | 1328.00 | 200.35 | .60 | 10.37 | 134.00 | 207.00 |

## BASIC STATISTICS OF ENVIRONMENTAL COMPONENT (M)

| | Mean Level For Total Suspended Particulates IA1 | Mean Level for Sulfur Dioxide IA2 | Mean Annual Inversion Frequency IB1 | % of Housing Units Dilapidated IB2 | Park and Recreation Acres/ 1,000 Pop. IB3 | Pop. Density in Central City IC1 | Motor Vehicle Registrations/ 1,000 Pop. IC2 | Motorcycle Registrations/ 1,000 Pop. IC3 | Solid Waste Generated by Manufacturing ID | Water Pollution Index IE |
|---|---|---|---|---|---|---|---|---|---|---|
| 66 ALB | 92.33 | 56.00 | 37.50 | 2.30 | 5.70 | 2965.00 | 654.00 | 32.00 | 668.40 | .79 |
| 67 ANN | 73.95 | 308.00• | 32.50 | 1.60 | 60.10 | 4578.00 | 494.00 | 25.00 | 301.10 | 1.10• |
| 68 APP | 91.63• | 124.00• | 32.50 | 1.40 | 12.50 | 4905.00 | 472.00 | 13.00 | 550.40 | 1.50 |
| 69 AUG | 62.86• | 16.00 | 42.50 | 3.40 | 3.60 | 3938.00 | 532.00 | 8.00 | 445.80 | .89 |
| 70 AUS | 69.74 | 16.00 | 22.50 | 2.20 | 7.70 | 3492.00 | 565.00 | 23.00 | 1172.50 | 1.11 |
| 71 BAK | 135.19• | 19.00• | 37.50 | 3.20 | 64.20 | 2684.00 | 643.00 | 43.00 | 664.60 | .54 |
| 72 BAT | 61.22 | 91.00 | 32.50 | 2.80 | 7.30 | 4108.00 | 584.00• | 18.00• | 295.40 | .59 |
| 73 BEA | 59.98 | 52.00 | 27.50 | 3.40 | 4.80 | 1489.00 | 594.00 | 14.00 | 222.80 | 2.55 |
| 74 BIN | 57.77 | 67.00• | 32.50 | 3.20 | 5.80 | 5829.00 | 470.00 | 8.00 | 629.70 | 4.84 |
| 75 BRI | 57.24 | 90.00 | 22.50 | 3.90 | 11.00 | 9723.00 | 603.00• | 10.00• | 443.50 | 2.65 |
| 76 CAN | 102.62 | 173.00 | 27.50 | 1.50 | 4.90 | 5792.00 | 565.00 | 12.00 | 502.70 | 5.33 |
| 77 CHA | 46.72 | 18.00 | 37.50 | 2.90 | 5.40 | 3892.00 | 453.00 | 12.00 | 1078.80 | 2.05 |
| 78 CHA | 104.65 | 120.00 | 42.50 | 2.20 | 8.60 | 2629.00 | 500.00 | 33.00 | 213.20 | 12.28 |
| 79 CHA | 98.97 | 203.00 | 47.50 | 2.30 | 2.80 | 3173.00 | 629.00 | 17.00• | 727.70 | 2.28 |
| 80 CHA | 105.55 | 92.00 | 37.50 | 2.50 | 6.60 | 2268.00 | 552.00 | 15.00 | 532.80 | .80 |
| 81 COL | 96.56 | 26.00• | 37.50 | 1.70 | 16.40 | 2221.00 | 609.00 | 28.00 | 805.20 | .91 |
| 82 COL | 62.86 | 62.00 | 42.50 | 2.30 | 6.40 | 3399.00 | 536.00 | 8.00 | 914.00 | 2.84 |
| 83 COL | 50.08 | 87.00 | 37.50 | 3.30 | 11.40 | 2218.00 | 509.00 | 17.00 | 658.20 | .89 |
| 84 COH | 103.71 | 10.00 | 22.50 | 3.10 | 53.00 | 2033.00 | 570.00 | 13.00 | 339.30 | 1.05 |
| 85 DAV | 127.16 | 28.00• | 32.50 | 1.30 | 26.60 | 3022.00 | 574.00 | 20.00 | 443.20 | .86 |
| 86 DES | 85.23 | 28.00 | 32.50 | 1.20 | 12.90 | 3174.00 | 621.00 | 31.00 | 450.00 | .84 |
| 87 DUL | 71.51 | 66.00 | 27.50 | 1.30 | 45.50 | 1264.00 | 538.00 | 26.00 | 712.20 | 1.01 |
| 88 ELP | 142.42 | 119.00 | 37.50 | 1.60 | 3.70 | 2724.00 | 512.00 | 16.00 | 713.30 | 1.10 |
| 89 ERI | 104.43 | 106.00 | 22.50 | 3.50 | 3.70 | 6838.00 | 481.00• | 12.00 | 531.20 | 1.42 |
| 90 EUG | 85.52• | 99.00• | 32.50 | 2.30 | 53.50 | 2925.00 | 615.00 | 36.00 | 660.90 | 1.07 |
| 91 EVA | 75.25 | 97.00 | 32.50 | 2.20 | 10.90 | 3855.00 | 585.00 | 19.00 | 421.00 | 2.71 |
| 92 FAY | 65.18 | 52.00 | 32.50 | 2.30 | 1.50 | 2287.00 | 431.00 | 17.00• | 1071.40 | .74 |
| 93 FLI | 130.10 | 71.00 | 32.50 | 1.80 | 27.40 | 5894.00 | 523.00 | 26.00 | 514.80 | 1.34 |
| 94 FOR | 75.41 | 56.00 | 32.50 | 1.50 | 4.90 | 3450.00 | 556.00 | 16.00 | 464.00 | 2.30 |
| 95 FRE | 114.98 | 12.00 | 42.50 | 2.80 | 1133.00 | 3971.00 | 632.00 | 29.00 | 532.20 | .59 |
| 96 GRE | 76.65 | 55.00 | 47.50 | 2.70 | 19.40 | 2957.00 | 575.00 | 7.00 | 750.80 | 2.51 |
| 97 HAM | 81.28 | 24.00 | 27.50 | 1.70 | 10.80 | 3313.00 | 549.00 | 15.00 | 603.10 | 3.07 |
| 98 HAR | 77.44 | 14.00• | 32.50 | 3.90 | 7.40 | 6955.00 | 481.00• | 12.00 | 584.40 | 2.44 |
| 99 HUN | 96.35 | 120.00• | 42.50 | 2.00 | 20.50 | 4562.00 | 509.00 | 18.00 | 448.70 | 9.26 |
| 100 HUN | 63.06 | 105.00• | 37.50 | 1.80 | 11.50 | 1263.00 | 617.00 | 21.00 | 642.10 | .73 |
| 101 JAC | 105.33• | 12.00 | 32.50 | 3.10 | 17.70 | 3067.00 | 573.00 | 16.00 | 620.00 | 1.25 |
| 102 JOH | 102.76 | 4.00 | 32.50 | 3.60 | 109.90 | 7452.00 | 481.00• | 12.00 | 782.40 | 5.87 |
| 103 KAL | 58.93 | 43.00 | 32.50 | 1.50 | 22.80 | 3492.00 | 520.00 | 24.00 | 393.20 | 1.44 |
| 104 KNO | 99.42 | 47.00 | 42.50 | 2.10 | 236.80 | 2267.00 | 546.00 | 16.00• | 584.90 | 1.19 |
| 105 LAN | 107.58 | 89.00 | 32.50 | 3.30 | 2.00 | 8013.00 | 481.00• | 12.00 | 570.80 | 1.50 |
| 106 LAN | 77.93 | 62.00 | 32.50 | 1.50 | 13.90 | 3939.00 | 518.00 | 29.00 | 384.70 | 1.76 |
| 107 LAS | 100.42 | 19.00• | 47.50 | 1.90 | 2680.10 | 2438.00 | 698.00 | 36.00 | 480.40 | .97 |
| 108 LAW | 65.08 | 293.00 | 27.50 | 4.50 | 19.60 | 2891.00 | 481.00• | 10.00• | 677.50 | 1.07 |
| 109 LIT | 73.88• | 18.00 | 37.50 | 2.30 | 15.40 | 2449.00 | 589.00 | 13.00 | 697.40 | 1.42 |
| 110 LOR | 200.26• | 113.00• | 22.50 | 1.50 | 17.40 | 3307.00 | 572.00 | 15.00 | 580.90 | 4.44 |
| 111 LOW | 50.31 | 414.00 | 27.50 | 4.00 | 14.70 | 6929.00 | 481.00• | 10.00• | 818.60 | 1.54 |
| 112 MAC | 81.63• | 16.00 | 37.50 | 3.20 | 5.20 | 2498.00 | 547.00 | 16.00 | 568.20 | 2.36 |
| 113 MAD | 73.84 | 37.00 | 32.50 | 1.30 | 6.50 | 3572.00 | 494.00 | 16.00 | 615.40 | .59 |
| 114 MOB | 106.27 | 71.00 | 32.50 | 3.50 | 21.60 | 1630.00 | 561.00 | 14.00 | 722.00 | 9.43 |
| 115 MON | 96.99 | 25.00 | 37.50 | 3.10 | 27.10• | 2875.00 | 572.00 | 14.00 | 853.90 | .89 |
| 116 NEW | 59.72 | 75.00 | 22.50 | 4.20 | 7.60 | 7484.00 | 553.00• | 10.00• | 461.90 | 2.64 |
| 117 NEW | 61.81• | 75.00• | 22.50 | 3.90 | 16.30 | 2269.00 | 574.00• | 10.00• | 531.10 | 3.38 |
| 118 NEW | 53.84 | 14.00 | 22.50 | 2.20 | 34.10 | 2092.00 | 456.00 | 17.00• | 713.00 | .73 |
| 119 ORL | 75.40• | 73.00• | 32.50 | 2.30 | 19.60 | 3600.00 | 701.00 | 14.00 | 629.70 | 1.46 |
| 120 OXN | 118.49• | 52.00• | 37.50 | 2.30 | 32.20 | 3640.00 | 594.00 | 35.00 | 1107.60 | .80 |
| 121 PEN | 106.27• | 71.00• | 32.50 | 2.80 | 5.90 | 2479.00 | 595.00 | 17.00 | 451.90 | 3.77 |
| 122 PEO | 77.71 | 126.00 | 32.50 | 1.50 | 27.70 | 3395.00 | 562.00 | 17.00 | 455.60 | 1.87 |
| 123 RAL | 54.91 | 51.00 | 32.50 | 2.00 | 26.80 | 2708.00 | 741.00 | 17.00 | 719.70 | 2.27 |
| 124 REA | 117.29 | 141.00 | 32.50 | 3.20 | 44.60 | 8853.00 | 481.00• | 12.00 | 737.70 | 1.98 |
| 125 ROC | 105.13• | 23.00 | 32.50 | 1.70 | 27.60 | 4309.00 | 548.00• | 13.00 | 462.80 | 1.04 |
| 126 SAG | 130.10 | 38.00 | 32.50 | 2.20 | 3.50 | 5309.00 | 517.00 | 24.00 | 404.50 | 1.86 |
| 127 SAL | 114.98• | 12.00 | 37.50 | 2.90 | 154.80 | 4019.00 | 549.00 | 25.00 | 465.90 | 1.13 |
| 128 SAN | 118.49• | 52.00• | 37.50 | 2.20 | 16.70 | 3344.00 | 600.00 | 34.00 | 826.00 | .59 |
| 129 SAN | 118.49• | 52.00• | 37.50 | 2.80 | 78.90 | 2513.00 | 684.00 | 34.00 | 820.60 | .74• |
| 130 SCR | 188.75 | 93.00 | 32.50 | 3.30 | 3.10 | 4030.00 | 481.00• | 12.00 | 875.00 | 1.62 |
| 131 SHR | 105.33 | 143.00 | 32.50 | 3.20 | 9.50 | 3200.00 | 584.00• | 18.00• | 840.70 | 2.46 |
| 132 SOU | 75.41 | 152.00 | 32.50 | 1.70 | 5.70 | 4301.00 | 530.00 | 15.00 | 618.50 | 1.40 |
| 133 SPO | 97.91 | 19.00 | 37.50 | 2.10 | 101.30 | 3357.00 | 652.00 | 24.00 | 476.70 | .78 |
| 134 STA | 57.24 | 90.00• | 22.50 | 3.40 | 7.70 | 2856.00 | 603.00• | 10.00• | 389.20 | 2.16 |
| 135 STO | 59.83• | 36.00• | 42.50 | 2.70 | 1.00 | 3600.00 | 623.00 | 27.00 | 376.00 | 1.53 |
| 136 TAC | 93.89 | 73.00 | 32.50 | 2.10 | 483.30 | 3241.00 | 573.00 | 19.00 | 645.40 | 1.07 |
| 137 TRE | 71.05 | 74.00 | 22.50 | 4.70 | 5.00 | 13952.00 | 481.00• | 10.00• | 513.40 | .60 |
| 138 TUC | 98.08 | 12.00 | 42.50 | 2.50 | 41.10 | 3287.00 | 656.00 | 24.00 | 788.40 | 1.22 |
| 139 TUL | 83.13 | 464.00 | 37.50 | 2.00 | 57.10 | 2369.00 | 672.00 | 29.00 | 571.50 | 3.50 |
| 140 UTI | 71.67 | 67.00 | 32.50 | 3.30 | 21.60 | 2704.00 | 444.00 | 7.00 | 485.40 | 2.02 |
| 141 VAL | 59.83• | 36.00• | 37.50 | 2.30 | 136.20 | 3629.00 | 604.00 | 32.00 | 1180.90 | 1.10 |
| 142 WAT | 80.53 | 33.00 | 27.50 | 4.60 | 29.50 | 3914.00 | 553.00• | 10.00• | 561.40 | 1.88 |
| 143 WES | 61.80• | 12.00• | 17.50 | 2.80 | 5.40 | 4182.00 | 704.00 | 24.00 | 665.70 | 13.89 |
| 144 WIC | 142.33 | 22.00 | 37.50 | 2.30 | 17.80 | 3197.00 | 655.00 | 34.00 | 420.40 | .79 |
| 145 WIL | 127.44 | 141.00• | 32.50 | 3.50 | 49.90 | 7086.00 | 481.00• | 12.00 | 906.60 | 1.16 |
| 146 WIL | 125.19 | 104.00 | 22.50 | 1.70 | 7.40 | 6231.00 | 579.00• | 17.00• | 557.90 | .77 |
| 147 WOR | 72.43 | 210.00 | 27.50 | 4.60 | 13.30• | 4721.00 | 481.00• | 10.00• | 577.40 | 2.22 |
| 148 YOR | 84.58 | 14.00 | 32.50 | 3.50 | 28.50 | 9497.00 | 481.00• | 12.00 | 669.90 | 3.69 |

| | | Mean Annual Inversion Frequency IIA1 | Possible Annual Sunshine Days IIA2 | No. of Days With Thunder-Storms IIA3 | No. of Days With Temp. 90° or Above IIA4 | No. of Days With Temp. 32° or Below IIA5 | Park and Recreation Acres/1,000 Pop. IIB1 | Miles of Trails/ 100,000 Pop. IIB2 |
|---|---|---|---|---|---|---|---|---|
| 66 | ALB | 37.50 | 77.00 | 43.00 | 62.00 | 128.00 | 5.70 | 148.70 |
| 67 | ANN | 32.50 | 54.00 | 34.00 • | 14.00 • | 130.00 • | 60.10 | 192.30 |
| 68 | APP | 32.50 | 53.00 • | 29.00 • | 12.00 • | 138.00 • | 12.50 | 111.90 |
| 69 | AUG | 42.50 | 64.00 • | 77.00 | 62.00 | 56.00 | 3.60 | 197.60 |
| 70 | AUS | 22.50 | 61.00 | 48.00 | 98.00 | 18.00 | 7.70 | 70.90 |
| 71 | BAK | 37.50 | 83.00 • | 3.00 | 123.00 | 4.00 | 64.20 | 1164.10 |
| 72 | BAT | 32.50 | 60.00 • | 80.00 | 90.00 | 21.00 | 7.30 | 10.50 |
| 73 | BEA | 27.50 | 59.00 • | 75.00 | 50.00 | 25.00 | 4.80 | 50.60 |
| 74 | BIN | 32.50 | 51.00 • | 38.00 | 0.00 | 126.00 | 5.80 | 56.10 |
| 75 | BRI | 22.50 | 61.00 • | 24.00 | 10.00 | 89.00 | 11.00 | 92.50 |
| 76 | CAN | 27.50 | 52.00 • | 40.00 | 10.00 | 105.00 | 4.90 | 34.90 |
| 77 | CHA | 37.50 | 63.00 | 58.00 | 60.00 | 36.00 | 5.40 | 131.60 |
| 78 | CHA | 42.50 | 48.00 • | 51.00 | 22.00 | 93.00 | 8.60 | 243.50 |
| 79 | CHA | 47.50 | 66.00 | 45.00 | 25.00 | 69.00 | 2.80 | 0.00 |
| 80 | CHA | 37.50 | 58.00 | 60.00 | 37.00 | 72.00 | 6.60 | 134.40 |
| 81 | COL | 37.50 | 70.00 • | 56.00 | 17.00 | 168.00 | 16.40 | 288.10 |
| 82 | COL | 42.50 | 64.00 | 67.00 | 64.00 | 62.00 | 6.40 | 71.20 |
| 83 | COL | 37.50 | 59.00 • | 62.00 | 70.00 | 42.00 | 11.40 | 62.80 |
| 84 | COR | 22.50 | 64.00 | 33.00 | 102.00 | 13.00 | 53.00 | 7.00 |
| 85 | DAV | 32.50 | 54.00 | 45.00 | 21.00 | 107.00 | 26.60 | 322.30 |
| 86 | DES | 32.50 | 60.00 | 54.00 | 23.00 | 107.00 | 12.90 | 97.90 |
| 87 | DUL | 27.50 | 55.00 | 38.00 | 2.00 | 188.00 | 45.50 | 1101.80 |
| 88 | ELP | 37.50 | 83.00 | 22.00 | 108.00 | 73.00 | 3.70 | 136.40 |
| 89 | ERI | 22.50 | 53.00 • | 41.00 | 0.00 | 111.00 | 3.70 | 53.00 |
| 90 | EUG | 32.50 | 47.00 • | 1.00 | 16.00 | 47.00 | 53.50 | 3535.20 |
| 91 | EVA | 32.50 | 63.00 | 46.00 | 39.00 | 86.00 | 10.90 | 201.70 |
| 92 | FAY | 32.50 | 61.00 • | 48.00 • | 17.00 • | 76.00 • | 1.50 | 47.10 |
| 93 | FLI | 32.50 | 54.00 • | 30.00 | 9.00 | 119.00 | 27.40 | 175.00 |
| 94 | FOR | 32.50 | 58.00 | 42.00 | 17.00 | 115.00 | 4.90 | 82.10 |
| 95 | FRE | 42.50 | 83.00 | 8.00 | 106.00 | 11.00 | 1133.00 | 4401.90 |
| 96 | GRE | 47.50 | 59.00 | 46.00 | 24.00 | 61.00 | 19.40 | 70.00 |
| 97 | HAM | 27.50 | 57.00 • | 48.00 • | 21.00 • | 101.00 • | 10.80 | 435.00 |
| 98 | HAR | 32.50 | 58.00 | 28.00 | 24.00 | 95.00 | 7.40 | 878.30 |
| 99 | HUN | 42.50 | 48.00 • | 46.00 | 30.00 | 89.00 | 20.50 | 118.10 |
| 100 | HUN | 37.50 | 58.00 • | 71.00 | 35.00 | 54.00 | 11.50 | 276.30 |
| 101 | JAC | 32.50 | 60.00 | 76.00 | 83.00 | 40.00 | 17.70 | 0.00 |
| 102 | JOH | 32.50 | 52.00 • | 38.00 • | 17.00 • | 101.00 • | 109.90 | 634.90 |
| 103 | KAL | 32.50 | 51.00 • | 36.00 • | 14.00 • | 124.00 • | 22.80 | 49.50 |
| 104 | KNO | 42.50 | 56.00 | 48.00 | 10.00 | 60.00 | 236.80 | 350.00 |
| 105 | LAN | 32.50 | 57.00 • | 28.00 • | 24.00 • | 95.00 • | 2.00 | 78.10 |
| 106 | LAN | 32.50 | 54.00 | 34.00 | 14.00 | 130.00 | 13.90 | 84.60 |
| 107 | LAS | 47.50 | 86.00 | 15.00 | 141.00 | 36.00 | 2680.10 | 688.60 |
| 108 | LAW | 27.50 | 60.00 • | 17.00 • | 19.00 • | 76.00 • | 19.60 | 500.00 |
| 109 | LIT | 37.50 | 62.00 | 77.00 | 60.00 | 56.00 | 15.40 | 108.30 |
| 110 | LOR | 22.50 | 52.00 | 40.00 | 11.00 | 94.00 | 17.40 | 73.90 |
| 111 | LOW | 27.50 | 60.00 • | 17.00 | 19.00 | 76.00 | 14.70 | 267.60 |
| 112 | MAC | 37.50 | 62.00 | 52.00 | 96.00 | 42.00 | 5.20 | 43.60 |
| 113 | MAD | 32.50 | 58.00 | 39.00 | 13.00 | 132.00 | 6.50 | 48.20 |
| 114 | MOB | 32.50 | 60.00 | 95.00 | 98.00 | 21.00 | 21.60 | 21.20 |
| 115 | MON | 37.50 | 59.00 | 81.00 | 98.00 | 37.00 | 27.10 • | 237.50 • |
| 116 | NEW | 22.50 | 61.00 | 24.00 • | 10.00 • | 89.00 • | 7.60 | 73.00 |
| 117 | NEW | 22.50 | 61.00 | 24.00 • | 10.00 • | 89.00 • | 16.30 | 33.60 |
| 118 | NEW | 22.50 | 63.00 | 24.00 • | 10.00 • | 89.00 • | 34.10 | 191.70 |
| 119 | ORL | 32.50 | 64.00 • | 85.00 | 113.00 | 2.00 | 19.60 | 144.80 |
| 120 | OXN | 37.50 | 73.00 • | 1.00 | 21.00 • | 0.00 • | 32.20 | 2287.20 |
| 121 | PEN | 32.50 | 60.00 | 84.00 | 82.00 | 15.00 | 5.90 | 164.60 |
| 122 | PEO | 32.50 | 58.00 | 56.00 | 12.00 | 104.00 | 27.70 | 67.20 |
| 123 | RAL | 32.50 | 61.00 | 48.00 | 17.00 | 76.00 | 26.80 | 192.90 |
| 124 | REA | 32.50 | 57.00 | 28.00 • | 24.00 • | 95.00 • | 44.60 | 429.00 |
| 125 | ROC | 32.50 | 58.00 • | 43.00 | 13.00 | 109.00 | 27.60 | 213.20 |
| 126 | SAG | 32.50 | 54.00 • | 34.00 • | 14.00 • | 130.00 • | 3.50 | 63.60 |
| 127 | SAL | 37.50 | 67.00 • | 2.00 • | 6.00 • | 2.00 • | 154.80 | 1840.00 |
| 128 | SAN | 37.50 | 73.00 • | 1.00 • | 21.00 • | 0.00 • | 16.70 | 3102.20 |
| 129 | SAN | 37.50 | 67.00 • | 2.00 • | 6.00 | 2.00 | 78.90 | 404.80 |
| 130 | SCR | 32.50 | 53.00 | 31.00 | 6.00 | 120.00 | 3.10 | 59.80 |
| 131 | SHR | 32.50 | 64.00 | 62.00 | 57.00 | 32.00 | 9.50 | 128.80 |
| 132 | SOU | 32.50 | 57.00 • | 42.00 | 14.00 | 94.00 | 5.70 | 53.50 |
| 133 | SPO | 37.50 | 57.00 | 5.00 | 29.00 | 131.00 | 101.30 | 512.10 |
| 134 | STA | 22.50 | 61.00 • | 24.00 • | 10.00 • | 89.00 • | 7.70 | 48.50 |
| 135 | STO | 42.50 | 79.00 • | 5.00 | 80.00 | 9.00 | 1.00 | 17.20 |
| 136 | TAC | 32.50 | 48.00 | 4.00 • | 1.00 • | 17.00 • | 483.30 | 1214.10 |
| 137 | TRE | 22.50 | 59.00 | 33.00 | 24.00 | 63.00 | 5.00 | 3.20 |
| 138 | TUC | 42.50 | 86.00 | 28.00 | 135.00 | 18.00 | 41.10 | 1758.50 |
| 139 | TUL | 37.50 | 62.00 | 70.00 | 52.00 | 64.00 | 57.10 | 33.50 |
| 140 | UTI | 32.50 | 51.00 • | 33.00 • | 15.00 • | 111.00 • | 21.60 | 8.80 |
| 141 | VAL | 37.50 | 67.00 | 2.00 • | 6.00 | 2.00 | 136.20 | 409.60 |
| 142 | WAT | 27.50 | 57.00 | 28.00 • | 30.00 | 113.00 • | 29.50 | 224.80 |
| 143 | WES | 17.50 | 64.00 • | 92.00 | 70.00 | 0.00 | 5.40 | 120.30 |
| 144 | WIC | 37.50 | 65.00 | 53.00 | 61.00 | 100.00 | 17.80 | 38.50 |
| 145 | WIL | 32.50 | 53.00 | 31.00 | 6.00 | 120.00 | 49.90 | 230.90 |
| 146 | WIL | 22.50 | 58.00 | 27.00 | 24.00 | 76.00 | 7.40 | 68.10 |
| 147 | WOR | 27.50 | 57.00 • | 24.00 | 5.00 | 128.00 | 13.30 • | 261.90 • |
| 148 | YOR | 32.50 | 57.00 • | 28.00 • | 24.00 • | 95.00 • | 28.50 | 360.60 |

## BASIC STATISTICS OF HEALTH AND EDUCATION COMPONENT (M)

| | | Infant Mortality Rate/1,000 Live Births IA1 | Death Rate/ 1,000 pop. IA2 | Median Schools Years Completed IB1 | % of Persons 25+, Completed 4 yrs. High School or more IB2 | % of Males 16-21 not High School Graduates IB3 | % of pop., 3-34 Enrolled in Schools IB4 |
|---|---|---|---|---|---|---|---|
| US | | 21.20 | 9.50 | 12.10 | 52.30 | 15.20 | 54.30 |
| 66 | ALB | 20.70 | 6.30 | 12.50 | 66.20 | 11.00 | 55.90 |
| 67 | ANN | 22.10 | 5.90 | 12.60 | 67.50 | 9.10 | 61.10 |
| 68 | APP | 19.00 | 7.50 | 12.20 | 56.20 | 6.20 | 59.10 |
| 69 | AUG | 25.40 | 8.60 | 11.50 | 46.30 | 22.60 | 45.90 |
| 70 | AUS | 18.70 | 6.50 | 12.40 | 60.90 | 11.60 | 54.50 |
| 71 | BAK | 21.60 | 8.30 | 12.10 | 51.70 | 17.10 | 55.10 |
| 72 | BAT | 19.80 | 7.30 | 12.30 | 59.10 | 13.00 | 55.60 |
| 73 | BEA | 21.30 | 8.20 | 11.60 | 46.30 | 11.50 | 57.00 |
| 74 | BIN | 16.20 | 9.50 | 12.20 | 58.90 | 10.40 | 55.10 |
| 75 | BRI | 18.10• | 8.70 • | 12.10 | 51.90 | 11.50 | 57.50 |
| 76 | CAN | 19.00 | 9.90 | 12.10 | 52.40 | 12.80 | 53.80 |
| 77 | CHA | 25.60 | 7.50 | 11.80 | 48.40 | 19.10 | 48.30 |
| 78 | CHA | 22.00 | 10.20 | 12.10 | 52.80 | 15.20 | 52.40 |
| 79 | CHA | 22.20 | 7.80 | 12.00 | 50.80 | 17.20 | 51.00 |
| 80 | CHA | 24.00 | 9.70 | 11.60 | 47.60 | 21.10 | 49.80 |
| 81 | COL | 28.30 | 5.70 | 12.60 | 72.90 | 19.50 | 45.90 |
| 82 | COL | 23.60 | 7.30 | 12.00 | 50.60 | 21.00 | 48.30 |
| 83 | COL | 23.40 | 7.90 | 11.50 | 46.60 | 26.20 | 42.50 |
| 84 | COR | 21.00 | 6.90 | 11.50 | 47.10 | 19.20 | 53.10 |
| 85 | DAV | 27.00 | 9.60 | 12.10 | 55.60 | 9.70 | 55.10 |
| 86 | DES | 19.20 | 9.10 | 12.40 | 68.00 | 10.70 | 52.60 |
| 87 | DUL | 19.00 | 11.40 | 12.20 | 56.20 | 6.70 | 59.70 |
| 88 | ELP | 17.40 | 6.20 | 12.00 | 51.10 | 15.70 | 52.90 |
| 89 | ERI | 19.60 | 10.20 | 12.20 | 58.40 | 8.30 | 56.50 |
| 90 | EUG | 14.40 | 6.90 | 12.30 | 61.90 | 7.10 | 59.80 |
| 91 | EVA | 19.40 | 10.60 | 12.10 | 52.00 | 15.30 | 53.10 |
| 92 | FAY | 25.30 | 5.20 | 12.20 | 55.10 | 26.30 | 37.00 |
| 93 | FLI | 22.60 | 7.50 | 12.10 | 52.30 | 13.80 | 55.50 |
| 94 | FOR | 22.00 | 8.10 | 12.20 | 59.40 | 14.50 | 54.90 |
| 95 | FRE | 20.40 | 8.60 | 12.10 | 52.70 | 12.90 | 59.50 |
| 96 | GRE | 25.20 | 8.60 | 10.90 | 41.00 | 18.70 | 50.60 |
| 97 | HAM | 15.40 | 8.10 | 11.70 | 47.80 | 11.40 | 56.60 |
| 98 | HAR | 21.20 | 9.90 | 12.10 | 55.40 | 13.00 | 54.30 |
| 99 | HUN | 17.90 | 10.40 | 11.40 | 46.10 | 19.50 | 49.90 |
| 100 | HUN | 19.20 | 6.30 | 12.30 | 58.30 | 17.50 | 51.30 |
| 101 | JAC | 28.00 | 8.50 | 12.20 | 56.10 | 17.10 | 54.40 |
| 102 | JOH | 20.00 | 11.60 | 10.90 | 44.10 | 8.60 | 57.10 |
| 103 | KAL | 22.10 | 7.30 | 12.30 | 60.70 | 10.80 | 59.10 |
| 104 | KNO | 21.50 | 8.90 | 12.00 | 50.70 | 14.50 | 53.00 |
| 105 | LAN | 18.10 | 8.80 | 11.10 | 43.90 | 20.80 | 52.80 |
| 106 | LAN | 16.80 | 7.00 | 12.40 | 63.10 | 7.50 | 60.10 |
| 107 | LAS | 27.20 | 6.70 | 12.40 | 65.20 | 14.00 | 47.70 |
| 108 | LAW | 20.10• | 8.10• | 12.10 | 53.70 | 15.00 | 54.90 |
| 109 | LIT | 21.30 | 9.30 | 12.20 | 56.50 | 15.80 | 48.60 |
| 110 | LOR | 22.70 | 8.20 | 12.10 | 52.60 | 13.00 | 55.10 |
| 111 | LOW | 20.10• | 8.10• | 12.10 | 54.50 | 15.40 | 54.60 |
| 112 | MAC | 23.30 | 9.00 | 11.60 | 47.40 | 19.70 | 50.90 |
| 113 | MAD | 14.20 | 6.90 | 12.60 | 71.20 | 5.10 | 59.00 |
| 114 | MOB | 22.80 | 8.60 | 11.00 | 42.30 | 18.40 | 54.00 |
| 115 | MON | 31.20 | 10.70 | 12.10 | 51.60 | 23.80 | 52.90 |
| 116 | NEW | 20.80• | 9.40• | 12.20 | 56.80 | 10.50 | 58.20 |
| 117 | NEW | 21.80• | 8.20• | 12.10 | 54.10 | 11.20 | 52.10 |
| 118 | NEW | 23.50 | 6.50 | 12.10 | 52.10 | 18.90 | 49.40 |
| 119 | ORL | 26.10 | 8.60 | 12.20 | 56.10 | 18.30 | 55.00 |
| 120 | OXN | 23.80 | 6.10 | 12.40 | 63.80 | 13.80 | 56.90 |
| 121 | PEN | 24.20 | 7.30 | 12.00 | 51.00 | 15.90 | 50.00 |
| 122 | PEO | 23.90 | 9.10 | 12.10 | 53.70 | 11.90 | 56.10 |
| 123 | RAL | 21.80 | 7.30 | 12.20 | 53.60 | 14.30 | 54.20 |
| 124 | REA | 21.00 | 11.00 | 11.10 | 43.30 | 14.50 | 54.40 |
| 125 | ROC | 18.50 | 8.10 | 12.10 | 52.20 | 18.70 | 53.20 |
| 126 | SAG | 23.20 | 8.30 | 12.00 | 50.60 | 13.20 | 55.70 |
| 127 | SAL | 20.70 | 6.90 | 12.40 | 62.50 | 22.70 | 47.20 |
| 128 | SAN | 17.50 | 7.50 | 12.60 | 71.30 | 8.40 | 58.00 |
| 129 | SAN | 20.00 | 10.70 | 12.40 | 63.60 | 12.10 | 55.20 |
| 130 | SCR | 20.00 | 13.50 | 11.70 | 48.00 | 10.90 | 56.50 |
| 131 | SHR | 24.10 | 9.70 | 12.00 | 50.90 | 15.80 | 53.00 |
| 132 | SOU | 20.20 | 9.40 | 12.10 | 54.20 | 14.00 | 57.40 |
| 133 | SPO | 19.60 | 10.40 | 12.40 | 65.30 | 6.90 | 57.00 |
| 134 | STA | 18.10• | 8.70• | 12.60 | 68.10 | 6.70 | 62.60 |
| 135 | STO | 15.50 | 9.40 | 11.90 | 49.40 | 14.20 | 57.30 |
| 136 | TAC | 21.60 | 8.60 | 12.30 | 60.70 | 20.00 | 49.20 |
| 137 | TRE | 25.80 | 9.60 | 12.10 | 52.80 | 11.00 | 57.20 |
| 138 | TUC | 17.50 | 8.40 | 12.40 | 63.10 | 10.90 | 56.70 |
| 139 | TUL | 19.80 | 9.00 | 12.20 | 58.20 | 13.20 | 53.10 |
| 140 | UTI | 18.10 | 10.80 | 12.00 | 49.90 | 12.20 | 55.80 |
| 141 | VAL | 23.40 | 8.00 | 12.30 | 62.90 | 9.10 | 52.00 |
| 142 | WAT | 20.80• | 9.40 • | 12.00 | 49.90 | 16.00 | 56.50 |
| 143 | WES | 28.00 | 11.60 | 12.20 | 55.70 | 20.30 | 55.10 |
| 144 | WIC | 22.60 | 8.00 | 12.40 | 63.20 | 11.10 | 55.30 |
| 145 | WIL | 19.10 | 12.90 | 11.50 | 46.90 | 12.90 | 54.70 |
| 146 | WIL | 19.20 | 8.80 | 12.10 | 54.40 | 13.50 | 54.90 |
| 147 | WOR | 21.20 • | 10.30• | 12.10 | 53.70 | 10.60 | 59.40 |
| 148 | YOR | 17.10 | 9.60 | 11.20 | 44.70 | 13.50 | 52.40 |

| | Dentists/ 100,000 pop. IIA1 | Hospital Beds/ 100,000 pop. IIA2 | Hospital Occupancy Rates IIA3 | Physicians/ 100,000 pop. IIA4 | Per Capita Local Gov't Expend. on Health IIA5 | Per Capita Local Gov't Expend. on Educ. IIB1 | % of Persons, 25+, Completed 4 yrs. College or more IIB2 |
|---|---|---|---|---|---|---|---|
| US | 59.50 | 414.90 | 79.80 | 153.80 | 2.96 | 145.69 | 10.70 |
| 66 ALB | 53.20 | 363.60 | 77.00 | 218.50 | 1.70 | 152.43 | 16.90 |
| 67 ANN | 111.50 | 772.30 | 78.00 | 557.00 | 3.01 | 175.06 | 27.40 |
| 68 APP | 53.80 | 535.60 | 73.30 | 99.00 | 4.16 • | 226.68• | 9.50 |
| 69 AUG | 55.60 | 464.40 | 82.30 | 217.80 | 2.23 | 105.28 | 10.50 |
| 70 AUS | 56.50 | 312.30 | 81.40 | 162.10 | 1.71 | 132.93 | 19.50 |
| 71 BAK | 38.60 | 342.10 | 69.80 | 107.80 | 5.93 | 218.27 | 8.90 |
| 72 BAT | 53.30 | 425.40 | 73.20 | 142.70 | 1.72 | 145.98 | 16.60 |
| 73 BEA | 41.10 | 434.30 | 81.40 | 105.10 | 2.27 | 133.11 | 8.80 |
| 74 BIN | 53.20 | 462.20 | 87.60 | 150.00 | 4.61 | 222.52 | 10.50 |
| 75 BRI | 80.50• | 324.30• | 83.70 • | 187.70• | 4.02 | 138.73 | 10.80 |
| 76 CAN | 46.70 | 401.10 | 82.80 | 108.50 | 1.56 | 121.86 | 7.10 |
| 77 CHA | 42.50 | 400.20 | 77.10 | 185.30 | 1.84 | 88.52 | 10.10 |
| 78 CHA | 51.80 | 619.10 | 83.70 | 144.70 | 2.16 | 119.83 | 9.90 |
| 79 CHA | 42.00 | 443.10 | 82.60 | 127.00 | 4.67 | 142.27 | 12.80 |
| 80 CHA | 48.90 | 435.50 | 78.90 | 137.40 | 4.23 | 121.88 | 9.30 |
| 81 COL | 61.00 | 307.70 | 74.90 | 110.20 | 2.20 | 184.42 | 16.50 |
| 82 COL | 47.40 | 409.40 | 80.60 | 131.90 | 1.89 | 94.23 | 14.40 |
| 83 COL | 23.50 | 347.00 | 101.50 | 75.40 | 2.27 | 105.90 | 9.00 |
| 84 COR | 42.50 | 441.30 | 69.60 | 125.00 | 2.10 | 163.98 | 9.80 |
| 85 DAV | 45.20 | 488.90 | 78.10 | 86.00 | .84 | 142.52 | 8.90 |
| 86 DES | 65.40 | 517.60 | 88.60 | 133.50 | 1.96 | 161.59 | 12.80 |
| 87 DUL | 69.70 | 764.70 | 75.90 | 121.00 | 2.05 | 171.10 | 9.20 |
| 88 ELP | 33.40 | 419.70 | 77.20 | 98.00 | 2.62 | 122.75 | 11.40 |
| 89 ERI | 58.00 | 397.50 | 84.00 | 99.00 | 1.21 | 124.67 | 8.80 |
| 90 EUG | 68.90 | 296.20 | 72.00 | 128.40 | 2.31 | 184.50 | 14.20 |
| 91 EVA | 47.30 | 634.10 | 81.70 | 134.50 | 1.60 | 121.46 | 8.10 |
| 92 FAY | 22.20 | 183.00 | 89.80 | 46.20 | 2.23 | 100.51 | 10.00 |
| 93 FLI | 46.10 | 382.80 | 89.70 | 100.10 | 2.84 | 199.60 | 7.20 |
| 94 FOR | 44.90 | 519.50 | 86.40 | 116.20 | 1.27 | 129.62 | 10.20 |
| 95 FRE | 56.20 | 393.40 | 67.30 | 135.80 | 6.90 | 187.01 | 10.20 |
| 96 GRE | 36.10 | 331.90 | 85.00 | 109.80 | 1.76 | 89.06 | 10.20 |
| 97 HAM | 33.20 | 523.90 | 75.80 | 92.00 | 2.02 | 131.49 | 8.50 |
| 98 HAR | 52.80 | 463.90 | 86.40 | 155.40 | .45 | 154.58 | 9.40 |
| 99 HUN | 45.30 | 593.50 | 77.20 | 101.70 | 2.08 | 104.60 | 7.50 |
| 100 HUN | 34.60 | 416.20 | 81.40 | 71.40 | 1.23 | 103.13 | 16.40 |
| 101 JAC | 44.80 | 493.20 | 85.00 | 229.00 | 1.88 | 102.64 | 14.00 |
| 102 JOH | 45.70 | 552.50 | 82.30 | 94.00 | .17 | 113.32 | 5.10 |
| 103 KAL | 59.50 | 368.10 | 77.90 | 165.20 | 1.92 | 153.13 | 14.50 |
| 104 KNO | 50.70 | 535.80 | 81.90 | 149.90 | 1.77 | 114.42 | 11.30 |
| 105 LAN | 46.90 | 321.90 | 76.70 | 100.10 | .46 | 157.20 | 8.20 |
| 106 LAN | 52.10 | 348.00 | 77.20 | 107.80 | 1.82 | 193.34 | 14.90 |
| 107 LAS | 44.60 | 299.70 | 72.20 | 99.90 | 2.94 | 158.33 | 10.00 |
| 108 LAW | 82.50• | 466.80• | 80.00 • | 274.00• | 2.56 | 132.41 | 9.40 |
| 109 LIT | 46.70 | 556.10 | 82.10 | 224.60 | 1.63 | 105.01 | 10.70 |
| 110 LOR | 42.00 | 358.60 | 88.60 | 96.90 | 2.62 | 135.06 | 7.10 |
| 111 LOW | 82.50• | 466.80• | 80.00 • | 274.00• | 2.94 | 129.99 | 9.10 |
| 112 MAC | 35.40 | 374.10 | 75.50 | 111.00 | 2.31 | 115.52 | 9.30 |
| 113 MAD | 72.00 | 624.20 | 75.40 | 363.10 | 2.94 | 171.42 | 23.10 |
| 114 MOB | 33.70 | 382.30 | 86.40 | 102.70 | 1.92 | 93.66 | 7.30 |
| 115 MON | 40.70 | 457.00 | 81.30 | 105.80 | 2.06 | 89.40 | 11.50 |
| 116 NEW | 67.80• | 377.10• | 81.40 • | 267.80• | 3.22 | 148.31 | 14.40 |
| 117 NEW | 48.90• | 244.00• | 73.40 • | 135.30• | 1.54 | 144.96 | 11.30 |
| 118 NEW | 39.40 | 395.00 | 80.20 | 94.50 | 1.84 | 123.90 | 11.50 |
| 119 ORL | 53.00 | 448.80 | 78.10 | 149.50 | .65 | 126.11 | 11.20 |
| 120 OXN | 52.10 | 341.10 | 66.00 | 146.40 | 3.37 | 231.74 | 12.30 |
| 121 PEN | 34.60 | 396.20 | 82.50 | 93.40 | 1.34 | 145.95 | 9.30 |
| 122 PEO | 44.70 | 606.20 | 81.80 | 118.70 | 2.09 | 134.75 | 9.30 |
| 123 RAL | 53.80 | 394.00 | 81.80 | 130.90 | 2.60 | 121.97 | 17.10 |
| 124 REA | 54.30 | 380.60 | 88.70 | 127.90 | .70 | 141.16 | 6.60 |
| 125 ROC | 47.00 | 402.50 | 75.90 | 119.10 | .83 | 131.29 | 8.30 |
| 126 SAG | 46.90 | 364.50 | 84.90 | 93.70 | 2.35 | 148.52 | 7.40 |
| 127 SAL | 68.80 | 308.70 | 102.30 | 147.20 | 5.56 | 183.43 | 15.00 |
| 128 SAN | 81.70 | 452.10 | 67.20 | 212.60 | .25 | 173.92 | 17.90 |
| 129 SAN | 77.10 | 328.50 | 78.90 | 173.80 | 8.13 • | 118.34• | 11.10 |
| 130 SCR | 62.40 | 553.60 | 77.10 | 108.50 | .43 | 96.81 | 6.00 |
| 131 SHR | 52.90 | 641.00 | 74.40 | 144.20 | 1.90 | 159.44 | 10.60 |
| 132 SOU | 52.10 | 322.80 | 88.70 | 108.20 | 1.80 | 137.00 | 9.30 |
| 133 SPO | 73.70 | 468.20 | 75.20 | 169.70 | 2.45 | 147.32 | 11.90 |
| 134 STA | 80.50• | 324.30• | 83.70 • | 187.70• | 3.27 | 196.13 | 25.40 |
| 135 STO | 55.10 | 342.90 | 68.80 | 137.50 | 9.78 | 173.78 | 8.00 |
| 136 TAC | 54.30 | 280.80 | 76.00 | 108.30 | 2.27 | 176.64 | 10.10 |
| 137 TRE | 57.20 | 525.10 | 76.50 | 216.10 | 4.05 | 144.20 | 14.10 |
| 138 TUC | 54.00 | 358.90 | 74.40 | 207.00 | 3.32 | 167.66 | 15.70 |
| 139 TUL | 51.80 | 415.80 | 77.10 | 118.50 | 2.69 | 132.99 | 11.70 |
| 140 UTI | 51.40 | 399.40 | 82.00 | 123.90 | 2.59 | 192.35 | 8.70 |
| 141 VAL | 60.60 | 388.60 | 63.80 | 163.00 | 4.20 | 170.44 | 10.00 |
| 142 WAT | 67.80• | 377.10• | 81.40 • | 267.80• | 2.29 | 113.54 | 9.60 |
| 143 WES | 78.60 | 393.40 | 77.00 | 182.10 | 1.49 | 174.89 | 11.90 |
| 144 WIC | 47.30 | 527.50 | 81.70 | 131.00 | 4.05 | 149.55 | 12.00 |
| 145 WIL | 56.40 | 469.50 | 79.70 | 102.20 | .41 | 95.06 | 5.50 |
| 146 WIL | 44.40 | 340.70 | 78.40 | 141.90 | 1.23 | 147.13 | 13.00 |
| 147 WOR | 56.30• | 474.50• | 84.70 • | 132.00• | 2.63 | 136.43 | 10.10 |
| 148 YOR | 47.90 | 253.40 | 81.80 | 94.70 | .28 | 123.22 | 7.00 |

## BASIC STATISTICS OF SOCIAL COMPONENT (M)

| | Labor Force Participation Rate (%) IA1 | % of Labor Force Employed IA2 | Mean Income Per Family Member 1A3 | % of Children Under 18 Living With Both Parents IA4 | % of Married Couples Without Own Household IA5 | Per Capita Local Gov't Expend. on Education IB1 | % of Persons 25+, Completed 4 yrs High School or More IB2 | % of Males,16-64 Less Than 15 yrs School But Vocational Training IB3a | % of Females 16-64 Less Than 15 yrs School But Vocational Training IB3b | Motor Vehicle Registrations/ 1,000 pop. IC1a |
|---|---|---|---|---|---|---|---|---|---|---|
| US | 66.00 | 95.60 | 3092.00 | 82.70 | 1.30 | 145.69 | 52.30 | 28.70 | 21.90 | 551.00 |
| 66 ALB | 61.70 | 94.50 | 2787.00 | 80.80 | 1.00 | 152.43 | 66.20 | 31.50 | 24.70 | 654.00 |
| 67 ANN | 65.60 | 95.00 | 3983.00 | 86.80 | 1.00 | 175.06 | 67.50 | 26.20 | 25.00 | 494.00 |
| 68 APP | 68.40 | 96.70 | 3006.00 | 91.60 | .60 | 226.68 • | 56.20 | 26.90 | 18.60 | 472.00 |
| 69 AUG | 55.40 | 96.10 | 2551.00 | 73.80 | 1.80 | 105.28 | 46.30 | 29.50 | 19.90 | 532.00 |
| 70 AUS | 64.20 | 96.90 | 3133.00 | 79.00 | 1.20 | 132.93 | 60.90 | 28.70 | 24.60 | 565.00 |
| 71 BAK | 60.30 | 93.30 | 2757.00 | 80.30 | 1.10 | 218.27 | 51.70 | 24.80 | 18.40 | 643.00 |
| 72 BAT | 61.50 | 95.50 | 2879.00 | 78.10 | 1.40 | 145.98 | 59.10 | 30.80 | 26.20 | 584.00 • |
| 73 BEA | 63.50 | 95.60 | 2845.00 | 83.20 | 1.00 | 133.11 | 46.30 | 30.40 | 22.30 | 594.00 |
| 74 BIN | 68.80 | 96.30 | 3022.00 | 86.90 | 1.10 | 222.52 | 58.90 | 27.80 | 20.10 | 470.00 |
| 75 BRI | 71.70 | 96.20 | 3691.00 | 86.10 | 1.40 | 138.73 | 51.90 | 35.30 | 27.40 | 603.00 • |
| 76 CAN | 66.80 | 95.70 | 3162.00 | 87.50 | 1.00 | 121.86 | 52.40 | 27.50 | 22.30 | 565.00 |
| 77 CHA | 53.00 | 95.90 | 2317.00 | 72.50 | 1.70 | 88.52 | 48.40 | 33.70 | 21.20 | 453.00 |
| 78 CHA | 60.60 | 95.90 | 2805.00 | 82.00 | 1.10 | 119.83 | 52.80 | 22.30 | 18.80 | 500.00 |
| 79 CHA | 72.80 | 97.30 | 3172.00 | 80.70 | 1.20 | 142.27 | 50.80 | 29.50 | 24.70 | 629.00 |
| 80 CHA | 67.60 | 97.00 | 2791.00 | 78.80 | 1.50 | 121.88 | 47.60 | 25.30 | 21.20 | 552.00 |
| 81 COL | 44.10 | 94.50 | 2899.00 | 83.30 | .70 | 184.42 | 72.90 | 36.30 | 26.50 | 609.00 |
| 82 COL | 57.50 | 97.00 | 2683.00 | 76.60 | 1.70 | 94.23 | 50.60 | 26.50 | 14.20 | 536.00 |
| 83 COL | 50.30 | 95.30 | 2430.00 | 71.80 | 1.70 | 105.90 | 46.60 | 26.20 | 18.40 | 509.00 |
| 84 COR | 61.20 | 95.70 | 2376.00 | 81.80 | 2.00 | 163.98 | 47.10 | 26.80 | 20.10 | 570.00 |
| 85 DAV | 70.00 | 95.50 | 3259.00 | 88.00 | .60 | 142.52 | 55.60 | 32.10 | 22.20 | 574.00 |
| 86 DES | 73.70 | 97.20 | 3397.00 | 84.50 | .80 | 161.59 | 68.00 | 26.90 | 21.80 | 621.00 |
| 87 DUL | 64.70 | 92.70 | 2696.00 | 86.20 | .80 | 171.10 | 56.20 | 25.90 | 19.70 | 538.00 |
| 88 FLP | 54.60 | 94.80 | 2283.00 | 80.90 | 2.00 | 122.75 | 51.10 | 28.50 | 20.50 | 512.00 |
| 89 FRI | 66.50 | 95.90 | 2831.00 | 86.40 | 1.00 | 124.67 | 58.40 | 30.10 | 19.50 | 481.00 • |
| 90 EUG | 64.10 | 91.90 | 3047.00 | 86.80 | .50 | 184.50 | 61.90 | 29.60 | 22.80 | 615.00 • |
| 91 EVA | 68.60 | 95.60 | 2835.00 | 84.20 | 1.10 | 121.46 | 52.00 | 24.10 | 16.60 | 585.00 |
| 92 FAY | 36.50 | 94.80 | 2199.00 | 74.90 | 1.20 | 100.51 | 55.10 | 32.90 | 21.10 | 431.00 |
| 93 FLI | 65.30 | 94.70 | 3199.00 | 84.50 | 1.10 | 199.60 | 52.30 | 27.20 | 20.10 | 523.00 |
| 94 FOR | 72.00 | 96.90 | 3329.00 | 86.90 | .50 | 129.62 | 59.40 | 30.20 | 22.70 | 556.00 |
| 95 FRE | 61.90 | 92.00 | 2707.00 | 79.10 | 1.30 | 187.01 | 52.70 | 23.40 | 18.20 | 632.00 |
| 96 GRE | 69.40 | 97.40 | 2718.00 | 81.30 | 1.40 | 89.06 | 41.00 | 22.60 | 17.70 | 575.00 |
| 97 HAM | 63.50 | 96.30 | 3121.00 | 86.40 | 1.20 | 131.49 | 47.80 | 26.70 | 20.00 | 549.00 |
| 98 HAR | 70.10 | 97.80 | 3241.00 | 85.00 | 1.20 | 154.58 | 55.40 | 33.10 | 23.50 | 481.00 • |
| 99 HUN | 57.90 | 94.90 | 2613.00 | 82.30 | 1.50 | 104.60 | 46.10 | 23.70 | 14.90 | 509.00 |
| 100 HUN | 62.30 | 95.60 | 2925.00 | 83.60 | 1.50 | 103.13 | 58.30 | 26.20 | 18.50 | 617.00 |
| 101 JAC | 65.80 | 96.60 | 2558.00 | 73.30 | 1.90 | 102.64 | 56.10 | 21.90 | 19.90 | 573.00 |
| 102 JOH | 59.00 | 95.10 | 2563.00 | 87.60 | 1.70 | 113.32 | 44.10 | 23.30 | 16.50 | 481.00 • |
| 103 KAL | 66.40 | 95.30 | 3492.00 | 86.10 | 1.00 | 153.13 | 60.70 | 30.00 | 22.60 | 520.00 |
| 104 KNO | 62.20 | 96.10 | 2748.00 | 81.20 | 1.70 | 114.42 | 50.70 | 22.50 | 17.60 | 546.00 |
| 105 LAN | 74.50 | 97.90 | 3101.00 | 88.80 | 1.00 | 157.20 | 43.90 | 22.70 | 16.50 | 481.00 • |
| 106 LAN | 67.40 | 94.90 | 3415.00 | 86.10 | .70 | 193.34 | 63.10 | 28.10 | 22.20 | 518.00 |
| 107 LAS | 67.10 | 94.80 | 3364.00 | 81.50 | 1.30 | 158.33 | 65.20 | 38.20 | 24.40 | 698.00 |
| 108 LAW | 76.10 | 95.90 | 3376.00 | 87.50 | 1.30 | 132.41 | 53.70 | 32.30 | 24.30 | 481.00 • |
| 109 LIT | 64.90 | 96.70 | 2753.00 | 78.70 | 1.10 | 105.01 | 56.50 | 27.40 | 22.40 | 589.00 |
| 110 LOR | 66.40 | 96.30 | 3145.00 | 88.60 | 1.40 | 135.06 | 52.60 | 30.10 | 22.50 | 572.00 |
| 111 LOW | 71.70 | 95.90 | 2978.00 | 88.70 | 1.40 | 129.99 | 54.50 | 33.20 | 24.90 | 481.00 • |
| 112 MAC | 64.20 | 96.10 | 2704.00 | 76.10 | 1.70 | 115.52 | 47.40 | 26.50 | 19.40 | 547.00 |
| 113 MAD | 70.20 | 97.10 | 3541.00 | 88.20 | .40 | 171.42 | 71.20 | 29.40 | 22.90 | 494.00 |
| 114 MOB | 61.80 | 94.70 | 2372.00 | 77.20 | 1.70 | 93.66 | 42.30 | 22.90 | 17.30 | 561.00 |
| 115 MON | 65.00 | 96.20 | 2535.00 | 72.80 | 1.90 | 89.40 | 51.60 | 24.30 | 22.60 | 572.00 |
| 116 NEW | 70.80 | 96.60 | 3627.00 | 83.20 | 1.40 | 148.31 | 56.80 | 30.40 | 26.70 | 553.00 • |
| 117 NEW | 60.00 | 96.10 | 3179.00 | 82.80 | .80 | 144.96 | 54.10 | 41.10 | 27.40 | 574.00 • |
| 118 NEW | 54.40 | 96.40 | 2958.00 | 80.70 | 1.20 | 123.90 | 52.10 | 39.70 | 23.10 | 456.00 |
| 119 ORL | 65.20 | 95.20 | 2949.00 | 60.00 | 1.30 | 126.11 | 56.10 | 34.90 | 25.70 | 701.00 |
| 120 OXN | 64.20 | 94.10 | 3196.00 | 85.50 | 1.30 | 231.74 | 63.80 | 35.30 | 24.90 | 594.00 |
| 121 PEN | 53.00 | 95.00 | 2513.00 | 78.70 | 1.40 | 145.95 | 51.00 | 33.40 | 22.10 | 595.00 |
| 122 PEO | 69.20 | 96.80 | 3362.00 | 88.00 | .70 | 134.75 | 53.70 | 30.00 | 22.30 | 562.00 |
| 123 RAL | 67.60 | 97.50 | 3074.00 | 80.90 | 1.20 | 121.97 | 53.60 | 27.70 | 26.00 | 741.00 |
| 124 REA | 73.90 | 97.60 | 3274.00 | 86.80 | 1.80 | 141.16 | 43.30 | 26.50 | 19.00 | 481.00 • |
| 125 ROC | 73.00 | 96.00 | 3386.00 | 86.60 | .70 | 131.29 | 52.20 | 28.20 | 19.40 | 548.00 • |
| 126 SAG | 65.30 | 95.10 | 3080.00 | 85.70 | 1.00 | 148.52 | 50.60 | 27.60 | 19.40 | 517.00 |
| 127 SAL | 52.80 | 93.00 | 3077.00 | 78.90 | 1.20 | 183.43 | 62.50 | 28.40 | 23.90 | 549.00 |
| 128 SAN | 62.00 | 93.60 | 3359.00 | 82.50 | 1.00 | 173.92 | 71.30 | 34.60 | 25.70 | 600.00 |
| 129 SAN | 61.90 | 92.70 | 3217.00 | 80.30 | .90 | 118.34 • | 63.60 | 30.20 | 25.10 | 644.00 |
| 130 SCR | 68.30 | 94.80 | 2741.00 | 88.10 | 2.20 | 96.81 | 48.00 | 30.50 | 21.40 | 481.00 • |
| 131 SCH | 62.70 | 95.00 | 2518.00 | 74.10 | 1.30 | 159.44 | 50.90 | 28.90 | 22.90 | 584.00 • |
| 132 SOU | 69.50 | 95.30 | 3190.00 | 87.00 | .90 | 137.00 | 54.20 | 30.50 | 22.30 | 530.00 |
| 133 SPO | 62.90 | 93.10 | 3030.00 | 83.00 | .80 | 147.32 | 65.30 | 32.20 | 26.10 | 652.00 |
| 134 STA | 70.10 | 97.70 | 6289.00 | 87.70 | 1.50 | 196.13 | 68.10 | 34.50 | 28.90 | 603.00 • |
| 135 STO | 64.20 | 91.80 | 3063.00 | 79.30 | 1.10 | 173.78 | 49.40 | 27.10 | 21.90 | 623.00 |
| 136 TAC | 52.70 | 91.60 | 3193.00 | 83.40 | .60 | 176.64 | 60.70 | 37.20 | 28.30 | 573.00 |
| 137 TRE | 69.80 | 96.50 | 3672.00 | 81.70 | 2.00 | 144.20 | 52.80 | 32.50 | 24.90 | 481.00 • |
| 138 TUC | 58.40 | 96.00 | 2921.00 | 82.50 | 1.70 | 167.66 | 63.10 | 31.40 | 23.60 | 656.00 |
| 139 TUL | 68.90 | 95.40 | 3187.00 | 82.30 | .80 | 132.99 | 58.20 | 31.90 | 23.60 | 672.00 |
| 140 UTI | 66.70 | 94.30 | 2955.00 | 86.70 | 1.30 | 192.35 | 49.90 | 29.50 | 24.60 | 444.00 |
| 141 VAL | 55.90 | 93.30 | 3165.00 | 82.00 | .80 | 170.44 | 62.90 | 41.70 | 24.90 | 604.00 |
| 142 WAT | 72.40 | 95.20 | 3453.00 | 87.20 | 1.40 | 113.54 | 49.90 | 33.40 | 26.10 | 553.00 • |
| 143 WES | 69.40 | 97.00 | 3809.00 | 78.00 | 1.30 | 174.89 | 55.70 | 30.20 | 24.50 | 704.00 |
| 144 WIC | 69.10 | 92.90 | 3105.00 | 84.30 | .70 | 149.55 | 63.20 | 32.80 | 24.10 | 655.00 |
| 145 WIL | 66.80 | 96.00 | 2685.00 | 86.80 | 2.50 | 95.06 | 46.90 | 30.60 | 19.50 | 481.00 • |
| 146 WIL | 66.40 | 96.20 | 3397.00 | 83.50 | 1.50 | 147.13 | 54.40 | 32.30 | 25.40 | 579.00 • |
| 147 WOR | 71.40 | 96.40 | 3300.00 | 87.40 | 1.00 | 136.43 | 53.70 | 33.50 | 27.90 | 481.00 • |
| 148 YOR | 72.80 | 97.70 | 3240.00 | 87.50 | 1.30 | 123.22 | 44.70 | 29.20 | 19.90 | 481.00 • |

| | Motorcycle Registrations/ 1,000 pop. IC1b | % of Households With One or More Automobiles IC1c | Local Sunday Newspaper Circ./ 1,000 pop. IC2a | % Occupied Housing With TV IC2b | Local Radio Stations/ 100,000 pop. IC2c | Population Density In SMSA IC3a | % Pop. Under 5 and 65+ in Central City IC3b | Negro to Total Pop. Median Family Income Adj. For Education IIA1 | Negro to Total Pop. Professional Emp. Adj. For Education IIA2 | Negro Males To Total Males Unemployment Rate Adj. For Education IIA3 |
|---|---|---|---|---|---|---|---|---|---|---|
| US | 16.00 | 82.50 | 243.00 | 95.50 | .03 | 360.00 | 18.30 | .78 | .07 | 2.08 |
| 66 ALB | 32.00 | 89.70 | 376.00 | 95.00 | 4.43 | 270.00 | 15.20 | .74 | .01 | 2.12 |
| 67 ANN | 25.00 | 91.20 | 363.00 | 95.00 | 1.28 | 329.00 | 13.40 | .95 | .04 | 1.77 |
| 68 APP | 13.00 | 89.70 | 844.00 | 98.50 | .72 | 197.00 | 18.00 | 1.00• | 1.00• | 1.00• |
| 69 AUG | 8.00 | 82.30 | 1133.00 | 94.60 | 3.95 | 180.00 | 19.80 | .86 | .20 | 2.35 |
| 70 AUS | 23.00 | 90.40 | 341.00 | 94.30 | 3.71 | 292.00 | 15.60 | .72 | .05 | 1.67 |
| 71 BAK | 43.00 | 89.20 | 703.00 | 94.90 | 3.34 | 40.00 | 17.60 | .67 | .08 | 3.17 |
| 72 BAT | 18.00• | 88.10 | 540.00 | 96.50 | 3.15 | 621.00 | 15.60 | .73 | .20 | 2.63 |
| 73 BEA | 14.00 | 88.10 | 666.00 | 95.90 | 1.58 | 241.00 | 17.40 | .77 | .11 | 3.12 |
| 74 BIN | 8.00 | 85.40 | 1266.00 | 96.60 | 1.32 | 146.00 | 23.10 | .97 | .01 | 2.75 |
| 75 BRI | 10.00• | 85.20 | 565.00 | 97.50 | 1.54 | 2016.00 | 20.60 | .79 | .03 | 1.81 |
| 76 CAN | 12.00 | 88.00 | 778.00 | 97.10 | .80 | 646.00 | 21.40 | .91 | .02 | 3.88 |
| 77 CHA | 12.00 | 80.10 | 1323.00 | 94.80 | 1.97 | 148.00 | 17.80 | .85 | .23 | 2.85 |
| 78 CHA | 33.00 | 80.30 | 1488.00 | 95.40 | 3.47 | 253.00 | 18.90 | .77 | .04 | 1.29 |
| 79 CHA | 17.00• | 84.90 | 852.00 | 95.90 | 2.20 | 350.00 | 16.30 | .74 | .13 | 2.27 |
| 80 CHA | 15.00 | 82.70 | 1021.00 | 96.10 | 2.95 | 306.00 | 19.40 | .74 | .10 | 2.62 |
| 81 COL | 28.00 | 92.80 | 602.00 | 95.50 | 5.93 | 109.00 | 16.80 | .73 | .02 | 1.88 |
| 82 COL | 8.00 | 85.20 | 1067.00 | 95.40 | 2.47 | 220.00 | 13.40 | .84 | .16 | 2.52 |
| 83 COL | 17.00 | 82.10 | 390.00 | 95.30 | 3.34 | 217.00 | 15.60 | .88 | .26 | 2.16 |
| 84 COR | 13.00 | 88.50 | 425.00 | 94.30 | 2.10 | 187.00 | 15.70 | .72 | .03 | 1.31 |
| 85 DAV | 20.00 | 87.80 | 835.00 | 97.00 | 1.37 | 213.00 | 20.00 | .76 | .02 | 2.79 |
| 86 DES | 31.00 | 86.90 | 2421.00 | 96.70 | 2.44 | 495.00 | 19.70 | .71 | .03 | 2.80 |
| 87 DUL | 26.00 | 81.40 | 820.00 | 96.00 | 3.01 | 36.00 | 21.00 | .82 | .01 | 1.67 |
| 88 ELP | 16.00 | 84.20 | 267.00 | 95.60 | 2.78 | 340.00 | 16.10 | .83 | .03 | 1.66 |
| 89 ERI | 12.00 | 86.10 | 752.00 | 97.50 | 1.13 | 324.00 | 20.10 | .87 | .02 | 4.09 |
| 90 EUG | 36.00 | 91.10 | 713.00 | 93.70 | 4.69 | 47.00 | 15.80 | .80 | .01 | 1.43 |
| 91 EVA | 19.00 | 84.40 | 811.00 | 97.50 | 1.71 | 219.00 | 19.80 | .76 | .03 | 4.36 |
| 92 FAY | 17.00• | 87.40 | 789.00 | 95.90 | 1.41 | 324.00 | 15.10 | .85 | .22 | 1.52 |
| 93 FLI | 26.00 | 91.00 | 583.00 | 97.50 | 1.20 | 382.00 | 19.40 | .90 | .06 | 1.81 |
| 94 FOR | 16.00 | 88.90 | 604.00 | 96.80 | 2.50 | 418.00 | 19.30 | .90 | .03 | 2.95 |
| 95 FRE | 29.00 | 88.20 | 856.00 | 95.00 | 2.90 | 69.00 | 18.90 | .73 | .03 | 3.54 |
| 96 GRE | 7.00 | 85.80 | 1631.00 | 95.90 | 2.33 | 233.00 | 17.90 | .82 | .08 | 1.84 |
| 97 HAM | 15.00 | 88.70 | 453.00 | 97.20 | 1.32 | 480.00 | 19.40 | .87 | .03 | 2.11 |
| 98 HAR | 12.00 | 85.00 | 2487.00 | 96.50 | 1.45 | 253.00 | 22.80 | .76 | .03 | 2.82 |
| 99 HUN | 18.00 | 79.00 | 762.00 | 95.90 | 1.96 | 180.00 | 20.50 | .80 | .02 | 1.00 |
| 100 HUN | 21.00 | 89.40 | 385.00 | 96.80 | 2.63 | 169.00 | 14.10 | .70 | .08 | 2.94 |
| 101 JAC | 16.00• | 83.80 | 722.00 | 95.00 | 1.93 | 157.00 | 16.90 | .76 | .24 | 2.74 |
| 102 JOH | 12.00 | 82.20 | 1377.00 | 96.70 | 1.52 | 148.00 | 20.90 | .83 | .01 | 1.74 |
| 103 KAL | 24.00 | 90.90 | 723.00 | 97.30 | 2.97 | 359.00 | 17.70 | .85 | .03 | 3.60 |
| 104 KNO | 16.00 | 84.90 | 936.00 | 95.80 | 2.75 | 282.00 | 17.70 | .76 | .04 | 2.48 |
| 105 LAN | 12.00 | 84.70 | 2043.00 | 89.30 | 1.56 | 338.00 | 21.40 | .76 | .01 | 4.82 |
| 106 LAN | 29.00 | 91.40 | 611.00 | 96.50 | 2.11 | 222.00 | 18.90 | .84 | .03 | 2.26 |
| 107 LAS | 36.00 | 92.80 | 802.00 | 96.10 | 3.29 | 35.00 | 15.00 | .72 | .03 | 1.13 |
| 108 LAW | 10.00• | 81.10 | 712.00 | 97.30 | .86 | 1119.00 | 23.30 | .77 | .01 | .32 |
| 109 LIT | 13.00 | 84.60 | 1705.00 | 95.90 | 2.16 | 217.00 | 19.00 | .70 | .11 | 2.71 |
| 110 LOR | 15.00 | 91.20 | 501.00 | 97.70 | .38 | 519.00 | 17.80 | .91 | .03 | 2.14 |
| 111 LOW | 10.00• | 82.50 | 454.00 | 97.90 | 1.87 | 1397.00 | 21.10 | .49 | .01 | 1.03 |
| 112 MAC | 16.00 | 81.90 | 604.00 | 95.50 | 2.42 | 325.00 | 17.70 | .79 | .16 | 2.92 |
| 113 MAD | 16.00 | 85.90 | 642.00 | 95.00 | 2.41 | 242.00 | 15.30 | .66 | .01 | 2.37 |
| 114 MOB | 14.00 | 83.10 | 501.00 | 94.20 | 2.65 | 134.00 | 17.40 | .75 | .20 | 2.13 |
| 115 MON | 14.00 | 79.70 | 595.00 | 95.20 | 4.47 | 142.00 | 17.80 | .72 | .26 | 2.71 |
| 116 NEW | 10.00• | 81.90 | 940.00 | 96.70 | 1.12 | 1450.00 | 20.70 | .73 | .06 | 1.96 |
| 117 NEW | 10.00• | 89.00 | 1228.00 | 96.40 | .48 | 562.00 | 20.50 | .84 | .02 | 1.25 |
| 118 NEW | 17.00• | 85.50 | 584.00 | 95.90 | .34 | 1150.00 | 14.30 | .86 | .16 | 2.08 |
| 119 ORL | 19.00 | 88.40 | 1655.00 | 95.60 | 2.33 | 352.00 | 20.40 | .72 | .08 | 2.04 |
| 120 OXN | 35.00 | 93.80 | 311.00 | 96.60 | .53 | 202.00 | 15.50 | .74 | .01 | 1.95 |
| 121 PEN | 17.00 | 86.40 | 1075.00 | 94.70 | 3.29 | 143.00 | 17.60 | .75 | .09 | 2.97 |
| 122 PEO | 17.00 | 88.50 | 898.00 | 96.00 | 1.16 | 190.00 | 19.40 | .81 | .02 | 3.61 |
| 123 PAL | 17.00• | 87.10 | 1268.00 | 95.80 | 3.07 | 266.00 | 14.90 | .72 | .11 | 2.86 |
| 124 HEA | 12.00 | 82.80 | 1048.00 | 96.50 | 1.68 | 344.00 | 23.10 | .76 | .03 | 5.42 |
| 125 ROC | 13.00 | 88.90 | 567.00 | 96.50 | 1.83 | 339.00 | 19.90 | .85 | .02 | 2.50 |
| 126 SAG | 24.00 | 89.30 | 664.00 | 97.90 | 1.81 | 270.00 | 19.60 | .88 | .06 | 1.52 |
| 127 SAL | 25.00 | 90.40 | 372.00 | 93.80 | 1.60 | 75.00 | 17.10 | .74 | .02 | 1.10 |
| 128 SAN | 34.00 | 90.40 | 639.00 | 93.30 | 3.40 | 97.00 | 24.70 | .67 | .01 | 2.09 |
| 129 SAN | 34.00 | 89.40 | 1069.00 | 93.70 | 1.46 | 128.00 | 22.20 | .66 | .01 | 1.35 |
| 130 SCR | 12.00 | 78.90 | 944.00 | 98.10 | 2.13 | 516.00 | 21.30 | .90 | .01 | 2.49 |
| 131 SCH | 18.00• | 81.90 | 648.00 | 95.20 | 3.05 | 169.00 | 19.10 | .76 | .21 | 2.74 |
| 132 SOU | 15.00 | 87.80 | 1014.00 | 97.30 | 1.78 | 308.00 | 19.80 | .87 | .04 | 3.65 |
| 133 SPO | 24.00 | 85.30 | 752.00 | 95.50 | 5.57 | 164.00 | 21.60 | .77 | .01 | 1.64 |
| 134 STA | 10.00• | 89.50 | 292.00 | 98.00 | .48 | 1702.00 | 17.40 | .57 | .03 | 2.73 |
| 135 STO | 27.00 | 85.80 | 464.00 | 94.00 | 2.41 | 206.00 | 20.00 | .73 | .04 | 2.12 |
| 136 TAC | 19.00 | 88.40 | 663.00 | 95.40 | 2.18 | 245.00 | 20.50 | .79 | .02 | 1.42 |
| 137 TRE | 10.00• | 82.60 | 1046.00 | 97.00 | .98 | 1333.00 | 20.80 | .79 | .08 | 2.75 |
| 138 TUC | 24.00 | 90.00 | 333.00 | 94.60 | 3.69 | 38.00 | 18.60 | .78 | .01 | 1.82 |
| 139 TUL | 29.00 | 88.40 | 541.00 | 95.70 | 1.67 | 126.00 | 17.50 | .61 | .04 | 2.20 |
| 140 UTI | 7.00 | 83.80 | 634.00 | 97.20 | 2.05 | 128.00 | 23.10 | .86 | .01 | 2.27 |
| 141 VAL | 32.00 | 90.70 | 412.00 | 95.80 | 0.00 | 155.00 | 17.80 | .78 | .04 | 1.55 |
| 142 WAT | 10.00• | 84.40 | 539.00 | 97.60 | 1.43 | 968.00 | 21.10 | .78 | .03 | 2.04 |
| 143 WES | 24.00 | 87.50 | 1294.00 | 95.10 | .85 | 172.00 | 24.60 | .83 | .11 | 2.15 |
| 144 WIC | 34.00 | 90.80 | 643.00 | 95.80 | 2.82 | 159.00 | 17.40 | .72 | .04 | 1.61 |
| 145 WIL | 12.00 | 79.80 | 947.00 | 97.60 | 1.75 | 386.00 | 21.30 | .62 | .01 | 4.57 |
| 146 WIL | 17.00• | 87.20 | 1156.00 | 97.40 | 1.20 | 429.00 | 22.33 | .78 | .06 | 3.03 |
| 147 WOR | 10.00• | 82.30 | 610.00 | 97.80 | 2.03 | 727.00 | 22.00 | .75 | .01 | 2.77 |
| 148 YOR | 12.00 | 87.90 | 901.00 | 96.00 | 1.21 | 230.00 | 23.30 | .73 | .02 | 3.03 |

# TABLE B-5 (Continued)

| | Negro Females To Total Females Unemployment Rate Adj. For Education IIA4 | Male to Female Unemployment Rate Adj. For Education IIB1 | Male to Female Professional Emp. Adj. For Education IIB2 | % Working Outside County of Residence IIC1 | Central City & Suburban Income Dist. IIC2 | Housing Segregation Index IIC3 | % Families With Income Above Poverty Level IIIA1 | % Occupied Housing With Plumbing IIIA2 | % Occupied Housing With 1.01 or More Persons Per Room IIIA3 | % Occupied Housing With Telephone IIIA4 |
|---|---|---|---|---|---|---|---|---|---|---|
| US | 1.79 | .75 | 1.49 | 17.80 | .06 | .27 | 89.30 | 94.50 | 8.20 | 87.30 |
| 66 ALB | .74 | .72 | 1.91 | 2.80 | -.12 | .08 | 87.00 | 97.50 | 10.30 | 85.60 |
| 67 ANN | 1.96 | 1.12 | 1.47 | 12.10 | -.08 | .09 | 94.90 | 97.90 | 5.90 | 95.00 |
| 68 APP | 1.00 • | .55 | 1.43 | 15.80 | -.04 | .86 | 94.50 | 96.30 | 7.90 | 95.50 |
| 69 AUG | 2.05 | .53 | 1.14 | 14.20 | .04 | .75 | 84.60 | 93.10 | 10.40 | 81.30 |
| 70 AUS | 1.44 | .70 | 1.63 | 2.90 | 0.00 | .10 | 89.20 | 97.50 | 8.90 | 88.10 |
| 71 BAK | 1.92 | .75 | 1.72 | 3.70 | -.06 | 1.22 | 87.40 | 98.60 | 10.90 | 85.70 |
| 72 BAT | 2.18 | .75 | 1.47 | 9.60 | -.08 | .04 | 86.40 | 97.50 | 10.80 | 90.50 |
| 73 BEA | 2.08 | .48 | 1.42 | 10.00 | 0.00 | .53 | 88.40 | 96.90 | 9.60 | 88.30 |
| 74 BIN | 1.06 | .77 | 1.98 | 13.00 | -.02 | 2.16 | 92.70 | 97.30 | 5.10 | 92.00 |
| 75 BRI | 1.39 | .80 | 1.83 | 12.00 | .10 | 1.13 | 94.80 | 97.40 | 6.20 | 92.70 |
| 76 CAN | 2.43 | .71 | 1.45 | 11.30 | .04 | 1.15 | 94.20 | 97.40 | 5.90 | 93.60 |
| 77 CHA | 2.01 | .48 | .96 | 11.60 | -.06 | .43 | 79.40 | 88.60 | 11.40 | 79.80 |
| 78 CHA | 1.49 | .89 | 1.63 | 4.60 | -.12 | .72 | 87.00 | 93.70 | 7.10 | 85.40 |
| 79 CHA | 2.16 | .46 | 1.26 | 7.90 | -.02 | .32 | 90.10 | 96.10 | 7.80 | 85.80 |
| 80 CHA | 1.62 | .57 | 1.23 | 12.50 | .08 | 1.39 | 86.70 | 95.90 | 8.30 | 82.90 |
| 81 COL | 2.11 | .65 | 1.32 | 1.80 | -.04 | .02 | 90.80 | 98.40 | 5.90 | 90.20 |
| 82 COL | 1.90 | .50 | 1.20 | 18.80 | 0.00 | .15 | 85.70 | 91.70 | 9.00 | 84.30 |
| 83 COL | 1.90 | .49 | .71 | 34.20 | -.10 | .07 | 81.30 | 93.30 | 11.40 | 80.80 |
| 84 COR | .76 | .65 | 1.25 | 7.90 | -.06 | .28 | 81.60 | 93.10 | 16.70 | 79.40 |
| 85 DAV | 2.52 | .70 | 1.52 | 16.60 | -.04 | .47 | 93.30 | 96.10 | 6.70 | 93.40 |
| 86 DES | 1.94 | .89 | 1.26 | 2.90 | 0.00 | .30 | 93.90 | 96.80 | 6.00 | 93.00 |
| 87 DUL | .84 | .92 | 1.29 | 7.40 | -.06 | .87 | 91.70 | 91.70 | 7.40 | 93.10 |
| 88 FLP | 1.65 | .80 | 1.26 | 4.00 | -.04 | .22 | 82.60 | 92.10 | 18.30 | 80.10 |
| 89 FRI | 1.60 | .39 | 1.53 | 2.80 | .02 | .82 | 93.20 | 97.50 | 5.90 | 90.30 |
| 90 FUG | 1.00 • | .86 | 1.41 | 4.10 | -.06 | 1.29 | 92.10 | 98.40 | 5.50 | 91.00 |
| 91 FVA | 2.24 | .56 | 1.37 | 12.40 | -.02 | .29 | 90.90 | 95.00 | 8.70 | 89.30 |
| 92 FAY | 1.46 | .47 | .72 | 2.40 | -.08 | .54 | 82.90 | 92.50 | 10.80 | 75.10 |
| 93 FLI | 1.94 | .54 | 1.39 | 7.60 | 0.00 | 1.27 | 93.10 | 97.60 | 8.70 | 90.70 |
| 94 FOR | 1.98 | .82 | 1.76 | 3.00 | .04 | .57 | 94.90 | 97.90 | 5.90 | 91.10 |
| 95 FRE | 1.41 | .74 | 1.34 | 4.10 | -.04 | .99 | 85.80 | 98.30 | 10.80 | 88.00 |
| 96 GRE | 1.69 | .46 | 1.25 | 9.40 | -.04 | 1.08 | 88.20 | 92.20 | 8.30 | 81.30 |
| 97 HAM | 2.35 | .54 | 1.58 | 22.50 | -.02 | .76 | 93.00 | 94.50 | 8.50 | 90.80 |
| 98 HAR | 2.51 | .70 | 1.66 | 24.00 | .04 | 3.53 | 93.40 | 95.60 | 4.00 | 92.00 |
| 99 HUN | 1.87 | .93 | 1.25 | 24.10 | -.10 | .65 | 85.20 | 90.10 | 7.80 | 82.70 |
| 100 HUN | 2.00 | .62 | 2.65 | 9.20 | -.18 | .24 | 86.50 | 91.70 | 8.30 | 83.90 |
| 101 JAC | 2.39 | .63 | 1.19 | 11.90 | -.14 | .07 | 81.40 | 92.10 | 12.90 | 80.50 |
| 102 JOH | 3.85 | 1.14 | 1.20 | 14.10 | 0.00 | 3.70 | 90.30 | 91.60 | 6.50 | 89.70 |
| 103 KAL | 2.02 | .80 | 1.40 | 6.50 | .04 | 1.76 | 94.20 | 97.40 | 5.40 | 94.50 |
| 104 KNO | 1.83 | .63 | 1.58 | 12.80 | 0.00 | .80 | 85.70 | 92.50 | 7.30 | 84.60 |
| 105 LAN | 3.07 | .38 | 1.52 | 9.80 | .04 | 3.42 | 93.50 | 94.60 | 4.30 | 90.90 |
| 106 LAN | 2.02 | 1.06 | 1.59 | 23.20 | 0.00 | 1.29 | 93.90 | 97.00 | 6.20 | 93.70 |
| 107 LAS | 1.18 | .67 | 1.60 | 4.60 | -.02 | .21 | 93.00 | 99.20 | 8.90 | 81.80 |
| 108 LAW | 1.31 | .98 | 1.65 | 21.40 | .04 | 1.05 | 94.20 | 96.80 | 5.70 | 91.20 |
| 109 LIT | 2.05 | .70 | 1.19 | 6.30 | -.14 | .21 | 86.60 | 95.80 | 8.50 | 85.70 |
| 110 LOR | 1.34 | .60 | 1.59 | 18.00 | .02 | .57 | 94.30 | 97.50 | 8.50 | 90.80 |
| 111 LOW | 1.00 • | .93 | 1.79 | 14.10 | .04 | .57 | 93.90 | 96.90 | 8.10 | 92.90 |
| 112 MAC | 1.90 | .44 | 1.10 | 13.90 | 0.00 | .29 | 84.90 | 93.40 | 11.00 | 83.90 |
| 113 MAD | .87 | 1.18 | 1.56 | 3.40 | -.02 | .13 | 84.60 | 96.10 | 6.40 | 95.80 |
| 114 MOB | 1.83 | .62 | 1.30 | 10.00 | -.12 | .19 | 81.40 | 93.00 | 12.00 | 82.30 |
| 115 MON | 2.08 | .58 | 1.01 | 10.60 | -.12 | .05 | 80.80 | 89.50 | 11.00 | 82.90 |
| 116 NEW | 2.25 | .84 | 1.53 | 5.90 | .10 | 1.21 | 92.70 | 98.30 | 5.40 | 93.90 |
| 117 NEW | 1.58 | .64 | 1.56 | 8.00 | 0.00 | 1.03 | 91.70 | 97.50 | 5.50 | 93.70 |
| 118 NEW | 1.64 | .49 | 1.64 | 34.10 | .06 | .05 | 89.90 | 97.70 | 7.20 | 87.70 |
| 119 ORL | 1.78 | .67 | 1.54 | 14.70 | 0.00 | 1.02 | 88.70 | 96.50 | 7.10 | 83.50 |
| 120 OXN | 1.37 | .75 | 2.10 | 18.30 | -.02 | 1.21 | 92.60 | 99.40 | 8.40 | 91.20 |
| 121 PEN | 1.87 | .51 | 1.23 | 9.70 | -.04 | .93 | 84.50 | 93.10 | 9.30 | 83.20 |
| 122 PEO | 1.84 | .51 | 1.52 | 26.00 | -.04 | 1.51 | 94.30 | 96.70 | 6.50 | 92.50 |
| 123 PAL | 2.53 | .51 | 1.72 | 7.90 | -.10 | .01 | 88.80 | 93.20 | 7.90 | 87.10 |
| 124 PEA | 1.05 | .67 | 1.44 | 14.20 | .06 | 2.36 | 95.00 | 95.50 | 3.70 | 93.30 |
| 125 ROC | 2.19 | .61 | 1.63 | 9.50 | -.04 | .39 | 93.60 | 97.30 | 7.10 | 90.60 |
| 126 SAG | 2.26 | .71 | 1.42 | 8.30 | .04 | .95 | 92.30 | 96.90 | 8.80 | 92.20 |
| 127 SAL | 1.52 | .68 | 1.21 | 3.50 | -.06 | .71 | 90.40 | 98.80 | 10.20 | 87.10 |
| 128 SAN | 1.56 | .84 | 1.66 | 3.50 | -.06 | .26 | 92.40 | 99.00 | 6.70 | 91.00 |
| 129 SAN | .75 | .95 | 1.21 | 15.50 | -.08 | .39 | 89.60 | 98.90 | 6.50 | 89.40 |
| 130 SCR | 1.00 • | 1.47 | 1.40 | 9.10 | -.02 | 1.29 | 92.20 | 95.90 | 4.70 | 93.00 |
| 131 SCH | 2.33 | .65 | 1.09 | 15.70 | -.12 | .03 | 81.80 | 91.20 | 11.40 | 83.80 |
| 132 SOU | 1.85 | .65 | 1.81 | 12.20 | -.04 | 1.10 | 94.10 | 97.50 | 6.20 | 92.70 |
| 133 SPO | 1.39 | .88 | 1.29 | 2.40 | -.02 | .11 | 91.40 | 97.20 | 5.30 | 91.80 |
| 134 STA | 1.41 | .98 | 1.85 | 21.30 | .26 | .64 | 96.00 | 98.50 | 4.80 | 96.40 |
| 135 STO | 2.22 | .76 | 1.34 | 5.60 | -.02 | .98 | 88.80 | 97.40 | 9.30 | 87.70 |
| 136 TAC | 1.32 | 1.00 | 1.28 | 9.40 | 0.00 | .47 | 92.00 | 98.30 | 5.20 | 90.00 |
| 137 TRE | 1.57 | .76 | 1.83 | 14.00 | .18 | 1.26 | 93.60 | 98.30 | 4.90 | 90.80 |
| 138 TUC | .86 | .71 | 1.59 | 3.00 | .09 | .20 | 89.20 | 97.50 | 10.50 | 84.60 |
| 139 TUL | 1.91 | .58 | 1.95 | 8.20 | -.12 | .29 | 90.20 | 97.10 | 5.80 | 88.70 |
| 140 UTI | 2.61 | .76 | 1.62 | 10.10 | .02 | 1.14 | 92.60 | 96.00 | 5.20 | 91.60 |
| 141 VAL | 1.36 | .67 | 1.20 | 19.40 | -.08 | .49 | 91.20 | 99.20 | 6.70 | 91.30 |
| 142 WAT | 1.56 | .59 | 1.34 | 16.90 | .06 | .76 | 94.50 | 98.10 | 7.60 | 94.60 |
| 143 WES | 2.31 | .91 | 1.55 | 4.20 | .04 | .40 | 89.80 | 95.60 | 8.80 | 82.60 |
| 144 WIC | 1.75 | .85 | 1.49 | 5.00 | -.06 | .35 | 92.00 | 98.10 | 6.90 | 90.30 |
| 145 WIL | 2.37 | 1.43 | 1.31 | 11.50 | 0.00 | 1.14 | 91.10 | 95.10 | 4.40 | 91.40 |
| 146 WIL | 1.64 | .62 | 2.02 | 14.60 | .04 | 2.64 | 92.90 | 97.30 | 5.10 | 91.60 |
| 147 WOR | 1.18 | .97 | 1.36 | 8.30 | 0.00 | .46 | 94.60 | 96.90 | 5.60 | 94.20 |
| 148 YOR | 1.65 | .52 | 1.61 | 15.40 | .04 | 3.96 | 94.10 | 93.90 | 4.70 | 90.90 |

| | % Workers Who Use Public Transport To Work IIIA5 | Total Crime Rate/ 100,000 pop. IIIA6 | Cost of Living Index IIIA7 | Public Swimming Pools/ 100,000 pop. IIIB1a | Public Camping Sites/ 100,000 pop. IIIB1b | Public Tennis Courts/ 100,000 pop. IIIB1c | Miles of Trails/ 1,000 pop. IIIB1d | Banks and S&L Assoc./ 1,000 pop. IIIB2 | Retail Trade Establishments/ 1,000 pop. IIIB3 | Selected Service Establishments/ 1,000 pop. IIIB4 |
|---|---|---|---|---|---|---|---|---|---|---|
| US | 8.90 | 2829.50 | 100.00 | N.A. | N.A. | N.A. | N.A. | N.A. | 8.68 | 5.85 |
| 66 ALH | 2.50 | 5910.20 | 87.60 | 28.50 | 598.10 | 253.20 | 148.70 | .03 | 6.91 | 5.15 |
| 67 ANN | 2.40 | 4990.00 | 106.70• | 12.80 | 1341.90 | 123.90 | 192.30 | .05 | 5.70 | 4.47 |
| 68 APP | 1.90 | 1461.00 | 95.00 | 28.90 | 584.80 | 151.60 | 111.90 | .15 | 9.17 | 5.23• |
| 69 AUG | 3.50 | 1820.10 | 94.60• | 23.70 | 2.40 | 71.10 | 197.60 | .07 | 7.87 | 4.86 |
| 70 AUS | 3.60 | 3116.20 | 102.50 | 3.00 | 523.60 | 4.80 | 70.90 | .06 | 7.66 | 5.95 |
| 71 HAK | 1.10 | 4223.00 | 92.00 | 57.80 | 3984.80 | 60.80 | 1164.10 | .05 | 9.48 | 6.67 |
| 72 BAT | 3.40 | 5229.20 | 104.00• | 14.00 | 49.10 | 115.80 | 10.50 | .05 | 6.67 | 4.95 |
| 73 HEA | 2.50 | 2528.90 | 95.10 | 22.20 | 753.20 | 85.40 | 50.60 | .09 | 9.41 | 6.33 |
| 74 HIN | 2.60 | 1322.10 | 113.00• | 16.50 | 940.60 | 49.50 | 56.10 | .06 | 8.68 | 5.56 |
| 75 BPI | 7.50 | 2964.50• | 118.70• | 10.30 | 359.90 | 141.40 | 92.50 | .04 | 8.67 | 5.27 |
| 76 CAN | 2.50 | 2174.10 | 100.10• | 3.00 | 137.10 | 16.10 | 34.90 | .07 | 8.05 | 5.63 |
| 77 CHA | 5.10 | 3079.80 | 100.30 | 13.20 | 421.10 | 55.90 | 131.60 | .04 | 6.81 | 4.20 |
| 78 CHA | 5.80 | 1862.30 | 104.10 | 17.40 | 195.70 | 108.70 | 243.50 | .08 | 7.94 | 5.27 |
| 79 CHA | 6.90 | 3109.90 | 101.40 | 12.20 | 48.90 | 200.50 | 3.20 | .05 | 7.55 | 6.07 |
| 80 CHA | 4.30 | 3443.00 | 97.00 | 26.20 | 108.20 | 98.40 | 134.40 | .03 | 8.97 | 5.93 |
| 81 COL | 1.40 | 3454.10 | 100.20 | 4.20 | 97.50 | 105.90 | 288.10 | .10 | 6.80 | 6.53 |
| 82 COL | 3.80 | 3650.60 | 97.40• | 12.40 | 863.20 | 117.60 | 71.20 | .05 | 7.48 | 4.92 |
| 83 COL | 3.60 | 1904.20 | 95.50 | 66.90 | 2.40 | 33.50 | 62.80 | .06 | 7.56 | 4.23 |
| 84 COW | 2.40 | 3812.80 | 99.30• | 10.50 | 1491.20 | 7.00 | 7.00 | .11 | 4.30 | 6.22 |
| 85 DAV | 2.40 | 2039.60 | 106.40• | 24.80 | 3325.10 | 206.60 | 322.30 | .15 | 8.18 | 5.72 |
| 86 DES | 4.70 | 2564.50 | 107.80 | 24.40 | 2167.80 | 234.20 | 97.90 | .10 | 8.35 | 7.17 |
| 87 DUL | 5.70 | 1996.40 | 99.90 | 3.00 | 2603.70 | 52.80 | 1101.80 | .16 | 9.46 | 5.43 |
| 88 ELP | 8.50 | 3100.00 | 91.00 | 3.00 | 440.10 | 16.70 | 136.40 | .04 | 7.09 | 4.31 |
| 89 FHI | 3.50 | 1972.30 | 101.80 | 3.00 | 2.40 | 4.80 | 53.00 | .05 | 8.56 | 5.83 |
| 90 EUG | 1.00 | 3844.30 | 87.30• | 4.60 | 8666.60 | 23.40 | 3535.20 | .05 | 8.10 | 5.56 |
| 91 EVA | 2.10 | 2552.40 | 96.00 | 51.50 | 85.80 | 120.10 | 201.70 | .11 | 8.69 | 6.84 |
| 92 FAY | 3.00 | 3527.50 | 99.00 | 9.40 | 47.10 | 89.60 | 47.10 | .04 | 5.60 | 3.47 |
| 93 FLI | 1.40 | 3422.00 | 98.50• | 10.00 | 710.20 | 154.90 | 175.00 | .03 | 6.41 | 4.09 |
| 94 FOR | 3.00 | 3076.30 | 91.00• | 35.70 | 153.50 | 225.00 | 82.10 | .04 | 6.68 | 5.66 |
| 95 FRE | 1.50 | 5318.80 | 99.50 | 19.30 | 4428.50 | 101.60 | 4401.90 | .04 | 9.42 | 6.55 |
| 96 GRE | 2.50 | 3620.70 | 95.20 | 13.30 | 696.60 | 50.00 | 70.00 | .07 | 8.87 | 6.11 |
| 97 HAM | 2.40 | 2361.10• | 98.70 | 44.20 | 243.30 | 212.30 | 438.00 | .07 | 7.07 | 4.99 |
| 98 HAM | 4.70 | 1509.90 | 104.30• | 21.80 | 2.40 | 143.50 | 878.30 | .09 | 8.72 | 6.04 |
| 99 HUN | 3.70 | 1796.00 | 101.80 | 7.80 | 594.40 | 82.60 | 118.10 | .11 | 8.63 | 5.09 |
| 100 HUN | .70 | 1912.20 | 95.00 | 13.10 | 26.30 | 122.80 | 276.30 | .04 | 6.80 | 4.14 |
| 101 JAC | 2.90 | 2287.70 | 96.90 | 15.40 | 2.40 | 84.90 | 3.20 | .05 | 7.84 | 5.03 |
| 102 JOH | 5.80 | 709.80 | 95.20• | 15.20 | 2908.70 | 57.00 | 634.90 | .12 | 9.28 | 5.27 |
| 103 KAL | 2.50 | 3574.60 | 98.00• | 4.90 | 108.90 | 183.10 | 49.50 | .03 | 6.15 | 4.76 |
| 104 KNO | 3.90 | 1880.20 | 93.20 | 17.50 | 1442.50 | 267.50 | 350.00 | .05 | 7.67 | 5.66 |
| 105 LAN | 2.50 | 943.20 | 103.90• | 18.70 | 2.40 | 81.20 | 78.10 | .08 | 9.12 | 5.59 |
| 106 LAN | 1.70 | 3967.90 | 101.10 | 7.90 | 2.40 | 79.30 | 84.60 | .05 | 6.48 | 4.44 |
| 107 LAS | 4.90 | 4732.40 | 112.10 | 51.20 | 4717.90 | 54.90 | 688.60 | .03 | 6.90 | 7.42 |
| 108 LAW | 3.10 | 3404.00• | 109.80• | 8.60 | 1336.20 | 56.00 | 500.00 | .09 | 8.79 | 5.51 |
| 109 LIT | 3.90 | 3619.10 | 98.50 | 18.50 | 18.50 | 185.70 | 108.30 | .06 | 8.88 | 6.19 |
| 110 LOR | 1.70 | 1962.70 | 105.60• | 31.10 | 1225.60 | 124.50 | 73.90 | .05 | 6.72 | 4.56 |
| 111 LOW | 4.70 | 3404.00• | 112.90• | 32.80 | 2.40 | 352.10 | 267.60 | .06 | 6.03 | 3.66 |
| 112 MAC | 5.50 | 3324.60 | 94.20 | 24.20 | 2.40 | 116.50 | 43.60 | .07 | 8.22 | 5.03 |
| 113 MAD | 6.70 | 2885.90 | 100.70 | 20.60 | 727.50 | 55.10 | 48.20 | .14 | 7.94 | 4.70 |
| 114 MOB | 3.10 | 2642.20 | 89.10 | 21.20 | 2.40 | 169.70 | 21.20 | .05 | 7.56 | 4.83 |
| 115 MON | 5.80 | 1842.90• | 104.20 | 36.60• | 791.80• | 117.60• | 237.50• | .06 | 8.20 | 4.39 |
| 116 NEW | 9.50 | 2841.30• | 121.80• | 5.60 | 384.80 | 58.90 | 73.00 | .06 | 8.68 | 5.99 |
| 117 NEW | 3.20 | 2238.00• | 124.90• | 4.80 | 1230.70 | 86.50 | 33.60 | .08 | 7.99 | 4.37 |
| 118 NEW | 7.70 | 2392.20 | 97.50• | 6.80 | 647.20 | 109.50 | 191.70 | .05 | 5.18 | 3.84 |
| 119 ORL | 3.50 | 3598.10 | 100.10 | 18.60 | 700.90 | 100.40 | 144.80 | .08 | 7.80 | 5.90 |
| 120 OXN | 1.30 | 3800.80 | 105.30• | 23.90 | 3494.60 | 98.40 | 2287.20 | .04 | 6.82 | 4.81 |
| 121 PEN | 1.90 | 3654.80 | 97.50• | 4.10 | 1576.10 | 74.00 | 164.60 | .07 | 7.34 | 4.87 |
| 122 PEO | 2.70 | 2619.10 | 106.10 | 29.20 | 1154.90 | 84.70 | 67.20 | .17 | 8.25 | 6.24 |
| 123 RAL | 3.80 | 2632.30 | 96.00 | 8.70 | 2057.00 | 184.20 | 192.90 | .06 | 8.37 | 5.66 |
| 124 REA | 6.80 | 1000.80 | 101.50• | 10.10 | 378.30 | 57.40 | 429.00 | .06 | 9.66 | 6.27 |
| 125 ROC | 2.20 | 1990.10 | 102.00 | 22.00 | 1845.50 | 224.20 | 213.20 | .10 | 7.37 | 5.78 |
| 126 SAG | 1.40 | 3878.30 | 96.50• | 9.00 | 2.40 | 45.40 | 63.60 | .05 | 6.59 | 3.91 |
| 127 SAL | 2.10 | 3564.30 | 108.40• | 4.00 | 4812.00 | 84.00 | 1840.00 | .04 | 8.57 | 5.63 |
| 128 SAN | .90 | 3291.60 | 106.00• | 15.10 | 4765.10 | 60.60 | 3102.20 | .07 | 8.59 | 6.53 |
| 129 SAN | 1.80 | 4320.90 | 103.10• | 19.50 | 1658.50 | 4.80 | 404.80 | .07 | 10.04 | 6.91 |
| 130 SCR | 7.50 | 1053.80 | 97.10• | 42.70 | 2.40 | 94.00 | 59.80 | .10 | 11.50 | 6.10 |
| 131 SCH | 5.30 | 2320.10 | 94.50 | 5.00 | 471.10 | 233.80 | 128.80 | .05 | 8.57 | 5.48 |
| 132 SOU | 3.60 | 2862.50 | 90.40 | 14.20 | 21.40 | 346.40 | 53.50 | .08 | 8.28 | 6.01 |
| 133 SPO | 4.10 | 2870.80 | 104.10 | 52.20 | 480.80 | 289.10 | 512.10 | .05 | 7.57 | 6.14 |
| 134 STA | 16.10 | 2964.50• | 131.20• | 9.70 | 19.40 | 165.00 | 48.50 | .05 | 9.14 | 7.53 |
| 135 STO | 1.70 | 5470.10 | 96.40 | 6.80 | 224.10 | 34.40 | 17.20 | .06 | 8.64 | 5.87 |
| 136 TAC | 2.90 | 3234.70 | 113.60• | 12.10 | 2525.50 | 58.30 | 1214.10 | .04 | 6.70 | 4.42 |
| 137 TPE | 8.00 | 3854.90 | 128.80• | 6.50 | 2.40 | 111.80 | 3.20 | .08 | 8.68 | 5.84 |
| 138 TUC | 1.60 | 3291.60 | 106.50 | 53.90 | 1619.30 | 125.00 | 1758.50 | .03 | 7.29 | 5.78 |
| 139 TUL | 2.30 | 3021.30 | 96.90 | 27.20 | 471.60 | 218.00 | 33.50 | .10 | 9.68 | 7.60 |
| 140 UTI | 4.60 | 1054.80 | 110.50• | 23.50 | 1005.80 | 26.40 | 8.80 | .05 | 9.92 | 5.89 |
| 141 VAL | 2.40 | 3800.10 | 103.10• | 28.10 | 546.10 | 152.60 | 409.60 | .05 | 7.52 | 5.03 |
| 142 WAT | 6.60 | 2841.30• | 111.10• | 14.30 | 1755.90 | 129.10 | 224.80 | .06 | 8.45 | 4.76 |
| 143 WES | 3.80 | 4428.50 | 105.20• | 11.40 | 830.90 | 65.90 | 120.30 | .11 | 9.59 | 7.43 |
| 144 WIC | 2.40 | 3133.30 | 90.20• | 41.10 | 439.50 | 35.90 | 38.50 | .12 | 9.56 | 7.11 |
| 145 WIL | 6.50 | 985.90 | 97.90 | 11.60 | 298.20 | 4.80 | 230.90 | .09 | 12.01 | 6.09 |
| 146 WIL | 4.60 | 3148.20 | 111.40• | 22.00 | 354.70 | 32.00 | 68.10 | .07 | 6.99 | 3.93 |
| 147 WOR | 7.90 | 3618.60• | 119.30• | 15.30• | 373.50• | 86.10• | 261.90• | .06 | 7.95 | 5.28 |
| 148 YOR | 1.40 | 1460.40 | 101.90 | 3.00 | 1684.80 | 66.60 | 360.60 | .08 | 9.21 | 5.89 |

| | Hospital Beds/ 100,000 pop. IIIB5 | Vols. of Books in Main Public Library/ 1,000 pop. IIIB6 | Death Rate/ 1,000 pop. IIIC1 | Birth Rate/ 1,000 pop. IIIC2 | Sports Events IIIC3 | Dance Drama and Music Events IIIC4a | Cultural Institutions IIIC4b | Fairs and Festivals Held IIIC4c |
|---|---|---|---|---|---|---|---|---|
| US | 486.00 | 1568.40 | 9.50 | 17.50 | N.A. | N.A. | N.A. | N.A. |
| 66 ALB | 363.60 | 953.50 | 6.30 | 18.90 | 0.00 • | 2.00 • | 0.00 • | 0.00 • |
| 67 ANN | 772.30 | 653.00 | 5.90 | 19.10 | 12.00 | 51.00 | 4.00 | 6.00 |
| 68 APP | 535.60 | 429.00 | 7.50 | 18.00 | 12.00 | 84.00 | 3.00 | 6.00 |
| 69 AUG | 464.40 | 903.60 | 8.60 | 20.40 | 2.00 | 33.00 | 2.00 | 2.00 |
| 70 AUS | 312.30 | 961.20 | 6.50 | 18.90 | 4.00 | 45.00 | 0.00 | 6.00 |
| 71 BAK | 342.10 | 1513.80 | 8.30 | 17.90 | 0.00 • | 2.00 • | 0.00 • | 0.00 • |
| 72 BAT | 425.40 | 834.50 | 7.30 | 21.80 | 4.00 | 70.00 | 14.00 | 18.00 |
| 73 BEA | 434.30 | 291.50 | 8.20 | 16.70 | 3.00 | 32.00 | 4.00 | 6.00 |
| 74 BIN | 462.20 | 773.30 | 9.50 | 18.20 | 5.00 | 32.00 | 8.00 | 3.00 |
| 75 BRI | 324.30 • | 1145.50 | 8.70 • | 15.90 • | 7.00 | 18.00 | 3.00 | 3.00 |
| 76 CAN | 401.10 | 1009.90 | 9.90 | 17.10 | 3.00 | 17.00 | 2.00 | 3.00 |
| 77 CHA | 400.20 | 754.10 | 7.50 | 22.30 | 4.00 | 30.00 | 2.00 | 7.00 |
| 78 CHA | 619.10 | 1244.20 | 10.20 | 16.70 | 3.00 | 12.00 | 2.00 | 2.00 |
| 79 CHA | 443.10 | 1236.70 | 7.80 | 19.80 | 10.00 | 35.00 | 10.00 | 6.00 |
| 80 CHA | 435.50 | 679.40 | 9.70 | 18.10 | 0.00 • | 2.00 • | 0.00 • | 0.00 • |
| 81 COL | 307.70 | 832.60 | 5.70 | 18.90 | 5.00 | 14.00 | 3.00 | 0.00 |
| 82 COL | 409.40 | 733.10 | 7.30 | 17.90 | 5.00 | 43.00 | 4.00 | 6.00 |
| 83 COL | 347.00 | 1276.20 | 7.90 | 21.20 | 5.00 | 27.00 | 2.00 | 6.00 |
| 84 COH | 441.30 | 903.00 | 6.90 | 21.40 | 0.00 | 21.00 | 2.00 | 12.00 |
| 85 DAV | 488.90 | 552.50 | 9.60 | 18.40 | 5.00 | 18.00 | 2.00 | 4.00 |
| 86 DES | 517.60 | 1309.00 | 9.10 | 18.20 | 6.00 | 35.00 | 3.00 | 7.00 |
| 87 DUL | 764.70 | 632.50 | 11.40 | 15.40 | 9.00 | 38.00 | 3.00 | 6.00 |
| 88 FLP | 419.70 | 960.60 | 6.20 | 28.90 | 7.00 | 39.00 | 4.00 | 8.00 |
| 89 FRI | 397.50 | 950.50 | 10.20 | 18.80 | 10.00 | 42.00 | 1.00 | 15.00 |
| 90 FUG | 296.20 | 569.80 | 6.90 | 16.20 | 5.00 | 28.00 | 4.00 | 2.00 |
| 91 EVA | 634.10 | 1841.40 | 10.60 | 17.10 | 5.00 | 24.00 | 1.00 | 5.00 |
| 92 FAY | 183.00 | 404.20 | 5.20 | 23.40 | 0.00 • | 2.00 • | 0.00 • | 0.00 • |
| 93 FLI | 382.80 | 689.40 | 7.50 | 20.20 | 10.00 | 50.00 | 6.00 | 8.00 |
| 94 FOR | 519.50 | 4882.20 | 8.10 | 20.00 | 9.00 | 12.00 | 2.00 | 3.00 |
| 95 FRE | 393.40 | 1565.30 | 8.60 | 18.30 | 8.00 | 51.00 | 3.00 | 6.00 |
| 96 GRE | 331.90 | 634.80 | 8.60 | 18.40 | 6.00 | 30.00 | 2.00 | 10.00 |
| 97 HAM | 523.90 | 897.10 | 8.10 | 17.50 | 2.00 | 4.00 | 1.00 | 4.00 |
| 98 HAR | 463.90 | 548.30 | 9.90 | 15.60 | 4.00 | 29.00 | 7.00 | 9.00 |
| 99 HUN | 593.50 | 537.30 | 10.40 | 16.90 | 3.00 | 39.00 | 3.00 | 2.00 |
| 100 HUN | 416.20 | 582.70 | 6.30 | 20.60 | 0.00 | 30.00 | 2.00 | 1.00 |
| 101 JAC | 493.20 | 669.20 | 8.50 | 20.50 | 3.00 | 39.00 | 3.00 | 6.00 |
| 102 JOH | 552.50 | 248.60 | 11.60 | 14.40 | 6.00 | 20.00 | 4.00 | 5.00 |
| 103 KAL | 368.10 | 992.60 | 7.30 | 17.60 | 4.00 | 46.00 | 2.00 | 5.00 |
| 104 KNO | 535.80 | 1027.00 | 8.90 | 15.60 | 4.00 | 71.00 | 6.00 | 4.00 |
| 105 LAN | 321.90 | 559.70 | 8.80 | 17.10 | 4.00 | 32.00 | 4.00 | 3.00 |
| 106 LAN | 348.00 | 606.60 | 7.00 | 19.70 | 5.00 | 27.00 | 3.00 | 4.00 |
| 107 LAS | 299.70 | 257.60 | 6.70 | 20.70 | 6.00 | 27.00 | 7.00 | 8.00 |
| 108 LAW | 466.80 • | 824.20 | 8.10 • | 16.70 • | 3.00 | 20.00 | 3.00 | 4.00 |
| 109 LIT | 556.10 | 597.10 | 9.30 | 19.20 | 5.00 | 55.00 | 7.00 | 6.00 |
| 110 LOH | 358.60 | 808.70 | 8.20 | 19.20 | 0.00 | 2.00 | 0.00 | 2.00 |
| 111 LOW | 466.80 • | 1278.60 | 8.10 • | 16.70 • | 0.00 • | 2.00 • | 0.00 • | 0.00 • |
| 112 MAC | 374.10 | 1550.00 | 9.00 | 19.20 | 0.00 • | 2.00 • | 0.00 • | 0.00 • |
| 113 MAD | 624.20 | 1071.20 | 6.90 | 18.00 | 5.00 | 77.00 | 4.00 | 3.00 |
| 114 MOH | 382.30 | 600.80 | 8.60 | 18.90 | 2.00 | 24.00 | 1.00 | 6.00 |
| 115 MON | 457.00 | 790.50 | 10.70 | 19.10 | 0.00 • | 2.00 • | 0.00 • | 0.00• |
| 116 NEW | 377.10 • | 1266.50 | 9.40• | 16.80 • | 14.00 | 40.00 | 5.00 | 5.00 |
| 117 NEW | 244.00 • | 276.00 | 8.20• | 18.70 • | 0.00 • | 2.00• | 0.00 • | 0.00 • |
| 118 NEW | 395.00 | 429.10 | 6.50 | 20.30 | 11.00 | 49.00 | 10.00 | 7.00 |
| 119 ORL | 448.80 | 743.40 | 8.60 | 17.20 | 0.00 • | 2.00 • | 0.00 • | 0.00 • |
| 120 OXN | 341.10 | 236.20 | 6.10 | 18.80 | 0.00 | 28.00 | 0.00 | 2.00 |
| 121 PEN | 396.20 | 520.00 | 7.30 | 20.50 | 1.00 | 28.00 | 6.00 | 3.00 |
| 122 PEO | 606.20 | 1085.80 | 9.10 | 17.80 | 4.00 | 54.00 | 11.00 | 9.00 |
| 123 RAL | 394.00 | 828.30 | 7.30 | 18.10 | 7.00 | 59.00 | 4.00 | 2.00 |
| 124 REA | 380.60 | 714.00 | 11.00 | 13.90 | 4.00 | 26.00 | 1.00 | 4.00 |
| 125 ROC | 402.50 | 886.00 | 8.10 | 19.80 | 0.00 • | 2.00 • | 0.00 • | 0.00 • |
| 126 SAG | 364.50 | 1300.70 | 8.30 | 20.60 | 2.00 | 40.00 | 2.00 | 2.00 |
| 127 SAL | 308.70 | 374.50 | 6.90 | 18.80 | 2.00 | 11.00 | 1.00 | 5.00 |
| 128 SAN | 452.10 | 897.70 | 7.50 | 17.70 | 0.00 • | 2.00 • | 0.00 • | 0.00 • |
| 129 SAN | 328.50 | 1123.80 | 10.70 | 16.00 | 0.00 • | 2.00 • | 0.00 • | 0.00 • |
| 130 SCR | 553.60 | 752.60 | 13.50 | 13.80 | 8.00 | 52.00 | 1.00 | 6.00 |
| 131 SCH | 641.00 | 738.50 | 9.70 | 20.90 | 4.00 | 32.00 | 6.00 | 4.00 |
| 132 SOU | 322.80 | 928.30 | 9.40 | 16.70 | 9.00 | 82.00 | 8.00 | 6.00 |
| 133 SPO | 468.20 | 1356.50 | 10.40 | 16.00 | 6.00 | 11.00 | 3.00 | 3.00 |
| 134 STA | 324.30 • | 1302.60 | 8.70 • | 15.90 • | 0.00 | 32.00 | 1.00 | 16.00 |
| 135 STO | 342.90 | 2141.50 | 9.40 | 17.30 | 6.00 | 19.00 | 2.00 | 5.00 |
| 136 TAC | 280.80 | 1158.50 | 8.60 | 18.90 | 5.00 | 45.00 | 4.00 | 7.00 |
| 137 TRE | 525.10 | 750.20 | 9.60 | 16.70 | 5.00 | 20.00 | 5.00 | 2.00 |
| 138 TUC | 358.90 | 1005.80 | 8.40 | 16.90 | 0.00 • | 2.00• | 0.00 • | 0.00 • |
| 139 TUL | 415.80 | 1127.50 | 9.00 | 17.00 | 9.00 | 55.00 | 4.00 | 15.00 |
| 140 UTI | 399.40 | 323.80 | 10.80 | 17.50 | 0.00 • | 2.00 • | 0.00 • | 0.00 • |
| 141 VAL | 388.60 | 479.90 | 8.00 | 18.10 | 0.00 | 9.00 | 1.00 | 4.00 |
| 142 WAT | 377.10 • | 752.50 | 9.40 • | 16.80 • | 2.00 | 7.00 | 1.00 | 3.00 |
| 143 WES | 393.40 | 143.30 | 11.60 | 14.70 | 0.00 • | 2.00 • | 0.00 • | 0.00 • |
| 144 WIC | 527.50 | 742.20 | 8.00 | 19.50 | 4.00 | 33.00 | 4.00 | 3.00 |
| 145 WIL | 469.50 | 380.20 | 12.90 | 13.60 | 5.00 | 79.00 | 1.00 | 10.00 |
| 146 WIL | 340.70 | 793.00 | 8.80 | 18.00 | 6.00 | 31.00 | 6.00 | 2.00 |
| 147 WOR | 474.50 • | 1927.10 | 10.30 • | 15.80 • | 5.00 | 35.00 | 5.00 | 5.00 |
| 148 YOR | 253.40 | 331.90 | 9.60 | 16.90 | 3.00 | 16.00 | 1.00 | 2.00 |

# LIST C

## SMSA'A WITH POPULATION LESS THAN 200,000 (S)

| | SMSA | Code | Population, 1970 (in 1,000) |
|---|---|---|---|
| 149 | Abilene, Texas | ABI | 114 |
| 150 | Albany, Ga. | ALB | 90 |
| 151 | Altoona, Pa. | ALT | 135 |
| 152 | Amarillo, Texas | AMA | 144 |
| 153 | Anderson, Ind. | AND | 138 |
| 154 | Asheville, N.C. | ASH | 145 |
| 155 | Atlantic City, N.J. | ATL | 175 |
| 156 | Bay City, Mich. | BAY | 117 |
| 157 | Billings, Mont. | BIL | 87 |
| 158 | Biloxi-Gulfport, Miss. | BIL | 135 |
| 159 | Bloomington-Normal, Ill. | BLO | 104 |
| 160 | Boise City, Idaho | BOI | 112 |
| 161 | Bristol, Conn. | BRI | 66 |
| 162 | Brockton, Mass. | BKI | 190 |
| 163 | Brownsville-Harlingen-San Benito, Texas | BRO | 140 |
| 164 | Bryan-College Station, Texas | BRY | 58 |
| 165 | Cedar Rapids, Iowa | CED | 163 |
| 166 | Champaign-Urbana, Ill. | CHA | 163 |
| 167 | Columbia, Mo. | COL | 81 |
| 168 | Danbury, Conn. | DAN | 79 |
| 169 | Decatur, Ill. | DEC | 125 |
| 170 | Dubuque, Iowa | DUB | 91 |
| 171 | Durham, N.C. | DUR | 190 |
| 172 | Fall River, Mass.-R.I. | FAL | 150 |
| 173 | Fargo-Moorhead, N. Dak.-Minn. | FAR | 120 |
| 174 | Fitchburg-Leominster, Mass. | FIT | 97 |
| 175 | Fort Smith, Ark.-Okla. | FOR | 160 |
| 176 | Gadsden, Alabama | GAD | 94 |
| 177 | Gainesville, Fla. | GAI | 105 |
| 178 | Galveston-Texas City, Texas | GAL | 170 |
| 179 | Great Falls, Mont. | GRE | 82 |
| 180 | Green Bay, Wis. | GRE | 158 |
| 181 | Jackson, Mich. | JAC | 143 |
| 182 | Kenosha, Wis. | KEN | 118 |
| 183 | La Crosse, Wis. | LAC | 80 |
| 184 | Lafayette, La. | LAF | 110 |
| 185 | Lafayette-West Lafayette, Ind. | LAF | 109 |
| 186 | Lake Charles, La. | LAK | 145 |
| 187 | Laredo, Texas | LAR | 73 |
| 188 | Lawton, Okla. | LAW | 108 |
| 189 | Lewiston-Auburn, Maine | LEW | 73 |
| 190 | Lexington, Ky. | LEX | 174 |
| 191 | Lima, Ohio | LIM | 171 |
| 192 | Lincoln, Nebraska | LIN | 168 |
| 193 | Lubbock, Texas | LUB | 179 |
| 194 | Lynchburg, Va. | LYN | 123 |
| 195 | Manchester, N.H. | MAN | 108 |
| 196 | Mansfield, Ohio | MAN | 130 |
| 197 | McAllen-Pharr-Edinburg, Texas | MCA | 182 |
| 198 | Meriden, Conn. | MER | 56 |

| | SMSA | Code | Population, 1970 (in 1,000) |
|---|---|---|---|
| 199 | Midland, Texas | MID | 65 |
| 200 | Modesto, Calif. | MOD | 195 |
| 201 | Monroe, La. | MON | 115 |
| 202 | Muncie, Ind. | MUN | 129 |
| 203 | Muskegon-Muskegon Heights, Mich. | MUS | 157 |
| 204 | Nashua, N.H. | NAS | 67 |
| 205 | New Bedford, Mass. | NEW | 153 |
| 206 | New Britain, Conn. | NEW | 145 |
| 207 | Norwalk, Conn. | NOR | 120 |
| 208 | Odessa, Texas | ODE | 92 |
| 209 | Ogden, Utah | OGD | 126 |
| 210 | Owensboro, Ky. | OWE | 79 |
| 211 | Petersburg-Colonial Heights, Va. | PET | 129 |
| 212 | Pine Bluff, Ark. | PIN | 85 |
| 213 | Pittsfield, Mass. | PIT | 80 |
| 214 | Portland, Maine | POR | 142 |
| 215 | Provo-Orem, Utah | PRO | 138 |
| 216 | Pueblo, Colo. | PUE | 118 |
| 217 | Racine, Wis. | RAC | 171 |
| 218 | Reno, Nev. | REN | 121 |
| 219 | Roanoke, Va. | ROA | 181 |
| 220 | Rochester, Minn. | ROC | 84 |
| 221 | St. Joseph, Mo. | STJ | 87 |
| 222 | Salem, Oreg. | SAL | 187 |
| 223 | San Angelo, Texas | SAN | 71 |
| 224 | Savannah, Ga. | SAV | 188 |
| 225 | Sherman-Denison, Texas | SHE | 83 |
| 226 | Sioux City, Iowa-Nebraska | SIO | 116 |
| 227 | Sioux Falls, S. Dak. | SIO | 95 |
| 228 | Springfield, Ill. | SPR | 161 |
| 229 | Springfield, Mo. | SPR | 153 |
| 230 | Springfield, Ohio. | SPR | 156 |
| 231 | Steubenville-Weirton, Ohio-W. Va. | STE | 166 |
| 232 | Tallahassee, Fla. | TAL | 103 |
| 233 | Terre Haute, Ind. | TER | 175 |
| 234 | Texarkana, Texas-Ark. | TEX | 101 |
| 235 | Topeka, Kans. | TOP | 155 |
| 236 | Tuscaloosa, Alabama | TUS | 116 |
| 237 | Tyler, Texas | TYL | 97 |
| 238 | Vineland-Millville-Bridgeton, N.J. | VIN | 121 |
| 239 | Waco, Texas | WAC | 147 |
| 240 | Waterloo, Iowa | WAT | 133 |
| 241 | Wheeling, W. Va.-Ohio | WHE | 183 |
| 242 | Wichita Falls, Texas | WIC | 126 |
| 243 | Wilmington, N.C. | WIL | 107 |

## TABLE C-1

## BASIC STATISTICS OF ECONOMIC COMPONENT (S)

| | | Personal Income Per Capita IA | Savings Per Capita IB1 | Property Income/ Personal Income IB2 | % Owner-Occupied Housing Units IB3 | % Households With One Or More Automobiles IB4 | Median Value, Owner Occupied Single Family Housing (in $1,000) IB5 | Percent of Families With Income Above Poverty Level IIA | Degree of Economic Concentration IIB |
|---|---|---|---|---|---|---|---|---|---|
| US | | 3139.00 | 702.00 | .14 | 62.90 | 82.50 | 17.10 | 89.30 | .00 |
| 149 | ABI | 2524.00 | 733.00 | .16 | 66.60 | 91.30 | 9.80 | 86.70 | .25 |
| 150 | ALB | 2467.00 | 439.00 | .10 | 49.60 | 81.30 | 16.30 | 81.40 | .06 |
| 151 | ALT | 2631.00 | 537.00 | .10 | 73.50 | 83.10 | 9.10 | 91.60 | .08 |
| 152 | AMA | 3006.00 | 667.00 | .21 | 68.10 | 92.00 | 12.30 | 90.90 | .24 |
| 153 | AND | 3259.00 | 1228.00 | .12 | 74.10 | 89.00 | 13.60 | 93.80 | .12 |
| 154 | ASH | 2671.00 | 441.00 | .15 | 71.80 | 82.20 | 14.00 | 86.50 | .15 |
| 155 | ATL | 3083.00 | 891.00 | .16 | 62.20 | 72.40 | 14.90 | 90.10 | .03 |
| 156 | BAY | 3065.00 | 806.00 | .14 | 81.30 | 89.80 | 15.20 | 92.40 | .06 |
| 157 | BIL | 2855.00 | 623.00 | .15 | 63.50 | 90.30 | 17.20 | 90.60 | .37 |
| 158 | BIL | 2319.00 | 324.00 | .10 | 60.80 | 86.60 | 14.90 | 82.70 | .17 |
| 159 | BLO | 3195.00 | 1394.00 | .15 | 64.80 | 88.90 | 17.40 | 93.80 | .31 |
| 160 | BOI | 3144.00 | 914.00 | .15 | 71.20 | 91.40 | 16.40 | 91.40 | .30 |
| 161 | BRI | 3509.00 | 6.00 | .15 | 65.60 | 90.60 | 20.80 | 96.10 | .01 |
| 162 | BRO | 3073.00 | 379.00 | .15 | 68.50 | 86.60 | 18.30 | 94.80 | .09 |
| 163 | BRO | 1580.00 | 345.00 | .15 | 67.40 | 80.50 | 7.20 | 61.50 | .28 |
| 164 | BRY | 2669.00 | 1043.00 | .15 | 56.30 | 88.50 | 12.90 | 83.40 | .36 |
| 165 | CED | 3208.00 | 791.00 | .15 | 71.90 | 88.70 | 18.00 | 94.30 | .06 |
| 166 | CHA | 3230.00 | 613.00 | .14 | 53.90 | 89.50 | 19.00 | 92.80 | .46 |
| 167 | COL | 2963.00 | 223.00 | .13 | 57.10 | 87.30 | 19.20 | 91.30 | .56 |
| 168 | DAN | 3610.00 | 140.00 | .22 | 69.70 | 90.60 | 28.20 | 95.40 | .09 |
| 169 | DEC | 3356.00 | 946.00 | .14 | 71.60 | 86.00 | 14.60 | 93.20 | .09 |
| 170 | DUB | 2696.00 | 321.00 | .15 | 73.20 | 85.90 | 17.70 | 92.40 | .05 |
| 171 | DUR | 2909.00 | 804.00 | .13 | 53.90 | 83.50 | 16.30 | 87.70 | .12 |
| 172 | FAL | 2859.00 | 302.00 | .12 | 48.30 | 77.20 | 18.40 | 91.10 | .08 |
| 173 | FAR | 2868.00 | 1979.00 | .15 | 62.50 | 88.00 | 18.30 | 92.70 | .49 |
| 174 | FIT | 3152.00 | 532.00 | .13 | 60.70 | 84.30 | 17.50 | 93.70 | .03 |
| 175 | FOR | 2222.00 | 783.00 | .14 | 70.10 | 81.70 | 9.40 | 80.30 | .04 |
| 176 | GAD | 2419.00 | 422.00 | .10 | 70.10 | 85.50 | 11.30 | 82.60 | .20 |
| 177 | GAI | 2717.00 | 704.00 | .09 | 60.80 | 88.00 | 14.50 | 84.70 | .46 |
| 178 | GAL | 3036.00 | 719.00 | .15 | 62.50 | 85.20 | 13.30 | 88.90 | .07 |
| 179 | GRE | 2864.00 | 708.00 | .13 | 56.90 | 89.20 | 16.40 | 91.70 | .30 |
| 180 | GRE | 2866.00 | 467.00 | .14 | 73.20 | 90.70 | 17.10 | 93.90 | .09 |
| 181 | JAC | 3218.00 | 486.00 | .13 | 78.90 | 90.60 | 14.70 | 93.40 | .03 |
| 182 | KEN | 3072.00 | 456.00 | .11 | 70.10 | 88.50 | 17.00 | 94.30 | .03 |
| 183 | LAC | 2771.00 | 1295.00 | .16 | 70.30 | 85.00 | 17.00 | 93.50 | .10 |
| 184 | LAF | 2454.00 | 1093.00 | .09 | 68.80 | 88.00 | 16.80 | 80.70 | .45 |
| 185 | LAF | 3106.00 | 439.00 | .14 | 62.20 | 88.80 | 17.60 | 93.90 | .27 |
| 186 | LAK | 2480.00 | 768.00 | .11 | 71.10 | 86.90 | 13.30 | 83.50 | .07 |
| 187 | LAR | 1573.00 | 146.00 | .10 | 59.00 | 74.70 | 7.90 | 61.60 | .44 |
| 188 | LAW | 2569.00 | 262.00 | .08 | 57.50 | 91.00 | 13.40 | 85.70 | .46 |
| 189 | LEW | 2616.00 | 262.00 | .13 | 53.90 | 76.30 | 15.90 | 91.60 | .09 |
| 190 | LEX | 3154.00 | 394.00 | .12 | 55.30 | 84.40 | 19.10 | 90.30 | .15 |
| 191 | LIM | 2953.00 | 770.00 | .13 | 75.10 | 89.40 | 13.90 | 92.80 | .07 |
| 192 | LIN | 3180.00 | 1492.00 | .17 | 61.90 | 88.10 | 16.20 | 94.10 | .32 |
| 193 | LUB | 2720.00 | 695.00 | .16 | 60.60 | 92.00 | 13.20 | 86.60 | .26 |
| 194 | LYN | 2710.00 | 763.00 | .10 | 68.30 | 80.20 | 14.40 | 89.10 | .19 |
| 195 | MAN | 2990.00 | 1044.00 | .12 | 56.70 | 78.50 | 17.70 | 93.20 | .02 |
| 196 | MAN | 3077.00 | 423.00 | .12 | 72.70 | 88.20 | 16.00 | 92.90 | .15 |
| 197 | MCA | 1523.00 | 255.00 | .16 | 70.50 | 81.40 | 6.40 | 58.00 | .46 |
| 198 | MER | 3379.00 | 1541.00 | .16 | 59.30 | 84.30 | 21.80 | 95.20 | .05 |

| | Personal Income Per Capita IA | Savings Per Capita IB1 | Property Income/ Personal Income IB2 | % Owner-Occupied Housing Units IB3 | % Households With One Or More Automobiles IB4 | Median Value, Owner Occupied Single Family Housing (in $1,000) IB5 | Percent of Families With Income Above Poverty Level IIA | Degree of Economic Concentration IIB |
|---|---|---|---|---|---|---|---|---|
| 199 MID | 3500.00 | 986.00 | .20 | 73.80 | 93.50 | 14.00 | 90.20 | .40 |
| 200 MOD | 2924.00 | 68.00 | .12 | 63.60 | 89.30 | 16.30 | 88.20 | .16 |
| 201 MON | 2372.00 | 859.00 | .12 | 66.10 | 82.50 | 13.60 | 79.20 | .05 |
| 202 MUN | 3052.00 | 1105.00 | .13 | 70.60 | 88.50 | 13.30 | 92.70 | .09 |
| 203 MUS | 2889.00 | 378.00 | .12 | 78.70 | 89.10 | 12.90 | 92.20 | .12 |
| 204 NAS | 3252.00 | 7.00 | .14 | 62.40 | 84.40 | 19.20 | 95.50 | .08 |
| 205 NEW | 2872.00 | 24.00 | .12 | 53.60 | 75.30 | 17.60 | 89.90 | .01 |
| 206 NEW | 3538.00 | 279.00 | .15 | 57.60 | 85.10 | 22.90 | 95.20 | .02 |
| 207 NOR | 4992.00 | 416.00 | .22 | 67.80 | 91.20 | 41.30 | 95.60 | .20 |
| 208 ODE | 2919.00 | 642.00 | .11 | 72.70 | 94.20 | 10.80 | 90.10 | .25 |
| 209 OGD | 2973.00 | 586.00 | .13 | 69.60 | 90.00 | 17.00 | 92.60 | .45 |
| 210 OWE | 2672.00 | 881.00 | .13 | 70.20 | 85.60 | 14.00 | 88.10 | .10 |
| 211 PET | 2602.00 | 646.00 | .09 | 59.60 | 82.00 | 14.80 | 88.30 | .10 |
| 212 PIN | 2189.00 | 635.00 | .14 | 63.70 | 75.90 | 10.80 | 77.00 | .05 |
| 213 PIT | 3333.00 | 1676.00 | .15 | 64.30 | 84.10 | 18.20 | 94.60 | .09 |
| 214 POR | 3047.00 | 558.00 | .15 | 60.60 | 80.00 | 17.00 | 92.60 | .12 |
| 215 PRO | 2221.00 | 26.00 | .11 | 67.00 | 93.20 | 16.20 | 88.30 | .23 |
| 216 PUE | 2546.00 | 474.00 | .13 | 72.80 | 86.50 | 12.70 | 88.80 | .18 |
| 217 RAC | 3260.00 | 743.00 | .14 | 69.60 | 87.80 | 17.90 | 94.40 | .06 |
| 218 REN | 3898.00 | 1349.00 | .15 | 57.40 | 88.70 | 23.60 | 94.10 | .42 |
| 219 ROA | 3052.00 | 625.00 | .14 | 69.50 | 83.50 | 15.50 | 91.40 | .08 |
| 220 ROC | 3292.00 | 644.00 | .12 | 69.40 | 89.10 | 20.40 | 94.60 | .15 |
| 221 STJ | 2747.00 | 666.00 | .16 | 67.80 | 80.30 | 11.30 | 90.50 | .02 |
| 222 SAL | 2851.00 | 535.00 | .15 | 67.80 | 88.40 | 15.50 | 90.10 | .27 |
| 223 SAN | 2656.00 | 914.00 | .17 | 67.40 | 90.20 | 10.20 | 85.40 | .18 |
| 224 SAV | 2671.00 | 512.00 | .13 | 57.30 | 78.00 | 13.50 | 83.10 | .03 |
| 225 SHE | 2668.00 | 458.00 | .14 | 68.20 | 85.10 | 10.10 | 87.90 | .06 |
| 226 SIO | 2853.00 | 909.00 | .15 | 69.60 | 84.70 | 13.20 | 90.80 | .16 |
| 227 SIO | 2771.00 | 781.00 | .14 | 66.90 | 89.00 | 15.40 | 91.80 | .16 |
| 228 SPR | 3432.00 | 773.00 | .15 | 66.50 | 85.80 | 15.70 | 93.30 | .27 |
| 229 SPR | 2800.00 | 962.00 | .15 | 68.50 | 86.30 | 14.20 | 89.70 | .07 |
| 230 SPR | 3084.00 | 935.00 | .11 | 68.00 | 88.50 | 16.40 | 92.70 | .11 |
| 231 STE | 2887.00 | 626.00 | .12 | 74.20 | 83.70 | 14.60 | 92.10 | .02 |
| 232 TAL | 2887.00 | 853.00 | .14 | 60.00 | 87.50 | 16.20 | 86.30 | .51 |
| 233 TER | 2823.00 | 506.00 | .11 | 75.90 | 83.40 | 8.90 | 90.50 | .11 |
| 234 TEX | 2479.00 | 433.00 | .11 | 70.00 | 81.50 | 10.40 | 84.00 | .02 |
| 235 TOP | 3152.00 | 3224.00 | .17 | 64.30 | 88.20 | 14.90 | 93.10 | .31 |
| 236 TUS | 2253.00 | 573.00 | .12 | 60.60 | 82.20 | 13.80 | 80.10 | .00 |
| 237 TYL | 2767.00 | 1116.00 | .18 | 70.60 | 86.00 | 11.60 | 87.10 | .09 |
| 238 VIN | 2902.00 | 900.00 | .10 | 68.30 | 85.10 | 13.70 | 90.80 | .02 |
| 239 WAC | 2561.00 | 960.00 | .17 | 65.60 | 86.10 | 9.60 | 85.20 | .03 |
| 240 WAT | 3013.00 | 1092.00 | .13 | 73.40 | 89.50 | 16.20 | 92.70 | .03 |
| 241 WHE | 2732.00 | 834.00 | .13 | 69.70 | 78.90 | 12.40 | 89.80 | .06 |
| 242 WIC | 2785.00 | 786.00 | .18 | 66.20 | 89.70 | 10.00 | 89.10 | .28 |
| 243 WIL | 2591.00 | 1053.00 | .11 | 66.60 | 82.20 | 13.50 | 83.80 | .12 |

## TABLE C-1 (Continued)

| | | Value Added/ Worker in Manufacturing (in $1,000) IIC1 | Value of Construction/ Worker (in $1,000) IIC2 | Sales/ Employee in Retail Trade (in $1,000) IIC3 | Sales/ Employee in Wholesale Trade (in $1,000) IIC4 | Sales/ Employee in Selected Services (in $1,000) IIC5 | Total Bank Deposits Per Capita IID | Central City and Suburban Income Distribution IIE1 | Percent of Families With Income Below Pov. Level or Greater Than $15,000 IIE2 | Unemployment Rate IIF | Chamber of Commerce Employees/ 100,000 Pop. IIG |
|---|---|---|---|---|---|---|---|---|---|---|---|
| US | | 13.50 | 4.30 | 33.00 | 130.60 | 15.80 | 2492.00 | .06 | 31.30 | 4.40 | NA |
| 149 | ABI | 15.50 | .64 | 30.90 | 94.30 | 11.00 | 1872.00 | -.02 | 24.30 | 3.60 | 15.80 |
| 150 | ALB | 11.70 | 5.19 | 30.80 | 90.20 | 11.60 | 1241.00 | .02 | 32.70 | 4.30 | 2.20 • |
| 151 | ALT | 11.90 | 3.24 | 32.50 | 82.60 | 13.20 | 1396.00 | .02 | 29.30 | 3.50 | 1.50 • |
| 152 | AMA | 11.40 | 1.52 | 30.80 | 96.40 | 14.60 | 2441.00 | -.02 | 25.20 | 3.40 | 6.90 |
| 153 | AND | 15.90 | 3.88 | 32.50 | 72.60 | 13.40 | 975.00 | -.02 | 27.30 | 5.30 | 3.60 |
| 154 | ASH | 9.90 | .70 | 32.90 | 66.30 | 12.40 | 1495.00 | -.09 | 25.30 | 3.90 | 9.70 |
| 155 | ATL | 14.70 | 3.68 | 32.80 | 85.50 | 14.80 | 1872.00 | .08 | 27.40 | 5.70 | 2.30 • |
| 156 | RAY | 15.40 | 3.66 | 35.10 | 90.00 | 12.50 | 1578.00 | .00 | 27.50 | 6.70 | 1.70 |
| 157 | MIL | 26.50 | 2.00 | 32.80 | 103.40 | 11.50 | 2417.00 | -.08 | 25.40 | 5.80 | 6.90 |
| 158 | BIL | 13.30 | 4.01 | 30.20 | 69.70 | 9.60 | 1268.00 | -.06 | 27.60 | 4.20 | 3.70 |
| 159 | BLO | 15.30 | 7.74 | 30.20 | 123.60 | 19.00 | 1952.00 | -.04 | 27.80 | 3.50 | 1.90 |
| 160 | BOI | 10.30 | 3.32 | 31.00 | 84.80 | 13.40 | 2458.00 | -.06 | 27.90 | 3.70 | 7.10 |
| 161 | BRI | 11.20 | 4.37 | 34.30 • | 98.50 | 14.20 | 1722.00 • | -.02 | 30.10 | 4.10 | 6.10 |
| 162 | BRO | 9.50 | 6.08 | 30.70 | 59.70 | 15.30 | 1672.00 | .00 | 27.40 | 3.70 | 1.10 |
| 163 | BRO | 8.40 | 1.64 | 28.40 | 78.50 | 11.80 | 1117.00 | .02 | 46.10 | 6.60 | 1.40 |
| 164 | BRY | 8.40 | 0.00 | 31.90 | 91.60 | 13.20 | 1694.00 | -.04 | 33.20 | 2.60 | 3.40 |
| 165 | CED | 14.90 | 3.49 | 30.10 | 82.20 | 13.10 | 1906.00 | -.06 | 26.50 | 4.00 | 8.60 |
| 166 | CHA | 10.80 | 3.12 | 30.50 | 179.90 | 13.40 | 1528.00 | -.06 | 30.80 | 3.80 | 3.10 |
| 167 | COL | 10.60 | 3.10 • | 30.60 | 86.70 | 11.40 | 1491.00 | -.06 | 29.30 | 2.40 | 3.70 |
| 168 | DAN | 13.40 • | 4.37 | 34.30 | 98.50 | 14.20 | 1722.00 • | -.04 | 34.30 | 4.20 | 5.10 |
| 169 | DEC | 20.10 | 4.22 | 31.30 | 142.70 | 12.20 | 2104.00 | -.04 | 27.60 | 4.30 | 6.40 |
| 170 | DUB | 16.40 | 2.60 | 33.10 | 82.40 | 11.30 | 2292.00 | -.08 | 26.30 | 2.70 | 5.50 |
| 171 | DUR | 16.30 | 6.87 | 29.40 | 83.10 | 12.30 | 1253.00 | .02 | 29.00 | 2.80 | 4.20 |
| 172 | FAL | 7.20 | 2.93 | 31.40 | 81.70 | 11.50 | 2225.00 | .08 | 22.00 | 4.80 | 6.00 |
| 173 | FAR | 12.70 | 6.05 | 30.40 | 159.00 | 13.80 | 2348.00 | -.06 | 25.90 | 4.60 | 6.70 |
| 174 | FIT | 11.50 | 3.08 | 30.60 | 59.60 | 13.60 | 2282.00 | .00 | 25.80 | 4.20 | 2.10 |
| 175 | FOR | 11.60 | 2.25 | 30.90 | 77.80 | 13.10 | 1384.00 | -.22 | 27.00 | 4.80 | 4.40 |
| 176 | GAD | 18.00 | 1.88 | 34.30 | 71.60 | 11.20 | 2223.00 | -.10 | 27.40 | 7.30 | 4.30 |
| 177 | GAI | 9.50 | 3.10 • | 32.40 | 71.10 | 11.30 | 1319.00 | -.06 | 32.90 | 3.40 | 7.60 |
| 178 | GAL | 49.30 | 1.06 | 32.00 | 78.60 | 11.40 | 1254.00 | .00 | 30.00 | 3.70 | 1.20 |
| 179 | GRE | 18.10 | 1.90 | 35.50 | 161.20 | 12.20 | 2147.00 | -.10 | 23.70 | 6.50 | 4.90 |
| 180 | GRE | 17.40 | 6.40 | 29.60 | 120.30 | 14.00 | 2066.00 | .04 | 24.23 | 4.00 | 8.20 |
| 181 | JAC | 14.30 | 3.75 | 32.20 | 106.00 | 13.30 | 1657.00 | .00 | 30.10 | 5.60 | 3.50 |
| 182 | KEN | 12.90 | 3.73 | 29.10 | 75.30 | 14.00 | 1332.00 | .02 | 25.10 | 4.30 | 1.70 |
| 183 | LAC | 13.80 | 3.61 • | 28.50 | 89.10 | 14.40 | 1767.00 | -.06 | 21.40 | 5.70 | 5.00 |
| 184 | LAF | 11.50 | 4.10 | 29.70 | 85.00 | 16.20 | 1298.00 | .06 | 34.60 | 4.10 | 5.50 |
| 185 | LAF | 15.70 | 2.62 | 30.90 | 63.80 | 11.20 | 2223.00 | -.10 | 26.30 | 3.40 | 4.60 |
| 186 | LAK | 22.40 | 1.66 | 34.30 | 78.10 | 12.10 | 1319.00 | -.02 | 30.10 | 5.70 | 5.50 |
| 187 | LAR | 7.60 | 3.15 | 27.40 | 62.00 | 7.50 | 1254.00 | -.04 | 45.50 | 6.80 | 6.80 |
| 188 | LAW | 9.60 | 5.56 | 32.60 | 61.70 | 10.60 | 966.00 | .02 | 24.30 | 7.00 | 3.70 |
| 189 | LEW | 7.50 | 2.00 | 32.80 | 78.50 | 14.00 | 2875.00 | .00 | 28.80 | 4.50 | 4.10 |
| 190 | LEX | 21.40 | 8.96 | 28.20 | 99.20 | 12.30 | 1945.00 | .08 | 30.00 | 3.10 | 6.90 |
| 191 | LIM | 15.70 | 2.54 | 32.70 | 111.50 | 14.20 | 1483.00 | .00 | 24.80 | 4.10 | 1.20 |
| 192 | LIN | 12.70 | 2.59 | 26.10 | 111.50 | 12.10 | 2292.00 | -.02 | 25.40 | 2.90 | 11.90 |
| 193 | LUB | 11.10 | 4.22 | 31.30 | 102.50 | 13.00 | 2415.00 | -.06 | 29.40 | 3.60 | 10.10 |
| 194 | LYN | 11.00 | 5.80 | 29.80 | 86.30 | 10.40 | 1921.00 | -.10 | 25.40 | 2.30 | 1.60 |
| 195 | MAN | 9.30 | 1.95 | 32.00 | 101.10 | 14.50 | 4712.00 | .02 | 24.00 | 3.20 | 4.60 |
| 196 | MAN | 16.30 | 5.32 | 31.20 | 66.00 | 12.40 | 1915.00 | -.02 | 25.50 | 3.90 | 1.50 |
| 197 | MCA | 9.00 | 1.68 | 28.40 | 43.50 | 12.30 | 1019.00 | -.12 | 47.90 | 5.90 | 7.10 |
| 198 | MEM | 13.10 | 1.95 | 35.50 | 76.40 | 13.90 | 2891.00 | .00 | 28.70 | 4.30 | 3.60 |

| | Value Added/ Worker in Manufacturing (in $1,000) IIC1 | Value of Construction/ Worker (in $1,000) IIC2 | Sales/ Employee in Retail Trade (in $1,000) IIC3 | Sales/ Employee in Wholesale Trade (in $1,000) IIC4 | Sales/ Employee in Selected Services (in $1,000) IIC5 | Total Bank Deposits Per Capita IID | Central City and Suburban Income Distribution IIE1 | Percent of Families With Income Below Pov. Level or Greater Than $15,000 IIE2 | Unemployment Rate IIF | Chamber of Commerce Employees/ 100,000 Pop. IIG |
|---|---|---|---|---|---|---|---|---|---|---|
| 199 MID | 10.60 | 1.46 | 35.20 | 120.30* | 13.00 | 3741.00 | -.04 | 35.20 | 3.50 | 7.70 |
| 200 MOD | 16.50 | 7.19* | 40.50 | 94.80 | 12.10 | 1842.00 | -.10 | 28.50 | 9.40 | 2.10 |
| 201 MON | 15.20 | 1.79 | 34.60 | 97.70 | 12.00 | 1244.00 | .00 | 32.70 | 5.40 | 4.30 |
| 202 MUN | 14.20 | 5.58 | 28.60 | 80.50 | 13.00 | 1446.00 | .06 | 25.00 | 5.00 | 3.90 |
| 203 MUS | 13.50 | 5.81 | 34.20 | 73.10 | 14.80 | 1590.00 | -.04 | 24.90 | 6.70 | 1.30* |
| 204 NAS | 9.80* | 3.43* | 35.30 | 87.90* | 16.30* | 1388.00* | -.02 | 26.60 | 2.80 | 3.00* |
| 205 NEW | 8.50 | 3.10 | 30.20 | 82.10 | 13.50 | 3079.00 | -.10 | 24.00 | 5.10 | 1.40 |
| 206 NEW | 13.80 | 3.48 | 31.50 | 96.20 | 13.30 | 3111.00 | .00 | 30.10 | 4.00 | 1.40* |
| 207 NOR | 13.10 | 2.63 | 39.80 | 80.00 | 20.30 | 3545.00 | -.24 | 51.10 | 2.70 | 3.30 |
| 208 ODE | 27.70 | 1.46 | 34.30 | 88.40 | 15.00 | 1320.00 | -.02 | 25.40 | 4.30 | 10.90 |
| 209 OGD | 13.10 | 8.23 | 30.20 | 110.10 | 11.20 | 1614.00 | .00 | 28.80 | 6.00 | 1.60* |
| 210 OWE | 11.50 | 2.63* | 32.00 | 97.00 | 11.20 | 1628.00 | -.00 | 25.40 | 4.90 | 3.00 |
| 211 PET | 12.00* | 4.39* | 31.30 | 108.70* | 11.80* | 1014.00 | -.04 | 40.90 | 3.00 | 1.60 |
| 212 PIN | 16.20 | 1.66 | 31.40 | 171.40 | 11.30 | 1487.00 | -.10 | 33.20 | 6.20 | 4.70 |
| 213 PIT | 15.50 | 3.64 | 30.90 | 64.50 | 12.90 | 3506.00 | .00 | 28.10 | 4.10 | 2.50* |
| 214 POR | 12.90 | 3.16 | 30.90 | 106.10 | 14.10 | 3461.00 | -.08 | 24.60 | 3.20 | 12.70 |
| 215 PRO | 18.20 | 6.41 | 27.70 | 59.80 | 11.30 | 1054.00 | -.02 | 22.80 | 6.70 | 1.40 |
| 216 PUE | 12.40 | 5.26 | 29.90 | 107.10 | 12.30 | 1321.00 | -.04 | 23.20 | 5.90 | 5.90 |
| 217 RAC | 16.20 | 5.12 | 31.10 | 77.60 | 15.90 | 1694.00 | -.02 | 28.10 | 4.60 | 2.30 |
| 218 REN | 14.80 | 8.88 | 35.70 | 86.90 | 15.10 | 2916.00 | -.04 | 33.50 | -6.20 | 24.80 |
| 219 ROA | 11.40 | 6.30 | 29.70 | 75.10 | 11.60 | 2026.00 | .04 | 25.00 | 2.30 | 3.90 |
| 220 ROC | 12.60 | 4.70 | 30.30 | 65.00 | 11.00 | 1883.00 | -.08 | 25.00 | 3.40 | 6.00 |
| 221 STJ | 12.80 | 4.02 | 34.80 | 200.10 | 12.20 | 2559.00 | -.06 | 21.20 | 3.90 | 9.20* |
| 222 SAL | 12.80 | 6.16 | 32.10 | 87.80 | 14.70 | 1552.00 | -.00 | 26.00 | 6.70 | 14.10* |
| 223 SAN | 13.70 | 3.56 | 30.50 | 80.60 | 11.80 | 2166.00 | -.08 | 27.30 | 3.80 | 5.30 |
| 224 SAV | 15.90 | 4.45 | 32.90 | 97.80 | 11.30 | 1679.00 | -.00 | 31.30 | 4.30 | 3.60 |
| 225 SHE | 14.00 | 3.90 | 30.60 | 81.70 | 13.70 | 1937.00 | -.08 | 23.70 | 4.40 | 6.00 |
| 226 SIO | 12.70 | 2.16 | 29.80 | 220.70 | 13.50 | 2252.00 | -.06 | 24.70 | 2.60 | 6.00 |
| 227 SIO | 10.20 | 5.07 | 29.80 | 167.30 | 14.50 | 2405.00 | -.08 | 23.40 | 4.40 | 6.30 |
| 228 SPR | 14.40 | 2.74 | 32.50 | 117.10 | 12.60 | 2471.00 | -.08 | 28.20 | 4.20 | 3.70 |
| 229 SPR | 12.70 | 4.77 | 31.00 | 98.80 | 12.80 | 1727.00 | -.06 | 23.10 | 4.10 | 6.50 |
| 230 SPR | 12.00 | 5.22 | 35.10 | 88.90 | 11.40 | 1388.00 | -.05 | 26.40 | 3.90 | 1.30* |
| 231 STE | 17.70 | 1.98 | 31.80 | 76.10 | 14.50 | 5142.00 | -.03 | 22.50 | 3.70 | 1.80 |
| 232 TAL | 8.90 | 10.89 | 30.50 | 55.10 | 11.70 | 1492.00 | -.02 | 24.10 | 3.00 | 12.60 |
| 233 TER | 13.20 | 0.49 | 34.40 | 71.90 | 12.50 | 1982.00 | -.00 | 24.70 | 4.20 | 2.30 |
| 234 TEX | 4.80 | 1.98 | 34.50 | 45.10 | 11.40 | 1641.00 | -.04 | 26.60 | 5.50 | 8.90 |
| 235 TOP | 20.30 | 3.90 | 29.30 | 87.60 | 10.70 | 2187.00 | -.08 | 24.70 | 2.70 | 6.50 |
| 236 TUS | 11.90 | 5.38 | 30.90 | 76.00 | 11.50 | 962.00 | -.08 | 32.20 | 4.00 | 1.70* |
| 237 TYL | 12.80 | 2.66 | 37.30 | 74.80 | 11.80 | 1963.00 | -.16 | 26.70 | 3.60 | 7.20 |
| 238 VIN | 10.50 | 8.03 | 36.80 | 95.90 | 15.50 | 1407.00 | -.04 | 25.80 | 5.70 | 1.70 |
| 239 WAC | 13.80 | 3.54 | 29.40 | 69.90 | 10.60 | 2112.00 | -.02 | 26.90 | 4.10 | 6.80 |
| 240 WAT | 14.80 | 4.52 | 31.10 | 61.40 | 11.50 | 1446.00 | -.04 | 25.60 | 6.00 | 7.50 |
| 241 WHE | 12.10 | 1.19 | 30.70 | 77.20 | 12.20 | 1737.00 | -.06 | 21.80 | 4.20 | 2.20 |
| 242 WIC | 9.60 | 2.83 | 34.40 | 121.80 | 11.50 | 2267.00 | -.04 | 24.10 | 4.00 | 7.90 |
| 243 WIL | 10.80 | 6.77 | 35.60 | 87.70 | 12.60 | 1127.00 | -.00 | 28.60 | 3.30 | 4.70 |

## TABLE C-2

## BASIC STATISTICS OF POLITICAL COMPONENT (S)

| | Local Sun. newspaper circ./ 1,000 pop. IA1 | % occupied housing with TV IA2 | Local radio stations/ 1,000 pop. IA3 | Pres. vote cast/voting age pop. IB | Avg. monthly earnings of teachers IIA1 | Avg. monthly earnings of other employees IIA2 | Entrance salary of patrolmen IIA3 | Entrance salary of firemen IIA4 | Total municipal employment/ 1,000 pop. IIA5 |
|---|---|---|---|---|---|---|---|---|---|
| US | 243.00 | 95.50 | .03 | 39.10 | 642.00 | 515.00 | 6848.00 | 6569.00 | 15.80 |
| 149 ABI | 620.00 | 95.80 | 1.75 | 44.90 | 557.00 | 375.00 | 6420.00 | 6300.00 | 9.50 |
| 150 ALB | 492.00 | 94.40 | 3.33 | 34.50 | 571.00 | 341.00 | 5400.00 | 5400.00 | 9.90 |
| 151 ALT | 571.00 | 96.80 | 3.70 | 56.50 | 593.00 | 385.00 | 5800.00 | 5200.00 | 8.60 |
| 152 AMA | 600.00 | 96.70 | 3.47 | 54.10 | 616.00 | 367.00 | 5850.00 | 5850.00 | 10.20 |
| 153 AND | 314.00 | 97.20 | 1.44 | 71.10 | 707.00 | 433.00 | 6550.00 | 6750.00 | 11.00 |
| 154 ASH | 1248.00 | 92.90 | 3.44 | 51.60 | 641.00 | 386.00 | 5590.00 | 5590.00 | 15.20 |
| 155 ATL | 1363.00 | 96.40 | .57 | 68.40 | 721.00 | 407.00 | 7900.00 | 7905.00 | 46.30 |
| 156 BAY | 917.00 | 98.40 | 3.41 | 65.20 | 573.00 | 479.00 | 7805.00 | 7505.00 | 11.00 |
| 157 BIL | 907.00 | 95.10 | 6.89 | 64.00 | 633.00 | 434.00 | 6900.00 | 6758.00 | 7.70 |
| 158 BIR | 899.00 | 94.20 | .74 | 39.20 | 442.00 | 302.00 | 4432.00 | 4432.00 | 8.10 |
| 159 BLO | 1143.00 | 95.60 | 1.92 | 62.30 | 796.00 | 463.00 | 6888.00 | 6888.00 | 8.10 |
| 160 BOI | 826.00 | 96.40 | 8.03 | 72.70 | 557.00 | 389.00 | 5340.00 | 5340.00 | 7.40 |
| 161 BRI | 317.00 | 98.70 | 1.51 | 67.30 | 752.00 | 530.00 | 7300.00 | 7300.00 | 25.40 |
| 162 BRO | 637.00 | 98.20 | 1.57 | 66.00 | 629.00 | 483.00 | 7200.00 | 7700.00 | 23.90 |
| 163 BRO | 268.00 | 88.70 | .71 | 41.70 | 488.00 | 312.00 | 5520.00 | 4800.00 | 11.70 |
| 164 BRY | 388.00 | 92.20 | 6.89 | 48.50 | 566.00 | 384.00 | 5484.00 | 4968.00 | 26.20 |
| 165 CED | 742.00 | 97.00 | 4.90 | 66.70 | 673.00 | 449.00 | 6894.00 | 6762.00 | 9.40 |
| 166 CHA | 1238.00 | 93.80 | 2.45 | 53.30 | 683.00 | 456.00 | 6900.00 | 6600.00 | 10.90 |
| 167 COL | 406.00 | 94.50 | 7.40 | 56.50 | 606.00 | 423.00 | 5929.00 | 5929.00 | 8.40 |
| 168 DAN | 635.00 | 97.00 | 5.06 | 68.20 | 752.00 | 530.00 | 6587.00 | 6588.00 | 21.60 |
| 169 DEC | 578.00 | 96.10 | 1.60 | 65.80 | 766.00 | 472.00 | 7112.00 | 7255.00 | 4.10 |
| 170 DUB | 681.00 | 97.20 | 5.49 | 71.40 | 617.00 | 454.00 | 6918.00 | 6918.00 | 7.70 |
| 171 DUR | 546.00 | 93.20 | 1.57 | 53.00 | 625.00 | 391.00 | 6516.00 | 5628.00 | 10.90 |
| 172 FAL | 440.00 | 98.30 | 1.39 | 61.20 | 612.00 | 435.00 | 6525.00 | 6525.00 | 24.60 |
| 173 FAR | 1111.00 | 98.70 | 2.54 | 60.90 | 698.00 | 461.00 | 7056.00 | 7056.00 | 7.50 |
| 174 FIT | 708.00 | 97.50 | 5.83 | 66.00 | 671.00 | 464.00 | 5889.00 | 5889.00 | 34.00 |
| 175 FOR | 476.00 | 98.00 | 2.06 | 67.60 | 491.00 | 342.00 | 4649.00 | 4649.00 | 7.60 |
| 176 GAD | 572.00 | 92.60 | .62 | 53.50 | 678.00 | 376.00 | 6900.00 | 6758.00 | 11.70 |
| 177 GAI | 468.00 | 95.40 | 4.25 | 55.10 | 600.00 | 417.00 | 6323.00 | 6032.00 | 14.90 |
| 178 GAL | 367.00 | 89.10 | 3.80 | 46.70 | 600.00 | 376.00 | 6756.00 | 6756.00 | 18.30 |
| 179 GRE | 777.00 | 96.00 | 7.31 | 57.40 | 651.00 | 461.00 | 6300.00 | 6300.00 | 7.90 |
| 180 GRE | 695.00 | 98.50 | 3.16 | 65.10 | 705.00 | 516.00 | 6690.00 | 6690.00 | 26.80 |
| 181 JAC | 887.00 | 97.10 | 1.39 | 61.20 | 779.00 | 448.00 | 8740.00 | 7947.00 | 8.10 |
| 182 KEN | 370.00 | 97.90 | 2.54 | 60.90 | 782.00 | 542.00 | 6900.00 | 6758.00 | 29.60 |
| 183 LAC | 708.00 | 97.50 | 3.75 | 66.00 | 658.00 | 497.00 | 5760.00 | 6140.00 | 21.50 |
| 184 LAF | 377.00 | 96.20 | 2.72 | 51.70 | 557.00 | 344.00 | 7125.00 | 7125.00 | 11.90 |
| 185 LAF | 1007.00 | 94.70 | 3.66 | 65.10 | 684.00 | 417.00 | 4800.00 | 4800.00 | 9.30 |
| 186 LAK | 460.00 | 96.50 | 2.75 | 55.10 | 547.00 | 343.00 | 6900.00 | 6758.00 | 6.30 |
| 187 LAR | 262.00 | 91.60 | 1.36 | 31.60 | 552.00 | 293.00 | 4800.00 | 4800.00 | 9.10 |
| 188 LAW | 357.00 | 95.30 | 2.77 | 37.70 | 682.00 | 360.00 | 4800.00 | 4800.00 | 5.00 |
| 189 LEW | 770.00 | 97.00 | 5.47 | 65.90 | 519.00 | 395.00 | 5200.00 | 5200.00 | 18.70 |
| 190 LEX | 692.00 | 95.80 | 4.59 | 42.00 | 579.00 | 391.00 | 6561.00 | 6561.00 | 11.00 |
| 191 LIM | 861.00 | 97.40 | 2.33 | 64.60 | 578.00 | 420.00 | 6552.00 | 5949.00 | 7.20 |
| 192 LIN | 416.00 | 95.40 | 4.76 | 59.40 | 638.00 | 448.00 | 6562.00 | 5949.00 | 13.70 |
| 193 LUB | 476.00 | 96.00 | 3.35 | 50.00 | 542.00 | 363.00 | 6630.00 | 6630.00 | 10.80 |
| 194 LYN | 596.00 | 94.70 | 3.25 | 69.20 | 629.00 | 361.00 | 5850.00 | 5850.00 | 28.50 |
| 195 MAN | 628.00 | 96.80 | 3.70 | 57.10 | 562.00 | 449.00 | 7254.00 | 5980.00 | 21.40 |
| 196 MAN | 837.00 | 96.40 | .76 | 40.70 | 613.00 | 459.00 | 7030.00 | 7030.00 | 8.80 |
| 197 MCA | 466.00 | 90.20 | .54 | | 528.00 | 277.00 | 5220.00 | 4584.00 | 18.90 |
| 198 MER | 379.00 | 97.50 | 5.35 | 67.80 | 780.00 | 504.00 | 6716.00 | 6716.00 | 26.30 |

| | | Local Sun. newspaper circ./1,000 pop. IA1 | % occupied housing with TV IA2 | Local radio stations/100,000 pop. IA3 | Pres. vote cast/voting age pop. IB | Avg. monthly earnings of teachers IIA1 | Avg. monthly earnings of other employees IIA2 | Entrance salary of patrolmen IIA3 | Entrance salary of firemen IIA4 | Total municipal employment/1,000 pop. IIA5 |
|---|---|---|---|---|---|---|---|---|---|---|
| 199 | MID | 341.00 | 96.40 | 7.69 | 62.20 | 630.00 | 385.00 | 6900.00 | 6758.00 | 9.60 |
| 200 | MOD | 843.00 | 94.70 | 4.10 | 53.40 | 880.00 | 650.00 | 8479.00 | 7565.00 | 7.40 |
| 201 | MON | 830.00 | 95.20 | 1.73 | 49.20 | 755.00 | 319.00 | 5700.00 | 4800.00 | 17.80 |
| 202 | MUN | 519.00 | 46.30 | 2.32 | 67.60 | 709.00 | 413.00 | 7480.00 | 7480.00 | 6.60 |
| 203 | MUS | 1158.00 | 97.40 | 2.54 | 66.30 | 726.00 | 484.00 | 8250.00 | 8250.00 | 9.50 |
| 204 | NAS | 365.00 | 98.60 | 2.98 | 67.00 | 545.00 | 405.00 | 5760.00 | 4992.00 | 18.10 |
| 205 | NEW | 690.00 | 97.10 | 2.61 | 66.20 | 622.00 | 406.00 | 7575.00 | 7575.00 | 24.80 |
| 206 | NEW | 402.00 | 47.10 | 0.00 | 67.30 | 725.00 | 524.00 | 6900.00 | 6758.00 | 21.30 |
| 207 | NOR | 294.00 | 97.90 | 1.66 | 68.20 | 870.00 | 564.00 | 6900.00 | 6758.00 | 24.50 |
| 208 | ODE | 469.00 | 95.90 | 5.43 | 48.10 | 620.00 | 410.00 | 6150.00 | 5550.00 | 6.50 |
| 209 | OGD | 629.00 | 96.80 | 3.96 | 72.90 | 589.00 | 469.00 | 6120.00 | 6120.00 | 8.00 |
| 210 | OWE | 534.00 | 97.30 | 1.26 | 50.00 | 577.03 | 347.00 | 5473.00 | 5573.00 | 26.60 |
| 211 | PET | 620.00 | 95.90 | 2.32 | 43.40 | 627.00 | 388.00 | 5512.00 | 5512.00 | 30.50 |
| 212 | PIN | 383.00 | 93.00 | 3.52 | 50.00 | 470.00 | 312.00 | 5220.00 | 5256.00 | 5.20 |
| 213 | PIT | 1691.00 | 96.90 | 5.00 | 69.60 | 649.00 | 524.00 | 6916.00 | 6916.00 | 28.20 |
| 214 | POR | 1752.00 | 96.40 | 5.63 | 66.70 | 603.00 | 442.00 | 5376.00 | 5637.00 | 34.30 |
| 215 | PRO | 342.00 | 93.50 | 2.17 | 69.40 | 575.00 | 404.00 | 5916.00 | 5634.00 | 6.70 |
| 216 | PUE | 479.00 | 96.10 | 5.08 | 69.60 | 601.00 | 473.00 | 6528.00 | 6246.00 | 7.30 |
| 217 | RAC | 427.00 | 97.40 | .58 | 64.90 | 655.00 | 513.00 | 8886.00 | 8298.00 | 9.40 |
| 218 | REN | 479.00 | 92.60 | 8.26 | 56.60 | 728.00 | 509.00 | 7176.00 | 7176.00 | 9.80 |
| 219 | ROA | 1189.00 | 96.70 | 2.76 | 44.30 | 560.00 | 368.00 | 6156.00 | 6156.00 | 33.70 |
| 220 | ROC | 620.00 | 95.80 | 3.57 | 66.70 | 681.00 | 490.00 | 7236.00 | 7236.00 | 10.60 |
| 221 | STJ | 712.00 | 96.70 | 4.59 | 63.60 | 548.00 | 360.00 | 5436.00 | 5436.00 | 7.70 |
| 222 | SAL | 576.00 | 94.30 | 1.06 | 60.20 | 654.00 | 443.00 | 7020.00 | 6690.00 | 9.70 |
| 223 | SAN | 672.00 | 95.00 | 7.04 | 46.50 | 674.00 | 337.00 | 5952.00 | 5748.00 | 8.30 |
| 224 | SAV | 601.00 | 44.40 | 4.25 | 44.20 | 553.00 | 366.00 | 5789.00 | 5520.00 | 9.70 |
| 225 | SHE | 602.00 | 95.40 | 3.61 | 44.20 | 566.00 | 344.00 | 5400.00 | 5424.00 | 10.80 |
| 226 | SIO | 664.00 | 97.50 | 3.44 | 66.70 | 581.00 | 460.00 | 6714.00 | 6714.00 | 10.30 |
| 227 | SIO | 745.00 | 96.80 | 10.52 | 70.40 | 575.00 | 446.00 | 6444.00 | 6204.00 | 8.00 |
| 228 | SPR | 779.00 | 95.10 | 2.48 | 73.00 | 632.00 | 460.00 | 6900.00 | 7500.00 | 12.00 |
| 229 | SPR | 625.00 | 95.30 | 5.22 | 62.10 | 575.00 | 422.00 | 6000.00 | 5712.00 | 10.70 |
| 230 | SPR | 541.00 | 97.40 | 1.92 | 58.10 | 599.00 | 460.00 | 7539.00 | 7539.00 | 8.10 |
| 231 | STE | 1015.00 | 97.50 | 1.20 | 69.60 | 613.00 | 420.00 | 6236.00 | 6672.00 | 12.50 |
| 232 | TAL | 476.00 | 90.80 | 4.85 | 80.50 | 661.00 | 369.00 | 6300.00 | 6300.00 | 24.40 |
| 233 | TER | 645.00 | 96.10 | 4.00 | 69.70 | 679.00 | 380.00 | 6270.00 | 6270.00 | 7.20 |
| 234 | TEX | 1022.00 | 95.00 | 1.98 | 48.40 | 497.00 | 391.00 | 5700.00 | 5415.00 | 7.40 |
| 235 | TOP | 572.00 | 96.80 | 4.51 | 63.80 | 625.00 | 415.00 | 6900.00 | 6758.00 | 9.20 |
| 236 | TUS | 347.00 | 92.40 | 2.58 | 40.00 | 545.00 | 330.00 | 5807.00 | 5807.00 | 21.40 |
| 237 | TYL | 624.00 | 94.90 | 3.09 | 52.50 | 579.00 | 373.00 | 5340.00 | 5340.00 | 9.00 |
| 238 | VIN | 336.00 | 97.00 | .82 | 60.80 | 781.00 | 499.00 | 7250.00 | 7250.00 | 20.20 |
| 239 | WAC | 546.00 | 96.00 | 4.08 | 51.10 | 543.00 | 365.00 | 6120.00 | 5790.00 | 10.10 |
| 240 | WAT | 734.00 | 97.40 | 3.00 | 65.80 | 659.00 | 479.00 | 6804.00 | 6804.00 | 8.40 |
| 241 | WHE | 1298.00 | 97.20 | 3.27 | 71.60 | 631.00 | 381.00 | 6000.00 | 5700.00 | 13.40 |
| 242 | WIC | 483.00 | 96.40 | 3.17 | 47.40 | 559.00 | 368.00 | 6108.00 | 5370.00 | 15.20 |
| 243 | WIL | 789.00 | 93.80 | 4.67 | 56.20 | 611.00 | 356.00 | 5628.00 | 5628.00 | 11.90 |

TABLE C-2 (Continued)

| | Police protection employment/ 1,000 pop. IIA6 | Fire protection employment/ 1,000 pop. IIA7 | Violent Crime rate/ 100,000 pop. IIB1 | Property Crime rate/ 100,000 pop. IIB2 | Local govt. revenue per capita IIB3 | % of revenue from federal govt. IIB4 | Per capita local govt. Expend. on public welfare IIC1 | Avg. monthly retiree benefits IIC2 | Avg. monthly payments to families w/dependent children IIC3 |
|---|---|---|---|---|---|---|---|---|---|
| US | 2.50 | 1.40 | 397.70 | 2431.80 | 329.86 | 2.70 | 11.88 | 132.00 | 190.00 |
| 149 ABI | 1.50 | 1.50 | 144.00 | 1277.30 | 204.61 | 3.00 | 1.17 | 120.00 | 114.00 |
| 150 ALB | 1.30 | 1.60 | 377.60• | 2091.30• | 277.14 | 2.90 | 2.22 | 109.00 | 106.00 |
| 151 ALT | 1.70 | 2.10 | 81.00 | 1012.30 | 203.01 | .70 | 6.27 | 119.00 | 202.00 |
| 152 AMA | 1.90 | 1.50 | 237.00 | 2736.00 | 278.24 | 3.50 | .63 | 126.00 | 114.00 |
| 153 AND | 1.90 | 2.00 | 210.50 | 1357.40 | 289.75 | 5.70 | 10.80 | 143.00 | 139.00 |
| 154 ASH | 2.20 | 2.20 | 154.40 | 1737.70 | 262.08 | .40 | 14.77 | 120.00 | 123.00 |
| 155 ATL | 6.30 | 4.90 | 437.50 | 3935.00 | 337.60 | 1.10 | 46.15 | 133.00 | 253.00 |
| 156 BAY | 1.90 | 2.40 | 188.70 | 2069.40 | 307.02 | 1.10 | 10.05 | 142.00 | 235.00 |
| 157 BIL | 1.30 | 1.20 | 150.10 | 1776.60• | 290.36 | 1.90 | 5.41 | 131.00 | 159.00 |
| 158 BIL | 1.50 | 1.20 | 146.40 | 1355.60 | 412.32• | 22.80• | 38.36• | 111.00 | 58.00 |
| 159 BLO | 1.40 | 1.20 | 199.60 | 1600.00 | 264.30 | 1.00 | 3.18 | 134.00 | 184.00 |
| 160 BOI | 1.40 | 1.90 | 224.40 | 2476.30 | 225.06 | 1.50 | 4.55 | 130.00 | 206.00 |
| 161 BRI | 1.30 | 1.40 | 238.20 | 2015.30• | 506.90• | 12.30• | 37.29• | 149.00• | 264.00• |
| 162 BRO | 1.90 | 2.40 | 295.20 | 3096.20• | 325.87 | 2.50 | 50.25 | 137.00 | 231.00 |
| 163 BRO | 2.20 | 1.60 | 350.90 | 2304.70• | 239.79 | 2.00 | 1.09 | 113.00 | 117.00 |
| 164 BRY | 1.00 | 1.10 | 350.40 | 2304.70 | 430.61• | 15.90• | 27.70• | 115.00 | 114.00 |
| 165 CED | 1.50 | 1.30 | 44.70 | 1356.80 | 282.79 | 1.70 | 2.88 | 140.00 | 196.00 |
| 166 CHA | 1.30 | 1.10 | 336.80 | 2039.60 | 281.56 | 4.30 | 5.22 | 131.00 | 237.00 |
| 167 COL | 1.10 | .90 | 383.40• | 2270.80• | 447.71• | 16.60• | 38.51• | 128.00 | 98.00 |
| 168 DAN | 1.70 | 1.40 | 201.70 | 2762.80• | 506.90• | 12.30• | 37.29• | 150.00• | 259.00 |
| 169 DEC | 1.10 | 1.10 | 293.80 | 1518.10 | 252.45 | .20 | 1.86 | 134.00 | 198.00 |
| 170 DUB | 1.20 | 1.80 | 87.60 | 1374.00 | 180.61 | 1.30 | 7.47 | 137.00 | 195.00 |
| 171 DUR | 1.80 | 1.60 | 362.60 | 2242.90 | 254.54 | 2.50 | 30.45 | 125.00 | 124.00 |
| 172 FAL | 3.10 | 3.20 | 36.30 | 3362.00• | 246.52 | 1.20 | 71.46 | 128.00• | 214.00• |
| 173 FAR | 1.60 | 1.60 | 209.70 | 1745.30 | 352.01 | 3.50 | 11.15 | 127.00 | 207.00 |
| 174 FIT | 1.60 | 2.90 | 36.30 | 3408.90• | 323.22 | 3.60 | 37.07 | 139.00• | 219.00• |
| 175 FOR | 1.40 | 1.40 | 144.50 | 925.30 | 179.25 | 4.00 | .52 | 112.00 | 120.00 |
| 176 GAD | 1.80 | 1.80 | 313.20• | 1529.00• | 191.33 | 2.60 | .32 | 123.00 | 61.00 |
| 177 GAI | 1.80 | 1.50 | 684.80• | 3707.50• | 467.56• | 13.10• | 23.84• | 115.00 | 85.00 |
| 178 GAL | 1.50 | 2.00 | 432.40 | 2641.30 | 311.40 | 2.60 | 1.15 | 131.00 | 113.00 |
| 179 GRE | 1.10 | 1.10 | 150.10• | 1776.60• | 311.47 | 4.80 | 4.67 | 138.00 | 160.00 |
| 180 GRE | 1.80 | 1.80 | 28.60 | 1233.50 | 292.62 | .10 | 12.69 | 136.00 | 215.00 |
| 181 JAC | 1.90 | 1.80 | 487.50 | 2647.70 | 280.59 | 1.60 | 14.77 | 143.00 | 223.00 |
| 182 KEN | 2.00 | 1.70 | 215.70 | 3208.50• | 309.37 | 3.00 | 33.98 | 150.00 | 239.00 |
| 183 LAC | 1.90 | 2.00 | 96.40• | 1686.70• | 544.23• | 11.00• | 40.00• | 134.00 | 193.00 |
| 184 LAF | 1.30 | 1.30 | 430.90 | 2008.90 | 266.73 | .50 | .17 | 106.00 | 90.00 |
| 185 LAF | 2.00 | 2.00 | 58.20 | 1423.80 | 217.89 | .30 | 8.88 | 140.00 | 136.00 |
| 186 LAK | .90 | 1.30 | 263.70 | 1475.40 | 273.62 | 1.70 | .25 | 127.00 | 85.00 |
| 187 LAR | 1.00 | 1.30 | 350.90• | 2304.70• | 199.21 | 6.50 | 2.32 | 103.00 | 120.00 |
| 188 LAW | 1.30 | 1.00 | 426.00 | 2409.60 | 177.25 | 9.60 | .12 | 114.00 | 137.00 |
| 189 LEW | 2.00 | 2.10 | 103.80• | 1414.30• | 149.80 | .50 | 3.14 | 124.00• | 141.00 |
| 190 LEX | 2.80 | 2.20 | 352.50 | 3179.00 | 198.42 | 4.10 | 2.73 | 124.00 | 122.00 |
| 191 LIM | 1.70 | 1.60 | 249.60 | 1700.60 | 231.20 | 1.20 | 8.07 | 130.00 | 164.00 |
| 192 LIN | 1.40 | 1.50 | 192.00 | 1944.40 | 368.79 | 3.80 | 20.39 | 134.00 | 147.00 |
| 193 LUR | 1.80 | 1.40 | 383.00• | 2969.50 | 223.11 | 1.80 | 1.94 | 124.00 | 120.00 |
| 194 LYN | 2.20 | 1.70 | 177.20 | 1180.20 | 197.90 | 1.30 | 14.48 | 123.00 | 147.00 |
| 195 MAN | 1.60 | 2.40 | 64.90• | 1378.40• | 194.62 | 4.40 | 2.96 | 135.00• | 226.00• |
| 196 MAN | .90 | 1.70 | 228.00 | 1602.60 | 248.16 | .90 | 11.33 | 141.00 | 138.00 |
| 197 MCA | .90 | 1.10 | 76.20 | 1177.50 | 215.51 | 1.70 | 1.17 | 107.00 | 118.00 |
| 198 MER | 1.90 | 1.60 | 178.80• | 2662.50• | 268.74 | 5.70 | 2.68 | 148.00• | 269.00• |

| | Police protection employment/ 1,000 pop. IIA6 | Fire protection employment/ 1,000 pop. IIA7 | Violent Crime rate/ 100,000 pop. IIB1 | Property Crime rate/ 100,000 pop. IIB2 | Local govt. revenue per capita IIB3 | % of revenue from federal govt. IIB4 | Per capita local govt. Expend. on public welfare IIC1 | Avg. monthly retiree benefits IIC2 | Avg. monthly payments to families w/dependent children IIC3 |
|---|---|---|---|---|---|---|---|---|---|
| 199 MID | 2.10 | 1.70 | 350.90 • | 2304.70 • | 279.57 | 0.00 • | 1.64 | 129.00 | 116.00 |
| 200 MOD | 1.60 | 1.20 | 378.30 | 3526.80 | 753.58 • | 15.70 • | 86.25 • | 123.00 | 239.00 • |
| 201 MON | 1.90 | 2.50 | 335.60 | 1120.10 | 250.31 | 1.10 | .03 | 116.00 | 85.00 |
| 202 MUN | 1.80 | 1.80 | 231.60 | 2136.30 | 212.31 | .30 | 13.38 | 140.00 | 136.00 |
| 203 MUS | 1.50 | 2.00 | 501.40 • | 2593.50 | 321.67 | 2.20 | 13.57 | 147.00 | 230.00 |
| 204 NAS | 2.60 | 2.00 | 64.90 | 1378.40 • | 486.38 | 13.30 • | 31.13 | 134.00 | 218.00 |
| 205 NEW | 2.20 | 2.70 | 250.60 | 3362.00 • | 300.58 | 5.80 | 74.28 | 128.00 | 214.00 • |
| 206 NEW | 2.20 | 2.00 | 238.20 | 2015.80 • | 309.96 | 9.20 | 1.82 | 149.00 | 264.00 • |
| 207 NOR | 2.20 | 2.10 | 201.70 • | 2762.80 • | 390.60 | 5.40 | 4.38 | 150.00 | 259.00 • |
| 208 ODE | 1.40 | 1.50 | 350.90 | 2304.70 | 323.83 | 1.40 | 1.42 | 130.00 | 112.00 |
| 209 OGD | 2.00 | 1.60 | 221.80 | 2290.80 • | 284.42 | 6.90 | .24 • | 123.00 | 186.00 |
| 210 OWE | 1.80 | 1.90 | 225.70 | 1541.00 | 425.32 | 24.70 • | 40.32 • | 121.00 | 123.00 |
| 211 PET | 2.00 | 1.60 | 272.00 • | 1203.80 • | 427.56 | 15.80 • | 15.88 • | 126.00 | 170.00 |
| 212 PIN | 1.30 | 1.30 | 244.70 • | 1362.10 | 157.91 | 9.90 | .31 | 105.00 | 98.00 |
| 213 PIT | 1.90 | 2.70 | 64.40 • | 1841.50 • | 289.86 | 4.00 | 53.81 • | 139.00 | 226.00 • |
| 214 POR | 2.10 | 3.50 | 144.90 • | 2311.00 | 242.83 | 2.40 | 3.97 | 130.00 | 143.00 • |
| 215 PRO | 1.10 | .80 | 93.50 | 1349.30 | 249.02 | .80 | .43 | 140.00 | 186.00 |
| 216 PUE | 1.50 | 1.50 | 628.10 | 2985.60 • | 310.70 | 2.70 | 58.14 • | 130.00 | 179.00 |
| 217 RAC | 2.10 | 1.80 | 362.50 | 2088.60 | 310.63 | .20 | 19.81 | 149.00 | 259.00 |
| 218 REN | 3.20 | 2.20 | 362.80 | 4323.00 | 447.96 | 1.50 | 3.55 | 132.00 | 91.00 |
| 219 ROA | 1.80 | 2.00 | 354.60 | 2265.20 | 243.90 | 2.90 | 19.02 | 124.00 | 174.00 • |
| 220 ROC | 2.00 | 1.60 | 555.20 • | 3264.30 • | 596.82 | 14.50 • | 46.58 • | 132.00 | 221.00 |
| 221 STJ | 1.60 | 1.70 | 383.40 | 2270.80 • | 190.43 | .60 | 2.25 | 130.00 | 100.00 |
| 222 SAL | 2.10 | 1.70 | 176.10 | 2263.50 | 269.79 | 3.70 | 1.15 | 132.00 | 182.00 |
| 223 SAN | 1.70 | 1.60 | 350.90 | 2304.70 | 198.29 | 4.30 | 1.58 | 117.00 | 111.00 |
| 224 SAV | 1.80 | 1.60 | 811.80 • | 3750.10 • | 279.49 | 4.70 | 7.41 | 120.00 | 146.00 |
| 225 SHE | 1.50 | 1.60 | 370.50 | 2165.20 | 430.61 | 15.90 • | 27.70 • | 112.00 | 106.00 |
| 226 SIO | 1.50 | 1.40 | 121.20 | 2078.60 | 278.66 | 2.00 | 11.77 | 133.00 | 102.00 |
| 227 SIO | 1.40 | 1.40 | 111.30 | 1167.50 | 253.92 | .50 | 3.11 | 132.00 | 177.00 |
| 228 SPR | 1.50 | 1.40 | 380.80 | 2111.80 | 278.50 | 3.40 | 2.30 | 135.00 | 179.00 |
| 229 SPR | 1.30 | 1.20 | 151.30 | 2791.70 | 319.84 | .60 | 1.73 | 120.00 | 95.00 |
| 230 SPR | 1.50 | 1.70 | 174.50 | 1741.40 | 229.06 | 2.80 | 7.83 | 135.00 | 145.00 |
| 231 STE | 1.60 | 2.10 | 299.40 • | 2061.70 | 202.82 | 2.70 | 9.37 | 147.00 | 134.00 |
| 232 TAL | 1.80 | 1.40 | 424.70 • | 2743.90 | 373.71 | 1.20 | 1.06 | 125.00 | 78.00 |
| 233 TER | 2.00 | 2.10 | 104.40 | 1768.70 • | 275.01 | 2.90 | 27.74 | 132.00 | 146.00 |
| 234 TEX | 1.60 | 1.60 | 350.90 | 2304.70 | 187.10 | 8.30 | .16 | 520.00 | 106.00 |
| 235 TOP | 1.60 | 1.60 | 370.50 | 2434.50 | 337.97 | 5.10 | 25.85 | 132.00 | 172.00 |
| 236 TUS | 1.60 | 1.60 | 326.10 | 1502.50 | 186.44 | 1.00 | 0.00 | 118.00 | 177.00 |
| 237 TYL | 1.30 | 1.50 | 219.80 | 1823.50 | 229.38 | 1.20 | .89 | 114.00 | 64.00 |
| 238 VIN | 1.50 | .30 | 208.20 | 2264.90 | 498.22 | 9.80 • | 24.55 • | 134.00 | 235.00 |
| 239 WAC | 1.80 | 1.70 | 632.70 | 2599.30 | 204.14 | 5.00 | 1.56 | 113.00 | 108.00 |
| 240 WAT | 1.90 | 1.60 | 149.80 | 1640.80 | 295.22 | 5.90 | 5.53 | 142.00 | 198.00 |
| 241 WHE | 2.00 | 2.20 | 87.40 | 982.10 | 204.21 | 3.10 | 10.10 | 135.00 | 118.00 |
| 242 WIC | 1.40 | 1.40 | 238.20 | 1522.10 | 245.36 | 4.00 | .84 | 123.00 | 111.00 |
| 243 WIL | 1.80 | 2.20 | 582.20 | 2456.60 | 295.30 | 2.40 | 24.09 | 116.00 | 120.00 |

TABLE C-3

## BASIC STATISTICS OF ENVIRONMENTAL COMPONENT (S)

| | Mean Annual Inversion Frequency IB1 | % of Housing Units Dilapidated IB2 | Park and Recreation Acres/ 1,000 Pop. IB3 | Pop. Density in Central City IC1 | Motor Vehicle Registrations/ 1,000 Pop. IC2 | Motorcycle Registrations/ 1,000 Pop. IC3 | Solid Waste Generated by Manufacturing ID | Water Pollution Index IE | Park and Recreation Acres/1,000 Pop. IIB1 | Miles of Trails/ 100,000 Pop. IIB2 |
|---|---|---|---|---|---|---|---|---|---|---|
| 149 ABI | 32.50 | 3.20 | 13.80 | 1197.00 | 649.00 | 16.00 | 552.50 | .87 | 13.80 | 0.00 |
| 150 ALB | 37.50 | 3.30 | 26.30 | 2470.00 | 524.00 | 14.00 | 672.70 | .98 | 26.30 | 55.50 |
| 151 ALT | 32.50 | 4.00 | 8.10 | 6912.00 | 481.00 | 12.00 | 639.80 | 1.61 | 8.10 | 237.00 |
| 152 AMA | 37.50 | 2.00 | 281.00 | 2092.00 | 707.00 | 27.00 | 963.00 | 4.40 | 281.00 | 48.60 |
| 153 AND | 32.50 | 2.10 | 5.40 | 1904.00 | 552.00 | 20.00 | 444.10 | 2.24 | 5.40 | 0.00 |
| 154 ASH | 47.50 | 1.90 | 76.20 | 2587.00 | 573.00 | 10.00 | 688.00 | 1.11 | 76.20 | 13.70 |
| 155 ATL | 17.50 | 5.30 | 1.60 | 3860.00 | 481.00 | 10.00 | 547.00 | 1.72 | 1.60 | 120.00 |
| 156 BAY | 32.50 | 1.70 | 9.30 | 4145.00 | 522.00 | 30.00 | 641.00 | 1.66 | 9.30 | 8.50 |
| 157 BIL | 42.50 | 1.80 | 10.40 | 4189.00 | 689.00 | 39.00 | 306.40 | 1.78 | 10.40 | 0.00 |
| 158 BIL | 32.50 | 2.80 | 10.70 | 2419.00 | 507.00 | 14.00 | 819.70 | 1.62 | 10.70 | 22.20 |
| 159 BLO | 32.50 | 1.50 | 25.70 | 4256.00 | 548.00 | 17.00 | 553.30 | .66 | 25.70 | 182.60 |
| 160 BOI | 42.50 | 2.00 | 41.60 | 3205.00 | 613.00 | 52.00 | 897.40 | .70 | 41.60 | 26.70 |
| 161 BRI | 27.50 | 3.40 | 78.60 | 2086.00 | 586.00 | 10.00 | 868.10 | 1.32 | 78.60 | 484.80 |
| 162 BRO | 27.50 | 3.50 | 1.10 | 4200.00 | 481.00 | 10.00 | 1103.80 | .78 | 1.10 | 226.30 |
| 163 BRO | 32.50 | 3.60 | 6.90 | 2264.00 | 485.00 | 10.00 | 568.20 | 1.18 | 6.90 | 292.80 |
| 164 BRY | 22.50 | 3.10 | 5.60 | 1539.00 | 536.00 | 16.00 | 1023.80 | 1.11 | 5.60 | 17.20 |
| 165 CED | 32.50 | 1.20 | 10.00 | 2182.00 | 606.00 | 23.00 | 414.40 | 1.38 | 10.00 | 36.80 |
| 166 CHA | 32.50 | 1.90 | 10.20 | 6667.00 | 464.00 | 20.00 | 676.60 | 1.96 | 10.20 | 0.00 |
| 167 COL | 37.50 | 2.10 | 10.50 | 1410.00 | 470.00 | 32.00 | 792.10 | .94 | 10.50 | 111.10 |
| 168 DAN | 27.50 | 3.40 | 20.00 | 1157.00 | 603.00 | 10.00 | 518.60 | 1.32 | 20.00 | 126.50 |
| 169 DEC | 32.50 | 1.50 | 25.10 | 2954.00 | 575.00 | 18.00 | 332.70 | 1.74 | 25.10 | 328.00 |
| 170 DUB | 32.50 | 1.40 | 6.90 | 3799.00 | 515.00 | 25.00 | 407.40 | 1.02 | 6.90 | 175.80 |
| 171 DUR | 37.50 | 2.50 | 13.60 | 2608.00 | 545.00 | 17.00 | 509.40 | 1.57 | 13.60 | 12.10 |
| 172 FAL | 32.50 | 7.30 | 13.30 | 6190.00 | 481.00 | 10.00 | 1270.90 | 1.14 | 13.30 | 261.90 |
| 173 FAR | 32.50 | 1.50 | 22.40 | 4614.00 | 610.00 | 94.00 | 694.00 | 1.36 | 22.40 | 125.00 |
| 174 FIT | 27.50 | 4.50 | 37.10 | 1355.00 | 481.00 | 10.00 | 620.30 | 1.28 | 37.10 | 1072.10 |
| 175 FOR | 37.50 | 3.10 | 199.20 | 1396.00 | 633.00 | 17.00 | 764.20 | 1.63 | 199.20 | 187.50 |
| 176 GAD | 37.50 | 3.00 | 27.10 | 1664.00 | 667.00 | 14.00 | 390.90 | .81 | 27.10 | 237.50 |
| 177 GAI | 32.50 | 2.60 | 6.20 | 2477.00 | 588.00 | 29.00 | 662.80 | .59 | 6.20 | 57.10 |
| 178 GAL | 22.50 | 3.90 | 19.50 | 1572.00 | 550.00 | 16.00 | 201.50 | 26.40 | 19.50 | 5.80 |
| 179 GRE | 37.50 | 1.90 | 13.20 | 4088.00 | 639.00 | 39.00 | 536.40 | .68 | 13.20 | 1512.10 |
| 180 GRE | 32.50 | 1.50 | 5.40 | 2106.00 | 474.00 | 14.00 | 420.00 | 2.74 | 5.40 | 322.70 |
| 181 JAC | 32.50 | 1.60 | 89.20 | 4251.00 | 526.00 | 24.00 | 508.80 | 1.32 | 89.20 | 559.40 |
| 182 KEN | 32.50 | 1.50 | 9.80 | 5752.00 | 493.00 | 13.00 | 699.20 | .90 | 9.80 | 177.10 |
| 183 LAC | 32.50 | 1.60 | 14.20 | 3365.00 | 489.00 | 12.00 | 605.10 | .82 | 14.20 | 62.50 |
| 184 LAF | 27.50 | 2.80 | 5.70 | 3445.00 | 603.00 | 18.00 | 660.90 | 3.97 | 5.70 | 9.00 |
| 185 LAF | 32.50 | 1.70 | 6.20 | 5170.00 | 501.00 | 19.00 | 367.70 | 1.91 | 6.20 | 36.60 |
| 186 LAK | 27.50 | 3.30 | 3.00 | 3391.00 | 603.00 | 18.00 | 372.10 | 6.52 | 3.00 | 0.00 |
| 187 LAR | 27.50 | 4.10 | 9.60 | 3367.00 | 533.00 | 15.00 | 1717.00 | .87 | 9.60 | 0.00 |
| 188 LAW | 32.50 | 2.20 | 9.50 | 2347.00 | 495.00 | 23.00 | 921.70 | 5.13 | 9.50 | 27.70 |
| 189 LEW | 32.50 | 3.50 | 11.30 | 957.00 | 481.00 | 10.00 | 916.70 | 1.68 | 11.30 | 41.00 |
| 190 LEX | 32.50 | 1.60 | 14.90 | 4702.00 | 562.00 | 14.00 | 262.10 | 1.03 | 14.90 | 0.00 |
| 191 LIM | 27.50 | 1.90 | 2.20 | 4593.00 | 597.00 | 16.00 | 499.30 | 7.23 | 2.20 | 5.80 |
| 192 LIN | 37.50 | 1.20 | 60.00 | 3033.00 | 574.00 | 23.00 | 541.50 | 1.02 | 60.00 | 0.00 |
| 193 LUB | 32.50 | 2.40 | 10.00 | 1970.00 | 619.00 | 17.00 | 464.00 | 1.25 | 10.00 | 33.50 |
| 194 LYN | 32.50 | 2.10 | 33.20 | 2155.00 | 524.00 | 10.00 | 663.50 | 1.48 | 33.20 | 56.90 |
| 195 MAN | 32.50 | 4.00 | 5.90 | 2734.00 | 481.00 | 21.00 | 664.30 | 1.03 | 5.90 | 1111.10 |
| 196 MAN | 27.50 | 1.60 | 1.80 | 2284.00 | 595.00 | 8.00 | 437.50 | 1.70 | 1.80 | 23.00 |
| 197 MCA | 27.50 | 3.60 | 5.30 | 2695.00 | 493.00 | 10.00 | 1331.80 | .97 | 5.30 | 186.80 |
| 198 MER | 22.50 | 3.90 | 48.50 | 2361.00 | 553.00 | | 710.50 | .59 | 48.50 | 464.20 |

| | | Mean Annual Inversion Frequency IB1 | % of Housing Units Dilapidated IB2 | Park and Recreation Acres/ 1,000 Pop. IB3 | Pop. Density in Central City IC1 | Motor Vehicle Registrations/ 1,000 Pop. IC2 | Motorcycle Registrations/ 1,000 Pop. IC3 | Solid Waste Generated by Manufacturing ID | Water Pollution Index IE | Park and Recreation Acres/1,000 Pop. IIB1 | Miles of Trails/ 100,000 Pop. IIB2 |
|---|---|---|---|---|---|---|---|---|---|---|---|
| 199 | MID | 32.50 | 2.30 | 1.50 | 2036.00 | 723.00 | 23.00 | 1648.60 | 1.08 | 1.50 | 0.00 |
| 200 | MOD | 42.50 | 2.70 | 56.50 | 6496.00 | 667.00 | 33.00 | 419.40 | 1.04 | 56.50 | 25.60 |
| 201 | MON | 32.50 | 3.20 | 19.00 | 2539.00 | 603.00• | 18.00• | 432.60 | 6.14 | 19.00 | 34.70 |
| 202 | MUN | 32.50 | 2.10 | 27.60• | 5397.00 | 536.00 | 16.00 | 536.60 | 2.24• | 27.60• | 170.80• |
| 203 | MUS | 32.50 | 2.30 | 20.90 | 3800.00 | 513.00 | 28.00 | 491.60 | .82 | 20.90 | 191.00 |
| 204 | NAS | 32.50 | 3.80 | 1.50 | 1778.00 | 481.00• | 10.00 | 848.20• | 1.54 | 1.50 | 134.30 |
| 205 | NEW | 22.50 | 6.80 | .90 | 5219.00 | 481.00 | 10.00 | 899.80 | 1.23 | .90 | 281.00 |
| 206 | NEW | 27.50 | 4.40 | 12.00 | 6274.00 | 586.00• | 10.00 | 482.90 | .83 | 12.00 | 82.70 |
| 207 | NOR | 22.50 | 3.50 | 13.10 | 3596.00 | 603.00• | 10.00 | 451.60 | 1.14 | 13.10 | 83.30 |
| 208 | ODE | 32.50 | 2.50 | 3.00 | 4260.00 | 721.00 | 23.00 | 347.10 | 1.11 | 3.00 | 119.50 |
| 209 | OGD | 42.50 | 1.80 | 24.70 | 3293.00 | 656.00 | 40.00 | 625.80 | .91 | 24.70 | 436.50 |
| 210 | OWE | 32.50 | 1.60 | 7.00 | 5921.00 | 608.00 | 14.00 | 573.30 | 1.20 | 7.00 | 25.30 |
| 211 | PET | 27.50 | 2.30 | 8.10 | 3200.00 | 430.00 | 17.00• | 717.50• | 1.84 | 8.10 | 410.80 |
| 212 | PIN | 32.50 | 3.70 | 26.40 | 3565.00 | 475.00 | 11.00 | 550.90 | .90 | 26.40 | 0.00 |
| 213 | PIT | 32.50 | 3.20 | 8.40 | 1411.00 | 481.00• | 10.00 | 352.60 | 1.85 | 8.40 | 2425.00 |
| 214 | POR | 32.50 | 3.10 | 14.20 | 3015.00 | 481.00• | 10.00 | 460.70 | 1.57 | 14.20 | 98.50 |
| 215 | PRO | 42.50 | 1.80 | 11.30 | 2178.00 | 578.00 | 31.00 | 490.60 | 2.12 | 11.30 | 4485.50 |
| 216 | PUE | 37.50 | 2.30 | 11.90 | 4331.00 | 620.00 | 29.00 | 545.30 | .75 | 11.90 | 186.40 |
| 217 | RAC | 32.50 | 1.50 | 6.00 | 7264.00 | 478.00 | 11.00 | 515.10 | .90• | 6.00 | 105.20 |
| 218 | REN | 42.50 | 1.90 | 27.80 | 2405.00 | 773.00 | 45.00 | 735.50 | 2.09 | 27.80 | 603.30 |
| 219 | ROA | 37.50 | 1.30 | 23.80 | 3463.00 | 589.00 | 17.00• | 624.20 | 1.22 | 23.80 | 71.80 |
| 220 | ROC | 32.50 | 1.10 | 21.30 | 4012.00 | 561.00 | 26.00 | 544.00 | .94 | 21.30 | 547.60 |
| 221 | STJ | 37.50 | 1.90 | 252.80 | 2533.00 | 539.00 | 32.00 | 497.80 | 1.47 | 252.80 | 0.00 |
| 222 | SAL | 37.50 | 2.50 | 62.80 | 2776.00 | 615.00• | 31.00 | 701.00 | 1.48 | 62.80 | 1352.90 |
| 223 | SAN | 32.50 | 3.20 | 187.80 | 1896.00 | 658.00 | 19.00 | 521.70 | 8.66 | 187.80 | 1126.70 |
| 224 | SAV | 37.50 | 4.00 | 30.80 | 4416.00 | 512.00 | 13.00 | 393.80 | 1.06 | 30.80 | 5.30 |
| 225 | SHE | 32.50 | 3.60 | 364.30 | 1736.00 | 663.00 | 25.00 | 758.80 | 8.38 | 364.30 | 132.50 |
| 226 | SIO | 32.50 | 1.60 | 11.20 | 1652.00 | 600.00 | 24.00 | 518.80 | 1.26 | 11.20 | 534.40 |
| 227 | SIO | 32.50 | 1.30 | 1.30 | 2900.00 | 614.00 | 22.00 | 647.70 | .67 | 1.30 | 0.00 |
| 228 | SPR | 32.50 | 1.50 | 8.40 | 3641.00 | 581.00 | 18.00 | 466.80 | 1.28 | 8.40 | 304.30 |
| 229 | SPR | 37.50 | 2.30 | 10.20 | 1953.00 | 580.00 | 32.00• | 538.30 | .70 | 10.20 | 183.00 |
| 230 | SPR | 27.50 | 2.10 | .30 | 4906.00 | 568.00 | 17.00 | 679.50 | 1.51 | .30 | 6.40 |
| 231 | STE | 27.50 | 1.40 | 7.60 | 2129.00 | 497.00 | 18.00 | 375.20 | 3.65 | 7.60 | 120.40 |
| 232 | TAL | 32.50 | 9.30 | 38.10 | 2755.00 | 447.00 | 15.00 | 1176.10 | .90 | 38.10 | 436.80 |
| 233 | TER | 32.50 | 1.80 | 12.60 | 2693.00 | 559.00 | 19.00 | 704.60 | 10.56 | 12.60 | 428.50 |
| 234 | TEX | 32.50 | 3.20 | 13.50 | 2138.00 | 616.00 | 16.00 | 1306.60 | 1.11• | 13.50 | 0.00 |
| 235 | TOP | 37.50 | 1.90 | 6.90 | 2632.00 | 637.00 | 28.00 | 387.20 | .65 | 6.90 | 19.30 |
| 236 | TUS | 37.50 | 2.70 | 19.00 | 2400.00 | 512.00 | 16.00 | 609.80 | 1.25 | 19.00 | 103.40 |
| 237 | TYL | 32.50 | 3.40 | 66.80 | 2501.00 | 640.00 | 15.00 | 621.90 | .92 | 66.80 | 587.60 |
| 238 | VIN | 17.50 | 4.60 | 16.20 | 1093.00 | 441.00• | 10.00 | 583.20 | .59 | 16.20 | 99.10 |
| 239 | WAC | 27.50 | 3.80 | 26.10 | 1624.00 | 611.00 | 17.00 | 567.40 | 1.29 | 26.10 | 0.00 |
| 240 | WAT | 32.50 | 1.40 | 20.70 | 1636.00 | 592.00 | 27.00 | 373.20 | 1.40 | 20.70 | 285.70 |
| 241 | WHE | 32.50 | 1.90 | 8.30 | 3623.00 | 482.00 | 15.00 | 691.80 | 3.76 | 8.30 | 103.80 |
| 242 | WIC | 32.50 | 3.20 | 48.00 | 2312.00 | 645.00 | 18.00 | 904.30 | 8.12 | 48.00 | 293.60 |
| 243 | WIL | 32.50 | 3.50 | 4.40 | 2638.00 | 594.00 | 17.00• | 921.80 | 1.81 | 4.40 | 1046.70 |

## TABLE C-4

## BASIC STATISTICS OF HEALTH AND EDUCATION COMPONENT (S)

| | Infant Mortality Rate/1,000 Live Births IA1 | Death Rate/ 1,000 pop. IA2 | Median Schools Years Completed IB1 | % of Persons, 25+, Completed 4 yrs. High School or more IB2 | % of Males 16-21 not High School Graduates IB3 | % of pop., 3-34 Enrolled in Schools IB4 |
|---|---|---|---|---|---|---|
| US | 21.20 | 9.50 | 12.10 | 52.30 | 15.20 | 54.30 |
| 149 ABI | 13.50 | 9.10 | 12.10 | 52.50 | 12.70 | 51.70 |
| 150 ALB | 20.00 | 7.20 | 11.80 | 48.30 | 19.30 | 48.30 |
| 151 ALT | 22.40 | 12.60 | 11.90 | 49.00 | 10.80 | 54.10 |
| 152 AMA | 15.60 | 8.10 | 12.30 | 59.20 | 11.50 | 54.00 |
| 153 AND | 18.40 | 8.80 | 12.00 | 51.40 | 16.50 | 50.80 |
| 154 ASH | 27.10 | 10.00 | 11.60 | 46.70 | 19.00 | 48.40 |
| 155 ATL | 29.60 | 14.70 | 11.20 | 44.40 | 16.40 | 56.00 |
| 156 BAY | 18.30 | 9.20 | 11.70 | 47.80 | 10.90 | 55.80 |
| 157 BIL | 14.30 | 8.10 | 12.40 | 64.30 | 6.70 | 57.60 |
| 158 BIL | 22.40 | 9.10 | 12.10 | 54.70 | 12.90 | 44.80 |
| 159 BLO | 13.50 | 9.40 | 12.30 | 60.90 | 4.00 | 64.00 |
| 160 BOI | 17.90 | 8.20 | 12.50 | 69.50 | 9.00 | 55.60 |
| 161 BRI | 19.00• | 8.50• | 11.50 | 46.80 | 12.90 | 54.60 |
| 162 BRO | 15.80• | 9.20• | 12.20 | 59.40 | 13.20 | 54.20 |
| 163 BRO | 18.00 | 7.30 | 8.50 | 34.90 | 27.00 | 55.60 |
| 164 BRY | 15.40 | 6.90 | 12.20 | 54.50 | 4.60 | 63.00 |
| 165 CED | 22.10 | 8.50 | 12.40 | 67.70 | 8.20 | 51.30 |
| 166 CHA | 18.60 | 6.10 | 12.60 | 70.00 | 5.50 | 60.40 |
| 167 COL | 12.20 | 7.00 | 12.70 | 68.20 | 4.90 | 64.90 |
| 168 DAN | 18.10• | 8.70• | 12.20 | 55.30 | 16.70 | 54.90 |
| 169 DEC | 31.90 | 9.30 | 12.10 | 53.00 | 13.70 | 54.60 |
| 170 DUB | 24.40 | 9.00 | 12.10 | 54.60 | 8.60 | 56.90 |
| 171 DUR | 19.10 | 8.00 | 12.00 | 50.00 | 10.10 | 59.00 |
| 172 FAL | 17.90• | 10.80• | 9.40 | 31.90 | 24.70 | 53.40 |
| 173 FAR | 19.00 | 7.10 | 12.40 | 63.90 | 2.70 | 62.10 |
| 174 FIT | 21.20• | 10.30• | 11.90 | 49.20 | 15.30 | 55.70 |
| 175 FOR | 24.30 | 10.50 | 10.80 | 41.90 | 21.40 | 47.80 |
| 176 GAD | 28.80 | 10.40 | 10.80 | 40.80 | 19.20 | 50.50 |
| 177 GAI | 13.70 | 7.20 | 12.40 | 59.80 | 10.00 | 62.60 |
| 178 GAL | 20.40 | 8.60 | 11.50 | 45.90 | 14.60 | 55.50 |
| 179 GRE | 13.10 | 8.10 | 12.40 | 65.30 | 7.70 | 51.80 |
| 180 GRE | 19.30 | 7.30 | 12.20 | 58.40 | 9.40 | 56.40 |
| 181 JAC | 24.80 | 9.40 | 12.10 | 52.20 | 14.00 | 54.70 |
| 182 KEN | 21.00 | 8.10 | 11.80 | 48.80 | 13.10 | 56.80 |
| 183 LAC | 14.80 | 8.70 | 12.30 | 60.00 | 4.10 | 60.30 |
| 184 LAF | 11.90 | 6.30 | 11.70 | 48.30 | 14.20 | 57.60 |
| 185 LAF | 14.50 | 6.50 | 12.50 | 67.70 | 5.00 | 63.20 |
| 186 LAK | 20.00 | 7.80 | 11.70 | 48.30 | 18.90 | 55.50 |
| 187 LAR | 18.00 | 7.20 | 7.60 | 32.10 | 24.70 | 53.50 |
| 188 LAW | 23.50 | 5.50 | 12.30 | 62.10 | 23.60 | 37.40 |
| 189 LEW | 21.50• | 11.00• | 10.80 | 42.90 | 16.90 | 52.70 |
| 190 LEX | 19.70 | 7.80 | 12.30 | 60.10 | 16.40 | 51.50 |
| 191 LIM | 21.40 | 10.20 | 12.10 | 53.80 | 11.40 | 55.00 |
| 192 LIN | 12.40 | 7.80 | 12.60 | 71.90 | 4.40 | 59.20 |
| 193 LUB | 23.20 | 6.50 | 12.20 | 55.10 | 11.40 | 55.30 |
| 194 LYN | 26.20 | 9.90 | 10.70 | 41.00 | 26.60 | 51.20 |
| 195 MAN | 18.80• | 10.30• | 11.90 | 49.40 | 16.60 | 53.80 |
| 196 MAN | 22.80 | 9.20 | 12.00 | 51.20 | 21.80 | 51.60 |
| 197 MCA | 19.10 | 6.60 | 7.30 | 30.30 | 28.80 | 57.60 |
| 198 MER | 20.80• | 9.40• | 11.40 | 45.70 | 18.90 | 54.60 |

270

| | Infant Mortality Rate/1,000 Live Births IA1 | Death Rate/ 1,000 pop. IA2 | Median Schools Years Completed IB1 | % of Persons, 25+, Completed 4 yrs. High School or more IB2 | % of Males 16-21 not High School Graduates IB3 | % of pop., 3-34 Enrolled in Schools IB4 |
|---|---|---|---|---|---|---|
| 199 MID | 15.40 | 5.70 | 12.60 | 66.60 | 16.80 | 56.60 |
| 200 MOD | 16.60 | 9.60 | 12.00 | 50.40 | 14.00 | 56.30 |
| 201 MON | 20.80 | 9.60 | 11.70 | 47.80 | 16.90 | 53.90 |
| 202 MUN | 21.20 | 8.90 | 12.10 | 52.00 | 11.00 | 57.10 |
| 203 MUS | 23.80 | 8.50 | 11.60 | 46.50 | 14.80 | 58.60 |
| 204 NAS | 18.80• | 10.30• | 12.20 | 57.20 | 18.30 | 50.50 |
| 205 NEW | 17.90• | 10.80• | 9.50 | 33.70 | 24.90 | 54.40 |
| 206 NEW | 19.00• | 8.50• | 11.50 | 46.50 | 13.50 | 56.40 |
| 207 NOR | 18.10• | 8.70• | 12.50 | 65.50 | 11.40 | 60.60 |
| 208 ODE | 28.80 | 6.00 | 12.10 | 52.40 | 18.20 | 51.20 |
| 209 OGD | 13.30 | 7.20 | 12.40 | 64.80 | 9.90 | 61.20 |
| 210 OWE | 16.20 | 9.10 | 11.80 | 48.90 | 15.20 | 51.60 |
| 211 PET | 28.40 | 8.20 | 11.00 | 42.80 | 30.30 | 40.70 |
| 212 PIN | 18.90 | 10.60 | 11.10 | 43.90 | 19.80 | 54.10 |
| 213 PIT | 21.00• | 10.90• | 12.30 | 60.60 | 8.60 | 58.80 |
| 214 POR | 21.70• | 10.90• | 12.40 | 65.60 | 11.50 | 55.90 |
| 215 PRO | 11.20 | 5.50 | 12.60 | 72.70 | 5.50 | 66.60 |
| 216 PUE | 27.00 | 9.20 | 12.00 | 51.20 | 8.00 | 60.40 |
| 217 RAC | 19.40 | 8.30 | 12.10 | 52.10 | 13.90 | 57.80 |
| 218 REN | 22.60 | 8.70 | 12.50 | 68.70 | 11.30 | 54.60 |
| 219 ROA | 20.30 | 9.20 | 12.10 | 52.20 | 19.10 | 50.40 |
| 220 ROC | 13.70 | 6.80 | 12.60 | 70.20 | 5.80 | 52.20 |
| 221 STJ | 26.90 | 14.00 | 12.00 | 50.30 | 16.50 | 53.00 |
| 222 SAL | 15.80 | 9.40 | 12.30 | 60.60 | 12.70 | 54.80 |
| 223 SAN | 16.20 | 9.80 | 11.80 | 48.60 | 11.50 | 52.40 |
| 224 SAV | 21.90 | 11.00 | 11.80 | 48.20 | 21.00 | 50.20 |
| 225 SHE | 12.80 | 11.90 | 11.70 | 47.30 | 14.80 | 50.30 |
| 226 SIO | 21.70 | 10.70 | 12.20 | 58.70 | 9.40 | 56.10 |
| 227 SIO | 11.80 | 8.40 | 12.30 | 62.50 | 7.30 | 57.50 |
| 228 SPR | 17.40 | 11.00 | 12.20 | 56.60 | 11.10 | 56.60 |
| 229 SPR | 23.80 | 10.30 | 12.20 | 58.40 | 11.50 | 53.30 |
| 230 SPR | 16.10 | 9.50 | 12.00 | 50.80 | 11.00 | 54.40 |
| 231 STE | 22.70 | 10.50 | 11.30 | 45.50 | 10.60 | 54.90 |
| 232 TAL | 18.20 | 6.80 | 12.60 | 64.50 | 7.90 | 64.50 |
| 233 TER | 23.30 | 13.40 | 12.00 | 50.00 | 8.10 | 57.20 |
| 234 TEX | 23.70 | 10.60 | 11.30 | 44.40 | 18.60 | 48.20 |
| 235 TOP | 14.40 | 8.80 | 12.40 | 64.80 | 8.80 | 52.40 |
| 236 TUS | 18.00 | 8.30 | 11.30 | 44.80 | 13.10 | 56.60 |
| 237 TYL | 25.00 | 9.30 | 12.00 | 50.80 | 13.20 | 54.30 |
| 238 VIN | 19.00 | 10.40 | 10.70 | 40.00 | 19.60 | 52.90 |
| 239 WAC | 26.50 | 11.50 | 11.40 | 45.10 | 10.80 | 57.20 |
| 240 WAT | 17.20 | 7.90 | 12.30 | 62.40 | 7.90 | 57.60 |
| 241 WHE | 18.20 | 12.50 | 11.20 | 45.00 | 10.20 | 54.60 |
| 242 WIC | 24.30 | 8.70 | 12.10 | 54.40 | 10.40 | 46.70 |
| 243 WIL | 24.70 | 10.30 | 11.40 | 45.50 | 22.70 | 48.00 |

TABLE C-4 (Continued)

| | | Hospital Beds/ 100,000 pop. IIA2 | Hospital Occupancy Rates IIA3 | Per Capita Local Gov't Expend. on Health IIA5 | Per Capita Local Gov't Expend. on Educ. IIB1 | % of Persons, 25+, Completed 4 yrs. College or more IIB2 |
|---|---|---|---|---|---|---|
| US | | 486.00 | 79.80 | 2.96 | 145.69 | 10.70 |
| 149 | ABI | 563.60 | 74.40 | .16 | 109.31 | 10.90 |
| 150 | ALB | 433.30 | 76.20 | 3.49 | 128.53 | 9.50 |
| 151 | ALT | 691.20 | 81.00 | .41 | 117.88 | 5.20 |
| 152 | AMA | 555.90 | 76.70 | 1.97 | 128.22 | 12.30 |
| 153 | AND | 442.60 | 77.60 | .47 | 139.82 | 6.70 |
| 154 | ASH | 804.70 | 92.10 | 5.24 | 102.25 | 10.00 |
| 155 | ATL | 350.00 | 90.90 | 3.25 | 113.74 | 6.20 |
| 156 | BAY | 573.70 | 79.70 | 3.33 | 148.08 | 6.20 |
| 157 | BIL | 495.10 | 75.60 | 1.64 | 170.53 | 13.10 |
| 158 | BIL | 1324.30 | 87.20 | 3.88• | 147.50• | 9.50 |
| 159 | BLO | 582.60 | 77.80 | 1.72 | 127.08 | 15.20 |
| 160 | BOI | 493.10 | 81.10 | .26 | 110.76 | 13.60 |
| 161 | BRI | 466.70• | 84.20• | 5.60• | 175.53• | 6.80 |
| 162 | BRO | 238.80• | 71.50• | 2.10 | 147.22 | 8.20 |
| 163 | BRO | 252.10 | 75.60 | 1.24 | 125.22 | 7.40 |
| 164 | BRY | 200.00 | 81.10 | 2.90• | 177.24• | 22.80 |
| 165 | CED | 583.60 | 74.70 | 1.68 | 163.42 | 11.90 |
| 166 | CHA | 486.60 | 79.60 | .12 | 177.59 | 24.30 |
| 167 | COL | 970.70 | 73.50 | 4.69• | 171.72• | 27.20 |
| 168 | DAN | 323.40• | 83.70• | 5.60• | 175.53• | 11.40 |
| 169 | DEC | 678.10 | 77.40 | 1.96 | 142.56 | 8.90 |
| 170 | DUB | 613.30 | 75.90 | 2.71 | 70.10 | 10.10 |
| 171 | DUR | 1116.10 | 81.60 | 2.50 | 103.07 | 20.00 |
| 172 | FAL | 383.90• | 82.20• | 3.18 | 94.04 | 5.30 |
| 173 | FAR | 842.20 | 75.40 | 2.30 | 199.92 | 13.60 |
| 174 | FIT | 515.40• | 84.70• | 2.54 | 129.82 | 7.20 |
| 175 | FOR | 532.70 | 77.90 | 1.04 | 93.58 | 5.90 |
| 176 | GAD | 392.50 | 86.80 | 1.64 | 85.33 | 5.20 |
| 177 | GAI | 961.40 | 79.30 | 7.26• | 163.41• | 23.10 |
| 178 | GAL | 1102.40 | 76.00 | 2.04 | 157.70 | 10.40 |
| 179 | GRE | 766.70 | 72.30 | 2.49 | 141.39 | 12.90 |
| 180 | GRE | 572.90 | 77.20 | 1.89 | 128.94 | 9.60 |
| 181 | JAC | 372.10 | 79.30 | .25 | 170.95 | 7.60 |
| 182 | KEN | 465.20 | 73.40 | 1.78 | 151.79 | 6.80 |
| 183 | LAC | 961.50 | 73.20 | 4.16• | 226.68• | 11.20 |
| 184 | LAF | 601.90 | 76.50 | 1.53 | 138.33 | 13.50 |
| 185 | LAF | 574.80 | 85.70 | .30 | 145.13 | 20.60 |
| 186 | LAK | 523.00 | 70.00 | 2.10 | 138.32 | 9.10 |
| 187 | LAR | 320.50 | 82.80 | 1.37 | 110.31 | 6.90 |
| 188 | LAW | 513.60 | 84.90 | .66 | 111.65 | 11.30 |
| 189 | LEW | 557.30 | 75.80 | .80 | 61.02 | 6.40 |
| 190 | LEX | 671.20 | 84.30 | 2.27 | 103.25 | 17.20 |
| 191 | LIM | 505.00 | 71.40 | 1.86 | 111.44 | 6.30 |
| 192 | LIN | 640.20 | 75.80 | 1.82 | 138.99 | 17.50 |
| 193 | LUB | 398.00 | 78.80 | 4.03 | 112.23 | 14.00 |
| 194 | LYN | 399.20 | 82.80 | 2.09 | 105.04 | 9.30 |
| 195 | MAN | 565.40• | 77.60• | 1.64 | 124.66 | 8.20 |
| 196 | MAN | 517.70 | 83.50 | 1.90 | 125.55 | 6.40 |
| 197 | MCA | 210.60 | 75.70 | .92 | 128.71 | 7.30 |
| 198 | MER | 477.50• | 81.40• | 2.82 | 94.15 | 6.70 |

| | Hospital Beds/ 100,000 pop. IIA2 | Hospital Occupancy Rates IIA3 | Per Capita Local Gov't Expend. on Health IIA5 | Per Capita Local Gov't Expend. on Educ. IIB1 | % of Persons, 25+, Completed 4 yrs. College or more IIB2 |
|---|---|---|---|---|---|
| 199 MID | 361.20 | 57.00 | .42 | 159.36 | 21.20 |
| 200 MOD | 534.90 | 64.20 | 8.13• | 118.34• | 8.20 |
| 201 MON | 555.60 | 70.60 | 1.74 | 135.41 | 10.60 |
| 202 MUN | 431.10 | 85.90 | .70 | 117.32 | 9.80 |
| 203 MUS | 420.10 | 84.90 | 1.73 | 201.41 | 6.80 |
| 204 NAS | 393.50• | 81.30• | 6.22• | 179.53• | 11.20 |
| 205 NEW | 383.90• | 82.20• | 1.97 | 101.68 | 5.50 |
| 206 NEW | 466.70• | 84.20• | 2.05 | 142.93 | 7.30 |
| 207 NOR | 323.40• | 83.70• | 2.88 | 230.06 | 23.20 |
| 208 ODE | 393.20 | 78.60 | 1.10 | 165.95 | 8.40 |
| 209 OGD | 533.30 | 92.90 | 2.46 | 164.70 | 11.50 |
| 210 OWE | 789.70 | 88.00 | 5.63• | 160.15• | 8.70 |
| 211 PET | 621.30 | 73.60 | 5.86• | 163.48• | 8.30 |
| 212 PIN | 425.80 | 82.10 | .94 | 92.98 | 7.60 |
| 213 PIT | 538.80• | 78.00• | 2.05 | 143.60 | 11.90 |
| 214 POR | 504.60• | 80.60• | 1.89 | 120.72 | 12.10 |
| 215 PRO | 358.30 | 71.20 | 1.40 | 176.07 | 16.10 |
| 216 PUE | 621.70 | 81.20 | 2.56 | 142.36 | 8.10 |
| 217 RAC | 358.40 | 72.40 | 1.49 | 161.80 | 8.80 |
| 218 REN | 750.00 | 81.00 | 3.96 | 161.20 | 13.60 |
| 219 ROA | 633.70 | 98.10 | 2.32 | 111.38 | 10.20 |
| 220 ROC | 2102.70 | 79.60 | 3.73• | 235.54• | 18.00 |
| 221 STJ | 761.60 | 83.70 | 3.59 | 108.10 | 6.40 |
| 222 SAL | 240.00 | 77.80 | 3.18 | 174.81 | 12.50 |
| 223 SAN | 476.00 | 74.80 | 3.04 | 163.05 | 10.10 |
| 224 SAV | 593.70 | 85.10 | 5.34 | 101.82 | 8.80 |
| 225 SHE | 690.40 | 90.60 | 2.90• | 177.24• | 8.70 |
| 226 SIO | 730.80 | 74.60 | 4.03 | 121.96 | 9.40 |
| 227 SIO | 927.40 | 90.40 | 3.18 | 138.50 | 10.40 |
| 228 SPR | 782.10 | 79.90 | .21 | 100.82 | 10.40 |
| 229 SPR | 792.50 | 93.40 | 2.05 | 123.07 | 9.80 |
| 230 SPR | 416.40 | 82.20 | 1.91 | 120.52 | 7.20 |
| 231 STE | 315.30 | 99.60 | 1.67 | 103.33 | 5.10 |
| 232 TAL | 370.60 | 79.50 | 5.67 | 158.44 | 24.10 |
| 233 TER | 484.40 | 84.20 | .60 | 126.74 | 7.80 |
| 234 TEX | 364.50 | 87.40 | .45 | 140.28 | 6.70 |
| 235 TOP | 522.60 | 84.70 | 3.92 | 153.72 | 13.30 |
| 236 TUS | 367.20 | 84.80 | .67 | 93.01 | 10.90 |
| 237 TYL | 499.00 | 83.20 | 1.36 | 138.97 | 10.10 |
| 238 VIN | 384.90 | 75.90 | 4.91• | 166.14• | 5.70 |
| 239 WAC | 360.90 | 82.00 | 2.06 | 105.84 | 10.30 |
| 240 WAT | 734.50 | 73.30 | 2.21 | 128.04 | 10.10 |
| 241 WHE | 675.30 | 84.00 | 1.02 | 93.30 | 5.80 |
| 242 WIC | 606.30 | 84.70 | 1.72 | 96.99 | 10.60 |
| 243 WIL | 499.00 | 80.80 | 3.31 | 119.62 | 8.40 |

## TABLE C-5

## BASIC STATISTICS OF SOCIAL COMPONENT (S)

| | Labor Force Participation Rate (%) IA1 | % of Labor Force Employed IA2 | Mean Income Per Family Member IA3 | % of Children Under 18 Living With Both Parents IA4 | % of Married Couples Without Own Household IA5 | Per Capita Local Gov't Expend. on Education IB1 | % of Persons 25+, Completed 4 yrs High School or More IB2 | % of Males, 16-64 Less Than 15 yrs School But Vocational Training IB3a | % of Females 16-64 Less Than 15 yrs School But Vocational Training IB3b | Motor Vehicle Registration/ 1,000 pop. IC1a |
|---|---|---|---|---|---|---|---|---|---|---|
| US | 66.00 | 95.60 | 3092.00 | 82.70 | 1.30 | 145.69 | 52.30 | 28.70 | 21.90 | 551.00 |
| 149 ABI | 63.20 | 96.40 | 2583.00 | 80.20 | .90 | 109.31 | 52.50 | 29.10 | 22.40 | 649.00 |
| 150 ALB | 60.40 | 95.70 | 2411.00 | 71.00 | 1.40 | 128.53 | 48.30 | 28.40 | 21.60 | 524.00 |
| 151 ALT | 64.60 | 96.50 | 2629.00 | 85.50 | 1.90 | 117.88 | 49.00 | 31.00 | 21.70 | 481.00• |
| 152 AMA | 69.30 | 96.60 | 2984.00 | 83.70 | .90 | 128.22 | 59.20 | 25.40 | 20.80 | 707.00 |
| 153 AND | 67.50 | 94.70 | 3256.00 | 87.30 | .80 | 139.82 | 51.40 | 30.00 | 19.70 | 552.00 |
| 154 ASH | 69.00 | 96.10 | 2620.00 | 79.80 | 1.70 | 102.25 | 46.70 | 28.80 | 22.20 | 573.00 |
| 155 ATL | 70.40 | 94.30 | 3032.00 | 76.90 | 1.50 | 113.74 | 44.40 | 31.10 | 23.80 | 481.00• |
| 156 BAY | 65.70 | 93.30 | 3010.00 | 89.00 | 1.00 | 148.08 | 47.80 | 26.80 | 21.40 | 522.00 |
| 157 BIL | 67.30 | 94.20 | 2809.00 | 86.20 | .90 | 170.53 | 64.30 | 25.80 | 17.60 | 689.00 |
| 158 BIL | 48.80 | 95.80 | 2234.00 | 79.30 | 1.30 | 147.50• | 54.70 | 32.30 | 19.40 | 507.00 |
| 159 BLO | 69.20 | 96.50 | 3346.00 | 88.30 | .70 | 127.08 | 60.90 | 26.30 | 18.90 | 548.00 |
| 160 BOI | 71.20 | 96.30 | 3115.00 | 86.00 | .70 | 110.76 | 69.50 | 28.60 | 22.40 | 613.00 |
| 161 BRI | 74.40 | 95.90 | 3458.00 | 90.50 | 1.20 | 175.53• | 46.80 | 34.20 | 27.10 | 586.00• |
| 162 BRO | 71.30 | 96.30 | 3074.00 | 87.20 | 1.30 | 147.22 | 59.40 | 36.20 | 25.20 | 481.00• |
| 163 BRO | 58.10 | 93.40 | 1528.00 | 78.50 | 3.40 | 125.22 | 34.90 | 17.70 | 14.70 | 485.00 |
| 164 BRY | 59.50 | 97.40 | 2818.00 | 79.60 | 1.20 | 177.24 | 54.50 | 23.50 | 22.90 | 536.00 |
| 165 CED | 72.60 | 96.00 | 3162.00 | 88.80 | .60 | 163.42 | 67.00 | 25.50 | 18.00 | 606.00 |
| 166 CHA | 58.20 | 96.20 | 3393.00 | 86.50 | .50 | 177.59 | 70.00 | 35.10 | 22.90 | 464.00 |
| 167 COL | 59.00 | 97.60 | 3264.00 | 86.20 | .50 | 171.72 | 68.20 | 22.80 | 18.80 | 470.00• |
| 168 DAN | 73.30 | 95.80 | 3566.00 | 89.10 | 1.10 | 175.53• | 55.30 | 37.70 | 25.90 | 603.00 |
| 169 DEC | 72.20 | 95.70 | 3357.00 | 84.10 | .80 | 142.56 | 53.00 | 31.40 | 19.30 | 575.00 |
| 170 DUB | 69.40 | 97.30 | 2711.00 | 91.60 | .70 | 70.10 | 54.60 | 16.60 | 13.20 | 515.00 |
| 171 DUR | 65.30 | 97.20 | 3000.00 | 76.10 | 1.30 | 103.07 | 50.00 | 25.30 | 24.30 | 545.00 |
| 172 FAL | 74.20 | 95.20 | 2850.00 | 86.60 | 1.30 | 94.04 | 31.90 | 28.20 | 19.40 | 481.00• |
| 173 FAR | 65.80 | 95.40 | 2938.00 | 91.70 | .70 | 199.92 | 63.90 | 22.60 | 21.80 | 610.00• |
| 174 FIT | 71.90 | 95.80 | 3142.00 | 87.60 | .90 | 129.82 | 49.20 | 31.50 | 21.20 | 481.00• |
| 175 FOR | 63.70 | 95.20 | 2204.00 | 82.20 | 1.40 | 93.58 | 41.90 | 22.10 | 15.70 | 633.00 |
| 176 GAD | 61.40 | 92.70 | 2402.00 | 79.50 | .50 | 85.33 | 40.80 | 23.80 | 16.50 | 667.00 |
| 177 GAI | 60.30 | 96.60 | 2915.00 | 75.90 | 1.30 | 163.41 | 59.80 | 25.60 | 18.20 | 588.00 |
| 178 GAL | 66.70 | 96.30 | 2943.00 | 81.30 | 1.00 | 157.70 | 45.90 | 31.00 | 22.90 | 550.00 |
| 179 GRE | 59.60 | 93.50 | 2803.00 | 85.90 | .40 | 141.39 | 65.30 | 34.70 | 21.50 | 639.00 |
| 180 GRE | 68.20 | 96.00 | 2829.00 | 91.00 | .70 | 178.94 | 58.40 | 29.10 | 23.20 | 474.00 |
| 181 JAC | 65.50 | 94.40 | 3286.00 | 87.40 | 1.20 | 170.95 | 52.20 | 27.30 | 19.00 | 526.00 |
| 182 KEN | 70.10 | 95.70 | 3037.00 | 88.30 | .80 | 151.79 | 48.80 | 32.50 | 23.50 | 493.00 |
| 183 LAC | 68.10 | 94.30 | 2840.00 | 87.40 | .70 | 226.68• | 60.00 | 27.30 | 23.50 | 489.00 |
| 184 LAF | 60.90 | 95.90 | 2468.00 | 82.40 | 1.70 | 138.33 | 48.30 | 19.70 | 15.00 | 603.00• |
| 185 LAF | 63.90 | 96.60 | 3273.00 | 88.10 | .50 | 145.13 | 67.70 | 22.60 | 18.80 | 501.00 |
| 186 LAK | 60.70 | 94.30 | 2441.00 | 81.60 | 1.10 | 138.32 | 48.30 | 25.60 | 18.20 | 603.00• |
| 187 LAR | 52.60 | 93.20 | 1498.00 | 80.40 | 3.50 | 110.31 | 32.10 | 21.40 | 12.20 | 533.00 |
| 188 LAW | 37.10 | 93.00 | 2423.00 | 75.80 | .90 | 111.65 | 62.10 | 31.30 | 20.20 | 495.00 |
| 189 LEW | 75.60 | 95.50 | 2606.00 | 84.00 | 1.30 | 61.02 | 42.90 | 21.80 | 16.90 | 481.00• |
| 190 LEX | 66.40 | 96.40 | 3201.00 | 78.60 | 1.20 | 103.25 | 60.10 | 25.20 | 20.10 | 562.00 |
| 191 LIM | 69.10 | 95.90 | 2946.00 | 88.20 | .80 | 111.44 | 53.80 | 24.80 | 17.90 | 597.00 |
| 192 LIN | 73.60 | 97.10 | 3286.00 | 87.10 | .70 | 138.99 | 71.90 | 24.50 | 20.50 | 574.00 |
| 193 LUB | 63.10 | 96.40 | 2753.00 | 82.20 | .90 | 112.23 | 55.10 | 23.10 | 16.10 | 619.00 |
| 194 LYN | 68.00 | 97.70 | 2794.00 | 78.50 | 2.60 | 105.04 | 41.00 | 24.60 | 16.90 | 524.00 |
| 195 MAN | 73.00 | 96.80 | 2995.00 | 85.90 | 1.20 | 124.66 | 49.40 | 19.50 | 16.90 | 481.00• |
| 196 MAN | 68.80 | 96.10 | 3076.00 | 86.40 | .80 | 125.55 | 51.20 | 26.00 | 19.80 | 595.00 |
| 197 MCA | 57.30 | 94.10 | 1479.00 | 81.60 | 3.80 | 128.71 | 30.30 | 14.60 | 11.70 | 493.00 |
| 198 MER | 72.70 | 95.70 | 3290.00 | 86.10 | 1.20 | 94.15 | 45.70 | 33.20 | 24.70 | 553.00• |

| | Labor Force Participation Rate (%) IA1 | % of Labor Force Employed IA2 | Mean Income Per Family Member IA3 | % of Children Under 18 Living With Both Parents IA4 | % of Married Couples Without Own Household IA5 | Per Capita Local Gov't Expend. on Education IB1 | % of Persons 25+, Completed 4 yrs High School or More IB2 | % of Males, 16-64 Less Than 15 yrs School But Vocational Training IB3a | % of Females 16-64 Less Than 15 yrs School But Vocational Training IB3b | Motor Vehicle Registration/ 1,000 pop. IC1a |
|---|---|---|---|---|---|---|---|---|---|---|
| 199 MID | 69.20 | 96.50 | 3407.00 | 85.60 | 1.00 | 159.36 | 66.60 | 26.10 | 24.20 | 723.00 |
| 200 MOD | 63.20 | 90.60 | 2886.00 | 81.10 | 1.10 | 118.34• | 50.40 | 24.10 | 17.70 | 667.00 |
| 201 MON | 62.70 | 94.60 | 2360.00 | 72.70 | 1.70 | 135.41 | 47.80 | 25.30 | 18.80 | 603.00• |
| 202 MUN | 65.00 | 95.00 | 3150.00 | 85.00 | .70 | 117.32 | 52.00 | 26.00 | 18.00 | 536.00 |
| 203 MUS | 67.40 | 93.30 | 2856.00 | 84.00 | .90 | 201.41 | 46.50 | 28.00 | 22.10 | 513.00 |
| 204 NAS | 73.70 | 97.20 | 3176.00 | 89.00 | .80 | 179.53• | 57.20 | 31.00 | 20.60 | 481.00• |
| 205 NEW | 72.20 | 94.90 | 2823.00 | 83.00 | 1.60 | 101.68 | 33.70 | 28.80 | 21.10 | 481.00• |
| 206 NEW | 73.30 | 96.00 | 3495.00 | 87.80 | 1.20 | 142.93 | 46.50 | 32.50 | 23.10 | 586.00• |
| 207 NOR | 73.60 | 97.30 | 4923.00 | 75.90 | 1.40 | 230.06 | 65.50 | 33.40 | 29.80 | 603.00• |
| 208 ODE | 67.90 | 95.70 | 2861.00 | 83.80 | 1.00 | 165.95 | 52.40 | 22.40 | 22.50 | 721.00 |
| 209 OGD | 70.80 | 94.00 | 2956.00 | 86.80 | .60 | 164.70 | 64.80 | 33.10 | 23.60 | 656.00 |
| 210 OWE | 68.90 | 95.10 | 2632.00 | 85.10 | .90 | 160.15• | 48.90 | 23.70 | 17.30 | 608.00 |
| 211 PET | 54.30 | 97.00 | 2666.00 | 75.20 | 2.20 | 163.43• | 42.80 | 26.00 | 14.90 | 430.00 |
| 212 PIN | 60.40 | 93.80 | 2199.00 | 72.90 | 1.70 | 92.98 | 43.90 | 20.60 | 16.10 | 475.00 |
| 213 PIT | 71.10 | 95.90 | 3280.00 | 87.50 | .80 | 143.60 | 60.60 | 32.50 | 25.50 | 481.00• |
| 214 POR | 72.00 | 96.80 | 3005.00 | 83.80 | 1.20 | 120.72 | 65.60 | 21.40 | 18.40 | 481.00• |
| 215 PRO | 59.00 | 93.30 | 2305.00 | 89.20 | .80 | 176.07 | 72.70 | 24.50 | 18.90 | 578.00 |
| 216 PUE | 53.80 | 94.10 | 2523.00 | 83.10 | 1.10 | 142.36 | 51.20 | 23.30 | 19.30 | 620.00 |
| 217 RAC | 70.80 | 95.40 | 3240.00 | 87.40 | .70 | 161.80 | 52.10 | 31.80 | 23.60 | 478.00 |
| 218 REN | 74.00 | 93.80 | 3802.00 | 81.10 | .90 | 161.20 | 68.10 | 33.90 | 28.20 | 773.00• |
| 219 ROA | 69.40 | 97.70 | 3041.00 | 81.70 | 1.80 | 111.38 | 52.20 | 24.90 | 18.00 | 589.00 |
| 220 ROC | 75.00 | 96.60 | 3228.00 | 91.40 | .30 | 235.54• | 70.20 | 26.70 | 23.70 | 568.00 |
| 221 STJ | 54.80 | 96.10 | 2738.00 | 83.80 | .80 | 108.10 | 50.30 | 31.00 | 23.20 | 539.00 |
| 222 SAL | 64.80 | 93.30 | 2897.00 | 83.20 | .80 | 174.81 | 60.60 | 28.60 | 21.60 | 615.00• |
| 223 SAN | 64.30 | 96.20 | 2641.00 | 81.20 | 1.10 | 163.05 | 48.60 | 29.10 | 19.30 | 658.00 |
| 224 SAV | 61.60 | 95.70 | 2612.00 | 72.70 | 1.50 | 101.82 | 48.20 | 27.10 | 22.20 | 512.00 |
| 225 SHE | 66.70 | 97.40 | 2667.00 | 82.60 | 1.50 | 177.24• | 47.30 | 29.30 | 20.90 | 663.00 |
| 226 SIO | 69.70 | 95.60 | 2826.00 | 87.00 | .80 | 121.96 | 58.70 | 23.90 | 18.80 | 600.00 |
| 227 SIO | 72.20 | 95.80 | 2776.00 | 88.10 | .80 | 138.50 | 62.50 | 25.30 | 21.50 | 614.00 |
| 228 SPR | 74.50 | 97.00 | 3361.00 | 86.30 | .50 | 100.82 | 56.60 | 31.00 | 22.10 | 581.00 |
| 229 SPR | 56.80 | 95.90 | 2838.00 | 83.60 | .70 | 123.07 | 58.40 | 26.30 | 17.20 | 580.00 |
| 230 SPR | 66.30 | 96.10 | 3077.00 | 85.30 | 1.50 | 120.52 | 50.80 | 28.70 | 19.80 | 568.00 |
| 231 STE | 60.00 | 96.30 | 2866.00 | 87.30 | 1.00 | 103.33 | 45.50 | 24.00 | 16.60 | 497.00 |
| 232 TAL | 66.20 | 97.00 | 3065.00 | 76.20 | 1.00 | 158.44 | 64.50 | 26.60 | 22.10 | 447.00 |
| 233 TER | 65.70 | 95.80 | 2892.00 | 85.00 | 1.00 | 126.74 | 50.00 | 25.60 | 16.10 | 559.00 |
| 234 TEX | 67.20 | 94.50 | 2467.00 | 78.10 | 1.60 | 140.28 | 44.40 | 21.30 | 17.80 | 616.00 |
| 235 TOP | 67.40 | 97.30 | 3128.00 | 84.80 | .90 | 153.72 | 64.80 | 36.90 | 24.80 | 637.00 |
| 236 TUS | 56.20 | 96.00 | 2429.00 | 73.30 | 1.50 | 93.01 | 44.80 | 21.10 | 18.10 | 512.00 |
| 237 TYL | 70.20 | 96.40 | 2793.00 | 80.60 | 1.60 | 138.97 | 50.80 | 23.10 | 20.00 | 640.00 |
| 238 VIN | 70.40 | 94.30 | 2910.00 | 78.70 | 1.60 | 166.14• | 40.00 | 27.10 | 20.10 | 481.00• |
| 239 WAC | 67.00 | 95.90 | 2610.00 | 77.60 | 1.20 | 105.84 | 45.10 | 26.50 | 20.40 | 611.00 |
| 240 WAT | 69.20 | 94.00 | 3045.00 | 86.20 | .90 | 128.04 | 62.40 | 23.30 | 16.70 | 592.00 |
| 241 WHE | 63.30 | 95.80 | 2747.00 | 87.10 | 1.30 | 93.30 | 45.00 | 26.60 | 17.70 | 482.00 |
| 242 WIC | 55.10 | 96.00 | 2811.00 | 81.90 | 1.10 | 96.99 | 54.40 | 29.80 | 22.30 | 645.00 |
| 243 WIL | 65.60 | 96.70 | 2550.00 | 75.90 | 1.90 | 119.62 | 45.50 | 23.50 | 15.30 | 594.00 |

TABLE C-5 (Continued)

| | Motorcycle Registrations/ 1,000 pop. IC1b | % of Households With One or More Automobiles IC1c | Local Sunday Newspaper Circ./ 1,000 pop. IC2a | % Occupied Housing With TV IC2b | Local Radio Stations/ 1,000 pop. IC2c | Population Density In SMSA IC3a | % Pop. under 5 and 65+ in Central City IC3b | Negro to Total Pop. Median Family Income Adj. For Education IIA1 | Negro to Total Pop. Professional Emp. Adj. For Education IIA2 | Negro Males To Total Males Unemployment Rate Adj. For Education IIA3 |
|---|---|---|---|---|---|---|---|---|---|---|
| US | 16.00 | 82.50 | 243.00 | 95.50 | .03 | 360.00 | 18.30 | .78 | .07 | 2.08 |
| 149 ABI | 16.00 | 91.30 | 620.00 | 95.80 | 1.75 | 61.00 | 17.00 | .75 | .03 | 3.61 |
| 150 ALB | 14.00 | 81.30 | 492.00 | 94.40 | 3.33 | 277.00 | 17.10 | .86 | .33 | 2.92 |
| 151 ALT | 12.00 | 83.10 | 571.00 | 96.80 | 3.70 | 255.00 | 22.60 | .90 | .01 | 3.15 |
| 152 AMA | 27.00 | 92.00 | 600.00 | 96.70 | 3.47 | 80.00 | 17.20 | .77 | .03 | 1.39 |
| 153 AND | 20.00 | 89.00 | 314.00 | 97.20 | 1.44 | 306.00 | 18.90 | .89 | .02 | 2.67 |
| 154 ASH | 15.00 | 82.20 | 1248.00 | 92.90 | 3.44 | 221.00 | 21.40 | .73 | .07 | 2.32 |
| 155 ATL | 10.00* | 72.40 | 1363.00 | 96.40 | .57 | 308.00 | 31.20 | .79 | .12 | 2.00 |
| 156 BAY | 30.00 | 89.80 | 917.00 | 98.40 | 3.41 | 263.00 | 19.70 | .75 | .01 | 1.67 |
| 157 BIL | 39.00* | 90.30 | 907.00 | 95.10 | 6.89 | 33.00 | 16.10 | 1.00* | .01 | 1.00* |
| 158 BIL | 14.00 | 86.60 | 899.00 | 94.20 | .74 | 230.00 | 14.60 | .79 | .12 | 2.72 |
| 159 BLO | 17.00 | 88.90 | 1143.00 | 95.60 | 1.92 | 89.00 | 20.40 | .66 | .01 | .37 |
| 160 BOI | 52.00 | 91.40 | 826.00 | 96.40 | 8.03 | 108.00 | 18.50 | 1.00* | .01 | 1.00* |
| 161 BRI | 10.00* | 90.60 | 317.00 | 98.70 | 1.51 | 1349.00 | 17.00 | 1.02 | .01 | 2.56 |
| 162 BRO | 10.00* | 86.60 | 637.00 | 98.20 | 1.57 | 1170.00 | 21.40 | .81 | .01 | 2.88 |
| 163 BRO | 10.00 | 80.50 | 268.00 | 88.70 | .71 | 157.00 | 18.80 | 1.00* | 1.00* | 1.00* |
| 164 BRY | 16.00 | 88.50 | 388.00 | 92.20 | 6.89 | 99.00 | 19.20 | .75 | .04 | 2.90 |
| 165 CED | 23.00 | 88.70 | 742.00 | 97.00 | 4.90 | 229.00 | 18.90 | .78 | .01 | 2.12 |
| 166 CHA | 20.00 | 89.50 | 1238.00 | 93.80 | 2.45 | 163.00 | 13.30 | .73 | .03 | 2.73 |
| 167 COL | 32.00* | 87.30 | 406.00 | 94.50 | 7.40 | 118.00 | 13.20 | .79 | .03 | 3.04 |
| 168 DAN | 10.00* | 90.60 | 635.00 | 97.00 | 5.06 | 775.00 | 18.80 | .78 | .02 | 1.25 |
| 169 DEC | 18.00 | 86.00 | 578.00 | 96.10 | 1.60 | 216.00 | 20.50 | .85 | .03 | 2.17 |
| 170 DUB | 25.00 | 85.90 | 681.00 | 97.20 | 5.49 | 148.00 | 20.60 | 1.00* | 1.00* | 1.00* |
| 171 DUR | 17.00* | 83.50 | 546.00 | 93.20 | 1.57 | 274.00 | 17.00 | .86 | .16 | 2.00 |
| 172 FAL | 10.00* | 77.20 | 440.00 | 98.30 | 1.33 | 1051.00 | 22.20 | 1.00* | .03 | 1.00* |
| 173 FAR | 94.00 | 88.00 | 1111.00 | 95.60 | 5.83 | 43.00 | 17.40 | 1.00* | .01 | 3.54 |
| 174 FIT | 10.00* | 84.30 | 476.00 | 98.00 | 2.06 | 581.00 | 20.60 | .93 | 1.00* | 1.62 |
| 175 FOR | 17.00 | 81.70 | 572.00 | 92.60 | .62 | 47.00 | 19.80 | .68 | .01 | 1.82 |
| 176 GAD | 14.00 | 85.50 | 468.00 | 95.40 | 4.25 | 170.00 | 18.30 | .79 | .04 | 1.97 |
| 177 GAI | 29.00 | 88.00 | 367.00 | 89.10 | 3.80 | 114.00 | 13.20 | .78 | .10 | 1.24 |
| 178 GAL | 16.00 | 85.20 | 436.00 | 95.40 | 1.17 | 426.00 | 19.10 | .68 | .10 | 1.86 |
| 179 GRE | 39.00 | 89.20 | 777.00 | 96.00 | 7.31 | 31.00 | 17.60 | .56 | .01 | 1.00* |
| 180 GRE | 14.00 | 90.70 | 695.00 | 98.50 | 3.16 | 302.00 | 19.00 | 1.00* | 1.00* | 1.00* |
| 181 JAC | 24.00 | 90.60 | 887.00 | 97.40 | 1.39 | 205.00 | 22.30 | .80 | .03 | 2.65 |
| 182 KEN | 13.00 | 88.50 | 370.00 | 97.90 | 2.54 | 434.00 | 19.10 | .87 | .01 | 1.61 |
| 183 LAC | 12.00 | 85.00 | 708.00 | 97.50 | 3.75 | 178.00 | 19.50 | 1.00* | 1.00* | 1.00* |
| 184 LAF | 18.00* | 88.00 | 377.00 | 96.20 | 2.72 | 388.00 | 15.30 | .97 | .16 | 3.92 |
| 185 LAF | 19.00 | 88.80 | 1007.00 | 94.70 | 3.66 | 219.00 | 19.40 | .88 | .01 | 1.37 |
| 186 LAK | 18.00* | 86.90 | 460.00 | 96.50 | 2.75 | 132.00 | 16.20 | .86 | .14 | 2.61 |
| 187 LAR | 15.00 | 74.70 | 262.00 | 91.60 | 1.36 | 22.00 | 19.40 | 1.00* | 1.00* | 1.00* |
| 188 LAW | 23.00 | 91.00 | 357.00 | 95.30 | 2.77 | 100.00 | 15.60 | .75 | .06 | 1.80 |
| 189 LEW | 10.00* | 76.30 | 770.00 | 97.00 | 5.47 | 604.00 | 21.50 | 1.00* | .01 | 1.00* |
| 190 LEX | 14.00 | 84.40 | 692.00 | 95.80 | 4.59 | 623.00 | 17.00 | .68 | .05 | 1.70 |
| 191 LIM | 16.00 | 89.40 | 861.00 | 97.40 | 2.33 | 131.00 | 21.20 | .91 | .02 | 3.05 |
| 192 LIN | 23.00 | 88.10 | 410.00 | 95.40 | 4.76 | 199.00 | 17.70 | .72 | .01 | 2.41 |
| 193 LUB | 23.00 | 92.00 | 476.00 | 96.00 | 3.35 | 201.00 | 15.30 | .74 | .05 | 2.15 |
| 194 LYN | 17.00* | 80.20 | 596.00 | 94.70 | 3.25 | 121.00 | 19.30 | .85 | .10 | 3.19 |
| 195 MAN | 10.00* | 78.50 | 628.00 | 96.80 | 3.70 | 742.00 | 21.00 | 1.00* | .01 | 3.12 |
| 196 MAN | 21.00 | 88.20 | 837.00 | 96.40 | .76 | 262.00 | 19.30 | .91 | .03 | 3.12 |
| 197 MCA | 8.00 | 81.40 | 466.00 | 90.20 | .54 | 118.00 | 19.40 | 1.00* | 1.00* | 1.00* |
| 198 MER | 10.00* | 84.30 | 379.00 | 97.50 | 5.35 | 2361.00 | 19.20 | .74 | .01 | .65 |

| | Motorcycle Registrations/ 1,000 pop. IC1b | % of Households With One or More Automobiles IC1c | Local Sunday Newspaper Circ./ 1,000 pop. IC2a | % Occupied Housing With TV IC2b | Local Radio Stations/ 100,000 pop. IC2c | Population Density In SMSA IC3a | % Pop. under 5 and 65+ in Central City IC3b | Negro to Total Pop. Median Family Income Adj. For Education IIA1 | Negro to Total Pop. Professional Emp. Adj. For Education IIA2 | Negro Males To Total Males Unemployment Rate Adj. For Education IIA3 |
|---|---|---|---|---|---|---|---|---|---|---|
| 199 MID | 23.00 | 93.50 | 341.00 | 96.40 | 7.69 | 70.00 | 13.60 | .61 | .03 | 4.41 |
| 200 MOD | 33.00 | 89.30 | 343.00 | 94.70 | 4.10 | 129.00 | 18.70 | .89 | .01 | 5.45 |
| 201 MON | 18.00 | 82.50 | 330.00 | 95.20 | 1.73 | 181.00 | 19.50 | .77 | .20 | 1.62 |
| 202 MUN | 16.00* | 88.50 | 519.00 | 96.30 | 2.32 | 326.00 | 17.80 | .88 | .02 | 2.94 |
| 203 MUS | 28.00 | 89.10 | 1158.00 | 97.40 | 2.54 | 314.00 | 21.50 | .95 | .05 | 1.96 |
| 204 NAS | 10.00* | 84.40 | 365.00 | 98.60 | 2.98 | 1093.00 | 19.10 | 1.00* | .01 | 1.00* |
| 205 NEW | 10.00* | 75.30 | 590.00 | 97.10 | 2.61 | 1076.00 | 22.40 | .68 | .02 | 1.66 |
| 206 NEW | 10.00* | 85.10 | 402.00 | 97.10 | 0.00 | 1674.00 | 18.80 | .82 | .01 | 2.07 |
| 207 NOR | 10.00* | 91.20 | 294.00 | 97.90 | 1.66 | 1798.00 | 17.60 | .59 | .03 | 1.29 |
| 208 ODE | 23.00 | 94.20 | 469.00 | 95.90 | 5.43 | 101.00 | 14.00 | .69 | .06 | 1.40 |
| 209 OGD | 40.00 | 90.00 | 529.00 | 96.80 | 3.96 | 217.00 | 20.00 | .77 | .01 | 2.93 |
| 210 OWE | 14.00 | 85.60 | 534.00 | 97.30 | 1.26 | 172.00 | 19.20 | .74 | .01 | 2.90 |
| 211 PET | 17.00* | 82.00 | 520.00 | 95.90 | 2.32 | 159.00 | 19.20 | .96 | .24 | 2.38 |
| 212 PIN | 11.00* | 75.90 | 383.00 | 93.00 | 3.52 | 98.00 | 19.80 | .73 | .35 | 2.52 |
| 213 PIT | 10.00* | 84.10 | 1591.00 | 96.90 | 5.00 | 570.00 | 20.00 | .71 | .01 | .75 |
| 214 POR | 10.00* | 80.00 | 1752.00 | 96.40 | 5.63 | 591.00 | 22.80 | 1.00* | .01 | 10.94 |
| 215 PRO | 31.00 | 93.20 | 342.00 | 93.50 | 2.17 | 68.00 | 14.70 | 1.00* | 1.00* | 1.00* |
| 216 PUE | 29.00 | 86.60 | 479.00 | 96.10 | 5.08 | 49.00 | 16.00 | .94 | .01 | 2.20 |
| 217 RAC | 11.00* | 87.80 | 427.00 | 97.40 | .58 | 507.00 | 19.80 | .84 | .02 | 2.75 |
| 218 REN | 45.00 | 88.70 | 479.00 | 92.60 | 8.26 | 19.00 | 16.70 | .67 | .02 | 1.20 |
| 219 ROA | 17.00* | 83.50 | 1189.00 | 96.70 | 2.76 | 571.00 | 21.10 | .80 | .06 | 1.92 |
| 220 ROC | 26.00 | 89.10 | 520.00 | 95.80 | 3.57 | 128.00 | 19.20 | 1.00* | .01 | 1.00* |
| 221 STJ | 32.00* | 80.30 | 712.00 | 96.70 | 4.59 | 215.00 | 23.50 | .96 | .02 | 1.73 |
| 222 SAL | 31.00 | 88.40 | 576.00 | 94.30 | 1.06 | 98.00 | 15.90 | .82 | .01 | 3.07 |
| 223 SAN | 19.00 | 90.20 | 501.00 | 95.00 | 7.04 | 47.00 | 18.70 | .80 | .04 | 3.26 |
| 224 SAV | 13.00 | 78.00 | 502.00 | 94.40 | 4.25 | 422.00 | 16.60 | .78 | .23 | 2.68 |
| 225 SHE | 25.00 | 85.70 | 502.00 | 95.40 | 3.61 | 89.00 | 19.80 | .87 | .04 | 2.56 |
| 226 SIO | 24.00 | 84.70 | 564.00 | 97.50 | 3.44 | 103.00 | 20.80 | .77 | .01 | 2.32 |
| 227 SIO | 22.00 | 89.00 | 745.00 | 96.80 | 10.52 | 117.00 | 16.40 | 1.00* | .01 | 3.42 |
| 228 SPR | 18.00 | 85.80 | 779.00 | 95.10 | 2.48 | 184.00 | 21.00 | .73 | .02 | 2.20 |
| 229 SPR | 32.00* | 86.30 | 625.00 | 95.30 | 5.22 | 226.00 | 19.60 | .79 | .01 | 1.48 |
| 230 SPR | 17.00 | 88.60 | 541.00 | 97.40 | 1.92 | 391.00 | 20.90 | .89 | .07 | 2.17 |
| 231 STE | 18.00 | 83.70 | 1015.00 | 97.50 | 1.20 | 285.00 | 20.00 | .80 | .02 | 2.54 |
| 232 TAL | 15.00 | 87.50 | 476.00 | 90.80 | 4.85 | 154.00 | 13.10 | .72 | .16 | 2.63 |
| 233 TER | 19.00 | 83.40 | 645.00 | 96.10 | 4.00 | 117.00 | 21.00 | .80 | .01 | 2.27 |
| 234 TEX | 16.00 | 81.50 | 1022.00 | 95.00 | 1.98 | 67.00 | 22.60 | .79 | .14 | 2.95 |
| 235 TOP | 28.00 | 88.20 | 572.00 | 96.80 | 4.51 | 283.00 | 19.70 | .74 | .04 | 2.97 |
| 236 TUS | 16.00 | 82.20 | 387.00 | 92.80 | 2.58 | 87.00 | 16.10 | .73 | .15 | 2.52 |
| 237 TYL | 15.00 | 86.00 | 624.00 | 94.90 | 3.09 | 104.00 | 18.80 | .74 | .17 | 1.95 |
| 238 VIN | 10.00* | 85.10 | 336.00 | 97.00 | .82 | 243.00 | 19.10 | .83 | .05 | 2.26 |
| 239 WAC | 17.00 | 86.10 | 546.00 | 96.00 | 4.08 | 148.00 | 20.00 | .68 | .12 | 2.26 |
| 240 WAT | 27.00 | 89.50 | 734.00 | 97.40 | 3.00 | 234.00 | 19.60 | .82 | .02 | 2.92 |
| 241 WHE | 15.00 | 78.90 | 1298.00 | 97.20 | 3.27 | 194.00 | 21.90 | .73 | .01 | 2.43 |
| 242 WIC | 18.00* | 49.70 | 483.00 | 96.40 | 3.17 | 84.00 | 16.90 | 1.39 | .10 | 2.62 |
| 243 WIL | 17.00* | 82.20 | 789.00 | 93.80 | 4.67 | 103.00 | 18.50 | .71 | .15 | 2.07 |

TABLE C-5 (Continued)

| | Negro Females To Total Females Unemployment Rate Adj. For Education IIA4 | Male to Female Unemployment Rate Adj. For Education IIB1 | Male to Female Professional Emp. Adj. For Education IIB2 | % Working Outside County of Residence IIC1 | Central City & Suburban Income Dist. IIC2 | Housing Segregation Index IIC3 | % Families With Income Above Poverty Level IIIA1 | % Occupied Housing With Plumbing IIIA2 | % Occupied Housing With 1.01 or More Persons Per Room IIIA3 | % Occupied Housing With Telephone IIIA4 |
|---|---|---|---|---|---|---|---|---|---|---|
| US | 1.79 | .75 | 1.49 | 17.80 | .06 | .27 | 89.30 | 94.50 | 8.20 | 87.30 |
| 149 ABI | 2.46 | .52 | 1.16 | 5.50 | -.02 | .07 | 86.70 | 97.80 | 7.90 | 85.90 |
| 150 ALB | 2.08 | .42 | .92 | 4.00 | .02 | .07 | 81.40 | 91.80 | 13.70 | 81.10 |
| 151 ALT | .39• | 1.09 | 1.14 | 5.20 | .02 | .72 | 91.60 | 94.80 | 4.60 | 92.70 |
| 152 AMA | 1.45 | .64 | 1.38 | 31.30 | -.02 | .13 | 90.90 | 99.10 | 7.10 | 87.90 |
| 153 AND | 2.89 | .46 | 1.41 | 12.00 | -.02 | .94 | 93.80 | 97.30 | 6.50 | 91.20 |
| 154 ASH | 1.17 | .64 | 1.27 | 4.00 | -.09 | 1.11 | 86.50 | 92.00 | 7.10 | 83.60 |
| 155 ATL | 1.32 | .69 | 1.34 | 14.60 | -.08 | 1.55 | 90.10 | 97.60 | 5.30 | 88.90 |
| 156 BAY | 4.43 | .85 | 1.47 | 21.70 | 0.00 | 1.38 | 93.40 | 96.50 | 7.90 | 93.10 |
| 157 BIL | 1.00• | .73 | 1.23 | 2.20 | -.08 | .39 | 90.60 | 96.70 | 6.70 | 89.70 |
| 158 BIL | 1.57 | .52 | 1.26 | 5.40 | -.06 | .07 | 82.70 | 95.30 | 11.00 | 76.90 |
| 159 BLO | 1.95 | 1.00 | 1.33 | 6.90 | -.04 | .10 | 93.80 | 96.40 | 4.80 | 92.10 |
| 160 BOI | 6.92 | .78 | 1.78 | 4.40 | -.06 | .50 | 91.40 | 98.50 | 5.70 | 90.70 |
| 161 BRI | 1.00• | .64 | 1.54 | 13.80 | -.02 | .20 | 96.10 | 98.40 | 7.90 | 95.60 |
| 162 BRO | 2.47 | .88 | 1.55 | 37.80 | 0.00 | .42 | 94.80 | 97.50 | 7.00 | 93.60 |
| 163 BRO | .93 | .81 | .81 | 4.00 | -.02 | .63 | 61.50 | 78.70 | 28.70 | 64.90 |
| 164 BRY | 2.23 | .56 | 2.20 | 4.50 | -.04 | .46 | 83.40 | 92.20 | 8.80 | 81.00 |
| 165 CED | 1.79 | .46 | 1.71 | 3.50 | -.06 | .46 | 94.30 | 96.40 | 6.30 | 94.70 |
| 166 CHA | 1.80 | .64 | 1.77 | 3.10 | -.06 | 2.13 | 92.80 | 96.90 | 5.30 | 94.10 |
| 167 COL | 4.14 | 1.03 | 1.50 | 8.00 | -.04 | .40 | 91.30 | 94.80 | 5.70 | 88.70 |
| 168 DAN | 1.31 | 1.03 | 1.79 | 9.80 | -.04 | .55 | 95.40 | 98.50 | 6.30 | 95.70 |
| 169 DEC | 2.00• | .52 | 1.30 | 4.70 | -.04 | .37 | 93.20 | 95.00 | 6.90 | 92.10 |
| 170 DUB | 1.00• | .63 | 1.07 | 3.70 | -.08 | .45 | 92.40 | 95.80 | 11.70 | 95.60 |
| 171 DUR | 1.95 | .88 | 1.34 | 16.40 | -.02 | .40 | 87.70 | 93.90 | 7.40 | 88.50 |
| 172 FAL | 1.00• | 1.66 | 1.14 | 19.10 | .08 | .55 | 91.10 | 96.20 | 6.70 | 91.70 |
| 173 FAR | 1.00• | 1.08 | 1.34 | 18.90 | -.06 | .50 | 92.70 | 94.10 | 7.40 | 94.70 |
| 174 FIT | 1.00• | .67 | 1.47 | 11.20 | 0.00 | .23 | 93.70 | 96.70 | 7.10 | 93.00 |
| 175 FOR | 1.21 | .72 | .53 | 21.10 | -.22 | .81 | 80.30 | 89.10 | 9.90 | 74.70 |
| 176 GAD | 2.16 | .80 | .95 | 10.00 | -.06 | .47 | 82.60 | 90.20 | 7.40 | 84.40 |
| 177 GAI | 1.69 | .64 | 1.49 | 5.00 | -.04 | .08 | 84.70 | 92.20 | 7.90 | 83.50 |
| 178 GAL | 1.96 | .69 | 1.49 | 15.30 | -.04 | .34 | 88.90 | 97.00 | 9.60 | 84.80 |
| 179 GRE | 1.76 | .66 | 1.20 | 2.20 | -.10 | .59 | 91.70 | 95.60 | 8.10 | 89.30 |
| 180 GRE | 1.00• | .57 | 1.31 | 4.90 | 0.00 | .68 | 93.90 | 96.40 | 9.90 | 96.00 |
| 181 JAC | 1.58 | .82 | 1.63 | 9.30 | 0.00 | 1.38 | 93.40 | 96.30 | 6.70 | 92.20 |
| 182 KEN | 1.73 | .61 | 1.39 | 26.20 | -.02 | .50 | 94.30 | 97.70 | 8.80 | 93.00 |
| 183 LAC | 1.00• | .82 | 1.21 | 4.90 | -.02 | .54 | 93.50 | 96.40 | 5.90 | 93.90 |
| 184 LAF | 2.02 | .60 | 1.54 | 6.30 | -.06 | .13 | 80.70 | 93.10 | 15.10 | 87.40 |
| 185 LAF | 1.81 | .64 | 1.77 | 6.10 | -.10 | .18 | 93.90 | 97.60 | 6.50 | 90.50 |
| 186 LAK | 2.42 | .82 | 1.16 | 6.20 | -.10 | .44 | 83.50 | 95.30 | 12.40 | 86.00 |
| 187 LAR | 1.00• | .81 | .77 | 2.70 | -.04 | .05 | 61.60 | 83.30 | 31.40 | 71.70 |
| 188 LAW | 1.62 | .45 | .94 | 2.00 | -.02 | .05 | 85.70 | 98.30 | 8.70 | 85.40 |
| 189 LEW | 1.00• | .91 | 1.01 | 9.60 | 0.00 | 0.00 | 91.60 | 95.30 | 6.80 | 85.90 |
| 190 LEX | 2.14 | .62 | 1.43 | 5.30 | -.08 | .38 | 90.30 | 96.90 | 7.20 | 84.40 |
| 191 LIM | 2.88 | .60 | 1.29 | 18.10 | 0.00 | 1.82 | 92.80 | 95.70 | 7.00 | 90.40 |
| 192 LIN | 2.10 | .76 | 1.43 | 4.00 | -.02 | .12 | 94.10 | 97.90 | 4.20 | 94.20 |
| 193 LUB | 1.53 | .62 | 1.26 | 3.10 | -.06 | .02 | 86.60 | 98.90 | 11.40 | 84.90 |
| 194 LYN | 2.33 | .75 | 1.43 | 33.30 | -.10 | .09 | 89.10 | 88.50 | 7.80 | 84.50 |
| 195 MAN | 1.00• | .96 | 1.30 | 10.50 | 0.00 | .21 | 93.20 | 97.00 | 6.80 | 88.10 |
| 196 MAN | 2.96 | .66 | 1.48 | 6.20 | -.02 | 1.10 | 92.90 | 96.10 | 6.40 | 90.60 |
| 197 MCA | 1.00• | .65 | .84 | 3.80 | -.12 | .27 | 58.00 | 74.90 | 33.00 | 63.90 |
| 198 MER | 5.24 | .82 | 1.46 | 19.10 | 0.00 | 0.00 | 95.20 | 97.90 | 6.90 | 93.50 |

| | Negro Females To Total Females Unemployment Rate Adj. For Education IIA4 | Male to Female Unemployment Rate Adj. For Education IIB1 | Male to Female Professional Emp. Adj. For Education IIB2 | % Working Outside County of Residence IIC1 | Central City & Suburban Income Dist. IIC2 | Housing Segregation Index IIC3 | % Families With Income Above Poverty Level IIIA1 | % Occupied Housing With Plumbing IIIA2 | % Occupied Housing With 1.01 or More Persons Per Room IIIA3 | % Occupied Housing With Telephone IIIA4 |
|---|---|---|---|---|---|---|---|---|---|---|
| 199 MID | 1.96 | .46 | 2.43 | 5.50 | -.04 | .08 | 90.20 | 99.30 | 8.80 | 90.00 |
| 200 MOD | 2.19 | .62 | 1.15 | 8.50 | -.10 | .56 | 88.20 | 99.00 | 9.10 | 87.40 |
| 201 MON | 1.81 | .78 | 1.13 | 4.20 | 0.00 | .46 | 79.20 | 89.70 | 11.90 | 84.80 |
| 202 MUN | 1.39 | .48 | 1.34 | 9.40 | .06 | .87 | 92.70 | 96.90 | 7.10 | 88.80 |
| 203 MUS | 2.16 | .84 | 1.44 | 6.00 | .04 | 1.38 | 92.20 | 97.60 | 9.20 | 90.90 |
| 204 NAS | 4.99 | .63 | 2.05 | 13.60 | -.02 | .20 | 95.50 | 97.70 | 7.60 | 90.10 |
| 205 NEW | 1.92 | 1.21 | 1.14 | 7.90 | .10 | .13 | 89.90 | 96.30 | 5.60 | 90.60 |
| 206 NEW | 1.88 | .80 | 1.43 | 8.30 | 0.00 | .31 | 95.20 | 97.60 | 7.00 | 93.50 |
| 207 NOR | 1.53 | .95 | 1.78 | 14.20 | .24 | .37 | 95.60 | 98.10 | 5.30 | 95.50 |
| 208 ODE | 1.65 | .61 | 1.25 | 7.20 | -.02 | .18 | 90.10 | 99.20 | 11.80 | 85.60 |
| 209 OGD | 1.28 | .82 | 1.37 | 24.90 | 0.00 | .82 | 92.60 | 97.90 | 8.40 | 92.30 |
| 210 OWE | 1.52 | .59 | 1.26 | 10.70 | -.10 | .58 | 88.10 | 92.40 | 10.40 | 85.60 |
| 211 PET | 1.77 | .49 | 1.19 | 42.40 | -.04 | .23 | 88.30 | 89.60 | 10.30 | 80.50 |
| 212 PIN | 1.87 | .65 | 1.09 | 5.20 | -.10 | .02 | 77.00 | 83.40 | 12.50 | 77.20 |
| 213 PIT | 1.05 | .64 | 1.80 | 2.20 | 0.00 | .40 | 94.60 | 97.60 | 4.70 | 94.90 |
| 214 POR | 1.00• | .74 | 1.09 | 3.50 | .08 | 1.19 | 92.60 | 95.30 | 5.60 | 90.20 |
| 215 PRO | 1.00• | .96 | 1.88 | 10.10 | -.02 | .50 | 88.30 | 99.40 | 12.10 | 93.20 |
| 216 PUE | .64 | .88 | 1.14 | 3.70 | -.04 | .22 | 88.80 | 96.10 | 11.50 | 87.50 |
| 217 RAC | 2.70 | .61 | 1.50 | 16.80 | -.02 | .64 | 94.40 | 97.30 | 8.10 | 93.80 |
| 218 REN | 1.24 | .95 | 1.34 | 3.20 | -.04 | .66 | 94.10 | 96.70 | 6.30 | 84.60 |
| 219 ROA | 1.54 | .59 | 1.26 | 43.70 | .04 | .69 | 91.40 | 96.50 | 4.70 | 89.20 |
| 220 ROC | 1.00• | 1.10 | 1.38 | 3.90 | -.08 | .54 | 94.60 | 96.30 | 6.20 | 94.90 |
| 221 STJ | .92 | .67 | 1.14 | 6.30 | .02 | .19 | 90.50 | 94.50 | 7.40 | 90.30 |
| 222 SAL | 1.00• | .74 | 1.32 | 18.90 | .06 | 1.05 | 90.10 | 98.10 | 5.70 | 89.20 |
| 223 SAN | 2.04 | .58 | 1.08 | 2.60 | 0.00 | .11 | 85.40 | 96.80 | 9.40 | 81.30 |
| 224 SAV | 2.11 | .52 | .96 | 2.50 | .08 | .34 | 83.10 | 93.70 | 9.60 | 83.40 |
| 225 SHE | 1.74 | .61 | 1.50 | 6.30 | -.08 | .32 | 87.90 | 95.60 | 6.80 | 83.90 |
| 226 SIO | 1.77 | .55 | .97 | 10.80 | -.08 | .35 | 90.80 | 95.90 | 7.30 | 91.90 |
| 227 SIO | 2.70 | .71 | 1.11 | 2.80 | -.08 | .33 | 91.80 | 96.10 | 7.10 | 93.10 |
| 228 SPR | 2.02 | 1.27 | 1.48 | 6.10 | -.02 | .53 | 93.30 | 96.30 | 7.00 | 91.50 |
| 229 SPR | .84 | .62 | 1.15 | 3.50 | -.06 | .27 | 89.70 | 95.80 | 6.20 | 89.60 |
| 230 SPR | 1.49 | .57 | 1.42 | 23.50 | .06 | .90 | 92.70 | 96.20 | 6.30 | 91.70 |
| 231 STE | 2.00 | .71 | 1.27 | 28.50 | -.08 | 1.04 | 92.10 | 94.60 | 7.70 | 90.70 |
| 232 TAL | 2.41 | .70 | 1.50 | 4.10 | -.02 | 1.02 | 86.30 | 91.20 | 7.70 | 82.20 |
| 233 TER | 2.26 | .87 | 1.18 | 16.90 | 0.00 | 1.08 | 90.50 | 88.90 | 6.80 | 87.20 |
| 234 TEX | 2.12 | .50 | 1.15 | 21.00 | -.04 | .15 | 84.00 | 89.20 | 9.50 | 78.90 |
| 235 TOP | 1.66 | .86 | 1.30 | 2.40 | -.04 | .13 | 93.10 | 97.70 | 5.50 | 92.50 |
| 236 TUS | 1.94 | .72 | 1.19 | 5.20 | -.08 | .07 | 80.10 | 88.50 | 9.00 | 82.50 |
| 237 TYL | 1.27 | .34 | 1.37 | 6.80 | -.16 | .13 | 87.10 | 91.40 | 8.90 | 83.10 |
| 238 VIN | 2.11 | .49 | 1.05 | 12.20 | -.04 | .20 | 90.80 | 95.50 | 7.60 | 89.50 |
| 239 WAC | 1.89 | .80 | 1.11 | 3.80 | .02 | .29 | 85.20 | 96.40 | 7.70 | 85.30 |
| 240 WAT | 2.28 | .82 | 1.20 | 3.20 | -.04 | .52 | 92.70 | 96.60 | 7.70 | 94.40 |
| 241 WHE | 1.99 | .87 | 1.16 | 29.30 | -.06 | .90 | 89.80 | 92.60 | 6.50 | 88.70 |
| 242 WIC | 1.84 | .59 | 1.24 | 3.30 | -.04 | .31 | 89.10 | 98.20 | 7.00 | 88.10 |
| 243 WIL | 1.76 | .51 | 3.16 | 11.10 | 0.00 | .43 | 83.80 | 92.50 | •8.10 | 80.20 |

279

TABLE C-5 (Continued)

| | % Workers Who Use Public Transport To Work IIIA5 | Total Crime Rate/ 100,000 pop. IIIA6 | Cost of Living Index IIIA7 | Public Swimming Pools/ 100,000 pop. IIIB1a | Public Camping Sites/ 100,000 pop. IIIB1b | Public Tennis Courts/ 100,000 pop. IIIB1c | Miles of Trails/ 1,000 pop. IIIB1d | Retail Trade Establishments/ 1,000 pop. IIIB3 | Selected Service Establishments/ 1,000 pop. IIIB4 | Hospital Beds/ 100,000 pop. IIIB5 |
|---|---|---|---|---|---|---|---|---|---|---|
| US | 8.90 | 2829.50 | 100.00 | N.A. | N.A. | N.A. | N.A. | 8.68 | 5.85 | 414.90 |
| 149 ABI | 1.20 | 1421.30 | 89.50 | 17.50 | 1289.40 | 149.10 | 5.30 | 11.61 | 8.58 | 563.60 |
| 150 ALB | 2.60 | 2469.90• | 103.70 | 44.40 | 455.50 | 66.60 | 55.50 | 8.42 | 5.18 | 433.30 |
| 151 ALT | 4.20 | 1093.20 | 96.80• | 7.40 | 7.60 | 6.10 | 237.00 | 9.27 | 5.44 | 691.20 |
| 152 AMA | 1.40 | 2972.90 | 91.20 | 27.70 | 2541.60 | 326.30 | 48.60 | 12.37 | 10.07 | 555.90 |
| 153 AND | 1.00 | 1567.90 | 86.60 | 21.70 | 144.90 | 65.20 | 13.70 | 8.12 | 6.09 | 442.60 |
| 154 ASH | 4.50 | 1892.20 | 93.20 | 27.50 | 1055.10 | 48.20 | 120.00 | 8.90 | 5.97 | 804.70 |
| 155 ATL | 10.00 | 4372.50 | 120.60• | 5.80 | 297.10 | 57.10 | 8.50 | 13.89 | 8.94 | 350.00 |
| 156 BAY | .90 | 2258.10 | 93.70• | 5.80 | 2435.80 | 59.80 | | 8.07 | 4.55 | 573.70 |
| 157 BIL | 1.00 | 1926.70• | 98.10 | 34.40 | 7.60 | 241.30 | 5.30 | 9.24 | 6.05 | 495.10 |
| 158 BIL | 2.80 | 1502.00 | 100.30• | 5.80 | 162.90 | 6.10 | 22.20 | 9.45 | 6.10 | 1324.30 |
| 159 BLO | 1.80 | 1799.70 | 107.10• | 28.80 | 1365.30 | 115.30 | 182.60 | 8.42 | 6.55 | 582.60 |
| 160 BOI | .60 | 2703.70 | 101.10 | 35.70 | 89.20 | 195.40 | 26.70 | 9.85 | 7.79 | 493.10 |
| 161 BRI | .90 | 2253.50• | 116.00• | 166.60 | 3515.10 | 772.70 | 484.80 | 7.11 | 5.35• | 466.70 |
| 162 BRO | 3.30 | 3391.40 | 121.50• | 10.50 | 436.80 | 63.70 | 226.30 | 7.79 | 4.79 | 238.80 |
| 163 BRO | 2.80 | 2655.60• | 89.10• | 28.50 | 7742.80 | 42.80 | 292.60 | 9.79 | 4.78 | 252.10 |
| 164 BRY | .90 | 1401.50 | 88.80• | 51.70 | 1982.70 | 120.60 | 17.20 | 9.02 | 6.48• | 200.00 |
| 165 CED | 2.50 | 2376.40 | 107.60 | 5.80 | 1153.30 | 6.10 | 36.80 | 7.73 | 5.76 | 583.60 |
| 166 CHA | 3.30 | 2954.20• | 111.70• | 30.60 | 7.60 | 233.10 | 5.30 | 6.29 | 6.42 | 486.60 |
| 167 COL | 2.00 | | 99.10 | 24.60 | 12.30 | 74.00 | 111.10 | 7.41 | 5.42 | 970.70 |
| 168 DAN | 2.20 | | 119.10 | 25.30 | 50.60 | 430.30 | 126.50 | 8.34 | 5.35• | 323.40• |
| 169 DEC | 2.50 | 1811.80 | 102.50• | 16.00 | 1352.00 | 256.00 | 328.00 | 7.74 | 6.47 | 678.10 |
| 170 DUB | 4.50 | 1461.30• | 100.00 | 21.90 | 7.60 | 197.80 | 175.80 | 8.74 | 4.99 | 613.30 |
| 171 DUR | 5.70 | 2605.50 | 95.60 | 31.50• | 578.90 | 115.70 | 142.10 | 7.38 | 4.63 | 1116.10 |
| 172 FAL | 3.50 | 3512.60 | 109.90• | 15.30• | 373.50• | 86.10• | 261.90• | 8.81 | 5.29 | 388.90• |
| 173 FAR | 1.10 | 1781.50 | 110.00 | 41.60 | 891.60 | 158.30 | 125.00 | 9.05 | 5.78 | 842.20 |
| 174 FIT | 3.60 | 3618.60• | 106.30• | 92.70 | 7.60 | 855.60 | 1072.10 | 8.68 | 5.25 | 515.40• |
| 175 FOR | 1.00 | 1069.80 | 95.00 | 31.20 | 1975.00 | 87.50 | 187.50 | 10.69 | 6.84 | 532.70 |
| 176 GAD | 1.70 | 1842.20• | 94.00 | 36.60• | 791.80• | 117.60• | 237.50• | 10.07 | 5.51 | 392.50 |
| 177 GAI | 1.90 | 4392.30 | 102.30 | 19.00 | 7.60 | 28.50 | 57.10 | 8.20 | 4.80 | 961.40 |
| 178 GAL | 4.70 | 3113.60 | 87.90• | 29.40 | 500.00 | 76.40 | 5.80 | 9.39 | 5.75 | 1102.40 |
| 179 GRE | .50 | 1926.70• | 117.10 | 48.70 | 426.80 | 85.30 | 1512.10 | 8.13 | 5.09 | 766.70 |
| 180 GRE | 3.00 | 1262.10 | 97.20 | 31.60 | 7.60 | 215.10 | 322.70 | 8.75 | 4.17 | 572.90 |
| 181 JAC | 1.40 | 3135.30 | 95.50• | 5.80 | 3000.00 | 104.80 | 559.40 | 7.16 | 5.23 | 372.10 |
| 182 KEN | 1.90 | 3424.30 | 95.50• | 5.80 | 423.70 | 6.10 | 127.10 | 8.54 | 3.95 | 465.20 |
| 183 LAC | 4.00 | 2439.80 | 94.40 | 5.80 | 5625.00 | 87.50 | 62.50 | 10.56 | 5.84 | 461.50 |
| 184 LAF | 3.00 | 1482.00 | 97.70 | 18.10 | 9.00 | 154.50 | 9.00 | 9.39 | 6.37 | 601.90 |
| 185 LAF | 1.60 | 2239.10 | 100.60• | 36.60 | 7.60 | 110.00 | 36.60 | 6.24 | 5.30 | 574.80 |
| 186 LAK | 2.40 | 2655.60• | 95.90 | 55.10 | 7.60 | 68.90 | 5.30 | 8.75 | 5.33 | 523.00 |
| 187 LAR | 8.00 | 2835.50 | 89.50 | 13.60 | 616.40 | 27.30 | 5.30 | 8.93 | 3.63 | 320.50 |
| 188 LAW | 18.60 | | 98.80• | 27.70 | 37.00 | 111.10 | 27.70 | 7.97 | 5.15 | 513.60 |
| 189 LEW | 4.30 | 1518.10• | 107.10• | 5.80 | 13.60 | 123.20 | 41.00 | 9.95 | 6.81 | 557.30 |
| 190 LEX | 5.70 | 3531.50 | 98.70 | 51.70 | 7.60 | 172.40 | 5.30 | 7.61 | 5.92 | 671.20 |
| 191 LIM | 1.10 | 1950.20 | 99.80• | 17.50 | 7.60 | 99.40 | 5.80 | 9.22 | 6.42 | 505.00 |
| 192 LIN | 3.70 | 2136.50 | 96.20 | 5.40• | 3720.20 | 6.10 | 5.30 | 7.54 | 6.08 | 640.20 |
| 193 LUB | .90 | 3352.50 | 95.60 | 33.50 | 754.10 | 162.00 | 33.50 | 10.37 | 7.49 | 398.00 |
| 194 LYN | 5.80 | 1357.50 | 89.60• | 16.20 | 967.40 | 699.10 | 46.90 | 7.78 | 5.23 | 399.20 |
| 195 MAN | 5.90 | 1443.20• | 105.80• | 74.00 | 7.60 | 185.10 | 111.10 | 9.20 | 7.03 | 517.40• |
| 196 MAN | 2.60 | 1829.90 | 100.80• | 15.30 | 7.60 | 169.20 | 23.00 | 8.28 | 6.02 | 567.60 |
| 197 MCA | 1.20 | 1253.60 | 88.70• | 27.40 | 2148.30 | 76.90 | 186.80 | 9.38 | 4.70 | 210.60 |
| 198 MER | 3.10 | 2841.30• | 114.50• | 35.70 | 2446.40 | 375.00 | 464.20 | 8.61 | 4.91 | 477.50• |

| | % Workers Who Use Public Transport To Work IIIA5 | Total Crime Rate/ 100,000 pop. IIIA6 | Cost of Living Index IIIA7 | Public Swimming Pools/ 100,000 pop. IIIB1a | Public Camping Sites/ 100,000 pop. IIIB1b | Public Tennis Courts/ 100,000 pop. IIIB1c | Miles of Trails/ 1,000 pop. IIIB1d | Retail Trade Establishments/ 1,000 pop. IIIB3 | Selected Service Establishments/ 1,000 pop. IIIB4 | Hospital Beds/ 100,000 pop. IIIB5 |
|---|---|---|---|---|---|---|---|---|---|---|
| 199 MID | 1.10 | 2655.60• | 88.20• | 61.50 | 1015.30 | 184.60 | 5.30 | 10.06 | 9.75 | 361.20 |
| 200 MOD | .30 | 3905.00 | 95.10 | 10.20 | 1153.80 | 10.20 | 25.60 | 9.77 | 5.79 | 534.90 |
| 201 MON | 3.90 | 1455.70 | 91.40 | 26.00 | 60.80 | 86.90 | 34.70 | 9.77 | 5.30 | 555.60 |
| 202 MUN | 1.50 | 2367.90 | 86.90 | 20.00• | 1463.60• | 116.90• | 170.80• | 7.64 | 5.93 | 431.10 |
| 203 MUS | 1.20 | 3094.90 | 91.40 | 6.30 | 8299.30 | 229.20 | 191.00 | 7.13 | 4.78 | 420.10 |
| 204 NAS | 2.20 | 1443.20 | 112.90 | 14.90 | 7.60 | 119.40 | 134.30 | 6.90• | 7.16• | 393.50• |
| 205 NEW | 4.80 | 3612.60 | 111.60 | 19.60 | 542.40 | 58.80 | 281.00 | 9.57 | 5.92 | 383.90 |
| 206 NEW | 4.70 | 2253.50 | 122.80 | 68.90 | 13.70 | 317.10 | 82.70 | 8.00 | 4.76 | 466.70 |
| 207 NOR | 10.30 | 2955.60 | 128.40 | 16.50 | 33.30 | 283.30 | 83.30 | 9.46 | 7.57 | 323.40 |
| 208 ODE | .50 | 2655.60 | 83.90 | 54.30 | 347.80 | 206.50 | 119.50 | 11.59 | 9.46 | 393.20 |
| 209 OGD | 1.70 | 2512.60 | 96.80 | 23.80 | 3539.60 | 47.60 | 436.50 | 7.01 | 5.40 | 533.30 |
| 210 OWE | .80 | 1766.70 | 95.30 | 25.30 | 7.60 | 151.80 | 25.30 | 8.91 | 6.05 | 789.70 |
| 211 PET | 4.30 | 1475.90 | 95.70 | 15.50 | 1317.80 | 217.00 | 410.80 | 6.65 | 4.30• | 621.30 |
| 212 PIN | 3.40 | 1606.80 | 91.80 | 23.50 | 352.90 | 35.20 | 5.30 | 9.46 | 4.89 | 425.80 |
| 213 PIT | 3.20 | 1905.90 | 116.90 | 62.50 | 5537.50 | 62.50 | 2425.00 | 8.83 | 6.19 | 508.80• |
| 214 POR | 6.50 | 2455.90 | 114.30 | 7.00 | 2422.50 | 133.80 | 98.50 | 8.87 | 6.48• | 504.60• |
| 215 PRO | .70 | 1442.80 | 96.10 | 21.70 | 5094.20 | 217.30 | 4485.50 | 6.26 | 4.28 | 358.30 |
| 216 PUE | 2.20 | 3613.60 | 88.50 | 33.80 | 7.60 | 101.60 | 186.40 | 8.55 | 5.51 | 621.70 |
| 217 RAC | 3.80 | 2451.10 | 96.50 | 5.80 | 7.60 | 29.20 | 105.20 | 8.15 | 4.39 | 358.40 |
| 218 REN | 1.70 | 4665.80 | 102.90 | 41.30 | 1057.80 | 297.50 | 603.30 | 8.48 | 8.27 | 750.00 |
| 219 ROA | 6.60 | 2619.80 | 91.30 | 22.00 | 560.10 | 187.80 | 71.80 | 7.56 | 5.88 | 633.70 |
| 220 ROC | 2.50 | 3819.50 | 118.60 | 23.80 | 440.40 | 404.10 | 547.60 | 7.56 | 5.21 | 2102.70 |
| 221 STJ | 5.10 | 2654.20 | 93.20 | 5.80 | 344.80 | 6.10 | 5.30 | 10.76 | 7.41 | 761.60 |
| 222 SAL | 1.30 | 2439.50 | 84.90 | 37.40 | 5219.20 | 90.90 | 1352.90 | 8.48 | 5.33 | 240.00 |
| 223 SAN | 1.30 | 2655.60 | 83.90 | 42.20 | 4563.30 | 295.70 | 1126.70 | 10.87 | 8.99 | 476.00 |
| 224 SAV | 9.30 | 4561.90 | 100.30 | 15.90 | 106.30 | 58.50 | 132.50 | 8.16 | 5.12 | 593.70 |
| 225 SHE | 1.00 | 2655.60 | 85.30 | 60.20 | 2867.40 | 132.50 | 534.40 | 10.27 | 6.75 | 690.40 |
| 226 SIO | 3.40 | 2286.40 | 102.00 | 60.30 | 1862.00 | 181.00 | 5.30 | 9.99 | 7.07 | 730.80 |
| 227 SIO | 2.60 | 1278.80• | 105.20 | 5.80 | 7.60 | 6.10 | 304.30 | 9.91 | 7.47 | 927.40 |
| 228 SPR | 4.00 | 2492.60 | 103.20 | 12.40 | 534.10 | 118.00 | | 9.24 | 8.07 | 782.10 |
| 229 SPR | 2.80 | 2942.90 | 87.30 | 39.20 | 7.60 | 39.20 | 183.00 | 10.54 | 7.75 | 792.50 |
| 230 SPR | 1.70 | 1915.90 | 99.50 | 5.80 | 7.60 | 12.80 | 6.40 | 6.77 | 4.53 | 416.40 |
| 231 STE | 6.80 | 2361.10• | 102.70 | 42.10 | 584.30 | 48.10 | 120.40 | 8.88 | 5.16 | 315.30 |
| 232 TAL | 2.80 | 3148.50 | 102.30 | 9.70 | 1097.00 | 80.00 | 436.80 | 6.93 | 5.51 | 370.60 |
| 233 TER | 2.10 | 1873.10 | 85.70 | 22.80 | 4120.00 | 49.50 | 428.50 | 9.74 | 6.33 | 484.40 |
| 234 TEX | 1.70 | 2265.60 | 81.30 | 19.80 | 3712.80 | 219.30 | 5.30 | 10.68 | 6.54 | 364.50 |
| 235 TOP | 3.30 | 2805.10 | 93.50 | 38.70 | 645.10 | 6.10 | 19.30 | 8.83 | 5.54 | 522.60 |
| 236 TUS | 1.40 | 1828.60 | 101.90 | 17.20 | 1775.80 | 92.70 | 103.40 | 7.27 | 3.84 | 367.20 |
| 237 TYL | .90 | 2043.30 | 82.70 | 20.60 | 3587.60 | 214.40 | 587.60 | 10.78 | 6.94 | 499.00 |
| 238 VIN | 1.90 | 2473.00 | 122.10 | 91.30 | 7.60 | | 99.10 | 10.42 | 5.94 | 384.90 |
| 239 WAC | 2.20 | 3232.00 | 87.60 | 6.80 | 1360.50 | 6.10 | 5.30 | 11.74 | 7.07 | 360.90 |
| 240 WAT | 2.20 | 1790.60 | 103.50 | 7.50 | 3857.10 | 308.00 | 285.70 | 8.41 | 5.69 | 734.50 |
| 241 WHE | 7.60 | 1069.50 | 95.50 | 21.80 | 409.80 | 49.10 | 103.80 | 9.44 | 5.60 | 675.30 |
| 242 WIC | 1.80 | 1760.20 | 89.90 | 12.60 | 1277.70 | 468.20 | 293.60 | 10.75 | 8.63 | 606.30 |
| 243 WIL | 3.30 | 3038.80 | 103.70 | 5.80 | 355.10 | 6.10 | 1046.70 | 10.73 | 6.26 | 499.00 |

TABLE C-5 (Continued)

| | Vols. of Books in Main Public Library/ 1,000 pop. IIIB6 | Death Rate/ 1,000 pop. IIIC1 | Birth Rate/ 1,000 pop. IIIC2 | Sports Events IIIC3 | Dance Drama and Music Events IIIC4a | Cultural Institutions IIIC4b | Fairs and Festivals Held IIIC4c |
|---|---|---|---|---|---|---|---|
| US US | 1568.40 | 9.50 | 17.50 | N.A. | N.A. | N.A. | N.A. |
| 149 ABI | 916.60 | 9.10 | 17.70 | 3.00 | 17.00 | 4.00 | 5.00 |
| 150 ALB | 1022.20 | 7.20 | 20.80 | 0.00 | 0.00 | 0.00 | 0.00 |
| 151 ALT | 444.40 | 12.60 | 15.70 | 0.00 | 0.00 | 0.00 | 0.00 |
| 152 AMA | 1289.30 | 8.10 | 18.60 | 6.00 | 22.00 | 3.00 | 9.00 |
| 153 AND | 808.40 | 8.80 | 17.90 | 3.00 | 21.00 | 1.00 | 5.00 |
| 154 ASH | 932.30 | 10.00 | 16.90 | 7.00 | 27.00 | 1.00 | 12.00 |
| 155 ATL | 383.10 | 14.70 | 16.10 | 3.00 | 43.00 | 0.00 | 1.00 |
| 156 HAY | 820.50 | 9.20 | 19.70 | 3.00 | 10.00 | 4.00 | 1.00 |
| 157 BIL | 1781.60 | 8.10 | 16.80 | 5.00 | 22.00 | 7.00 | 3.00 |
| 158 BIL | 169.10 | 9.10 | 23.20 | 0.00 | 23.00 | 2.00 | 4.00 |
| 159 BLO | 891.00 | 9.40 | 15.90 | 0.00 | 0.00 | 0.00 | 0.00 |
| 160 BOI | 1131.40 | 8.20 | 16.60 | 3.00 | 10.00 | 2.00 | 2.00 |
| 161 BRI | 1992.50 | 8.50 | 16.60 | 2.00 | 5.00 | 1.00 | 1.00 |
| 162 BRO | 1004.00 | 9.20 | 18.30 | 5.00 | 5.00 | 2.00 | 6.00 |
| 163 BRO | 376.20 | 7.30 | 31.90 | 0.00 | 0.00 | 0.00 | 0.00 |
| 164 BRY | 1034.50 | 6.90 | 20.10 | 0.00 | 0.00 | 0.00 | 0.00 |
| 165 CED | 1124.40 | 8.50 | 21.30 | 9.00 | 30.00 | 3.00 | 7.00 |
| 166 CHA | 564.00 | 6.10 | 17.70 | 5.00 | 62.00 | 6.00 | 4.00 |
| 167 COL | 1411.60 | 7.00 | 17.10 | 4.00 | 22.00 | 11.00 | 1.00 |
| 168 DAN | 766.50 | 8.70 | 15.90 | 4.00 | 38.00 | 2.00 | 6.00 |
| 169 DEC | 1518.50 | 9.30 | 16.70 | 7.00 | 13.00 | 3.00 | 7.00 |
| 170 DUB | 1285.70 | 9.00 | 19.90 | 3.00 | 23.00 | 0.00 | 3.00 |
| 171 DUB | 871.70 | 8.00 | 18.20 | 4.00 | 18.00 | 2.00 | 3.00 |
| 172 FAL | 1387.30 | 10.80 | 16.40 | 3.00 | 5.00 | 2.00 | 6.00 |
| 173 FAR | 736.20 | 7.10 | 16.80 | 5.00 | 15.00 | 3.00 | 0.00 |
| 174 FIT | 1420.20 | 10.30 | 15.80 | 0.00 | 0.00 | 0.00 | 6.00 |
| 175 FOR | 324.90 | 10.50 | 17.20 | 3.00 | 66.00 | 5.00 | 12.00 |
| 176 GAD | 1053.70 | 10.40 | 17.90 | 1.00 | 38.00 | 1.00 | 4.00 |
| 177 GAI | 723.10 | 7.20 | 19.30 | 4.00 | 38.00 | 2.00 | 2.00 |
| 178 GAL | 847.30 | 8.60 | 16.50 | 0.00 | 0.00 | 0.00 | 0.00 |
| 179 GRE | 1819.00 | 8.10 | 20.30 | 5.00 | 70.00 | 2.00 | 7.00 |
| 180 GRE | 1806.80 | 7.30 | 18.80 | 11.00 | 14.00 | 2.00 | 5.00 |
| 181 JAC | 780.10 | 9.40 | 17.50 | 3.00 | 7.00 | 2.00 | 6.00 |
| 182 KEN | 1639.80 | 8.10 | 16.90 | 0.00 | 0.00 | 0.00 | 0.00 |
| 183 LAC | 1612.90 | 8.70 | 17.00 | 4.00 | 36.00 | 0.00 | 12.00 |
| 184 LAF | 921.50 | 6.30 | 20.50 | 3.00 | 27.00 | 4.00 | 5.00 |
| 185 LAF | 847.50 | 6.50 | 18.90 | 9.00 | 84.00 | 2.00 | 1.00 |
| 186 LAK | 642.10 | 7.80 | 20.40 | 5.00 | 60.00 | 5.00 | 10.00 |
| 187 LAK | 305.40 | 7.20 | 42.10 | 3.00 | 22.00 | 1.00 | 9.00 |
| 188 LAW | 470.40 | 5.50 | 24.10 | 3.00 | 41.00 | 5.00 | 2.00 |
| 189 LEW | 1301.40 | 11.00 | 17.10 | 7.00 | 27.00 | 2.00 | 4.00 |
| 190 LEX | 577.50 | 7.80 | 19.20 | 5.30 | 30.00 | 0.00 | 3.00 |
| 191 LIM | 1133.30 | 10.20 | 18.70 | 0.00 | 7.00 | 0.00 | 0.00 |
| 192 LIN | 2088.10 | 7.80 | 17.50 | 3.00 | 31.00 | 5.00 | 10.00 |
| 193 LOR | 761.70 | 6.50 | 21.50 | 3.00 | 41.00 | 3.00 | 2.00 |
| 194 LYN | 297.50 | 9.90 | 17.10 | 0.00 | 0.00 | 0.00 | 5.00 |
| 195 MAN | 1805.30 | 10.30 | 18.90 | 7.00 | 25.00 | 5.00 | 5.00 |
| 196 MAN | 1461.10 | 9.20 | 17.80 | 0.00 | 0.00 | 1.00 | 7.00 |
| 197 MCA | 227.40 | 6.60 | 30.10 | 2.00 | 24.00 | 3.00 | 7.00 |
| 198 MER | 2041.00 | 9.40 | 16.80 | 0.00 | 5.08 | 1.06 | 0.00 |

| | Vols. of Main Public Library, 1,000 pop. IIIB6 | Death Rate 1,000 pop. IIIC1 | Birth Rate 1,000 pop. IIIC2 | Sports Events IIIC3 | Dance Drama and Music Events IIIC4a | Cultural Institutions IIIC4b | Fairs and Festivals Held IIIC4c |
|---|---|---|---|---|---|---|---|
| 199 MID | 1411.40 | 5.70 | 16.80 | 0.00 | 12.00 | 3.00 | 0.00 |
| 200 MOD | 1152.00 | 9.60 | 18.90 | 5.00 | 4.00 | 2.00 | 1.00 |
| 201 MON | 1176.60 | 9.60 | 23.00 | 3.00 | 20.00 | 2.00 | 2.00 |
| 202 MUN | 1614.90 | 8.90 | 19.00 | 3.00 | 11.00 | 1.00 | 1.00 |
| 203 MUS | 697.90 | 8.50 | 18.50 | 0.00 | 0.00 | 0.00 | 0.00 |
| 204 NAS | 2076.30 | 10.30 | 17.30 | 0.00 | 0.00 | 0.00 | 0.00 |
| 205 NEW | 260.50 | 10.80 | 16.40 | 0.00 | 0.00 | 0.00 | 0.00 |
| 206 NEW | 1178.20 | 8.50 | 16.60 | 0.00 | 0.00 | 0.00 | 0.00 |
| 207 NOR | 455.70 | 8.70 | 15.90 | 4.00 | 20.00 | 2.00 | 0.00 |
| 208 ODE | 1195.70 | 6.00 | 18.10 | 2.00 | 27.00 | 12.00 | 15.00 |
| 209 OGD | 928.00 | 7.20 | 22.00 | 0.00 | 0.00 | 0.00 | 0.00 |
| 210 OWE | 746.60 | 9.10 | 18.80 | 2.00 | 14.00 | 3.00 | 9.00 |
| 211 PET | 436.30 | 8.20 | 19.10 | 6.00 | 9.00 | 2.00 | 3.00 |
| 212 PIN | 1112.90 | 10.60 | 18.50 | 3.00 | 24.00 | 2.00 | 2.00 |
| 213 PIT | 1638.60 | 10.90 | 14.50 | 2.00 | 30.00 | 6.00 | 0.00 |
| 214 POR | 1475.50 | 10.90 | 17.20 | 3.00 | 25.00 | 8.00 | 6.00 |
| 215 PRO | 466.30 | 5.50 | 24.80 | 4.00 | 25.00 | 6.00 | 3.00 |
| 216 PUE | 932.40 | 9.20 | 17.30 | 5.00 | 39.00 | 5.00 | 6.00 |
| 217 RAC | 1325.40 | 8.30 | 18.40 | 5.00 | 22.00 | 2.00 | 5.00 |
| 218 REN | 1542.50 | 8.70 | 16.60 | 7.00 | 20.00 | 7.00 | 10.00 |
| 219 ROA | 1147.50 | 9.20 | 16.40 | 6.00 | 69.00 | 2.00 | 6.00 |
| 220 ROC | 1393.70 | 6.80 | 20.60 | 3.00 | 17.00 | 3.00 | 3.00 |
| 221 STJ | 1883.80 | 14.00 | 15.30 | 3.00 | 7.00 | 4.00 | 1.00 |
| 222 SAL | 555.40 | 9.40 | 15.30 | 0.00 | 0.00 | 0.00 | 0.00 |
| 223 SAN | 1298.70 | 9.80 | 18.30 | 2.00 | 13.00 | 3.00 | 5.00 |
| 224 SAV | 1525.60 | 11.00 | 19.80 | 4.00 | 17.00 | 4.00 | 13.00 |
| 225 SHE | 362.90 | 11.90 | 16.00 | 3.00 | 15.00 | 0.00 | 2.00 |
| 226 SIO | 1535.30 | 10.70 | 18.20 | 5.00 | 40.00 | 4.00 | 4.00 |
| 227 SIO | 1111.50 | 8.40 | 17.80 | 5.00 | 23.00 | 3.00 | 4.00 |
| 228 SPR | 1478.90 | 11.00 | 16.70 | 5.00 | 14.00 | 4.00 | 12.00 |
| 229 SPR | 1359.30 | 10.30 | 16.40 | 5.00 | 18.00 | 1.00 | 5.00 |
| 230 SPR | 2819.60 | 9.50 | 16.60 | 0.00 | 8.00 | 0.00 | 3.00 |
| 231 STE | 808.70 | 10.50 | 15.60 | 4.00 | 14.00 | 5.00 | 4.00 |
| 232 TAL | 1868.70 | 6.80 | 16.90 | 3.00 | 10.00 | 2.00 | 3.00 |
| 233 TER | 1164.50 | 13.40 | 15.30 | 3.00 | 12.00 | | 2.00 |
| 234 TEX | 37.00 | 10.60 | 18.80 | 0.00 | 52.00 | 9.00 | 10.00 |
| 235 TOP | 1422.20 | 8.80 | 17.80 | 6.00 | 0.00 | 0.00 | 0.00 |
| 236 TUS | 703.10 | 8.30 | 17.50 | 0.00 | 18.00 | 2.00 | 9.00 |
| 237 TYL | 601.50 | 9.30 | 17.30 | 3.00 | 20.00 | 1.00 | 6.00 |
| 238 VIN | 341.00 | 10.40 | 19.00 | 4.00 | | | |
| 239 WAC | 987.10 | 11.50 | 15.30 | 3.00 | 16.00 | 2.00 | 4.00 |
| 240 WAT | 1313.00 | 7.90 | 19.30 | 7.00 | 18.00 | 5.00 | 4.00 |
| 241 WHE | 557.00 | 12.50 | 15.30 | 5.00 | 56.00 | 1.00 | 15.00 |
| 242 WIC | 674.00 | 8.70 | 16.80 | 3.00 | 43.00 | 3.00 | 5.00 |
| 243 WIL | 960.50 | 10.30 | 17.70 | 3.00 | 11.00 | 9.00 | 5.00 |

CHART 1

DATA SOURCES - ECONOMIC COMPONENT

| Factor | Sources | Year |
|--------|---------|------|
| IA | COP, T. 89 and COP, US, T. 105 | 1969 |
| IB1 | C&C, Item 120 | 1970 |
| IB2 | U.S. Department of Commerce, Survey of Current Business, May 1974, Part II, Tables 1 and 2 | 1972 |
| IB3 | C&C, Item 87 | 1970 |
| IB4 | C&C, Item 101 | 1970 |
| IB5 | C&C, Item 88 | 1970 |
| IIA | COP, US, Tables 141 and 184 | 1969 |
| IIB | C&C, Items 39 and 41 | 1970 |
| IIC1 | C&C, Item 129 | 1967 |
| IIC2 | COP, T. 87; SA, 1971, T. 1098; U.S. Department of Commerce, Construction Reports - Housing Authorized by Building Permits and Public Contracts, 1970 | 1970 |
| IIC3 | C&C, Items 135 and 148 | 1967 |
| IIC4 | C&C, Items 160 and 162 | 1967 |
| IIC5 | C&C, Items 151 and 158 | 1967 |
| IID | C&C, Item 118 | 1970 |
| IIE1 | COP, Tables 81 and 89 and COP, US, Tables 107 and 116 | 1969 |
| IIE2 | COP, US, Tables 141 and 184 | 1969 |
| IIF | C&C, Item 37 | 1970 |
| IIG | MRI Questionnaire | 1970 |

CHART 2

DATA SOURCES - POLITICAL COMPONENT

| Factor | Sources | Year |
|--------|---------|------|
| IA1 | Ayer Directory of Newspapers and Periodicals | 1971 |
| IA2 | U.S. Department of Commerce, Census of Housing, Housing Characteristics for States, Cities, and Counties, Table 41 | 1970 |
| IA3 | The Working Press of the Nation, Vol III, 1974 Edition and SA, 1972, T. 801 | 1974 |
| IB | C&C, Item 102; SA, 1973, Section 33; COP, T. 24 | 1968 and 1972 |
| IIA1 | COG, Vol 5, Tables 5 and 8; COG, State Parts, T. 13 | 1967 |
| IIA2 | Same as IIA1 | |
| IIA3 | International City Management Association, Municipal Yearbook (Washington, D.C., 1971), Tables C 4/6 and C 4/11 | 1971 |
| IIA4 | International City Management Association, Municipal Yearbook (Washington, D.C., 1971), Tables C 4/7 and C 4/12 | 1971 |
| IIA5 | International City Management Association, Municipal Yearbook (Washington, D.C., 1971), Tables E 1/2 and E 1/7 | 1971 |
| IIA6 | Same as IIA5 | 1971 |
| IIA7 | Same as IIA5 | 1971 |
| IIA8 | U.S. Department of Labor, Manpower Report of the President, 1972, Tables D6 and D10 | 1970 |
| IIB1 | U.S. Federal Bureau of Investigation, Uniform Crime Reports for the United States, 1972 | 1972 |
| IIB2 | Same as IIB1 | 1972 |
| IIB3 | COG, Vol 5, Tables 9 and 12; COG, State Parts, T.18; SA, 1971, T.12 | 1967 |
| IIB4 | Same as IIB3 | 1967 |
| IIC1 | Same as IIB3 | 1967 |
| IIC2 | C&C, Item 70 | 1971 |
| IIC3 | C&C, Item 76 | 1972 |

CHART 3

DATA SOURCES - ENVIRONMENTAL COMPONENT

| Factor | Sources | Year |
|--------|---------|------|
| IA1 | Air Quality Data - 1972 Annual Statistics | 1972 |
| IA2 | Same as IA1 | 1970 |
| | | |
| IB1 | Same as IA1, Figure D-1 | 1973 |
| IB2 | U.S. Department of Commerce, Census of Housing, Plumbing Facilities and Estimates of Dilapidated Housing | 1970 |
| IB3 | Bureau of Outdoor Recreation, Public Outdoor Recreation Acres and Facilities Inventory | 1972 |
| | | |
| IC1 | COP, US, T.35 | 1970 |
| IC2 | U.S. Department of Transportation, Federal Highway Administration, Motor Vehicle Registration by Standard Metropolitan Statistical Areas-1971 and SA, 1972, Table 889 | 1971 |
| IC3 | Same as IC2 | 1971 |
| | | |
| ID | Brian J., L. Berry, et.al; Land Use, Urban Form and Environmental Quality (The University of Chicago; Department of Geography Research Paper No. 155, 1974), page 268; COP, Table 87; C&C, Item 129 | 1970 |
| | | |
| IE | The Mitre Corporation, The PDI Index (Working Paper 7963) Table IV, September 1971 | 1971 |
| | | |
| IIA1 | See IB1 | 1973 |
| IIA2 | C&C, Item 493 | 1970 |
| IIA3 | U.S. Department of Commerce, Local Climatological Data | 1973 |
| IIA4 | Same as IIA3 | 1973 |
| IIA5 | Same as IIA3 | 1973 |
| | | |
| IIB1 | Same as IB3 | 1972 |
| IIB2 | Same as IB3 | 1972 |

CHART 4

DATA SOURCES - HEALTH AND EDUCATION COMPONENT

| Factor | Sources | Year |
|--------|---------|------|
| IA1 | U.S. Department of Health Education and Welfare, Vital Statistics of the U.S., 1968, Vol I, Tables 1-53 and 2-1 and Vol II, Part B, Tables 7-1 and 7-4 | 1968 |
| IA2 | C&C, Item 22 | 1969 |
| IB1 | COP, US, Tables 140 and 183 | 1970 |
| IB2 | Same as IB1 | 1970 |
| IB3 | COP, T.83 and COP, US, T.99 | 1970 |
| IB4 | Same as IB3 | 1970 |
| IIA1 | SA, 1972, Section 33 | 1970 |
| IIA2 | SA, 1972, Section 33 and Hospitals: A County and Metropolitan Area Data Book | 1969 and 1970 |
| IIA3 | Hospitals: A County and Metropolitan Area Data Book | 1969 |
| IIA4 | SA, 1972, Section 33 | 1971 |
| IIA5 | COG, Vol 5, Tables 9 and 12; COG, State Parts, T. 18; SA, 1971, T. 12 | 1967 |
| IIB1 | Same as IIA5 | 1967 |
| IIB2 | C&C, Item 27 | 1970 |

CHART 5

## DATA SOURCES - SOCIAL COMPONENT

| Factor | Sources | Year |
|--------|---------|------|
| IA1 | C&C, Item 34; COP, T. 24; COP, US, T. 96 | 1970 |
| IA2 | C&C, Item 37 | 1970 |
| IA3 | COP, T.89; COP, US, T. 105 | 1969 |
| IA4 | COP, US, T. 140 and 183 | 1970 |
| IA5 | Same as IA4 | 1970 |
| | | |
| IB1 | See Health and Education Component IIB1 | 1967 |
| IB2 | Same as IA4 | 1970 |
| IB3a | COP, T. 83 and COP, US, T. 99 | 1970 |
| IB3b | Same as IB3a | 1970 |
| | | |
| IC1a | See Environmental Component IC2 | 1971 |
| IC1b | See Environmental Component IC3 | 1971 |
| IC1c | C&C, Item 101 | 1970 |
| IC2a | See Political Component IA1 | 1971 |
| IC2b | See Political Component IA2 | 1970 |
| IC2c | See Political Component IA3 | 1974 |
| IC3a | COP, US, Table 35 | 1970 |
| IC3b | C&C, Items 12 and 14 | 1970 |
| | | |
| IIA1 | C&C, Items 51 and 68; COP, T. 91; COP, US, Tables 75, 119, 183 | 1969 |
| IIA2 | COP, Tables 86, 91, 93 and COP, US, Tables 75, 91, 119, 183 | 1970 |
| IIA3 | COP, Tables 83, 85, 91, 92 and COP, US, Tables 75, 101, 119, 120 | 1970 |
| IIA4 | Same as IIA3 | 1970 |
| | | |
| IIB1 | COP, Tables 83 and 85 and COP, US, Tables 75 and 101 | 1970 |
| IIB2 | COP, Tables 83 and 86 and COP, US, Tables 75 and 91 | 1970 |
| | | |
| IIC1 | C&C, Item 49 | 1970 |
| IIC2 | See Economic Component IIE1 | 1969 |
| IIC3 | COP, Tables 81 and 91 and COP, US, Tables 107 and 124 | 1970 |

| | | |
|---|---|---|
| IIIA1 | <u>COP</u>, <u>US</u>, Tables 141 and 184 | 1970 |
| IIIA2 | <u>C&C</u>, Item 96 | 1970 |
| IIIA3 | <u>C&C</u>, Item 91 | 1970 |
| IIIA4 | <u>C&C</u>, Item 100 | 1970 |
| IIIA5 | <u>C&C</u>, Item 48 | 1970 |
| IIIA6 | U.S. Federal Bureau of Investigation, <u>Uniform Crime Reports for the United States</u>, 1972 | 1972 |
| IIIA7 | American Chamber of Commerce Researchers Association, "Cost of Living Indicators" | 1970 |
| | | |
| IIIB1a-d | See Environmental IB3 | 1972 |
| IIIB2 | <u>SA</u>, 1972, Section 33 | 1972 |
| IIIB3 | <u>C&C</u>, Item 135 | 1967 |
| IIIB4 | <u>C&C</u>, Item 15 | 1967 |
| IIIB5 | See Health and Education Component IIA2 | 1969 and 1970 |
| IIIB6 | <u>American Library Directory</u>, 1970-1971 | 1970 |
| | | |
| IIIC1 | <u>C&C</u>, Item 22 | 1969 |
| IIIC2 | <u>C&C</u>, Item 21 | 1968 |
| IIIC3 | MRI Questionnaire | 1970 |
| IIIC4 | MRI Questionnaire | 1970 |

## Metropolitan Areas
## Chambers of Commerce Questionnaire

Name of Respondent _____ Title _____

Organization _____

Address _____

_____ Zip Code _____

Telephone No.  Area Code (   ) _____

1. Number of full-time employees on the staff of your Metropolitan Chamber of Commerce in 1970 _____

2. What is the dollar amount of the Chamber of Commerce budget in 1970  $ _____

3. Please check the appropriate columns for those cultural events which were held on a regular basis in the metropolitan area in 1970:

| Event | Professional | Semi-Professional | University or College | Touring Groups |
|---|---|---|---|---|
| **Dance** | | | | |
| Ballet | | | | |
| Modern | | | | |
| Folk/Ethnic | | | | |
| **Drama** | | | | |
| Plays | | | | |
| Stage Productions | | | | |
| Opera | | | | |
| **Music** | | | | |
| Symphonic/Philharmonic | | | | |
| Chamber Music Groups | | | | |
| Choirs | | | | |
| Country-Western-Bluegrass | | | | |
| Rock Concerts | | | | |
| Jazz | | | | |

Class of Event (check where applicable)

4.  Please indicate the number of the following cultural institutions located in the metropolitan area in 1970:

| Institutions | Number |
|---|---|
| Art Museums | _____ |
| Science Museums | _____ |
| History Museums | _____ |
| Natural Science Museums | _____ |

5.  Please indicate the size and scope of fairs and festivals held in the metropolitan area in 1970:

| Event | Local Importance | Regional Importance | National Importance |
|---|---|---|---|
| Fairs: (please list) | | | |
| _____ | | | |
| _____ | | | |
| Festivals: (please list) | | | |
| _____ | | | |
| _____ | | | |

6.  Please check the appropriate columns for those sports events which were played on a regular season basis in the metropolitan area in 1970:

| | Class of Team | | |
|---|---|---|---|
| Event | Major League | Minor League | College or University |
| a. Football | | | |
| b. Baseball | | | |
| c. Basketball | | | |
| d. Hockey | | | |
| e. Soccer | | | |

# REFERENCES

Addman, Irma and Cynthia T. Morris, "A Factor Analysis of the Inter-relationship Between Social and Political Variables and Per Capita Gross National Product," Quarterly Journal of Economics (November 1965).

Advisory Commission on Intergovernmental Relation, City Financial Emergencies (Washington, D.C.: U.S. Government Printing Office, 1973).

Allardt, Erik. "About Dimensions of Welfare: An Exploratory Analysis of a Comparative Scandinavian Survey" (Monography, Helsinki: University of Helsinki, 1973).

American Academy of Arts and Sciences, Daedalus (Fall 1973).

American Statistical Association, Proceedings of the Social Statistics Section, 1974.

Anderson, James, "Causal Models and Social Indicators: Toward the Development of Social Systems Models," American Sociological Review, Vol. 38, No. 3 (June 1973).

Arrow, Kenneth, "Limited Knowledge and Economic Analysis," American Economic Review (March 1974).

Ball, S. J. and M. Rokeach, "Value and Violence: A Test of the Sub-culture of Violence Thesis," American Sociological Review, Vol. 38, No. 6 (December 1973).

Barrett, Larry and Thomas Waddell, Cost of Air Pollution Damage: A Status Report (Research Triangle Park, North Carolina: National Environmental Research Center, 1973).

Bauer, Raymond (ed.), Social Indicators (Cambridge: MIT Press, 1966).

Bauer, Raymond, "Social Indicators and Sample Surveys," in <u>Public Opinion Quarterly,</u> Vol. 30, No. 3 (Fall 1966).

Becker, G., <u>The Economics of Discrimination</u> (Chicago: University of Chicago Press, 1957).

Becker, G., <u>Human Capital</u> (New York: Columbia University Press, 1964).

Bell, W. H. and D. W. Stevenson, "An Index of Economics Health for Ontario Counties and Districts," <u>Ontario Economic Review</u>, 2 (1964).

Berendt, John, "The Worst American State," <u>Lifestyle Magazine</u> (November 1972).

Bergmann, B., "The Effects on White Incomes of Discrimination in Employment," <u>Journal of Political Economy</u> (August 1967).

Berry, J. L. et al., <u>Land Use, Urban Form and Environmental Quality</u> (Chicago: The University of Chicago, Department of Geography Research Paper No. 155, 1974).

Borts, G. H. and J. L. Stein, <u>Economic Growth in a Free Market</u> (New York: Columbia University Press, 1964).

Bradburn, Norman, <u>The Structure of Psychological Well-Being</u> (Chicago: Aldine Publishing Company), 1969.

Brown, Lester R., <u>In the Human Interest</u> (New York: W. W. Norton and Company, 1974).

Bullard, J. L. and R. Stith, <u>Community Conditions in Charlotte 1970</u> (Charlotte, North Carolina: The Charlotte-Mecklenburg Community Relations Committee, 1974).

Campbell, A., "Measuring the Quality of Life," <u>Michigan Business Review</u>, 261 (January 1974).

Campbell, Angus and Philip Converse, <u>The Human Meaning of Social Change</u> (New York: Russell Sage Foundation, 1972).

Campbell, H. J., <u>The Pleasure Areas</u> (New York: Delacorte Press, 1973).

Cantril, A. H. and C. W. Roll, Jr., _Hopes and Fears of the American People_ (New York:  Universe Books, 1971).

Cantril, Hadley, _The Patterns of Human Concerns_ (New Brunswick:  Rutgers University Press, 1965).

Castle, E. N., "Economics and the Quality of Life," _American Journal of Agricultural Economics_ (December 1972).

Christakis, Alexander, "Limits of Systems Analysis of Economic and Social Development Planning," _Existics 200_ (July 1972).

Christian, David E., _Social Indicators, the OECD Experience_ (Paris:  OECD, June 1974).

Citizens Advisory Committee on Environmental Quality, _Annual Report to the President and to the Council on Environmental Quality 1972_ (Washington, D.C.:  Government Printing Office, 1972).

Citizens Conference on State Legislature, _State Legislatures:  An Evaluation of Their Effectiveness_ (New York:  Prager Publishers, 1971).

Coates, Joseph F., "Some Methods and Techniques for Comprehensive Impact Assessment," _Technological Forecasting and Social Changes_ 6 (1974).

Cohn, Wilbur, _Toward A Social Report_ (Washington, D.C.:  U.S. Government Printing Office, 1969).

Cole, R., _Errors in Provisional Estimates of Gross National Product_ (New York:  National Bureau of Economic Research, 1969).

Committee for Economic Development, _Building a National Health-Care System_ (New York:  Committee for Economic Development, April 1973).

Coughlin, R., "Attainment Along Goal Dimensions in 101 Metropolitan Areas," _Journal of the American Institute of Planners_, Vol. 39, No. 6 (November 1973).

Council of Municpal Performance, _City Crime_, Municipal Performance Report, 1:1 (May-June 1973).

Council of Municipal Performance, The Wealth of Cities, Municipal Performance Report, 1:3 (April 1974).

Crew, Robert E., "Dimensions of Public Policy: A Factor Analysis of State Expenditures," Social Science Quarterly (September 1969).

Crittenden, John, "Dimensions of Modernization in the American States," American Political Science Review, Vol. 61, No. 4 (1967).

Dalkey, N. C., Studies in the Quality of Life--Delphi and Decision Making (Lexington, Massachusetts: D.C. Heath Company, 1972).

Dalkey, Norman and Daniel Rourke, "The Delphi Procedure and Rating Quality of Life Factors," in Experimental Assessments of Delphi Procedures with Group Value Judgments (California: Rand Corporation, 1971).

Daniere, Andre and Jerry Mechling, "Direct Marginal Productivity of College Education in Relation to College Aptitude of Students and Production Costs of Institution," The Journal of Human Resources, Vol. 5, No. 1 (Winter 1970).

Denison, Edward, "Welfare Measurement and the GNP," in Survey of Current Business (January 1971).

Denison, Edward F., Why Growth Rates Differ (Washington, D.C.: The Brooking Institution, 1967).

Department of the Treasury of New Jersey, Seventh Annual Report (Trenton, 1974).

Ditton, Robert and Thomas Goodale (eds.), Environmental Impact Analysis: Philosophy and Methods (Madison, Wisconsin: University of Wisconsin, Sea Grant Publication, 1972).

Dorfman, Robert, Models for Water Quality Management (Cambridge: Howard University Press, 1973).

Dorfman, Robert and Henry Jacoby, "A Public Decision Model Applied to a Local Pollution Problem," Economics of the Environment, R. and N. Dorfman (eds.) (New York: W. W. Norton and Company, 1972).

Easterlin, R. A., "Does Money Buy Happiness?" The Public Interest, 30 (Winter 1973).

Easton, David, A System Analysis of Political Life (New York, 1965).

Economic Planning Center. "Quality of Life, Social Goals and Measurement." (Monography, Division of the Economic Council of Finland 1973).

Ehrlich, P. R., A. H. Ehrlich, and J. P. Holdren, Human Ecology (San Francisco: W. H. Freeman and Company, 1973).

Elgin, Duane, City Size and the Quality of Life (Menlo Park, California: Stanford Research Institute, 1974).

Elmhorm, Kerstin, "Life Quality and Environmental Investigation." (Monography, the Swedish National Board of Health and Social Welfare, July 1974).

Environmental Protection Agency, The Quality of Life Concept (Washington, D.C.: U.S. Government Printing Office, 1973).

Faris, R. E. (ed.), Handbook of Modern Sociology (Chicago: Rand McNally, 1964).

Flaming, K. H. and J. N. Ong, Mr., A Social Report for Milwaukee: Trends and Indicators (Milwaukee: Milwaukee Urban Observatory, 1973).

Flax, M., A Study in Comparative Urban Indicators: Conditions on 18 Large Metropolitan Areas (Washington, D.C.: The Urban Institute, 1972).

Fox, Karl A., Social Indicators and Social Theory (New York: John Wiley and Sons, 1974).

Francis, Wayne, Legislative Issues in the Fifty States (Chicago: Rand-McNally, 1967).

Forrester, Jay, Urban Dynamics (Cambridge: The MIT Press, 1969).

Galbraith, John K., The Affluent Society (Boston: Houghton Mifflin Company, 1958).

Galbraith, John K., "Power and the Useful Economist," American Economic Review (March 1973).

Garn, H., M. Flax, M. Springer, and J. Taylor, "Social Indicator
Models for Urban Policy--Five Specific Applications" (Washington,
D.C.: The Urban Institute, 1973).

Gautrin, Jean-Francois, "An Evaluation of the Impact of Aircraft Noise
on Property Values," Land Economics ,Vol. 51, No. 1 (February 1975).

Gehrmann, Freidhelm, "The Definition of Fundamental Indicators for
Employment and Services," paper presented at the second meeting
of the OECD Working Group on Environmental Indicators (Paris:
October 3-4, 1974).

Gehrman, Freidhelm, "Überblick über den Stand der Forschung auf den
Gebiet: Quantifizierungsversuche der (städtischen) Lebensqualität.
(Monographie, Universität Augsburg, Augsburg, July 1974).

Gehrman, Freidhelm, "Vorschläge zu Forschungsstrategien in Rahmen der
Quantifizierung der städtischen Lebensqualität" (Paris: OECD Sector
Group on the Urban Envrionment, Vol. 25-26, July 1974).

Ginsburg, Helen (ed.), Poverty, Economics, and Society (Boston: Little,
Brown and Company, 1972).

Government Statistics Service, Social Trends, No. 4 (December 1974),
London.

Graves, Clare, W. Huntley and Douglas Bier, "Personality Structure and
Perceptual Readings: An Investigation of Their Relationship to
Hypothesized Levels of Human Existence," Mimeographed paper, 1965.

Grieson, Ronald E., Urban Economics: Readings and Analysis (Boston:
Little, Brown and Company, 1973).

Grumm, John, "Structural Determinates of Legislative Output," in
Legislatures in Developmental Perspective, A. Kronberg and L.
Musolf (eds.) (Durham: Duke University Press, 1970).

Guertin, W. H. and J. P. Bailey, Introduction to Modern Factor Analysis
(Ann Arbor, Michigan: Edward Brothers, Inc., 1970).

Haber, A. and R. P. Runyon, General Statistics (Reading, Massachusetts:
Addison-Wesley Company, 1969).

Hamilton, Mary, "Sex and Income Inequality Among the Employed," The Annals of the American Academy of Political and Social Science (September 1973).

Hanayama, Yuzuru, "Development and Environment in Japan," Internationales Asienforum, Vol. 4, 1973.

Harman, H. H., Modern Factor Analysis (Chicago: Chicago University Press, 1966).

Hawley, Amos, "Community Power and Urban Renewal Success," American Journal of Sociology (January 1963).

Herzberg, F., B. Mansner, and B. Snyderman, The Motivation to Work (New York: Wiley, 1959).

Hoel, P. G. and R. J. Jessen, Basic Statistics for Business and Economics (New York: Wiley and Sons, 1959).

Hofferbert, Richard, "The Relation Between Public Policy and Some Structural and Environmental Variables in the American States," American Political Science Review, Vol. 60, No. 1 (1966).

Homans, George, Social Behavior: Its Elementary Forms (New York: Harcourt, Brace and Company, 1961).

Horn, Patrice (ed.), Behavior Today, Vol. 61, No. 5 (February 3, 1975).

Inhaber, H., "Environmental Quality: Outline for a National Index for Canada," in Science, Vol. 186, No. 4166 (November 29, 1974).

Japanese Economic Planning Agency. White Paper on National Life: The Life and Its Quality in Japan, Minister of State, Japan, 1973.

Johnson, G. E. and F. P. Stafford, "The Economics and Promotion of Women Faculty," American Economics Review.

Johnson, J. M. and G. P. Johnson, "Cross-Impact Dynamic Modeling for Policy Analysis," Monography (Washington, D.C.: National Science Foundation, 1974).

Kamrany, N. M. and A. N. Christakis, "Social Indicators in Perspective," Socioeconomic Planning Sciences, 4, 1970.

Keynes, John Maynard, _Essays in Persuasion_ (London:  MacMillan and Company, 1933).

Kneese, Allen, "Analysis of Environmental Pollution," _The Swedish Journal of Economics_ (March 1971).

Koelle, H. H., "Entwurf eines zielorientierten, gesamtgesellschaftlichen Simulations Modells zur Unterstutzung der Ziel-, Aufgaben- und Finanzplanung," Monographie, Zentrum Berlin für Zukunftsforschung e.v., 1974.

Kunkel, John and Richard Nagasawa, "A Behavioral Model of Man:  Propositions and Implications," _American Sociological Review_, Vol. 38, No. 5 (October 1973).

Kuznets, Simon, _National Product Since 1869_ (New York:  National Bureau of Economic Research, 1946).

Land, Kenneth C., "Social Indicators," in R. B. Smith (ed.), _Social Science Methods_ (New York:  The Free Press, 1970).

Land, Kenneth C., "On the Definition of Social Indicators," _American Sociology_ (November 1971).

Lave, Lester and Eugene Seskin, "Air Pollution and Human Health," in _Science_, Vol. 169 (August 21, 1970).

Leftvich, R. H. and A. M. Sharp, _Economics of Social Issues_ (Dallas, Texas:  Business Publications, Inc., 1974).

Lenski, Gerhard, _Power and Privilege:  A Theory of Stratification_ (New York:  McGraw-Hill, 1966).

Leontief, Wassily, "Environmental Repercussions and the Economic Structure:  An Input-Output Approach," in _The Review of Economics and Statistics_, Vol. 53, No. 3 (August 1970).

Leontief, Wassily, "Theoretical Assumptions and Nonobserved Facts," _American Economic Review_ (March 1971).

Leopold, Luna, Danke Frank, Bruce Hanshaw, and James Balsley, _A Procedure for Evaluating Environmental Impact_, U.S. Department of the Interior, Geological Survey Circular 645, 1971.

Lineberry, R., A. Mandel, and P. Shoemaker, Community Indicators:
    Improving Communities Management (Austin, Texas:  Lyndon B. Johnson
    School of Public Affairs, The University of Texas, 1974).

Liu, B. C., "Impact of Local Government on Regional Growth," Proceedings
    of the American Statistical Association, Business and Economics
    Section, 1973.

Liu, B. C., Quality of Life in the U.S., 1970 (Kansas City:  Midwest
    Research Institute, 1973).

Liu, B. C., "Variations in the Quality of Life in the U.S. by State,
    1970, in Review of Social Economy, Vol. 32, No. 2 (October 1974).

Liu, B. C., "Quality of Life Indicators:  A Preliminary Investigation,"
    Social Indicators Research Journal, Vol. 1, No. 2 (September 1974).

Liu, B. C., "Quality of Life:  Concept, Measure and Results," in The
    American Journal of Economics and Sociology, Vol. 34, No. 1
    (January 1975).

Liu, B. C., "Net Migration Rate and the Quality of Life," Review of
    Economics and Statistics, Vol. 57, No. 3 (August 1975).

Lockard, Duane, "State Party Systems and Policy Output," in Political
    Research and Political Theory, Oliver Garceau (ed.) (Cambridge:
    Howard University Press, 1968).

Louis, Arthur, "The Worst American City," Harper's Magazine (January 1975).

Lowenthal, David (ed.), Environmental Perception and Behavior (Chicago:
    Chicago University Department of Geography, 1967).

Lowry, M., "Race and Socioeconomic Well-Being:  A Geographical Analysis
    of the Mississippi Case," Geographical Review, 60, 1970.

Lyle, John and Mark von Wodtke, "Information System for Environmental
    Planning," in Journal of the American Institute of Planners,
    Vol. 40, No. 6 (November 1974).

Macy, Bruce and Robert Foster, "A Tentative Comparison of Metropolitan
    Quality of Life," paper presented at the Conference on Growth Centers
    and Development Policy, Halifax, Nova Scotia, Canada, April 9-10,
    1975.

Marlin, John, "Jobs and Well-Being: Which Cities Perform the Best," _Business and Society Review_ (Summer 1974).

Marshall, H., Jr., "Black/White Economic Participation in Large U.S. Cities," _The American Journal of Economics and Sociology_, Vol. 31, No. 4 (October 1972).

Maruo, Naoni, "Measuring Welfare of the Japanese People--Including International Comparisons," _Internationales Asienforum_, Vol. 4, 1973.

Maslow, Abraham, _Motivation and Personality_ (New York: Harper and Row, 1970).

Maslow, Abraham, _Toward a Psychology of Being_ (New York: Van Nostrand Reinhold, 1962).

McGinnies, Elliott, _Social Behavior: A Functional Analysis_ (Boston: Houghton Mifflin, 1970).

Meadows, D. H., D.L. Meadows, Jorgen Randers, and W. W. Behrens, III, _The Limits to Growth_ (New York: Universe Books, 1972).

Michalos, Alex, "Methods of Developing Social Indicators," paper presented at the Conference Growth Centers and Development Policy, Halifax, Nova Scotia, Canada, April 9-10, 1975.

Mills, Edwin S., "Economic Incentives in Air Pollution Control," _Economics of Air Pollution,_ Harold Wolzin (ed.) (New York: W. W. Norton and Company, Inc., 1966).

Mishan, E. J., _The Costs of Economic Growth_ (New York, 1967).

Mitchell, A., T. Logothetti, and R. Canton, "An Approach to Measuring Quality of Life," (Menlo Park, California: Stanford Research Institute, 1971).

Moore, W. and S. Maxine, "New Development in Labor Statistics," _Monthly Labor Review_ (March 1972).

Myrdal, G., _Economic Theory and Underdeveloped Regions_ (London: Duckworth, 1957).

National Advisory Commission on Criminal Justice Standards and Goals.
    A National Strategy to Reduce Crime, Washington, D.C. (January 1973).

National Goals Research Staff, Report to the President, Washington,
    D. C., 1970.

National Wildlife Federation, "1971 National Environmental Quality
    Index," National Wildlife (October-November 1971).

Nordhaus, W. and J. Tobin, "Is Growth Obsolete?" in Economic Growth,
    50th Anniversary Colloquium V, New York.

North, Douglas and Roger Miller, The Economics of Public Issues
    (New York:  Harper and Row, 1973).

Office for Planning and Programming, Iowa, The Quality of Life in
    Iowa:  An Economic and Social Report to the Governor for 1973,
    Des Moines, 1973.

Olson, M., "Social Indicators and Social Accounts," Socioeconomics
    Planning Sciences, 2, 1969.

Parsons, Talcott, The Social System (Glencoe:  Free Press, 1951).

Patterson, Samuel, "The Political Cultures of the American States,"
    in Journal of Politics, Vol. 30, No.1 (February 1968).

Pennings, Johannes, "Measures of Organizational Structure:  A Methodolog-
    cal Note," American Journal of Sociology, Vol. 79, No. 3 (November
    1973).

Perloff, Harvey, "A Framework for Dealing with Urban Environment:
    Introductory Statement," in Harvey Perloff (ed.), The Quality of
    the Urban Environment (Washington, D.C.:  Resources for the Future,
    Inc., 1969).

President's Commission on National Goals, Goals for Americans
    (Englewood Cliffs, New Jersey:  Prentice Hall, 1960).

President's Council on Environmental Quality, Environmental Quality
    1972:  Third Annual Report (Washington, D.C., 1972).

President's Science Adviory Committee, Strengthening the Behavioral Science: Statement by the Behavioral Science Subpanel, Washington, D. C., April 20, 1962.

Psacharopoulos, George, "Estimating Shadow Rates of Return to Investment in Education," Journal of Human Resources, Vol. 5, No. 1 (Winter 1970).

The Quality of Life and Social Indicators, New York, National Bureau of Economic Research, 1972.

Quinn, Robert and Linda Shepard, The 1972-73 Quality of Employment Survey (Ann Arbor, Michigan: University Institute for Social Research, 1974).

Real Estate Research Company. The Costs of Sprawl (Chicago: Real Estate Research Company, 1974).

Robbins, L., An Essay on the Nature and Significance of Economics Science (London, 1932).

Rockfeller, John, III., The Second American Revolution (New York: Harper and Row, 1973).

Rokeach, M. and S. Parker, The Nature of Human Values (New York: Free Press, 1973).

Rokeach, M. and S. Parker, "Values as Social Indicators of Poverty and Race Relations in America," The Annals of the American Academy of Political and Social Science, 388, March 1970.

Romans, J. T., Capital Exports and Growth Among U.S. Regions (Middletown, Connecticut: Weslayan University, 1965).

Ruggles, N. and R. Ruggles, The Design of Economic Accounts (New York: National Bureau of Eoonomic Research, 1970.

Ruggles, R. and H. Ruggles, "Social Indicators and a Framework for Social and Economic Accounts," presented at Annual Meeting of the American Statistical Association, St. Louis, 1974.

Rummel, R. J., "Indicators of Cross-National and International Patterns," The American Political Science Review, Vol. 63, No. 1 (March 1969).

Sackrey, Charles, The Political Economy of Urban Poverty (New York: W. W. Norton Company, 1973).

Samuelson, Paul, Economics, 8th Edition (New York: McGraw-Hill, 1970).

Samuelson, Paul, Foundations of Economic Analysis (New York: Harvard University Press, 1965).

Samuelson, Paul, "Maximum Principles in Analytical Economics," Science, Vol. 173, September 10, 1972.

Sawhill, I. V., "The Role of Social Indicators and Social Reporting in Public Expenditure Decisions," in The Analysis and Evaluation of Public Expenditures: The System, papers submitted to the Joint Economic Committee of the U.S. Congress,(Washington, D.C.: U.S. Government Printing Office, 1969).

Schlesinger, Joseph, "The Politics of the Executive," in Politics in the American States, H. Jacob and K. Vines (eds.) (Boston: Little, Brown, and Company, 1965).

Scott, Edward, An Arena for Happiness (Springfield, Illinois: Charles C. Thomas, 1971).

Seashore, Stanley, "Job Satisfaction as an Indicator of the Quality of Employment," Social Indicator Research, Vol. 1, No. 2 (September 1974).

Sharkansky, Ira, "Regionalism, Economic Status and the Public Policies of American States," The Social Science Quarterly (June 1968).

Sheldon, Eleanor and Howard Freedman, "Notes on Social Indicators: Promises and Potential," Policy Sciences, 1,1970.

Sheldon, Eleanor and Wilbert Moore, Indicators of Social Change: Concepts and Measurements (New York: Russell Sage Foundation, 1968).

Shelly, Penelope and Maynard Shelly, Sources of Satisfaction (Lawrence, Kansas: The Key Press, 1973).

Simon, Herbert, Models of Man (New York: Wiley and Sons, 1957).

Skinner, B. F., Beyond Freedom and Dignity (New York: Knopf, 1971).

Smith, David M., The Geography of Social Well-Being in the U.S. (New York: McGraw-Hill, 1973).

Stone, Richard, Towards a System of Social and Demographic Statistics (New York: United Nations, ST/Stat 68, July 1973).

Taeuber, Richard, "Social Indicators and Policy Making," Proceedings of the American Statistical Association, Social Statistics Section, 1974.

Terleckyz, Nestor, "Measuring Progress Towards Social Goals: Some Possibilities at National and Local Levels," Management Science, Vol. 16, No. 12 (August 1970).

Thomas, Harold, Jr., "The Animal Farm: A Mathematical Model for the Discussion of Social Standards for Control of the Environment," in Quarterly Journal Economics (February 1963).

Thorndike, E. L., 144 Smaller Cities (New York: Harcourt, Brace and Company, 1940).

Thorndike, E. L., Your City (New York: Harcourt, Brace and Company, 1939).

Torres, Juan, "The Quality of Life in America's Major Metropolitan Areas," The Conference Board Record, Vol. 11, No. 2, 1974.

Tunstall, Daniel B., Social Indicators, 1973 (Washington, D.C.: Office of Management and Budget, 1974).

Ullman, Edward L., "Regional Development and the Geography of Concentration," Papers and Proceedings of the Regional Science Association, Vol. 4 (1958).

U.S. Department of Commerce, Bureau of the Census, Statistical Abstract of the U.S., 1971 (Washington, D.C.: U.S. Government Printing Office, 1972).

U.S. Department of Health, Education and Welfare, Toward a Social Report (Washington, D.C.: U.S. Government Printing Office, 1969).

U.S. Department of Housing and Urban Development, *International Information Series*, 26, February 5, 1974.

Urban Institute and International City Management Association, *Measuring the Effectiveness of Basic Municipal Sciences* (Washington, D.C.: The Urban Institute, 1974).

Van Dusen, Roxann, "Problems of Measurement in Areas of Social Concerns," *Monthly Labor Review* (September 1974).

Waddell, Thomas, *The Economic Damages of Air Pollution* (Washington, D.C.: EPA Washington Environmental Research Center, 1974).

Walker, Jack, "The Diffusion of Innovations Among the American States," *American Political Science Review* (September 1969).

Welch, F., "Black/White Differences in Returns to Schooling," *American Economic Review* (December 1973).

"What America Thinks of Itself," *Newsweek* (December 10, 1973).

Whitman, Ira et al., *Design of An Environmental Evaluation System* (Columbus, Ohio: Battelle Columbus Laboratories, June 1971).

Wilson, John, *The Quality of Life in America* (Kansas City: Midwest Research Institue, 1967).

Wilson, John, *The Quality of Life in the U.S.--An Excursion Into the New Frontier of Socioeconomic Indicators* (Kansas City: Midwest Research Institute, 1970).

Wingo, Lowdon, "The Quality of Life: Toward a Microeconomic Definition," *Urban Studies* (October 1973).

Wolf, C. P., "Social Impact Assessment: The State of the Art," (Fort Belvior, Virginia: Institute for Water Resources, U.S. Army Corps, 1974).

Numbers refer to the pages in the content of the report.

Effects,
   adverse and beneficial, 17, 18,
      26, 98, 99, 156, 228
   factor, 57, 60, 64, 68, 75, 76,
      77
Employment, 6, 7, 10, 32, 33, 35,
   36, 69, 75, 82, 129, 164,
   204, 210
Environment,
   individual and institutional,
      2, 6, 10, 17, 18, 32, 37, 38,
      39, 51, 62-66, 70, 73, 76, 78,
      112, 113, 116, 128, 185
   natural, 2, 6, 10, 17, 18, 32,
      33, 36, 37, 38, 39, 51, 62,
      63, 64, 65, 66, 73, 74, 77,
      78, 111, 112, 113, 115, 116,
      119, 128, 154, 156, 158, 185,
      211
Environmental component, 62-66,
   78, 93, 111-119, 128, 136,
   151-158, 185-191, 198, 207,
   211, 219, 227
Equilibrium, 43, 44, 45, 46, 47,
   48, 49, 51, 203

### F

Factor and component analysis, 82,
   83, 88-92, 101, 137
Free market mechanism, 1, 2, 17,
   36, 152, 228

### G

Gini coefficient, 55
Goods and services, 56, 57, 58, 59,
   93, 103, 111, 128, 164, 170,
   218, 220
Government performance, 58, 59,
   103, 104, 107, 110, 128, 137,
   145, 149, 181, 182, 211

Gross national product, 6, 12, 13,
   17, 37, 38, 50, 210, 218

### H

Health and education component,
   59, 60, 66-68, 78, 85, 93,
   119-127, 128, 136, 137, 158-
   163, 164, 169, 170, 171, 191-
   197, 198, 211, 219, 220
Health and medical care, 6, 10,
   19, 24, 28, 32, 33, 59, 60,
   63, 66, 67, 68, 69, 70, 74,
   75, 82, 103, 120, 121, 123,
   124, 129, 162, 163, 169, 182,
   191, 192, 195, 221
Homogeneity, 121, 151
Housing, 6, 10, 24, 32, 33, 55,
   57, 64, 71, 72, 76, 77, 78,
   86, 100, 115, 129, 141, 156,
   166, 175, 188, 202

### I

Income distribution, 2, 6, 24,
   32, 37, 39, 55, 56, 57, 70,
   71, 72, 74, 86, 94, 98, 100,
   121, 127, 133, 141, 143, 175
Index,
   air pollution, 63, 64, 65, 115
   cardinal and ordinal, 211
   composite, 145, 147, 158, 171,
      202, 211, 218, 222
   cost of living, 72, 77, 79, 82,
      97, 103, 104, 131, 134, 164
   crime, 82, 103, 107, 129, 149,
      166, 181, 182, 202
   economic concentration, 56, 57
   environmental quality, 18, 81
      115, 116, 137, 152, 156, 185, 188
   housing segregation, 71, 72, 76,
      133, 166, 202

Social,
  component, 69-79, 85, 93, 128-
    138, 164-169, 170, 171, 198-
    204, 206, 211, 219, 221
  disorder, 6, 10, 19, 23, 32, 33
  economic system, 5
  indicators, 6-12, 38, 69, 85,
    129, 208, 210, 218, 227, 228
  mobility, 32, 33, 127, 164, 204,
    221
  statistics and accounts, 3, 7,
    12, 208, 210, 228
  welfare function, 3, 8, 25, 26,
    28, 36, 38, 85, 222, 223
  well-being, 2, 3, 5, 6, 7, 9,
    16, 38, 40, 50, 69, 72, 79,
    82, 121, 127, 136, 138, 163,
    164, 166, 169, 218, 228
Solid waste generation, 39, 63,
    64, 65, 113, 115, 137, 152,
    154, 185, 188, 191, 227
Sports, 73, 77, 129, 131, 166
Standard,
  deviation, 83, 84, 87, 88, 92,
    94, 95, 101, 124, 129, 131,
    139, 141, 143, 145, 147, 152,
    156, 158, 163, 164, 169, 175,
    178, 181, 182, 185, 192, 195,
    198, 202, 204, 206, 211
  economic areas (SEA), 61, 62,
    65, 69
  of living, 10, 39, 58, 59, 93,
    128
Standardized additive method, 83-
    87, 89, 91, 101, 137, 218
Static analysis, 79, 99, 121, 124,
    227
Subjective arguments and measures,
    6, 80, 81

T

Technology, 2, 5, 23, 24, 98, 221
Trade-offs, 51, 116, 137, 152,
    156, 170, 171, 185, 220

Transitional society, 1, 2, 3,
    14, 15

U

Unemployment rate, 55, 57, 60,
    62, 70, 71, 75, 76, 82, 86,
    94, 98, 99, 131, 134, 141,
    143, 164, 175, 204
Unit of measurement, 79, 80, 83,
    84, 97
Urban renewal/blight, 2, 55, 64,
    78
Urbanization, 2, 32, 55, 70, 76,
    78, 111

V

Value system, 1, 2, 3, 10, 13,
    15, 24, 25, 36, 37, 38, 39,
    62
Variables,
  flow and stock, 54, 79, 80, 86,
    88, 99, 120, 198, 211, 218
  input and output, 88, 91, 93,
    103, 129, 131, 172
Vehicle ownership registration,
    55, 57, 64, 65, 70, 75, 100,
    115, 154, 188

W

Wealth status, 54, 55, 56, 57,
    143, 175, 198, 219
Welfare payment and assistance,
    2, 6, 10, 24, 28, 32, 59, 60,
    62, 103, 104, 108, 110, 149,
    151, 211
Widening opportunity for individual
    choice, 41, 45, 69, 70, 75

Z

Z-score, 83, 84, 86, 87, 90, 101,
    143, 145, 147

315

## ABOUT THE AUTHOR

Dr. Ben-chieh Liu ( 劉 本 傑 ) is the Principal Economist at Midwest Research Institute and adjunct professor at University of Missouri, Kansas City, Missouri. A native of Chungking, China, he received his B.A. degree from National Taiwan University, M.A. from Memorial University of Newfoundland, and Ph.D. in Economics from Washington University (St. Louis). He has directed and conducted extensive research in the field of applied econometrics, particularly on urban and regional economics, health and manpower, public finance and social indicators, and pollution and environmental studies. He has published numerous articles in many leading professional journals such as: Journal of American Statistical Association, Review of Economics and Statistics, National Tax Journal, Land Economics, and the American Journal of Economics and Sociology, etc., and presented papers at meetings of the Economic Society, the International Statistical Institute, tha Allied Social Sciences, the Operations Research Society, and other professional organizations.

While in graduate schools, Dr. Liu was a recipient of many fellowships, including the World University Services Fellowship in Canada and the Economic Development Administration Fellowship in the United States. He has taught at Washington University, University of Missouri and the Graduate Engineering Center in St. Louis, and served as a consultant to the Chinese Government and the United Nations. In addition, he has reviewed research proposals to the National Science Foundation and articles submitted to many professional journals and is a member of the American Economic Association, the American Statistical Association, the Air Pollution Control Association, the Econometric Society, the Regional Science Association, and the National Tax Association--Tax Institute of America.

THE EFFECTS OF URBAN GROWTH:  A Population Impact Analysis
Richard P. Appelbaum
Jennifer A. Bigelow
Henry P. Kramer
Harvey L. Motlotch
Paul Relis

INDUSTRIAL INVASION OF NONMETROPOLITAN AMERICA:  A Quarter
Century of Experience
Gene F. Summers
E.M. Beck
Frank Clemente
Sharon D. Evans
Jon Minkoff

POLICY EVALUATION FOR COMMUNITY DEVELOPMENT:  Decision
Tools for Local Government
Shimon Awerbuch
William A. Wallace

SOCIAL INDICATORS OF WELL-BEING IN AMERICA
Frank M. Andrews
Stephen B. Withey

SYSTEMIC URBAN PLANNING
Darwin G. Stuart

URBAN PROBLEMS AND PUBLIC POLICY CHOICES
edited by
Joel Bergsman and
Howard L. Wiener